The essays included here are the best-sellers of recent American economic history: the articles and chapters from the books that most frequently appear on the syllabi of American economic history courses. The readings are organized chronologically and thematically, covering such topics as the colonial and early national economy, slavery and indentured servitude, the South since the Civil War, the origins of American industrial success, the causes of farm protest in the late nineteenth century, the role of women in the economy, and the Great Depression. The introductions to each essay, written by Robert Whaples and Dianne C. Betts, add context, provide critical questions about the arguments and evidence, note important subsequent works, and suggest additional readings. Also included are an appendix that provides a clear, simple introduction to regression analysis and a glossary.

HISTORICAL PERSPECTIVES ON THE AMERICAN ECONOMY

HISTORICAL PERSPECTIVES ON THE AMERICAN ECONOMY

SELECTED READINGS

Edited by

Robert Whaples
Wake Forest University

Dianne C. Betts
Southern Methodist University

CAMBRIDGE
UNIVERSITY PRESS

Published by the Press Syndicate of the University of Cambridge
The Pitt Building, Trumpington Street, Cambridge CB2 1RP
40 West 20th Street, New York, NY 10011-4211, USA
10 Stamford Road, Oakleigh, Melbourne 3166, Australia

First published 1995

Library of Congress Cataloging-in-Publication Data

Historical perspectives on the American economy: selected readings/
edited by Robert Whaples, Dianne C. Betts.

p. cm.

Includes index.

ISBN 0-521-46107-3 (hard). – ISBN 0-521-46648-2 (pbk.)

1. United States – Economic conditions.

HC103.H57 1995
330.973–dc20 93-49100
CIP

A catalog record for this book is available from the British Library.

ISBN 0-521-46107-3 hardback
ISBN 0-521-46648-2 paperback

Transferred to digital printing 2002

Contents

Acknowledgments

We would like to thank Martin Eisenberg, Stanley Engerman, and David Mitch, who helped us with this project by sending several pages of comments. We received additional help from Farley Grubb, Dennis Halcoussis, Winifred Rothenberg, Faye Kisel, and Marilyn Coopersmith.

Introduction to students

Critics argue that textbooks are intellectual fast food, lacking in both flavor and nutrition. They charge that textbooks alone cannot adequately capture the complexity of issues, the subtlety of argument, and the richness of evidence needed to convey the character of the discipline of economic history (Mitch, 1990). We agree.

The purpose of a college education is to search for truth while exercising the mind's powers of reasoning and analysis. In using this reader, you will discover how professional economic historians search for truth, and will be compelled to exert your intellect far more than if you only read a textbook. You will discover that history is not written in stone, that there is an ongoing, never-ending debate about the meaning of the past. You will discover the methods and sources used by economic historians. You will have to grapple with the structure of arguments, the meaning of evidence, the applicability of theories, and the rhetorical devices used in persuasion.

The essays included here are widely used in American economic history classes and could be considered best-sellers. We think highly of each one, but do not necessarily agree with the conclusions of any of the works and do not mean to imply that they are the final or official interpretations, nor that they are the "truth." Each of these essays demonstrates the craftsmanship, ingenuity, and skill involved in drawing conclusions given limited historical evidence. On the other hand, there is almost inevitably some weakness in any argument or set of evidence presented. We encourage you to look for both the strengths and weaknesses in them as you develop your critical skills, expand your intellectual powers, and learn more about the history of the American economy.

The text is organized chronologically and thematically, as are most economic history classes. We provide introductions to each essay or group of essays. Our purpose is not to judge the essays or give away the plot, but to provide additional context where necessary, pose critical questions about the arguments and evidence advanced, note important works that have subsequently been published, and suggest additional readings. Make sure to take advantage of the appendix on statistics and regression analysis, as well as the glossary.

References

David Mitch, "The Role of the Textbook in Undergraduate Economic History Courses: Indispensable Tool or Superficial Convenience?" *Journal of Economic History*, 50 (June 1990), 428–31.

Introduction to instructors

The field of American economic history is fortunate to have a wide range of quality textbooks. However, two out of three economic historians feel that a textbook unaccompanied by any other type of reading is unsatisfactory. The majority feel that journal articles and selections from monographs should be used as complements to or substitutes for textbooks (Mitch, 1990). An alternative to the standard textbook is needed, but as we all know, customizing a set of readings can be difficult. We hope that this collection of readings fills the void identified by economic history teachers.

In 1991, the Committee on Education in Economic History organized a syllabus exchange. The response was overwhelming, and many of the syllabi included extensive reading lists. Although the reading lists demonstrate the great variety in what economic historians teach, they also reflect the core readings economic historians assign to their students. The chapters we have included in *Historical Perspectives on the American Economy* come from this collection of reading lists. They are, in essence, the best-sellers of American economic history, the articles and chapters from the books that most frequently appear on the reading lists in American economic history courses.

A recent quantitative history of the *Journal of Economic History* reveals the wide range of the topics and time periods examined by American economic historians (Whaples, 1991). Among the topics economic historians have explored most thoroughly are economic growth, money and banking, transportation, technological change, agriculture, slavery and servitude, and labor markets. Each of these themes is examined in this reader. The bulk of the profession's attention has been turned to the nineteenth century and the twentieth century before World War II, and the essays found here follow the same chronological pattern. Cliometrics has become the field's primary method, and many, but not all, of the readings included here are cliometric. Thus, the readings in this book are not only a good reflection of what economic historians teach, but are also indicative of mainstream research in economic history.

The text is organized chronologically and thematically, as are most economic history classes. We provide introductions to each essay or group of essays. Our purpose is not to judge the essays or give away the plot, but to provide additional context where necessary, pose critical questions about the arguments and evidence advanced, note important works that have subsequently been published, and suggest additional readings. We also provide an appendix on regression analysis and a glossary.

References

David Mitch, "The Role of the Textbook in Undergraduate Economic History Courses: Indispensable Tool or Superficial Convenience?" *Journal of Economic History*, 50 (June 1990), 428–31.

Robert Whaples, "A Quantitative History of the *Journal of Economic History* and the Cliometric Revolution," *Journal of Economic History*, 51 (June 1991), 289–302.

Contributors

Jeremy Atack is Professor of Economics at Vanderbilt University.

Alfred D. Chandler, Jr., is Professor of Business History, Emeritus, Harvard School of Business.

Paul A. David is Professor of Economics at Stanford University.

Marc Egnal is Professor of History at Atkinson College, York University.

Stanley L. Engerman is Professor of Economics at the University of Rochester.

Joseph A. Ernst is Professor of History at Atkinson College, York University.

Robert W. Fogel is Director of the Center for Population Economics at the University of Chicago.

Milton Friedman is a fellow at the Hoover Institute.

David W. Galenson is Professor of Economics at the University of Chicago.

Claudia Goldin is Professor of Economics at Harvard University.

Donald N. McCloskey is Professor of Economics and History at the University of lowa.

Anne Mayhew is Professor of Economics at the University of Tennessee.

Roger L. Ransom is Professor of Economics and History at the University of California, Riverside.

Hugh Rockoff is Professor of Economics at the Rutgers University.

Winifred B. Rothenberg is Associate Professor of Economics at Tufts University.

Anna Jacobson Schwartz is a fellow at the Hoover Institute.

Richard Sutch is Professor of Economics at the University of California, Berkeley.

Richard Sylla is Professor of Economics at the Leonard Stern School of Business, New York University.

Peter Temin is Professor of Economics at the Massachusetts Institute of Technology.

Gavin Wright is Professor of Economics at Stanford University.

I

Introduction

"Does the past have useful economics?"

by Donald N. McCloskey

The quick answer to McCloskey's question is "Yes" or an emphatic "Of course!" Many would consider it bizarre that this question should even be posed, but McCloskey documents the fact that economic historians are unread by mainstream economists. His audience in the *Journal of Economic Literature* is primarily these sinners, the academic economists whom he wishes to pull back from the road to hell. Many of these professional economists are in the same position as students reading this collection. They are uninformed about economic history and need to be shown its merits. This is McCloskey's task.

McCloskey demonstrates his points convincingly, and his sermon is splendidly written. Among the strengths of economic history that he illustrates is its ability to provide researchers with "more economic facts" and even "better economic facts" than are currently available from modern data. Had he written the piece more recently, he might have added that historical data are a marvelous teaching device as well. For example, the state Bureau of Labor Statistics data computerized by Susan Carter, Roger Ransom, and Richard Sutch have proven to be excellent for classroom use in economic history or quantitative methods courses (Whaples, 1992).

While his jeremiad is principally directed at economists, McCloskey additionally confirms that economic history is an indispensable part of good history. To study the past without examining economic events or using the tools of economics is to ignore an essential dimension of history.

Additional Reading

Robert W. Fogel and G. R. Elton, *Which Road to the Past?* New Haven: Yale University Press, 1983.

Donald N. McCloskey, *Second Thoughts: Myths and Morals of U.S. Economic History*, New York: Oxford University Press, 1993.

Robert Solow, "Economic History and Economics," *American Economic Review: Papers and Proceedings*, 75 (May 1985), 328–31.

Richard Sutch, "All Things Reconsidered: The Life-Cycle Perspective and the Third Task of Economic History," *Journal of Economic History*, 51 (June 1991), 271–88.

Robert Whaples, "Using Historical State Bureau of Labor Statistics Reports in Teaching," *Historical Methods*, 25 (Summer 1992), 132–36.

Gavin Wright, "History and the Future of Economics," in *Economic History and the Modern Economist*, edited by William Parker. New York: Basil Blackwell, 1986, 77–82.

1

Does the past have useful economics?

DONALD N. McCLOSKEY

It is not mere convention that impels me to thank the many colleagues who have commented on earlier drafts of this essay. I have received from them in writing the equivalent of over 100 typed pages, and many hours of conversation as well. This itself measures the vigor of historical economics, one theme here, but their contribution to the product is immeasurable. I would like to thank, therefore, the seminars in economic history at Chicago and at Northwestern; and R. Cameron, M. Edelstein, S. L. Engerman, R. W. Fogel, R. Gallman, H. Gemery, C. D. Goldin, G. Gunderson, G. Hawke, R. Higgs, G. Hueckel, J. R. T. Hughes, H. G. Johnson, E. L. Jones, A. Kahan, C. P. Kindleberger, A. Leijonhufvud, P. Lindert, P. McClelland, M. McInnis, J. Mokyr, L. D. Neal, A. Olmstead, D. Perkins, J. D. Reid, N. Rosenberg, W. W. Rostow, A. J. Schwartz, B. Solow, G. Walton, D. Whitehead, and J. G. Williamson. And I would like to apologize to George Stigler for inverting for my own purposes the title of his fine essay, "Does Economics Have a Useful Past?" {107, 1969}, and for ignoring the useful lemma illustrated there (p. 226): "there are not ten good reasons for anything."

The answer, of course, is "yes," and at one time the very question would have seemed impertinent. Smith, Marx, Mill, Marshall, Keynes, Heckscher, Schumpeter, and Viner, to name a few, were nourished by historical study and nourished it in turn. Gazing down from Valhalla it would seem to them bizarre that their heirs would study economics with the history left out, stopping their desultory search for facts in time series at the last 25 years and in cross sections at the latest tape from the Bureau of the Census, passing by the experiments of history with little regard for their place in a nonexperimental science, distrusting old facts as error-ridden intrusions from another structure, abandoning historical perspectives on their political economy, and basing their theory and policy on stylized nonfacts about economic development, fairy tales remembered from their youth.

Yet this is what has happened. It began in the 1940s, in some respects earlier, as young American economists bemused by revolutions

Source: Donald N. McCloskey, "Does the Past Have Useful Economics?" *Journal of Economic Literature* (June 1976), 434–61. Reprinted with permission of the author and the American Economic Association.

in the substance and method of economics neglected the reading of history in favor of macroeconomics, mathematics, and statistics. The low opportunity cost of such specialization reinforced it: American economic history by that time was, albeit with a few brilliant exceptions, neither good economics nor good history, a dim echo of the American institutionalists and through them of the German historical school. It is not surprising that immature scholars undervalued history then, still less surprising in a decade in which economists were having difficulty understanding macroeconomic policy even in the short run, mathematical maximization even under narrow constraints, and statistical inference even with a simple structure. What is more surprising is that the reading and using of history was not taken up again in the early 1950s, as economists rediscovered economic growth, surprise which turns to astonishment when the neglect of history persisted into the 1970s, as they rediscovered property rights, inheritance, educational investment, social class, income distribution, and other pieces of history in economics. And what is most astonishing in this – what must make Schumpeter, say, turn back in disgust to his horn of mead and his dialogue with Marx and Smith on the historical dynamics of capitalism – is that in the late 1950s a throng of historical economists equipped with Lagrangean multipliers and Durbin-Watson statistics poured out of Purdue, Harvard, Washington, Columbia, Johns Hopkins, and a widening array of new factories at home and abroad to reshape economic history into a form suited to the tastes of their colleagues in economics, yet their colleagues did not buy. The identification problem is solved: it was the demand curve, not the supply curve, that moved back. At the same price measured in an hour of reading or a month of writing, economists nowadays demand less economic history.

The result is apparent in those periodical declarations of what it is that real economists do, the general interest journals of the profession. From 1925 to 1944 the pages of the *American Economic Review*, the *Quarterly Journal of Economics*, and the *Journal of Political Economy* taken together contained 6.5 percent (as weighted by size) of articles on economic history; from 1945 to 1974 they contained 3.3 percent (similarly weighted).[1] For the three journals taken separately the drift

1. This difference, treating each of the 50 years as an observation, is significant at the .00003 level. Because the distribution for the earlier period was bimodal, and plainly therefore non-normal, I used the Mann-Whitney U test. The underlying evidence is available on request. Briefly, for 1925–1963 the number of pages in articles on history in the three journals was calculated from all their appearances in the various history classifications in the *Index of Economic Journals* [1, 1961–1965]. Its definition of "history" is "articles concerned primarily with a period 20 years or more earlier than the beginning date of the volume" [1, 1961, p. xi]. The definition imparts a downward bias to the number of pages recorded as history in earlier years, because the volumes

away from history was as shown in Table I, and more detailed statistics tell a similar story. The *JPE* was for a long time the most historical of the journals, reflecting perhaps the reluctance with which Chicago embraced the view that economics is applied mathematics and statistics and that in the long run we are all dead. From 1929 to 1944, with a remarkable devotion to intellectuality in the face of world depression and war, the *JPE* devoted 11 percent of its pages to economic history, many of them the products of Earl Hamilton and John Nef. By 1970–74, however, the heirs of Jacob Viner and Paul Douglas devoted 2.8 percent of the pages of their journal to it. They were merely joining the trend. The journals of 1935–1939, when economists were obsessed (properly) with last year's unemployment and trade statistics, contained proportionately 2.7 times more economic history than the journals of 1970–1974, when economists were instead obsessed (again properly) with the origins in the very long run of growth, discrimination, legal change, and the historic evils of capitalism.

These contrasts will surprise no one familiar with the literature of economics over the last fifty years, confirmed as they are in other ways.[2] To be sure, specialized journals of economic history drew off historical articles from the three major journals, as did specialized journals in other fields. The composition of the general journals is nonetheless a measure

of the *Index* for those years cover a wider span: to qualify as history an article in 1939 had to concern events 34 years before; one in 1949, 29 years before; one in 1963, 23 years; and one in 1974, only 20. A correction would accentuate the postwar fall. For 1964–1974 the number of pages in articles on history was calculated from the journals themselves, classifying doubtful cases as history. The total number of pages available for all subjects was calculated from the journals, including supplements sent to subscribers and excluding advertisements, administrative matter, and book reviews in book review sections (not classified in the *Index*). The AER after 1969 is not defined to include this *Journal*; if one were to adopt the alternative definition, the recent evaporation of history from the journals would be somewhat more pronounced. The percentages divide the pages of history by total pages, weighting journals in the total by their number of total pages. Unweighted averages of the three behave in much the same way.

2. Martin Bronfenbrenner would not agree [7, 1966]. He measured the column inches of Class 5 (Economic History) relative to the total in the *Index* volumes, arriving at:

1886–1924	1.21%	1950–1954	1.44%
1925–1939	1.49	1955–1959	1.64
1940–1949	1.49	1960–1963	1.47

This he described as an "upturn . . . with some slight decline since 1960" [7, 1966, p. 544]. In this calculation, however, he neglects the articles classified as History but appearing in other parts of the index (such as 9.51, Security and Money Markets, History), which are, ignoring the double-counting, 80 percent of the total; and he does not notice the sharp downward bias in the earlier volumes imparted by the definition of "history" in the index (an article appearing 1924 would have to be concerned chiefly with events before 1866, 58 years before, to qualify as history). A. W. Coats' assertion that economic history has occupied "an increasing share of the total periodical literature'; [12, 1971, p. 32] is based on Bronfenbrenner's figures.

Table 1. *Summary of the percent of pages devoted to economic history, 1925–1974*

	AER	*QJE*	*JPE*
1925–44	4.4	5.4	9.9
1945–74	2.2	3.3	5.4
Level at which the differences are significant (Mann-Whitney test)	.011	.021	.020

of what those who write for, edit, and referee them believe is of general interest to economists. They believe history to be of small and diminishing interest. That the general journals have little economic history in view of the existence of specialized journals in economic history read exclusively by economic historians does not contradict the observation that economists are increasingly ahistorical. It restates it. Indeed, even if one were to suppose that economists read at random in all the 200-odd journals indexed in this *Journal*, the probability of them stumbling on an article on economic history in 1973–1974 would have been .028, and the number of encounters with history in the journals, like the number of deaths from horse kicks in the cavalry, would approximate a Poisson distribution.[3] Of course, economists in other fields do not in fact consult specialized journals of economic history. The drift of economic history into specialized journals and of economists out of reading these journals is doubtless attributable to the widening gap in method, closing only comparatively recently, between economics and history. In 1926 the editors of the *JPE* believed, no doubt correctly, that their subscribers would read B. J. Hovde, "French Socialism and the Triple Entente, 1893–1914," the first of three long articles cast in narrative. What is most significant, though, and least quantifiable, is the drift in economics away from using history, as distinct from merely reading it. Whether or not an economist specialized in, say, international trade reads for himself a seminal article on distributed lags in *Econometrica* or on portfolio analysis in the *Journal of Finance*, he will use their results, distilled in survey articles and in textbooks. The same cannot be said at present for economic history. Does the past have useful economics? The average American economist nowadays answers, "No."

The exceptions are notable, in more ways than one. It will come as a surprise to many economists that among others Armen Alchian, E. Cary

3. The figure is the share of column inches of history titles in the index of the *Journal*. In 1973–1974 these included all articles in history, not merely those fitting into Class 5 of the *Index*. Highly specialized journals of economic history, such as *Agricultural History*, are not indexed in the *Journal*; they were in the *Index*.

Brown, Richard Caves, Donald Gordon, Reuben Kessel, Marc Nerlove, Mancur Olson, Albert Rees, Stanley Reiter, and Arnold Zellner, none of whom do their main work in history, have in fact made contributions to it.[4] Turning away for a moment from the subject here, American economics and its relations with American history, it might be noted that in Britain such traditions of a serious amateur interest in economic history are strong: Mark Blaug, A. K. Cairncross, J. R. Hicks, R. C. O. Matthews, E. H. Phelps-Brown, R. S. Sayers, Brinley Thomas, and John Vaizey, for example, are well-known in Britain as economists dealing with contemporary problems of policy and theory, yet all of them have contributed to British economic history at a high level. The postwar officers of the American Economic Association, members of the older generation trained to place history as Schumpeter did with theory and statistics at the foundation of economic science, can provide a comparable list. Among recent vice-presidents, Moses Abramovitz, Evsey Domar, Charles Kindleberger, W. Arthur Lewis, and Robert Triffin show no signs of forsaking history. Nor do the words and works of postwar presidents reflect the dominant opinion of their constituents that economic history is a frill, useless to the hard, important business of formalizing another economic idea, of refining the techniques for exploiting a given set of statistics, or of deflecting current policy from a third into a second best configuration. In his presidential address to the Association in 1970, Wassily Leontief scolded those who had elected him for ignoring empirical work in favor of ever more mechanical theory and scholastic econometrics [66, 1971, p. 3]:

> Devising a new statistical procedure, however tenuous, that makes it possible to squeeze out one more unknown parameter from a given set of data, is judged a greater scientific achievement than the successful search for additional information that would permit us to measure the magnitude of the same parameter in a less ingenious, but more reliable way.

He applauded agricultural economists for a long tradition in another style, and might as well have applauded historical economists for a younger tradition in the same style [66, 1971, p. 5]:

> An exceptional example of a healthy balance between theoretical and empirical analysis and of the readiness of professional economists to cooperate with experts in the neighboring disciplines is offered by Agricultural Economics as it developed in this country over the last fifty years.

4. [60 Kessel and Alchian, 1959; 8, Brown, 1956; 10, Caves, 1971; 11, Chambers and Gordon, 1966; 77, Nerlove, 1965; 81, Olson, 1963; 90, Rees, 1961; 54, Hughes and Reiter, 1958; 137, Zellner and Murphy, 1959.] It was Reiter who invented the word "cliometrics," a joke that caught on.

One of the agricultural economists whom Leontief undoubtedly had in mind, Theodore W. Schultz, himself a past president of the Association, regretted in 1974 that he himself had not studied economic history more diligently in his youth and argued that "there is a strong tendency on the part of virtually all economists to undervalue the history of the economy of both high and low income countries. I doubt the wisdom of this tendency to concentrate on the immediate present" [101, 1974, p. 12]. Another postwar president, Milton Friedman, in collaboration with Anna J. Schwartz, carried a high valuation of economic history to the point of making a seminal contribution to it, as in a less extended way did Paul Douglas, John Kenneth Galbraith, Robert Aaron Gordon, and J. H. Williams. And still others, such as Schumpeter, Harold Innis, and Simon Kuznets, valued economic history to the point of devoting sustained effort over long careers to its enrichment.

It is apparent, however, that this older generation of American economists did not persuade many of the younger that history is essential to economics. Those they did persuade – the "new" economic historians or "cliometricians" – ignored the task of persuading their doubting colleagues and directed their rhetorical energies instead towards non-economists, chiefly historians. This choice of audience had the advantage of imparting emotional cohesion to the cliometricians, filling them with the enthusiasm and energy of convinced imperialists. The result was a series of conquests beginning, as I have said, in the late 1950s and widening further with each year that sharply revised American economic history and has begun recently to revise other economic histories as well. Being intellectual imperialists, however, the cliometricians forgot, as many imperialists do, that foreign adventures require domestic support, and by neglecting to solicit it, they lost it. Were other economists so disregarding of their self-interests [that] they would court a similar fate? For thirty years after the first stirrings in the 1930s, mathematical and statistical economists pointed out to everyone who would listen that one or another piece of economics is essentially mathematical or essentially statistical until at last no one remained to be convinced. Historical economists could have pointed out with equal force that one or another piece, in some cases the same piece claimed by their more aggressive colleagues, is essentially historical. But they seldom did. Socialized inside economics as it developed after the War, they were apologetic and deferential towards their colleagues, to the point at times of imitating their colleagues' low standards of factual accuracy and wider social relevance along with their high standards of logical cogency and statistical grace. Lacking the self-confidence of the mathematical or statistical economists, the new historical economists have neglected the task of persuading others of the worth of history in economics.

I. The value of economic history

It is not because it is difficult to do that the task has been neglected. The lines of argument are opened with little effort. For the professional economic historian the worth of economic history is that of general history, to which it contributes, and it is because he puts a high value on history, economic or not, that he chooses to study it. This justification suffices for him and for any economist who believes that history, whether or not it is directly useful in testing economic laws or framing economic policy, is collective memory fruitful of wisdom. At the least pragmatic level, indeed, the worth of economic history is that of intellectual activity generally, and nothing should be easier than convincing professional intellectuals that such activity is worthwhile. G. M. Trevelyan put the point gracefully [117, 1942, pp. viii, x]:

> Disinterested intellectual curiosity is the lifeblood of real civilization. . . . There is nothing that more divides civilised from semi-savage man than to be conscious of our forefathers as they really were, and bit by bit to reconstruct the mosaic of the long-forgotten past. To weigh the stars, or to make ships sail in the air or below the sea, is not a more astonishing and ennobling performance on the part of the human race in these latter days, than to know the course of events that had long been forgotten, and the true nature of men and women who were here before us.

One can admire historically important and economically perceptive histories of Southern slaves, nineteenth-century businessmen, or medieval peasants in the same way that one admires a mathematically beautiful and elegantly proven theorem in the theory of optimal control, whether or not the histories or the theorem have any practical use.

In this respect, indeed, by their attachment to the ivory tower, historical economists have much in common with mathematical economists. Further, though in their fascination with markets both activities are recognizably economic, both practitioners are likely to be met with a glassy stare and a change of subject when they speak of probate records or fixed point theorems to their colleagues in the coffee room. There remains, to be sure, one conspicuous point of asymmetry: forty years of investment in mathematizing economics and of disinvestment in historicizing economics has made it less acceptable among economists to admit ignorance of mathematics than to admit ignorance of history. The days are passing when the social sciences bridged the two cultures, literary and scientific, and economics burned the bridge long ago. Comfortable ignorance, to be sure, is not a monopoly of economists. A culture is a definition of barbarians, a definition of which people one may safely ignore; an intellectual culture is a definition of which classes of knowledge one may safely ignore. A social historian dealing habitually with inherently quantitative issues would be deeply ashamed to admit that he is ignorant of the languages, literature, or political history of the societies he studies; yet admits cheerfully, with no apparent resolve to amend his ignorance, that his mathematical and statistical sophistication is that of a ten year old child. It is meritorious in such circles to be innocent of numbers as to be free from some mental defect. Economists have not usually carried the parallel attitude so far. It is true, nonetheless, that an applied economist dealing habitually with inherently historical issues would be ashamed to admit that he is ignorant of differential equations or identifiability, yet admits with no sense of loss that he is entirely ignorant of what occurred in the economy he studies before 1929 or 1948 or 1970.

What, then, do economists lose by their increasing inclination to define their intellectual culture to involve ignorance of the past? Why, even if they choose not to heed the lofty call of disinterested intellectual curiosity, should economists read and write economic history?

II. The pragmatic value of economic history

A. More economic facts

The pragmatic answers are straightforward, the first and most obvious being that history provides the economist with more information with which to put his propositions in jeopardy. The volume of information available will come as a surprise to most economists, consumers as they are. The National Bureau of Economic Research is unusual in this, and its half-century of tillage of the past, harvested as data in thousands of regressions by economists otherwise uninterested in history, amply nourished the new historical economists of the last fifteen years. During the 1950s and 1960s many of them served an apprenticeship in economic observation, to change the metaphor, at the Bureau's social observatory in New York, contributing heavily to the two catalogues of historical objects produced in the late 1950s and the early 1960s (edited by W. N. Parker [82, 1960] and D. S. Brady [6, 1966]).[5] The publication in 1960 of another work in which the historians at the NBER had a hand, together with the Bureau of the Census and the Social Science Research Council [118, 1960], can mark the beginning of the Keplerian stage of the new economic history. The National Bureau's interests were more nomothetic than historical – an interest in quantitative history for the light it could cast on regularities and (eventually) predictabilities of the economic system rather than for the light it could

5. The earlier volume contains most of the papers delivered to the joint meeting of the Conference on Income and Wealth and the American Economic History Association at Williamstown in 1957, a meeting that celebrated the marriage between the NBER and the new economic history. Recently, it is sad to report, the marriage has been drifting towards separation.

cast on history itself – but it would be churlish as well as inaccurate to discount for that reason the role Moses Abramovitz, Arthur Burns, Solomon Fabricant, Raymond Goldsmith, and John Kendrick among many others played in encouraging historical economics. In a discipline increasingly bored by history the Bureau was from the beginning, as Wesley Clair Mitchell put it in 1927, committed to the notion that [74, 1927, p. x]:

> Business cycles consist of exceedingly complex interactions among a considerable number of economic processes, that to gain insight into the interactions one must combine historical studies with quantitative and qualitative analysis, that the phenomena are peculiar to a certain form of economic organization, and that understanding of this scheme of institutions is prerequisite to an understanding of cyclical fluctuations.

Thirty-six years later the commitment to history lived on in the ambition of Milton Friedman and Anna J. Schwartz to write an "analytical narrative" as "a prologue and background for a statistical analysis of the secular and cyclical behavior of money in the United States" [33, 1963, pp. xxi–xxii].

This governing idea of the Bureau – that one could in empirical work go beyond consuming historical facts to producing them, embedding the output in its appropriate historical milieu – was seized on and expanded by the young historical economists of the 1950s and 1960s. It occurred to them that the statistics most economists are content to receive from clean-looking columns of reference books could in fact be constructed for much earlier times than had been thought possible and could be brought to bear after their construction on important historical issues. Brimming from their other courses in graduate school with the new mathematical, statistical, and computational techniques that flowed into the curriculum in the 1950s, they had the tools with which to reshape the historical object. To use symbolically the names of three men whose influence was more than symbolic, the students of Alexander Gerschenkron, Simon Kuznets, and Douglass North were quick learners and saw that if the masters could push measures of American income or Italian industrial output or the American balance of payments back to 1869 or 1881 or 1790, they could too, and more. Robert Gallman, a student of Kuznets, laboriously reconstructed first American commodity output then GNP back to the 1830s [34, 1960; 35, 1966]; he later joined with William Parker, a student of A. P. Usher at Harvard and of Gerschenkron, Usher's successor, in a large-scale sampling of the handwritten manuscripts of the 1860 agricultural census. Richard Easterlin, another student of Kuznets, reconstructed income by state back to 1840, then turned, by way of the long swing, to the analysis of American population back to the middle of the nineteenth century [21, 1960; 22,

1961; 23, 1968]. Alfred Conrad, Paul David, Albert Fishlow, John Meyer, Goran Ohlin, Henry Rosovsky, and Peter Temin, all students of Gerschenkron, made Harvard for a time in the late 1950s and early 1960s a center of research in the new economic history by exploring with economists' eyes the voluminous quantitative records, hitherto neglected, of slavery, agricultural machinery, railways, schooling, and iron and steel in nineteenth-century America, agriculture and governmental finance in nineteenth-century Japan, and population in medieval Europe.[6] At about the same time, another example of simultaneous discovery so common when an idea's time has come, similar centers had sprung up at Rochester (where two students of Kuznets, Robert Fogel and Stanley Engerman, were exploring the records of American railways, slavery, and agriculture in the nineteenth century) and at Purdue (where Jonathan Hughes and Lance Davis, students of North, together with Edward Ames, Nathan Rosenberg, and a startlingly large number of other economists were reinterpreting the record of finance, business cycles, and technological change from the twentieth century to the fourteenth).[7] From 1960 on, these groups gathered annually at a conference at Purdue, transferred to Wisconsin after 1969.[8] Elsewhere Gary Walton [121, 1967] and other students of North joined with North himself in a reconstruction of ocean shipping rates back to the seventeenth century [78, 1968]; Matthew Simon, also working with the fact-makers at Columbia and the NBER in the 1950s, developed balance of payments accounts for 1861–1900 [104, 1960]. Stanley Lebergott examined anew the record of American labor back to 1800 [65, 1964]. Gary Walton in collaboration with James Shepherd [102, 1972], another student of North, constructed trade accounts for the American colonies, and still another student of North, and of R. P. Thomas, Terry Anderson [2, 1972], constructed income and population statistics of New England in the seventeenth century..Roger Weiss estimated the supply of money in the American colonies [122, 1970; 123, 1974]. So it went, and goes.

To some degree these waves of fact originated inside economics. Yet once transferred to specialized historical economists such work developed

6. The monument to this work is Part One of Rosovsky, ed. [96, 1966]. Conrad and Meyer's work is collected in [14, 1964].

7. The products of the Purdue school (*floruit* 1958–1966) are gathered in *Purdue Faculty Papers in Economic History* [88, 1967].

8. The role of foundation financing for this and other projects in cliometrics was critical. The Ford Foundation supported the Purdue meetings for a time, and the Rockefeller Foundation supported a generation of Gerschenkron's students at Harvard. A brief gap in the middle 1960s was filled after 1968 by the National Science Foundation, which has continued since then to encourage cliometrics. When some future historian of economic thought applies refined measures to this history, he will find, I think, that the intellectual marginal product of these grants was extraordinarily high.

a momentum of its own. To take a recent example, the successes of Friedman and Schwartz with the American monetary statistics for 1867 to 1960 inspired historical work on earlier American statistics, then on British, and now on other countries [111, Temin, 1969; 103, Sheppard, 1971]. The historical study of productivity change is another recent example of transferred momentum.[9] The early work by Abramovitz and Solow was, like that of Friedman and Schwartz, nomothetic rather than historical. In the hands of historical economists, however, it gave impetus to the construction of historical series on the quantities and prices of inputs and outputs useful far beyond their initial purpose. Whether or not the theories tested by such economic studies survive the next twist in intellectual fashion – theories of business cycles, consumption, investment behavior, growth, money, or productivity change – the urge to implement them historically continues to generate new and lasting facts.

It will seem strange to economists exposed only to older writing on history or to no writing on history at all to assert that history is a rich mine of statistical information. Badly educated economists believe there are "no data" before the year in which the reference book nearest to hand begins its series on income or wages or exports, and twenty years ago most historians, even economic historians, would have agreed with them. Some still do, dropping with relief the task of measurement before 1900 as soon as they hit on one or another specious reason for doing so: that perfect accuracy is not attainable (estimates have errors), that no individual possesses the attributes of the average individual (distributions have variances), or that statistics dehumanize history (sets are defined for limited characteristics of the objects included). The economist should be aware that the case against statistics in history rests on such pitiable foundations, however pleasing it may be for him to suppose that the historian possesses special tools of insight superior to the spirit-killing tools of his own trade. The computer and the resulting advance in quantitative history, led by the new economic historians, have in any case given statistical agnosticism in history a quaint look.

The historical facts available for the economist's work, in truth, are voluminous beyond the wildest dreams of intellectual avarice, extending back in diminishing volume to the Middle Ages. They require only work and imagination. No Ministry of Agriculture in the thirteenth

9. It is not widely appreciated outside British economic history that the "residual" (in its price dual form) was invented in the 1920s for a historical study of British and American industry by G. T. Jones in his posthumous book *Increasing Returns: A Study of the Relation Between the Size and Efficiency of Industries, with Special Reference to the History of Selected British and American Industries, 1850–1910* [57, 1933, p. 33]. As we shall see again below, reading history has even its theoretical rewards.

century collected statistics on English agricultural output for the benefit of twentieth-century students of agricultural economics. Yet medievalists realized long ago that the annual account of the bailiff to his lord could yield such statistics for the lands farmed by the lord himself; and they have realized more recently that all the land, farmed by the lord or by the peasants, paid tithes to the Church, itself a literate and methodical bureaucracy with a strong self-interest in examining and preserving the records of the tithe from year to year, from which output can be estimated.[10]

A large investment, of course, is necessary to put such collections of facts into usable form, and relative to the size of the investment economic historians, for all their energy, have just begun. A case in point is the astoundingly large collection of genealogical records held for baptizing the dead by the Mormon Church in Salt Lake City, records yielding detailed family histories for many generations.[11] But the student of inherited and acquired human capital could find material for his work that is less difficult than this to handle in the historical record were he to look into it. Surveys, for example, are not a recent invention. The history of Europe and its offshoots from 1086 to the present is littered with them. To take a comparatively recent example, in 1909 the United States Immigration Commission collected questionnaires from over half a million wage earners, some 300,000 of them foreign born, and from 14,000 families totalling 60,000 people, asking them about their occupation, wage income, employment, property income, earnings of the household, housing, rent paid, children, schooling, literacy, languages, money remitted abroad, money when first landed, and many other matters. The Commission surveyed employers on a comparably large scale. The results were published in 42 volumes, which still await the curiosity of economists interested in the accumulation of human capital, the life cycle of income, the participation of women in the labor force, migration, and discrimination.[12] Whenever men write down accounts of their own or others' economic activities the economist has

10. Skeptics will find a look at J. Z. Titow convincing on the wealth of data derivable from bailiffs' accounts [116, 1972]. There does not appear to be a use of the tithe in the English literature, but it has become a commonplace in the French, as in J. Goy and E. Le Roy Ladurie [41, 1972].

11. See the article by Clayne Pope and Larry Wimmer on these records, forthcoming in *Historical Methods Newsletter*.

12. See R. Higgs [50, 1971] for a brief description and use of the *Report*. Higgs used the published volumes, but the manuscript questionnaires, if they have survived, would be still more revealing. The *Report*, incidentally, is a good example of the need for historical sophistication in interpreting historical statistics. It was a nativist and racist document, in the candid style of the age of the Big Stick and the White Man's Burden.

more observations for his science. Economic historians realize that men have been doing this for a long time.

B. Better economic facts

The inspiration for reconstructing the statistics of the past has not come from economics alone, with the result that economic historians can present to economists new classes of facts, richer in many dimensions than modern facts. The very deadness of the men and companies of the nineteenth century and before opens to view records closed to an economist who insists that his subjects be alive or recently deceased. Only a successful antitrust suit pries loose the records of General Electric's conspiracies in restraint of trade, yet the student of industrial organization could if he wished turn to business historians for information on the costs and benefits of collusion that would bring statistical life to his speculations on their magnitudes. The Department of Commerce, the SEC, and the self-interest of the companies expose to public view some scraps of information about the costs, profits, and investments of industrial firms; yet the student of investment and finance could turn to work such as Paul F. McGouldrick's *New England Textiles in the Nineteenth Century: Profits and Investment* [70, 1968] for much richer information.[13] Even for firms that have come now under close and inquisitive government regulation, such as banks, old records, once confidential and therefore candid and complete, are better than new [80, Olmstead, 1974].

Demographic history, long practiced outside of economic history but now influencing it heavily, provides still more examples of the virtues of the dead as objects of economic study. The very records of death, probate inventories and wills are rich sources of facts (see A. H. Jones [56, 1972]). So too are counts of the once living. The 100-year rule of disclosure in, say, Britain makes it possible to do for the 1871 census of population what is impossible for the 1971 census, to scrutinize samples or, if one wishes, the entire population of all coal-mining towns (with their startlingly high fertility) or of all industrial villages (with their startlingly wide variation in family structure).[14] The critical item that is

13. Gavin Wright described this impressive study as "the most 'vertically integrated' study of econometric history to date. McGouldrick has performed every 'stage of production' himself, from the basic source work with a sample of Waltham-Lowell type textile firms (1836–86) to sorting out the various conceptual problems involved in measuring the capital stock, output, capacity, etc., and finally, to regression analysis of dividend and investment behavior" [132, 1971, p. 440].

14. See E. A. Wrigley [135, 1972], especially the essay by Michael Anderson on the use of the British census manuscripts for the study of family structure.

missing in any modern sample from the census is the person's name, for without his name one is unable to link the record of the census to other records. To appreciate the significance of this fact, one has only to reflect that men and governments are more methodical in their record-keeping and more bold – one might say impertinent – in their curiosity today than they were once, and when some future economic historian is able to trace people by their name (or social security number) through all the records of families, businesses, the IRS, the credit bureaus, the schools, the hospitals, and the courts, our knowledge of economic behavior will, to put it mildly, increase. It has occurred to historical demographers that we need not wait until the twenty-first century (and if we wait we are liable in fact to be disappointed, for the cheapening of travel and the spread of the telephone – *sans* tap and tape – has impoverished the written record). If it is important for certain issues in labor economics, for example, to have collections of economic biographies of people, the historian stands ready to supply them in detail. The work of the Cambridge Group for the History of Population and Social Structure, building on the work of French historical demographers after the War, has developed two centuries of family histories in Britain from "nominal record linkage," to use the jargon, applied to birth, death, and marriage registers back to the sixteenth century.[15] In what is perhaps the most ambitious project of this sort to date, scholars at the University of Montreal are reconstituting the entire population of Quebec from the beginning of the colony to the French and Indian War, recording every notice of every person in the remarkably complete records of French Canada and linking them. As the age of economists and calculators dawns, statistics such as these can be linked with a widening array of records on income, property holdings, business, education, and the like to provide life histories much superior to the recent samples worked over so lovingly in any current issue of the *Journal of Political Economy* or the *American Economic Review*.

The census is, of course, a survey on a massive scale, and when the manuscripts are open – *i.e.*, when the census is old – there are few limits on economic curiosity. The Parker-Gallman work mentioned earlier, for example, matched the manuscripts of the American census of agriculture in 1860 with those of the census of population – matching that cannot be done on recent, closed censuses, that is, without the name of the respondent – and produced a full profile of those involved in farming enterprises. Because the 1860 census inquired into the wealth of those it

15. A selection from the work of the Cambridge Group is worth including in any reading list for the new labor economics. For a nontechnical summary, see E. A. Wrigley [134, 1969], and for a recent example in detail of such work, T. P. R. Laslett [64, 1972].

surveyed, it is possible to examine the determinants of the distribution of wealth in 1860 at a level of detail unattainable with modern records, and Lee Soltow is currently exploiting these possibilities [106, 1975]. Roger Ransom and Richard Sutch were able to extract from the manuscript census of 1880 intimate details on a random sample of 5,283 farms in the South and to confront the issue of racial discrimination more directly than is typically possible with modern data [89, forth.]. By comparison with such rich and varied facts, the economist's usual store looks pitiably thin.

Nor are the errors in these facts larger than those in modern facts. It is naive on two counts to believe that historical statistics have larger errors, naive both in overestimating the quality of modern statistics and in underestimating the quality of historical statistics. When pressed an economist will usually admit that his data on, say, prices in the American economy over the last twenty years are in error to some large and unknown degree because the quality of the goods in question has improved, because the list prices correspond poorly with the transaction prices, because the definition and relevance of the sample is in doubt, or because the price index used corresponds poorly with the conceptually correct definition. He will admit, too, that these errors introduce biases of unknown sign into his multivariate regressions containing prices as an independent variable. He will run the regressions anyway, comforting himself with the mistaken reflections that his data are as good as one can get and that his estimates are in any case consistent.

Confronted on both sides by skepticism, from his colleagues in history that statistical demonstrations in history are persuasive and from his colleagues in economics that historical statistics are reliable, the historical economist cannot take this line. He has in fact developed an art of creative self-doubt that is practiced in some other fields of economics and might be with profit practiced more widely. The habit of testing the sensitivity of one's argument to possible errors in its data or possible mistakes in its analytical assumptions is widespread among scientists and historians, but is not among economists. Many, of course, understand the frailty of "data" and act on this understanding. The tradition of the National Bureau and of the more careful empiricists outside it of publishing a full description of how data were made and where they might be wrong, in the hope (so often vain) that users will read it, fits well with historiographic traditions: in his preface to Albert Fishlow's *American Railroads and the Transformation of the Ante-Bellum Economy*, Alexander Gerschenkron drew special attention to "the statistical appendixes in which the author offers a full insight into his laboratory and without which no real appreciation of the importance of the study and the validity of its interpretative results is possible" [27,

Fishlow, 1965, p. viii]. Yet it is rare for the major journals in general economics to publish factual revisionism such as Robert J. Gordon's "$45 Billion of U.S. Private Investment Has Been Mislaid," perhaps because it is rare for economists to write it [39, 1969].[16] Zvi Griliches put his finger on the reason many economists are uninterested in the sources of data and their errors [42, 1974, p. 973]:

> Much of the problem, I think, arises because of the separation in economics between data producers and data analyzers. By and large, we do not produce our own data and, hence, do not feel responsible for it.[17]

For economic historians, required to collect their own materials and imbued with the historian's rather than the economist's attitude toward their handling, the buck stops here. Robert Fogel's *Railroads and American Economic Growth* [28, 1964] is perhaps the fullest example to date of this attitude.[18] Combining the traditions of creative self-doubt in economic history and in project evaluation, its 260 pages are directed at producing essentially one number, the benefit half of a cost-benefit study of nineteenth-century investment in American railways. Fogel began this research believing that he would confirm the assumption of the indispensability of the railways underlying earlier treatments (by Schumpeter and Rostow, for example), but found to his surprise that the facts cast doubt on it. To test this doubt, therefore, he directed his energies to estimating an upper bound on the contribution of railroads to national income and found it low; therefore, he concluded that railroads were far from indispensable for American economic growth. Historical facts are often better for economists' purposes than recent facts: they are often more detailed, voluminous, and accurate, and what errors they contain are treated with respect.

But there is, of course, another sense in which they are "better," for history performs experiments: history provides the economist not only

16. That George Jaszi of the U.S. Department of Commerce was able to argue in a comment that Gordon had discovered nothing new makes the other point: details of data, even important details, are not interesting to economists [55, 1970]. In his reply to Jaszi, Gordon asserts that "the economics profession and particularly production function investigators had remained ignorant of government owned, privately operated capital" [40, 1970, p. 945] before his article. This appears to be correct.
17. Having drawn on Griliches's thinking here, it would be impolite to add that, the studies on which he comments make no attempt to remove errors by remeasurement and embark instead, to repeat Leontief's acerbic remark quoted earlier, on "devising a new statistical procedure, however tenuous, that makes it possible to squeeze out one more unknown parameter from a given set of data" [66, 1971, p. 3].
18. Fogel's calculations were for 1890. Fishlow's *American Railroads* is a similar study for the early nineteenth century [27, 1965]. Together they constitute a brilliant reinterpretation of the role of transportation in American growth, for which they were awarded in 1971 the Schumpeter Prize. The account of Fogel's experience derives from conversations with him.

with more rich and accurate facts but also with more variable facts. A macabre example of the point is T. W. Schultz's use of Indian statistics of agricultural output and population during the influenza epidemic of 1918–1919 to argue that the marginal product of labor was positive and roughly equal to the going wage: output fell as the working population did, and labor therefore was not "surplus," contrary to the assumption of much work on economic development, particularly Indian economic development [100, 1964, pp. 63–70]. An equally dismal experiment, the Great Depression, will remain for a long time to come the great testing ground for theories of aggregate economics, as monetarists, fiscalists, and others have on occasion realized. The appreciation of the pitfalls of monetary policy was much increased by the argument of Friedman and Schwartz that, far from having little impact, it was powerfully mishandled in the 1930s; and the appreciation of the potential of fiscal policy was much increased by the argument of E. Cary Brown that, far from failing, it was not in fact tried [8, 1956] (see also L. C. Peppers [85, 1973]).

That history has performed the very experiment he wishes had been performed must occur from time to time to every economist. He must realize, too, that economics is like astronomy an observational science, taking its data and its controls, alas, as it finds them. Yet he fixes his telescope (during his infrequent trips to the observatory) on the sun, moon, and nearer planets alone, for two reasons: first, he believes that these objects close to home are the only ones that provide insight into how the home planet behaves; and, second, he believes that to look beyond the near solar system, not to speak of the galaxy, is to look into another structure, where familiar laws (*e.g.*, there are six planets, stars are little points fixed to a sphere, and light moves in straight lines) might not apply. The belief that history is irrelevant to public policy will be examined below and will prove to be incorrect. The incorrectness of the belief that history might come from a different structure than the quarterly national income figures since the War and is therefore to be ignored is plain enough. To those who adopt the argument in order to limit the amount of empirical work they have to do, one can only sigh and turn back to scholars who take scholarship seriously. These innocents will always believe that "empirical work" is a conflation of the appendix to the *Economic Report of the President* and Johnston's *Econometric Methods*. Even serious and sophisticated economic scholars are prone to adopt the assumption that the past has a different structure without testing it. The cliometricians have been forced to test the assumption at every turn, facing as they do scholars in both economics and in history who adopt it as a matter of course. Indeed, if the findings of the new economic history of the last fifteen years or so had to be put in one sentence, it would be this: in the eighteenth and nineteenth centuries men sought profit in as clear-headed and competitive a way as an economist dreaming of auctioneers and perfect markets might wish. Following Lenin and Veblen, of course, one is free to assert that the atomistic competition of the age of Smith and Mill is dead, that simple models of competitive behavior might apply to the nineteenth century but not to the twentieth. This variant assertion, however, merely reinforces the point, for it has never been tested, at any rate not in a way that would convince someone who did not believe it to begin with, despite its large role in the political economy of the last fifty years. Even if one could show that for a particular experiment (the effect of government spending on employment, say) the environment of the nineteenth century was so different from that of the 1970s that little could be learned about the present structure from the comparison, it would remain true that structures continue to change, as the often discouraging and sometimes comical results of large scale econometric models suggest. History, like the study of other countries and cultures, is an education in structural change. A familiar example of the more usual practice is that of dropping the War years from regressions, as intrusions from another structure. Wars, however, recur, and it behooves the economic scientist, even if his interests in science extend only to its uses for today's public policy, to understand how war changes the way economies behave (see, for example, D. F. Gordon and G. M. Walton [38, 1974] and Mancur Olson [81, 1963]). Paul David put a similar point in the following way [15, 1975, p. 14]:

> An equation that fits the data well for half the available run of time-series observations and not for the rest is, for the ordinary applied economist, a failure; he will have to resist the impulse to discard the recalcitrant data in presenting his results. By contrast . . . the economic historian may hail the half-failed regression equation as nothing less than a triumph – in the sense that by uncovering the occurrence of a change in economic structure, it signals him to set to work to learn what happened in history.

Limiting one's field of vision to close objects, in any case, is as peculiar in economics as it would be in astronomy. Examples of historical experiments larger, clearer, and more decisive than most that could be framed on the basis of recent experience can be generated at will. The migrations from one country or another in the last twenty years that have alarmed modern governments are dwarfed by the migrations of the nineteenth century.[19] The same can be said of the migrations of capital:

19. There is a voluminous literature by historical economists on these: B. Thomas [114, 1954], R. A. Easterlin [22, 1961], and many more, among them P. Hill [52, 1970], L. Neal and P. Uselding [75, 1972], and A. C. Kelley [58, 1965].

if one wishes to measure the effects of foreign investment on the sending or receiving country, the British, French, Argentinian and Canadian experiences of the late nineteenth century are the best available cases in point.[20] From 1870 to 1913 Britain sent one-third of her savings abroad. If one wishes to measure the effects, burdensome or otherwise, of government debt, the British experience with the debt from the Napoleonic War or the American experience with the debt from the Civil War are the clearest experiments, taking place as they did before the Internal (or Inland) Revenue codes among other disturbing influences reached their present chaotic state (for the American case see J. G. Williamson [130, 1974]). In the 1820s the British government debt was on the order of two and a half times national income, about the same as the present ratio in the United States.[21] If one wishes to measure the impact of legal changes, the experiences in the nineteenth century and before with laws of incorporation, school attendance, child labor, and the like are large and varied experiments [109, Sylla, 1969; 63, Landes and Solmon, 1972; 124, West, 1975; 99, Sanderson, 1974]. So too, if one wishes to measure the impact of floating exchange rates, are the experiences of the United States in the 1860s and 1870s, of Britain from 1914 to 1925, or of China in the 1930s. In a time of free banking, as in the United States before the Civil War, one can examine the consequences of free entry [92, Rockoff, 1974]; in a time of war and unfettered capital markets, as during the Civil War, one can examine the responsiveness of expectations to events [94, Roll, 1972]; in a time of massive new investment in public hygiene, as in American cities after the Civil War, one can examine the value of health [71, Meeker, 1972; 72, 1974]. History is society's laboratory.

20. See Michael Edelstein [24, 1974] and works cited there. The seminal work on the case of a receiving country is Jacob Viner [120, 1924]. The other books from the Taussig school of international finance published at Harvard in the 1920's and 1930's were also richly historical: J. H. Williams [128, 1920], H. D. White [126, 1933], and W. F. Beach [4, 1935]. Taussig himself as a young man wrote history [101, 1888].

21. One must include gross social security wealth, gross of the present value of social security taxes (as estimated by Martin Feldstein [26, 1974, p. 915, col. 3]). In 1971 GNP was on the order of $1,000 billion, the gross government debt $400 billion, and Feldstein's estimate of gross social security wealth $2,000 billion, for a ratio of about 2.4. In 1821 the GNP of the United Kingdom was on the order of £340 millions (based on the P. Deane and W. A. Cole [19, 1962] estimate for Great Britain increased by an estimate of Irish income at two-thirds the British level *per capita*) and the funded and unfunded government debt £840 million [73, Mitchell, 1962, pp. 8, 366, 402], for a ratio of about 2.5. The ratio of payments of interest to GNP in the U.K. in 1821 was 9 percent, about the same as interest, income security, and veterans benefits and services to GNP in the U.S.A. in 1971, namely, 8 percent [73, Mitchell, 1962, p. 396; 119, *Economic Report of the President*, 1975, p. 325]. These-comparisons could be refined to include local governments and non-interest-bearing debt.

C. *Better economic theory*

The products of this laboratory affect economic ideas in ways that few economists recognize. The headline of today's newspaper, to be sure, has an effect, the more so as money for research follows the headline with a short lag. But historical findings, true or false, underlie the reaction to the headline. To pick some influential historical findings that have recently been shown to be false by cliometricians, the finding that the increase in the capital stock per man left much of the increase in income per man unexplained set off in the late 1950s an intellectual explosion in models of growth with technological change. The historical finding that the rate of savings was constant over a long period set off in the early 1950s a somewhat smaller explosion in the theory of the consumption function. The historical finding that the share of labor in income has been constant set off in the 1930s still another in the theory of the production function. The influence of economic theory on the writing of history is apparent in most pieces of new economic history, but the influence of economic history on the writing of theory is apparent only in the seminal pieces, to be forgotten in the sequel. The high ratio of historical reserves to theoretical deposits in the work of Robert Solow, Milton Friedman, or Paul Douglas is not maintained in the work of their intellectual customers, with the result that the intellectual money supply is a large multiple of the factual base and subject to violent fluctuations. Rondo Cameron put the point well:

> In analogous discussions concerning the role of theory in historical research the argument is frequently made (perhaps because it is valid) that the historian will inevitably be guided by some a priori ideas. It is desirable, therefore, that these ideas be made explicit and systematized if possible. The choice, in other words, is not between theory and no theory, but explicit, consciously formulated theory and implicit, unconscious theorizing. Much the same can be said for the use of history by theorists. Even the most scornful ahistorical economist makes some use of history: his own experience, the experience of his generation, or the loose historical generalizations which abound in the folklore of even highly sophisticated societies. [9, 1965, p. 112; *cf.* 74, Mitchell, 1927, p. 59]

The obvious case in point is the theory of economic growth, in which a particular set of historical conventions dominate the argument. These conventions – described by Nicholas Kaldor in 1958 as "stylized facts," a defensive usage that has been adopted widely – were developed in the 1950s, once intellectual putty but now clay, before new economic historians had begun in earnest to announce the unstylized facts. It is at least uncertain that their work will confirm the constancy of the capital/output ratio, of the rate of profit, or of the rate of growth of output per man and of the capital stock. As Robert Solow remarks at the conclusion of a brief inquiry into the factual relevance of these elements in the steady state of economic growth, "the steady state is not a bad place for the theory of growth to start, but may be a dangerous place for it to end" [105, 1970, p. 7]. From the historical work by economists over the last two decades or so, ignored by growth theorists, it would seem so. During the second half of the nineteenth century, for example, the capital/output ratio in America rose by a factor of two, while falling by a third in Britain; during the first half of the twentieth century, the ratio in America fell 22 percent, while remaining roughly constant in Britain.[22] It may be that a fuller definition of "capital" to include acquired human skills and a fuller definition of "output" to include production in the household would yield different results. Economic historians, facing long periods of history in which the relation of the narrow to the full definitions have changed radically, are forced routinely to consider refinements of this sort. Whether refined or not the facts accumulated by them for the study of economic growth warrant a second look. This is perhaps most clear in the matter of technological change, the chief jewel and the chief embarrassment of the modern theory of growth. As R. R. Nelson and S. G. Winter have recently emphasized [76, 1974], historians of technology such as Paul David, Peter Temin, and Nathan Rosenberg have much to tell the theorists, but the theorists' minds are fixed on other things (see, *e.g.*, Rosenberg [95, 1972] or David [15, 1975]).

The sins of pseudo-history are not, of course, confined to mathematical theorists of economic growth. There is nothing in words as distinct from equations, however frequent the appeals in the words to the alleged experience of history, that protects looser theorizers from the error of irrelevancy. Ricardo's notion of rising land rents, Marx's of immiseriza-tion of the industrial proletariate, Lenin's of the profits from imperialism, Dennis Robertson's of foreign trade as an engine of growth, Harold Innis's of staple products as centers of growth, W. A. Lewis's of development with unlimited supplies of labor, or W. W. Rostow's of a

22. For the United Kingdom this is the ratio in 1855, 1900, and 1958 of fixed reproducible capital net of depreciation to net domestic product (see C. H. Feinstein, Tables 43 and 20, with an allowance for capital consumption based on Table 1 [25, 1972]); for the United States the ratios in 1844–53, 1894–1903, and 1958 of depreciable capital to net national product (Gallman's Table 2.9 in Davis *et al.* [18, 1972]). The two books from which these figures come, incidentally, illustrate the role of social observatories in the encouragement of new economic history: Feinstein's is one of a series published under the auspices of the National Institute of Economic and Social Research (the British equivalent of the NBER) and the Cambridge Department of Applied Economics (an interpretive volume by Feinstein and R. C. O. Matthews is to follow); eight of the twelve authors of the Davis *et al.* book have worked at the NBER, and the book itself amounts to an interpretive summary of the long inquiry by them and others (notably Simon Kuznets) at the Bureau into trends in American economic growth.

take-off induced by great inventions and a sharp rise in the savings rate, to name a few, have not fared well in confrontation with historical fact.[23] This is not to say that theorists should forsake their blackboards or their typewriters for the nearest archive. An occasional trip to the library might help. And they should be doubtful of their own unassisted ability to summarize historical experience in a few stylized facts.

The contribution of history to theory is not confined to a supply of factual grist for the theorists' mill. The use of theory in economic history illuminates the theory and tests it, and in this respect economic history is no different from other applied economics. An application of input-output analysis to the measurement of effective protection in nineteenth-century America tests the usefulness of this tool in the same way as does an application to the measurement of effective protection in present-day Pakistan [127, Whitney, 1968; 43, Guisinger, 1970]. An agricultural economist, at least, would be comfortable with the use of simple models of supply and demand to explore the growth of the American ship-building, cotton textile, or iron industries, and would not be surprised that use deepens them.[24] Nor would the student of international trade, aggregate economics, or labor markets find anything strange in applications of models of two sector general equilibrium to the American economy before and after the Civil War or to the British economy during the Napoleonic War,[25] of money and prices to the British and American business cycle in the early nineteenth century [113, Temin, 1974], or of marginal productivity to slavery or post-bellum sharecropping.[26] He might be a little surprised that such remote issues can be reached with tools perfected in the middle of the twentieth century and might, too, admire the skill with which issues long cut off from

23. See, in order, P. Lindert [68, 1974]; R. M. Hartwell [46, 1970]; R. P. Thomas [115, 1968]; I. B. Kravis [62, 1970]; E. J. Chambers and D. F. Gordon [11, 1966]; A. C. Kelley, J. G. Williamson, and R. J. Cheetham [59, 1972]; and W. W. Rostow, ed. [97, 1963]. The work by Fishlow and Fogel on the American railway in the nineteenth century was in part motivated by Rostow's large claims for it as the critical innovation in American growth.

24. See among many others C. K. Harley [45, 1973]; R. B. Zevin [138, 1971]; and R. W. Fogel and S. L. Engerman [29, 1969], reprinted in Fogel and Engerman [30, 1971]. This book [30, 1971], incidentally, is a good selection of work on America by new economic historians, as is P. Temin [112, 1973].

25. See C. Pope [87, 1972]; P. Passell and G. Wright [84, 1972]; P. Passell and M. Schmundt [83, 1971]; G. Hueckel [53, 1973]; and, the most ambitious work to date along these lines, J. G. Williamson [130, 1974]. Cliometricians have been among the few economists to use non-linear general equilibrium models empirically.

26. C. D. Goldin [36, 1973; 37, 1976] and Fogel and Engerman [31, 1974] are recent examples of a large literature on slavery deriving from the early work of Conrad and Meyer [13, 1958]. J. D. Reid, Jr. [91, 1973] is an example of an equally large literature on sharecropping by cliometricians, among them Rogert Higgs [51, 1974], Stephen DeCanio [20, 1974], and Roger Ransom and Richard Sutch [89, forth.].

economic thinking are brought back to it. But on the whole he would perceive good economic history to be simply good applied economics.

It should be pointed out, parenthetically, that in an important sense his perception would be wrong, for good economic history must also be good history. It is this requirement that puts economic history at the highest levels on a par of difficulty with, say, econometrics at the highest levels, which requires a mastery of statistics, or mathematical economics at the highest levels, which requires a mastery of mathematics.[27] True, some new economic historians believe that economic history consists of the application of production theory or econometrics to a more or less vague notion of what happened in history, just as other economists believe that economic thinking consists of the application of Lagrangean multipliers or optimal control theory to a more or less vague notion of what is to be maximized. But the best new economic historians are historians as well as economists, just as the best economists are social scientists as well as applied mathematicians.

Even at the lower levels of historical as distinct from economic sophistication, however, reforming the economic history of the late 1950s into good applied economics, exhibiting in the reformation the power of modern economic theory, was a remarkable achievement, comparable with the reformations over the last decade in the economics of politics, property rights, labor markets, and the household. For a time the new economic historians, like the new labor economists and the rest, devoted themselves to this task of intellectual arbitrage. But the theoretical rewards of economic history are greater. Any extension of economics to new subjects sets new questions with which existing theory cannot deal, and for which new theory must be created. Economic historians have been bold in this. Their theoretical boldness arises in part from the recalcitrance of the world: when the scholar's chief purpose is to understand a piece of behavior, historical or current, rather than to test a familiar economic idea (still less to develop its logic), he takes his insights from wherever he can get them, whether or not they bear the *imprimatur* of an economic bishop.[28] It arises, too, from the unusually close contact that historical economists have with another discipline,

27. Any economic historian has had the experience of colleagues announcing to him that they, too, are economic historians. It usually develops that they have run a regression back to 1929. The effect is similar to that of an economist who uses arithmetic announcing to his colleagues in mathematical economics that he, too, is a mathematical economist.

28. A good example is J. G. Williamson, especially Chapter V [129, 1964]. After using without success the usual theories to explain the American balance of payments in the nineteenth century, he developed finally what is now known as the monetary theory, anticipating by several years its first theoretical statement. P. B. Whale, beginning with a similar historical problem, had done the same in 1937 [125, 1937].

history. They have internalized the intellectual values of historians more than sociological economists have internalized those of sociologists or legal economists those of lawyers, and in consequence are peculiarly inclined to face questions for which economics has no ready answer. A case in point is the question of why political and social revolutions occur, a question that even most political scientists and sociologists, contrary to what one might expect, carefully avoid. It is impossible for a historian who wishes to write coherent history to avoid the question, even if he wished to, for revolutions, such as the American Revolution and the Civil War, are the stuff of change and change the stuff of history.[29] For this reason a good deal of the new economic history in America has centered around the causes of the Revolution and the Civil War, approaching the causes (as comparative advantage dictates) with the characteristically economic assumption of rational and informed self-interest. The new economic history made a contribution, albeit a modest one, to the understanding of the American Revolution by measuring the economic burden of the Navigation Acts and finding it small (see P. D. McClelland [69, 1969] and works cited there); it made a contribution to the understanding of the Civil War by measuring the economic burden on the South of the tariff or of the restrictions on the expansion of slavery and finding these also to be small [87, Pope, 1972; 84, Passell and Wright, 1972]. If one believes that economic interests determine political behavior, then, one can look to new economic historians for measurements of these interests. If one does not believe it, one can look to new economic historians for whatever economic measure is to the point: by showing, for example, that slavery was not economically moribund on the eve of the Civil War, the new economic historians were able to reject the theme of many historians sympathetic with the South that military intervention to abolish slavery was unnecessary.[30] In any case, the application of economics to politics raises the theoretical issue, neglected by most economists (namely, most economists to the left of Milton Friedman and to the right of Paul Sweezy), of bringing politics into economic models.[31]

29. Coherence was sacrificed for the gains from specialization in the collective volume by Davis, Easterlin, Parker, and others [18, 1972], in so many other ways such a fine summary of the work of the cliometricians. Its focus on the economic revolution (its subtitle was "An Economist's History of the United States") required it to bypass the contributions of new economic history to political history. The Revolution, Jackson and the Second Bank, the tariff, slavery, the Civil War, and the free coinage of silver occupy, according to the index, 20 pages in total, smaller than the single entry "Canals."

30. This was explicit in Conrad and Meyer [13, 1958], although it was not put on a firm base until Y. Yasuba [136, 1961]. *Cf.* G. Gunderson [44, 1974].

31. Violent revolution and civil war are not the only political events to attract the attention of new

The new economic history has turned increasingly in the past few years to issues such as this, central to the development of economics as a social science. The deepening of the study of American slavery, for example, notably by Fogel and Engerman in their recent book [31, 1974], has opened the issue of the role of coercion in economic society. Outside the growing band of Marxist economists, who are like their colleagues on the right unusually historically-minded, the limit of thinking on the matter in economics has been an occasional remark on command compared with market economies, assuming in the background that market economies use little coercion beyond taxes, enforcement of contract, and the criminal law. The assumption has never been appropriate for that quarter of the population under the age of responsibility, and in a slave society, of course, it is still less appropriate. Fogel and Engerman were able to show, however, that Southern slaveowners, capitalistic as they were, used market mechanisms as well as the whip to manipulate their slaves. In "Slavery: The Progressive Institution?" a long review of the book, two other economic historians, Paul David and Peter Temin, argued that the economic theory to deal with such mixed systems of enticement and coercion does not exist [16, 1974, esp. pp. 778–83]. It may not, and this is the challenge to theory.

The challenges arise from the wide perspective forced on the economic historian by his subject. Obviously, one cannot study the long swing, if one wishes to, without long swings in income [61, Klotz and Neal, 1973]; one cannot study the long-run determinants of city size without long runs of city sizes [108, Swanson and Williamson, 1974]. But the point goes deeper than this. An economist whose attention is riveted on the present cannot be expected to ask why the institutions of the labor and capital markets change, as Lance Davis and Douglass North did in *Institutional Change and American Economic Growth* [17, 1971], still less to ask why fundamental social arrangements rise and decay, as North and Robert Thomas did in *The Rise of the Western World* [79, 1973]. At a more modest level, few economists outside of agricultural economics and economic history have given serious attention to measuring (as distinct from theorizing about) managerial ability or, in more elaborate language, entrepreneurship, that phantom of the theory of the firm. The measurement was forced on economists studying agriculture by the insistence of government planners who were not economists that farmers are irrational;

economic historians: see J. Pincus [86, 1972] on the causes of early nineteenth-century tariffs; E. P. LeVeen [67, 1971] on the British suppression of the slave trade; R. B. Freeman [32, 1972] – an example of fine historical work by a non-historian – on the rise of educational discrimination in the South; R. Higgs [49, 1971, chap. IV] and J. Bowman and R. H. Keehn [5, 1974] on agrarian protest in the late nineteenth century; and G. Wright [133, 1974] on the political economy of New Deal spending.

it was forced on economists studying the Victorian economy by the insistence of historians who were not economists that British businessmen in the late nineteenth century were irrational as well [98, Sandberg, 1974]. And even agricultural economists, on the whole exceptional among economists for their long historical perspective, cannot be expected to ask why the peculiarities of peasant land tenure have survived in many countries for centuries and why they were dissolved in land reform.

The Icelandic poet Einor Benediktsson put it this way: "To the past you must look/ If originality you wish to build;/ Without the teaching of the past/ You see not what is new."[32]

D. Better economic policy

Few intellectual activities are more mischievous when done poorly than economics or history. The power of fallacious economic reasoning or fallacious historical example to damage society is obvious: the pseudo-economics of mercantilism has been reducing trade and protecting vested interests for many centuries; the pseudo-history of the Aryan "race" lent dignity to German fascism. The combination of bad economics and bad history in bad economic history is pernicious. To be sure, the makers of economic policy have ample opportunity for falling into error without the excuse of economic history poorly grasped. Yet, to specialize Keynes's frequently quoted remarks on the subject – frequently quoted, perhaps, because they are correct – the ideas of economic historians, both when they are right and when they are wrong, are more powerful than is commonly understood. Madmen in authority, who hear voices in the air, are distilling their frenzy from an understanding of the economic events of a few years back. Practical men, who believe themselves to be quite exempt from any historical influences, are usually the slaves of historical example.

The industrial revolution, it is said, came to Britain suddenly and simply around 1760 in a wave of gadgets, justifying policies for growth that equip illiterate peasants with computers. Foreign trade, it is said, was an engine of economic growth in Britain (and, lately, Japan), justifying a policy of impoverishing one's citizens in the pursuit of exports. Floating exchange rates, it is said, added to the chaos of the international economy in the 1930s, justifying the sacrifice of employment to the maintenance of $4.86, $2.80, $2,40, or (most recently) $2.00 to the pound sterling. Railways, it is said, were crucial to industrialization in the nineteenth century, justifying policies in non-

32. I owe this quotation to Jon Sigurdsson of the Icelandic Economic Development Institute.

industrial countries in the twentieth of shoring up railways with subsidies and of eliminating trucking competition. Industrialization, it is said, brutalized the working class, justifying among most educated people a deep suspicion of capitalism. Labor unions, it is said, were responsible for a good part of the increase in wages since 1900, justifying government protection of extortionate plumbers, electricians, and butchers. The competitive supply of professional services in the nineteenth century, it is said, grieviously injured consumers, justifying official cartels of doctors and undertakers. Business monopoly, it is said, has spread greatly during the last century, justifying public hostility towards big business. The payment of competitive interest on demand or time deposits, it is said, created instability in the banking system, justifying laws to forbid it. Air pollution, it is said, is worse now than it was once, justifying draconic policies to combat it. Fossil fuel, it is said, is being used at a faster rate relative to proven reserves now than fifty years ago, justifying national goals of subsidizing new fuels and abandoning international trade in oil. Whether these are good or bad policies, to the extent that their public propaganda and their private inspiration rest on false historical premises – and most of them to a large extent do – their rationale is full of doubt.

One could add cases in point without limit, but two of the more important will suffice. The muddle of exchange rates in the 1920's and 1930's led to the development of the elasticities approach to the balance of payments, which to this day dominates theory and policy. The approach has been under attack now for several years on logical ground, but the development of an alternative will depend on a reinterpretation of past experience with exchange rates.[33] The muddle of employment in the 1930s and the interpretation of the muddle by Keynes and others led to the postwar policy of full employment and to a concentration on fiscal methods to achieve it. Their interpretation bears rethinking. As Hugh Rockoff remarked in a recent survey of the American experience with free entry to banking, "One purpose of history is to broaden our conception of the possible" [93, 1975, p. 176]. The apprehension of true history as well as the correction of false contributes to public policy because an economist whose memory is limited to the recent past has a narrow conception of the possible. We may in our praise and criticism of present governments be willing or unwilling slaves of historical example, but slaves we are.

33. Presently much of the effort of the International Trade Workshop at the University of Chicago is devoted to applying the "monetary" approach to the experience of England, France, and Japan before the Second World War.

E. *Better economists*

In the light of all this, it is not surprising that Smith and Marshall, Schumpeter and Keynes were deeply historical in their thinking. An economist, least of all a cliometrician, cannot argue that there are no substitutes for history in the production of important economics, no more than he can argue that there was no substitute for the railway in American economic growth. Some important economics has been written by historical illiterates, although it must be admitted that cases are difficult to find. The work of Edgeworth as distilled in modern textbooks, for example, seems a likely candidate until one reads the work itself and stumbles over tags from Herodotus. In much of the work of J. R. Hicks it is not obvious that history plays a part, yet he lectured on medieval history in one of his early academic appointments, has been by his own account a lifelong reader of the *Economic History Review*, and published in 1969 *A Theory of Economic History* [48, 1969, p. v] (see also [47, 1953]). History is a stimulus to the economic imagination, defining and stretching the limits of economic craft. An economist learns from his other studies how to see, to label, and to repair the pieces of the economic building. From history he learns whence the building came, how its neighbors were built, and why a building in one place was and will be built differently from one in another. The wider questions that face economics are historical. If history is useful to an economist's work, it is still more useful to his education.

It would be unreasonable to propose in the style of the German historical school that history dominate the education of economists, that abstractions of maximization be abandoned in favor of the concreteness (or, more commonly in practice, the verbal abstractions) of history. The reaction to this unreasonable proposal, indeed, explains some of the drift towards present-mindedness in modern economics. Yet, as the English economic historian T. S. Ashton said [3, (1946) 1971, p. 177]:

> The whole discussion as to whether deduction or induction is the proper method to use in the social sciences is, of course, juvenile: it is as though we were to debate whether it were better to hop on the right foot or on the left. Sensible men with two feet know that they are likely to make better progress if they walk on both.

An economist hopping along without a historical leg, unless he is a decathalon athlete, has a narrow perspective on the present, shallow economic ideas, little appreciation for the strengths and weaknesses of economic data, and small ability to apply economics to large issues. If we interrogate our students, we will find that they believe economic research to consist chiefly of a passing acquaintance with the latest pronouncement of the Council of Economic Advisors, the latest assumption relaxed in an economic model, and the latest revision in the local canned regression program. One does not have to look beyond their teachers to find where they acquired this peculiar set of notions.

For fifteen years or so cliometricians have been explaining to their colleagues in history the wonderful usefulness of economics. It is time they began explaining to their colleagues in economics the wonderful usefulness of history. Wonderfully useful it is, a storehouse of economic facts tested by skepticism, a collection of experiments straining the power of economics in every direction, a fount of economic ideas, a guide to policy, and a school for social scientists. It is no accident that some of the best minds in economics value it highly. What a pity, then, that the rest have drifted away. Does the past have useful economics? Of course it does.

References[34]

1. American Economic Association. *Index of economic journals*. Vols. I–VI. Homewood, Ill.: Irwin, 1961–65.
2. Anderson, T., "The Economic Growth of Seventeenth-Century New England: A Measurement of Regional Income," unpublished doctoral dissertation, University of Washington, 1972.
3. Ashton, T. S., "The Relation of Economic History to Economic Theory," *Economica, N. S.*, May 1946, *13*, pp. 81–96; reprinted in *The study of economic history*. Edited by N. B. Harte. London: Frank Cass, 1971, pp. 161–80.
4. Beach, W. F., *British international gold movements and banking policy, 1881–1913*. Cambridge: Harvard University Press, 1935.
5. Bowman, J. and Keehn, R. H., "Agricultural Terms of Trade in Four Midwestern States, 1870–1900," *J. Econ. Hist.*, Sept. 1974, *34*, pp. 592–609.
6. Brady, D. S., ed. *Output, employment, and productivity in the United States after 1800*. Conference on Research in Income and Wealth, Studies in Income and Wealth, Vol. 30. New York: National Bureau of Economic Research; distributed by Columbia University Press, 1966.
7. Bronfenbrenner, M., "Trends, Cycles, and Fads in Economic Writing," *Amer. Econ. Rev.*, Supplement, May 1966, *56*(2), pp. 538–52.
8. Brown, E. C., "Fiscal Policy in the 'Thirties: A Reappraisal," *Amer. Econ. Rev.*, Dec. 1956, *46*(5), pp. 857–79.
9. Cameron, R., "Has Economic History a Role in an Economist's Education?" *Amer. Econ. Rev.*, Supplement, May 1965, *55*(2), pp. 112–15.
10. Caves, R., "Export-Led Growth and the New Economic History," in *Trade, balance of payments and growth*. Edited by J. N. Bhagwati *et al.* Amsterdam: North Holland, 1971.
11. Chambers, E. J. and Gordon, D. F., "Primary Products and Economic Growth: An Empirical Measurement," *J. Polit. Econ.*, Aug. 1966, *74*(4), pp. 315–32.

34. A complete bibliography on American economic history useful to economics, even if confined to "cliometrics" in its recent incarnation, would run to many hundreds of items. This selection misses much important work. Items 18, 30, 49, 88, 112, 130, and 132 contain alternative selections.

12. Coats, A. W., "The Role of Scholarly Journals in the History of Economics: An Essay," *J. Econ. Lit.*, March 1971, *9*(1), pp. 29–44.
13. Conrad, A. H. and Meyer, J. R., "The Economics of Slavery in the Ante-Bellum South," *J. Polit. Econ.*, April 1958, *66*, pp. 95–130; reprinted in [14, 1964].
14. ———. *The economics of slavery and other studies in econometric history*. Chicago: Aldine, 1964.
15. David, P. A., *Technical choice, innovation and economic growth: Essays on American and British experience in the nineteenth century*. New York and London: Cambridge University Press, 1975.
16. ——— and Temin, P., "Slavery: The Progressive Institution?" *J. Econ. Hist.*, Sept. 1974, *34*, pp. 739–83.
17. Davis, L. E. and North, D. C., *Institutional change and American economic growth*. Cambridge: Cambridge University Press, 1971.
18. Davis, L. E., Easterlin, R. A., Parker, W. N. and Others, *American economic growth: An economist's history of the United States*. New York: Harper and Row, 1972.
19. Deane, P. and Cole, W. A., *British economic growth, 1688–1959*. Cambridge: Cambridge University Press, 1962.
20. DeCanio, S., *Agricultural production, supply and institutions in the post-Civil War South*. Cambridge: M.I.T. Press, 1974.
21. Easterlin, R. A., "Interregional Differences in Per Capita Income, Population, and Total Income, 1840–1950," in [82, Parker, 1960].
22. ———. "Influences in European Overseas Emigration before World War I." *Econ. Dev. Cult. Change*, April 1961, *9*, pp. 331–51.
23. ———. *Population, labor force, and long swings in economic growth: The American experience*. New York: NBER; distributed by Columbia University Press, 1968.
24. Edelstein, M., "The Determinants of U. K. Investment Abroad, 1870–1913: The U.S. Case," *J. Econ. Hist.*, Dec. 1974, *34*(4), pp. 980–1007.
25. Feinstein, C. H., *National income, expenditure and output of the United Kingdom, 1855–1956*. Cambridge: Cambridge University Press, 1972.
26. Feldstein, M., "Social Security, Induced Retirement, and Aggregate Capital Accumulation," *J. Polit. Econ.*, Sept./Oct. 1974, *82*(5), pp. 905–26.
27. Fishlow, A., *American railroads and the transformation of the Antebellum economy*. Cambridge: Harvard University Press, 1965.
28. Fogel, R. W., *Railroads and American economic growth: Essays in econometric history*. Baltimore: Johns Hopkins Press, 1964.
29. ——— and Engerman, S. L., "A Model for the Explanation of Industrial Expansion during the Nineteenth Century: With an Application to the American Iron Industry," *J. Polit. Econ.*, May/June 1969, *77*(3), pp. 306–28.
30. ——— and Engerman, S. L., eds., *The reinterpretation of American economic history*. New York: Harper and Row, 1971.
31. ——— and Engerman, S. L., *Time on the cross: The economics of American negro slavery*. 2 vols. Boston: Little, Brown, 1974.
32. Freeman, R. B., "Black-White Income Differences: Why Did They Last So Long?" unpublished manuscript, Harvard University, 1972.
33. Friedman, M. and Schwartz, A. J., *A monetary history of the United States 1867–1960*, Princeton: Princeton University Press for the NBER, 1963.
34. Gallman, R. E., "Commodity Output, 1839–1899," in [82, Parker, 1960].
35. ———. "Gross National Product in the United States, 1834–1909," in [6, Brady, 1966].
36. Goldin, C. D., "The Economics of Emancipation," *J. Econ. Hist.*, March 1973, *33*(1), pp. 66–85.

37. ———. Unpublished manuscript on urban slavery, forthcoming, Chicago: University of Chicago Press, 1976.
38. Gordon, D. F. and Walton, G. M., "A New Theory of Regenerative Growth and the Experience of Post World War II West Germany," unpublished manuscript, Oct. 1974, University of Indiana.
39. Gordon, R. J., "$45 Billion of U.S. Private Investment Has Been Mislaid," *Amer. Econ. Rev.*, June 1969, *59*(3), pp. 221–38.
40. ———. "Reply to Comment by G. Jaszi," *Amer. Econ. Rev.*, Dec. 1970, *60*(5), pp. 940–45 (see [55, Jaszi, 1970]).
41. Goy, J. and Le Roy Ladurie, E., *Les fluctuations du produit de la Dîme.* Paris: Mouton, 1972.
42. Griliches, Z., "Errors in Variables and Other Unobservables," *Econometrica*, Nov. 1974, *42*(6), pp. 971–98.
43. Guisinger, S. E., "The Theory and Measurement of Effective Protection – The Case of Pakistan," unpublished doctoral dissertation, Harvard University, 1970.
44. Gunderson, G., "The Origin of the American Civil War," *J. Econ. Hist.*, Dec. 1974, *34*(4), pp. 915–50.
45. Harley, C. K., "On the Persistence of Old Techniques: The Case of North American Wooden Shipbuilding," *J. Econ. Hist.*, June 1973 *33*(2), pp. 372–98.
46. Hartwell, R. M., "The Standard of Living Controversy: A Summary," in *The Industrial Revolution.* Edited by R. M. Hartwell. Oxford: Basil Blackwell, 1970.
47. Hicks, J. R., "An Inaugural Lecture," *Oxford Econ. Pap., N.S.*, June 1953, *5*, pp. 117–35.
48. ———. *A theory of economic history.* Oxford: Clarendon Press, 1969.
49. Higgs, R., *The transformation of the American economy, 1865–1914: An essay in interpretation.* New York: Wiley, 1971.
50. ———. "Race, Skills, and Earnings: American Immigrants in 1909," *J. Econ. Hist.*, June 1971, *31*(2), pp. 420–8.
51. ———. "Patterns of Farm Rental in the Georgia Cotton Belt, 1880–1900," *J. Econ. Hist.*, June 1974, *34*(2), pp. 468–82.
52. Hill, P., "The Economic Impact of Immigration into the United States," unpublished doctoral dissertation, University of Chicago, 1970.
53. Hueckel, G., "War and the British Economy, 1793–1815, A General Equilibrium Analysis," *Explor. Econ. Hist.*, Summer 1973, *10*(4), pp. 365–96.
54. Hughes, J. R. T. and Reiter, S., "The First 1,945 British Steamships," *J. Amer. Statist. Assoc.*, June 1958, *53*, pp. 360–81.
55. Jaszi, G., "$45 Billion of U.S. Private Investment Has Been Mislaid: Comment," *Amer. Econ. Rev.*, Dec. 1970, *60*(5), pp. 934–9 (see R. J. Gordon's "Reply" [40, 1970]).
56. Jones, A. H., "Wealth Estimates for the New England Colonies about 1770," *J. Econ. Hist.*, March 1972, *32*(1), pp. 98–127.
57. Jones, G. T., *Increasing returns.* Cambridge: Cambridge University Press, 1933.
58. Kelley, A. C., "International Migration and Economic Growth: Australia, 1865–1935," *J. Econ. Hist.*, Sept. 1965, *25*(3), pp. 333–54.
59. ———, Williamson, J. G. and Cheetham R. J., *Dualistic economic development: Theory and history.* Chicago: University of Chicago Press, 1972.
60. Kessel, R. A. and Alchian, A. A., "Real Wages in the North during the Civil War: Mitchell's Data Reinterpreted," *J. Law Econ.*, Oct. 1959, *2*, pp. 95–113.
61. Klotz, B. P. and Neal, L. D., "Spectral and Cross-Spectral Analysis of the Long Swing Hypothesis," *Rev. Econ. Statist.*, August 1973, *55*(3), pp. 291–8.
62. Kravis, I. B., "Trade as a Handmaiden of Growth: Similarities between the

Nineteenth and Twentieth Centuries," *Econ. J.*, Dec. 1970, *80*(320), pp. 850–72.

63. Landes, W. M. and Solmon, L. C., "Compulsory Schooling Legislation: An Economic Analysis of Law and Social-Change in the Nineteenth Century," *J. Econ. Hist.*, March 1972, 32(1), pp. 54–91.
64. Laslett, T. P. R., *Household and family in past time.* Cambridge: Cambridge University Press, 1972.
65. Lebergott, S., *Manpower in economic growth: The American record since 1800.* New York: McGraw-Hill, 1964.
66. Leontief, W., "Theoretical Assumptions and Nonobserved Facts," *Amer. Econ. Rev.*, March 1971, *61*(1), pp. 1–7.
67. LeVeen, E. P., "British Slave Trade Suppression Policies 1821–1865: Impact and Implications," unpublished doctoral dissertation, University of Chicago, 1971.
68. Lindert, P. H., "Land Scarcity and American Growth," *J. Econ. Hist.*, Dec. 1974, *34*(4), pp. 851–84.
69. McClelland, P. D., "The Cost to America of British Imperial Policy," *Amer. Econ. Rev.*, Supplement, May 1969, *59*(2), pp. 370–81.
70. McGouldrick, P. F., *New England textiles in the nineteenth century: Profits and investment.* Cambridge, Mass.: Harvard University Press, 1968.
71. Meeker, E., "The Improving Health of the United States, 1850–1915," *Explor. Econ. Hist.*, Summer 1972, 9(4), pp. 353–74.
72. ———. "The Social Rate of Return on Investment in Public Health, 1880–1910," *J. Econ. Hist.*, June 1974, *34*(2), pp. 392–421.
73. Mitchell, B. R. with Deane, P., *Abstract of British historical statistics.* Cambridge: Cambridge University Press, 1962.
74. Mitchell, W. C., *Business cycles: The problem and its setting.* New York: NBER, 1927.
75. Neal, L. and Uselding, P., 'Immigration, A Neglected Source of American Economic Growth: 1790–1912," *Oxford Econ. Pap., N. S.*, March 1972, *24*(1), pp. 68–88.
76. Nelson, R. R. and Winter, S. G., "Neoclassical vs. Evolutionary Theories of Economic Growth: Critique and Prospectus," *Econ. J.*, Dec. 1974, *84*(336), pp. 886–905.
77. Nerlove, M., "Two Models of the British Economy: A Fragment of a Critical Survey," *Int'l. Econ. Rev.*, May 1965, 6(2), pp. 127–81.
78. North, D. C., "Sources of Productivity Change in Ocean Shipping, 1600–1850," *J. Polit. Econ.*, Sept./Oct. 1968, 76(5), pp. 953–70.
79. ——— and Thomas, R. P., *The rise of the Western World.* Cambridge: Cambridge University Press, 1973.
80. Olmstead, A. L., "New York City Mutual Savings Bank Portfolio Management and Trustee Objectives," *J Econ. Hist.*, Dec. 1974, *34*(4), pp. 815–34.
81. Olson, M., *The economics of wartime shortage, a history of British food supplies in the Napoleonic Wars and in World Wars I and II.* Durham: Duke University Press, 1963.
82. Parker, W. N., ed., *Trends in the American economy in the nineteenth century.* Conference on Research in Income and Wealth, Studies in Income and Wealth, Vol. 24. Princeton: Princeton University Press, 1960.
83. Passell, P. and Schmundt, M., "Pre–Civil War Land Policy and the Growth of Manufacturing," *Explor. Econ. Hist.*, Fall 1971, 9(1), pp. 35–48.
84. ——— and Wright, G., "The Effects of Pre–Civil War Expansion on the Price of Slaves," *J. Polit. Econ.*, Nov./Dec. 1972, *80*(6), pp. 1188–1202.

85. Peppers, L. C., "Full-Employment Surplus Analysis and Structural Change: The 1930s," *Explor. Econ. Hist.*, Winter 1973, *10*(2), pp. 197–210.
86. Pincus, J., "A Positive Theory of Tariff Formation Applied to the 19th-Century United States," unpublished doctoral dissertation, Stanford University, 1972.
87. Pope, C., "The Impact of the Ante-Bellum Tariff on Income Distribution," *Explor. Econ. Hist.*, Summer 1972, *9*(4), pp. 375–421.
88. *Purdue faculty papers in economic history 1956–1966*. Homewood, Ill.: Irwin, 1967.
89. Ransom, R. and Sutch, R., Unpublished book manuscript on post-bellum Southern agriculture, forthcoming.
90. Rees, A. E., *Real wages in manufacturing, 1890–1914*. Princeton: Princeton University Press, 1961.
91. Reid, J. D., Jr., "Sharecropping as an Understandable Market Response: The Post-Bellum South," *J. Econ. Hist.*, March 1973, *33*(1), pp. 106–30.
92. Rockoff, H. T., "The Free Banking Era: A Reexamination," *J. Money, Credit, Banking*, May 1974, *6*(2), pp. 141–67.
93. ———. "Varieties of Banking and Regional Economic Development in the United States, 1840–1860," *J. Econ. Hist.*, March 1975, *35*(1), pp. 160–81.
94. Roll, R., "Interest Rates and Price Expectations During the Civil War," *J. Econ. Hist.*, June 1972, *32*(2), pp. 476–98.
95. Rosenberg, N., *Technology and American economic growth*. New York: Harper and Row, 1972.
96. Rosovsky, H., ed., *Industrialization in two systems: Essays in honor of Alexander Gerschenkron, by a group of his students*. New York: Wiley, 1966.
97. Rostow, W. W., ed., *The economics of take-off into sustained growth*. New York: St. Martin's, 1963.
98. Sandberg, L. G., *Lancashire in decline: A study in entrepreneurship, technology and international trade*. Columbus: Ohio State University Press, 1974.
99. Sanderson, A. R., "Child-Labor Legislation and the Labor Force Participation of Children," *J. Econ. Hist.*, March 1974, *34*(1), pp. 297–9.
100. Schultz, T. W., *Transforming traditional agriculture*. New Haven: Yale University Press, 1964.
101. ———. "Lingering Doubts About Economics," unpublished paper, University of Chicago, 1974; *Amer. Econ. Rev.*, forthcoming.
102. Shepherd, J. F. and Walton, G. M., *Shipping, maritime trade, and the economic development of colonial North America*. Cambridge: Cambridge University Press, 1972.
103. Sheppard, D. K., *The growth and role of U.K. financial institutions, 1880–1962*. London: Methuen, 1971.
104. Simon, M., "The United States Balance of Payments, 1861–1900," in [82, Parker, 1960].
105. Solow, R. M., *Growth theory: An exposition*. Oxford: Clarendon Press, 1970.
106. Soltow, L., *Men and wealth in the United States, 1850–1870*. New Haven: Yale University Press, 1975.
107. Stigler, G. J., "Does Economics Have a Useful Past?" *Hist. Pol. Econ.*, Fall 1969, *1*(2), pp. 217–30.
108. Swanson, J. A. and Williamson, J. G., "Firm Location and Optimal City Size in American History," in *The new urban history: Quantitative explorations by American historians*. Edited by L. F. Schnore. Princeton: Princeton University Press, 1974.
109. Sylla, R., "Federal Policy, Banking Market Structure and Capital Mobilization in the United States, 1863–1913," *J. Econ. Hist.*, Dec. 1969, *29*(4), pp. 657–86.
110. Taussig, F. W., *The tariff history of the United States*. New York: Putnam, 1888.

111. Temin, P., *The Jacksonian economy*. New York: Norton, 1969.
112. ———, ed. *New economic history: Selected Readings*. Harmondsworth, England: Penguin, 1973.
113. ———. "The Anglo-American Business Cycle, 1820–1860," *Econ. Hist. Rev.*, 2nd ser., May 1974, *27*(2), pp. 207–21.
114. Thomas, B., *Migration and economic growth*. Cambridge: Cambridge University Press, 1954.
115. Thomas, R. P., "The Sugar Colonies of the Old Empire: Profit or Loss for Great Britain?" *Econ. Hist. Rev.*, 2nd ser., April 1968, *21*(1), pp. 30–45.
116. Titow, J. Z., *Winchester yields*. Cambridge: Cambridge University Press, 1972.
117. Trevelyan, G. M., *English social history*. London and New York: Longmans, Green, 1942.
118. U.S. Bureau of the Census., *Historical statistics of the United States, Colonial times to 1957*. Washington: U.S.G.P.O., 1960.
119. U.S. President., *Economic report of the President*. Washington, D.C., U.S.G.P.O., 1975.
120. Viner, J., *Canada's balance of international indebtedness, 1900–1913*. Cambridge, Mass.: Harvard University Press, 1924.
121. Walton, G. M., "Sources of Productivity Change in American Colonial Shipping, 1675–1775," *Econ. Hist. Rev.*, 2nd ser., April 1967, *20*(1), pp. 67–78.
122. Weiss, R. W., "The Issue of Paper Money in the American Colonies, 1720–1774," *J. Econ. Hist.*, Dec. 1970, *30*(4), pp. 770–84.
123. ———. "The Colonial Monetary Standard of Massachusetts," *Econ. Hist. Rev.*, 2nd ser., Nov. 1974, *27*(4), pp. 577–92.
124. West, E. G., "Educational Slowdown and Public Intervention in 19th-Century England: A Study in the Economics of Bureaucracy," *Explor. Econ. Hist.*, Jan. 1975, *12*(1), pp. 61–87.
125. Whale, P. B., "The Working of the Pre-War Gold Standard," *Economica, N.S.*, Feb. 1937, *4*, pp. 18–32.
126. White, H. D., *The French international accounts, 1880–1913*. Cambridge, Mass.: Harvard University Press, 1933.
127. Whitney, W. G., "The Structure of the American Economy in the Late 19th Century," unpublished doctoral dissertation, Harvard University, 1968.
128. Williams, J. H., *Argentine international trade under inconvertible paper money: 1880–1900*. Cambridge, Mass.: Harvard University Press, 1920.
129. Williamson, J. G., *American growth and the balance of payments, 1820–1913*. Chapel Hill: University of North Carolina Press, 1964.
130. ———. *Late nineteenth-century American development: A general equilibrium history*. London and New York: Cambridge University Press, 1974.
131. ———. "Watersheds and Turning Points: Conjectures on the Long-Term Impact of Civil War Financing," *J. Econ. Hist.*, Sept. 1974, *34*(3), pp. 636–61.
132. Wright, G., "Econometric Studies of History," in *Frontiers of quantitative economics*. Edited by M. D. Intriligator. Amsterdam: North Holland, 1971.
133. ———. "The Political Economy of New Deal Spending: An Econometric Analysis," *Rev. Econ. Statist.*, Feb. 1974, *56*(1), pp. 30–8.
134. Wrigley, E. A., *Population and history*, London: Weidenfeld and Nicolson; New York: McGraw-Hill, 1969.
135. ———, ed., *Nineteenth-century society: Essays in the use of quantitative methods for the study of social data*. Cambridge: Cambridge University Press, 1972.
136. Yasuba, Y., "The Profitability and Viability of Plantation Slavery in the United States," *Econ. Stud. Quart.*, Sept. 1961, *12*, pp. 60–7; reprinted in [30, Fogel and Engerman, 1971].

137. Zellner, A. and Murphy, G., "Sequential Growth, the Labor-Safety-Valve Doctrine and the Development of American Unionism," *J. Econ. Hist.*, Sept. 1959, *19*(3), pp. 402–21.
138. Zevin, R. B., "The Growth of Cotton Textile Production after 1815," in [30, Fogel and Engerman, 1971].

II

Colonial and early national economy

"An economic interpretation of the American Revolution"

by Marc Egnal and Joseph A. Ernst

Although "An Economic Interpretation of the American Revolution" was written over two decades ago, it remains "the best starting point for historians interested in the role of the economy in the Revolution" (McCusker and Menard, 352). The essay concerns questions of profound importance to historians of all types. What role did economic forces play in the founding of this country? Or, more broadly, how did the American economy and American society become the way they are today? Our history matters. And this was a critical episode.

The essay is an excellent example of how historians convince one another. It opens with a review of the historiographical debate between Whig and Progressive historians. Marc Egnal and Joseph Ernst must recapitulate the ideas that have come before theirs, because there is no consensus on this subject and so that their original contributions can be highlighted and put in context. The historiography is also necessary to show the weaknesses of earlier theories, to understand better what needs patching up. In addition, the historiography reminds us of the complexity of the roots of the Revolution. The authors stress that there is no monocausal explanation, and they implicitly recognize that theirs will not be the final word. Notice that the article is titled "an" economic interpretation, not "the" economic interpretation.

Next, they lay out their hypothesis. Much scholarly writing, including this essay, proceeds somewhat like a mathematical proof. Egnal and Ernst present "necessary and sufficient conditions" for the revolutionary movement and then align three distinct building blocks supporting their argument. How do the three blocks support one another? Are there gaps where they abut? (The bulk of the essay focuses on the validity of just one part of the argument.)

Then they turn to their sources. Historical data are not handed down from the heavens; they must be scoured out from a wide variety of archival sources.

New sources are continually coming to light. Half of the job of the historian is digging up the evidence, the other half is interpreting it.

The key point of Egnal and Ernst concerns broad economic changes between 1745 and 1775. Is the argument put forward convincing?

- Are you convinced by the evidence about changes in freedom to conduct business? What kinds of freedom did these elite merchants want?
- What is profit? Do the sources adequately measure it? Is the evidence on changing profit rates convincing?
- Is the evidence on the link between imperial policies and local economic development convincing? What is "economic sovereignty?"

Notice the differing interests of the groups examined by Egnal and Ernst. Much of the profit seeking they describe is called "rent seeking" by economists. Rent seeking occurs when high profits are protected not by reducing one's own costs but by favorable government decisions, often those that increase the costs of competitors.

Egnal and Ernst discuss producers and merchants extensively but say little about consumers.

- How did the changing market structure and the boycotts affect the consumers and consumer surplus? In what ways were the "lower orders" hurt and helped by imperial policies?

An excellent summary of work published after this essay is bound in John McCusker and Russell Menard's *The Economy of British America, 1607–1789* (1985). They agree that economic matters were central to the Revolution and that the colonials had many economic grievances with the British government, but they argue that "the progress of the early British American economy over the colonial period had been sufficient to make independence thinkable by the 1770s." Instead of an economy in crisis, they argue that "Americans could look around and see great increases in output and settled area, large and busy port cities dispatching ships throughout the Atlantic world, substantial accumulations of wealth by those at the top, prosperous farms and great plantations, and, especially, a stunning enlargement of the population. Americans perceived this as evidence of their rapid rise to 'wealth and greatness' which they extrapolated into the future. . . . Such a perception shaped the hopes and aspirations of many Americans . . . persuading them that they had a bountiful future. . . . That bounty could be captured faster . . . some Americans thought, if they were freed of the constraints of the Old Empire and took firm control of their destiny" (McCusker and Menard, 353).

Additional Reading

Gordon Bjork, "The Weaning of the American Economy," *Journal of Economic History*, 24 (December 1964), 541–60.

Marc Egnal, *A Mighty Empire: The Origins of the American Revolution*, Ithaca, NY: Cornell University Press, 1988.

Peter McClelland, "The Cost to America of British Imperial Policy," *American Economic Review*, 59 (May 1969), 370–81.

John McCusker and Russell Menard, *The Economy of British America, 1607–1789*, Chapel Hill, NC: University of North Carolina Press, 1985.

Joseph D. Reid, Jr., "Economic Burden: Spark to the Revolution?" *Journal of Economic History*, 38 (March 1978), 81–100.

2

An economic interpretation of the American Revolution

MARC EGNAL and JOSEPH A. ERNST

The Atlantic economy in the half century before American Independence underwent deep, wrenching changes. As a result, English capital and English decisions increasingly dominated the colonial economy. The freedom of the wealthy colonists, merchants and planters alike, to conduct business as they chose was restricted. Profit margins were lessened and possibilities for local development sacrificed. These broad, structural changes, and the accompanying short-run economic crises, troubled the colonial elite at least as much as did the parliamentary enactments which followed the Seven Years War. These new British measures remain one ostensible cause of revolt. But the colonial reaction to them was determined in large part by a growing concern for the economy and for economic sovereignty, a concern that only coincidentally reinforced the dictates of patriotic principle.

This transformation of the colonial business world is the framework for the following broad and tentative reinterpretation of the American Revolution. Our reinterpretation, however, does not argue a monocausal explanation for the colonies' struggle with Britain. Consequently, an examination of the strengths and weaknesses of earlier writers provides a necessary introduction to the presentation of a new hypothesis.

Modern historians of the American Revolution conveniently fall into two schools: the Progressive and the neo-whig. In seeking to explain the colonists' break with the mother country, Progressive authors wrestled with two stubborn problems for which they never achieved a happy resolution. One was the question of the impact of the Navigation Acts. At the turn of the century, the architects of the so-called "Imperial

Mr. Egnal and Mr. Ernst are members of the Department of History, York University, Toronto, Ontario.

Source: Marc Egnal and Joseph A. Ernst, "An Economic Interpretation of the American Revolution," *William and Mary Quarterly*, 3rd Ser. (January 1972), 3–32. Reprinted with permission of the authors and the *William and Mary Quarterly*.

School" of British-American history, George Beer and Charles M. Andrews, pronounced the administration of the empire from Whitehall and Westminister remarkably evenhanded.[1] Some progressive historians, including Arthur Schlesinger and Carl Becker, went along with this interpretation. For these writers no fundamental conflict existed between English and American societies. There was only a series of unwise measures passed by Parliament after 1763.[2]

Other Progressives found this analysis of colonial–metropolitan relations less satisfactory. Charles A. Beard, and later Louis Hacker, saw the rending of empire in 1776 as the product of long-standing conflicts between Britain and America, confiicts embodied in the Acts of Trade. Their condemnation of the Navigation Acts sits uneasily, however, and seems a weak foundation for any "economic interpretation." Hacker, for instance, dwelt on the restrictions on manufacture and trade before 1763.[3] Yet these regulations either were ignored by the colonists (as in the case of the Molasses Act of 1733) or touched only the periphery of trade. The ambivalence of these historians' explanation is best illustrated by Beard's comment:

> Modern calculators have gone to some pains to show that on the whole American colonists derived benefits from English policy which greatly outweighed their losses from the restraints laid on them. For the sake of argument the case may be conceded; it is simply irrelevant to the uses of history. The origins of the legislation are clear; and the fact that it restricted American economic enterprise in many respects is indisputable.[4]

In addition to the difficulties raised by the Navigation Acts, the Progressives wrestled with a second problem: the complex nature of the Revolutionary movement in the decade before Independence. Seeking to answer the "why" of the Revolution, men like Becker, Andrews, and Schlesinger came up with two hypotheses. First, while dismissing the idea of long-standing conflict between Britain and the colonies, these

1. For a recent and suggestive discussion of these schools, see Gordon S. Wood, "Rhetoric and Reality in the American Revolution," *William and Mary Quarterly*, 3rd Ser., XXIII (1966), 3–32. Concerning the views of the "Imperial School," see esp. Charles M. Andrews, *The Colonial Period of American History*, IV (New Haven, Conn., 1938); Andrews, *The Colonial Background of the American Revolution: Four Essays in American Colonial History* (New Haven, Conn., 1924); and George Louis Beer, *British Colonial Policy 1754–1765* (New York, 1907). See also, A. S. Eisenstadt, *Charles McLean Andrews: A Study in American Historical Writing* (New York, 1956).
2. See Arthur Meier Schlesinger, *The Colonial Merchants and the American Revolution 1763–1776* (New York, 1918); and Carl Lotus Becker, *The History of Political Parties in the Province of New York, 1760–1776* (Madison, Wis., 1909).
3. Louis M. Hacker, "The First American Revolution," *Columbia University Quarterly*, XXVII (1935), 29.
4. Charles A. and Mary R. Beard, *The Rise of American Civilization*, I (New York, 1927), 196.

historians argued that the measures adopted by Britain after the end of the French and Indian War in 1763, coupled with the postwar colonial depression, caused the ruling classes, the merchants in the North, the planters in the South, to take the lead in opposing British policy.[5] And in sharp distinction to what neo-whig historians contend, this hostility to British measures stemmed not from whiggish constitutional principles, but from economics. Restrictive commercial regulations were imposed by the British upon colonies whose merchants were suffering in the depths of depression and whose large land- and slaveholders were groaning under a burden of indebtedness. This "economic interpretation" of the Progressives was narrowly focused upon the years after 1763 and was based upon an analysis which went little beyond the depiction of "hard times." Questions of the structure of the economy, or of long-term developments within the merchant and planting communities, were foreign to the concerns of these historians. The conclusion that merchants and wealthy planters sought imperial reform but shunned rebellion seems almost dictated by the limits of the economic analysis.

Since economic concerns did not make the merchants or planters into full-fledged revolutionaries, a different dynamic must have carried the movement of protest to fruition. Accordingly, an examination of the behavior of the "lower orders" provided the Progressives with their second, complementary hypothesis. During the decade before Independence, the argument ran, the lower classes of the cities fought to gain greater rights for themselves in what was essentially an undemocratic society. These "lower orders" supposedly joined the Revolutionary movement both because of a desire for greater power and because of a dedication to constitutional and democratic principles – the latter point strangely sounding more neo-whiggish than Progressive.[6] With their adherence to the cause, the Revolutionary movement was transformed, in Carl Becker's famous phrase, into a two-fold contest: a struggle not only over "home rule" but also over "who shall rule at home." Furthermore, in the course of the Revolutionary struggle, these "radicals" (i.e., in the North, the "lower orders" of the cities and their leaders, and in the South, certain of the debt-ridden tobacco and rice planters) came

5. See n. 2 and Charles M. Andrews, *The Boston Merchants and the Non-Importation Movement* (New York, 1968). Reprinted from Colonial Society of Massachusetts, *Publications*, XIX (1916–1917), 159–259.

6. The democratic ethos of the lower classes is explored by Jesse Lemisch, "The American Revolution Seen from the Bottom Up," in Barton J. Bernstein, ed., *Towards a New Past: Dissenting Essays in American History* (New York, 1968), 3–45. See also the earlier statement by Merrill Jensen, "Democracy and the American Revolution," *Huntington Library Quarterly*, XX (1957), 321–341; as well as Jensen's recent essay, "The American People and the American Revolution," *Journal of American History*, LVII (1970), 5–35.

to dominate the protests against Great Britain. The radicals were now opposed in their desire for imperial change by their natural enemies, the "conservatives" – wealthy merchants of northern cities and Charles Town and certain of the aristocratic planters. The two theses offered by Progressive historians were tied together by a transition in the nature of the protest movement during 1770. Pinpointing this change, Charles M. Andrews stated, "The non-importation movement [against the Townshend Acts] began as a merchant's device wherewith to obtain a redress of trade grievances; it ended as an instrument in the hands of political agitators and radicals for the enforcement of their claims of constitutional liberty and freedom."[7]

The Progressives did not, however, cut short their analysis with the break from England in 1776. Instead, led by the logic of their explanation, they mapped out a broad interpretation of events through the adoption of the Constitution in 1789. The Revolution (at least in the North) was of the lower classes against a plutocracy. This implied serious social change after Independence, a theory the Progressive scholar, J. Franklin Jameson, sought to defend.[8] The Constitution then became the quintessential counterrevolutionary document, a position ably presented in Beard's *Economic Interpretation*.[9] But such a tidy and sweeping account of the Revolutionary era rested on weak grounds. Research into areas such as the confiscation of loyalist estates, the nature of the new state governments, and so on has shown that there was no social overturn accompanying the American Revolution and that what change did come about in the nature of society was most moderate.[10] It was just these preoccupations and weaknesses of the Progressive approach that helped determine much of the content of the neo-whig scholarship that was to follow and that was to reshape the history of the Revolution.

Neo-whig critics have explicitly denied the existence of those internal conflicts so central to the Progressive view. For these historians, an understanding of the American Revolution rests in the realm of ideas and principles as opposed to economics or social classes. Both in the

7. Andrews, *Boston Merchants and Non-Importation*, 101. In his writings on the Revolutionary years, Andrews easily fits the Progressive pattern.

8. *The American Revolution Considered as a Social Movement* (Princeton, N.J., 1926).

9. *An Economic Interpretation of the Constitution of the United States* (New York, 1913).

10. Compare Elisha P. Douglass, *Rebels and Democrats: The Struggle for Equal Political Rights and Majority Rule During the American Revolution* (Chapel Hill, N.C., 1955); James T. Lemon and Gary B. Nash, "The Distribution of Wealth in Eighteenth-Century America: A Century of Change in Chester County, Pennsylvania, 1693–1802," *Journal of Social History*, II (1968–1969), 1–24; Jackson Turner Main, *The Social Structure of Revolutionary America* (Princeton, N.J., 1965); and Frederick B. Tolles, "The American Revolution Considered as a Social Movement: A Re-Evaluation," *American Historical Review*, LX (1954–1955), 1–12.

North and South, their argument goes, American society was dominated by consensus and ruled in the interests of a property-holding middle class.[11] It follows that only minor social change accompanied Independence. Most important, the Revolutionary movement appeared to be conservative in the fullest sense of the word. A trend toward greater colonial sovereignty had been underway since the time of the first settlements. The colonists had indeed acquired more and more of the "rights of Englishmen" and a stronger dedication to these principles. After 1763, British measures threatened American liberty, leading colonists to react both to preserve their formal rights and to protect themselves against what they felt to be a genuine threat of British conspiracy, corruption, and enslavement. Declaring Independence merely confirmed trends dating back a century or more.[12]

For the neo-whigs, an examination of the colonial economy only strengthens their argument. The abundance of cheap land and the richness of the soil underscore a picture of contented, middle-class farmers. More recently, and with perhaps some contradiction, writers such as Bernard Bailyn and Gordon Wood have noted the economic uncertainties that beset debt-ridden planters and struggling merchants. For neo-whigs, however, such commercial problems do not form the basis of an interest-oriented interpretation. Rather, instabilities in the economy are only part of the troubling ambience that led colonists to credit all the more reports of ministerial plots against their freedom.[13]

The "consensus" or neo-whig approach of many recent writers does

11. For a more complete bibliography of the neo-whig literature than is offered here, see Jack P. Greene, ed., *The Reinterpretation of the American Revolution 1763–1789* (New York, 1968), 2–59.

12. See esp. Wood, "Rhetoric and Reality," *Wm. and Mary Qtly.*, 3rd Ser., XXIII (1966), 3–32; Edmund S. Morgan, "The American Revolution Considered as an Intellectual Movement," in Arthur M. Schlesinger, Jr., and Morton White, eds., *Paths of American Thought* (Boston, 1963), 11–33; and Bernard Bailyn, "Political Experience and Enlightenment Ideas in Eighteenth-Century America," *Amer. Hist. Rev.*, LXVII (1961–1962), 339–351.

13. Bernard Bailyn, *The Origins of American Politics* (New York, 1967); and Wood,, "Rhetoric and Reality," *Wm. and Mary Qtly.*, 3rd Ser., XXIII (1966), 25–32. It is suggested that Bailyn's *The Origins of American Politics* represents a half-step back to the realities of the Progressives and away from the idealist approach offered in his introduction to the *Pamphlets of the American Revolution 1750–1776*, I (Cambridge, Mass., 1965). While Bailyn continues to locate motivation firmly in the realm of ideas, these ideas have their roots in social reality, or in the formal and informal structures that made up the colonial political and economic system. But this social reality is, for Bailyn, one typified by inherent uncertainty and instability, a view which seemingly derives from Parsonian sociology and equilibrium theory. What is interesting about the Bailyn model, however, is that it attempts to incorporate elements behind the instabilities in the life of early America that led to social disequilibrium and ultimately the social breakdown which was the Revolution. For a general discussion of this view of reality see C. Wright Mills, *The Sociological Imagination* (New York, 1959), Chap. 2.

rectify some of the more blatant shortcomings of the Progressive reading of the Revolutionary era. It helps explain, for instance, the achievement of Independence with only minor changes in the structure of society. It avoids as well the contorted explanation of the Progressives, with first the upper classes, then a noble-minded lower class, leading the Revolution. And the neo-whig approach readily incorporates the conclusion of the Imperial School that the Navigation Acts did not constitute a long-standing grievance.

But criticism may be directed at the neo-whigs even more devastating than that levelled at the Progressives. Basically they do not explain what happened. They do not explain, for example, why protests against the important Revenue Acts of 1764 and 1766 were so mild, and why colonists duly complied with these measures down to the eve of Independence. These laws placed a duty on West Indian goods but explicitly declared in their preambles their purpose of raising a revenue to support English placemen in the colonies rather than merely regulating trade. And if neo-whig emphasis on principle and consensus makes plausible the leading role played by certain merchants in the Revolutionary movement, it fails to explain the large tory element among the traders and the subsequent loyalist exodus. The conflicts in the years after 1763 seem either inexplicable or irrelevant as a result. The forward part played by the Northern Neck of Virginia in pushing that colony toward Independence demands an investigation of colonial society far beyond treatises on whig ideologies, just as the presentation of America as a nation of prosperous middle-class farmers overlooks a diversity of sharply differing regional economies. Similarly, the treatment of economic problems in psychological terms can be misleading if done in the context of the most facile economic analysis. At least the Progressives tried to grapple with these economic questions. If they failed to clarify the issue in every case, they nonetheless realized the problems involved.

Finally, the debates between the defenders of the several schools have a fixed and unproductive air about them. As in the case of the interminable disagreement over perennials such as "Was plantation slavery profitable?" attackers and defenders of the Progressive or neo-whig positions concern themselves with equally hoary questions such as "Were the Navigation Acts a burden?" and "Were the ideas of the Revolution radical or conservative?" A new approach is in order.

This discussion of the historiography of the Revolution points up the contributions of earlier interpretations as well as the problems with which any new explanation must deal. The following discussion addresses itself to these considerations and focuses on three broad interrelated developments in the decades preceding 1776. Together, the three, in the light of post-1763 British policies, form the necessary and sufficient conditions for the Revolutionary movement. Two of the developments have received lengthy treatment by other historians and, while an important part of this reinterpretation, will be mentioned only briefly in this paper.

The first of these is the growth of a self-conscious, powerful colonial elite composed of merchants and wealthy landowners in the North, and planters and merchants in the South.[14] At odds with themselves on some issues, on most questions touching local control these colonial elites had successfully asserted their autonomy from the crown.[15] Further, the whig elite had developed an ideology, a widely-held set of political and constitutional beliefs, that had been shaped and tested in colonial resistance to British men and measures in the past. This ideology became in turn an important element in later conflicts as a means of uniting and motivating the elite, as well as other members of the colonial middle classes. By the eve of the Revolution, a class or group consciousness that had evolved was essential to the mentality of the whig elite.[16]

The second development was the active and self-conscious involvement of the "lower orders" in the Revolutionary movement. The "mob" had been an element in the volatile mix of colonial politics dating back at least to the early eighteenth century. But the decade or two before Independence saw the "poorer sort" of the city and the less wealthy landowners articulating their own interests and seriously questioning long-held assumptions about society and politics. The "lower orders," to be sure, never gained control in a society that was always dominated by the upper classes. However, the new demands they voiced, and the important role they played in the Revolutionary movement, frightened many of the wealthy. This will be touched on later.[17]

14. See esp. Leonard Woods Labaree, *Conservatism in Early American History* (New York, 1948).

15. Much of this story is told in the rise of the popular branches of the several provincial legislatures. See the earlier study of Mary Patterson Clarke, *Parliamentary Privilege in the American Colonies* (New Haven, Conn., 1943); and the more detailed and recent account by Jack P. Greene, *The Quest for Power: The Lower Houses of Assembly in the Southern Royal Colonies, 1689–1776* (Chapel Hill, N.C., 1963). A more theoretical consideration of both the nature and aspirations of the colonial elite is Robert K. Lamb, "Political Elites and the Process of Economic Development," in Bert F. Hoselitz, ed., *The Progress of Underdeveloped Areas* (Chicago, 1952).

16. For a useful discussion of the problem of ideology as used here, see H. Stuart Hughes, *Consciousness and Society: The Reorientation of European Social Thought 1890–1930* (New York, 1958).

17. See n. 6 above and Jesse Lemisch, "Jack Tar in the Streets: Merchant Seamen in the Politics of Revolutionary America," *Wm. and Mary Qtly.*, 3rd Ser., XXV (1968), 371–407; Lemisch,

The third development forms the heart of this paper. During the eighteenth century, broad economic changes transformed the Atlantic economy. The impact of these changes on the several colonial regions and classes of people forms a crucial background for an understanding of the Revolution. Only from this vantage does the actual response of the colonists to British measures, from the Currency Act of 1751 to the Tea Act of 1773 and beyond, become intelligible.

The fundamental change affecting the Atlantic economy was that during the period 1720 to 1775 trade grew in two long swings. The areas involved included the British Isles, the slave coast of Africa, the British West Indies, and the American mainland colonies. These swings may be roughly dated 1720 to 1745 and 1745 to 1775. The first wave of growth was gradual, the second marked by an unprecedented expansion. Not all flows of goods took part in these two waves of growth, but the areas and trades included were significant: the export of British manufactures to Africa and the American colonies; the export to the West Indies of slaves from Africa and provisions from the mainland colonies; and the flow of sugar products to Britain. Exceptions to this pattern of growth were exports of tobacco and, in general, shipments from the American colonies to Britain. This rapid expansion after 1745 seems to have been produced by the strong growth of the British economy which was able to transmit significant new purchasing power to its trading partners across the Atlantic.[18]

The impact of this commercial expansion on the American colonies is best considered by regions. There are, of course, several ways in which the North American colonies may be grouped, but with respect to the

"Listening to the 'Inarticulate': William Widger's Dream and the Loyalties of American Revolutionary Seamen in British Prisons," *Jour. Soc. Hist.*, III (1969–1970), 1–29; and James H. Hutson, "An Investigation of the Inarticulate: Philadelphia's White Oaks," *Wm. and Mary Qtly.*, 3rd Ser., XXVIII (1971), 3–25.

18. The authors' arguments generally follow those presented in Phyllis Deane and W. A. Cole, *British Economic Growth 1688–1959: Trends and Structure* (Cambridge, Eng., 1962), Chaps. 1–3. There are several strong indications that imperial growth from 1745 to 1783 was based primarily on developments in Great Britain and only secondarily on developments overseas. One is the similar growth patterns evidenced by England's commerce with East Asia, Ireland, Africa, the West Indies, and America. Another is the generally adverse movement of terms of trade during periods of expansion. Terms of trade for Britain are presented *ibid.*, while those for North America are derived by the authors. See also K. Berrill, "International Trade and the Rate of Economic Growth," *Economic History Review*, 2nd Ser., XII (1959–1960), 351–359; R. B. Sheridan, "The Wealth of Jamaica in the Eighteenth Century," *ibid.*, XVIII (1965), 292–311; Robert Paul Thomas, "The Sugar Colonies of the Old Empire: Profit or Loss for Great Britain?" *ibid.*, XXI (1968), 30–45; and Sheridan, "The Wealth of Jamaica in the Eighteenth Century: A Rejoinder," *ibid.*, 46–61.

impact of British export policies a twofold division seems most useful. First are those areas in which the distribution of British goods was handled by an urban center controlled by a strong native merchant community. Four colonial ports with their respective hinterlands may be singled out in this regard: Boston, New York, Philadelphia, and Charles Town. Baltimore joined this list at the very end of the colonial period. Second, one may delineate that region where the distribution of British goods occurred within a decentralized marketing and credit structure – namely, the broad area of tobacco cultivation that included Virginia and parts of North Carolina and Maryland.[19]

Before examining more closely the economic and political impact of this post-1745 expansion, we must turn briefly to the sources of this study, for the question may well be asked: Is there sufficient evidence to depict short- and long-run economic changes in colonial America? The answer is an unequivocal yes. Indeed, what is surprising given the excellent work being done by scholars on the nineteenth-century United States is the almost complete lack of detailed analysis of the eighteenth-century economy.

Of first importance are the extensive collections of business letters, journals, and diaries that give an excellent day to day picture of colonial economic life. Of the commercial centers, only Baltimore and possibly Charles Town in the late colonial period lack a solid run of documents. For the tobacco colonies, letters and diaries of planters, and letterbooks and ledgers of both British factors and local merchants, offer a solid basis

19. Unlike "sectionalism," "regionalism" has not attracted much attention among colonial scholars. And those few who have adopted the regional approach have focused almost entirely on the "formal" or "homogeneous" region – a region defined by "uniformity of characteristics, or homogeneity of content," such as the Tobacco Coast, the Tidewater, the Low Country, and the Wheat Belt. Of another regional concept as used here – the "functional" region, a region identified by an "interdependence of parts," by its economic connections and coherence – students of early America remain largely ignorant. For a general discussion of the problem and a definition of terms, see G. W. S. Robinson, "The Geographical Region: Form and Function," *Scottish Geographical Magazine*, LXIX (1953), 49–57. See also the important use of the concept by James T. Lemon, "Urbanization and the Development of Eighteenth-Century Southeastern Pennsylvania and Adjacent Delaware," *Wm. and Mary Qtly.*, 3rd Ser., XXIV (1967), 501–542; and William S. Sachs, "Interurban Correspondents and the Development of a National Economy before the Revolution: New York as a Case Study," *New York History*, XXXVI (1955), 320–335. The approach has also been employed by Joseph A. Ernst and H. Roy Merrens in two joint papers, "The View from Philadelphia: An Interdisciplinary Approach to the South Carolina Economy of the Middle Eighteenth Century," Southern Historical Association Meeting, Oct. 31, 1969, Washington, D.C.; and "Southern 'Worlds' in the Atlantic Economy," South Carolina Tricentennial Commission Meeting, Mar. 21, 1970, Columbia, S.C.

for an economic study.[20] The exception is North Carolina, for which we have little business correspondence.[21]

In addition to these sources, there is a surprising abundance of quantitative data which allows for a more precise demarcation of short-run changes. Price series for North American and West Indian goods, for instance, are available, or easily derivable, for most of the regional economies.[22] Data for overseas trade is provided by both British customs records and by an examination of the ship movements recorded in most colonial newspapers.[23] Indeed, the newspapers are a virtual mine of information for examining fluctuations in the economy. Changes

20. For Baltimore the single most important source remains the Letterbook of William Lux, 1763–1768, New-York Historical Society, New York. There are any number of smaller collections of business letters and the like that touch on Baltimore's economic life, virtually all of which have been successfully exploited by Ronald Hoffman in his recent study of "Economics, Politics and the Revolution in Maryland" (unpubl. Ph.D. diss., University of Wisconsin, 1969). The Charles Town picture is less bleak. Even here, however, the available collections can hardly be compared with materials, either in quantity or quality, available for cities to the north. A major exception to this would be Philip M. Hamer and George C. Rogers, Jr., ed., *The Papers of Henry Laurens*, 2 vols. (Columbia, S.C., 1968–). The letters covering the Revolutionary period have yet to be published; however, they may be found in the South Carolina Historical Society, Charleston, and in the Historical Society of Pennsylvania, Philadelphia. A further exception would be the Peter Manigault Letterbook, covering the years 1763 to 1776, which is to be published this year by the South Carolina Tricentennial Commission. Interested readers are also referred to the Josiah Smith, Jr., Letterbook for the period just prior to Independence, in the Southern Historical Collection at the University of North Carolina, Chapel Hill. Nor is the Letterbook of William Pollard, a Philadelphia merchant with trade connections in Charles Town, at the Hist. Soc. of Pa., to be overlooked. A sampling of the materials available for Virginia may be found in Joseph A. Ernst, "Genesis of the Currency Act of 1764: Virginia Paper Money and the Protection of British Investments," *Wm. and Mary Qtly.*, 3rd Ser., XXII (1965), 33–74; and Ernst, "The Robinson Scandal Redivivus: Money, Debts, and Politics in Revolutionary Virginia," *Virginia Magazine of History and Biography*, LXXVII (1969), 146–173. The best reference to the Maryland sources is the Hoffman study cited above.
21. The best guide to the North Carolina materials is H. Roy Merrens, *Colonial North Carolina in the Eighteenth Century: A Study in Historical Geography* (Chapel Hill, N.C., 1964). But see also Charles Christopher Crittenden, *The Commerce of North Carolina 1763–1789* (New Haven, Conn., 1936).
22. See, for instance, Anne Bezanson *et al.*, eds., *Prices in Colonial Pennsylvania* (Philadelphia, 1935); Arthur Harrison Cole, *Wholesale Commodity Prices in the United States 1700–1861* (Cambridge, Mass., 1938); and United States, Department of Commerce, Bureau of the Census, *Historical Statistics of the United States, Colonial Times to 1957* (Washington, D.C., 1960). It should also be noted that prices current are listed in colonial newspapers and very often in letterbooks.
23. There are several useful guides to the records on Britain's foreign trade. Most particularly, see G. N. Clark, *Guide to English Commercial Statistics 1696–1782* (London, 1938); T. S. Ashton's introduction to Elizabeth Boody Schumpeter, *English Overseas Trade Statistics 1697–1808* (Oxford, 1960); the introduction to the section on overseas trade in B. R. Mitchell and Phyllis Deane, *Abstract of British Historical Statistics* (Cambridge, 1962); and *Historical Statistics of the U.S.*

Average markup by Philadelphia importers: Eight linen and cotton checks, 1747 to 1774

Year	Per Cent	Year	Per Cent
1747–1749	39	1763–1765	13
1750–1753	29	1766–1768	28
1754–1757	27	1769–1770	42
1758–1759	33	1771–1773	16
1760–1762	16		

Sources: Selling prices in Philadelphia are culled from the daily entries in John Reynell Day Books, 1747–1773; Thomas Biddle Cash Book, 1772–1773; Henry Drinker Day Book, 1773. English prices, freight, and insurance rates are drawn from invoices in the following collections: Reynell Papers, 1747–1761; Wharton Manuscripts, 1754–1760; Richard Waln Invoice Book, 1763–1771; William Pollard Letterbook, 1772–1773. All manuscripts are in Hist. Soc. of Pa. Interpolations in the series for English prices are on the basis of fluctuations in the cost of other fabrics. Final calculations are in sterling, and Philadelphia prices are reduced by the exchange rates presented in Bezanson *et al.*, *Colonial Prices*, 431, as modified by the authors.

in merchant credit policy may be observed from a careful study of advertising, while sheriffs' sales and announcements of repossession are important indicators of periods of contraction and expansion.[24] Another valuable and generally unused source is merchants' account books. These make possible not only the calculation of the success of individual firms but also the derivation of the cost and selling price of dry goods. As an example, the chart above presents the changing markup in Philadelphia for linen and cotton checks. Reflected in the figures are the prosperity of the late 1740s, the depression of the first part of the 1750s, the flush times of the early war years, the depression of the 1760s, the recovery during nonimportation in the late 1760s, and the slump of 1772 to 1774.

These series amount to only a suggestion of the sources available for economic analysis. Wills, inventories, court records – both of the provinces and, later, of the early states and the federal government – and the various records of local chambers of commerce, poorhouses, insurance offices, and manufacturing establishments offer data of significant value for a detailed study of the colonial economy.

The sharp expansion of British commerce during the second long swing (1745–1775) was first felt in the colonial cities with the cessation of hostilities in 1748. British imports surged to record levels, increasing in the northern colonies by a full 40 per cent per capita between 1740 to

24. These sources have been largely ignored by researchers. See, however, William S. Sachs, The Business Outlook in the Northern Colonies (unpubl. Ph.D. diss., Columbia University, 1957), 132–133.

1744 and 1750 to 1754. The result, despite some improvement in the markets to which the colonists shipped their produce, was a depression of unprecedented magnitude. Dry goods piled up on shelves; profit margins for the merchants were small or nonexistent. Bankruptcies were common.[25] This was the beginning of a quarter century in which established merchants became increasingly concerned about their survival as a group.

Why, it may be asked, did merchants import such large quantities of goods when the results were so manifestly disastrous, and why did these importations persist at such high levels despite uniform complaints of depressed conditions? To some extent, established merchants were encouraged to take more goods by liberal offers of credit from the English suppliers, who, backed by a burgeoning economy, found that they could deal more generously.[26] But far more important in facilitating this swollen flow of goods were structural changes that threatened wholly to transform the trading communities in the colonial cities. Increasingly, British houses were bypassing the established colonial merchant to promote the sale of dry goods. This period was marked by the growth of vendue or auction sales. These sales had been an integral part of colonial life before 1748, but most often their role had been to aid in the disposal of damaged or outmoded goods rather than to serve as a major wholesale outlet. Now new merchants began importing directly for auctions to sell off large quantities of goods with only fractional profits on each sale.[27] A careful study of mercantile advertising in Boston indicates that during depressions there was a sharp rise in vendue sales and a parallel decline in the offerings of the established merchants.[28] Not surprisingly, the larger importers were angered by the new prominence of auctions and undertook campaigns to regulate public sales. Such regulation as was adopted, however, generally proved ineffective.[29]

25. *Ibid.*, Chap. 2; Arthur L. Jensen, *The Maritime Commerce of Colonial Philadelphia* (Madison, Wis., 1963), 116–117; *Historical Statistics of the U.S.*, 756–757. For economic conditions in Charles Town see the Laurens Papers and the Round Papers, D/DRC. B-26-29, Essex Record Office, Chelmsford, England.

26. Sachs, Business Outlook, 53–61; Jensen, *Maritime Commerce*, 98–101; Elias Bland to John Reynell, July 18, 1748, Richard Hillary to Reynell, Dec. 31, 1748, Reynell Papers. For conditions in England, see T. S. Ashton, *Economic Fluctuations in England 1700–1800* (Oxford, 1959).

27. Sachs, Business Outlook, 253–254. For an understanding of the operation of the vendue in Charles Town, as well as of the connection between depressed local markets for manufactures, vendue sales, and exports to Philadelphia, see Laurens Papers, Roll 2, no. 3, *passim*.

28. Dave Hutchinson, A Quantitative Approach to Business Cycles in Massachusetts, 1763–1774 (seminar paper, York University, 1971).

29. See n. 27 and Benjamin Fuller Letterbook, *passim*, Hist. Soc. of Pa.

British firms also increasingly entered into direct dealings with shopkeepers and other marginal importers in the urban centers, importers who normally would have bought from one of the established merchants. By the 1760s and 1770s it was not uncommon to find numerous English "agents" in any colonial city drumming up business for their parent firms and seeking liaisons with the smallest shopkeeper along with the largest importer. A major London house might have as many as one hundred fifty correspondents in a single northern port.[30] This practice of direct dealing riled the established merchants and provoked a stream of angry letters. "I would have you not bee too forward in pushing goods upon people," Philadelphia importer John Kidd wrote to the London house of Neate and Neave. "I shall also take the liberty to inform you that your supplying the shopkeepers at all is more harm than good to you, which I saw long ago but was afraid to mention it for fear you should think it was a sinister view for my own interest. For these merchants that probably might be inclined to correspond with you or at least say nothing to your disadvantage, take the liberty to ridicule you in all companies."[31]

Nonetheless such complaints counted little when weighed against the desire for profits on the part of the English exporters. Attempts of colonial legislatures to ease depressed conditions and to aid the merchants were checked by the tight hand the Privy Council and royal governors kept on colonial currency and banking practices. War proved to be, at least temporarily, more efficacious than any legislation in easing the trading community's plight. The prosperity that accompanied the campaigns of the French and Indian War assuaged the dissatisfaction and anger which had mounted among the merchants during the early 1750s. Good times, however, abruptly came to an end with Britain's victories in 1760 and the shifting of the theater of war.[32]

By 1763 a dark pall of depression hung over the commercial colonies. Creditors scrambled for liquidity, and commercial establishments from the largest British exporters to country storekeepers contracted their affairs. The colonial importers called in debts from shopkeepers and, at the same time, frantically sought to stave off English creditors. "Thus

30. See the discussion in Harry D. Berg, "The Organization of Business in Colonial Philadelphia," *Pennsylvania History*, X (1943), 157–166; James and Drinker Letterbook, 1762; William Pollard Letterbook, 1773; Testimony of Barlow Trecothick, Committee on the American Papers, Feb. 11, 1766, Additional Manuscript 33030, foll. 88–90, British Museum, London. Hereafter cited as Add. MS 33030: 88–90.

31. May 31, 1750, John Kidd Letterbook, Hist. Soc. of Pa.

32. Sachs, Business Outlook, Chaps. 3–4; Marc Egnal, Business Cycles in Pennsylvania, 1747 to 1774 (seminar paper, University of Wisconsin, 1968). The construction industry, however, evinced a countercyclical trend during the slump 1760 to 1763.

the consumers break the shopkeepers; they break the merchants," John Dickinson wrote, "and the stock must be felt as far as *London*."[33] Seemingly overnight, the hard money spent by the British forces drained back to the mother country.[34] Nor was this the only difficulty faced by the colonial merchants. The curtailment of British spending and the colonial need for bills of exchange drove up the exchange rate; debts collected within the colonies were translated into smaller sums of sterling. Furthermore, American merchants, confronted on the one hand by a debt-strapped countryside, and on the other by overstocked inventories, experienced a virtual disappearance of profits in the sale of imported wares.[35] However, neither reports of these conditions nor the difficulty of collecting debts from their colonial correspondents deterred British houses from renewing their former practices. Exports to the commercial provinces climbed sharply in 1764 despite a wave of bankruptcy that brought down some of the largest colonial houses.[36]

More and more the established merchants spoke of reasserting control over their commercial dealings and over the local economy in general. The strong repugnance voiced by colonial importers for British mercantile practices merged with other grievances to form an inseparable part of the protests against the new parliamentary enactments. The Currency Act of 1764 is a case in point. The emission of paper money had always been considered by the colonists as having importance far beyond the financing of government expenditures.[37] Bills of tender were often issued by a land bank which provided the money as a rotating mortgage fund, thus facilitating agricultural expansion.[38] In some colonies, such as Maryland,

33. *The Late Regulations respecting the British Colonies* . . . (Philadelphia, 1765), in Paul Leicester Ford, ed., *The Writings of John Dickinson* (Historical Society of Pennsylvania, *Memoirs*, XIV [Philadelphia, 1895]), 228, 227. See also the general discussions in Harry D. Berg, "Economic Consequences of the French and Indian War for the Philadelphia Merchants," *Pa. Hist.*, XIII (1946), 185–193; and Wilbur C. Plummer, "Consumer Credit in Colonial Philadelphia," *Pennsylvania Magazine of History and Biography*, LXVI (1942), 385–409.

34. An Account of the Bullion imported and brought to the Bank from the several colonies in North America . . . [1748–1765], Add. MS 32971: 64; Testimony of George Masterman, Comm. on Amer. Papers, Feb. 13, 1766, Add. MS 33030: 148–149; James and Drinker Letterbook, 1761–1764, *passim*.

35. An elaboration of this interpretation of rising exchange rates in the period is to be found in Ernst, "Currency Act of 1764," *Wm. and Mary Qtly.*, 3rd Ser., XXII (1965), 33–74. See n. 33 above for a detailed discussion on the plight of the merchants, and Sachs, Business Outlook, Chap. 4.

36. Sachs, Business Outlook, Chap. 4; Schlesinger, *Colonial Merchants*, 50–60; Andrews, *Boston Merchants and Non-Importation*, 22–32; *Historical Statistics of the U.S.*, 757.

37. An extensive bibliography concerning paper money is to be found in E. James Ferguson, "Currency Finance: An Interpretation of Colonial Monetary Practices," *Wm. and Mary Qtly.*, 3rd Ser., X (1953), 153–180.

38. See Theodore Thayer, "The Land-Bank System in the American Colonies;" *Journal of Economic History*, XIII (1953), 145–159.

these land bank loans directly provided businessmen with a source of working capital.[39] And, in general, local merchants saw a close link between fluctuations in the visible money supply (chiefly paper money and foreign coin) and American prosperity. While modern analysts may debate the wisdom of the varying colonial monetary practices and proposals, there is no doubt that Britain's constant and jealous supervision of the colonists' currency systems seriously weakened the American's ability to control their own economy. The reaction to the Currency Act of 1764 reflected only a new and extreme phase of a long struggle over this aspect of economic sovereignty.[40]

Control over currency and banking was for some in the commercial provinces the "sovereign remedy."[41] But this was not the only stratagem pursued by the beleaguered larger merchants to rectify structural imbalances in domestic and foreign trade. Testy letters to British houses berating them for crediting shopkeepers, or for shipping unsolicited goods, were a commonplace in the decade before Independence. The attempts of the large importers to regulate the vendues also continued, although the strenuous campaigns met with only partial success. In Massachusetts a move in 1773 to limit business to four licensed auctioneers in each town was vetoed by the Privy Council.[42]

Another recourse for the large merchants was the encouragement of manufactures. Declining profits in the dry goods trade made investment opportunities offered by domestic industries all the more appealing. British regulations had long been ignored, and despite prohibitive legislation, colonial hats, shoes, finished ironware, and furniture competed profitably in North America and the West Indies with English products.[43] Some industries, however, catered to, rather than competed

39. See Joseph A. Ernst, Currency in the Era of the American Revolution, 1764–1781 (unpubl. Ph.D. diss., University of Wisconsin, 1962), Chap. 8.

40. This is the subject of a forthcoming monograph, The Currency Act of 1764: A Study of the Political Economy of Revolution, by Joseph A. Ernst, to be published by the Institute of Early American History and Culture. Despite its New Deal bias and questionable assumptions about the quantity theory of money, Richard A. Lester's *Monetary Experiments: Early American and Recent Scandinavian* (Princenon, N.J., 1939) remains a useful introduction to the earlier struggle over this aspect of economic sovereignty.

41. This point is discussed in Joseph A. Ernst, "The Currency Act Repeal Movement: A Study in Imperial Politics and Revolutionary Crisis, 1764–1767," *Wm. and Mary Qtly.*, 3rd Ser., XXV (1968), 177–211.

42. The public auctions in Pennsylvania seemed almost untouched by the assembly's deliberations. In New York, a 5% tax on vendue sales proved generally ineffective. See Sachs, Business Outlook, 253–254; and Jensen, *Maritime Commerce*, 259ff.

43. For a general discussion of manufacturing in the period, see Sachs, Business Outlook, 254–255. An interesting contemporary commentary on the subjects is *The Commercial Conduct of the Province of New-York Considered, and The True Interest of that Colony attempted to be shewn In a Letter to The Society of Arts, Agriculture, and Economy* (New York, 1767), Bancroft Collection,

with, Great Britain. These offered the merchant the possibility of directly reducing his indebtedness to the mother country. Consequently, in the decades before Independence there was a spurt in the production and export to England of such goods as pig and bar iron, alkalines, and whale products. Wine, soap, hemp, and flax were also encouraged, although with poor results.[44] But the relationship of the merchants to domestic manufacturing went beyond questions of straightforward economic interest. Increasingly after the French and Indian War, the colonial importer looked upon the development of domestic industry as an integral part of a program to achieve economic sovereignty to counter the restrictions imposed by membership in the British Empire. "We are clearly of the opinion," wrote one importer in 1764, "that if our trade is obstructed or labors under any objection, it will more affect England than us, as it will put it out of our power to pay for such vast quantities of goods, as we have yearly imported from thence. And what we want more than we can pay for will be made among ourselves."[45] Reasoning in this manner, colonial merchants were willing to encourage native industries, such as the production of woolen and linen cloth, that directly competed with their importations.[46]

Still the encouragement of manufacturing, as important as it might have been in reflecting the outlook of the merchants, absorbed only limited amounts of capital and ultimately made only a small difference in the structure of foreign trade. Control over currency and banking, regulation of vendues, development of manufactures – the stratagems used by the established importers to ameliorate conditions of glutted

England and America, 1766–1767, New York Public Library, New York. On the question of ironware see Arthur C. Bining, *British Regulation of the Colonial Iron Industry* (Philadelphia, 1933). The trade in colonial hats is discussed in *Pennsylvania Chronicle* (Philadelphia), June 29, 1767; and the commerce in shoes and household furniture is mentioned in Lt. Gov. William Stuart to Lord Dartmouth, Dec. 24, 1733, Colonial Office, Class 71, Vol. 3, fol. 71, Public Record Office. Hereafter cited as C. O. 71/3: 71; Lord Dartmouth to Stuart, Apr. 6, 1774, C. O. 71/4: 118.

44. On pig and bar iron see Arthur C. Bining, *Pennsylvania Iron Manufacture in the Eighteenth Century* (Pennsylvania Historical Commission, *Publications*, IV [Harrisburg, Pa., 1938]). Otherwise see William S. Sachs and Ari Hoogenboom, *The Enterprising Colonials: Society on the Eve of the Revolution* (Chicago, 1965), 103–106; Sachs, Business Outlook, 259–269; and *Historical Statistics of the U.S.* 762–765, 771.

45. Richard Waln, Jr., to Nicholas Waln, June 25, 1764, Waln Collection, Box II, Hist. Soc. of Pa.

46. Certainly this was much in the minds of the New York affiliate of the London-based Society for the Promotion of Arts, Agriculture, and Economy, established in 1767 and revived in 1767 in an effort to encourage by private means the fabrication of cheap linen cloth for local consumption and the employment of the poor. See n. 43 above and *New-York Journal*, Dec. 24, 31, 1767, Jan. 14, 21, 1768; John Reynell to William Henry Reynell, May 15, 1769, Reynell Papers.

markets, overcompetition, lack of liquidity, and falling profits – for the most part proved unsuccessful despite the strong support of merchant communities. Nonetheless, these efforts sooner or later boded conflict with royal authority. The consciousness of a clash of interests made the merchants more aware of the identity of economic and political goals.

One course of action that did offer the larger merchants immediate benefits and tangible relief from depressed conditions – at least in the short run – was the nonimportation of British goods. Nonimportation permitted the merchants to dispose of their inventories at higher prices and to retrench. "You will have a good price for all your dead goods which have always been unprofitable," an anonymous writer reminded his merchant readers in the November 1767 issue of the *Pennsylvania Gazette*. "You will collect your debts and bring your debts in England to a close, so that balances would hereby be brought about in your favor, which without some such method must forever be against you."[47] Equally important, nonimportation meant the elimination, if only temporarily, of the upstart trader with his smaller stock of goods.[48] Finally, it meant that bills of exchange, the international currency of the eighteenth century, would be cheaper so that debts could be paid to England without a sharp discount.[49] As a consequence, merchants in the northern colonies adopted nonimportation in 1765 and again in 1768. In Charles Town's rice and naval stores economy, local conditions made for somewhat different timing, and there the second boycott was decided upon in 1769.[50]

In sum, nonimportation was only incidentally designed to compel Parliament to repeal obnoxious legislation. Without understanding the economic background, the timing and the nature of the boycotts is almost inexplicable. The agreements adopted in Boston in 1768 and Charles Town in 1769 were intended to run for no more than a year, even if Parliament took no action whatsoever.[51] Nonimportation was not applied to the West Indian trade until 1774, and the taxes on tropical

47. *Pennsylvania Gazette* (Philadelphia), Nov. 17, 1767.

48. The importers "got rid of their old Shop-Keepers," one editorialist observed in 1770. *Ibid.*, May 31, 1770. Henry Drinker to Abel James, Apr. 29, 1770, "Effects of the 'Non-Importation Agreement' in Philadelphia, 1769–1770," *Pa. Mag. Hist. Biog.*, XIV (1890), 42; *Pa. Gaz.* (Phila.), Aug. 23, 1770.

49. This point is discussed more in the forthcoming study of the Currency Act of 1764. See n. 40. Gen. Thomas Gage to William Melish, Dec. 20, 1765, Treasury Papers, Class 1, Vol. 442, fol. 219, Public Record Office; Samuel Coates to Noah Parker, Mar. 17, 1769, Coates Letterbook, Hist. Soc. of Pa.

50. However inadequate, the best account is still Leila Sellers, *Charleston Business on the Eve of the American Revolution* (Chapel Hill, N.C., 1934), 203–210.

51. See Merrill Jensen, *The Founding of a Nation: A History of the American Revolution 1763–1776* (New York, 1968), 283–284, 311, 500–506.

goods were always paid despite Britain's avowed intention of raising a revenue, rather than regulating commerce, with those duties. American merchants would not curtail their commerce with the Caribbean because in their dealing with the islands they enjoyed persistently favorable balances to pay for British goods.[52]

Nor were the merchants reluctant, at least in private correspondence, to express their reasons for supporting the boycott. John Chew frankly discussed the desire of Philadelphia merchants for nonimportation. In a letter of November 7, 1765, he wrote: "Indeed we are well convinced something of this sort is absolutely necessary at this time from the great much too large importation that has for sometime past been made. There will be no wanted goods for a twelve month."[53] The nonimportation agreements of 1765 and 1766 were short-lived, ending in the jubilation that accompanied the repeal of the Stamp Act. But they had beneficial results, bringing down exchange rates and clearing glutted inventories.[54] By 1767 and 1768, conditions had worsened once more, and importers were beset by the same broad spectrum of problems. Again, merchants turned to nonimportation for motives avowedly economic. "I believe the gentlemen in trade are one and all convinced," Thomas Cushing of Boston observed in 1768, "that it will be to no good purpose for them to import English goods as usual. They despair of ever selling them, and consequently of ever being able to pay for them."[55] His sentiments were echoed by a Philadelphia importer in April 1769: "A time of leisure seems now approaching and the commercial intercourse with Great Britain is inhibited for a season. It is a very general wish amongst the merchants that it may continue at least one year in order that they may dispose of the great quantity of goods on hand, and contract their affairs. This is agreeable to my private interest."[56]

52. Sachs, Business Outlook, 142–164, 170–172, and n. 18 above. James F. Shepherd and Gary M. Walton, "Estimate of 'Invisible' Earnings in the Balance of Payments of the British North American Colonies, 1768–1772," *Jour. Econ. Hist.*, XXIX (1969), 230–263. Walton and Shepherd's figures, however, appear to underestimate the illicit trade from the Caribbean to North America. See An Estimate of the Tea, Sugar, and Molasses illegally imported . . . , undated [ca. 1764], Add. MS 38335: 243.

53. To Samuel Galloway, Nov. 7, 1765, Galloway Papers, Library of Congress.

54. Sachs, Business Outlook, 193–195; Samuel Rhoads, Jr., to Richard Neave & Son, "Extracts from the Letter-Book of Samuel Rhoads, Jr., of Philadelphia," *Pa. Mag. Hist. Biog.*, XIV (1890), 425; exchange rates and dry goods price series for Philadelphia, compiled by the authors, indicate favorable movements during nonimportation.

55. To Denys DeBerdt, Mar. 4, 1768, quoted in Jensen, *Founding of a Nation*, 271.

56. R. Waln, Jr., to Harford & Powell, Apr. 18, 1769, Richard Waln Letterbook. Similar complaints could be heard in the other commercial centers as well. This is discussed in part in Sachs, Business Outlook, Chap. 7; and Virginia D. Harrington, *The New York Merchant on the Eve of the Revolution* (New York, 1935), Chap. 8. See also the entries for these years in the Laurens Papers, Roll 2, no. 3; and Philip L. White, ed., *The Beekman Merchantile Papers 1746–1799*, II (New York, 1956).

When the majority of the merchants sought to abandon nonimportation in 1770, charges of self-interest filled the press, and rightly so. As far as questions of principle were concerned, the only change occurring in 1770 was the partial repeal of the Townshend duties. There had been no serious revision of restrictive British legislation, and it could well be argued that the tax on tea was as serious an insult to Americans as the tax on painters' colors, glass, and tea. The point remains that merchants had instituted the boycott for reasons other than abstract principle and, having disposed of their inventories, easily separated themselves from the ideologues to resume trade at the end of 1770.

What was lost for the moment on those who railed at the merchants in 1770 was the profound and growing commitment of the colonial importers to the achievement of sovereignty, economic and political. It is in this light that many of the conflicts between the colonists and the British within the third quarter of the century must be viewed. The struggles over the Currency Act, the Stamp Act, the Revenue Act, and the Townshend Acts in the 1760s reflected a strengthened commitment to economic autonomy and an increased awareness of the close ties between the world of colonial business and imperial politics.

Although the nonimportation agreements of 1769 and 1770 significantly ameliorated depressed markets, as had the trade stoppage during 1766, by 1771 commercial centers from Charles Town to Boston were inundated by unprecedented quantities of English goods. The ensuing depression was the last, and perhaps the worst, of the colonial period. The proliferation of small importers, the wholesale dumping of goods by English houses, the sharp rise in vendue sales – all made American importers bitter once again. The fitful, angry reaction to the Tea Act of 1773 must be understood in this context. The East India Company's decision to sell directly to American agents was not viewed by the colonists as a chance to buy cheaper tea. Rather, for many colonial traders it was another instance of a British exporter seeking to swell his trade by dealing outside the established channels.[57]

In the swirl of events that followed the "tea parties," the established importers played a crucial role, both in positions of leadership and in the day to day administration of programs adopted by provincial and con-

57. A general discussion of the 1772 depression is to be found in Richard B. Sheridan, "The British Credit Crisis of 1772 and the American Colonies," *Jour. Econ. Hist.*, XX (1960), 161–186. For a closer evaluation of events in America, however, see Sachs, Business Outlook, 216–223. On the tea question, see Schlesinger, *Colonial Merchants*, Chaps. 6–8; see also, for instance, James and Drinker to Pigou and Booth, Nov. 18, 20, 1773, Henry Drinker Letterbook, Hist. Soc. of Pa.; and On the Tea Trade, Jan. 19, 1773, Wharton MSS. See also Benjamin Woods Labaree, *The Boston Tea Party* (New York, 1964), Chap. 5.

tinental congresses. Such vital, if secretive, actions as securing munitions and finding markets for America's cash crops performed by patriotic merchants made possible the final break from England. Hence, an understanding of the colonial merchants' long-term struggle for economic sovereignty is necessary to explain the nature of the Revolutionary movement in the commercial colonies and the leadership provided by the merchant class after Independence.[58]

Compared to those colonies with developed urban centers, the tobacco growing area – basically Virginia, along with adjacent regions in Maryland and North Carolina – was the more thoroughly penetrated by the British imperial system and the less able to adapt stratagems to counter the threatening developments in the Atlantic economy after 1745. The second long swing of trade from 1745 to 1775 brought to an end a lengthy period marked by a persistently favorable balance of trade with the mother country. After 1745, imports increased dramatically, facilitated by a heavy inflow of British capital.[59]

This inflow of capital was accompanied by far-reaching changes in the relations between colony and metropolis. The most striking aspect of these changes was the rapid growth of planter indebtedness. There was considerable alarm among colonial Virginians and Marylanders over the growing burden of debt, and Progressive historians such as Isaac Harrell and Schlesinger echoed this concern, seeing in the accumulated indebtedness grounds for revolution.[60] Neo-whig critics, however, have rejected that conclusion as a crude piece of "economic determinism" because there is scant evidence directly linking the debt question to Virginia's Revolutionary movement.[61] But if advocates of the "Planter Indebtedness" thesis failed to make a convincing case, it was only because they did not pursue their argument far enough. A detailing of debts reveals little by itself, for a debt may be either a boon or a disadvantage depending on the structure of the credit system and the dynamics of economic change. It is these latter questions that must be

58. See Jensen, *Founding of a Nation*, 632–633; Marc Egnal, Society and Politics in Massachusetts, 1774–1778 (unpubl. M.A. thesis, University of Wisconsin, 1967); Harrington, *New York Merchant*, 320–350.

59. The following analysis is based on the authors' works in progress. But for a more detailed discussion of certain aspects of the problem see Ernst, "Currency Act of 1764," *Wm. and Mary Qtly.*, 3rd Ser., XXII (1965), 33–74.

60. Isaac F. Harrell, *Loyalism in Virginia* (Philadelphia, 1926); and Schlesinger, *Colonial Merchants*, 38–39.

61. See the discussion in Thad W. Tate, "The Coming of the Revolution in Virginia: Britain's Challenge to Virginia's Ruling Class, 1763–1776," *Wm. and Mary Qtly.*, 3rd Ser., XIX (1962), 323–343.

investigated to understand fully the significance of the growing burden of debt.[62]

By the late 1740s, the intimate and relaxed relationship between the large planters and the English consignment merchants (to whom the planters shipped their tobacco to be sold on the English market) was breaking down. Replacing it was a new credit system managed by local factors of the great Glasgow tobacco houses. The distinguishing mark of the new system, whose real development accompanies the second period of imperial economic growth (1745–1775), was the establishment of chains of stores stretching along the great river valleys. These Scottish firms soon dominated the tobacco economy in the Piedmont and made serious inroads into the trade of the older Tidewater areas. The reason for the success of the Glasgow merchants was that they financed their exports to Virginia out of pocket by advancing the Virginians credit to make up trade deficits; the factor at each store bought tobacco, sold dry goods, and extended credit.[63]

The planters reacted with mixed emotions to the ever-expanding dealings of the Scots factors. On one hand, the credit these storekeepers proffered was the lifeblood of the plantation economy. It allowed the planter to defer payment for European goods and at the same time freed cash for the purchase of land and slaves, the basis of economic expansion and social position. The imperative to enlarge one's holdings remained constant and so did the demand for credit. On the other hand, the power of the Scottish merchants went far beyond these commercial dealings and threatened the planter elite on the most basic levels of political, social, and economic power. As James Madison once expressed it, the "essential legislation" of Virginia was passed by Scots traders at court days in Williamsburg, when they set tobacco prices, fixed exchange rates, and settled accounts.[64] In addition, the Scots challenged the planter elite's power even more directly. First in Whitehall, then in Virginia itself, the Scottish firms and their factors sought to block unfavorable legislation by the planter-dominated House of Burgesses. From 1759 on, for instance, the Scots, together with some of the larger London tobacco houses, persisted in using their influence on both sides of the Atlantic to regulate Virginia's paper money practices in their own

62. See esp. in this regard the exchange between Jackson T. Main and Forrest McDonald, *ibid.*, XVII (1960), 86–110.

63. See esp. Calvin B. Coulter, Jr., The Virginia Merchants (unpubl. Ph.D. diss., Princeton University, 1944); Jacob M. Price, "The Rise of Glasgow in the Chesapeake Tobacco Trade, 1707–1775," *Wm. and Mary Qtly.*, 3rd Ser., XI (1954), 179–199; James H. Soltow, *The Economic Role of Williamsburg* (Charlottesville, Va., 1965), Chap. 2.

64. Quoted in Fairfax Harrison, *Landmarks of Old Prince William: A Study of Origins in Northern Virginia*, II (Richmond, 1924), 390.

interest.[65] Thus members of the planting elite were faced with a dilemma: how to maintain their place in a society that valued social and economic independence without becoming pawns to that "plague of Egyptian locusts," the hated Scots.

Further, the Scottish factors' practice of dealing directly with the myriad of small tobacco producers threatened the sovereignty of the larger planters, who under the consignment system had handled the output of these smaller farmers, including it with their own consignments. A basis of unity was forged between the great planters and the farmers, both of whom now dealt directly with representatives of British capital.[66]

If these institutional shifts accompanying the transformation in the system of credit and trade elicited loud outcries against the Scots as well as imperial authorities, the sudden collapse of credit in 1762 produced even greater strains. At a time of general financial calamity in Europe, tobacco houses in Scotland and England began to cut back their short-term loans to Virginia and to press for payment of back debts. Meanwhile, the low price for tobacco and the prospect of an end to the French and Indian War, which was expected to lower prices even further, prompted a temporary abatement of tobacco imports. The overall effect was to reduce sharply the amount of credit and foreign exchange available in Virginia at the very moment the demand for sterling remittances was greatest. Many planters now refused to pay debts. General suspension of court proceedings involving debt cases soon followed, and public loans and similar expedients were urged.

Some of the cures posed were more radical. There was discussion, for instance, of exploiting new markets through the diversification of agriculture, and of encouraging secondary manufactures in items such as flour and bread. In addition, some planters raised anew the possibility of totally reorienting the local economy by accelerating the shift out of tobacco and into foodstuffs through the creation of a highly commercialized urban marketplace. The idea here was to lessen the dependence on resident Scots factors through the establishment of new urban-commercial hubs that would function as Philadelphia did in the North. Such centers were to be kept firmly in the hands of local Virginians. The outcome of these various schemes proved disheartening. Despite discouragements, the planters showed an increasing concern

65. See n. 59.

66. A different viewpoint is expressed in a recent article by Aubrey C. Land, "Economic Behavior in a Planting Society: The Eighteenth-Century Chesapeake," *Journal of Southern History*, XXXIII (1967), 469–485. But Land misreads the evidence regarding the credit structure of the Chesapeake region, and especially of Maryland.

with economic sovereignty. Furthermore, they came to feel that the restriction imposed by Parliament and the credit system of the Scots made changes in this direction unlikely. Economic strains in Virginia fast became an inseparable part of the struggle against the new British postwar policies.[67]

The economic situation worsened again after 1772 following the collapse of credit for the second time in a decade. The cry of the planters caught in a seemingly hopeless web of debt grew more shrill. With significant economic change an unrealized dream, the financial panic of 1772 and 1773 removed lingering hopes of a solution within the existing framework of the imperial system.[68]

Especially in those parts of Virginia, such as the Northern Neck bordering on the Potomac, where progressive planters were already making strenuous efforts to diversify their agriculture and establish commercial relations apart from the ubiquitous Scottish store system, more and more wealthy Virginians became convinced of the need for a radical change in imperial relations and for control of their own economic destiny.[69] Even planters who hoped for moderate reform within the empire were willing to take an active part in the frenzied politics that followed the depression of 1772 and 1773. Planters throughout the tobacco colonies stood shoulder to shoulder in a movement directed in large part against the Scottish mercantile community.[70] It is no surprise to find the planting elite in the forefront of Maryland's and Virginia's Revolutionary struggle.

If two developments – first, the long-term growth of the whig elite's self-conscious strength, and second, the increasing awareness of a need for economic sovereignty in the face of the post-1745 spurt in British exports and of new British policies after 1763 – called into existence the Revolutionary movement, a third factor, the involvement of the urban "lower orders" and the smaller farmers, was crucial in determining the nature of this movement.

The participation of the urban lower classes in the Revolution is a familiar theme; it was, of course, one of the Progressive historians' chief concerns. Most writing has stressed, with some validity, that tradesmen, sailors, and laborers were initially brought into political activity during

67. The foregoing analysis is based on the authors' work in progress. But for a brief discussion of some aspects of the problem see Ernst, "Robinson Scandal," *Va. Mag. Hist. Biog.*, LXXVIII (1969), 146–173.

68. See Sheridan, "British Credit Crisis of 1772," *Jour. Econ. Hist.*, XX (1960), 161–186.

69. Schlesinger, *Colonial Merchants*, 361–368.

70. See Robert P. Thomson, The Merchant in Virginia, 1700–1775 (unpubl. Ph.D. diss., University of Wisconsin, 1955).

the 1760s at the behest of the whig elite. The wealthier patriots in the cities, it has been argued, used the colonial "mob" to their own ends, directing its furies against stamp distributors and customs officials. What we emphasize here in addition is that to a great extent the involvement of these lower classes resulted from their own economic grievances. To begin with, city dwellers were the first to be encouraged to buy with liberal offers of credit, and the first to feel the bitterness of depression and debt contraction. Nor were tradesmen and artisans merely the first to be pressed for payment; they were also frequently the last to be paid in a time of stringency. "The poor industrious tradesmen, the needy mechanic, and all men of narrow circumstance," an observer of events reported to the readers of the *New-York Gazette* in November 1767, were facing "impending ruin." The "money'd men" were holding on to whatever cash came their way, refusing to pay their bills and bankrupting the small tradesman and artisan.[71] Also, during periods of business contraction, sailors and day laborers increasingly found themselves without work.[72] Thus beginning in the 1750s, and later paralleling the merchants' nonimportation movement in the 1760s, the urban lower classes organized and agitated for agreements promoting nonconsumption and domestic manufacturing. Such compacts served both to allow the debt-ridden citizenry to retrench as well as to boost local employment. For some among the urban "lower orders" these agreements marked their initial entry into active political life; for others they offered one additional, important reason for participation in the Revolutionary movement.[73]

As the urban lower classes became more involved in the pursuit of their own interests through such programs as nonconsumption and domestic manufacturing, they also became more vociferous in articulating other demands of their own, demands for the further democratization of colonial society. This new militancy frightened many of the merchants who now saw the threat of social upheaval. Admittedly, in historical

71. "Probus of the Printer," in *N.-Y. Jour.*, Nov. 19, 1767; Thomas Clifford to Thomas Penington, June 25, 1768, Clifford Letterbook, Hist. Soc. of Pa.; *Pa. Chron.* (Phila.), Oct. 10, 1768, Mar. 13, 1769; Sachs, Business Outlook, 254–256. See also Richard Walsh, *Charleston's Sons of Liberty: A Study of the Artisans 1763–1789* (Columbia, S.C., 1959).

72. This is a question that has yet to be fully researched. But see the suggestive note in Lemisch, "Jack Tar," *Wm. and Mary Qtly.*, 3rd Ser., XXV (1968), 397, n. 106. Unfortunately, Lemisch's concern with Revolutionary ideology among the "lower classes" has kept him from seriously investigating the economic conditions of ordinary life. See also Marcus Wilson Jernegan, *Laboring and Dependent Classes in Colonial America 1607–1783* (Chicago, 1931).

73. Schlesinger, *Colonial Merchants*, 106–115. Emphasizing the "lower orders'" involvement in nonconsumption (though in a different interpretative framework) in Jensen, *Founding of a Nation*, Chap. 10.

retrospect, there was little change in the structure of society though some in institutions. But there was ample justification for the fears of the wealthy, as numerous editorialists called for far-reaching changes in the nature of government. The mere airing of these demands was enough to convince many in the upper classes that the Revolution had gone too far and that it was better to bear the burdens of membership in the British Empire than to risk social disruption at home. This lower-class militancy helps explain the existence of important loyalist minorities in each of the port cities. On the other hand, most of the whig elite felt with some prescience that the situation could be kept well under control.[74]

Apart from the area of tobacco cultivation, the protests against Britain centered in the cities. Any recounting of the Revolutionary movement must necessarily focus on these centers and recognize the significance of the urban classes, merchant and laborer alike, which went far beyond the weight of their numbers. Yet, the bulk of the population was composed of farmers, and only with their involvement was war with Britain possible. Most farmers of the northern colonies and of the Appalachian plateau stood outside the Revolutionary movement until 1774. In part, this reflected the pacifism of certain religious sects as well as the difficulty of informing and organizing a population spread out over a large area. More significantly these farmers did not share the economic grievances of either merchants and tradesmen of the coastal cities or of the tobacco growing planters of Virginia and Maryland. The dry goods sector of the economy suffered from chronic depressions after 1745, strapping those who either handled goods or relied directly on British capital. However, those who raised wheat or other provisions experienced generally good times, selling their products to a constantly expanding world market and receiving prices which steadily appreciated in terms of West Indian and English goods. As the value of holdings constantly rose, it was only the improvident, or the heavily mortgaged, husbandman who suffered from the postwar contractions that beset the colonial credit supply and the dry goods sector.[75]

After 1774 the small farmer took a more active role in response to the increased presence of British forces and the impassioned pleas of continental and provincial congresses. His loyalty depended on a variety of considerations: the advantages offered by the new state governments, the

74. See the recent discussion in Jensen, "The American People," *Jour. Amer. Hist.*, LVII (1970), 5–35.

75. William S. Sachs, "Agricultural Conditions in the Northern Colonies Before the Revolution," *Jour. Econ. Hist.*, XIII (1953), 274–290. Concerning commodity prices see n. 22 above. The series for English goods were derived by the authors.

traditional relationship of the backcountry to the dominant groups on the coast, and often, simply the question of which army was in the neighborhood. In states like Pennsylvania, where Independence was accompanied by a new state constitution giving the back country more just apportionment and control over local affairs, the farmers became enthusiastic patriots. In the Carolinas, where the new government, like the old, showed less interest in mollifying back-country discontent, there were significant tory elements among the small farmers.[76]

One group of agriculturists serviced by an urban center had been active in the Revolutionary movement throughout the decade before Independence: the South Carolina rice and indigo planters. These slaveholders, like the wheat and provision farmers of the North, imported and exported their goods through a city and dealt with a merchant community composed predominantly of native merchants rather than foreign factors. Like northern farmers, rice planters sold to an expanding world market and enjoyed generally rising prices. But South Carolina planters differed in important ways from those who cultivated wheat and provisions, for rice and indigo planting required far greater inputs of capital, chiefly in the form of slaves, than did the production of grain. This means that rice and indigo planters were involved to a greater degree in local money markets than were northern farmers, and hence were more seriously affected by the currency and credit contractions that plagued the South Carolina economy in the 1760s and especially in the 1770s.[77] Also, planters of coastal South Carolina, as men of wealth and stature, had long been active in the struggles with royal governors and British policies.[78] This different background helps explain their more active role in the years before 1774.

The upper-class whigs who stood in the forefront of the Revolutionary movement retained their coherence and their momentum after 1776. Independence was no more their ultimate goal than was the repeal of any specific piece of British legislation. The control over the American economy that they sought required a restructuring of government and a

76 On this matter see the recent speculations of Merrill Jensen, "The American Revolution and American Agriculture," *Agricultural History*, XLIII (1969), 107–124. Noteworthy state studies include Robert J. Taylor, *Western Massachusetts in the Revolution* (Providence, R.I., 1954); and Irving Mark, *Agrarian Conflicts in Colonial New York, 1711–1775* (New York, 1940). See also Egnal, Society and Politics in Massachusetts, 1774–1778, Chaps. 1–2.

77. William Pollard Letterbook, 1774, esp. to Benjamin and John Bower, Jan. 25, 1774.

78. See M. Eugene Sirmans, *Colonial South Carolina: A Political History, 1663–1763* (Chapel Hill, N.C., 1966); and Joseph A. Ernst, Growth of the Commons House of Assembly of South Carolina 1761–1775 (unpubl. M.A. thesis, University of Wisconsin, 1958).

comprehensive program of legislation: for those in urban centers a national banking system and American navigation acts, and for the tobacco planters of the South, the encouragement of national cities. In addition, upper-class whigs showed a continued concern for challenges from the "lower orders." The Constitution of 1789, from the whig elite's viewpoint, was the culmination of the movement for Independence, not its antithesis.

Interpretations of the Revolutionary decades have changed much during the twentieth century. Progressive scholars offered a broad explanation which on closer scrutiny has been found wanting. Lower-class movements and social upheaval may in part characterize the Revolutionary movement; they do not explain it. Since the Second World War a generation of neo-whig scholars has completely rewritten the history of these years. Ideas rather than social classes, unreasoning fears rather than rational self-interest, have become keynotes of the Revolution. But if the pitfalls of the Progressive approach have been avoided, more glaring shortcomings have appeared. While neo-whig interpretations have shown an increasing concern for the "inner world" of a select group of publicists, they have at the same time shown less concern for the specific events, issues, and interests of the period. The time has come to reassert the essential reasonableness and necessity of the American Revolution in terms of the overall economic situation of the colonies and of the specific interests of the actors. In this way historians may be better able to explain both the ideas and the events that marked the decades of the American Revolution.

"The market and Massachusetts farmers, 1750–1855"

by Winifred B. Rothenberg

Throughout the seventeenth, the eighteenth, and much of the nineteenth centuries, most of America's work force was agricultural. Much of their output was consumed at home, but a proportion was traded.

Historians have debated what the precise patterns of production and exchange were and what they tell us about the *mentalité* of these farmers. This debate motivates Winifred Rothenberg in "The market and Massachusetts farmers, 1750–1855." Her first goal is to understand the process and timing of American economic growth. The second goal is to move the debate out of the realm of ideological discourse and into the realm of empirically testable propositions. Rothenberg wants to build a body of evidence that consists of observable behavior rather than unverifiable statements about "states of mind."

Note that Rothenberg focuses on the emergence of markets rather than on a "capitalist mind-set." She avoids the word "capitalism" because it is difficult, if not impossible, to define it in such a way that its presence can be distinguished from its absence. In many ways, it is one of many words that are "operationally meaningless." The framing of operationally meaningful, that is testable, hypotheses, more than mere quantification, is what distinguishes the methodology of social science history from that of many other kinds of history.

Rothenberg's argument proceeds by testing five indicators. Examine each of these indicators closely. Does each convince you that farmers were "embedded" in the market? Do they convince you that farmers responded to prices and profit opportunities? How do the building blocks of the argument support one another? Does the fact that these indicators lend themselves to quantification mean that only quantifiable magnitudes should be admissible as evidence in historical debates? How useful is quantification for unlocking the mysteries of human behavior?

In addition, consider these questions:

- How do transportation costs affect a farmer's outlook?
- Would farmers haul their products as far as they did, and to the locations they did, if they were not market oriented?

Rothenberg recognizes that the estimated relationship between the price of corn and the slaughter weight of hogs is "counter to intuition."

- What would you conclude if the signs had been reversed? What would you conclude if she had discovered no relationship?
- Can you reconcile this finding with a plausible model of the hog market? Is a single-equation model of this market appropriate?
- What does the elasticity of the supply curve imply about the values and attitudes of the producer?
- Are there other tests of whether or not a farmer was isolated from the market?

A market is considered "integrated" when the price of a product is uniform (or when differences are less than or equal to transport costs between locations). Rothenberg has not discovered uniform prices, but markets are not born full-blown from the head of Zeus. Market integration is a process that takes place over time as buyers and sellers locate each other, traveling farther afield to get a better price. In so doing, the differences in prices for the same good in different places are arbitraged away and prices converge toward uniformity. Rothenberg finds this process of price convergence in one period but discovers divergence in an earlier period. In fact, for most of the goods, the variation in prices is lowest in the earliest period.

- What do these differences in prices mean?
- Do you agree with Rothenberg's interpretation of the trend in the variation of prices?
- Were early price regulations good or bad for the economy?

Rothenberg takes up additional issues, especially the development and integration of labor and capital markets in her recent book, *From Market-Places to a Market Economy: The Transformation of Rural Massachusetts, 1750–1850* (1992). In addition, she elaborates on the argument that regulation and price fixing by Puritan church and town authorities initially constrained the movement of prices and wages, thus distorting the pattern of price convergence.

Additional Reading

Christopher Clark, *The Roots of Rural Capitalism: Western Massachusetts, 1780–1860*, Ithaca, NY: Cornell University Press, 1990.

James Henretta, "Families and Farms: *Mentalité* in Pre-Industrial America," *William and Mary Quarterly*, 3rd ser., 35 (January 1978), 3–32.

Joshua Rosenbloom, "Is Wage Rate Dispersion a Good Index of Labor Market Integration? A Comment on Rothenberg," *Journal of Economic History*, 49 (March 1989), 166–9.

Winifred Rothenberg, *From Market-Places to a Market Economy: The Transformation of Rural Massachusetts, 1750–1850*, Chicago: University of Chicago Press, 1992.

David Weiman, "Farmers and the Market in Antebellum America: A View from the Georgia Upcountry," *Journal of Economic History*, 47 (September 1987), 627–47.

3

The market and Massachusetts farmers, 1750–1855

WINIFRED B. ROTHENBERG

This paper attempts to make a contribution, both in method and in substance, to the debate about the timing and extent of market orientation in pre-industrial New England agriculture. The method consists in testing five quantifiable hypotheses, with data from manuscript account books and daybooks. The results, in repeated trials, confirm the influence of the market on the rural economy of Massachusetts from very early on.

Circumscribed as this subject is, its historiography in this century has followed a dialectic closely paralleling the dialectic of American history-writing generally. A preliminary survey of the debate will set the argument of this paper in its proper setting.

The debate began with Percy Bidwell. In all his work he described eighteenth- and early nineteenth-century farmers in New England as trapped by poor husbandry in chronically low-yield, subsistence agriculture, isolated by the lack of markets from the growth generated in the commercial sectors of the economy.[1]

Source: Winifred B. Rothenberg, "The Market and Massachusetts Farmers, 1750–1855," *Journal of Economic History* (June 1981), 283–314. Reprinted with permission of the author and the Economic History Association.

The author is a graduate student in American economic history at Brandeis University.

This article has been long in the making, and along the way much help has been received for which this acknowledgement is formal, but the gratitude is deep and enduring. There is a sense in which this has been a shared experience, shared with Stanley Engerman and Sarah F. McMahon above all, and with David Hackett Fisher, Jeremy Atack, Robert Margo, Claudia Goldin, Kenneth Sokoloff, Allan Kulikoff, Robert Fogel, Dan Scott Smith, Russell Menard, James T. Lemon, and Richard Sylla.

The author is also grateful to Etta Faulkner and Jay Adams of Old Sturbridge Village, Kathy Majors of the American Antiquarian Society, and the staffs of Baker Library Manuscripts Division (Harvard Business School), the Essex Institute, the Dedham Historical Society, and the Massachusetts State Archives.

1. Percy W. Bidwell, "Rural Economy in New England at the Beginning of the Nineteenth Century," *Transactions of the Connecticut Academy of Arts & Sciences*, Vol. 20 (April 1916), 241–399; Bidwell, "The Agricultural Revolution in New England," *American Historical Review*, 26 (July 1921), 683–702; Bidwell and John I. Falconer, *History of Agriculture in the Northern United States, 1620–1860* (New York, 1941, rpt.).

The point here is that Bidwell's perspective was fully consistent with the Progressive historiography of his own time. Substantively, he confirmed that conflicts of interest existed, in this case between farmers involved in the market and those locked outside it, between farmers with land who could remain and those without land who would have to move on, between farmers on the one hand and merchants and artisans on the other. In addition, the methodological consequences of putting about three quarters of New England's population beyond the reach of the market were congenial to the Progressives who wanted to limit the dominion of abstract theory over the rough texture of real life.

The reign of Progressive historians, and of Bidwell, was very long indeed, but "ideas have an inner dialectic of their own,"[2] and the pendulum eventually swung the other way. The same year that Hofstadter first developed the ideas that would henceforth be called Consensus History[3] – 1948 – Max George Schumacher finished his now-famous dissertation at Berkeley, "The Northern Farmer and his Markets During the Late Colonial Period." Drawing on British Public Record Office Customs Reports between 1768 and 1773, he showed the extent to which northern farmers participated in or were affected by imperial and coastwise trade.

Rodney C. Loehr's critique of Bidwell appeared in 1952.[4] Bidwell's argument for self-sufficiency, said Loehr, was inadequately supported and heavily deductive: from the small size of the non-farm sector the narrowness of the market had only been deduced; from the high level of mobility low productivity had only been deduced. Loehr, using contemporaneous travellers' diaries, had, on the other hand, found trade, exchange, and commerce ubiquitous. It was at this same time that Louis Hartz, in the articles on which he would base that "flagship" work of consensus history, *The Liberal Tradition*, wrote that from this nation's earliest years virtually everyone "had the mentality of an independent entrepreneur."[5]

The implications of this perspective were then elaborated by others, using different sources and boring back further and further in time. Charles S. Grant and James T. Lemon established the presence of farm surpluses from the difference between output (calculated from acreage and yield estimates) and family consumption (calculated from family size estimates and widows' portions at probate), and inferred from these surpluses the existence of markets for agricultural output in the

2. Richard Hofstadter, *The Progressive Historians* (New York, 1971), p. 439.
3. Ibid., p. 444n.
4. Rodney C. Loehr, "Self-Sufficiency on the Farm," *Agricultural History*, 26 (April 1952), 37–41.
5. Louis Hartz, *The Liberal Tradition in America* (New York, 1955), p. 89.

eighteenth century.[6] Grant's study of eighteenth-century Kent, Connecticut, went beyond marketing behavior to market *mentalité*, attributing to the early settlers an acquisitive yearning for speculative profits not unlike, he said, "perhaps the embryo John D. Rockefeller."[7] Richard Bushman found Connecticut farmers producing surpluses for a market as early as the mid-seventeenth century, and by 1690 tearing that Puritan commonwealth asunder in fierce struggles over land speculation, paper money, and the political representation of economic interests.[8] J. Emery Battis's remarkable study of the antinomian controversy pushes back even further, to 1637, the date when the market began to color values and attitudes otherwise so alien to it.[9] That the core support for Anne Hutchinson came overwhelmingly from the commercial interests of Boston confirms the curious link between the doctrine of predestination and capitalism, between free grace and free trade.[10]

It is as though the further back scholars were carried by the evidence, the fiercer they found the struggle for economic power and the more serious its threat to the social fabric.

True, strife like this does not sound much like "consensus," but it fits in this respect: what was "distinctively new" about consensus historiography was that "ideas and attitudes as *forces in history* have returned and are now being explored as *explanatory categories* in a novel way."[11] What Lemon, Grant, Bushman, and Battis were describing was a mind-set, the commercial *mentalité*, an attitude, a set of values and ideas that it would appear, existed – and had always existed – like noumena, independent of the phenomena of material life, and yet *predetermining its direction*. Was this, then, the "ineluctable singularity" of America – that it was, and always had been, "a democracy in cupidity?"[12]

The pendulum swung back hard, with the publication in 1967 of the New Left's *Towards A New Past*. Although it has taken longer to

6. Charles S. Grant, *Democracy in the Connecticut Frontier Town of Kent* (New York, 1961); and James T. Lemon, "Household Consumption in the Eighteenth Century and its Relationship to Production and Trade: The Situation among Farmers in Southeastern Pennsylvania," *Agricultural History*, 41 (Jan. 1967), 59–70.
7. Grant, *Democracy in Kent*, p. 53.
8. Richard L. Bushman, *From Puritan to Yankee: Character and the Social Order in Connecticut: 1690–1765* (Cambridge, MA, 1967).
9. J. Emery Battis, *Saints and Sectaries: Anne Hutchinson and the Antinomian Controversy in the Massachusetts Bay Colony* (Chapel Hill, 1962).
10. Larzer Ziff, in *Puritanism in America: New Culture in a New World* (New York, 1974), p. 76, put it this way: "Free grace struck a responsive, if inarticulate chord among those who felt the attractions of free trade."
11. Hofstadter, *Progressive Historians*, p. 443; emphasis added.
12. Hofstadter, *The American Political Tradition* (New York, 1948), p. viii.

formulate the New Left position on the market orientation of New England farmers, several articles have appeared in recent years, and the argument is now clear.[13] Drawing upon Marxist epistemology, Marxist analytical categories, and the wide cross-cultural perspective of Karl Polanyi, the new phase of the dialectic mounts a two-pronged attack: 1. It defines the realities of New England farmers' lives and work as "household mode of production," shared with others in the community in a "dense collective experience." Exchanges, when they took place – and they are acknowledged to have taken place – were governed by "need" and "use-value" rather than by price. The purpose of exchanges was not "to make a profit" but to weave a web of kin, community, and intergenerational reciprocity. 2. It rejects on principle the notion that onto this material substratum can be grafted an entrepreneurial ideology that is inconsistent with, and indeed dysfunctional to, it, for to do so violates the canons of Marxist epistemology in which the structure of "ideology" (beliefs, values, consciousness, *mentalité*) is functionally *rooted in* that material substratum. Ideas cut loose are never "forces in history," and ideas can never be "explanatory categories."

Instead, Henretta, Merrill, Mutch, and Clark find in eighteenth-century rural communities evidence of many kinds with which they deny the impact of markets, evidence such as the primacy of kin, forgiveness of debt, cooperative work practices, the absence of "innovative, risk-taking behavior," the persistence of subsistence agriculture and household manufactures, and, in the teeth of clear market signals, intransigent resistance to specialization.

Notice that in this form their argument is quite different from Bidwell's, even though the world they have reconstructed appears similar. Bidwell had in fact been speaking from a neoclassical set of assumptions: markets would have freed farmers trapped in suboptimal

13. Barton J. Bernstein, ed., *Towards a New Past: Dissenting Essays in American History* (New York, 1967); James Henretta, "Families and Farms: *Mentalité* in Pre-Industrial America," *William and Mary Quarterly*, 3rd Ser., 35 (Jan. 1978), 3–32; Robert E. Mutch, "Yeoman and Merchant in Pre-Industrial America: Eighteenth Century Massachusetts as a Case Study," *Societas*, 7 (Autumn 1977), 279–302; Michael Merrill, "Cash Is Good to Eat: Self-Sufficiency and Exchange in the Rural Economy of the United States," *Radical History Review*, 3 (Winter 1977), 42–71; Michael Merrill, "Agricultural Output, Innovation and Market Relations in the Hudson River Valley, 1785–1855," paper presented at the Newberry Library Conference on Economic Growth and Social Change in Early America, Chicago, April 1980; Christopher Clark, "Household Economy, Market Exchange, and the Rise of Capitalism in the Connecticut Valley, 1800–1860," *Journal of Social History*, 13 (Winter 1979). Clark appears to be writing about the early and rapid transformation of the Connecticut River Valley from a "household economy" to capitalist agriculture and industry, but his emphasis throughout is on the "bifurcation" between those who "continued willingly" in the quest for profits and those who "began to draw back," seeking refuge in what was left of "household values" from the repellent acquisitiveness of the new society.

equilibrium. The neo-Marxist–Polanyi argument finds the same absence of a market, but rather *celebrates* it, as it celebrates the integrity of pre-capitalist, cooperative societies generally.

There is much to praise in all this; it has the ring of authenticity. But there is also much to fault. At base the argument is tautological. We are told that the eighteenth-century rural *mentalité* was not – what for want of a better word I shall call, with them – capitalist.

— How do you know?
— From the KIND of transactions that took place.
— What about those transactions? They all involved, didn't they, the exchange of labor and commodities with prices for either cash, or equivalent value, or the assumption of a debt that had ultimately to be paid?
— Yes, but the money-of-account was not money,[14] and the price system was not sovereign,[15] "from which it follows that . . . the products we are dealing with are not commodities at all."[16]
— I don't follow you. Why not?
— Because the values attached to goods and services were use-values, not exchange values.
— How do you know that?
— Because the eighteenth-century rural *mentalité* was not capitalist.

There are, of course, ways of stepping outside the circle of tautology and developing sturdily empirical categories of "self-sufficiency" and "market orientation" in order to test these propositions. On a micro level, Clarence Danhof has suggested, in a recent study, a rule of thumb to identify as "market-integrated" any farm that consumes no more than 40 percent of its net product.[17] On a macro level two studies have come to my attention: Fred Bateman and Jeremy Atack have estimated the marketings of the rural economy of the North in 1860 from the surplus that remains after farm family consumption, seed and feed requirements are substracted from total output; Colleen Callahan and William K. Hutchinson estimate the part played by interregional trade (Northeast-West) in sustaining actual per capita consumption by adding imports from, or exports to, the West to per capita regional production of foodstuffs.[18]

14. Merrill, "Cash Is Good to Eat," 56.
15. Henretta, "Families and Farms," 16.
16. Merrill, "Cash Is Good to Eat," 53.
17. Clarence H. Danhof, "The Farm Enterprise: The Northern United States, 1820–1860," *Research in Economic History*, 4 (1979), 127–191.
18. Fred Bateman and Jeremy Atack, "The Profitability of Northern Agriculture in 1860," *Research in Economic History*, 4 (1979), 109–113; Colleen M. Callahan and William K. Hutchinson,

But I propose here to explore the timing and extent of market imbeddedness the other way 'round, through the behavior of farm prices and the movement in trade of farm products as recorded in farmers' own accounts.[19]

The argument will proceed by testing the following indicators:

Farmers' records of marketing trips. Farm account books and daybooks record the trips farmers actually took to buy and, far more often, to sell their output. From the records, histograms are constructed showing frequencies of miles travelled, origins, and destinations. Gini coefficients are calculated to measure, over time, the growing concentration of market destinations.

Farmers' records of transport costs. Any discussion of marketing must reckon with the high cost of overland transport, which has long been thought to have placed a prohibitive constraint on marketing, at least before 1820. The account books show how much the separate parts of the hauling package – wagon, team, driver – cost, and how much could be saved by using owned resources.

The convergence of farmers' prices. Economic theory recognizes the presence, in time and in space, of a market for a commodity when and where, through the unconstrained bargaining of buyers and sellers, the prices of that commodity tend toward uniformity. Thus it should be possible to test for market influences on farmers' own prices by testing for the convergence of those prices. A polynomial regression on time of the coefficient of variation (the standard deviation divided by the mean) of the prices of each of several farm outputs not only tests for that convergence, but also, by its inflection point, indicates when the narrowing process – the felt impact of the market – began.

The slaughter weight of hogs and feed and meat prices. It has proved possible to determine, at least to a first approximation, that feed (corn) and meat (pork) prices played a statistically significant role in farmers' decisions respecting the weight at which to slaughter hogs. If the method stands scrutiny it will be one of the few instances where a test of supply elasticity can be made for individual farmers in this period.

"Antebellum Interregional Trade in Agricultural Goods: Preliminary Results," this Journal, 40 (March 1980), 25–31. The method used by Callahan and Hutchinson to measure North-West trade was used earlier by Hutchinson and Samuel H. Williamson to measure South-West trade, in their "The Self-Sufficiency of the Antebellum South: Estimates of the Food Supply," this Journal, 31 (Sept. 1971), 591–612.

19. For the list of manuscript sources used, see Appendix.

The cyclical synchronicity of farm account book prices and big city prices. The price index constructed on Massachusetts farmers' prices is seen to exhibit, from 1760 on, a pattern of cycles and of responses to the major shocks of the period that is markedly and visibly synchronous with the pattern of the Bezanson index of Philadelphia prices and the Warren–Pearson index of New York City prices.[20]

Travelling to markets

In farm account books and daybooks are found the records of the trips farmers made to buy the things they did not produce – molasses, sugar, tea, rum, cloth, indigo, salt, fish, flour and meal, lime, shingles, iron, bricks – and to sell the things they did – grains, hay, meat, livestock, butter, cheese, vegetables, apples, cider, wool, hops, flax, wood and wood products, potash, and dung. Account books, as repositories of debt transactions, recorded only those trips that required the hiring of a wagon, team, or driver from someone else. As a consequence, transport services the farm family performed for itself went unrecorded, as probably did most completed cash or barter transactions. Furthermore, if the farmer sold "at the barn" to a buyer who hauled the goods back himself, the cost of that trip will not appear in either the seller's or the buyer's accounts. Thus, to an unknown but probably large extent, account books understate the movement and the volume of trade, serving to set only a lower bound to our estimates. Daybooks, diaries, and personal journals are far more generous; I have relied heavily on those I could find.

In the quantitative work that follows, only those trips are called "marketing trips" that specify hauling or carting a load off the farm, by cart, wagon, sled, or sleigh, with team and/or horses. Journeys by chaise, carriage, or on horseback were not included. I hoped thereby to exclude visiting, going to church or to meetings, settling disputes, attending to paupers, appraising inventories, administering estates, surveying, assessing – all the myriad responsibilities a farmer bore in his community that would have taken him away from home, but not to markets. In doing so, however, I am sure that I both excluded too much[21] and included too much.[22]

20. Winifred B. Rothenberg, "A Price Index for Rural Massachusetts, 1750–1855," this Journal, 39 (Dec. 1979), 975–1001.

21. Thus, Joseph Lee of Newton wrote: "Nov. 4, 1823: R.S. went to Boston *in the carriage* and . . . bot 113 lb beef @ 3, 28 lb Pot ashes @ 10. Bot at City Mills 2 bu rye meal 68, 2 bushels Indian meal 65." Emphasis added.

22. I assumed that all trips in which livestock were being hauled were to markets. Some of these, the daybooks make clear, were rather to winter the cattle or to have them mated.

The procedure with respect to trip data was first to measure on a map the mileages between towns of origin and towns of destination, in each case as straight-line distances, and then to multiply by 1.6, the ratio Robert Fogel found, from a random sample, to obtain between modern highway distances and bee-line distances.[23] Since old roads were far more winding than modern highways, all the mileages in the calculations that follow are probably understated.

Towns of origin and destination were then coded into two regions, East and West, as follows: towns in Essex, Middlesex, Suffolk, Norfolk, Plymouth, and Bristol counties in Massachusetts, and towns in Rhode Island, New Hampshire and Vermont were called East; towns in Worcester, Franklin, Hampshire, Hampden, and Berkshire counties in Massachusetts, and towns in Connecticut and New York were called West. The load being hauled, where given, was also coded. Year, and frequency of trips between origin-destination pairs were, of course, entered. The data were then placed in six time-period subfiles: 1750–1775, 1776–1790, 1791–1805, 1806–1820, 1821–1835, 1836–1855.[24]

The output relates to two questions: a) how far did farmers travel to market their goods? and b) to which principal market towns did they travel?

a. A frequency distribution of the distances farmers did in fact haul their loads in different time periods is presented in Figure 1. In light of transport cost constraints, the finding is of great interest. Although varying widely in length, the number of very long journeys is astonishing.[25] Table 1 presents mean and median distances for each period, first

23. Robert W. Fogel, *Railroads and American Economic Growth: Essays in Econometric History* (Baltimore, 1964), p. 67. Unfortunately, the 1789 *Survey of the Roads of the United States of America*, by Christopher Colles, is nothing of the sort: it contains no Massachusetts roads.

24. The periodization is not arbitrary. The first is the Colonial period, followed by the second, the years of Revolution and post-war depression and Constitutional crisis. The third, identified by David Hackett Fischer as the period of "Deep Change" in virtually every measurable social indicator, acquires thereby its coherent character as a time of pivotal transformation. The years 1806–1820 were dominated by the domestic consequences (among them, the so-called "first industrial revolution") of war in Europe – of isolation and neutrality from it, of involvement in it, and of panic and depression after it.

Although Bidwell himself dates the earliest transition to market agriculture at about 1810 (in his "Rural Economy," 245), most other writers use 1820 as their benchmark date; hence the fifth period begins in 1821. The year 1836 (actually the last half of 1835) marks the beginning of full-time freight and passenger railroad service from Boston to Worcester, a giant step on the road to Albany, an event of significance for Massachusetts agriculture. The sixth period is when the railroad came to most of the towns from which our farmers come. See footnote 26.

25. Clarence Danhof in his book, *Change in Agriculture: The Northern United States, 1820–1870* (Cambridge, MA, 1969), suggests a maximum distance of 12 to 15 miles. In his "The Farm

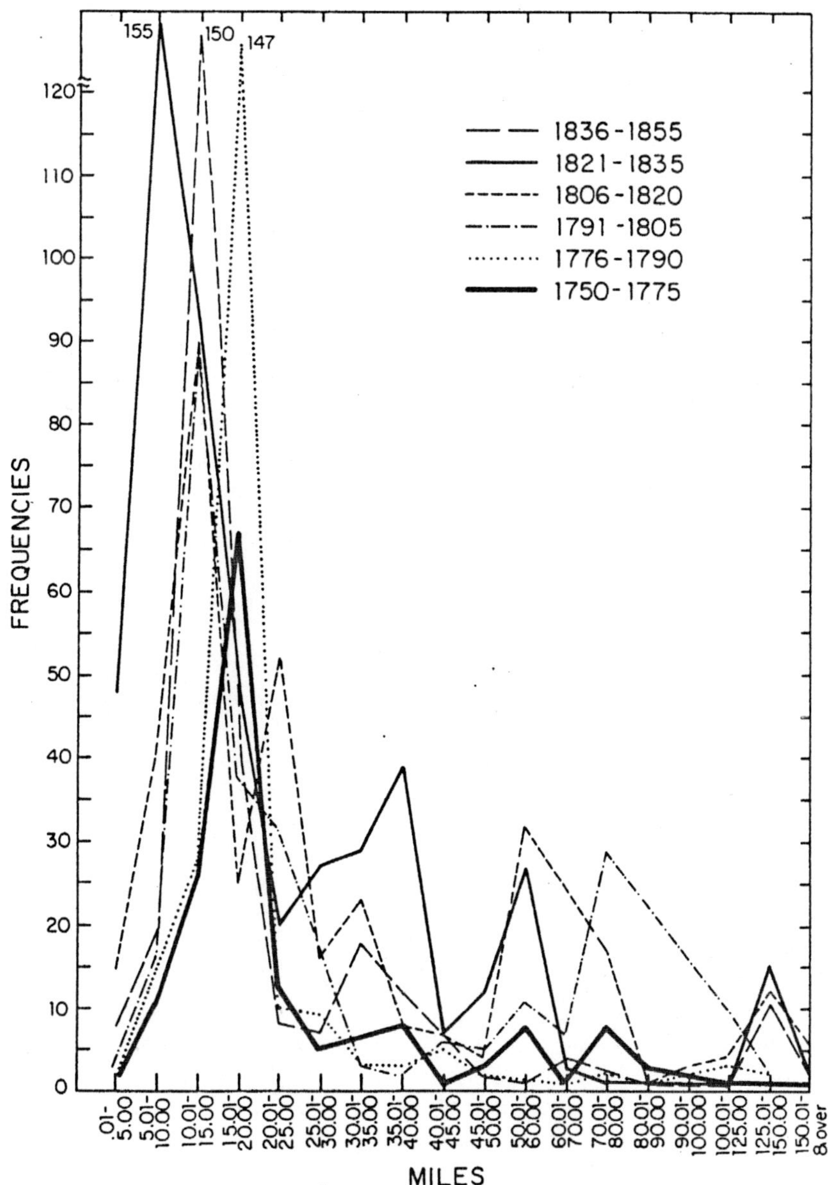

Figure 1. Frequency distribution of distances farmers traveled with loads.

Note: For method of measuring distances, see text.
Source: Farmers' accounts and daybooks.

Table 1. *Length of hauling trips*

Item	*Time Period* 1750–1775	1776–1790	1791–1805	1806–1820	1821–1835	1836–1855
A. All Trips						
Number of Trips	156	233	271	355	526	286
Average Mileage[a]	26.7	22.4	31.0	50.5	21.0	24.8
Median Mileage[b]	18.7	18.0	19.6	24.0	14.4	14.0
Range of Miles[c]	5–175	5–150	5–150	5–200+	5–200+	5–200+
Standard Deviation	22.2	18.0	27.0	165.4	26.9	33.0
B. Truncated Distribution						
Number of Trips	151	227	259	329	508	271
Average Mileage[a]	23.7	18.7	27.0	24.5	18.7	17.2
Median Mileage[b]	17.8	17.3	17.7	18.9	12.7	13.6
Range of Miles[c]	5–80	5–80	5–80	5–80	5–80	5–85

[a] The mean and median were calculated from mileage weighted by frequencies.
[b] The median is given because the distribution is so skewed to the right.
[c] Farm-to-town trips, the shortest, are assumed to be 5 miles.
Source: Account books and daybooks. The measurement of origin-to-destination distances is described in the text.

for the whole range of trips and second for the distribution curtailed to eliminate long-distance outlyers. This last was done on the hunch that many of the longest journeys, particularly in the fourth period, may have been one-of-a-kind, unlikely to have been part of a pattern. In fact, however, bricks, shingles, livestock, hay, barrels, "freight," ashes, corn, fish, molasses, and potatoes were all hauled 100 miles or more at one time or another on these trips, so trip length, though hardly typical, may deserve to influence the mean, after all.

From the pattern of mean distances over time it appears that marketing perimeters shortened during the Revolutionary and post-war depression years, widened markedly up until 1820, and shortened thereafter just as markedly. Because the fourth period, 1806–1820, witnessed an unusual number of very long trips – over 20 percent of the 355 origin–destination pairs for that period were between 50 and 300 miles apart – the dramatic drop in mean mileage between the fourth and fifth periods seems to demand an equally dramatic explanation. It is therefore worth emphasizing that it was not short hauls to the railroad depot that pulled the average mileage down from 50 to 21 (or from 24.5 to 18.7 in the truncated distribution). This discontinuity *predates* the arrival of

Enterprise," he puts it a bit differently: "Land lying within a few miles – a half-day return trip by road or water – of an urban market offered an acceptable cost of transportation . . ." (162).

railroads to Massachusetts towns.[26] Rather it was the growth – so I hypothesize – in first the number and then the size of market towns, each of which was developing in importance as a destination, and all of which, as a group, expanded the market options of an increasing number of farmers.

b. Can that hypothesis be tested? Which were the principal market towns in each period? This question may be approached at three approximations of increasing precision. When the trips are mapped from the point of view of the individual farmer, each place of *origin* appears like the hub of a large, eccentric wheel whose spokes of differing lengths radiate in a full circle from that farmer to a great number of destinations. To test the hypothesis of expanding market options, however, one needs, in a first approximation, to see the *destinations* as hubs, as Central Places. The first step, then, is Table 2, a list of the towns that served as markets for two or more origins.

The second approximation consists in weighting the principal origin–destination pairs by the frequency of trips made between them. Listed in Table 3 are the principal destinations defined in this way: those to which farmers came ten or more times during the time period.[27] The table

26. I am grateful to Prof. Charles J. Kennedy of the University of Nebraska for giving me the dates the railroad appeared in several Massachusetts towns. Framingham, 1835; Ipswich, 1839; Braintree, 1845; Westborough, 1835; Biddeford (now Maine), 1842; Oxford, 1840; Middleborough, 1846; Marlborough, 1855; Grafton, 1835; Springfield, 1841; Acton, 1844.

Allan R. Pred, in his *Urban Growth and the Circulation of Information: The U.S. System of Cities, 1790–1840* (Cambridge, MA, 1973), pp. 280–284, refers to a study by Julius Rubin that throws light on the late appearance of the railroad in Massachusetts. Contrasted with Philadelphia, which quickly built its own canal, and with Baltimore, which quickly built the B & O Railroad, Boston, says Rubin, met the challenge of the Erie Canal by "the common strategy of procrastination to cope with the uncertainty of the situation," a strategy conditioned by the history and traditions of Boston's conservative elites.

Stephen Salsbury, in *The State, the Investor and the Railroad: The Boston & Albany, 1825–1867* (Cambridge, MA, 1967), pp. 35–37, takes sharp issue with Rubin, claiming that the railroad in Massachusetts was not a response to the Erie Canal as much as it was a response to a developing need for markets and factory sites for Boston manufacturers. As such it was neither tardy nor conservative.

27. The persistent importance of Boston, the emergence of Concord and the retreat of Salem will come as no great surprise, but the importance of smaller towns may. In Shrewsbury, for example, Artemas Ward had a general store in the 1750s to which farm produce came from all over Worcester County and beyond. In Rainbow, Connecticut, there were, in the 1820s and 1830s, at least four grist mills, and it was to one of these mills that Horace Clark of East Granby sold about 500 bushels of corn and the same amount of rye each year. For a single mill regularly to buy such a large quantity from a single farmer suggests that trips to that tiny town (near the Connecticut River, midway between Springfield and Hartford), were not idiosyncratic, but that Rainbow had access to, or was itself, a regional entrepôt of importance for flour, meal and grain.

Table 2. *Destinations from two or more origins*

1750–1775		*1776–1790*		*1791–1805*		*1806–1820*		*1821–1835*		*1836–1855*	
Boston	4	Dedham	3	Northampton	5	Springfield	2	Springfield	2	Westfield	6
Shewsbury	18	Ipswich	3	Providence	3	Northampton	5	Northampton	7	Northampton	2
Springfield	2	Braintree	3	Woodstock, Ct.	2	Dedham	2	Roxbury	2	Roxbury	2
Leicester	5	Roxbury	2	Dedham	3	Acton	5	Acton	5	Boston	5
Hadley	2	Worcester	2	Boston	9	Boston	9	Boston	10	Mansfield	4
N =	114	Leicester	4	Ipswich	3	E. Cambridge	3	Harvard	3	Hadley	2
		Boston	2	Northborough	4	Charlestown	2	Concord	2	North Andover	4
		N =	116	Bolton	2	Concord	2	Littleton	2	Arlington	5
				Salem	2	Groton	2	Sudbury	2	Worcester	3
				Grafton	2	Harvard	3	Roxbury	2	Westborough	8
				Princeton	2	Littleton	2	Mansfield	6	N =	186
				Westborough	2	Lunenburg	2	Newton	2		
				Taunton	3	Ipswich	3	Hadley	2		
				N =	180	Hadley	2	Marlborough	2		
						Salem	2	Brighton	2		
						Leicester	2	Worcester	2		
						Sutton	2	Grafton	2		
						Worcester	3	Lancaster	2		
						Easthampton	2	South Hadley	2		
						South Hadley	2	Ware	2		
						Southampton	2	Duxbury	2		
						Wendell	2	N =	239		
						Williamsburg	2				
						Templeton	2				
						Pepperell	2				
						N =	218				

Source: Account books and daybooks.

Table 3. *Principal destinations, by frequency of trips*

Time Period and Destinations	*Number of Trips*	*Percent of Total Trips Made*
1750–1775 (N = 156)		
Boston	12	7.7
Salem	37	23.7
Shrewsbury	18	11.5
Percent of total		42.9
1776–1790 (N = 233)		
Boston	24	10.3
Salem	99	42.5
Percent of total		52.8
1791–1805 (N = 271)		
Boston	56	20.7
Salem	17	6.3
Kingston	17	6.3
Providence	13	4.8
Northampton	15	5.5
Northborough	15	5.5
Southampton	10	3.7
Roxbury	12	4.4
Ipswich	10	3.7
Percent of total		60.9
1806–1820 (N = 355)		
Boston	100	28.2
Concord	16	4.5
Kingston	17	4.8
Northampton	21	5.9
Harvard	12	3.4
Sutton	10	2.8
Waltham	12	3.4
Percent of total		53.0
1821–1835 (N = 526)		
Boston	74	14.1
Concord	27	5.1
Newton	37	7.0
Rainbow, Ct.	96	18.3
Grafton	33	6.3
Northampton	15	2.9
Petersham	13	2.5
Acton	10	1.9
Littleton	11	2.1
Percent of total		60.1
1836–1855 (N = 286)		
Springfield	112	39.2
Boston	20	7.0
Westfield	17	5.9
Suffield, Ct.	12	4.2
Westborough	10	3.5
Percent of total		59.8

Source: Account books and daybooks. See text and appendix.

shows both the percent of trips in each period going to each principal destination, and the percent of trips going to these principal centers as a group.

Changes in the concentration of market destinations can be most closely measured in the third approximation, Gini coefficients (G) that relate the percent of total trips (P) and the percent of total destinations (Y), as this relationship changes over time. For this calculation all origin–destination pairs were weighted by frequency and subdivided as to time period and region – East and West. The results are of great interest, as demonstrated graphically in the Lorenz curves of Figure 2. Trips to markets in the West become slowly but steadily more concentrated – from a G of .460 in the first period to a G of .755 in the last – in each successive period with the exception of the Revolution. The pattern of trips to markets in the East, on the other hand, was from the beginning dominated by the importance of Boston and Salem, that pattern of inequality in the distribution of trips as between destinations remaining much the same until the last period when, marked by the relative decline in the importance of Boston – Salem had waned earlier – we find a G of .487, very nearly the same as that for western Massachusetts a century earlier.

That the concentration of marketing trips proceeded at such different rates in East and West has implications that are in fact strongly confirmed in the price convergence regressions to be presented later.

Transport costs

It is difficult to understand how farmers could have afforded to haul their bulky, heavy farm produce as far as is shown in Table 1 if transport costs were as high as those found in published records.[28] In fact, so constraining have they been considered that most estimates of a feasible market range begin with, and are calculated from, given ton-mile

28. Twenty cents in Peter McClelland, "Railroads, American Growth, and the New Economic History, A Critique," this Journal, 28 (March 1968), 102–123. 30¢–70¢ for 1800–1819 in George R. Taylor, *Transportation Revolution* (New York, 1951), p. 133; 15¢ for 1853, ibid., p. 442; 30¢–70¢ in Allan Pred, *Urban Growth*, p. 112; 25¢ for 1906 reduced 17.6 percent for 1890 in Fogel, *Railroads and American Economic Growth*, p. 71; 12¢ during the cyclical decline in 1822, in Allan Pred, *Urban Growth*, p. 112; 50¢–20¢ by turnpike, 10¢–15¢ by macadam road in 1839, Pred, ibid., p. 112; 23½¢ Boston to Providence in the late 1820s, Pred, ibid., p. 113; 18¢ Boston to Worcester in 1832, Salsbury, *The State, the Investor, and the Railroad*, p. 122.

Some account books reveal ton-mile rates to have been just as high when a farmer is acting as teamster: Isaac Bullard of Dedham was a teamster and charged 20¢–25¢ between 1789 and 1803, but then so did John Baker of Ipswich in the 1790s (19¢–22¢), Robert Craig of Leicester in 1778 (21¢), and John Heald of Pepperell, in 1808–1813 (20¢).

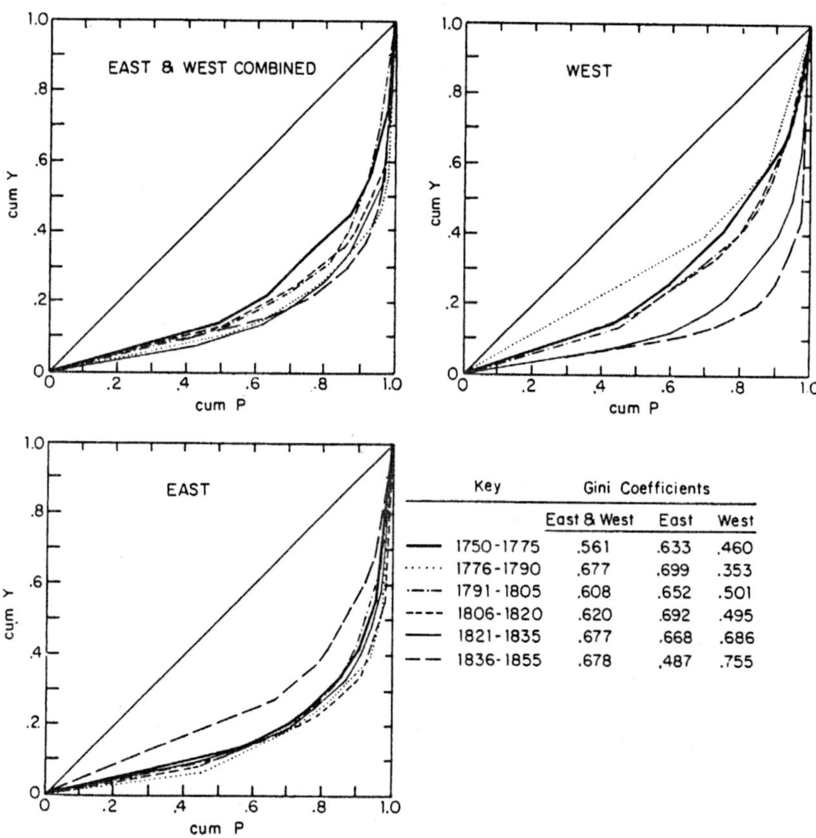

Figure 2. Measuring market concentration.

Note: Cum P measures the cumulative percent of total trips; Cum Y measures the cumulative percent of total destinations. The towns were divided as between East and West as described in the text.
Source: Farmers' accounts and daybooks.

wagon rates. Thus, when Danhof suggests that an "acceptable" cost of transportation must be less than 20 percent of the value of the produce, then, at hauling costs of 20¢ per ton-mile, the marketing perimeter for, say, a wagon load (40 bushels) of corn, which would sell for 50¢ a bushel, could not have exceeded 20 miles.[29] This is indeed a tight constraint: yet in the late eighteenth century, when corn did sell for 50¢ a bushel, nearly half our farmers' trips were longer than 20 miles.

29. Danhof, "The Farm Enterprise," 162.

To minimize high teamster rates farmers had at least three options: one was to sell "at the barn," in effect f.o.b. pricing, where the buyer assumes the hauling costs. One finds this fairly often in the sources, particularly with respect to meadow hay, a bulky thing and expensive to haul relative to its value. The second option was to "shop around," selling in markets where product price was highest, travel costs lowest, or both. Markets exist in space, which is to say that transport costs – whether borne by buyer or seller – will be a consideration in any market transaction.[30] Observing the multitude of destination vectors along which each farmer travelled, what we may be observing is the process of making distance into an economic variable (see Figure 3).

The third option was for the farmer to provide at least some of the transport inputs himself, borrowing or hiring the rest from neighbors. This is not new.[31] But what farm account books can tell us are the costs of the inputs when they are extracted, as it were, from the teamster package and hired separately, and their opportunity costs when they are owned.

The prices farmers charged each other for supplying one or another of these components – usually wagon and/or team – appear in the account books, along with clues like destination, mileage, or time, which allow us to calculate ton-mile transport rates. These rates can equally well be used to impute the value of the wagon and team when the farmer provided them for himself. The imputed value of the farmer's services when he does his own driving must also be calculated, and should in some sense be set equal to the value of his farm labor foregone.

Cognizant of these opportunity costs, most writers have assumed that market journeys were made in winter when the farmers were less occupied and the sledding was easy. At random, I made a note of the month of over 600 of the trips. One hundred seventy-two were made in the winter months of November, December, January, and February. Four hundred sixty-four were made between March and October. In fact, fewer trips were made in December and January than at any other time, and more trips – twice as many – were made during each harvest month than during any other month. And yet almost none of the transactions involved the hiring of a driver. In other words, opportunity costs must be taken into account in calculating the true cost of hauling.

One way to do this is to award to the farmer in each period the highest wage paid to hired farm labor in that period. Wages to hired farm labor differed by task, the highest wage going to hauling and carting labor between 1750 and 1810, and to haying and reaping labor

30. See Melvin L. Greenhut, *A Theory of the Firm in Economic Space* (New York, 1970), chap. 4.

31. See Fogel, *Railroads and American Economic Growth*, p. 71.

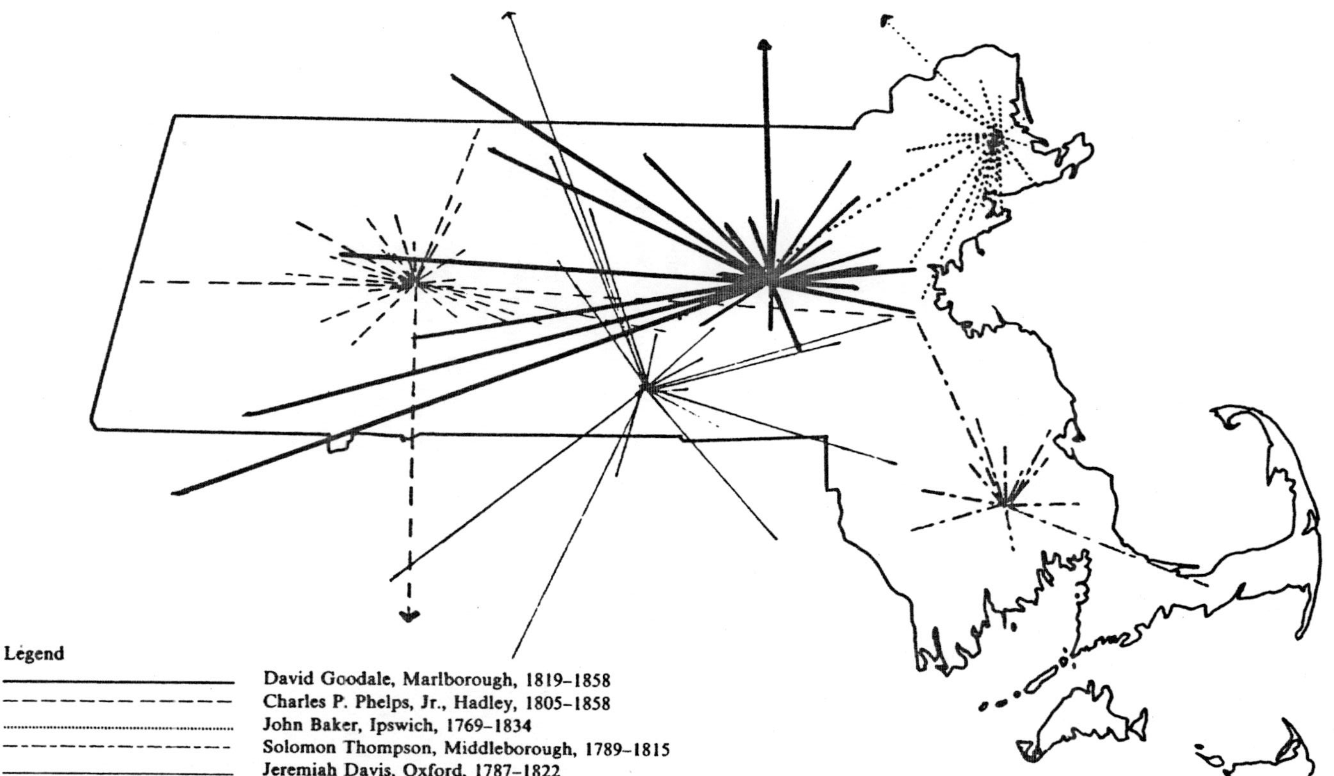

Figure 3. The pattern of marketing trips of five farmers.

Table 4. *Average per ton-mile costs of hauling, by component (dollars)*

Time Period	Yoke of Oxen[b,c]	Vehicle[b,c]	Driver[c,d]	Total Current	Total Constant[e]
1750–1775[a]	.031	.015	.049	.095	.151
1776–1790[a]	.049	.029	.073	.151	.177
1791–1805	.044	.032	.067	.143	.146
1806–1820	.083	.027	.072	.182	.156
1821–1835	.074	.033	.074	.181	.171
1836–1855	.085	.027	.108	.220	.180

[a] Currency: Old Tenor adjusted to Lawful Money at 7.5:1, adjusted to dollars at 1s = $0.1667.
[b] Costs of hiring wagons and yoke come from farm account books.
[c] Inputs hired by the trip adjusted to per-mile rate by dividing by straight line mileage between towns multiplied by 1.6. Ton-mile rates calculated from the assumption that a full load is 1 ton. Inputs hired by the day adjusted to per mile rate by assuming 10 miles travelled per day. To the extent that this assumption understates distance, the estimates overstate cost.
[d] Very few drivers were hired for hauling. This is the driving wage imputed to the farmer and calculated from the per-day wage for the highest paid labor hired on the firm—in early years carting, in later years haying.
[e] The total in current dollars is deflated by my price index, this JOURNAL, 39 (Dec. 1979), 983–85.
Source: Farm account books and daybooks (see Appendix).

thereafter.[32] Averaging these wages for each of the six periods, and assuming a 10-mile travelling day throughout (an assumption that remains to be discussed below), gives to farmers the per-mile imputed wage as drivers that is shown in Table 4.

The issue of opportunity costs applies not only to alternative uses of farmers' labor but to oxen power as well. It matters to the calculations in Table 4 whether the yoke being hired is the only animal power – as it would be for approximately one quarter of the farm families who, in 1771 at least, had no oxen – or whether the yoke is being hired to augment the farmer's own team for long, heavy trudges, in which case to the hired oxen's "wage" must be added the imputed return to owned oxen.[33] I have come across teams of as many as 18 oxen (in the diary of James Parker, Sr., of Shirley, in the 1770s), and clearly there is no provision for that in Table 4. Nor, I fear, can there be.

With that caveat, it is now possible to compare the ton-mile rates calculated here with teamster rates appearing in other sources. When the components are summed it appears that ton-mile rates in current dollars

32. I am engaged in a study of wage rates for hired farm labor, using farm account books.

33. Not all farm families had their own teams. A survey of the 1771 Valuations reveals that in most rural communities (that is, omitting Salem, Danvers, Newburyport and Boston), between 20 and 35 percent of farmers (defined as those reporting tillage acreage and bushels of grain) had no oxen, and that proportion went as high as 40 percent in Ipswich and 48 percent in Hadley.

approach 20¢ and climb above it in the sixth period, but that ton-mile rates in constant dollars stay well below 20¢ throughout. Because the deflator is an index of these same farmers' product prices, the costs in constant dollars are, it seems to me, the appropriate measure of the real burden of transport costs to Massachusetts farmers. That there was as high a level of market interaction as was demonstrated in the preceding section suggests that farmers made, in some sense, the same calculation.

It will undoubtedly strike the reader with some force that the cost of hauling, at least in real terms, fails to fall over this century of rapid change. To have made the assumption throughout the period, as I have, that no more than ten miles were travelled in a day injects into Table 4 a built-in bias against technological progress in road building. Is that assumption justified?

There were two bursts of road building in Massachusetts in our period: the private turnpike era of 1790–1808, and the public road building of the 1820s and 30s. The first of these brought major improvements in the straightening of roads, the second in the surfacing. Turnpikes strove for a Roman straightness that considerably shortened distance, but at the expense of steep grades which slowed the movement of heavy loads considerably, a grade of 5 percent adding 5 percent to the weight of the load. "Straight roads over high hills involved the expenditure of more horsepower in travelling than did winding roads over level ground between the same two points."[34]

The major innovation in road surfacing was macadam. Macadam roads were introduced in this country in 1820, but by 1851, "there were not a dozen miles of macadam road in all the New England states."[35] The diffusion of macadamizing had to await the invention of the mechanical stone crusher, and that was not until 1858. All Massachusetts country roads and most turnpikes were still, in our period, dirt roads requiring constant and expensive maintenance, and therefore, despite knowledge of the techniques of crowning and ditching, sluiceways and macadamizing, were allowed, up to the end of our period, to deteriorate.

Winter travel by sled or sleigh was, as a rule, faster and allowed the transport of much heavier loads. "On sleds drawn by two horses, farmers could carry 30 bushels of wheat (three quarters of a ton) 20 miles and return the same day."[36] But in this respect the improved turnpikes

34. P. E. Taylor, *The Turnpike Era in New England*, Ph.D. dissertation, Yale University, 1934, p. 173.

35. Roger Neal Parks, *The Roads of New England, 1790–1840*, Ph.D. dissertation, Michigan State University, 1966, p. 193.

36. Max George Schumacher, *The Northern Farmer and His Markets During the Late Colonial Period*, Ph.D. dissertation, University of California, Berkeley, 1948, p. 68.

could be worse for winter travel than the old country roads because their very straightness produced a wind-tunnel effect, blowing bare the high crowns and tracks, making them impassable for sleds.

Perhaps what speaks most unambiguously to the issue of road improvement is that, of the 1,827 trips analyzed in this paper, there is only one entry for a turnpike toll.

Price convergence

To use the narrowing of price differentials over time as a measure of the extent and timing of market-embeddedness is yet another way of inferring from available data behavioral characteristics of a sort for which there is no available data. But price convergence is more than a proxy for market-orientation: It is an experimental design, an operational formulation of an hypothesis which, if properly specified, can be confirmed or refuted by the results of the experiment.

"Economists understand by the term *market*," wrote Marshall in 1890, "the whole of any region in which buyers and sellers are in such free intercourse with one another that the prices of the same goods tend to equality easily and quickly."[37]

It is not hard to think of modern complexities that distort market outcomes and render Marshall's definition inadequate, but that is not, I think, true of the application we will make of it. In the rural commodity markets of New England in the century before the Civil War there were few, if any, oligopolistic elements. Transport costs, as we have seen, cannot be assumed away, but they can be added on top of that emerging uniform price, and their interaction with it will determine the equilibrium location of markets in space. A "good" for these farmers – as for most farmers – was a recognizable thing bounded by a gap in the chain of substitutes surrounding it; that is, there was, for farm commodities, little deliberate effort at product differentiation in order to introduce monopoly elements.

But here one must pause to note the product differentiation that did in fact exist. There were two grades or qualities or kinds of beef and of pork, salted and fresh; and there were two grades of cider, new and old (or water and clear). By 1762, two qualities of hay were being sold by these farmers, English and meadow, the price of one usually double the price of the other. In all the calculations to follow, each of the differentiated products has been treated as a separate good. Then, in the late 1840s, account books begin to distinguish several different quality grades of potatoes. I am not speaking here of the sort of thing one finds

37. Alfred Marshall, *Principles of Economics*, Eighth Ed. (London, 1946, reprint), p. 324.

in probate inventories – "a barrel of bad pork," "a firkin of rancid butter" – but of standardized grades of potatoes by size, by color ("blue potatoes"), and perhaps by other factors, all of which may have become feasible when, after the blight of 1843, potatoes became very expensive. Whatever the reason, the emergence of the price differentials that followed upon quality differentials plays havoc with the convergence of potato prices after 1840, though in so doing it points up the centrality of the definition of a good in Marshall's characterization of a market.[38]

The price data come from the 54 manuscript farm account books and daybooks (see Appendix), and from over 300 probate inventories. In addition, prices collected from inspection of over 600 inventories of Middlesex County, Massachusetts (200 gathered at random for each of the periods 1764–1776, 1789–1796, 1832–1835) were very generously made available to me by Sarah McMahon.

To test price convergence with a nonlinear time trend, a polynomial regression was fitted to the coefficient of variation (standard deviation divided by the mean) over time, of the prices of corn, potatoes, rye, oats, both hays, both kinds of beef, both kinds of pork, and both kinds of cider. The F levels on oats, meadow hay, beef, pork and cider were too low to justify their inclusion here, but the computer plots of regressions on corn, potatoes, rye and English hay are presented as Figure 4.[39]

Inspection of the regression plots reveals, first, that the negative slope of the regressions – that is, the impact of markets on the behavior of prices – began to happen decades before 1820, the date widely accepted as the pivot in the transformation of the rural economy of New England. Second, the hypothesis of price convergence stands confirmed in test after test, no matter from which source the data came (accounts or probates or both), no matter which the region (the price data were coded as to region, East or West), and no matter which the crop.

Two other scholars, whose work has recently been brought to my attention, have used price convergence to measure the impact of railroad building on the integration of national markets in developing countries:

38. Danhof, in *Change in Agriculture*, p. 43, footnote 61, says that the demand for higher quality both from abroad and from an increasingly urbanized population at home led to quality grading. Our butter, flour, cheese, wheat, pork, wool, and tobacco became graded, Danhof says, as early as the 1820s.

39. In an attempt to explain the rising portion of these time trends in the early years, I eliminated four Revolutionary War years with the greatest price variance and reran the regressions. A positively sloping time trend in the early years persists. I cannot explain it, unless it is that fewer price observations exist for the beginning of the period than for the later years. I am, in any case, loath to reverse the argument, that is, to find in the increasing coefficients of variation evidence of withdrawal from markets.

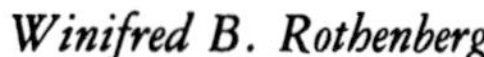

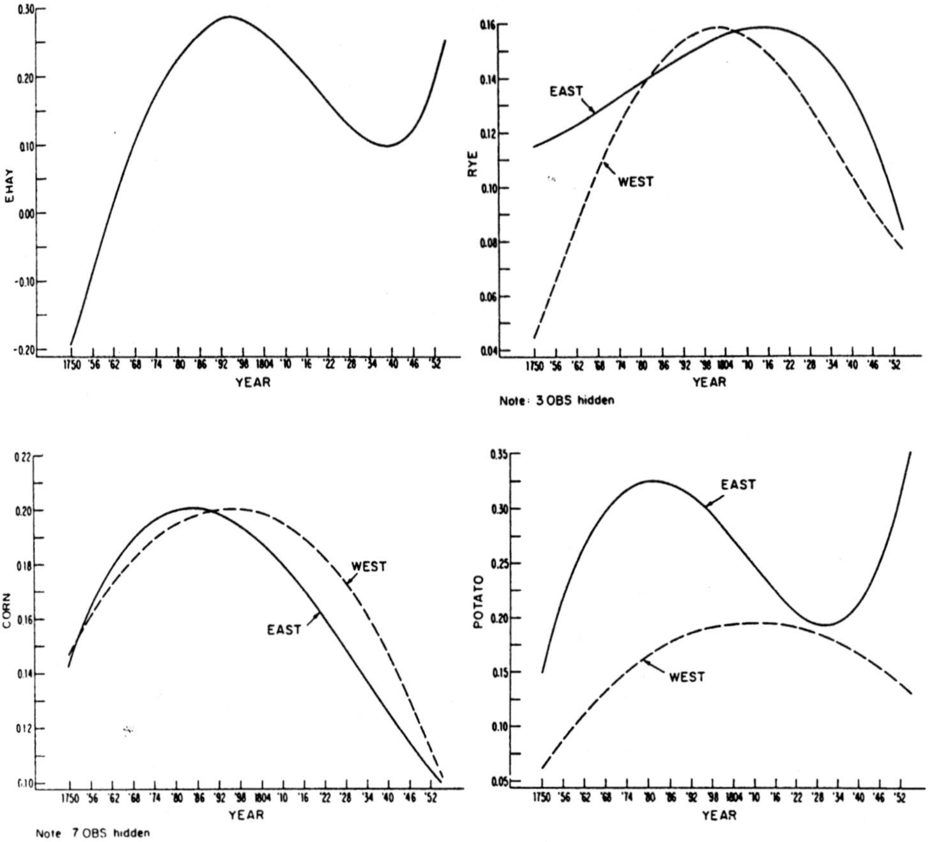

Note: 3 OBS hidden

Note 7 OBS hidden

Figure 4. Plotting the coefficient of variation of product prices over time for corn, rye, potatoes, and English hay.

Note: Preparation of data described in the text.
Source: Price data come from farm account books (see Appendix).

Michelle McAlpin's study of "Railroads, Prices and Peasant Rationality" in India (this Journal, 1974), and Jacob Metzer's dissertation, "Some Aspects of Railroad Development in Tsarist Russia" (University of Chicago, 1972). Both of them assert that price convergence, while a necessary condition, is not by itself sufficient proof of market embeddedness. It may only reflect the impact of the railroad in the lowering of transport cost differentials between markets without affecting the real terms of trade, or interregional specialization, or farmers' production decisions. In each case – late-nineteenth-century India and late-nineteenth-century Russia – what is being assessed is the impact of a sudden and major technological discontinuity: the railroad.

This was not the case in Massachusetts for the data with which this paper is concerned. Despite the presence of railroads in the later years, these were all wagon trips. Only once in over 1,800 journeys was there mention of a trip "to the depot." Although the period 1750–1855 saw some improvements in road construction, it is not clear how much of a difference they made. One may be justified then in eschewing the suggestion that there were innovation-induced transport cost reductions in Massachusetts, and that they were causing price convergence between regions.

But a test was made to see if, in Massachusetts, price convergence had in fact been accompanied by growing interregional specialization. Following the suggestion in Metzer's thesis, 1855 production figures for corn, rye, oats, and English hay were compared with 1801 production figures for the 48 different towns represented by the 54 farmers' accounts and journals.[40] The towns were grouped into counties, and the counties were used as surrogates for regions. Outputs by towns in 1801 and 1855 were averaged for each county and standard deviations and coefficients of variation calculated. If interregional specialization had been developing between 1801 and 1855, we should expect to see a larger coefficient of variation – an increased disparity in the production of the crop between counties – in 1855 than in 1801.

The results are given in Table 5. In the case of rye there is dramatic confirmation; corn and, to a lesser extent, English hay exhibit moderate increases; in the case of oats there is no change whatever. Perhaps there is not enough of a change to justify borrowing Metzer's sentence, but it is suggestive: "The observed increase in these dispersion measures between the two periods indicates that agricultural production in [Massachusetts] became indeed much more specialized in terms of its spatial distribution."[41] Well, perhaps not "much more," but "more."

It is now possible to bring together the marketing trip evidence and the price-behavior evidence and let them illuminate one another. It will be recalled that patterns of marketing trips differed as between East and West. Concentration – which in the terms of our earlier discussion meant a disproportionate frequency of trips to some destinations –

40. The 54 account and daybooks (footnote 19) come from 48 separate towns. The 1855 data for all 48 towns come from "The State of Industry in Massachusetts" (Boston, 1856), which is in effect a State Census. Only 45 of those towns appear in the 1801 Valuations. Although potatoes are counted in 1855, they were not enumerated in 1801.

41. Jacob Metzer, *Some Aspects of Railroad Development in Tsarist Russia*, Ph.D. dissertation, University of Chicago, 1972, p. 133. I am grateful to Professor Fogel for bringing this thesis to my attention and giving me access to it.

Table 5. *Regional specialization, 1801–1855, average production*

Region	Corn (bu.)	Rye (bu.)	Oats (bu.)	Potatoes (bu.)	English Hay (tons)
Berkshire					
1801 (2)[a]	6452.5	1524.5	2183.5	[b]	1082.00
1855 (2)	8196.0	787.0	6534.0	12822.5	2484.85
Essex					
1801 (5)	13416.2	1288.0	440.6		1057.80
1855 (6)	9768.0	1079.0	1616.5	13321.0	1598.18
Hampshire-Hampden-Franklin					
1801 (7)	8861.7	4316.0	1392.1		904.40
1855 (8)	21850.0	6979.0	4037.5	24233.0	2545.70
Middlesex					
1801 (10)	8074.7	2335.4	722.8		614.60
1855 (11)	11241.0	1180.0	3266.6	18504.0	1947.30
Norfolk					
1801 (4)	6917.0	528.0	169.2		593.40
1855 (4)	8090.0	481.7	484.5	12666.0	1457.20
Plymouth-Bristol					
1801 (5)	12739.2	2066.6	2158.0		1088.70
1855 (5)	6924.2	526.6	1581.0	12739.0	1019.50
Worcester					
1801 (12)	7447.7	1841.4	2531.4		698.25
1855 (12)	11108.0	963.0	6131.2	16885.0	2030.65
Mean of all regions					
1801	9129.9	1985.7	1371.1		862.70
1855	11025.3	1713.8	3378.8	15881.0	1869.05
Standard Deviation					
1801	2813.0	1183.5	944.8		223.60
1855	5037.3	2336.7	2334.2	4354.3	552.90
Coefficient of Variation					
1801	.31	.60	.69		.26
1855	.46	1.36	.69	.27	.30

[a] Numbers in parentheses are number of towns.
[b] Potatoes not included in 1801 Valuations.
Source: 1801 Valuations, "State of Industry in Massachusetts, 1855."

characterized Eastern marketing from the beginning, but emerged only slowly and late in the West. The implications of this are now visible in the respective patterns of price convergence in East and West. The narrowing of corn, potato, rye, and hay price differentials is not as statistically significant a proposition in the West as in the East. The early dominion of Boston and Salem contributed to the early conformity of prices throughout the East, but the tardy emergence of important regional market centers in the West is reflected in less reliable evidence of price convergence in the West. The mechanism that effected this link between observed travel patterns and the observed behavior of prices was not the sudden appearance of cheap transportation, but rather the arbitraging activity of the farmers themselves, each of whom (along with millers, merchants and itinerant peddlers) in moving out from his farm along a multitude of "destination vectors" served to transmit both the information and the behavior that brought about price convergence.

Supply elasticity: The case of hog weights

If it could be done, a most efficient test of market orientation would be to calculate supply elasticities of output, expected output, or output offered for sale. But the data for these calculations are so often just out of reach. The daybooks from which aggregate outputs can be derived seldom give prices; the account books from which prices can be derived seldom give outputs; and rarely do both sources exist for the same farmer.

It is presumably at planting time that one best captures the farmer in the act of responding to changes in relative prices, but even if it were possible to recover the record of a farmer's planting decisions, to which prices was he responding? Current price? Lagged price? Expected price? And in each case there is seldom a single price but rather a range, sometimes very wide, of seasonally fluctuating prices, the averaging of which might only obscure the very responses we are attempting to measure.[42]

Marc Nerlove has argued that farmers in fact do not respond, as is neoclassically assumed, to *all* price changes, but only to those they expect to be permanent, that is, to changes in what he calls the Expected Normal Price, defined as "the average level about which future prices are expected to fluctuate."[43] Expected normal price is arrived at by a progressive and cumulative learning process in which past expectations are regularly scrutinized and corrected against past realities.[44] But given the inadequacies in the data, one despairs of being able to use Nerlove's elegant model here.

There is a farm output that may lend itself to measuring price responsiveness without the complications separable expectations introduce, an output which, in a manner of speaking, *embodies* the farmer's

42. Marc Nerlove, *The Dynamics of Supply: Estimation of Farmers' Response to Price* (Baltimore, 1958).
43. Ibid., p. 25.
44. If P_t^* is the expected normal price in period t, then:
(1) $P_t^* - P_{t-1}^* = \beta[P_{t-1} - P_{t-1}^*]$, where β, the coefficient of expectation, lies between 0 and 1.
(2) $X_t = a_0 + a_1 P_t^* + u_t$, where u_t is a random residual and X_t is output in period t.
By substituting from equation (1) for P_t^*, the term $[\beta P_{t-1} + (1 - \beta)P_{t-1}^*]$ and introducing longer lags, Nerlove can, as it were, push back into insignificance the unobservable P^* term:
(3) $X_t = a_0 + a_1[\beta P_{t-1} + \beta(1 - \beta)P_{t-2} + \beta(1 - \beta)^2 P_{t-3} + \beta(1 - \beta)^3 P_{t-4}^* \ldots] + u_t$.

expectations. This is an output that does not ripen at a relentless moment in time; its growing season can be prolonged for years or cut short to a matter of days. Farmers are therefore in the position of being able to space the "harvest" in order to capture seasonal price advantages. True, it may have been customary to harvest this "crop" between Thanksgiving and Christmas, but that was never an imperative, at least in New England, and became less so over time.[45] I refer, of course, to the hog.

Although it is usually held that hogs were butchered at eighteen to twenty months of age, Bidwell and Falconer found, as early as 1800, that "some farmers kept their hogs over two winters, [while] others slaughtered at 8, 10, or 12 months."[46] Of the 556 slaughter weights of swine that I have collected from account and daybooks, 190 or 34 percent, were of young pigs, and a great many others were so heavy (450 to 600 pounds) that they must have been considerably older than 20 months. Clearly, it was the case that when to slaughter a hog could be a decision unconstrained by the inexorabilities of time or the weather, and we should, therefore, be able to locate the determinants of age at slaughter (that is, weight) in economic variables, perhaps in the price of corn (cost), the price of pork (revenue), and the interaction between them.

From the account books and daybooks the weights of 366 adult hogs were taken, with their year, town, and region – East or West.[47] In each case a determination first had to be made as to whether the weight given in the source was a live or dressed weight, and there are virtually no clues in the sources themselves. To do this, the per-pound price of the hog (usually given) was compared with the per-pound price of fresh pork for that region in that year. If the per-pound price of the hog was less than the price of fresh pork, the weight was called a live weight. If the per-pound price of the hog equalled or exceeded the price of fresh pork, the weight was called dressed weight and divided by 0.70 to standardize all weights as live weights.[48]

45. For the months in which butchering occurred, see Rothenberg, "A Price Index for Rural Massachusetts," 999.

46. Bidwell and Falconer, *History of Agriculture*, p. 111.

47. The fact that many small pigs were butchered at a very early age is certainly relevant to this inquiry, but because their presence would distort the results, pigs had to be removed from the sample. There is no line that separates pigs from hogs, and the decision had to be arbitrary: all swine whose live weight equaled or exceeded 200 pounds were included as hogs.

To the issue of the *timing* of market orientation in slaughtering decisions, it is relevant to state that only about one sixth of the hog weights in the sample appear before 1820; five sixths of the observations postdate 1820.

48. In all the calculations, a dressed weight-live weight ratio of 0.70 has been used, midway between the 0.75 or 0.76 used by Gallman, Atack and Bateman, and Battalio and Kagel, and

Regressions were then run of hog weights on corn prices, fresh pork, salt pork and combined pork prices, the ratio of corn to each pork price, and time, separately and in combination, in logs and not, deflated and undeflated, by region and for the aggregate sample, for the whole period, for time after 1820 as a dummy variable, and for a variety of period breakdowns. The best results can be read in the two parts of Table 6.

Table 6A presents nine regressions for the entire period 1750–1855, including the independent variables in the order in which they were entered, the proportion of variation in hog weights explained by the cumulative power of the variables (R^2), the coefficient on each variable (B), and lastly, the t-statistic for each B and the significance level of each completed regression, both of which test (and, fortunately, reject) the null hypothesis that these non-zero correlations are mere chance events.

Although the results in Table 6A indicate that corn and pork prices may have played a role in the slaughter decisions of farmers, it is evident that the most powerful explanatory variable in this table is time; hog weights were manifestly an increasing function of time. Time, in this case, however, is hardly neutral with respect to changes in relevant economic variables. "Time" conceals market-validated changes in animal husbandry such as the emphasis on manures which brought about stabling and penning, and the introduction of legumes and nonperishable root crops into swine feed enabling farmers to fatten them through the winter. "Time" conceals the impact a change in relative prices had on the allocation of corn between humans and animals. "Time" conceals the manifold effects of the proliferation, expansion, and accessibility of urban markets.

Pregnant with economic content as it is, however, "time" does not specify these variables, leaving us only the ones we have specified, and in Table 6A these make only a small contribution toward explaining hog weights at slaughter. Considerably stronger R^2s and more significant coefficients are obtained when the data are divided into time-period

the 0.65 used by several of my account books, and by Jay Adams, farmer at Old Sturbridge Village, whose job it is to replicate to the minutest detail the farming practices of central Massachusetts in 1800.

The procedure outlined here for distinguishing between dressed and live weight was generally followed, but exceptions were made. We know from records of a large-scale slaughterer in 1838–1839, that larger animals could command a higher per-pound price than smaller animals simply because they were fatter, not because they were dressed. That is, the higher price reflected a quality differential. Therefore, to avoid biasing the sample upward, swine weights were treated as live weights if to treat them as dressed would produce hogs weighing 700 pounds or more.

Table 6A. *Multiple regressions of hog weights on selected prices and time, 1750–1855*

	Regression Independent Variables	R^2	*B*	*t-statistic*	*Significance Level*
1.	Time ≧ 1820, EAST and WEST, N = 366	.27	.183	10.12	
	Corn Prices	.31	.354	5.04	
	Salt Pork Prices	.32	−.094	1.46	
	Constant		2.341		<.001
2.	Time ≧ 1820, EAST and WEST	.27	.201	11.66	
	Corn Price divided by Fresh Pork Price	.28	.149	2.60	
	Constant		2.218		<.001
3.	Time ≧ 1820, EAST and WEST	.27	.177	9.64	
	Corn Price divided by Salt Pork Price	.29	.200	3.34	
	Constant		2.230		<.001
4.	Combined Pork Prices, deflated, aggregate sample	.11	−.246	2.83	
	Corn Prices, deflated	.11	.157	1.64	
	Time	.32	.004	10.42	
	Constant		1.980		<.001
5.	Fresh Pork Prices, deflated, EAST, N = 179	.02	−.231	2.62	
	Time	.21	.004	6.58	
	Corn Prices, deflated	.22	.190	1.57	
	Constant		1.980		<.001
6.	Salt Pork Prices, deflated, EAST	.07	−.166	1.91	
	Corn Prices, deflated	.07	.233	1.88	
	Time	.20	.003	5.31	
	Constant		2.140		<.001
7.	Salt Pork Prices, deflated, WEST, N = 187	.16	−.148	1.38	
	Corn Prices, deflated	.17	.096	0.64	
	Time	.40	.005	8.53	
	Constant		2.060		<.001
8.	Ratio Corn Price/Salt Pork Price, EAST	.06	.186	2.47	
	Time	.20	.003	5.55	
	Constant		2.127		<.001
9.	Ratio Corn Price/Salt Pork Price, deflated, WEST	.15	.131	1.46	
	Time	.40	.005	8.78	
	Constant		2.080		<.001

Note: All hog weights and prices are entered in logs. Deflating is done by my price index (see Rothenberg, this JOURNAL, 39 [Dec. 1979], 975–1001). Hog weights adjusted to live weights as described in the text.

Source: Prices and hog weights are from account books and daybooks.

subfiles and time is entered as a polynomial to fit a nonlinear time trend.[49] The best of these results are shown in Table 6B.

In a different arrangement, selected variables are paired in order more clearly to expose the change over time in the price responsiveness of hog

49. There are *regional* differences in the explanatory power of these variables as well as temporal differences, and, in fact, the regional differences are more consistent. The time variables account for a smaller proportion of the change in hog weights, and price variables for a larger

Table 6B. *Multiple regressions of hog weights on selected prices, 1750–1855, in time-period breakdowns*

Independent Variable	R^2 *Change*	*B*	*t-statistic*
Corn Prices, EAST			
1750–1820	.006	−.690	1.36
1820–1835	.132	+.736	1.39
Salt Pork Prices, WEST			
1750–1810	.055	−.077	.20
1810–1830	.164	−.295	1.14
Corn Prices/Salt Pork Prices, WEST			
1750–1820	.012	+.496	1.65
1810–1820	.339	+1.222	2.13
T, EAST			
1750–1820	.523	+.010	.94
1820–1835	.017	−.287	4.32
T^4, EAST and WEST			
1750–1810	.206	+.464[a]	2.49
1830–1855	.005	+.345[b]	3.18

[a] Move decimal point six places to the left.
[b] Move decimal point seven places to the left.
Note: All hog weights and prices are handled as described in the notes to Table 6A.
Source: Underlying data from farmers' account books and daybooks (see Appendix).

weights. Because the variables in Table 6B are not presented in the order in which they were entered, a new column, R^2 Change, replaces R^2 to indicate the increase in explained variation accounted for by the addition of that variable.

The results suggest emphatically that the time variables in the later periods are losing to the price variables the dominance they had had in the early years. This shift of explanatory power from time trend to market factors can be seen in the later period in the much increased *t*-statistic on all coefficients, the sharply diminished R^2 change of all time variables, and the increased R^2 change of all price variables.

While the growing strength of the price variables supports the hypothesis of growing market involvement, that support remains modest. Unlike cattle, whose basic feed is hay, a diet rich in corn may have been

proportion, in the West than in the East. In view of our earlier findings of a slower pace of market development in the West than in the East, this deserves comment. We may be picking up the early specialization of Connecticut River Valley farms in livestock raising. According to Bidwell and Falconer, farms in and around Hadley were stall-feeding oxen for the Boston market as early as 1700 (Bidwell and Falconer, *History of Agriculture*, p. 109). Even if swine were not shipped to Boston, one imagines that the habit of responding to market signals would spill over from cattle raising to swine raising.

given to swine only for the brief fattening period.[50] If hog weights depended more on feeds other than corn, we have not captured that in these regressions.

In addition, the signs on the coefficients (and on the simple correlations not shown here) appear to run counter to intuition, at least for a static model. Ignoring expectations, one might suppose that the higher the price of corn, the earlier the farmer would butcher his corn-consuming animals; that the higher the price of pork, the fatter he would let his hogs become; that the higher the price of corn relative to the price of pork, the lower the weight of the butchered hog. Instead, the very opposite holds true, which suggests that expectations indeed played a decisive role here. A rise in the price of corn may have led to the anticipation of a rise in the price of pork fed on corn, and therefore to delayed butchering; a rise in the price of pork, which is expected to be short-lived, may have led to immediate "cashing-in"; alterations in the relative prices of corn and pork may have generated uncertainties that induced the farmer to salt and barrel his hogs where they could, without eating, await further price changes.

The time of killing beasts is to be regulated by the market, and the advantage and convenience of the farmer. And the same things must fix the time, if he sells them to the butchers. Beef that is only grass-fed must be killed as early as the beginning of November, because after this time, grass will not increase the fatness of cattle. This may be afforded at the lowest price, perhaps $2\frac{1}{2}$ pence per pound, without loss. Cattle that are fatted till December must have, besides grass or hay, corn or juicy vegetables, or both, to increase their fatness. The price of beef therefore ought to be higher, by about two farthings. If not killed till January, the price should continue rising at least in the same proportion; and so on, till the time of fatting by grazing returns.

This was written considerably before regressions, in 1803.[51]

Farmers' prices and the trade cycle

The final exhibit is, in a sense, the first, for it was the discovery of synchronous cycles in the behavior of Philadelphia prices, New York

50. Although cattle weights may be more nearly a function of the hay cattle consume than are hog weights of the corn hogs consume, it does not follow that a regression of the slaughter weights of cattle on hay prices would have given better results. Cattle, even if stall-fed in winter, grazed free for most of the year, free in the sense that pasture land was of such poor quality that it had virtually no alternative uses and therefore zero opportunity cost. In addition, cattle perform a wide variety of services throughout a long lifetime. It is unlikely that they were slaughtered for "light and transient causes" like a change in the relative prices of hay and beef.

51. Isaiah Thomas, Jr., "Agriculture: Killing of Beasts," in *Massachusetts, Connecticut, Rhode Island, New Hampshire and Vermont Almanack for the Year of Our Lord 1804* (Worcester, MA, 1803), n.p. I am grateful to Sarah McMahon for bringing this to my attention.

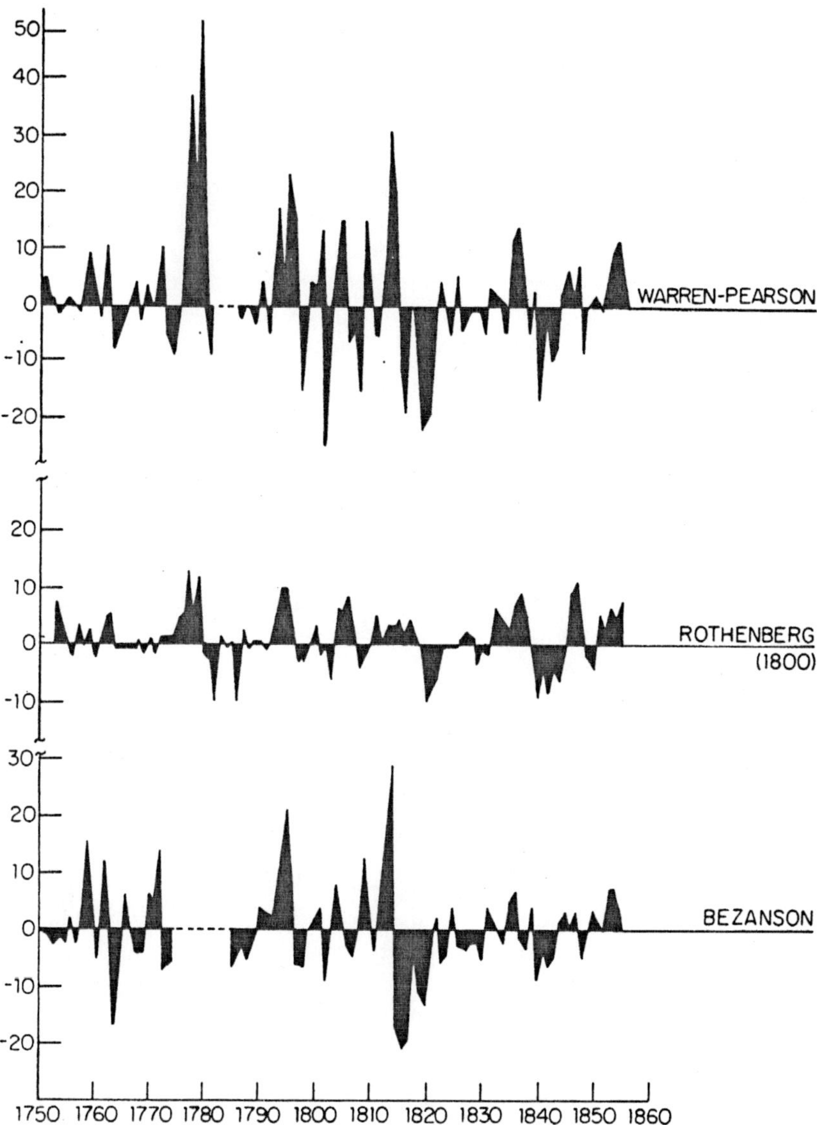

Figure 5. Cyclical synchronicity of the Massachusetts farm price index with the Bezanson index of Philadelphia prices and the Warren-Pearson index of New York City prices.

Note: Trend eliminated by calculation of first-differences. The Massachusetts index was first smoothed by a three-year moving average.
Source: Rothernberg, "A Price Index for Rural Massachusetts," this Journal, 39 (Dec. 1979), 975–1001. The Bezanson and Warren-Pearson indexes are presented and discussed in Arthur Harrison Cole. *Wholesale Commodity Prices in the United States, 1700–1861* (Cambridge, MA, 1938).

City prices, and Massachusetts farmers' account book prices that plunged me into the present investigation.

Examine Figure 5.[52] Visible in the behavior of all three indexes are the following events: some inflation in the French and Indian War; the depression that followed it and endured throughout most of the years of the imperial crisis; the Revolutionary War inflation and its deep post-war depression; the commercial shipping prosperity of the 1790s (in which Massachusetts prices led New York and Philadelphia prices by a year or two); the Embargo, registered on farms in Massachusetts in 1808, but felt far more keenly in urban markets than in rural; the high prices of the War of 1812, succeeded in all three indexes by the depression of 1819–1821; low prices throughout the decade of the 1820s; the dramatic boom of 1836, followed by steadily falling prices through the hungry forties, relieved momentarily in 1847 by the Mexican War prosperity; the assertive recovery in 1853 due to California gold – yes, even this is visible in Massachusetts farm prices; and the upsurge of prices the next year with the start of the Crimean War in Europe with its demands upon American foodstuffs.

The question for the skeptical to answer is this: If the farmers whose account books were used to build that index – middling farmers, widely scattered across the state, most from very small rural communities – were isolated from the market, then by what conduit were these macroeconomic shocks to the general price level communicated to them?

Conclusion

Massachusetts did not begin as an experiment in self-sufficiency. The people who settled this land came from a tradition of Market Crosses, Market Days, Corn Markets, cattle, wool, cheese, silk and produce markets, stalls, shops, fairs, itinerant peddlers, and cattle drovers. "Eight hundred fairs and markets were held regularly in every part of the English realm. Many a New England settlement was named after such a market town,"[53] and soon after founding, weekly market days

52. This paragraph is a brief recapitulation of pp. 981 and 985 of Rothenberg, "A Price Index for Rural Massachusetts." In that article, in order to isolate cyclical movements, I fitted trends to all three indexes and plotted deviations from trend. At Professor Engerman's suggestion I have revised these figures using first-differences instead of deviations from trend. It was his opinion that because I had used different trends for each of the indexes I had "implicitly assumed an independence of trend and cycle which is somewhat dubious." This is only one of his many suggestions for each of which I am deeply grateful. Also, my index of Massachusetts farmers' prices required some smoothing by a three-year moving average before first-differences were taken.

53. Howard S. Russell, *A Long, Deep Furrow: Three Centuries of Farming in New England* (Hanover, NH, 1976), p. 58.

and periodic fair days were authorized by the provincial government for the towns of Plymouth, Duxbury, Boston, Salem, Lynn, Charlestown, Watertown, Dorchester, New Haven, Hartford, New London, Fairfield, Newport (R.I.), and Providence. Then, as settlement spread, there were Fair Days as far north as New Castle in New Hampshire and as far west as Hardwick in western Worcester County.

The idea did not "take" in Massachusetts. A quick run-through of town and county histories shows, in almost every case, that after a decade or so no business relating to markets or fairs was taken up in town meetings.[54] They seem to have petered out.[55]

But this may speak less to a forced retreat into self-sufficiency than to its very opposite. In the seventeenth and early eighteenth centuries, the responsibility fell upon town government to legislate fixed prices, if only to stabilize the value in "country-pay" of ministers' salaries. To do this required laws against forestalling, engrossing and regrating, and a tight corpus of licensing, regulation, and surveillance to restrict supply and demand. Without this the statutory prices could not hold. This is easier to do when "the market" is in fact a particular place (stalls on the village green), and a particular time ("the fourth day of ye weeke commonly called Wednesday, from 9 a clock in the morning till 4 of the Clock after Noone"). It is harder to do if "the market" is a *process*, vaguely set in space and time, between autonomous buyers and sellers acting – at least more so than ever before – in their own interests.

Shall the case then be made that what prevailed in New England villages from the earliest decades of settlement was a commercial *mentalité*, an entrepreneurial spirit, an individualistic ethic of private gain? The

54. Boston was a special case in that the issue of establishing a market remained a heated controversy for well over a century. From Governor Winthrop's first declaration in 1633 setting Thursdays aside as market days, efforts were repeatedly made, but just as repeatedly foiled by opposition from several quarters. There were the country farmers who recognized the downward pressure such a market would place on prices, the householders who preferred the convenience of sellers coming to the door, the hucksters and other unsavory types who chafed against the regulations, and, lastly, there were the Puritan zealots who could not abide the association, from English days, of markets with Market Crosses. Unlikely as this last may sound, it is interesting that whoever it was that burned down the market in 1737 disguised themselves as clergymen ("stole the livery of heaven") to do so. See Abram English Brown. *Faneuil Hall and the Faneuil Hall Market* (Boston, 1900).

55. The same thing, apparently, happened in England. By the early eighteenth century, "Private bargaining between individuals characterized the [grain] trade; the regulated or 'open' market was insignificant." Dennis Baker, "The Marketing of Corn in the First Half of the 18th Century: North-East Kent," *Agricultural History Review*, 18 (1970), pt. 2, 139. Alan Everitt dates the privatization of trade in "corn" back to the early seventeenth century, with "yeomen, brewers, maltsters, millers, and the like negotiating and reaching agreement in numerous farmhouses, mills, barns, warehouses, corn-chambers, and inns" (quoted in Baker, "The Marketing of Corn," p. 139).

language is deliberately provocative to make the point that couched in those terms such a statement can neither be confirmed nor refuted. *Mentalité* may be relevant, it is certainly interesting, but its usefulness as an explanatory category in economic history lies, it seems to me, in finding and testing its correlates in observable behavior, more specifically, in testing those of its observable correlates that can be aggregated to describe whole relevant populations. The spatial pattern in which farmers moved their produce and the intricate behavior of their own prices are among such correlates.

Appendix: List of sources

In the following list of account books, diaries, journals and daybooks, OSV = Library of Old Sturbridge Village; HBS = Manuscript Division, Baker Library, Harvard Business School; DHS = Dedham Historical Society; EI = Essex Institute; and AAS = American Antiquarian Society.

Name	*Place*	*Date*	*Source*
John May	Woodstock, CT	1708–1766	AAS
Artemas Ward	Shrewsbury, MA	1750s	AAS
Henry Eames	Framingham, MA	1752–1762	HBS
William and Solomon Bartlett	Westhampton, MA	1753–1832	HBS
Robert Craig	Leicester, MA	1757–1781	OSV
James Emery	Biddeford, MA	1763–1802	HBS
John Baker	Ipswich, MA	1769–1834	HBS
Isaac Thayer	Braintree, MA	1769–1799	HBS
James Parker, Sr.	Shirley, MA	1770–1829	AAS
Nehemiah Stone	Charlton, MA	1772–1830	AAS
Samuel Sloper	Blandford, MA	1773–1802	HBS
Chapin Family	Springfield, MA	1782–1866	HBS
Joseph Hyde	Hopkinton, MA	1784–1791	HBS
Preserved Bartlett	Northampton, MA	1787–1832	OSV
Jeremiah Davis	Oxford, MA	1787–1822	HBS
Carpenter Family and Samuel Chamberlain	Westborough, MA	1788–1856	OSV
Aaron Everett	Wrentham, MA	1788–1795	HBS
Nahum Fay	Northborough, MA	1788–1832	HBS
Solomon Thompson	Middleborough, MA	1789–1815	HBS
Isaac Bullard	Dedham, MA	1789–1800	DHS
Jonathan Pierce	Lancaster, MA	1791	AAS
Aaron Cook	Harvard, MA	1794–1833	HBS
Alexander Smith	West Springfield, MA	1795–1844	HBS
Daniel Colman and D. Emery	Newburyport, MA	1796–1830	EI
Job Knapp	Douglas, MA	1803–1819	HBS

Name	*Place*	*Date*	*Source*
Ezekiel Bagg	West Springfield, MA	1803–1834	HBS
Charles P. Phelps, Jr.	Hadley, MA	1805–1858	HBS
Samuel Dike	Thompson, CT	1805–1830	HBS
Joseph Heald	Pepperell, MA	1808–1813	HBS
Timothy Allen	Sturbridge, MA	1811–1845	OSV
Asahel Smith	Dedham, MA	1811–1845	DHS
Richard Jaques	Newbury, MA	1814–1855	EI
Martin Brewer	Springfield, MA	1817–1840	OSV
Phineas Goodrich	Acton, MA	1818–1830	HBS
Thomas Walter Ward II	Shrewsbury, MA	1819–1820	AAS
David Goodale	Marlborough, MA	1819–1858	OSV
Nathaniel Brintnall	Mansfield, MA	1819–1840	HBS
Horace Clark	E. Granby, CT	1821–1834	OSV
Otis Sherman	Grafton, MA	1823–1834	HBS
Joseph Lee	Newton, MA	1823–1829	EI
Frederick Cone	Lee, MA	1825–1869	HBS
Nathan Atherton	Stoughton, MA	1825–1832	OSV
C. Adams	Kingston, MA	1825–1828	EI
Joseph Flagg	Boylston, MA	1825–1867	OSV
Hezekiah Allen	Sturbridge, MA	1826–1874	OSV
David S. Howes	Ashfield, MA	1830–1842	OSV
Harrison Howard	N. Bridgewater, MA	1830–1855	HBS
Edward Hale	Newbury, MA	1831–1855	EI
John Currier	Amesbury, MA	1833–1855	EI
Michael Jacobs	Plymouth, MA	1835–1859	OSV
Anonymous	West Cambridge, MA	1836–1850	OSV
William Hosmer	Westfield, MA	1842–1853	HBS
John Plummer Foster	North Andover, MA	1842–1891	EI
E. B. Ferguson and Parsons	Byfield (Newbury), MA	1848–1853	EI

III

Slavery and servitude

"The rise and fall of indentured servitude in the Americas: An economic analysis"

by David W. Galenson

The economic growth and development of the North American colonies depended on agriculture. To clear the abundant land and plant and harvest the crop, labor was needed. On small farms, the family supplied its own labor. The larger, commercial farms, however, demanded a greater labor supply. Because land was inexpensive, self-employment was common, and few laborers were willing to work for wages. Wage workers commanded relatively high compensation and often worked only long enough to save money to purchase their own land. A solution to this shortage was the importation of bound labor from the Old World.

While we all have some familiarity with the system of slavery, most of us are unfamiliar with another form of bound labor: indentured servitude. David Galenson demonstrates the importance of indentured servitude, noting that between the 1640s and the Revolution, over half of the European immigrants to the colonies arrived as indentured servants. Galenson's primary tasks in this essay are to explain the origins and early adaptations of indentured servitude, to unlock the economic logic of this institution, and to explain its rise, fall, rise, and fall in the Americas between 1620 and 1917.

The primary difference between slavery and indentured servitude was coercion. Indentured servitude was (almost always) entered into voluntarily; slavery was not. However, once the master–servant relationship was established, both systems developed an array of positive and negative incentives to elicit work from the servant. These issues of motivation and supervision fall into a broader class of problems collectively known as the *principal–agent* problem. The principal wants to get something done (like grow tobacco) and tries to get the agent to do it for him. Because the agent does not have the same goal as the principal, he will not do exactly what is desired. The principal must devise a set of incentives to elicit the behavior desired.

History is full of dead ends and mistakes. Notice that some of the early servitude arrangements failed to use compatible incentives, for example, the attempt of the Virginia Company to rent servants to local planters. The planters were not reliable agents for the company, did not have an incentive to look out for the company's interests, and drove the servants into poor health.

Indentured servitude illuminates a number of other economic issues, such as how labor markets equilibrate when there is no wage, how shifting supply and demand lead one input and then another to dominate a market, and how political changes have profound effects on economic institutions.

When Galenson tests one of the hypotheses quantitatively, lack of data forces him to test it indirectly. This example demonstrates the strengths and weaknesses of economic history. Galenson squeezes more out of the historical record by using two "proxies" for the variables he would prefer, but as he readily admits, his simple theory cannot fully explain some of the empirical findings. For example:

- Why wasn't there indentured servitude among Chinese immigrants in the United States?
- What explains the changes in servitude patterns among Europeans in the early 1800s?

Historians must keep digging in their never-ending quest to understand the past. Moreover, the scientific method requires that one amend a theory when its predictions fail, so researchers have attempted to tie up the loose ends in this essay. For example, since the publication of this essay, Patricia Cloud and David Galenson (1987) have made progress in explaining the anomalous situation of Chinese immigrants in the United States. Farley Grubb has gone far in analyzing the decline in servitude among European immigrants in the early 1800s. He measures the value of servants, looking for clues about shifting supply and demand, and concludes that "the disappearance of immigrant servitude must have been caused primarily by a fall in servant supply" (1992, 201).

Studying history expands the menu of choices available today. Would indentured servitude exist today if it were legal and immigration barriers did not forbid it? To answer this question, you could replicate Galenson's table and look for current average incomes in poorer countries and transportation costs from them to the United States. Why has society deemed indentured servitude unacceptable? What have we gained and given up by doing so?

Many young adults take the opportunity to attend college by agreeing to serve in the military for a few years. How is this similar to indentured servitude?

Additional Reading

Patricia Cloud and David Galenson, "Chinese Immigration and Contract Labor in the Late Nineteenth Century," *Explorations in Economic History*, 24 (January 1987), 22–42.

Ralph Gray and Betty Wood, "The Transition from Indentured to Involuntary Servitude in Colonial Georgia," *Explorations in Economic History*, 13 (October 1976), 353–70.

Farley Grubb, "The Long-Run Trend in the Value of European Immigrant Servants, 1654–1831: New Measurements and Interpretations," *Research in Economic History*, 14 (1992), 167–240.

Russell Menard, "From Servants to Slaves: The Transformation of the Chesapeake Labor System," *Southern Studies*, 16 (Winter 1977), 355–90.

Abbot Emerson Smith, *Colonists in Bondage: White Servitude and Convict Labor in America, 1607–1776*, Chapel Hill: University of North Carolina Press, 1947.

4

The rise and fall of indentured servitude in the Americas

An economic analysis

DAVID W. GALENSON

Indentured servitude appeared in Virginia by 1620. Initially a device used to transport European workers to the New World, over time servitude dwindled as black slavery grew in importance in the British colonies. Indentured servitude reappeared in the Americas in the mid-nineteenth century as a means of transporting Asians to the Caribbean sugar islands and South America following the abolition of slavery. Servitude then remained in legal use until its abolition in 1917. This paper provides an economic analysis of the innovation of indentured servitude, describes the economic forces that caused its decline and disappearance from the British colonies, and considers why indentured servitude was revived for migration to the West Indies during the time of the great free migration of Europeans to the Americas.

Indentured servitude appeared in use in Virginia by 1620, little more than a decade after the initial British settlement of North America at Jamestown. Servitude became a central institution in the economy and society of many parts of colonial British America; a leading historian of indentured servitude in the colonial period, Abbot Emerson Smith, estimated that between one-half and two-thirds of all white immigrants to the British colonies between the Puritan migration of the 1630s and the Revolution came under indenture.[1] Although it dwindled in im-

Source: David W. Galenson, "The Rise and Fall of Indentured Servitude in the Americas: An Economic Analysis," *Journal of Economic History* (March 1984), 1–26. Reprinted with permission of the author and the Economic History Association.

The author is Associate Professor of Economics, University of Chicago, Chicago, Illinois 60637, and is a Research Associate, National Bureau of Economic Research. He is grateful to Stanley Engerman for discussions of the issues treated in this paper, and to Andrew Abel, Yoram Barzel, James Buchanan, Charlotte Erickson, Robert Fogel, Alice Galenson, Robert Gallman, Farley Grubb, Jonathan Hughes, Michael Jensen, Douglass North, Jonathan Pincus, Joe Reid, Theodore W. Schultz, Gordon Tullock, and John Wallis for comments and suggestions. Patricia Cloud provided capable research assistance. Earlier versions of the paper were presented at a seminar at the Center for Study of Public Choice, Virginia Polytechnic Institute, at the Economic History Workshop, University of Chicago, and at the Liberty Fund Conference on Economic Organization in Theory and History, Port Ludlow, Washington, July, 1983.

1. Abbot Emerson Smith, *Colonists in Bondage: White Servitude and Convict Labor in America, 1607–1776* (Chapel Hill, 1947), p. 336.

portance over time, servitude continued to exist in mainland North America until at least the fourth decade of the nineteenth century. In that same decade, indentured servitude was brought back into large-scale use in the West Indies and parts of South America.[2] It remained in legal use in those areas until 1917.

This paper will consider some of the central economic factors underlying the appearance and disappearance of indentured servitude in the Americas. The following section will provide an economic analysis of the innovation of indentured servitude and of the problems the early English settlers solved in order to make servitude a useful institution. Subsequent sections will then consider how and why servitude declined in importance and disappeared from the English West Indies and mainland North America during the late eighteenth and early nineteenth centuries, as well as why the institution was revived in the Caribbean and South America in the mid-nineteenth century. The broad purpose of this paper is an economic interpretation of specific institutional changes; the paper seeks to provide a basis for understanding the economic forces that initially created and molded an institution that played a major role in American labor markets for three centuries, as well as the forces that later led to the disappearance of that institution.[3]

The seventeenth-century origins of indentured servitude in North America

Perhaps the most critical economic problem facing early investors in the Virginia Company and the settlers they sent to North America in the decade after 1607 was that of recruiting and motivating a labor force. An institutional solution to this problem, the system of indentured servitude, emerged after a series of experiments by the Company. A brief review of the historical context within which the settlement of Virginia

2. Indentured, or contract, labor was also used elsewhere in the nineteenth century, as, for example, significant movements of bound workers occurred within Asia. This paper will not treat these episodes, but will focus only on migrations to the Americas.

3. Throughout this paper, with reference to indentured servitude the term "institution" will be used broadly to refer to the sets of practices and rules – including both statute and common law – that governed the use of labor contracts written for specified periods and entered into by workers in order to finance migration. Contracts of servitude typically differed from hire labor contracts in specifying relatively long term – e.g., in the colonial period four years or more – and by involving a greater degree of control of the worker's living and working conditions by the employer, and from debt contracts of service in failing to provide for automatic dissolution of the agreement at any time upon repayment of a stated principal sum by the worker. These differences tended to make indentured servitude a distinctive status at most times and places, with a set of rules and practices specific to it, although of course these might differ among particular episodes, or for a single episode over time.

occurred, and of the sequence of adaptations introduced by the Company, will demonstrate how and why this solution was reached.

Recent estimates indicate that a majority of all hired labor in preindustrial England was provided by "servants in husbandry" – youths of both sexes, normally between the ages of 13 and 25, who lived and worked in the households of their masters, typically on annual contracts.[4] In view of the pervasiveness of service in husbandry as a source of labor supply in seventeenth-century England, it is not surprising that the notion of moving that institution to America occurred to members of the Virginia Company when the results of their initial efforts to recruit a sustained flow of adult workers to their colony proved disappointing.[5] Several problems had to be solved, however, before the English institution could be successfully transplanted to the New World; in their solution lay the origins of the system of indentured servitude.

The most obvious of these problems was that of the transportation costs of the settlers. Passage fares to Virginia in the early seventeenth century were high relative to the annual wages of English servants in husbandry or hired agricultural laborers, and few prospective migrants were able to pay the cost of their voyage out of their own accumulated savings or those of their families.[6] Existing English capital market institutions were patently inadequate to cope with the problem, considering difficulties that included the high transactions costs entailed in making loans to individuals and enforcing them at a distance of 3,000 miles. The Virginia Company's solution was to use its own funds to fill the gap left by this unavailability of capital from other sources – by advancing the cost of passage to prospective settlers. The Company's

4. Peter Laslett, *The World We Have Lost*, Second edition (London, 1971), Ch. 1; Ann Kussmaul, *Servants in Husbandry in Early Modern England* (Cambridge, 1981); also Alan Macfarlane, *The Origins of English Individualism* (New York, 1979).

5. On early attempts to attract settlers, and the Virginia Company's difficulties, see Sigmund Diamond, "From Organization to Society: Virginia in the Seventeenth Century," *American Journal of Sociology*, 63 (Mar. 1958), 457–475; Edmund S. Morgan, *American Slavery, American Freedom: The Ordeal of Colonial Virginia* (New York, 1975), Ch. 4.

6. The passage fare normally quoted until the middle of the seventeenth century was £6; for example, John Smith, *The Generall Historie of Virginia, New-England, and the Summer Isles* (London, 1624), p. 162. A Survey of wages in Cambridge, Canterbury, Dover, Exeter, Oxford. Westminster, Winchester, and Windsor for 1620 found a range of daily wages in skilled trades from 12–20d., and for unskilled laborers from 8–12d.; British Library of Political and Economic Science, Records of International Scientific Committee on Price History (Beveridge Price Commission). Implied annual wages for full-time skilled workers would be approximately £15–25, and for unskilled workers £10–15. The wages of unskilled servants in husbandry in the teen ages would presumably have been lower.

For further discussion of the influence of transportation costs relative to income and wealth on the form of migrations, see *infra*, "The Decline – and Revival – of Indentured Servitude in the Americas."

advance took the form of a loan to the migrants, who contracted to repay this debt out of their net earnings in America.[7]

Under the first scheme in which Company funds were used to pay transportation costs, the migrants were to work directly for the Company in Virginia. In return for passage to the colony and maintenance there during their terms of service to the Company, the workers were to become "adventurers" (investors) in the enterprise, with claim to a share in the division of the Company's profits that was to occur at the end of seven years. This system had appeared in use by 1609.[8] The arrangement, under which large groups of men lived and worked communally under quasi-military conditions, proved to be very unpopular with the recruits. Conditions for the workers were hard. One observer commented, in explaining the colony's high rate of mortality, that "the hard work and the scanty food, on public works kills them, and increases the discontent in which they live, seeing themselves treated like slaves, with great cruelty."[9] The response of some workers was to run away to live with the Indians. The Company clearly felt that this action threatened the continued survival of their enterprise, for they reacted forcefully to this crime. In 1612, the colony's governor dealt firmly with some recaptured laborers: "Some he apointed to be hanged Some burned Some to be broken upon wheles, others to be staked and some to be shott to death." The underlying motive of maintaining labor discipline was apparent to an observer, who remarked on the punishments that "all theis extreme and crewell tortures he used and inflicted upon them to terrify the reste for Attempting the Lyke." Another related problem perceived by Company managers was a lack of work effort by their bound workers.[10] These difficulties of supervising and motivating the discontented workers led the Company to seek a new solution to the labor problem.

By 1619 a new system had been introduced. New colonists bound for a term to the Company were sent over at the Company's expense, and the free planters of the colony were allowed to rent them from the Company for a year at a fixed rate, in addition to providing their

7. The large size of the debt meant that repayment would normally take longer than the single year that characterized the employment of farm servants in England. Thus although the early arrangements did not have all the characteristics of indentured servitude that would later develop, one important element of the indenture system – contracts binding the worker to a master for a number of years – appeared at an early stage.

8. Smith, *Colonists in Bondage*, p. 9. On this early scheme, see also J. R. T. Hughes, *Social Control in the Colonial Economy* (Charlottesville, 1976), pp. 55–57.

9. Alexander Brown, ed., *The Genesis of the United States* (Boston, 1890), Vol. II, p. 648.

10. Morgan, *American Slavery, American Freedom*, pp. 74, 78.

maintenance.[11] The Company believed that this system would yield them a number of advantages. The dispersal of the groups of new arrivals was expected to improve both their health and their industry, "for asmuch as wee find by experience, that were abundaunce of new men are planted in one body they doe overthrowe themselues . . . by Contagion of sicknes . . . and Cause thereof, ill example of Idlenes." The new migrants' placement with established planters would provide them with a place to live immediately after arrival, and the old planters would train them in the "vsuall workes of the Country," so that when their year of private service expired, they would "returne to the publique busines and be able to instructe other new Commers as they themselues had bine instructed."[12]

Yet this modification apparently aggravated some existing problems and created several new ones. By 1619 the tobacco boom had begun in Virginia, and the value of labor had risen sharply. The Company was acutely aware, in the celebrated words of the speaker of Virginia's first House of Burgesses, that "Our principall wealth . . . consisteth in seruants."[13] Enticement of servants by private employers seems to have occurred, for in 1619 the General Assembly ordered "that no crafty or advantagious means be suffered to be put in practise for the inticing awaye the Tenants or Servants of any particular plantation from the place where they are seatted;" in case of violations, the governor was "most severely to punish both the seducers and the seduced, and to returne these latter into their former places."[14] Perhaps more seriously, the rental arrangement introduced an additional principal–agent relationship, between the Company and the private planters, that became a source of concern to the Company. The Company ordered that planters were to be responsible for maintaining their servants if the latter fell ill, and were to be liable for rental payments to the Company for servants who died, with the amounts to be determined "proportionably for their

11. This system was clearly used in 1619; Susan Myra Kingsbury, ed., *The Records of the Virginia Company of London* (Washington, D.C., 1933), Vol. III. pp. 226–227. It is not clear whether it was in use earlier. A regulation of Virginia in 1616 mentions a covenanted obligation of "every farmer to pay yearly into the [Company's] magazine for himself and every man-servant, two barrels and a half a piece of their best Indian wheat"; Historical Manuscript Commission, *Eighth Report*, Vol. 2, No. 208, p. 31. The payment made by the farmer for himself was apparently a rental payment for an allotment of land from the Company (e.g., see Charles M. Andrews, *The Colonial Period of American History* [New Haven, 1934], Vol. I, p. 124), but it is not specified whether the payment to be made for each servant was a rental fee for a possible additional allotment of land or a rental payment to the Company for the services of the servant himself.

12. Kingsbury, *Records of the Virginia Company*, Vol. III, p. 226; also pp. 246, 257–258.

13. Ibid., p. 221.

14. Ibid., p. 167.

life time."[15] The speed with which the system of rental agreements was abandoned was probably a response to the Company's perception of the insufficient incentives of the planters to protect the Company's investment in the labor of their hired workers, not only in providing adequate maintenance and provision for health care in an environment where all settlers suffered extraordinarily high rates of mortality, but also in preventing runaways.[16]

The rapid termination of the use of this rental arrangement was apparently a result also of the Company's recognition of an alternative to the rental system that avoided the agency problem it had created. As part of an effort by a new group of Company officers to increase Virginia's population, transactions occurred in 1619 that contained the essential elements of the indenture system; migrants, transported at Company expense from England to Virginia and bound for fixed terms of years, were sold outright for the duration of these terms to planters upon the servants' arrival in the colony.[17] These bargains were enthusiastically received by the planters, and an early example of the indenture system's characteristic form on a quantitatively significant scale appeared in 1620, when the Company sent to Virginia "one hundred seruants to be disposed amongst the old *Planters*."[18] The cost of passage was advanced to the migrants by the Company, and the recruits in turn promised to work for stated periods; in Virginia, title to the migrants' labor during these periods was transferred to individual planters upon the planters' reimbursement of transportation costs to the Company. Thus by 1620 the development of the transaction that was to become prevalent for English indentured servants for nearly two centuries was complete as colonial planters obtained the services of immigrants for a specified time upon payment of a lump sum to an importer.

Institutional structure and work incentives under indentured servitude

Indentured servitude therefore emerged as a new institutional arrangement that was devised to increase labor mobility from England to

15. Ibid., p. 227.

16. The difficulties of devising rental agreements that would provide the proper incentives for planters would have been enormous in view of the problems involved in determining the presence of negligence by masters in the case of death or escape by servants under the conditions of high mortality and poor communications that existed in early Virginia. Sale of the contracts to masters was therefore superior to rental, and it appears that the Virginia Company realized this very quickly, as the only definite evidence of rentals dates from the same year – 1619 – in which the first outright sales of servants' contracts occurred. Rentals do not appear to have continued in later years.

17. Smith, *Colonists in Bondage*, p. 12. The contract that came to be used in these bargains was of a type commonly used in England for a variety of legal transactions, known as an indenture.

18. Kingsbury, *Records of the Virginia Company*, Vol. III, p. 313.

America.[19] The colonization of America made available for cultivation vast amounts of new land, and in those American regions where crops could be grown that used this land to satisfy the demands of both the large English market and the European markets that lay beyond it, the result was a marginal productivity of labor considerably higher than that found in English agriculture. Labor productivity in many parts of colonial America eventually proved to be sufficiently high to allow many bound European workers to repay the cost of passage to the colonies in periods of as little as four years. Yet when English colonization of North America began, a difficult problem existed, a problem of how workers unable to afford the cost of the passage fare out of their own savings could obtain the necessary funds. The requirements of the situation,

19. Lance E. Davis and Douglass C. North, *Institutional Change and American Economic Growth* (Cambridge, 1971), p. 211. Like its English counterpart, the system of service in husbandry, in the early British colonies indentured servitude increased labor mobility at a relatively low cost, for it involved the migration only of individual laborers who were currently in the labor force. Unlike most migratory movements, the system therefore did not have to bear the costs of transportation for "tied" movers in families, who would make no immediate contribution to production.

It might be argued that indentured servitude was adapted directly from the English system of apprenticeship. Some connections did exist. During 1619–1622 the Virginia Company sent several shipments of vagrant children to Virginia; their passage had been paid by the City of London, and in return the Company agreed to place them with planters as apprentices; see Robert C. Johnson, "The Transportation of Vagrant Children from London to Virginia, 1618–1622," in Howard S. Reinmuth, Jr., *Early Stuart Studies* (Minneapolis, 1970), pp. 137–151. This was an example of the compulsory power of parish apprenticeship, an institution distinct from the older system of craft apprenticeship; see Margaret Gay Davies, *The Enforcement of English Apprenticeship* (Cambridge, Massachusetts, 1956), pp. 12–13. Yet servitude, in which a capital sum was initially provided by the master to the servant (to be paid off by the servant's labor), posed very different problems of contract enforcement and labor motivation than did apprenticeship, in which the initial payment was made by the servant, with the master's obligation, in the form of training, to be paid over the course of the agreement. Thus, although some elements drawn from apprenticeship influenced the development of servitude, the incentives of both master and servant were quite different in the two systems, and servitude was more than a transfer of apprenticeship to the colonies.

Although indentured servitude was primarily used in order to facilitate migration, once the legal basis of the institution had been laid down it could also be used to improve the functioning of markets for credit for other purposes. Thus, for example, in 1640 a Barbados planter named Richard Atkinson borrowed the sum of 2,000 pounds of cotton from John Batt. The agreement provided "that if the said two thousand pounds of Cotton shall not be paid upon the day aforesaid, that then and immediately upon default of the said payment, it shall bee for the said John Batt, or his assigns, to take the body of me Richard Atkinson, servant for the terme of sixe yeares, without any further trouble or sute of law . . ."; quoted in Vincent T. Harlow, *A History of Barbados, 1625–1685* (Oxford, 1926), p. 294. Although indentured servitude could have been used in a wide variety of other situations involving debt, that it was overwhelmingly used for transportation was clearly because enforcing repayment of debts was relatively inexpensive when borrowing was done locally, and servitude was therefore unnecessary in these cases.

with the need for the emigrant to repay the funds over an extended period from a location far distant from England, posed enormous problems of enforcement for prospective British lenders, and it is not surprising that with the existing technology British financial institutions were inadequate to the task. As was seen in the above description of the Virginia Company's early experiments, the initial solution was for a large firm directly engaged in colonial production to advance the cost of passage to workers, who then became servants of the firm for a period agreed upon in advance, during which the loan would be repaid. The problems of motivation and supervision that resulted from this scheme soon led the Company to rent out the workers it transported to individual farmers who produced on a smaller scale. This modified scheme was itself short-lived, as the Company appears to have perceived quickly the advantages of simply selling the workers it imported to individual planters for the period necessary for repayment of their loans, as specified in the workers' contracts. By doing this, the Company unambiguously transferred all costs of labor supervision and enforcement of the contracts to the planters, including all risks of capital loss from such sources as the escape or death of the servant during the contract period.

Once the practice of outright sale of the contract had been established, a large firm no longer had any significant economic advantage in most aspects of servant transportation and supervision. The supervision and enforcement of the labor contracts could apparently be done quite efficiently by small planters responsible for only a small number of servants. The capital requirements for European merchants who advanced the funds to cover immigrant transportation were reduced from the full period of time specified by the contract to the time between the signing of the contract in England and its sale in the colonies (principally the two to three months during which the servant was on the ship). The cost of entry into the servant trade was low, and the industry soon became one in which many European merchants who traded with the colonies participated.

Work incentives for indentured servants appear to have been more varied in practice than a simple description of the system's form might imply. The question of incentives was a significant one, for the major benefit to the servant from the bargain – passage to America – was provided at the outset, before the servant had begun to work. Edmund Morgan concluded that physical violence was the principal means by which masters extracted work from servants in early Virginia; he argued that servants had little other reason to work hard, for few wished to be rehired at the end of their terms, while masters lacked an incentive to treat their servants well for precisely the same reason, since it was unlikely in any case that they could induce their servants to stay on after their terms ended.[20] And although colonial laws protected servants from excessive corporal punishment, and masters who killed their servants would be tried for murder, masters generally were permitted considerable latitude in beating their servants.[21] Yet it would be surprising if severe physical abuse had been very common, for it would obviously have interfered with servants' work capacity, to the detriment of their masters' profits. Significant positive work incentives clearly existed for servants, and a variety of scattered evidence suggests the potential flexibility of the system in practice. Colonial laws generally guaranteed servants access to adequate food, clothing, and lodging, but many planters exceeded the minimum required levels in providing for their servants.[22] Similarly masters could, and did, increase the freedom dues they gave to favored servants above the statutory minimum levels. Wages were sometimes paid to servants during their terms, and their amounts could be varied. Masters could make bargains with their servants under which the latter could be released early from their terms of servitude.[23] The frequency with which these positive incentives were used is difficult to determine, for within the operation of servitude it was only abuses by either masters or servants that were monitored by colonial courts, and therefore of which systematic legal records survive. Occasional references do show, however, that some servants were able to accumulate significant wealth during their terms.[24] The judgment of John Hammond, writing of the Chesapeake colonies in 1648, that "Those Servants that will be industrious may in their time of service gain a competent estate before their Freedomes, which is usually done by many," cannot be subjected to systematic test, and may have been overly optimistic. Yet it is likely that Hammond's description of the form of rewards given to some servants, including livestock and land on which to grow tobacco on their own account, came from actual observation, and it is also plausible that, as he admonished, these benefits "must be gained . . . by Industry and affability, not by sloth nor churlish behaviour."[25]

20. Morgan, *American Slavery, American Freedom*, p. 126.

21. Richard B. Morris, *Government and Labor in Early America* (New York, 1965), pp. 461–500.

22. Indeed, Gloria Main concluded that servants' material condition in seventeenth-century Maryland was typically no worse than that of many small planters; Main, *Tobacco Colony: Life in Early Maryland, 1650–1720* (Princeton, 1982), p. 113.

23. Russell R. Menard, "From Servant to Freeholder: Status Mobility and Property Accumulation in Seventeenth-Century Maryland," *William and Mary Quarterly* (Third series) 30 (Jan. 1973), 50.

24. Main, *Tobacco Colony*, p. 118.

25. Clayton Colman Hall, ed., *Narratives of Early Maryland, 1633–1684* (New York, 1946), p. 292.

The evolution of indentured servitude in colonial British America

Indentured servitude was an initial solution to an acute problem of obtaining a labor supply that existed in many regions of colonial America, and the basic form of the institution developed by the Virginia Company was widely adopted and used throughout the British colonies in the seventeenth and eighteenth centuries. Although precise estimates of the total numbers of servants are not available, an indication of their overall quantitative importance is given by Abbot Emerson Smith's judgment, noted earlier, that between half and two-thirds of all white immigrants to the American colonies after the 1630s came under indenture; their importance at times in particular regions was even greater, as is suggested by Wesley Frank Craven's estimate that 75 percent or more of Virginia's settlers in the seventeenth century were servants.[26] Although initially all the servants came from England, in the course of the colonial period migrants from other countries joined the flow of servants to British America, and especially in the eighteenth century sizeable numbers of Scottish, Irish, and German immigrants arrived in the colonies under indenture.

Active markets for indentured servants arose in Europe and in the colonies. Hundreds of English merchants in the major British ports participated in binding emigrants for servitude overseas. Transportation costs varied little across individuals or destinations, and differences in the emigrants' productivity, which affected the rate at which they could repay the implicit loans, were therefore reflected in variation in the length of the terms for which they were bound. Surviving collections of indentures clearly show that characteristics that raised the expected productivity of a servant tended to shorten the term for which the servant was indentured. Thus the length of indenture varied inversely with age, skill, and literacy, while servants bound for the West Indies received shorter terms in compensation for their undesirable destinations.[27] The presence of these markets provided a consistent link between European labor supply and the labor demand of colonial planters from the 1620s through the time of the American Revolution. The efficiency of the institution within the colonies was further increased by the fact that indentures were generally transferable, and masters could therefore freely buy and sell the remaining terms of servants already present in America in response to changes in economic circumstances.

26. Craven, *White, Red and Black: The Seventeenth-Century Virginian* (Charlottesville, 1971), p. 5.
27. David W. Galenson, *White Servitude in Colonial America: An Economic Analysis* (Cambridge, 1981), Ch. 7.

Even in those regions where it became quantitatively most important, however, indentured servitude was not the final solution to the problem of colonial American labor supply. For it was precisely in those regions that had initially depended most heavily on white servants for their labor needs – the West Indies, the Chesapeake, South Carolina, and Georgia – that planters eventually turned to black slaves as their principal source of bound labor. The transition from servants to slaves, which occurred at different times in these regions, and at different rates, appears explicable in terms of the changing relative costs of the two types of labor faced by colonial planters.[28]

Indentured servants were quantitatively most important in the early history of those colonies that produced staple crops for export. The primary demand was for workers to grow the staple, and initially planters relied on white indentured labor. In addition, as output increased there was an increasing demand for skilled workers to build houses and farm buildings, to make the hogsheads and barrels to pack and ship the sugar, tobacco, or rice, to make clothing for the planters and their labor forces, and to perform a variety of other crafts. Over time, in a number of colonial regions the price of indentured agricultural labor increased. In mid-seventeenth-century Barbados and later in the century elsewhere in the West Indies, this was the result of sugar cultivation, as the introduction of the valuable crop both greatly increased the demand for labor and produced harsh working conditions for field laborers that made Englishmen avoid the region.[29] In the Chesapeake colonies the cost of indentured labor rose by nearly 60 percent within a decade when white immigration to that region fell off during the 1680s, apparently as a result of improving conditions in the English labor market and the increasing attractiveness of Pennsylvania for new arrivals; the relative cost of bound white labor increased by an even greater amount, for the price of African slaves reached the bottom of a deep trough during the 1680s.[30] In South Carolina, high mortality rates and the rigors of rice cultivation combined to reduce the flows of

28. The following four paragraphs are based on the analysis in Galenson, *White Servitude in Colonial America*, Chs. 8–9.

29. Richard S. Dunn, *Sugar and Slaves: The Rise of the Planter Class in the English West Indies, 1624–1713* (Chapel Hill, 1972), pp. 59–72, 110–116, 301–334; Richard B. Sheridan, *Sugar and Slavery: An Economic History of the British West Indies, 1623–1775* (Barbados, 1974), pp. 131–133, 164, 194, 237–238.

30. Russell Menard, "From Servants to Slaves: The Transformation of the Chesapeake Labor System," *Southern Studies*, 16 (Winter 1977), 355–390; David W. Galenson, "The Atlantic Slave Trade and the Barbados Market, 1673–1723," this Journal, 42 (Sept. 1982), 491–511. For additional evidence and discussion of slave prices, see Galenson, *Traders, Planters and Slaves: The Atlantic Slave Trade and the English West Indies, 1673–1725* (forthcoming).

new white immigrants during the late seventeenth century, and the importance of rice as a staple crop later had the same effect in Georgia.[31] In each of these cases, the rising price of English servants tended to make the more elastically supplied African slaves a less expensive source of unskilled agricultural labor than additional indentured workers, and the majority of the bound labor force changed from white to black.

Yet the transition from servants to slaves was not a complete one at this stage, for newly arrived Africans normally did not have the traditional European skills required by planters in the colonies. Furthermore, colonial planters typically did not train adult Africans to do skilled jobs, preferring to wait and train either slaves imported as children or the American-born offspring of African adults in skilled crafts.[32] In an intermediate period in the growth of staple-producing colonies of the late seventeenth and early eighteenth centuries, a racial division of labor by skill therefore appeared; unskilled labor forces were increasingly made up of black slaves, while white servants continued to perform skilled crafts and services, and in many cases to act as plantation managers and supervisors of the slaves.

But this was not the final phase of development. As agricultural production continued to grow, the demand for both skilled and unskilled labor increased further. The price of skilled white servants tended to rise sharply. The result was investment in the training of slaves to take over the skilled jobs of the plantation. Although the dates at which labor supply conditions and the level of demand for skilled labor combined to produce this result differed across colonies, the tendency was present in all the British staple economies, as the relative price of skilled white servants apparently rose significantly over the course of the late seventeenth and eighteenth centuries. The differences in timing across colonies meant that the substitution of slaves for servants had not been completed throughout British America by the time of the Revolution, but the advance of the process described here was sufficient to make its result clearly visible in all the staple-producing colonies by the end of the mainland's colonial period, as in many

31. Peter H. Wood, *Black Majority: Negroes in Colonial South Carolina from 1670 through the Stono Rebellion* (New York, 1975), pp. 62–69.

32. Thus John Oldmixon noted in 1708 that slaves "that are born in *Barbadoes* are much more useful Men, than those that are brought from *Guinea*"; *The British Empire in America* (London, 1708), Vol. 2, pp. 121–122. On the relation between place of birth and training, see Russell R. Menard, "The Maryland Slave Population, 1658 to 1730," *William and Mary Quarterly* (Third Series), 32 (Jan. 1975), 36–37; Gerald W. Mullin, *Flight and Rebellion: Slave Resistance in Eighteenth-Century Virginia* (London, 1972), pp. 39, 47; John Donald Duncan, "Servitude and Slavery in Colonial South Carolina, 1670–1776" (Ph.D. dissertation, Emory University, 1971), pp. 436–437.

colonies significant numbers of plantations were based almost exclusively on black labor, with considerable numbers of skilled slaves as well as unskilled slave field hands.

The large-scale use of slaves as field laborers in those regions of British America that were characterized by plantation agriculture therefore did not bring a complete end to the immigration of white servants, but it did produce shifts in their composition by skill, and eventually in their principal regions of destination. By the time of the American Revolution, the British West Indian colonies had ceased to import white servants on a significant scale, and on the mainland only the colonies of the Chesapeake region and Pennsylvania continued to receive sizeable flows of indentured labor.[33]

In considering the career of indentured servitude in the British colonies, one characteristic that emerges is the flexibility of the institution. A single basic form of contract and method of enforcement proved useful in the colonies continuously between 1620 and the American Revolution in spite of major changes in the European places of origin of indentured labor, its colonial destinations, and its principal functions in the American labor market. Thus, from its beginnings as a supplier of unskilled labor to the southern mainland colonies and the islands of the West Indies, the indenture system ultimately evolved into a source of skilled labor to the Chesapeake region and the Middle Colonies of the mainland. The ability to satisfy the changing demands of the colonial labor market at critical periods helped make indentured servitude one of the central institutions of colonial American society.

The Revolution did not put an end to the importation of indentured servants. The war did disrupt the operation of the indenture system by temporarily curtailing immigration, but the servant trade revived in the early 1780s.[34] An apparent tendency for the postwar indenture system to rely even more heavily on German and Irish relative to English immigrants than before the war might have been due in part to English

33. For quantitative outlines of the servants' destinations over time, see Smith, *Colonists in Bondage*, pp. 307–337, and Galenson, *White Servitude in Colonial America*, Ch. 6.

During the eighteenth century a modification of indentured servitude appeared, particularly among German immigrants to Pennsylvania. Under the redemptioner system, a migrant would board a ship in Europe under a promise to pay for his passage after arriving in America. If he were unable to pay within two weeks after arrival, he would be indentured for a term sufficient to raise the fare. This arrangement is treated here as a variant of indentured servitude, for the basic form of the contract was similar, and there was no legal difference between indentured servants and redemptioners once the latter had been bound. For further discussion and references, see *Ibid.*, pp. 13–15.

34. Cheesman A. Herrick, *White Servitude in Pennsylvania* (Philadelphia, 1926), p. 254.

35. William Miller, "The Effects of the American Revolution on Indentured Servitude," *Pennsylvania History*, 7 (July 1940), 131–141.

legislation of the 1780s and 1790s aimed at preventing the emigration of artisans and of workers bound to servitude for debt. Legislation passed by individual American states in the aftermath of the Revolution affected the legal basis of servitude in only minor ways, and the system persisted in use, although apparently on only a limited scale, into the nineteenth century.[35]

The decline – and revival – of indentured servitude in the Americas in the nineteenth century

The history of the final disappearance of indentured servitude in the United States remains rather obscure. Although isolated cases of the indentured servitude of immigrants can be found as late as the 1830s, the system appears to have become quantitatively insignificant in mainland North America much earlier, perhaps by the end of the eighteenth century. It remains unclear whether indentured servitude dwindled in importance in the last quarter of the eighteenth century and the first quarter of the nineteenth primarily because of a general decline in the rate of immigration to the United States, or whether in the period the share of total immigration made up of servants declined. Nor does there appear to be a consensus on the role of legal changes in reducing the attractiveness of indentured servants to employers, as historians have variously cited English passenger acts and the legislation of American states abolishing imprisonment for debt as the system's "death blow."[36] It is known that by the time large-scale Atlantic migration revived, after 1820, indentured servitude was little used by Europeans, and the great nineteenth-century transatlantic migration from Europe to the United States was composed of free workers and their families.

The use of indentures to facilitate migration to the Americas had not ended, however. At the same time the indenture system was finally disappearing from the United States, the abolition of slavery in the British West Indies in the 1830s produced a renewed demand for indentured labor. Plantation owners there, primarily engaged in sugar

36. For a survey of these views, and a discussion of the timing and causes of the decline of indentured servitude for Europeans migrating to the United States – and its subsequent failure to revive – see Charlotte Erickson, "Why Did Contract Labour Not Work in the 19th Century USA?" (unpublished paper, London School of Economics, 1982). It might be noted that recent research has raised the possibility that the volume of immigration to the United States in the late eighteenth and early nineteenth centuries was substantially greater than has generally been believed; Henry A. Gemery, "European Emigration to the New World, 1700–1820: Numbers and Quasi-Numbers" (unpublished paper, Colby College, 1983). Both the overall magnitude of immigration and the role of indentured servitude during this period remain to be established firmly.

production, were unhappy with the large reduction of black labor supply that followed emancipation, as a large increase in wage rates was accompanied by greater irregularity in the blacks' hours of work and a perceived decline in the intensity of their labor. The planters lobbied the British government for a number of measures designed to promote immigration to their colonies in order to lower labor costs and allow them to recapture their positions in international sugar markets; one of these measures was the right to indenture their imported workers to prevent them from deserting their estates. After resisting this proposal for fear of creating the appearance of a new slave trade, the Colonial Office yielded, and finally agreed to permit the use of indentures under which immigrants were imported to work for specific employers for fixed terms.[37]

This nineteenth-century revival of the use of indentured labor in the British West Indian sugar colonies, and in parts of South America, constituted a historical episode quite different from the earlier use of bound workers in the British colonies of the seventeenth and eighteenth centuries. Whereas the indenture system had earlier involved the immigration of Europeans to America, in the nineteenth century it was Asia that furnished American planters with a supply of bound labor. Indentured Indians began to arrive in British Guiana in 1838, and that colony was soon joined as an importer by Trinidad and Jamaica. Shipments of indentured Chinese began to arrive in Cuba in 1847, and within a decade British Guiana, Trinidad, and Peru had also received cargoes of bound Chinese workers.[38]

The form of the contracts typically used in this nineteenth-century migration differed somewhat from that used in the earlier period; for example, wages were generally paid to the Asian servants, and their contracts often provided for their return passage to their country of

37. K. O. Laurence, "The Evolution of Long-Term Labour Contracts in Trinidad and British Guiana, 1834–1863," *Jamaican Historical Review*, 5 (May 1965), 9–27.

38. On the Indian indentured migration, see Alan H. Adamson, *Sugar Without Slaves: The Political Economy of British Guiana, 1838–1904* (New Haven, 1972); Donald Wood, *Trinidad in Transition: The Years After Slavery* (London, 1968); Hugh Tinker, *A New System of Slavery: The Export of Indian Labour Overseas, 1830–1920* (London, 1974). On Chinese indentured migration see Duvon Clough Corbitt, *A Study of the Chinese in Cuba, 1847–1947* (Wilmore, Kentucky, 1971); Watt Stewart, *Chinese Bondage in Peru: A History of the Chinese Coolie in Peru, 1849–1874* (Durham, North Carolina, 1951); Persia Crawford Campbell, *Chinese Coolie Emigration to Countries Within the British Empire* (London, 1923). In addition to these movements, during the nineteenth century relatively small migrations of indentured workers occurred from Africa and Madeira to the West Indies and South America. For an overview of these bound migrations, see Stanley L. Engerman, "Contract Labor, Sugar, and Technology in the Nineteenth Century," this Journal, 43 (Sept. 1983), 635–659; also G. W. Roberts and J. Byrne, "Summary Statistics on Indenture and Associated Migration Affecting the West Indies, 1834–1918," *Population Studies*, 20 (July 1966), 125–134.

origin upon completion of the term. Yet the immigrants normally worked for fixed terms of years, without the power to change employers, under legal obligation of specific performance of their contracts with penalties including imprisonment, and they were therefore bound under genuine contracts of servitude rather than simply service contracts of debt that could be terminated by repayment of a stated principal sum.[39]

In the second half of the nineteenth century another significant flow of migrants from Asia to the Americas occurred. Bound Chinese laborers were imported to work on the sugar plantations of Hawaii beginning in 1852, and they were joined there by a migration of Japanese workers that began in 1885. From 1852, Chinese workers also began to come to California to work as miners and to build the western railroads. The Asian migrants to Hawaii worked under true indentures, which bound them to work for specified planters for fixed periods of years, with legal provision for compulsion of specific performance or imprisonment.[40] Those bound for California immigrated under debt contracts, agreeing to repay the passage fare advanced to them out of their earnings in America; in principle they were free to change employers, or to repay their outstanding debt and become free.[41]

The question of why indentured servitude was revived for the facilitation of large-scale migration to the West Indies at the same time that it had finally disappeared from use for migration to the United States is of considerable historical significance; the arrival of Asians bound to servitude in the Caribbean had very different implications from the arrival of Europeans free to choose their jobs and places of residence in the nineteenth-century United States. These divergent outcomes resulted from the operation of powerful underlying economic forces, and a consideration of the economic basis of indentured rather than free migration can serve to suggest the source of the basic difference in the character of these two major nineteenth-century migrations to the Americas.[42]

39. For example, see Tinker, *A New System of Slavery*, Ch. 6. It might be noted that the Asian migrants to the West Indies often appear to have chosen not to return to their native countries after becoming free.

40. Katharine Coman, *The History of Contract Labor in the Hawaiian Islands*, Publications of the American Economic Association, Third series, 4 (Aug. 1903), 7–10; Clarence Glick, "The Chinese Migrant in Hawaii: A Study in Accommodation" (unpublished Ph.D. dissertation, University of Chicago, 1938), pp. 38–39.

41. Kil Young Zo, *Chinese Emigration into the United States, 1850–1880* (New York, 1978), pp. 95–96.

42. The magnitudes of these population movements were very different. Thus it has been estimated that 45.2 million free Europeans migrated to the Americas during 1846–1920, compared to a total of 775,000 bound Indians and Chinese who migrated to the West Indies and South America in the nineteenth century, and another 100,000 bound Chinese and Japanese who migrated to Hawaii; Stanley L. Engerman, "Servants to Slaves to Servants: Contract Labor and

Large-scale net migration may be warranted by economic conditions wherever sizeable differences in average labor productivity exist between two regions. An additional necessary condition for migration to occur in such situations is the absence of political barriers to migration. When a large-scale migration does occur, it will consist of free workers if the migrants can afford to pay the costs of migration out of their savings, or if existing sources of capital permit them to borrow these funds at a reasonable cost. As was seen in the discussion earlier in this paper, the migration will tend to be made up of bound workers if the migrants cannot readily pay the costs of migration out of their own wealth, or borrow the required funds; under these circumstances, the use of indentures can provide a new source of capital, as the intermediation of merchants can effectively allow migrants to borrow the cost of their passage from those who demand their services in their country of destination, in the form of advances against their future labor. Once again, it should be noted that existing political conditions in both sending and receiving areas must permit servitude in order for bound migration to occur.

This analysis suggests that a possible explanation for the contrast described above – a free European migration to the United States occurring coincidentally with a bound Asian migration to the West Indies, South America, Hawaii, and California – might lie in a differential ability of the two groups of migrants to bear the cost of migration. Precise empirical tests of this hypothesis are elusive because of the difficulties involved in measuring both the full costs of migration and the wealth of migrants. Examination of related evidence, however, can serve to indicate whether the explanation is plausible. Specifically, what can be done is to compare a major component of the cost of migration, the cost of passage, to a potential index of the wealth of migrants, the per capita income of their country of origin. Both of these variables are less than perfect proxies for the desired variables. Passage costs of course constituted only a share of the full cost of migration, and this share could vary from case to case. Nor can the relation of wealth to income be determined with precision in most instances. Yet these variables should generally have been correlated with the true variables of

European Expansion," in H. van den Boogart and P. C. Emmer, eds., *Colonialism and Migration: Indentured Labour Before and After Slavery* (The Hague, forthcoming), Table II. Yet in spite of the imbalance between these relative magnitudes, due to the enormity of the free European migration, the migration of bound Asians was clearly a significant one for the Americas. For some interesting recent comments on these nineteenth-century migrations, see William H. McNeill, *The Great Frontier: Freedom and Hierarchy in Modern Times* (Princeton, 1983), pp. 39–55.

interest here. Therefore if the analysis outlined above is valid, it would imply that the ratio of passage fare to per capita income should have been substantially higher for the bound Asian immigrants than for the free Europeans.[43] Although the test does have significant shortcomings, it can suggest whether the explanation suggested here is sufficiently plausible to be worth pursuing with measurements of greater precision.

Table 1 presents evidence on annual per capita income in a number of countries from which significant emigrations occurred in the nineteenth century, together with passage fares to some of the emigrants' principal countries of destination. Although the precision of both the estimates of income and the quotations of fares should not be exaggerated, most of the figures shown are drawn from careful studies, and should serve as reliable indicators of the relative magnitudes involved.

The most striking feature of the table is the contrast between the ratios of fares to per capita income for European and Asian countries of origin. During the nineteenth century, the evidence suggests that the cost of passage to America was consistently equivalent to less than one-half the level of per capita income in Great Britain, Scandinavia, and Germany, whereas potential Chinese and Japanese emigrants faced fares to the Americas of an amount consistently greater than three times the level of per capita income in their own countries. The absence of indentured servitude from the great nineteenth-century migration from Europe to the United States therefore appears understandable, for the cost of migration was apparently sufficiently low relative to the wealth of the migrants to render credit transactions unnecessary.[44] The contrasting

43. The test proposed here might be seen as an implication of a special case drawn from a more general analysis. In general, a migrant might choose between financing migration costs out of savings or by borrowing by comparing the levels of his income before and after the move; if income after moving is expected to be considerably higher than before, the migrant might prefer to repay moving costs out of the higher post-migration income, in order to smooth the path of his consumption over time. Therefore, if the question is simply one of whether the migrant will borrow in order to migrate, the answer would depend on a comparison of income levels in the countries of origin and destination. Yet although indentured servitude was a form of credit, it involved more than many credit transactions. For an indentured migrant not only agreed to repay his loan, but to give up much of his freedom during the period of repayment; thus servants typically gave up the freedom to marry during their terms, to engage in business on their own account, to determine where they would live, and so on. The assumption is therefore made here that given these conditions, migrants would strongly prefer not to borrow to migrate by indenturing themselves, but would instead prefer to save prior to migration in order to migrate as free workers. The test of the difficulty of doing this therefore involves a comparison of the wealth of migrants and the costs of migration; the variables examined in the text are intended to be considered as proxies for these less readily measurable variables.

44. An interesting feature of the fares shown in Table 1 is the significant decline in passage costs from Great Britain to the United States during the early nineteenth century. Although the greater regularity of the schedules of steamships apparently did reduce the variability of fares

Table 1. *Comparison of cost of passage to per capita income of sending countries: Selected countries and dates*

Sending Country	*Destination*	*Date*	*Form of Migration*	*Passage fare (current prices)*	*Per capita income, sending country (current prices)*	*Ratio of passage fare to per capita income*
(1) Great Britain	American colonies	1688	⅔ indentured, ⅓ free	£5	£9.8	.51
(2) Great Britain	United States	1816–1821	free	£10–12	£20.5	.49–.59
(3) Great Britain	United States	1831–1832	free	£4–6	£20.8	.19–.29
(4) Great Britain	United States	1841	free	£3–7	£24.4	.12–.29
(5) Great Britain	United States	1848–1851	free	£3.5–5	£25.1	.14–.20
(6) Great Britain	United States	1859–1861	free	£3.25	£28.8	.11
(7) Great Britain	Canada	1867–1871	free	£4.5	£35.0	.13
(8) Great Britain	United States	1881	free	£6–6.3	£35.3	.17–.18
(9) Great Britain	United States	1890–1891	free	£3.5	£38.9	.09
(1) Ireland	United States	1841	free	£3–7	£15	.20–.47
(1) Denmark	United States	1870	free	$24.33	$91.4	.27
(2) Denmark	United States	1880	free	$24.33	$105.3	.23
(3) Denmark	United States	1890	free	$24.33–36.50	$117.7	.21–.31
(4) Denmark	United States	1900	free	$36.50	$146.9	.25
(1) Norway	United States	1865	free	$24.33	$75.6	.32
(2) Norway	United States	1887	free	$24.33–36.50	$88.2	.28–.41
(3) Norway	United States	1899	free	$36.50	$127.3	.29
(1) Sweden	United States	1860	free	$24.33	$55.2	.44
(2) Sweden	United States	1870	free	$24.33	$57.6	.42
(3) Sweden	United States	1880	free	$24.33	$77.5	.31
(4) Sweden	United States	1890	free	$24.33–36.50	$86.3	.28–.42
(5) Sweden	United States	1900	free	$36.50	$124.4	.29
(1) Germany	United States	1880	free	$24.33	$104.5	.23
(2) Germany	United States	1890	free	$24.33–36.50	$133.8	.18–.27
(3) Germany	United States	1900	free	$36.50	$137.1	.27
(1) China	West Indies	1859–1880	indentured	$39–72	$7.3	5.3–9.9
(2) China	Hawaii	1852–1880	indentured	$50	$7.3	6.8
(3) China	California	1877–1880	contract labor	$40–50	$7.3	5.5–6.8
(1) India	West Indies	1859–1901	indentured	$35–77	$6.5–9.7	3.6–11.8

Sources: *Great Britain*

(1) GNP: Phyllis Deane and W. A. Cole, *British Economic Growth, 1688–1959*, Second ed. (Cambridge, 1967), p. 156. Population: E. A. Wrigley and R. S. Schofield, *The Population History of England, 1541–1871: A Reconstruction* (Cambridge, Massachusetts, 1981), p. 533. Fare: David W. Galenson, *White Servitude in Colonial America: An Economic Analysis* (Cambridge, 1981), pp. 251–252.

(2) GNP and population: Deane and Cole, *British Economic Growth*, pp. 8, 166. Fare: Marcus Lee Hansen, *The Atlantic Migration, 1607–1860* (Cambridge, Massachusetts, 1940), p. 198.

(3) GNP and population: see (2), above. Fare: see (2), above.

(4) GNP and population: see (2), above. Fare: Hansen, *The Atlantic Migration*, p. 249, also Philip Taylor, *The Distant Magnet: European Emigration to the U.S.A.* (New York, 1971), p. 94.

(5) GNP and population: see (2), above. Fare: Taylor, *The Distant Magnet*, p. 94; also Charlotte Erickson, ed., *Emigration from Europe, 1815–1914* (London, 1976), p. 248.

(6) GNP and population: see (2), above. Fare: Taylor, *The Distant Magnet*, p. 94.

(7) GNP and population: see (2), above. Fare: William Fraser, *The Emigrant's Guide* (Glasgow, 1867), p. 30.

(8) GNP and population: see (2), above. Fare: Evan R. Jones, *The Emigrant's Friend*, Revised edition (London, 1881), advertisements following p. 351.

(9) GNP and population: see (2), above. Fare: Taylor, *The Distant Magnet*, p. 94.

Ireland

(1) Per capita GNP: Joel Mokyr and Cormac O Grada, "Emigration and Poverty in Prefamine Ireland," *Explorations in Economic History*, 19 (Oct. 1982), 361; fare: see Great Britain, (4), above.

Denmark

(1) GNP: Kjeld Bjerke and Niels Ussing, *Studier over Danmarks Nationalprodukt 1870–1950* (Copenhagen, 1958), p. 146. Population: B. R. Mitchell, *European Historical Statistics* (London, 1975), p. 19. Exchange rate: Ainsworth R. Spofford, ed., *American Almanac . . . for the Year 1889* (New York, American News Company, 1889), p. 329. Fare: U.S. House of Representatives, *Reports of the Industrial Commission on Immigration*, 15 (Washington, D.C., 1901), p. 104.

(2)–(3) See Denmark (1).

(4) Per capita GNP and Fare: see Denmark (1). Exchange rate: *The Statesman's Yearbook: Statistical and Historical Annual of the States of the World for the Year 1899* (New York, 1899), p. clxxix.

Norway

(1) GNP: Juul Bjerke, *Trends in Norwegian Economy, 1865–1960* (Oslo, 1966), p. 38. Population: Mitchell, *European Historical Statistics*, p. 22. Exchange rate: Spofford, *American Almanac*, p. 329. Fare: U.S. House of Representatives, *Reports of the Industrial Commission on Immigration*, Vol. XV, p. 104.

(2) See (1), above.

(3) Per capita GNP and fare: see (1), above. Exchange rate: *Statesman's Yearbook . . . 1899*, p. clxxix.

Sweden

(1) GNP: Olle Krantz and Carl-Axel Nilsson, *Swedish National Product, 1861–1970* (Stockholm, 1975), pp. 150–151. Population: Mitchell, *European Historical Statistics*, p. 23. Exchange rate: Spofford, *American Almanac*, p. 329. Fare: U.S. House of Representatives, *Reports of the Industrial Commission on Immigration*, Vol. XV, p. 104.

TABLE 1 (Continued)

(2)–(4) See (1), above.

(5) Per capita GNP and Fare: see (1), above. Exchange rate: *Statesman's Yearbook . . . 1899*, p. clxxix.

Germany

(1) GNP: Walther G. Hoffmann, *Das Wachstum der Deutschen Wirtschaft Seit der Mitte des 19. Jahrhunderts* (Berlin, 1965), pp. 826–27. Population: Mitchell, *European Historical Statistics*, p. 20. Exchange rate: Spofford, *American Almanac*, p. 329. Fare: U.S. House of Representatives, *Reports of the Industrial Commission on Immigration*, Vol. XV, p. 104.

(2) See (1), above.

(3) Per capita GNP and Fare: see (1), above. Exchange rate: *Statesman's Yearbook . . . 1899*, p. clxxix.

China

(1) GNP and population: Albert Feuerwerker, *The Chinese Economy, 1870–1911* (Ann Arbor, 1969), pp. 2–3. Exchange rate: *The Daily News Almanac and Political Register for 1894* (Chicago, 1894), p. 125. Fare: Public Record Office, London, CO 386/179 and CO 386/188. The range of fares covers quotations from Hong Kong and Canton to British Guiana, Trinidad, and Grenada in the years 1859, 1860, 1861, 1864–1866, and 1868.

(2) Per capita GNP: see China (1). Fare: Katharine Coman, *The History of Contract Labor in the Hawaiian Islands*, Publications of the American Economic Association (Third Series), 4 (Aug. 1903), p. 11.

(3) Per capita GNP: see China (1). Fare: Kil Young Zo, *Chinese Emigration into the United States, 1850–1880* (New York, 1978), pp. 92, 185.

India

(1) Per capita GNP: M. Mukherjee, *National Income of India: Trends and Structure* (Calcutta, 1969), pp. 83–84. Exchange rate: Spofford, *American Almanac*, p. 329. Fare: Public Record Office, London, CO 386/179 and 386/188. The range of fares covers quotations from Calcutta and Madras to Jamaica, Trinidad, British Guiana, and Grenada in the years 1859–1862 and 1868–1870. Also see Panchanan Saha, *Emigration of Indian Labour, 1834–1900* (Delhi, 1970), p. 16, and I. M. Cumpston, *Indians Overseas in British Territories, 1834–1854* (London, 1953), p. 96.

ubiquity of indentured servitude in the Asian trans-Pacific migrations of the nineteenth century appears equally understandable, for the high passage fares facing emigrants from countries with very low levels of per capita income must have meant that few could afford to pay the cost of migration out of their savings.

The evidence of Table 1 nonetheless appears to raise several questions, as the result of apparent inconsistencies within these broad conclusions. One concerns the British migration to America in the colonial period: Why was a majority of the migration made up of bound workers when the ratio of passage fare to per capita income shown for the late seventeenth century, of about one-half, is not far above many of the ratios found for the free European migrations of the nineteenth century? Part of the explanation may lie in the demographic composition of the migrations. In the American colonial period, indentured servitude was strongly, although not exclusively, associated with the migration of unrelated individuals, most of whom were in their late teen ages and early twenties.[45] The European migration of the nineteenth century might have been made up to a greater extent of migrants in families than had generally been the case earlier.[46] The difference might have been important, for most migrating families began their voyages by liquidating the assets – most often land, homes, farm equipment, and livestock – they had accumulated over the course of the working lives of the parents. These family groups might as a result have had more capital

due to such factors as seasonality and the decisions of individual shipping agents – and the greater speed of the steamships reduced the full cost of passage by the opportunity cost of the saved time of passengers – the major decline in fares appears to have been complete by about 1830, well before steamships replaced sailing vessels in the Atlantic passenger trade in the 1860s. For discussion see J. D. Gould, "European InterContinental Emigration 1815–1914: Patterns and Causes," *Journal of European Economic History*, 8 (Winter 1979), 611–614; also see Douglass C. North, "Sources of Productivity Change in Ocean Shipping, 1600–1850," *Journal of Political Economy*, 76 (Sept. 1968), 953–970.

45. For example, see Galenson, *White Servitude in Colonial America*, Ch. 2.
46. For example, see Kristian Hvidt, *Flight to America: The Social Background of 300,000 Danish Emigrants* (New York, 1975), pp. 91–102; Charlotte Erickson, "Emigration from the British Isles to the U.S.A. in 1831," *Population Studies*, 35 (July 1981), 175–197; and Robert P. Swierenga, "International Labor Migration in the Nineteenth Century: The Dutch Example," paper presented to the Economic History Workshop, University of Chicago, May, 1979. During the colonial period, virtually all English indentured servants were unmarried (indeed, standard servant contracts in the eighteenth century included a declaration that the individual bound was single, as shown in Galenson, *White Servitude in Colonial America*, pp. 201–202). The same was not true for German redemptioners, who often came in families; quantitative information on their distribution by family status is poor, but the proportions in families generally appear to have been low. For a discussion of the evidence see Marianne Wokeck, "The Flow and the Composition of German Immigration to Philadelphia, 1727–1775," *Pennsylvania Magazine of History and Biography*, 105 (July 1981), 249–278.

on hand to pay for their voyages than the younger, single migrants who indentured themselves to gain passage to colonial America. Few of the latter would have had time to accumulate significant savings in their short working careers. Their families might in some cases have given them the capital necessary to pay their passage to America, but many may have found it difficult to raise the sums necessary without threatening the survival of their family farms or businesses. Demographic differences might therefore account in part for the apparent greater availability of capital among the migrants of the nineteenth century.[47] This hypothesis must be considered speculative, for information on the composition of both the colonial and the nineteenth-century migrations by family status of the migrants is incomplete. And even if present in some degree, these differences are unlikely to account fully for the nineteenth-century decline of indentures among Europeans, for many families had been indentured as redemptioners in the eighteenth century, and many young individuals without families were included in the transatlantic migration of the nineteenth century.

A more general factor might be of much greater importance in explaining this puzzle, for a likely solution lies in a significant discrepancy between the theoretical analysis suggested earlier and its implementation in Table 1. The analysis implied that the important variable determining migrants' ability to pay the costs of their migration was their wealth; Table 1 then presented evidence on per capita income as a proxy for wealth. National income and wealth are strongly and positively related over time, but during periods of transition from preindustrial to industrial economic conditions their relationship does not generally remain constant. Rather there is a long-run tendency for the share of savings in gross national product to rise, producing a tendency for the ratio of wealth to income to increase over time.[48] The significance of this for the empirical test considered here might be considerable in view of the substantial differences in per capita income and the level of industrialization among the economies examined, for

47. Farley Grubb has found that among German immigrants arriving in Philadelphia during 1785–1804, 51 percent of single males and 59 percent of single females were indentured, compared with only 35 percent of married adults and 40 percent of children traveling with parents; "Indentured Labor in Eighteenth-Century Pennsylvania" (dissertation in progress, University of Chicago). This result is consisent with the hypothesis that an increase in the importance of families in migration would have tended to reduce the amount of servitude.

48. Simon Kuznets, *Modern Economic Growth: Rate, Structure, and Spread* (New Haven, 1966), pp. 235–240. On the rising ratio of wealth to per capita output in Great Britain in the second half of the eighteenth century, see C. H. Feinstein, "Capital Formation in Great Britain," in Peter Mathias and M. M. Postan, eds., *The Cambridge Economic History of Europe*, Vol. VII. Part 1 (Cambridge, 1978), pp. 90–92.

potential migrants from countries in which many people are not far above what are considered to be subsistence levels might have relatively little ability to accumulate wealth in comparison with migrants from wealthier countries. Thus nineteenth-century Englishmen might have found it considerably easier on average to save an amount equivalent to one-half of annual per capita income than their poorer counterparts in England 200 years earlier, and this could well explain why the importance of indentured servitude among English and perhaps other European migrants to America declined so substantially in the long run.

A second question concerns the nineteenth-century Chinese migration to California. The quantitative evidence of Table 1 shows no obvious economic difference between this and the other Asian migrations to the Americas. Yet as discussed earlier, unlike the other Asian emigrants, the Chinese destined for California were not indentured. Why did similar economic conditions not lead to similar conditions of migration? A likely answer to this question appears to be that the conditions were in fact similar, and that a difference more apparent than real might have existed for political reasons. In practice it is not clear that the Chinese who migrated to California under debt contracts were actually able to take advantage of the fact that their contracts, unlike indentures, allowed them to repay their debts and become free workers before the end of the contracts' normal terms, nor is it clear that they were in fact free to choose their employers in America, and to change employers at will. Much remains unknown about the actual operation of the system under which Chinese, and later Japanese, migrants worked in the western United States, but many contemporaries believed these workers were effectively indentured, in being tied to specific employers for fixed terms. The question of why legal contracts of indenture were not used in these circumstances is an intriguing one; indentures for immigrants were not illegal in the United States when the Chinese migration to California first began in the 1850s, and indentures remained legal within some limits until 1885.[49] Yet the contemporary discussion of the Chinese migration appears to carry an implicit assumption that the use of indentured labor – or "servile" labor in the language of the day – was not acceptable in the United States on a large scale.[50] More work on

49. Charlotte Erickson, *American Industry and the European Immigrant, 1860–1885* (Cambridge, Massachusetts, 1957). The Act to Encourage Immigration of 1864 made it legal for immigrants to pledge their wages for a period of up to one year to repay costs of their migration that had been advanced to them. That indentures were not openly used for Chinese might have been due to the fact that in practice they were held for terms substantially longer than one year, but evidence on their actual terms is elusive.

50. For example, see the defense of the system by George F. Seward, *Chinese Immigration, In Its Social and Economical Aspects* (New York, 1881), pp. 136–158. For a brief but interesting

both the attitudes surrounding this episode and the Asians' conditions of work might prove rewarding, for it appears that even at a time when the U.S. government was encouraging the importation of indentured workers from Europe, Americans were not willing to tolerate the large-scale importation of indentured Asians. Thus in 1864 Congress passed the Act to Encourage Immigration, which attempted to revive the indenture system by providing for immigrant labor contracts to be registered with the U.S. Commissioner of Immigration, and for unfulfilled contracts to serve as a lien upon property acquired by the immigrant in the future. Yet this act was aimed at encouraging the immigration of skilled Europeans, and does not seem to have been intended in any way to promote the immigration of unskilled Asians.[51]

Conclusion: The economics and politics of indentured servitude in the Americas

Indentured servitude, as developed by the Virginia Company within little more than a decade after the first settlement at Jamestown, was an institutional response to a capital market imperfection. Designed for those without access to other suppliers of capital, the device of the indenture enabled prospective migrants to America to borrow against their future earnings in America in order to pay the high cost of passage across the Atlantic. After a series of unsuccessful early experiments, the Virginia Company solved a severe problem of enforcing the repayment of the initial capital outlay by selling the servant's contract outright to a colonial planter for a lump sum, thereby making the migrant's master at his destination also the source of his loan. The sale solved the agency problem that had existed when the Company had rented out servants for whom it had paid passage costs, for the colonial planter had then had insufficient incentive to protect the Company's investment in the worker.

The particular form of the solution devised by the Virginia Company to this problem of increasing long-distance labor mobility was of course not the only one possible. Other solutions to the problem of enforcing long-term labor contracts in order to facilitate migration have appeared,

discussion of the actual contractual agreements of the Chinese immigrants in California, see Elmer Clarence Sandmeyer, *The Anti-Chinese Movement in California* (Urbana, 1973), Ch. 2. I plan to present a further investigation of these arrangements, and of their deviation in practice from the descriptions given at the time by the "Chinese Six Companies" largely responsible for the importation of the Chinese, in a forthcoming paper coauthored by Patricia Cloud.

51. Erickson, *American Industry and the European Immigrant*, Ch. 1. On the politics of contract labor in the late nineteenth-century United States, and the opposition of unions, see Ibid., Chs. 8–10.

and some of these have been used successfully in significant historical episodes.[52] Yet the form originally used in early Virginia, in which an employer obtained the services of an immigrant for a specified period – usually a number of years – upon payment of a lump sum to the importer proved by far the most important quantitatively. Once introduced in the second decade of the seventeenth century, the indenture system in this same basic form remained in almost uninterrupted use on a significant scale in the Americas for nearly 300 years.

Entry into an indenture nearly always must have involved a substantial sacrifice of personal freedom for the migrant. Neither an Englishman bound to serve in colonial America nor a nineteenth-century Indian bound to labor in the West Indies would have much control over their conditions of work during the years in which their loan was repaid, and their ability to make decisions about most aspects of their lives in that time was severely circumscribed by the control of their masters. As a result, even many migrants accustomed to societies in which the rights of workers were less than those of their employers might have been reluctant to enter into long-term indentures. Yet the consequences of production that brought into use the natural resources of the Americas, with the resulting promise of economic opportunity for workers, provided a powerful attraction to prospective settlers drawn from the populations of Europe and Asia. The attraction was sufficient to prompt many migrants over the course of three centuries to enter indentures, giving up much of their freedom for a period of years "in hope thereby to amend theyr estates."[53]

52. The experience of the Chinese in California might offer an example of a significant additional means of enforcement. Gunther Barth wrote of the enforcement of their debt contracts that "the kinship system supplied an extra-legal control in a country where courts and customs failed to support any form of contract labor," as the families the migrants had left behind them in China remained "as hostages within the reach of their creditors;" Gunther Barth, *Bitter Strength: A History of the Chinese in the United States, 1850–1870* (Cambridge, Massachusetts, 1964), pp. 56, 86. Yet it might be noted that even in this case the ownership of the debt contract by the worker's immediate employer apparently remained typical; Ibid., pp. 55–56. The *padrone* system used in Italy and Greece in the late nineteenth century was based on securing the loan of passage money to the migrant through mortgages on land held by relatives who remained behind; Philip Taylor, *The Distant Magnet: European Emigration to the U.S.A.* (New York, 1971), p. 98. It might be noted here that the American Emigrant Company and the other companies that recruited laborers for northern manufacturers during the mid-1860s in effect operated on a basis similar to the English merchants who sent servants to colonial America, for these companies relied on American employers to provide the working capital to pay for transportation of workers, as well as to secure repayment from the wages of the contract laborers; Erickson, "Why Did Contract Labour Not Work in 19th Century USA?," p. 19.

53. The quotation is from the prophetic formulation of the indenture system of Sir George Peckham in 1583 in his *A True Reporte, of the late discoveries, and possessions, taken in the right of the Crowne of Englande, of the Newfound Landes, By that valiaunt and worthy Gentleman, Sir Humfrey Gilbert Knight*, Ch. 7.

But not all migrants to America during the colonial period and the nineteenth century entered indentures. The analysis presented in this paper suggested that flows of migrants would be composed of bound workers only when the migrants were unable to bear the costs of migration out of their accumulated wealth. Examination of empirical evidence supported the plausibility of this analysis, for the evidence suggested that indentured servitude assumed an important role in a migration when the direct cost of passage was high relative to the per capita income of the migrants' country of origin. Thus that the great nineteenth-century migration of Europeans to the Americas was composed of free individuals and families appears to have been a consequence of both falling transportation costs and rising European income levels.

The termination of the use of indentured labor in the Americas occurred as the result of political action. The use of indentured Asians in the West Indies, which originated with the abolition of slavery in the 1830s and continued into the twentieth century, had long been a source of concern to the governments of the sending countries, as well as the object of attacks by the same organized groups that had led the campaign to abolish slavery. A series of political actions, growing in intensity from the late nineteenth century, finally led to a decision by the British government in 1917 to prohibit further transportation of Indians for purposes of servitude for debt.

This legal abolition of the indentured emigration of Indians brought to an end a cycle in the use of bound labor in British America that had begun when indentured workers were used to provide an initial solution to the problem of labor shortage in the New World, then had seen the rise of slavery lead to an abandonment of servitude, and still later had seen the abolition of slavery produce a revival of servitude. In some of the phases of this cycle, economic forces determined outcomes with relatively little constraint from political considerations; such was the case, for example, in the original innovation of indentured servitude, in the substitution of slaves for servants in the sugar islands of the West Indies and the southern colonies of the British mainland in the course of the seventeenth century, and in the nineteenth-century revival of servitude in the West Indies. In another set of cases, political considerations appear to have dominated economic concerns; apparent examples include the decision of the British government to abolish slavery in its possessions during the 1830s, the termination of indentured servitude in Hawaii, imposed upon annexation to the United States, and the British government's later decision to abolish servitude for Indians. And in yet a third category of cases, a blend of significant economic and political forces appears to have produced outcomes that are less fully understood, and indeed in some instances have not even been fully described. Cases in point may include a number of episodes involving contract labor in the United States, such as the dwindling of importance of indentured servitude in the early national period, and the failure explicitly to use the common form of indentured servitude for the Chinese immigrants to California in the second half of the nineteenth century. Further study of this last group of phenomena might help to illuminate the ways in which economic and ideological forces contend when neither type clearly dominates, and thus might add to our understanding of how outcomes are determined when political attitudes and economic motivations collide.

The slavery debate

Robert W. Fogel and Stanley L. Engerman versus Paul A. David and Peter Temin

Slavery is an issue that has long dominated American economic history. Interest has been particularly strong since Alfred Conrad and John Meyer (1958) demonstrated that economic analysis could yield a significant reinterpretation of the slave system. Most scholars now agree that the slave economy was profitable for plantation owners and provided strong regional growth, as well as a relatively high standard of living for the free population of the South.

The debate over the economics of slavery reached a crescendo in the 1970s, with the publication of *Time on the Cross: The Economics of American Negro Slavery* by Robert Fogel and Stanley Engerman (1974) and the ensuing rounds of refutation and rebuttal. "The Anatomy of Exploitation" is a chapter from *Time on the Cross*, which was written for, and reached, a wide popular audience. The book's uniqueness lies in its assertions about the material treatment of slaves and the relative efficiency of agriculture based on slave labor. "Slavery: The Progressive Institution?" by Paul David and Peter Temin (1974) is a review of the entire book and part of the larger assessment of Fogel and Engerman's findings and interpretations. Many of these critical examinations were drawn together in the volume *Reckoning With Slavery* by David, Herbert Gutman, Richard Sutch, Temin, and Gavin Wright (1976). The third article in this set, "Explaining the Relative Efficiency of Slave Agriculture in the Antebellum South," by Fogel and Engerman (1977) is a technical response to some of these criticisms, especially those of David and Temin.

David and Temin's criticism is wide-ranging and systematically organized. It is the model of order. They identify the two crucial points of Fogel and Engerman and explain how these fit together. Then they attack the opponents' methods and measurement. Fogel and Engerman's reply is also a model of order and clarity. They systematically make each one of the adjustments their critics have proposed and gauge the cumulative impact on the crucial ratio that measures the relative efficiency of slave agriculture. Have they shifted their position at all after considering these criticisms?

Several subsequent rounds of refutation and rebuttal followed these essays. The March 1979 issue of the *American Economic Review* included four responses to Fogel and Engerman's article, including a comment by David and Temin. Fogel presents a deeper investigation of the issues and a more complete response to critics in *Without Consent or Contract: The Rise and Fall of American Slavery* (1989).

Many have interpreted *Time on the Cross* as an effort to rehabilitate slavery. This is a complete misreading and could not be further from Fogel and Engerman's intention. Their intention is to understand both the economic conditions under which slavery operated and the material circumstances of the lives of slaves. Therefore, when reading the three essays, be careful to determine the key issues and interpretations. It has been said that scholarship is a marketplace for ideas. These three essays lend credence to such a position. Which explanation do you buy? Why? Be aware that the profession itself has not reached a consensus on many of these issues. Note that points of disagreement are exaggerated and points of agreement are slighted. Finally, in your reading, be cognizant of the following:

- Slavery was a system that encompassed all aspects of life. For this reason, Fogel and Engerman must deal with a number of issues not usually addressed by economists, such as sexuality, punishment, and medical treatment.
- Knowledge of disciplines outside the purview of economics must be employed, such as human biology, nutrition, genetics, sociology, and probability theory.
- Cost-benefit analysis is a powerful tool that has been used in applications that extend from the field to the bedroom.
- A wide range of sources (the Census of Agriculture, plantation records, slave sale records) have been combined in ways nineteenth-century record keepers would never have foreseen.

This controversy is the most technical in the volume, especially the debate over slave efficiency. The authors assess efficiency by measuring total factor productivity. Total factor productivity, which the essays define mathematically, is simply a measure of how efficiently inputs (labor, land, livestock, machines, etc.) are used in producing output (cotton, corn, etc.). A higher total factor productivity figure means that one produces more output with the same amount of inputs. However, total factor productivity *cannot* be measured directly. It is a residual, the amount needed to balance the production function equation after everything else is measured. This is why the proper measure of inputs and outputs is crucial in this debate.

Additional Reading

Allan Bogue, "Fogel's Journey through the Slave States," *Journal of Economic History*, 50 (September 1990), 699–710.

Alfred Conrad and John Meyer, "The Economics of Slavery in the Antebellum South," *Journal of Political Economy*, 66 (April 1958), 95–130.

Paul David, Herbert Gutman, Richard Sutch, Peter Temin, and Gavin Wright, *Reckoning with Slavery: A Critical Study in the Quantitative History of American Negro Slavery*, New York: Oxford University Press, 1976.

Paul David and Peter Temin, "Explaining the Relative Efficiency of Slave Agriculture in the Antebellum South: Comment," *American Economic Review*, 69 (March 1979), 213–18.

Elizabeth Field, "The Relative Efficiency of Slavery Revisited: A Translog Production Function Approach," *American Economic Review*, 78 (June 1988), 543–9.

Robert Fogel, *Without Consent or Contract: The Rise and Fall of American Slavery*, New York: Norton, 1989.

Robert Fogel and Stanley Engerman, *Time on the Cross: The Economics of American Negro Slavery*, New York: Norton, 1974.

Richard Steckel, "A Peculiar Population: The Nutrition, Health, and Mortality of American Slaves from Childhood to Maturity," *Journal of Economic History*, 46 (September 1986), 721–41.

5

The anatomy of exploitation

ROBERT W. FOGEL and STANLEY L. ENGERMAN

Webster's Third New International Dictionary gives two definitions of personal exploitation. These are:

1. an unjust or improper use of another person for one's own profit or advantage;
2. utilization of the labor power of another person without giving a just or equivalent return.

Slaves were exploited in both of these senses. For the advantage of their masters, they were whipped, sold on the auction block, separated from loved ones, deprived of education, terrorized, raped, forced into prostitution, and worked beyond limits of human endurance. The labor power of slaves was also utilized without giving slaves an equivalent return. This aspect of their exploitation was most apparent in the case of hires. The man who rented a slave paid the full market value of the slave's services, but the slave received only part of that payment. The slave's income was the expenditure of the renter on his maintenance; the balance of the value produced by the slave went to the owner of the slave in the form of a rental fee.

While the existence of exploitation is beyond question, the extent of that exploitation is less clear. How frequent was the mean and improper use of slaves and how far did meanness go? How much of the income produced by slaves was expropriated from them?

The posing of these questions may seem irrelevant, even malicious. For many, it is enough merely to recognize the existence of 250 years of exploitation under slavery and to stress its horror. To haggle over the extent of the exploitation suggests callousness to the agony of human bondage and appears to diminish the significance of the moral issue.

If all that was at stake was the refinement of the historical image of

Source: "The Anatomy of Exploitation" is reprinted from TIME ON THE CROSS: The Economics of American Negro Slavery, by Robert William Fogel and Stanley L. Engerman, by permission of W. W. Norton & Company, Inc.

the slaveholding class, the issue of the extent of exploitation could be disregarded. Slaveholders have long been driven from the stage of American life, and the descendants of slaveholders generally do not wish to dwell on the meaner aspects of their ancestry. It is the need to arrive at an accurate historical image of the black man that gives urgency to the issue.

For it is widely assumed that the plantation regime under which most slaves lived was so cruel, the exploitation so severe, the repression so complete that blacks were thoroughly demoralized by it. In this view, blacks were virtually cultural ciphers until they obtained their freedom in 1865. Little positive development of black culture or personality was possible under the unbridled exploitation of slavery; those developments which did take place were largely negative. Under the regime of the lash the blacks had little incentive to improve themselves and "got into very bad habits of doing as little as possible." Undernourished, if not starved, they lacked both the physical capacity and the mental stamina to tackle any but the most routine tasks, and even these were poorly carried out. Forced or encouraged into promiscuity, blacks became extremely casual in their sexual relations: sexual rivalries threw "many slave quarters in constant turmoil"; "[c]hastity was 'out of the question'" and many girls became pregnant at twelve, thirteen, and fourteen years of age. Sexual laxity on the part of the slaves, combined with a wide array of policies pursued by masters, reduced the black family to "cultural chaos." Bereft of "deep and enduring affection," fathers and mothers not only came to regard their children with "indifference" but often neglected them in sickness and even practiced infanticide.

No one's personality could, according to this view, fail to be affected by a regime so brutal that some have compared plantations to concentration camps and others have compared them to prisons. In the daily fire of such "total" exploitation, masters and overseers fashioned a distinctive type of "slavish personality" that Stanley M. Elkins identified as "Sambo."

> Sambo, the typical plantation slave, was docile but irresponsible, loyal but lazy, humble but chronically given to lying and stealing; his behavior was full of infantile silliness and his talk was inflated by childish exaggeration. His relationship with his master was one of utter dependence and childlike attachment: it was indeed this childlike quality that was the very key to his being.

This, then, is the portrait contained in many current histories of the antebellum South. Both masters and slaves are painted as degraded brutes. Masters are vile because they are the perpetrators of unbridled exploitation; slaves are vile because they are the victims of it. How true to life is the portrait?

Food, shelter, and clothing

The belief that the typical slave was poorly fed is without foundation in fact. This mistaken view may have arisen from a misinterpretation of the instructions of masters to their overseers. For these documents often mention only corn and pork in outlining the rations that were to be distributed to Negroes. The typical daily ration described was two pounds of corn and one half pound of pork per adult. The misinterpretation stems from the incorrect assumption that the lack of reference to other foods meant that the slave diet was restricted largely to corn and pork.

Overseers' instructions, however, were not book-length manuals. They usually occupied just a few handwritten pages (generally ranging between one thousand and three thousand words in total) and were confined to outlining the major features of the routine the master wished to be pursued. They were not meant to be exhaustive documents, but to underscore those aspects of plantation management that particular owners held to be especially important. The incomplete nature of these widely quoted instructions is seen by the frequent omission of such important matters as rations for children, the disposition of wheat and other grain crops besides corn, the care of chickens and other small livestock, the production and disposition of dairy products, and the different feeds to be used for the various categories of livestock. The instructions to overseers are useful not because they contain a complete description of the plantation routine but because they reveal which aspects of that routine were uppermost in the minds of plantation owners.

The rationing of corn and pork to slaves was emphasized by slaveholders for two reasons. First, while corn and pork did not constitute the totality of the slave diet, they were the core of the diet on most plantations. Unlike other foods such as fruit and vegetables which were fed to slaves only in certain seasons, daily, weekly, or monthly rations of corn and pork were distributed throughout the year. Secondly, while beef, chicken, dairy products, and Irish potatoes had to be consumed soon after they were slaughtered or harvested (because they were difficult to preserve for later use), pork and corn were kept in store for the full year. Winter, especially January and February, was the season for killing, curing, and smoking pork, which could then be kept under lock and key in smoke houses until it was needed. Ensuring that the store of pork and corn was sufficient to last the entire year was one of the principal duties of the overseer, which is why explicit instructions on the disbursement of these two staples were common. The overseer, wrote one master, "must himself keep the keys of the keys of the [corn] cribs, smokehouses and all other buildings in which any property belonging to me is stored and must himself see to the giving out of food." Feed everyone "plentifully," wrote another, "but waste nothing."

More careful reading of plantation documents shows that the slave diet included many foods in addition to corn and pork. Among the other plantation products which slaves consumed were beef, mutton, chicken, milk, turnips, peas, squashes, sweet potatoes, apples, plums, oranges, pumpkins, and peaches. Certain foods not produced on most plantations were frequently purchased for slave consumption, including salt, sugar, and molasses. Less frequent, but not uncommon, purchases for slaves included fish, coffee, and whiskey. In addition to food distributed to them, slaves supplemented their diet, in varying degrees, through hunting and fishing, as well as with vegetables grown in the garden plots assigned to them.

Unfortunately, surviving plantation records are not complete enough to permit determination of the average amounts of each of the foods purchased for slaves or of the quantities of meats and fish that slaves obtained through hunting and fishing. However, on the basis of data obtained from the manuscript schedules of the 1860 census, it has been possible to compute the average amounts of eleven of the principal foods consumed by slaves who lived on the large plantations of the cotton belt. These eleven foods are beef, pork, mutton, milk, butter, sweet potatoes, white potatoes, peas, corn, wheat, and minor grains. While this list is short, it probably accounts for 80 percent of the caloric intake of slaves. Fish, fowl, game, sugar, as well as the various omitted vegetables and fruits, were choice items; but they did not constitute a large part of the diet for either whites or blacks during the middle of the nineteenth century.

Figure 1 shows that the average daily diet of slaves was quite substantial. The energy value of their diet exceeded that of free men in 1879 by more than 10 percent. There was no deficiency in the amount of meat allotted to slaves. On average, they consumed six ounces of meat per day, just an ounce lower than the average quantity of meat consumed by the free population. While pork was more important in the slave than in the free diet, the difference was not as large as is usually presumed. Slaves averaged 70 percent of the free population's consumption of beef. The milk consumption was low by free standards but still amounted to about one glass per day for each slave.

By weight, grains and potatoes dominated the diet of both the free and slave population. Much has been made of the fact that corn was the principal grain consumed by slaves, while wheat was the principal grain in the free diet. Yet from a nutritional standpoint, both are excellent foods, high in energy value and with substantial protein content. Wheat is richer in calcium and iron, but corn has more vitamin A. What has

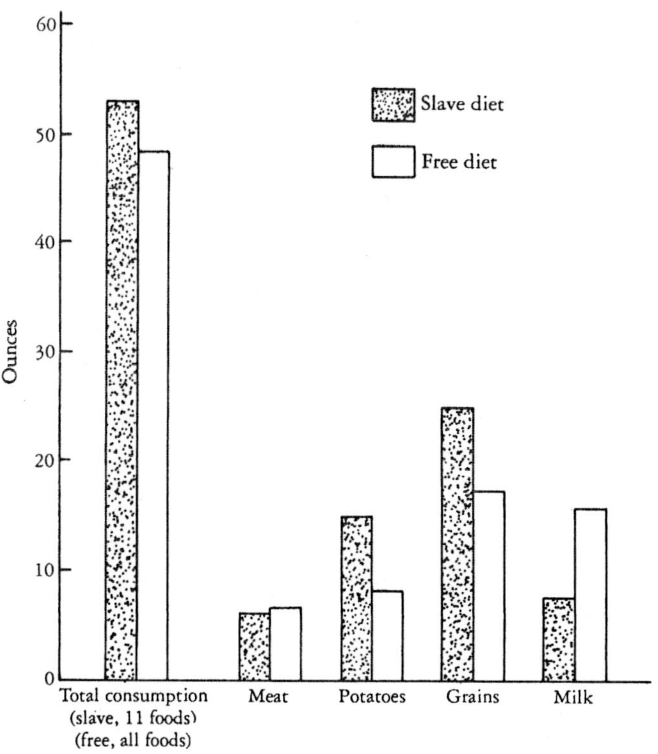

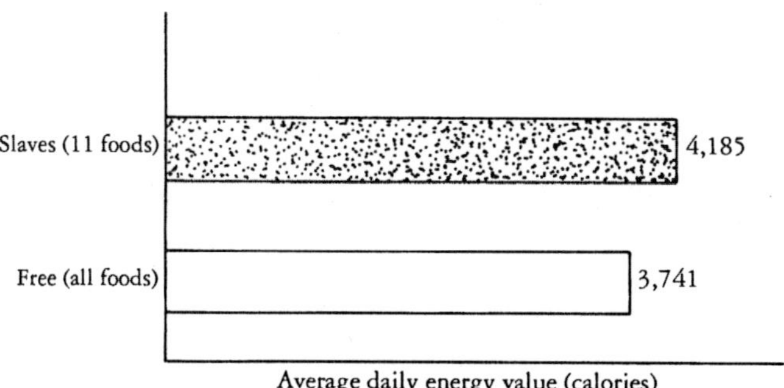

Figure 1. A comparison of the average daily food consumption of slaves in 1860 with the average daily food consumption of the entire population in 1879.

completely escaped attention is the fact that while both slaves and free men ate large quantities of potatoes, slaves consumed virtually nothing but sweet potatoes, although most of the potatoes consumed by free men were white. The significance of this dichotomy is that sweet potatoes are a much better food than white potatoes. Sweet potatoes are especially rich in vitamins A and C and are also fairly high in calcium.

The high slave consumption of meat, sweet potatoes, and peas goes a long way toward explaining the astounding results shown in Figure 2. The slave diet was not only adequate, it actually exceeded modern (1964) recommended daily levels of the chief nutrients. On average, slaves exceeded the daily recommended level of proteins by 110 percent, calcium by 20 percent, and iron by 230 percent. Surprisingly, despite the absence of citrus fruits, slaves consumed two and one half times the recommended level of vitamin C. Indeed, because of the large consumption of sweet potatoes, their intake of vitamin A was at the therapeutic level and vitamin C was almost at that level. Of course, the fact that the *average* daily nutrient content of the slave diet was good does not mean that it was good for all slaves. And even the best-fed slaves experienced seasonal variation in the quality of their diet, due to the limitations in the technology of food preservation during the antebellum era.

Data on slave housing are much more sparse than on slave diets. The most systematic housing information comes from the census of 1860, which included a count of slave houses. These census data show that on average there were 5.2 slaves per house on large plantations. The number of persons per free household in 1860 was 5.3. Thus, like free men, most slaves lived in single-family households. The sharing of houses by several families of slaves was uncommon. Occasionally, on very large plantations, there were dormitories for unmarried men and women. But these were exceptional. The single-family household was the rule.

Unfortunately, the census did not collect information on the size or the quality of slave houses. Descriptions in plantation records and in travelers' accounts are fragmentary. They suggest a considerable range in the quality of housing. The best were three- or four-room cottages, of wood frame, brick, or stone construction, with up to eight hundred square feet of space on the inside, and large porches on the outside. Such cottages had brick or stone chimneys and glazed windows. At the other pole were single-room log cabins without windows. Chimneys were constructed of twigs and clay; floors were either earthen or made of planks resting directly on the earth.

Comments of observers suggest that the most typical slave houses of the late antebellum period were cabins about eighteen by twenty feet. They usually had one or two rooms. Lofts, on which the children slept,

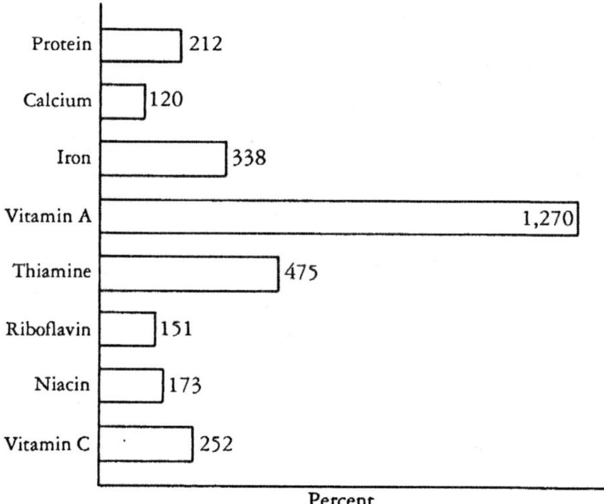

Figure 2. The nutritional value of the slave diet: average slave consumption of various nutrients in 1860 as a percentage of modern recommended daily allowances.

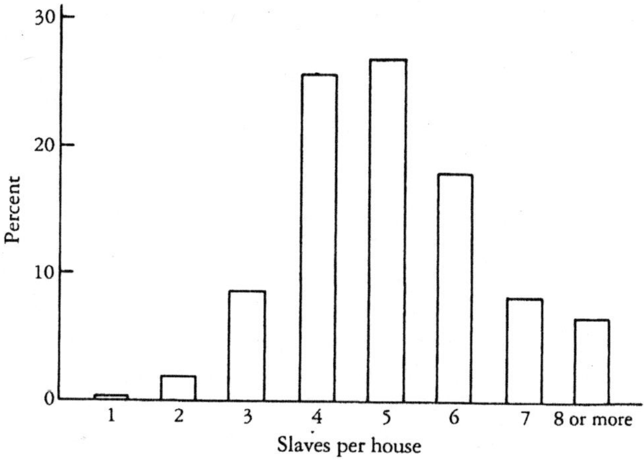

Figure 3. The distribution of slaves on large plantations, by persons per slave house, 1860.

were also quite common. Windows were not glazed, but closed by wooden shutters. Some houses also had rear doors. Chimneys were usually constructed of brick or stone. The building material was usually logs or wood. Seams in the log cabins were sealed by wooden splints and mud. Floors were usually planked and raised off the ground.

While such housing is quite mean by modern standards, the houses of slaves compared well with the housing of free workers in the antebellum era. It must be remembered that much of rural America still lived in log cabins in the 1850s. And urban workers lived in crowded, filthy tenements. One should not be misled by the relatively spacious accommodations in which U.S. working-class families live today. That is an achievement of very recent times. As late as 1893, a survey of the housing of workers in New York City revealed that the median number of square feet of sleeping space per person was just thirty-five. In other words, the "typical" slave cabin of the late antebellum era probably contained more sleeping space per person than was available to most of New York City's workers half a century later.

The best information on clothing comes from the records of large plantations. These indicate that a fairly standard annual issue for adult males was four shirts (of cotton), four pairs of pants (two of cotton and two of wool), and one or two pairs of shoes. Adult women were issued four dresses per year, or the material needed to make four dresses. Hats were also typically issued annually (women received head-kerchiefs). Blankets were issued once every two or three years. There seems to have been much more variability in the issue of socks and underclothes. Issues of petticoats to women are mentioned in a few records, but not in most. Mention of socks and underwear for men is also irregular. For winter months men had jackets, sometimes overcoats, although the frequency of their issue is unclear. Clothing for children showed some variation from estate to estate, but by far the most common issue was a one-piece garment which looked like an extra-long shirt.

Slave clothing was usually made of a coarse but durable cloth. The leather in slave shoes was of a high grade, but little attention was devoted to matters of fashion. Finer clothes were supplied to house servants and other favored slaves. Slaves also supplemented the standard issue by their own purchases. As indicated below, many slaves were able to earn substantial sums of money. Much of this was spent on such items of clothing as headkerchiefs and brightly colored cloth for dressmaking.

Medical care

While the quality of slave medical care was poor by modern standards, there is no evidence of exploitation in the medical care typically provided for plantation slaves. The inadequacy of the care arose not from intent or lack of effort on the part of masters, but from the primitive nature of medical knowledge and practices in the antebellum era.

That adequate maintenance of the health of their slaves was a central objective of most planters is repeatedly emphasized in instructions to

Table 1. *Clothing recommended for an adult worker by social-work agencies in New York City in 1907 compared with the "typical" clothing allotment for an adult male slave*

New York worker	"Typical" slave issue
2 hats or caps	1 hat
1 overcoat (every 2 or 3 years)	? overcoat
1 suit	1 jacket
1 pair pantaloons	4 pair pants
2 pair overalls	
5 shirts	4 shirts
6 collars	
4 ties	
4 handkerchiefs	
summer and winter underwear	? underwear
6 pair hose	? hose
2 pair shoes	1½ pair shoes
repair of shoes	
gloves or mittens	

The "typical" slave issue does not include purchases of clothing by slaves. The New York study in which the above list was published reported that the average expenditure of New York workers on clothes was below the recommended level.

overseers and in other records and correspondence of planters. "The preservation of the health of the negroes," wrote J. A. S. Acklen to his overseer, "and the care of them when sick, will require your best attention; and to be ignorant of the best mode of discharging your duties in these particulars, is to be unfit for the responsible station you hold." P. C. Weston charged his overseer "most distinctly to understand that his first object is to be, under all circumstances, the care and well being of the negroes." Consequently,

All sick persons are to stay in the hospital night and day, from the time they first complain to the time they are able to work again. The nurses are to be responsible for the sick not leaving the house, and for the cleanliness of the bedding, utensils, &c. The nurses are never to be allowed to give any medicine without the orders of the Overseer or Doctor. A woman, beside the plantation nurse, must be put to nurse all persons seriously ill. In all cases at all serious the Doctor is to be sent for, and his orders are to be strictly attended to; no alteration is to be made in the treatment he directs.

While planters worried about slaves who feigned illness to get out of work, they were generally more concerned about losing slaves or impairing their health through the neglect of real illness. Thus Bennet H. Barrow, owner of one of the largest Louisiana plantations, treated slaves as though they were sick even when he thought they were pretending. Nor was Barrow alone in this attitude. In their sick records planters sometimes described the malady which had removed a slave from production as "nothing," "complaining," and "more lazy and mad than sick." James Hammond insisted that, "[e]very reasonable complaint must be promptly attended to; and with any marked or general symptom of sickness, however trivial, a negro may lie up a day or so at least." "Unless it is a clear case of imposition," wrote still another planter, "a negro had better be allowed a day's rest when he lays up. A little rest often saves much by preventing serious illness."

Facilities for the treatment of the sick generally varied with the size of the plantations. The larger plantations maintained substantial hospitals. On one plantation with 168 slaves, for example, the hospital was a two-story brick building which had eight large rooms. Such hospitals usually contained separate rooms for men and women. A special room was often set aside for confinement cases. One or more of the rooms were "clinics" for the treatment of "outpatients." These rooms contained a pharmacy as well as other equipment needed for ministering to the sick. On smaller plantations, the "hospital" was merely an ordinary cabin reserved for the sick. In some instances, masters set aside several rooms in their own houses for use as a hospital. The rationale for hospitalizing slaves was twofold: it permitted the sick to receive special care including not only rest and medication but also special diets; it also isolated the sick slaves from the healthy ones and thus minimized the danger of contagion. Many planters insisted that slaves be removed from their cabins to hospitals as soon as their illness was made known.

Few plantations were large enough to justify the exclusive retention of a full-time physician. However, virtually all plantations of moderate or large size had at least one full-time nurse, usually an elderly slave, and many also had experienced midwives. The nurses and midwives worked under the direct supervision of the planter or his overseer. Planters sought to be, and overseers were expected to be, knowledgeable about current medical procedures and about drugs and their administration. Physicians were regularly brought onto the plantations to care for slaves whose health problems could not be treated adequately by the nurses, midwives, overseers, or planters. Some planters contracted for the physicians' services for a year at a time, paying a flat fee that was usually proportional to the number of persons covered by the contract. Others paid for services as rendered. In either case, the doctor attending to the slaves was usually the same doctor who ministered to the planter's family. Bills submitted by these physicians indicate, time after time, that they treated both slaves and members of the master's family during the same visit.

That it was generally the intent of planters to supply slaves with medical care of a relatively high quality does not imply that the objective was usually realized. Not only was the state of medical knowledge and arts quite primitive during the antebellum era, but the prevailing theory of disease frequently led to treatments which were inimical to the recovery of patients. Disease was assumed to be caused by "poisons emanating from decaying animal and vegetable matter," which were transmitted to human beings by "impure airs and waters." To rid the body of these poisons, doctors resorted to bleeding, blistering, and purging. Bleeding and purging were a standard treatment for such diseases as dysentery, cholera, and pleurisy. In each case, of course, the prescribed treatment removed from the body fluids that were vital to recovery. The therapy, no doubt, hurried to their graves many patients who might have survived if they were spared the services of doctors.

For many of the illnesses that afflicted slaves, especially pneumonia and diseases of the gastrointestinal tract, which were the greatest killers of blacks, the services of doctors were either useless or harmful. It was only in limited cases, such as smallpox and malaria (after the 1820s when sulphate of quinine became generally known), that doctors possessed effective pharmaceutical weapons. Beyond these, the useful medicines contained in the chests of doctors were primarily anodynes such as opium, paregoric, Dover's powder, and laudanum which, although they did not cure, at least served to relieve severe distress. Doctors were effective in cases requiring minor surgery, such as opening abscesses, removing teeth, and the setting of broken bones. They were also helpful in dealing with hernias, which were quite common among slaves. Although they lacked the surgical knowledge needed to repair the rupture, they did prescribe the use of trusses.

The prevailing theory of disease did have one quite salutary effect. It led many planters to adhere to a hygienic regimen. Few matters were more frequently emphasized in the instructions to overseers than the need to insure not only the personal cleanliness of slaves but also the cleanliness of their clothes, their bedding, and their cabins. Instructions required overseers "personally" to

> see that they keep their clothing mended and clean, and that they wash their clothes as often as once a week, for which purpose time must be regularly set apart the latter end of the week. He must see that they are clean on Sundays and not straggling about the country dirty and ragged, and he must see that they appear clean every Monday morning in the year, without any failure whatever.
>
> He must see that they keep their houses clean and their yards free from weeds and filth.

Some planters went even further. Hammond required a complete cleaning of slave cabins twice a year. During these spring and fall cleanings, all contents of the cabin were to be removed and sunned, all walls were to be washed, mattresses were to be restuffed, and the grounds under the houses were to be sprinkled with lime. Once a year every house was to be "whitewashed inside and out." The punishment for slaves who failed to keep themselves personally clean was a forced scrubbing by the driver and two other blacks. Another planter required the ground under the cabins to be swept every month and had cabins whitewashed twice a year. Charles Tait, a leading planter in Alabama, required the cabins of his slaves to be moved to new ground every fourth year "to prevent filth accumulations and cholera or diphtheria."

Slave health care was at its best for pregnant women. "Pregnant women," wrote one planter, "must be treated with great tenderness, worked near home and lightly." "Light work" was generally interpreted as 50 to 60 percent of normal effort and was to exclude activity which required heavy physical effort. During the last month of pregnancy work was further reduced, although various planters felt, as did P. C. Weston, that "pregnant women are always to do some work up to the time to their confinement, if it is only walking into the field and staying there." On large estates, women were usually confined in the "lying-in" ward of the plantation hospital. In normal cases the delivery was usually handled by a midwife. But if some difficulty in the delivery was anticipated, a doctor was called in. The period of confinement generally lasted about four weeks, during part of which time mothers were attended to by a midwife or a nurse. There frequently followed another two weeks of light work in the vicinity of the slave quarters. Women were expected to nurse their children, and hence were kept on relatively light work schedules for the balance of the year. Until the sixth or eighth month after birth, nursing took place four times per day during working hours, and nursing mothers were expected to work at only 50 to 60 percent of normal levels. For the balance of the first year infants were usually nursed twice a day during hours of work.

Demographic evidence gives strong support to descriptions of pre- and post-natal care contained in plantation rules, letters, and diaries. Computations based on data from the 1850 census indicate that the average death rate due to pregnancy among slave women in the prime childbearing ages, twenty to twenty-nine, was just one per thousand. This means that out of every 167 women in this age category who gave birth, only one died. The slave mortality rate in childbearing was not only low on an absolute scale, it was also lower than the maternal death rate experienced by southern white women.

The mortality rate for infants was less favorable than that of their mothers. Of every thousand slaves born in 1850, an average of 183 died before their first birthday. The death rate for white infants in the same year was 146 per thousand. In other words, the infant death rate for slaves was 25 percent higher than for whites. This finding appears to give credence to charges that mean treatment of infant slaves was widespread. In so doing it raises the strange paradox of planters who treated pregnant women and new mothers quite well while abusing their offspring.

Work on the demographic data for 1850 and 1860 has not proceeded far enough to permit a full resolution of this paradox. Definitive answers to many of the questions posed by the relatively high infant death rates experienced by slaves are at least several years off. The work thus far, however, has revealed little evidence to support the charge that masters neglected the care of infants. Most of the difference between the infant death rates of slaves and free persons appears to have been due to the fact that the South was less healthy than the North. The infant death rate of southern whites in 1850 was 177 per thousand – virtually the same as the infant death rate of slaves. Along this dimension, then, exploitation of blacks arose because slavery was confined to the South and because slaves were not free to choose where to live.

By and large, slave deaths during the first year of life, like those of free infants, were due to diseases such as whooping cough, croup, pneumonia, cholera, and various maladies of the gastrointestinal system – diseases about which the men of the antebellum era had little understanding and over which they had little control. Of those causes of death that apparently could be controlled, suffocation was most significant. About 9.3 percent of the slave infants who died in 1850 were reported to have succumbed from this cause. Among whites, only 1.2 percent of infants were reported to have died from suffocation. The excess of the slave suffocation rate over the white suffocation rate accounted for nearly fifteen deaths out of every thousand slave births.

There has been much debate among historians as to the causes of infant suffocations. Some have attributed them to infanticide, arguing that life was so unbearable for slaves that many mothers preferred to kill their young rather than to rear them in bondage. This argument is undermined by the extremely low suicide rate among slaves. Less than one slave in every ten thousand committed suicide in 1850. That was only one third of the suicide rate among the white population. Others have used suffocation as evidence that neglect of children by slave mothers was widespread. While one cannot rule out the possibility that deaths due to suffocation reflected neglect on the part of the mothers involved, the fact remains that out of every one hundred slaves born, less than two infants died of this cause. The mortality statistics, therefore,

Figure 4. The life expectation at birth for U.S. slaves and various free populations, 1830–1920.

leave plenty of room for slave mothers who gave their children tender care.

Nor should one necessarily accept the statistics on slave suffocations at face value. Many deaths that were interpreted as suffocation because of the absence of a prior fever or other then-accepted symptoms of illness could have been caused by undisclosed infections. That more such deaths were reported as suffocation for slaves than for free men might have been due to the jaundiced view of the overseers who reported the death statistics to the census takers.

Neither the 1850 nor the 1860 censuses collected information on morbidity. The only currently available data comes from a sample of 545 field hands who lived on fifteen plantations. This sample provides information on illness rates during 2,274 man years of labor time. It shows that on average each slave was sufficiently ill to be absent from work for just 12.0 days per year. This low illness rate tends to support the impression that slaves were well cared for. It also calls into question the widely asserted contention that slaves were always feigning illness. At the very least, the low absence rate shows that if pretense of illness was wide-spread, slaves were singularly unsuccessful in their deceptions.

For many, statistics on life expectancy are the ultimate measure of physical well-being. Figure 4 compares the life expectancy of U.S. slaves in 1850 with those of free men in various places between 1830 and 1920. Although the life expectation of slaves in 1850 was 12 percent below the average of white Americans, it was well within the range experienced by free men during the nineteenth century. It was, for example, nearly identical with the life expectation of countries as advanced as France and Holland. Moreover, U.S. slaves had much longer life expectations than free urban industrial workers in both the United States and Europe.

The family

The administration of most large plantations was based on two organizations. Fieldwork revolved around gangs. They were the vehicles through which planters were able to achieve a degree of specialization and efficiency that was unmatched elsewhere in agriculture. . . .

The other organization of central importance was the family. Planters assigned three functions to the slave family. First, it was the administrative unit for the distribution of food and clothing and for the provision of shelter. As we have already seen, the single-family house, not the dormitory, was almost the universal form of shelter on larger plantations. The records of planters also indicate that whether food was cooked in a common kitchen or in the house of individual families, allotments of rations were generally made by family. The same was true for clothing.

The family was also an important instrument for maintaining labor discipline. By encouraging strong family attachments, slaveowners reduced the danger that individual slaves would run away. By permitting families to have *de facto* ownership of houses, furniture, clothing, garden plots, and small livestock, planters created an economic stake for slaves in the system. Moreover, the size of the stake was variable. It was possible for some families to achieve substantially higher levels of income and of *de facto* wealth ownership than others. The size and quality of houses and the allotments of clothes as well as the size of the garden plots differed from family to family.

Third, the family was also the main instrument for promoting the increase of the slave population. Not only did planters believe that fertility rates would be highest when the family was strongest, but they relied on the family for the rearing of children. Although infants and very young children were kept in nurseries while mothers labored in the field, these supplemented rather than replaced the family. The central importance of the family in the rearing of slaves is revealed by the narratives of former slaves collected by the W.P.A. in the 1930s. In discussing their early upbringing and the influences on them, the former slaves frequently refer to what their parents taught them but rarely, if ever, invoke the names of women who ran the nurseries.

To promote the stability of slave families, planters often combined exhortations with a system of rewards and sanctions. The rewards included such subsidies as separate houses for married couples, gifts of household goods, and cash bonuses. They often sought to make the marriage a solemn event by embedding it in a well-defined ritual. Some marriage ceremonies were performed in churches, others by the planter in the "big house." In either case, marriages were often accompanied by feasts and sometimes made the occasion for a general holiday. The sanctions were directed against adultery and divorce. For many planters, adultery was an offense which required whippings for the guilty parties. Some planters also used the threat of the whip to discourage divorce.

Thus, while the existence of slave marriages was explicitly denied under the legal codes of the states, they were not only recognized but actively promoted under plantation codes. That the legal basis for slave marriage was derived from codes which held sway within the jurisdiction of the plantation, points to a much neglected feature of legal structure of the antebellum South. Within fairly wide limits the state, in effect, turned the definition of the codes of legal behavior of slaves, and of the punishment for infractions of these codes, over to planters. Such duality of the legal structure was not unique to the antebellum South. It existed in medieval Europe in the duality between the law of the manor and of the crown; it was a characteristic of the regimes under which the American colonies were governed; and in lesser degree, it exists with respect to certain large institutions today (for example, with respect to university regulations).

The importance of the dual legal structure of the ante-bellum South is that the latitude which the state yielded to the planter was quite wide. For most slaves it was the law of the plantation, not of the state, that was relevant. Only a small proportion of the slaves ever had to deal with the law-enforcement mechanism of the state. Their daily lives were governed by plantation law. Consequently, the emphasis put on the sanctity of the slave family by many planters, and the legal status given to the slave family under plantation law, cannot be lightly dismissed.

Recognition of the dualistic nature of the southern legal structure puts into a different perspective the emphasis which some historians have placed on the "pre-bourgeois" character of antebellum society. What made that society pre-bourgeois was not the absence of a commercial spirit among planters, but the wide area of legal authority which the state yielded to them. In Europe, the rise of capitalism was accompanied by a determined struggle to weaken the authority of the manor and to transfer its powers to the centralized state. This process was sharply curtailed in the South. While the South developed a highly capitalistic form of agriculture, and while its economic behavior was as strongly ruled by profit maximization as that of the North, the relationship between its ruling and its servile class was marked by patriarchal features which were strongly reminiscent of medieval life. Unlike the northern manufacturer, the authority of the planter extended not only to the conduct of business but to the regulation of the family lives of slaves, the control of their public behavior, the provision of their food and shelter, the care of their health, and the protection of their souls.

We do not mean to suggest that planters viewed the slave family purely as a business instrument. Victorian attitudes predominated in the planting class. The emphasis on strong, stable families, and on the limitation of sexual activity to the family, followed naturally from such attitudes. That morality and good business practice should coincide created neither surprise nor consternation among most planters.

Of course not all planters, and not all of their overseers, were men who lived by the moral codes of their day. That many of these men sought sex outside of the confines of their wives' beds is beyond question. To satisfy their desires they took on mistresses and concubines, seduced girls of tender ages, and patronized prostitutes. Such sexual exploitation was not limited to the South. And within the South, sexual exploitation by white men was not limited to black women.

The point at issue here is not whether the sexual exploitation of slave women by masters and overseers existed, but whether it was so frequent that it undermined or destroyed the black family. Let us pose the question somewhat more sharply: Are there reasons to believe that the degree of sexual exploitation which white men imposed on black women was greater than that imposed on white women? We put the issue in this way because while the sexual exploitation of white women was rife, few have gone so far as to claim that such exploitation destroyed the family institution among whites. Is the asymmetry in the presumed effects of sexual exploitation on the families of blacks and whites justified by available evidence?

Antebellum critics of slavery answered these questions in the affirmative. They accused slaveowners and overseers of turning plantations into personal harems. They assumed that because the law permitted slaveowners to ravish black women, the practice must have been extremely common. They also assumed that black women were, if not more licentious, at least more promiscuous than white women, and hence less likely to resist sexual advances by men, whether black or white. Moreover, the ravishing of black women by white men was not the only aspect of sexual exploitation which devastated the slave family. There was also the policy of deliberate slave-breeding, under which planters encouraged promiscuous relationships among blacks. Thus, economic greed and lust on the part of the planters, and submissiveness on the part of the slaves, combined to make the sexual exploitation of black women so extreme as to be beyond comparison with the situation of white women.

The evidence on which these assumptions and conclusions were based was extremely limited. While none of the various travelers through the South had seen deliberate slave-breeding practiced, they had all heard reports of it. Some travelers published conversations with men who admitted to fathering a large number of the slaves on their plantations. Others wrote of the special solicitude shown by one or another master to mulatto offspring, a solicitude which in their minds strongly implied parenthood. There were also the descriptions of the treatment of especially pretty slave women on the auction block and of the high prices at which such women sold, prices too high to be warranted by field labor and which could be explained only by their value as concubines or as prostitutes.

Even if all these reports were true, they constituted at most a few hundred cases. By themselves, such a small number of observations out of a population of millions, could just as easily be used as proof of the infrequency of the sexual exploitation of black women as of its frequency. The real question is whether such cases were common events that were rarely reported, or whether they were rare events that were frequently reported. The prevalence of mulattoes convinced not only the northern public of the antebellum era, but historians of today, that for each case of exploitation identified, there were thousands which had escaped discovery. For travelers to the South reported that a large proportion of the slaves were not the deep black of Africans from the Guinea coast but tawny, golden, and white or nearly white. Here was proof beyond denial of either the ubiquity of the exploitation of black women by white men, or of the promiscuity of black women, or of both.

But this seemingly irrefutable evidence is far from conclusive. It is not the eyesight of these travelers to the South which is questionable, but their statistical sense. For mulattoes were not distributed evenly through the Negro population. They were concentrated in the cities and especially among freedmen. According to the 1860 census, 39 percent of freedmen in southern cities were mulattoes. Among urban slaves the proportion of mulattoes was 20 percent. In other words, one out of every four Negroes living in a southern city was a mulatto. But among rural slaves, who constituted 95 percent of the slave population, only 9.9 percent were mulatto in 1860. For the slave population as a whole, therefore, the proportion of mulattoes was just 10.4 percent in 1860 and 7.7 percent in 1850. Thus it appears that travelers to the South greatly exaggerated the extent of miscegenation because they came into contact with unrepresentative samples of the Negro population. They appear to have had much more contact with the freedmen and slaves of the urban areas that with slaves living in the relative isolation of the countryside. Far from proving that the exploitation of black women was ubiquitous, the available data on mulattoes strongly militates against that contention.

The fact that during the twenty-three decades of contact between slaves and whites which elapsed between 1620 and 1850, only 7.7 percent of the slaves were mulattoes suggests that on average only a very small percentage of the slaves born in any given year were fathered by white men. This inference is not contradicted by the fact that the percentage of mulattoes increased by one third during the last decade of the antebellum era, rising from 7.7 to 10.4 percent. For it must be remembered that mulattoes were the progeny not just of unions between whites and pure blacks but also of unions between mulattoes and blacks. Under common definition, a person with one-eighth ancestry of another race was a mulatto. Consequently, the offspring of two slaves who were each one-eighth white was to be classified as a mulatto, as was the offspring of any slave, regardless of the ancestry of his or her mate, whose grandfather was a white.

A demographic model of the slave population, which is presented in the technical appendix, shows that the census data on mulattoes alone cannot be used to sustain the contention that a large proportion of slave children must have been fathered by white men. And other available bodies of evidence, such as the W.P.A. survey of former slaves, throw such claims into doubt. Of those in the survey who identified parentage, only 4.5 percent indicated that one of their parents had been white. But the work of geneticists on gene pools has revealed that even the last figure may be too high. Measurements of the admixture of "Caucasian" and "Negro" genes among southern rural blacks today indicate that the share of Negro children fathered by whites on slave plantations probably averaged between 1 and 2 percent.

That these findings seem startling is due in large measure to the widespread assumption that because the law permitted masters to ravish their slave women, they must have exercised that right. As one scholar recently put it, "Almost every [white] mother and wife connected with the institution [of slavery] either actually or potentially shared the males in her family with slave women." The trouble with this view is that it recognizes no forces operating on human behavior other than the force of statute law. Yet many rights permitted by legal statutes and judicial decisions are not widely exercised, because economic and social forces militate against them.

To put the issue somewhat differently, it has been presumed that masters and overseers must have ravished black women frequently because their demand for such sexual pleasures was high and because the cost of satisfying that demand was low. Such arguments overlook the real and potentially large costs that confronted masters and overseers who sought sexual pleasures in the slave quarters. The seduction of the daughter or wife of a slave could undermine the discipline that planters so assiduously strove to attain. Not only would it stir anger and discontent in the families affected, but it would undermine the air of mystery and distinction on which so much of the authority of large planters rested. Nor was it just a planter's reputation in the slave quarter of his plantation that would be at stake. While he might be able to prevent news of his nocturnal adventure from being broadcast in his own house, it would be more difficult to prevent his slaves from gossiping to slaves on other plantations.

Owners of large plantations who desired illicit sexual relationships were by no means confined to slave quarters in their quest. Those who owned fifty or more slaves were very rich men by the standards of their day. The average annual net income in this class was in excess of $7,500. That amount was more than sixty times per capita income in 1860. To have a comparable income today, a person would need an after-tax income of about $240,000 or a before-tax income of about $600,000. So rich a man could easily have afforded to maintain a mistress in town where his relationship could have been not only more discreet than in the crowded slave quarters of his own plantation, but far less likely to upset the labor discipline on which economic success depended.

For the overseer, the cost of sexual episodes in the slave quarter, once discovered, was often his job. Nor would he find it easy to obtain employment elsewhere as an overseer, since not many masters would be willing to employ as their manager a man who was known to lack self-control on so vital an issue. "Never employ an overseer who will equalize himself with the negro women," wrote Charles Tait to his children. "Besides the morality of it, there are evils too numerous to be now mentioned."

Nor should one underestimate the effect of racism on the demand of white males for black sexual partners. While some white men might have been tempted by the myth of black sexuality, a myth that may be stronger today than it was in the antebellum South, it is likely that far larger numbers were put off by racist aversions. Data on prostitution supports this conjecture. Nashville is the only southern city for which a count of prostitutes is available. The 1860 census showed that just 4.3 percent of the prostitutes in that city were Negroes, although a fifth of the population of Nashville was Negro. Moreover, all of the Negro prostitutes were free and light-skinned. There were no pure blacks who were prostitutes; nor were any slaves prostitutes. The substantial under-representation of Negroes, as well as the complete absence of dark-skinned Negroes, indicates that white men who desired illicit sex had a strong preference for white women.

The failure of Nashville's brothels to employ slave women is of special interest. For it indicates that supply as well as demand considerations served to limit the use of slaves as prostitutes. The census revealed that half of Nashville's prostitutes were illiterate – not functionally illiterate, but completely lacking in either the capacity to read, or to write, or both. In other words, the supply of prostitutes was drawn from poor, uneducated girls who could only command the wages of unskilled labor. Given such a supply, a slaveholder did not have to be imbued with Victorian morals to demur from sending his chattel into prostitution. He could clearly earn more on his slave women by working them in the fields where they would not be subject to the high morbidity and mortality rates which accompany the "world's oldest profession."

The contention that the slave family was undermined by the widespread promiscuity of blacks is as poorly founded as the thesis that masters were uninhibited in their sexual exploitation of slave women. Indeed, virtually no evidence, other than the allegations of white observers, has ever been presented which sustains the charge that promiscuity among slaves was greater than that found among whites. The question then arises, "Do the allegations reflect the reality of black behavior or are they merely reflections of the preconceptions of the observers?"

The allegations appeared creditable because they emanated not only from southern defenders of slavery but also from critics of the system. While the charges of Southerners could be set down as apologetics, one could not so easily dismiss the words of the abolitionists and other enemies of slavery. On the issue of promiscuity the antislavery forces differed from the apologists not in denying its existence but in the explanation of its extent. Slavery, the critics believed, worked to exacerbate rather than to hold in check the carnal instincts of blacks.

Unfortunately, abolitionists and other antislavery writers were not free of racism merely because they carried the banner of a moral struggle. With their greater physical separation from blacks, these writers were often more gullible and more quick in their acceptance of certain racial stereotypes than slaveholders. This, as we shall see, was a key factor in their underestimation of the efficiency of slave labor. Moreover, coming from the upper classes, as many of these writers did, they shared with slaveholders certain common conceptions regarding the behavior of all laboring folk. Thus, Fanny Kemble, whose descriptions of the family life of slaves is often quoted by historians, saw Irish peasants, English manufacturing workers, and American Negroes as all exhibiting the same "recklessness" toward human propagation.

The available demographic evidence on slaves suggests a picture of their sexual lives and family behavior that has little in common with that conveyed by the allegations. One of the most revealing pieces of information is the pattern of child spacing among mothers between the ages of eighteen and thirty. For those whose children were stillborn or who died within the first three months, the average elapsed time until the birth of the next child was slightly more than one year. However, for those mothers whose children survived the first year of life; the elapsed time before the birth of the next child was somewhat over two years. This is the pattern of child spacing that one would expect to find in a noncontraceptive population in which mothers engaged in breast feeding for the first year of their children's lives. For one of the effects of breast feeding is to reduce the likelihood of conception. In other words, the pattern of child spacing among slaves suggests that the nursing of infants by their mothers was widespread.

This finding hardly supports the charge that slave mothers were indifferent to their children, generally neglected them, and were widely engaged in infanticide. Quite the contrary, the ubiquity of the year-long pattern of breast feeding, combined with the nearly identical rate of infant mortality among slaves and southern whites, and with the rare occurrences of suffocation and other accidents as the cause of death of infant slaves, suggests that for the most part, black mothers cared quite well for their children.

An even more telling piece of information is the distribution of the ages of mothers at the time of the birth of their first surviving child. This distribution, which is shown in Figure 5, contradicts the charge that black girls were frequently turned into mothers at such tender ages as twelve, thirteen, and fourteen. Not only was motherhood at age twelve virtually unknown, and motherhood in the early teens quite uncommon, but the average age at first birth was 22.5 (the median age was 20.8). Thus the high fertility rate of slave women was not the consequence of the wanton impregnation of very young unmarried women by either white or black men, but of the frequency of conception after the first birth. By far the great majority of slave children were borne by women who were not only quite mature, but who were already married.

The high average age of mothers at first birth also suggests that slave parents closely guarded their daughters from sexual contact with men. For in a well-fed, noncontraceptive population in which women are quite fecund after marriage, only abstinence would explain the relative shortage of births in the late-teen ages. In other words, the demographic

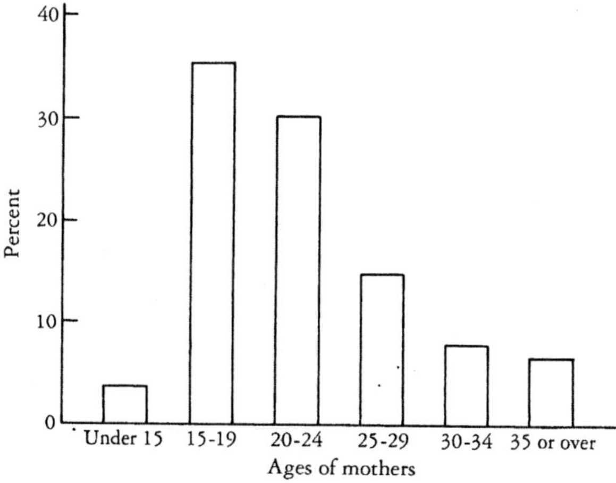

Figure 5. The distribution of first births, by the ages of slave mothers.

evidence suggests that the prevailing sexual mores of slaves were not promiscuous but prudish – the very reverse of the stereotype published by many in both the abolitionist and slaveholding camps and accepted in traditional historiography. Narratives collected from ex-slaves provide support for the prevalence of prudishness in the conduct of family life. "Dem's moral times," recollected Amos Lincoln, who was reared on a plantation in Louisiana. "A gal's twenty-one 'fore she marry. They didn't go wanderin' 'round all hours. They mammies knowed where they was. Folks nowadays is wild and weak."

That marriage altered the sexual behavior of slaves is clearly indicated by the difference between the seasonal pattern of first births and that of second and subsequent births (see Figure 6). Data culled from plantation records indicate that for second and subsequent births, roughly equal percentages of infants were born during every quarter of the year. But the seasonal pattern of first births shows a definite peak during the last quarter of the year – precisely the pattern to be expected in an agrarian society in which a large proportion of marriages took place soon after the harvest. Over twice as many first births took place during the last quarter of the year – roughly nine to thirteen months after the end of the harvest, depending on the region and crop – as took place during the first quarter of the year. This pattern cannot be attributed merely to the fact that slaves had more leisure time during the winter interstice, and hence, more opportunity for sexual intercourse. If that was all that had been involved, the peaking of births during the last quarter of

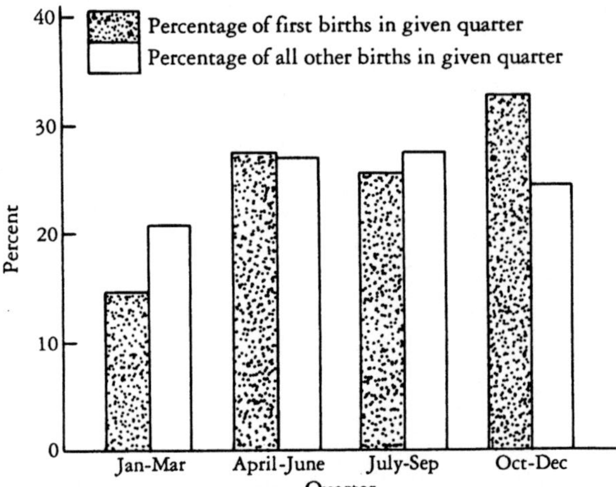

Figure 6. A comparison of the seasonal distribution of first births with that of all other births.

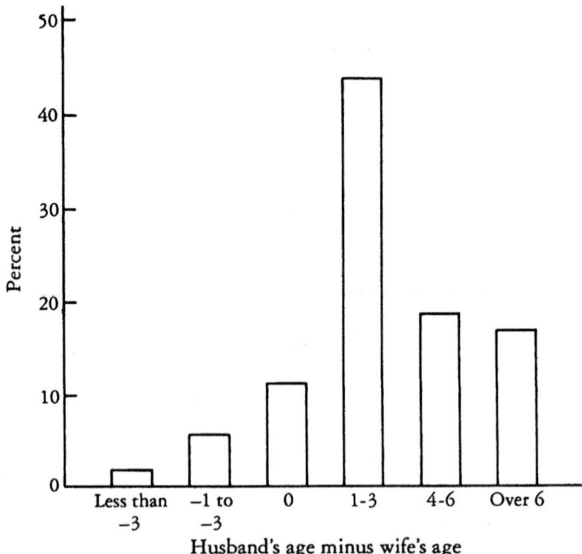

Figure 7. The distribution of age differences between slave husbands and wives.

the year would have occurred not only for first children but for subsequent children as well.

Also fallacious is the contention that slave marriages, since they were arbitrarily dictated by masters, frequently produced odd age combinations – young men married to old women and vice versa. Figure 7 shows that most marriages were contracted among partners quite close in age. The average age difference between husband and wife was just three years. In almost all cases, the man was the same age or older than the woman. Reversals in this pattern were quite uncommon.

That slave life pivoted around stable, nuclear families does not mean that the black family was merely a copy of the white family. No doubt the African heritage of blacks, as well as their particular socioeconomic circumstances, resulted in various characteristics which were, if not restricted to, at least more frequent among black than white families. For example, various bits of evidence suggest that wives tended to play a stronger role in black than in white families. Careful delineation of such special characteristics and the determination of their incidence is a task which has not yet been adequately essayed. The evidence already in hand, however, clearly invalidates many of the generalizations that now permeate history books.

It is not true that "the typical slave family was matriarchal in form" and that the "husband was at most his wife's assistant." Nor is it true that the "male slave's only crucial function within the family was that of siring offspring." For better or worse, the dominant role in slave society was played by men, not women. It was men who occupied virtually all of the managerial slots available to slaves. There were very few female overseers or drivers. Men occupied nearly all the artisan crafts; among them were carpentry, coopering and blacksmithing. In the city of Charleston in 1848, for example, all of the 706 slave artisans were male.

While females worked along with males in the field, their role was strictly delimited. Much has been made of the women who worked in plow gangs. But such participation was quite uncommon. Plow gangs were confined almost exclusively to men, and predominantly to young men. During the period of cultivation, women worked along with older men and children in the hoe gangs, where strength was not so important a factor. Only at harvesttime were women the equal of "any man" since dexterity, not strength, was the crucial characteristic of successful cotton picking. Just as some jobs on the plantation were confined strictly to men, others were confined strictly to women. Men were virtually never spinners, weavers, seamstresses, or nurses. The differentiation between male and female roles continued into the domestic staffs of plantations, although the division was somewhat less sharp. Gardeners and coachmen were jobs for males; laundresses and cooks, female jobs.

There was also a division of labor within the slave family, a division that began with courtship. It was the male who, at least on the surface, initiated the period of courtship. And it was the man who secured the permission of the planter to marry. After marriage, the tasks of cooking, ordinary household cleaning, laundering, and care of the children fell to the mother. Work in the garden patches of the slave household, hunting and fishing for extra food, and chopping wood were among the tasks of the father.

Planters recognized husbands as the head of the family. Slave families were listed in their record books with the husband at the top of the list. Houses were assigned by the names of husbands and the semiannual issues of clothing to families were made in the name of the husband. Garden patches were assigned to the husbands and the money earned from the sale of crops from these patches was held in his name. When slaves wanted advances of cash from these accounts, they were made to the men. Slave purchases of cloth and apparel (whether intended for men, women, or children) were charged against the names of the husbands, as were purchases of such other items as pails, pots, and special foods.

While both moral convictions and good business practice generally led planters to encourage the development of stable nuclear families, it would be a mistake to assume that the black family was purely, or even predominantly, the creation of white masters. The exact interplay of external and internal forces in shaping the black family is still unknown. But there is considerable evidence that the nuclear form was not merely imposed on slaves. Slaves apparently abandoned the African family forms because they did not satisfy the needs of blacks who lived and worked under conditions and in a society much different from those which their ancestors experienced. The nuclear family took root among blacks because it did satisfy those needs. Witness to the meaning which the family held for slaves is given by the deep anguish which they usually expressed on those occasions when their families were rent apart on the auction block. "Well, dey took us on up dere to Memphis and we was sold jest like cattle," said Nancy Gardner, a former slave who lived in Oklahoma. "Dey sold me and ma together and dey sold pa and de boys together. Dey was sent to Mississippi and we was sent to Alabama. My pa, O how my ma was grieved to death about him! She didn't live long after dat."

During the relatively infrequent instances when economic forces led the planter to destroy, rather than to maintain slave families, the *independent* striving of slaves to maintain their families came into sharp focus. Mrs. Josie Jordan, an ex-slave from Tennessee, reported that her mother "had two children while belonging to Mister Clark and he wouldn't let them go with mammy and pappy. That's what caused her misery. Pappy tried to ease her mind but she jest kept a'crying for her babies, Ann and Reuban, till Mister Lowery got Clark to leave them visit with her once a month." Further testimony to this striving is given by the ads which planters placed in newspapers advertising for the capture of runaways. These ads frequently indicate the planter's belief that his slave was attempting to reunite with the family from which the slave had recently been removed.

The abolitionist position on the black family, which has been accepted so uncritically by historians, was strikingly inconsistent. To arouse sentiment against the slave system they accurately portrayed the deep anguish which was caused by the forced breakup of slave families while simultaneously arguing that slavery had robbed black families of all meaning. This latter view was given vivid expression in Fanny Kemble's journal. The relationship between slave parents and children, she wrote, was reduced to the "connection between the animal and its young." In her view black families were stripped of "all the unspeakable tenderness and solemnity, all the rational, and all the spiritual grace and glory" which she associated with parenthood in upper-class English families. Under slavery, she concluded, parenthood became "mere breeding, bearing, suckling, and there an end." The anguish on the auction block as well as the struggle of blacks to reunite their severed families, both during and immediately after slavery, suggests that the love that permeated slave families eluded Fanny Kemble and most other white observers – perhaps because of a veil of racial and class biases which obscured their vision and prevented them from seeing the real content of black family life.

Punishment, rewards, and expropriation

The exploitative nature of slavery is most apparent in its system of punishment and rewards. Whipping was probably the most common punishment meted out against errant slaves. Other forms of punishment included the deprivation of various privileges (such as visits to town), confinement in stocks, incarceration, sale, branding, and the death penalty.

Whipping could be either a mild or a severe punishment, depending on how it was administered. Some whippings were so severe that they resulted in death. Indeed, in cases such as murder, the sentences of slaves who would otherwise have been executed were frequently converted to severe whipping, coupled with exportation to another state or a foreign country. For, by converting the death penalty to whipping and exportation, the state could recover a substantial part of the value of a slave that would have been lost through his execution. In other instances, whip-

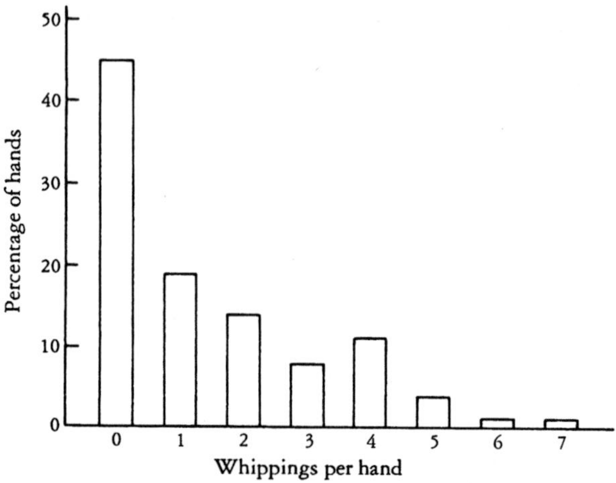

Figure 8. The distribution of whippings on the Bennet H. Barrow plantation during a two-year period beginning in December 1840.

ping was as mildly applied as the corporal punishment normally practiced within families today.

Reliable data on the frequency of whipping is extremely sparse. The only systematic record of whipping now available for an extended period comes from the diary of Bennet Barrow, a Louisiana planter who believed that to spare the rod was to spoil the slave. His plantation numbered about 200 slaves, of whom about 120 were in the labor force. The record shows that over the course of two years a total of 160 whippings were administered, an average of 0.7 whippings per hand per year. About half the hands were not whipped at all during the period.

There was nothing exceptional about the use of whipping to enforce discipline among slaves until the beginning of the nineteenth century. It must be remembered that through the centuries whipping was considered a fully acceptable form of punishment, not merely for criminals but also for honest men or women who in some way shirked their duties. Whipping of wives, for example, was even sanctified in some versions of the Scripture. The Matthew's Bible, which preceded the King James version, told the husband, in a note at 1 Pet. 3, that if his wife was "not obedient and healpfull vnto hym endeuoureth to beate the feare of God into her heade, and that therby she maye be compelled to learne her duitie and do it." During the seventeenth and most of the eighteenth centuries whipping was commonly employed as a punishment in the North as well as in the South. Not until the end of the eighteenth century and the beginning of the nineteenth century did whipping rapidly fall from favor in the free states.

To attribute the continuation of whipping in the South to the maliciousness of masters is naïve. Although some masters were brutal, even sadistic, most were not. The overwhelming majority of the ex-slaves in the W.P.A. narratives who expressed themselves on the issue reported that their masters were good men. Such men worried about the proper role of whipping in a system of punishment and rewards. Some excluded it altogether. Most accepted it, but recognized that to be effective whipping had to be used with restraint and in a coolly calculated manner. Weston, for example, admonished his overseer not to impose punishment of any sort until twenty-four hours after the offense had been discovered. William J. Minor, a sugar planter, instructed his managers "not [to] cut the skin when punishing, nor punish in a passion." Many planters forbade the whipping of slaves except by them or in their presence. Others limited the number of lashes that could be administered without their permission.

The decline of whipping as an instrument of labor discipline outside of the South appears to have been heavily influenced by economic considerations. With the rise of capitalism, impersonal and indirect sanctions were increasingly substituted for direct, personal ones. The hiring of free workers in the marketplace provided managers of labor with a powerful new disciplinary weapon. Workers who were lazy, indifferent, or who otherwise shirked their duties could be fired – left to starve beyond the eyesight or expense of the employer. Interestingly enough, denial of food was rarely used to enforce discipline on slaves. For the illness and lethargy caused by malnutrition reduced the capacity of the slave to labor in the fields. Planters preferred whipping to incarceration because the lash did not generally lead to an extended loss of the slave's labor time. In other words, whipping persisted in the South because the cost of substituting hunger and incarceration for the lash was greater for the slaveowner than for the northern employer of free labor. When the laborer owns his own human capital, forms of punishment which impair or diminish the value of that capital are borne exclusively by him. Under slavery, the master desired forms of punishment which, while they imposed costs on the slave, did so with minimum impairment to the human capital which the master owned. Whipping generally fulfilled these conditions.

While whipping was an integral part of the system of punishment and rewards, it was not the totality of the system. What planters wanted was not sullen and discontented slaves who did just enough to keep from getting whipped. They wanted devoted, hard-working, responsible slaves who identified their fortunes with the fortunes of their masters. Planters sought to imbue slaves with a "Protestant" work ethic and to transform that ethic from a state of mind into a high level of production. "My negros have their name up in the neighbourhood," wrote Bennet Barrow, "for making more than any one else & they think Whatever they do is better than any body Else." Such an attitude could not be beaten into slaves. It had to be elicited.

Much of the managerial attention of planters was focused on the problem of motivating their hands. To achieve the desired response they developed a wide-ranging system of rewards. Some rewards were directed toward improving short-run performance. Included in this category were prizes for the individual or the gang with the best picking record on a given day or during a given week. The prizes were such items as clothing, tobacco, and whiskey; sometimes the prize was cash. Good immediate performance was also rewarded with unscheduled holidays or with trips to town on weekends. When slaves worked at times normally set aside for rest, they received extra pay – usually in cash and at the rate prevailing in the region for hired labor. Slaves who were performing well were permitted to work on their own account after normal hours at such tasks as making shingles or weaving baskets, articles which they could sell either to their masters or to farmers in the neighborhood.

Some rewards were directed at influencing behavior over periods of intermediate duration. The rewards in this category were usually paid at the end of the year. Year-end bonuses, given either in goods or cash, were frequently quite substantial. Bennet Barrow, for example, distributed gifts averaging between $15 and $20 per slave family in both 1839 and 1840. The amounts received by particular slaves were proportional to their performance. It should be noted that $20 was about a fifth of national per capita income in 1840. A bonus of the same relative magnitude today would be in the neighborhood of $1,000.

Masters also rewarded slaves who performed well with patches of land ranging up to a few acres for each family. Slaves grew marketable crops on these lands, the proceeds of which accrued to them. On the Texas plantation of Julian S. Devereux, slaves operating such land produced as much as two bales of cotton per patch. Devereux marketed their crop along with his own. In a good year some of the slaves earned in excess of $100 per annum for their families. Devereux set up accounts to which he credited the proceeds of the sales. Slaves drew on these accounts when they wanted cash or when they wanted Devereux to purchase clothing, pots, pans, tobacco, or similar goods for them.

Occasionally planters even devised elaborate schemes for profit sharing with their slaves. William Jemison, an Alabama planter, entered into the following agreement with his bondsmen.

[Y]ou shall have two thirds of the corn and cotton made on the plantation and as much of the wheat as will reward you for the sowing it. I also furnish you with provisions for this year. When your crop is gathered, one third is to be set aside for me. You are then to pay your overseer his part and pay me what I furnish, clothe yourselves, pay your own taxes and doctor's fee with all expenses of the farm. You are to be no expense to me, but render to me one third of the produce and what I have loaned you. You have the use of the stock and plantation tools. You are to return them as good as they are and the plantation to be kept in good repair, and what clear money you make shall be divided equally amongst you in a fair proportion agreeable to the services rendered by each hand. There will be an account of all lost time kept, and those that earn most shall have most.

There was a third category of rewards. These were of a long-term nature, often requiring the lapse of a decade or more before they paid off. Thus, slaves had the opportunity to rise within the social and economic hierarchy that existed under bondage. Field hands could become artisans or drivers. Artisans could be allowed to move from the plantation to town where they would hire themselves out. Drivers could move up to the position of head driver or overseer. Climbing the economic ladder brought not only social status, and sometimes more freedom; it also had significant payoffs in better housing, better clothing, and cash bonuses.

Little attention has hitherto been paid to the manner in which planters selected the slaves who were to become the artisans and managers. In some cases boys were apprenticed to carpenters, blacksmiths, or some similar craftsmen when they were in their early teens, as was typically done with whites. For slaves, this appears to have been the exception rather than the rule. Analysis of occupational data derived from probate and plantation records reveals an unusual distribution of ages among slave artisans. Slaves in their twenties were substantially underrepresented, while slaves in their forties and fifties were overrepresented. This age pattern suggests that the selection of slaves for training in the crafts was frequently delayed until slaves reached their late twenties, or perhaps even into the thirties.

Normally this would be an uneconomical policy, since the earlier an investment is made in occupational training, the more years there are to reap the returns on that investment. Slavery altered this pattern by shifting the authority to determine occupational investments from the parents to the masters. In free societies, kinship is usually the primary basis for determining which members of the new generation are trained in skilled occupations. But the slaveholder lacked the vested interests of a parent. He could, therefore, treat entry into the skilled occupations as a prize that was to be claimed by the most deserving, regardless of family background. The extra effort put forth by young field hands who competed for these jobs appears to have more than offset the loss in returns due to the curtailed period over which the occupational investment was amortized. We do not mean to suggest that kinship played no role in the intergenerational transfer of skills among slaves. We merely wish to stress that its role was significantly reduced as compared with free society.

Another long-run reward was freedom through manumission. The chance of achieving this reward was, of course, quite low. Census data indicate that in 1850 the manumission rate was just 0.45 per thousand slaves. Manumission could be achieved either through the philanthropy of a master or through an agreement which permitted a slave to buy himself out. Sometimes gifts of freedom were bestowed while the master was still alive. More often it was a bequest set forth in a will. Self-purchase involved arrangements under which slaves were permitted to purchase themselves with money that they earned from work on their own account, or in the case of skilled urban slaves, by increasing the share of income which the artisan paid to his master. Some skilled slaves were able to accumulate enough capital to purchase their freedom within a decade. For others the period extended to two decades or more. Little information is currently available on the prices at which such transactions were concluded. It is not known whether slaves involved in self-purchase were generally forced to pay a price in excess of their market value.

From the foregoing it is clear that slaves did not all live at a uniform level of income. The elaborate system of rewards erected by planters introduced substantial variation in the slave standard of living. Much work remains to be done before it will be possible to reconstruct with reasonable accuracy the full range of the slave income distribution. It has been possible, however, to estimate the "basic income" of slaves in 1850. This, together with some fragmentary evidence on the higher incomes of slaves, will at least suggest the range of income variation that prevailed.

By "basic income" we mean the value of the food, clothing, shelter, and medical care furnished to slaves. The average value of the expenditure on these items for an adult male in 1850 was about $48.00. The most complete information on the extra earnings of field hands comes from several Texas plantations. The leading hands on these estates frequently earned between $40 and $110 per year above basic income through the sale of cotton and other products raised on their patches. This experience was not unique to Texas. On one Alabama plantation, eight hands produced cotton that earned them an average of $71 each, with the high man collecting $96. On still another plantation the average extra earnings of the thirteen top hands was $77. These scattered cases suggest that the ratio of high earnings to basic earnings among field hands was in the neighborhood of 2.5.

When the incomes of artisans are taken into account, the spread in slave earnings became still wider. The top incomes earned by craftsmen must have been several times basic income. This is implied by the high prices which artisans had to pay to buy themselves out. The average price of a prime-aged blacksmith was about $1,700 in 1850. Thus, a thirty-year-old man who was able to buy himself out in a decade probably earned in the neighborhood of $170 per year over subsistence. This suggests a ratio of artisan to basic income of about 4.5.

The highest annual figure we have been able to uncover for extra earnings by a field hand in a single year is $309. Aham, the Alabama slave whose sales of peaches, apples, and cotton yielded this sum, had accumulated enough capital over the years so that in 1860 he held notes on loans totaling over $2,400. The ratio of Aham's agricultural income to basic income is 7.4. If we assume that Aham earned 6 percent, or $144, on the loans, the ratio would rise to 10.4. The highest income above maintenance that we have found for an artisan is $500. In this case the ratio of earned to basic income is 11.4.

While the reward structure created much more room for upward mobility within the slave system than is usually supposed, the scope of opportunity should not be exaggerated. The highest levels of attainment were irrevocably foreclosed to slaves. The entrepreneurial talent obviously possessed by bondsmen such as Aham could not be used to catapult them into the stewardship of great businesses as long as they remained slaves. No slave, regardless of his gifts, could aspire to political position. No man of letters – there were slaves who acquired considerable erudition – could ever hold an appointment in the faculty of a southern university as long as he was a bondsman. The entrepreneurial genius had to settle for lingering in the shadow of the master on whose protection he was dependent. The man of letters could go no further than the position of tutor to the children of a benevolent and enlightened planter. It was on the talented, the upper crust of slave society, that deprivations of the peculiar institution hung most heavy. This, perhaps, explains why it was that the first to flee to northern lines as Yankee advances corroded the Rebel positions were not the ordinary field hands, but the drivers and the artisans.

As previously noted, a part of the income that slaves produced was expropriated from them. Determination of the average annual amount of this expropriation over the life cycle of the entire slave population is an extremely complex matter. For the rate of expropriation differed from slave to slave, as well as from year to year for particular slaves. Figure 9 presents the average accumulated value or, in the language of economists,

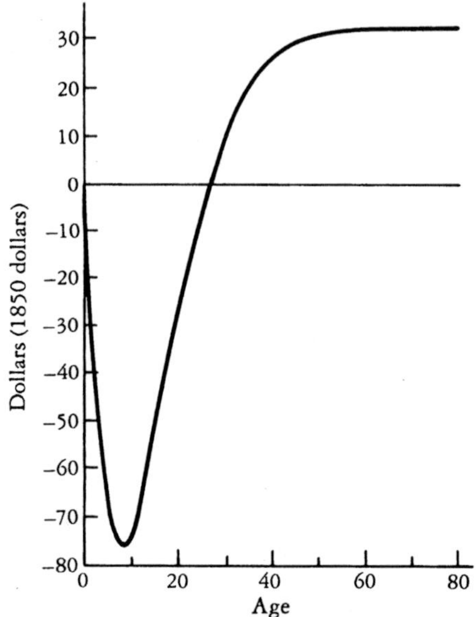

Figure 9. The average accumulated value (expected present value) of the income expropriated from slaves over the course of the life cycle.

the "expected present value" of the income that was expropriated at each age of the life cycle. Prior to age twenty-six, the accumulated expenditures by planters on slaves were greater than the average accumulated income which they took from them. After that age the reverse was true. Planters broke even early in the twenty-seventh year. Over the balance of the life cycle the accumulated or present value of the expropriation mounted, on average, to a total of $32. This last figure is 12 percent of the average present value of the income earned by slaves over their lifetimes. In other words, on average, 12 percent of the value of the income produced by slaves was expropriated by their masters.

The relatively late age at which planters broke even is of great significance and requires further discussion. Two factors are responsible for this lateness. The first is that the cost of capital was high in the South, and planters had to advance capital to cover the expense of rearing slaves for many years before they received a return from the labor of slaves. Second, because of the high mortality rates which prevailed for both black and white in the antebellum era, less than half the slaves lived to the break-even age. Fully 40 percent of the slaves died before age nineteen. Thus, a substantial part of the income taken from those slaves who survived into the later years was not an act of expropriation, but a payment required to cover the expenses of rearing children who failed to reach later ages. An additional part of the income taken from productive slaves, much smaller than that taken to cover child rearing, was used to sustain unproductive elderly slaves, as well as the incapacitated at all ages.

These intergenerational transfers of income were not, of course, limited to slave society. They took place among free men as well. For free men must also bear the cost of rearing the young, including those who fail to survive, as well as of supporting the sick and the aged. But among free men, the decision regarding the pattern of intergenerational transfers is made by parents rather than masters. The question thus arises, "How did masters alter the pattern of intergenerational transfers as compared to what it would have been if slaves had been free?" It is much easier to pose the question than to provide an answer. We do not yet have an answer to this question. We would, however, caution against two assumptions. It is not necessarily true that the substitution of planters for parents as decision makers on this issue had a large effect on the pattern of intergenerational transfers. Nor is it necessarily true that readers would consider all changes in the pattern of transfers made by the planters to have been negative. For example, planters spent more (a larger share of earnings) on the medical care of slave children than did the parents of freedmen during the decades following the Civil War.

The high break-even age also helps to explain why U.S. planters encouraged the fertility of slave women, while slaveowners in other parts of the hemisphere appear to have discouraged it. The crux of the matter is that child rearing was profitable only if the expected life of slaves at birth was greater than the break-even age. In the U.S., the life expectation of slaves exceeded the break-even age by more than a half decade. But in colonies such as Jamaica, available evidence suggests that life expectation fell below the break-even age, probably by at least a half decade.

Consequently, during most of the eighteenth century, masters in colonies such as Jamaica discouraged family formation and high fertility rates, preferring to buy adult slaves in Africa rather than to rear them. It was general policy to maintain an imbalance between the sexes with men outnumbering women by a ratio of 4 to 3. To further reduce the basis for stable families, planters encouraged polygamy among slaves by rewarding favored men with second and third wives. Thus, for the remainder of the population, the male-famale ratio was about 13 to 8. So large a disproportion between the sexes was bound to encourage sexual activity outside of the family and to reduce fertility. The care given to infants was quite poor compared with the South. Mothers were not encouraged to nurse their children; the southern practice of a 40 to 50 percent reduction of the workload of nursing mothers was not imitated in Jamaica. Further evidence of the neglect of pregnant women is to be found in the high rate of stillbirths. On one of the leading Jamaican plantations, 75 out of 345 births over a four-year period were stillborn. It has also been charged that abortion was both encouraged and widely practiced.

The 12 percent rate of expropriation reported on slave income falls well within the modern tax rate on workers. It has been estimated that about 30 percent of the income of workers at the poverty level is taken from them through sales, real estate, and income taxes. On the other hand, such workers, on average, receive payments and various services from the government which more than offset the tax burden. Were there any services received by slaves which offset the income expropriated from them? The answer is yes, but they cannot be quantified reliably at present. Slaves shared in the benefits of large-scale purchases made by the planter. Their clothing, for example, would have been more costly if purchased individually. Perhaps an even more important benefit was the saving on interest charges. Through the intervention of their masters slaves, in effect, were able to borrow at prime rates. Given the high interest charges which black sharecroppers suffered in the post–Civil War era, and the debt-peonage which enmeshed so many of them, the level of interest rates is not a small issue. Pending a more precise measurement of offsetting services, it seems warranted to place the average net rate of the expropriation of slave income at about 10 percent.

Expropriation is not, however, the only form of exploitation. As is shown in chapter 6, the *economic* burden imposed on slaves by other forms of exploitation probably exceeded that due to expropriation by a considerable margin.

6

Slavery

The progressive institution?

PAUL A. DAVID and PETER TEMIN

Time on the Cross[1] brings to a close an historiographic cycle that began with the publication of Ulrich Bonnell Phillips' *American Negro Slavery* (1918). According to Robert William Fogel and Stanley L. Engerman, the material conditions under which plantation slaves lived and worked compared favorably to those of free workers in the agriculture and industry of the time. Slavery, then, was not a physically harsh, labor-degrading regime. But neither was it an unprofitable system irrationally supported by paternalistic planters. It was good business practice in a highly competitive industry to care for and seek to make the most productive use of the competent and industrious workforce – particularly when abusive treatment of so valuable an asset would be at the economic expense of the slaveowners themselves. The system that had grown up around the holding of human chattels was not riddled with "internal economic contradictions" or verging upon "collapsing under its own weight." On the eve of the Civil War, slavery was a commercially vigorous and highly efficient mode of agricultural production, and the slave plantations formed the leading sector in the rapidly developing regional economy of the antebellum South.

Obviously, this is an ambitious and imposing book. Unlike most works of the new economic history, it has been featured in *Time*, *Newsweek* and many other popular journals and newspapers. The broad argument has been well projected to reach the general public, but the specific details of the authors' historical research are presented in a way

Source: Paul A. David and Peter Temin, "Slavery: The Progressive Institution?" *Journal of Economic History* (September 1974), 739–783. This article appears as a chapter of P. A. David et al., *Reckoning with Slavery: A Critical Study in the Quantitative History of American Negro Slavery*, New York: Oxford University Press, 1976. Reprinted with permission of the authors and the Economic History Association.

1. *Time on the Cross*, Vol. I: *The Economics of American Negro Slavery*, by Robert William Fogel and Stanley L. Engerman. 286 pp. Boston: Little, Brown and Company. $8.95; Vol. II; *Evidence and Methods – A Supplement*, by Robert William Fogel and Stanley L. Engerman, 267 pp. Boston: Little, Brown and Company, $12.50.

that precludes comprehension by that readership. Indeed, much of the underlying technical economic and statistical methodology has been made so unnecessarily difficult to follow that without further elucidation it will remain inaccessible to all but a tiny number of the book's readers.

It is obligatory upon our profession, therefore, to furnish general historians and other scholars with an appraisal of *Time on the Cross* as a technical work of economic history. This extended review essay is part of that process of evaluation. It contains four parts. The first undertakes to restate Fogel and Engerman's theses in the context of the recent literature on Negro slavery in America. Their arrestingly novel assertions about the material treatment of the slaves, and the relative efficiency of agriculture based on slave labor are shown to occupy a central place in the logical design, as well as in the rhetorical fabric of the book. The second and third parts of the review accordingly examine the evidence adduced in support of each of these assertions, taking them in turn. Although the authors' text forcefully argues that by comparison with free workers the plantation slaves were materially well-off and highly productive, both claims appear to lack an adequate scientific foundation. This is not just a matter of undue literary license having been taken in restating esoteric technical findings for popular consumption. The seemingly "neutral" numbers generated by Fogel and Engerman's quantitative methods carry a persistent bias, portraying slaveowners, and the conditions and work performance of the blacks they held in bondage, in a more favorable light than would be cast by a more complete analysis.

The fourth and concluding part of our review turns from technical criticism of the evidence actually adduced, and questions the basic conceptual approach Fogel and Engerman have applied in re-evaluating the economic performance of the peculiar institution. Paradoxically, the authors of *Time on the Cross* appear to have adopted a framework of analysis that leads them systematically to overlook the economic essence of slavery, namely that the slaves lost the freedom to exercise choices as producers and consumers.

The argument in context

Fogel and Engerman do not help the reader to place their work on the economics of American Negro slavery within its larger historiographic context. They do not suggest that many of the "corrections" they would make in the neoabolitionist portrayal of the peculiar institution form part of the broader reinterpretive trend in recent contributions to black history. The authors are promoting a particular methodological approach which they fervently oppose to the conventional, "un-social-scientific" study of history. This mission disposes them to gloss over the ebb and flow of debate in the historical literature of the last three decades, and to construct a fictitious protagonist against whom the arsenal of quantitative methods can be shown off as totally devastating, and hence "revolutionary" in its impact upon the interpretation of slavery. Even C. Vann Woodward has felt obliged to record, in an otherwise uncritical review,[2] that no historian has ever simultaneously held all the positions in "the traditional interpretation" against which Fogel and Engerman inveigh. Yet it is only against the actual historiographic background that the nature of their achievement can be properly grasped and assessed.

The considerable scholarship of Phillips and his followers was devoted to rehabilitating the progressive image of white supremacist society in the antebellum South; it provided a generally sympathetic and sometimes blatantly apologetic portrayal of slaveholders as a paternalistic breed of men. These planters, it turned out, had borne the economic (and ultimately the military) burden of trying to maintain a commercially moribund but socially benign institution; they had contributed to the making of America the control and instruction that was required for the gradual cultural and industrial acclimatization of inherently incompetent African savages. Through the perfection of plantation slavery the masters had managed a difficult problem of racial adjustment which had been thrust upon them by historical circumstances.

The reaction of the late 1930s and 1940s against the sort of racial bigotry which drew support from Phillips' work effected a complete reversal of the moral light in which the question of slavery was viewed. The vantage point correspondingly shifted from that of the master to that of his slave. The reversal culminated in Kenneth M. Stampp's *The Peculiar Institution* (1956), which rejected both the characterization of blacks as a biologically and culturally inferior, childlike people, and the depiction of the white planters as paternal Cavaliers coping with a vexing social problem that was not of their own making. The slaveholders, said Stampp, had built the system consciously, bit by bit, decision by decision. They had done so for profit, and they had been duly rewarded. Despite the unspeakable oppression to which the resulting regime had subjected the slaves held within it, American blacks somehow had remained uncrushed in spirit. Their resistance was not that of mass rebellion, of vain insurrection, but a day-to-day affair: the meek, smiling ones who many thought were "contented though irresponsible" had protested their bondage "by shirking their duties, injuring the crops, feigning illness, and disrupting the routine." In the end the slave had remained unbroken as a person, "a troublesome property."

In 1958 Alfred Conrad and John R. Meyer's now-renowned paper on

2. "The Jolly Institution," *New York Review of Books*, XXI (May 2, 1974), 3.

the economics of slavery provided rigorous support for Stampp's (and before him Lewis C. Gray's) insistence that the ownership of slaves represented a profitable private investment in the antebellum South. But it was Stanley Elkins' *Slavery: A Problem in American Institutional and Intellectual Life* (1959) that carried the rejection of Phillips still further. The personal and societal consequences flowing from the trauma of enslavement and the deprivations of slavery could not be comprehended within the terms of a mere point-by-point response to Phillips' account of a fundamentally genial regime rather like a boarding school. Think instead, suggested Elkins, of the phenomenon of mass personality distortion produced by a total institution like the Nazi concentration camp. Unfettered capitalism had created on the mainland of North America a peculiarly harsh and hopeless system of slavery, which left the typical bondsman broken in spirit – a psychologically "infantilized" inmate described by the stereotype of "Sambo."

From this high-water mark reached in the late 1950s, the tide of the anti-Phillips reaction began to recede. Comparative studies of slavery in the New World contradicted Elkins' presupposition that the Sambo stereotype was a peculiarity of the North American historical experience.[3] Doubts were raised about his assertion that the system of slavery developed there was – in its actual operation, as distinct from its legal provisions and restraints – significantly more "closed," and correspondingly more harsh than that which had evolved in Latin America. The a priori plausibility of this last comparative proposition appeared to be still further reduced by the results of Philip Curtin's (1969) meticulous examination of the available quantitative evidence relating to the Atlantic slave trade.[4] Of the Africans carried to the New World, all but a small fraction were absorbed in the comparatively high mortality environments of the Carribean sugar islands and Brazil; those brought to the northern mainland not only reproduced themselves, but grew in number at a rate not very different from the free, white population.

The emphasis given by Stampp and Elkins to the masters' systematic recourse to physical cruelty and unrelieved material deprivations – in pursuit of the related objectives of profit and psychological domination of the blacks – also came in for criticism from Eugene D. Genovese. In *The Political Economy of Slavery* (1965) he suggested that the former interpretive emphasis improperly deflected attention from the precapi-

3. Cf., e.g., the essays by Sidney W. Mintz, Marvin Harris, David Brion Davis, Arnold S. Sio, and others in Laura Foner and Eugene D. Genovese, eds., *Slavery in the New World* (Englewood Cliffs, N.J.: Prentice-Hall, 1969).
4. Phillip D. Curtin, *The Atlantic Slave Trade: A Census* (Madison: University of Wisconsin Press, 1969).

talistic, aristocratic, patriarchal aspects of the southern slaveowning class, and obscured the many paternalistic features of plantation life. Subsequently, in a bold reversal of Elkins, Genovese argued that paternalism constituted the more serious, more insidious mode of assault upon the autonomy of black culture and the slave's personality.

This broadening line of counter-argument indicated that Elkins, and perhaps also Stampp, had under-represented the extent of the psychological and cultural breathing-space which had been allowed American Negro slaves. J. W. Blassingame's *The Slave Community* (1972), based largely on a cautious re-examination of published slave narratives, portrays plantation life as holding out positive incentives as well as providing negative inducements to cooperate in the ostensible commercial undertakings of the organization. Within the structure of controls, moreover, the slaves found it possible to maintain greater stability of family life than has often been supposed, as well as to create and preserve their own religion, folklore and music.

However much the vantage point and the moral tone diverged from that of Phillips, the paternalistic aspects which were so prominent in his description of plantation life had thus begun to make their way back into the historical literature during the 1960's. Recognition of these outwardly more genial qualities of the peculiar institution now was enlisted in the effort to retrieve for American *blacks* some "usable past," some reconstruction of history that would leave them more than victims of a social tragedy, brutally infantilized, cut off from their cultural roots, dependent upon white society.[5]

For this purpose, however, a full rehabilitation of the system of slavery did not seem required. Indeed, Genovese's attention to planter paternalism was initially coupled with his dismissal of Stampp's and Conrad and Meyer's point about the private profitability of slaveownership as unilluminating; in *The Political Economy of Slavery* he sought to recast in Marxian terms the traditional Phillipsian representation of slavery as an economically dysfunctional system of production. In the resulting account of southern "backwardness," the derived precapitalist ideology of the ruling planter class, the unsuitability of the mode of plantation organization for the conduct of diversified farming, and slavery's distorting effects upon the distribution of income and the structure of demand within the region, all served to obstruct the economic modernization of the South. The slaveholders made, and ultimately fought vainly to preserve, a quasi-feudal political and social order based upon a distorted, non-progressive economy; the era of the planters' hegemony

5. Cf. David B. Davis, "Slavery and the Post-World War II Historians," *Daedalus* (Spring 1974), 9–10, for this imputation of purpose.

and tutelage could hardly have been expected to provide Afro-Americans any useful preparation for assuming a place in modern urban-industrial society, even if it had allowed them some considerable decency and dignity in the terms of their bondage.

Time on the Cross has finished the work of up-ending Elkins and Stampp. It asserts that through the unseen operation of competitive market forces a private vice, the planter's greed for profit, became a (comparative) social virtue. Unfettered capitalism in America led to a form of slavery which was peculiarly benign insofar as concerns the social and material circumstances of its human chattel. Equipped with this explanation for the manifestations of paternalism so central to Phillips' view of plantation life, the authors turn on Genovese and proceed to marshall the research of many other economic historians in order to contradict his representation of the antebellum southern economy as necessarily backward and stagnant.

Much of this second aspect of their thesis therefore should be familiar enough to professional readers. Richard Easterlin's (1961) compilation of regional income estimates for the United States had shown us that the South was not falling behind the rest of the nation in the period 1840–1860, and had attained high levels of GNP per capita on the eve of the Civil War. Charles Wesley's (1927) work on the urban Negro labor force, Robert Evans' (1962) study of the slave hire market, and, more recently, Robert Starobin's *Industrial Slavery in the Old South* (1970) provided ample evidence that slaves could be, and were, utilized in non-agrarian pursuits. Studies of the distribution of income and wealth in the antebellum period by Robert Gallman (1969) and Lee Soltow (1971) suggested that the degree of inequality among the free population was not notably greater in the South than in the North. The effect of the presence of the planter class in the rural South was counterbalanced by the comparative smallness of the southern urban population, urban wealth-holding being typically more concentrated than rural irrespective of region.[6]

To this sweeping revision of Genovese's picture of the slaveholders'

6. Cf. R. A. Easterlin, "Regional Income Trends, 1840–1950," in Seymour Harris, ed., *American Economic History* (New York: McGraw-Hill, 1961); C. H. Wesley, *Negro Labor in the United States, 1850–1925* (New York: Vanguard Press, 1927); R. Evans, Jr., "The Economics of American Negro Slavery," in *Aspects of Labor Economics* (Princeton: National Bureau of Economic Research, 1962); R. S. Starobin, *Industrial Slavery in the Old South* (New York: Oxford University Press, 1970); R. E. Gallman, "Trends in the Size Distribution of Wealth in the Nineteenth Century: Some Speculations," in *Six Papers on the Size Distribution of Wealth and Income*, ed. Lee Soltow (New York: Columbia University Press, 1969); L. Soltow, "Economic Inequality in the United States in the Period from 1790 to 1860," *Journal of Economic History*, XXXI (December 1971), 822–839.

economic milieu, *Time on the Cross* adds two arrestingly bold and essentially novel propositions. Both have a close connection with the authors' contention that the material conditions of life and labor were not especially harsh or degrading to the typical plantation slave. First, it is their view that the consumption standards at which slaves were maintained compared favorably with those of contemporaneous free agricultural labor in the South, and even approached the economic condition of urban industrial workers in the North during the latter half of the nineteenth century. Were this so, the direct transfer of income (to the free population as a whole) effected by slavery, itself could not have caused any very pronounced additional skewing of the overall distribution of income within the South.[7]

The second novel proposition is that as an agricultural system plantation slavery was more efficient in its use of the factors of production than the free family farm typical of the North. Fogel and Engerman assign economies of scale only partial responsibility for the greater measured productivity of southern plantation agriculture. Instead they argue that the comparative industriousness and personal efficiency of the Afro-American laborers vis-à-vis the free work force must have been the principal cause underlying their findings on this score. The conclusion complements the proposition that the typical slave was a well-cared-for productive asset.

Having stood both Elkins and Stampp on their heads as far as concerns the harshness of slavery under pure capitalism, and having concluded that black bondsmen must have been more efficient workers than free whites, Fogel and Engerman are thus in a position to dismiss the Sambo stereotype as utterly without objective basis in either the circumstances or behavior of the typical slave. They brand it as merely another pernicious myth, created as much by the latent prejudices of abolitionist propagandists as by the open bigotry of southern white supremacists. Even Frederick Law Olmsted gets some knocks here for "racial prejudices" and "northern chauvinism." Moreover, *Time on the Cross* is not above detecting subtle traces of lingering racism, or at best an insensitivity to the poisoning of race relations, in those neoabolitionist historians who would perpetuate the denigration of blacks' performance

7. The wealth distribution obviously was more concentrated than it would have been had the blacks owned themselves (had they not been the property of others), and been able to accumulate other forms of wealth. But it is usually argued that the effect on the level and composition of effective demand primarily are those exercised by the distribution of income. Fogel and Engerman's (Vol. I, pp. 253–254) brief discussion of slaves' consumption needs and the market for industrial goods seems to accept this emphasis on *income* distribution.

as slaves by attributing it not to biological inferiority but, alternatively, to mass infantilization or evasive non-collaboration.[8]

The paradox of *Time on the Cross* is that its laudable announced aim of rectifying a historiographic injustice and restoring to American Negroes today a source of justifiable pride in their cultural heritage has led the authors to the excesses of an utterly sanguine reappraisal of the peculiar institution. The commercial success of capitalistic slavery somehow emerges as the most fitting subject for modern black pride. Few readers will miss the irony that this book, whose passionate title is meant to convey the depth of the authors' moral condemnation of slavery, in substance actually transcends even U. B. Phillips' rehabilitative intentions. Cool, detached social science, we are told,[9] requires one to face up to the fact that Negro slavery in its time was a "vigorous, deeply entrenched, and rapidly growing economic system" – indeed, putting "purely moral" considerations aside, a comparatively benign institutional arrangement worthy of a progressive America. The revelation of what Fogel and Engerman construe to have been "the record of black achievement under adversity" seemingly demands nothing less than a historical work "which would," to quote David Brion Davis, "in most respects bring a smile of approval from the grim lips of John C. Calhoun."[10]

The keystones of this reinterpretive edifice, and the proximate sources of the rhetorical confusions which impart to the book a puzzling and paradoxical quality, are not hard to locate. They are found in the assertions Fogel and Engerman advance concerning the material conditions of the slaves' lives, and the latters' willing, industrious efficiency as workers. These two propositions, as we already have seen, underlie the truly novel arguments which *Time on the Cross* contributes to revising the macro-economic portrait of the antebellum South as a backward agrarian

8. "The principal cause of the persistence of the myth of black incompetence in American historiography is racism." Thus begins the section of the text headed "Toward an Explanation for the Persistence of the Myth of Black Incompetence," on p. 223 of Vol. I. Eight pages later: "What, of course, is common to Stampp and Elkins is agreement on the characteristics of slave behavior: slaves lie, steal, feign illness, behave childishly, and shirk their duties. Indeed, this characterization has been one of the enduring constants in the literature on slavery." The innuendos carried by the wording of Fogel and Engerman's excruciatingly labored critique of Stampp's *Peculiar Institution*, in Appendix C, are especially unfortunate:

> Stampp's inadequate definition of black accomplishments under slavery may have been related to his approach to the issue of racism. While Stampp unequivocally rejected the contention that Negroes were *biologically* inferior to whites, he did not consider how [racism] might have affected the views of both the "eyewitnesses" and the historians that he invoked as authorities....Stampp reported as fact, untinged by racism, Olmsted's description of slaves as "chronic" malingerers.... (Vol. II, pp. 234–235. Emphasis added.)

9. *Time on the Cross*, Vol. II, p. 16.
10. "Slavery and the Post-World War II Historians," p. 11.

region. Further, taken in combination with Stampp's and Conrad and Meyer's point about the private profitability of slaveownership, these same propositions form the empirical basis upon which Fogel and Engerman construct new characterizations for the *dramatis personae.* The patriarchal Cavalier has been turned into the shrewd master, an enlightened capitalistic manager of personnel. And Sambo's place is now occupied by the keen, "achieving" slave who strives for some measure of self-improvement within the considerable breathing space allowed him by competitive capitalism.[11]

What evidence and arguments support these two tenets of Fogel and Engerman's bold reinterpretation? Are these, perhaps, the "most telling revisions" which "turn on technical mathematical points, points which despite their obscurity are vital to the correct description and interpretation of the slave economy"? Just how have they been derived from "the new techniques and hitherto neglected sources" which the authors rather dauntingly allude to in their opening chapter on "Slavery and the Cliometric Revolution"?

Alas, the full text of *Time on the Cross* may be studied endlessly without learning the answers to these questions. To understand how this could be, one first must grasp the format of the book. It is presented in two volumes, the first (Volume I) being the text and an index thereto, the other (Volume II) comprising a bibliography and various appendices – including, as Appendix B, an extended set of technical notes pertinent to assertions made in the text.

Although the reader of the text is initially cautioned to "keep in mind [the] distinction between the principal findings of the cliometricians and our attempt to interpret them" (Vol. 1, p. 10), this is not so easily done when only "interpretations" are being presented. We do not allude here to the deep epistemological problems raised by Fogel and Engerman's desire to distinguish cleanly between findings of "fact" and their "interpretation." A more immediate difficulty is that the published findings of other historians, as well as their new empirical results described in Appendix B, are not invariably reported in the same terms by the narrative discussion of the text. The "primary volume" of *Time on the Cross* offers a popularized account, which has only slightly more of a claim to faithfully represent the nature of the authors' own research contributions than were it to have been prepared by someone else altogether.

11. The role of these new characterizations in the overall structure of *Time on the Cross*, as well as the evidence adduced for them, are discussed in P. A. David and P. Temin, "Capitalist Masters, Bourgeois Slaves," *Journal of Interdisciplinary History* (forthcoming, Winter 1975).

Fogel and Engerman's text itself is utterly unencumbered by documentation. Curiously, conventional historians who initially have reviewed the first volume seem to have been so unnerved by "the rattle of electronic equipment" and the tramping legions of research assistants "heard off stage" that they failed to complain of this omission. The absence of footnotes, bibliographic citations, discussion of sources, explicit mention of methodological problems, in short, of the standard critical apparatus of works of professional history is intended on this occasion "to encourage the widest possible discussion of the findings of the cliometricians" (Vol. I, pp. 11–12). But a heavy burden thereby has been placed upon any scholar who undertakes to inform "popular" discussions by critically examining these findings and relating them to the authors' conclusions.

The problem is that the second volume, subtitled *Evidence and Methods* simply does not set out the bushels of footnotes which, one might imagine, had studded an original, unpruned version of the text. The author's introductory essay (Appendix A) on the roles of ideology, humanism and science in the historical study of slavery discloses that only as much as they have been able to learn about slavery using the method of the social sciences, and no more, has been set down in Appendix B. Yet, to produce the reinterpretation offered by their first volume, something more was needed: "We were obliged to invoke assumptions which, though plausible, cannot be verified at present, and to rely on additional evidence which is too fragmentary to be subjected to systematic statistical tests" (Vol. II, 4). One has to turn to Appendix B remembering that it does not pretend to fully document the text, but only the portions (extensive as these are) for which Fogel and Engerman have felt able to present a suitably social-scientific basis.

And on these, Appendix B proves to be tough going indeed. Throughout the appendices the authors deploy an elaborate, sometimes bewildering system of internal cross-references and numerical bibliographic citations whose general effect is accurately conveyed by the following item.

> 4.11.1 The various points on the curve in figure 41 are the values of the right-hand terms of equation 4.7 for each value of t from 0 to 75. The values of the variables entering equation 4.7 were estimated in the manner described in 3.4.9 and 4.10.1 except that an allowance of 26 percent was added to basic income to cover the average amount of "extra" income received by slaves (see 6.7.1.2). The resulting figure ($42.99) was the average value of M. Atwater's weights [366, pp. 52–53] were used to convert the average value of *M* into age and sex specific values. (Vol. II, p. 120)

Quite obviously, Appendix B has not been written for anyone to sit down and read. It is neither a full set of conventional footnotes nor a self-contained technical monograph that can justly be evaluated on its own merits. It does not make available to other historians any of the original data from the probate records or the manuscript censuses upon which Fogel and Engerman have drawn. Far from undertaking to explain to conventional historians the cliometric methods which the authors espouse, the logic of their economic arguments (and their demographic analyses, about which we will say little) is made unnecessarily hard to follow, and the descriptions of the actual quantitative methods employed oscillate between the extremes of frustrating imprecision and ostentatious overformalism.

But, the details of Fogel and Engerman's difficult second volume, and the mysteries of Appendix B in particular, must be our main preoccupation. For it is to these that one is directed by the sorts of questions which the professional historian – and, most of all, the methodologically threatened "conventional" historian – will rightly want to have answered before he goes on to consider the more subtle problems of historical interpretation posed by *Time on the Cross.*[12] Clearly it is important to know how seriously to take the authors' prefatory admonitions to keep in mind the difference between the cliometric "findings" discussed by the supporting technical volume, and their attempt in the text at a broader interpretation of the historical experience of American Negro slavery. But it is no less vital to determine whether the claim implied in this warning can be safely accepted. Has cliometrics really provided startling "findings of fact" about which there is little room for argument? Do the key empirical propositions advanced by Fogel and Engerman – those regarding the comparatively favorable material conditions of life, and the greater efficiency of slave labor – possess an objective "scientific" status that derives from the methods employed in securing them?

The remainder of this review is geared to respond to these questions. From the detailed examination of the authors' evidence and methods on the material treatment and the productive efficiency of slaves, presented in the two following sections, we think it will become apparent just how unwarranted it is to accept their empirical "findings" as scientifically incontrovertible. But the closing section of the review takes up the still more fundamental point that many of the defects revealed by a close reading of the supporting, technical volume turn out to be conceptual rather than narrowly methodological. No greater degree of analytical

12. C. Vann Woodward, observing that Fogel and Engerman's second volume, *Evidence and Methods* "is given over to documentation, defense of method, algebraic equations, tables and graphs, and computer language [of which we find none] beyond the comprehension of laymen," voices this hope: "Their findings, their data, and their methods should have the most thorough and unsparing criticism . . . , especially [by] those who speak their own language," "The Jolly Institution," pp. 3, 6.

rigor or meticulousness of scholarship on the authors' part could really have redeemed the claim to have arrived at an ethically neutral economic appraisal of the "performance" of a social institution, let alone the institution of chattel slavery. The entire conception of producing a "scientifically objective" or "value free" reappraisal of the economic welfare consequences of slavery seems to us to be peculiarly ill-founded. For the ethical and behavioral premises upon which modern economic welfare analysis rests are immediately inconsonant with the degree of personal involition which remains the defining attribute of the institution in question. In this respect, we shall argue, the strain of paradox and confusion which runs through *Time on the Cross* involves more than a mere problem of rhetoric.

Methods and evidence on material treatment

The material side of the slaves' treatment is approached by Fogel and Engerman from three vantage points. First, indexes of the absolute standard of living are matched against those relating to free workers in other regions and periods during the nineteenth century. Second, the average income retained by slaves – which is to say the value of their consumption – is compared to the income of free agricultural workers. Finally, the relationship between the value of slave consumption and slave production is considered, indicating what part of the fruits of their labor was taken from them. In taking up these points in turn, fullest and most careful attention will be reserved for the third, since it best illustrates the way that the text of *Time on the Cross* simplifies for "popular" presentation some intricate, novel, and far from uncontroversial quantitative analyses which the authors report in their "secondary" volume.

The material conditions under which Negro slaves lived are suggested by several indexes: dietary standards, clothing allotments, housing space, medical care, and rates of mortality. The attempt at a systematic quantitative reappraisal is carried furthest in the case of the first of these, and the findings reported by Fogel and Engerman on this score are the most original as well as the most impressive. No serious historian of American Negro slavery has suggested that black bondsmen typically were kept at a starvation level. Stampp decided that instances "of deliberate stinting of rations were fortunately few; and the imbalance of the average slave's diet resulted from ignorance more often than penuriousness" on the master's part.[13] Still, one may be surprised by Fogel and Engerman's conclusion (Vol. I, pp. 113–114) that slaves in 1860 had excellent diets

13. *The Peculiar Institution*, p. 288.

by the standards of the time – nutritionally adequate even by modern standards (thanks in large measure to the richness of the sweet potato in calcium and vitamins A and C), and in caloric content surpassing by ten percent the average diet of free Americans in 1879.

Rather than relying on the information that can be culled from plantation records, instructions to overseers, or the southern agricultural press, the authors have developed figures for the food quantities comprising the average slave diet on a systematically selected sample of plantations, by making use of the so-called "disappearance method." In their variant of this statistical procedure, the total amount of each food item available for slave consumption is obtained as a residual from data on production and estimates of other utilization for the representative plantation, and the result is then divided by the representative number of resident plantation slaves. Thus "other utilization" should include not only what was set aside for seed and livestock feed and what was shipped from the plantation in processed or unprocessed form, but also some allowance for the "homegrown" foodstuffs retained for use at the table of the plantation's white residents. To deal with the difficult problems of estimating off-plantation sales of foodstuffs and non-slave consumption, Fogel and Engerman have selected (from the Parker-Gallman 1860 manuscript census sample) a sub-sample of plantations designed to minimize the quantitative importance to these non-slave consumption uses:

> In order to be able to separate free from slave consumption, we derived our estimates from a sample of large slave plantations (over 50 slaves). In order to separate consumption on these plantations from the sales of surpluses to cities, we further restricted the sample to plantations that were in counties at least 50 wagon miles away from the nearest cities. (Vol. II, p. 94)

For good measure, however, they reduce the estimated production of beef and pork, which well might have been salted and barrelled for shipment to more distant markets, and they deduct generous additional allowances for the consumption of meat and milk by the resident white population. (Cf. Vol. II, p. 95.)

Two questions about this procedure come immediately to mind. First, the derived figures purport to show the average slave diet. Not all slaves would have consumed this diet, and the relationship between the average diet and the diet of any particular slave is unclear. The procedures used by Fogel and Engerman could easily be extended to provide an estimate of variance in the average diet from one plantation to the next, but other methods would have to be employed to determine seasonal and longer temporal variations. Fogel and Engerman have followed Conrad and Meyer's methodological lead here, in concentrating on the slave *system* rather than individual slaves or plantations. Nonetheless, a little more attention to individual variations in the quality of slave life would have been illuminating.

Second, given that the authors make generous allowances for the food consumption of the resident whites, the rationale for restricting the sample to large plantations, holding more than 50 slaves, is not entirely persuasive. Less than one fourth of all slaves lived on plantations in this size class, according to the statistics compiled by Lewis C. Gray (cf. Vol. II, p. 144 for Gray's tabulations). Further work is needed to show that the average diet estimated by the disappearance method for this sample was typical of the standard at which the whole slave population lived. Since Fogel and Engerman find that there were considerable economies of scale in plantation agriculture (Vol. I, pp. 192–193), the suspicion may be entertained that slaves on large plantations ate better than some others.[14]

Such reservations notwithstanding, it would appear that the estimates Fogel and Engerman present for the diet of slaves in 1860 are considerably better grounded than the 1879 estimates for the free population with which they are compared. M. K. Bennett and R. H. Peirce, the authors of the study from which Fogel and Engerman obtained the latter figures, also employed the "disappearance method" in estimating per capita consumption of cereals and other vegetable foodstuffs from the United States. But 30 percent of the estimated calorie consumption was derived from estimated consumption of "major animal products" about which Bennett and Peirce themselves express the most serious reservations.[15] In approximating per capita consumption of beef, lean pork, and bacon and salt side around 1879, they simply extrapolated their 1909/1911 estimates on the per capita ratios of hogs on farms and cattle on farms without making any adjustments for changes in livestock weights or slaughter/inventory ratios. And in the case of whole milk consumption, a more important source of calories than any other among the animal products group, Bennett and Peirce have said that their figures (reproduced without comment by Fogel and Engerman, Vol. II, p. 94) represent "no more than reasoned conjectures" prepared "on the slenderest basis."

14. It may be noted that Fogel and Engerman's concentration on large plantations might have been suggested by Stampp's assertion that, in the quality or variety of food given, there were no "appreciable differences" in the practices of large and small slaveholders. But why take this for granted when all else is being cast into doubt?

15. Cf. Merrill K. Bennett and Rosamond H. Peirce, "Approximate Levels of Food Consumption Before 1909," [Food Research Institute (mimeo), Stanford, April 16, 1962] – A Supplement to "Change in the American National Diet, 1879–1959," *Food Research Institute Studies*, May 1961, pp. 95–119. The methodological supplement is referred to in the published Bennett–Peirce study which Fogel and Engerman cite in Vol. II, p. 98.

It is, therefore, somewhat unclear as to whether the figure of 4,100 calories given as the energy value of the typical slave diet and the 3,700 calories estimated for Americans in 1879 overstate or understate the actual average daily rates of food consumption. But the meaning one should attach to the results of this comparison – even if the true average calorie intakes of these two quite different populations had been established – is still less obvious than it might at first appear.

There is reason to suppose that on the average plantation slaves in every age- and sex-class (above age 10) were more active and consequently would have higher energy *requirements* than the corresponding groups in the free population.[16] This is so both because the age- and sex-specific labor force participation rates were higher for the slave population and because the kind of work in which rural, plantation slaves were engaged was physically more strenuous than that of the average member of the entire American workforce in 1879.[17] A modern textbook of physiology reports the following *occupational* differences in (adult male) energy requirements: 2,000–2,400 calories per day suffice for a shoemaker, 2,700–3,200 for a carpenter or mason, 3,200–4,100 for a (free) farm laborer, and so on, with over 5,000 calories being required by a lumberman.[18] Thus, after due adjustment for differences in demographic and occupational distributions it might well turn out that the averages reported by Fogel and Engerman are consistent with members of the slave population having a relatively *lower* caloric intake than comparable members of the free northern population.

Indeed, when caloric requirements are considered, it seems quite possible that southern slaves might have been suffering from some measure of food energy deprivation. Comparatively little seems to be known about the effect of food energy deprivation (calorie deficits) at levels which are neither drastic nor accompanied by serious shortage of essential nutrients. In some experiments made before World War I with healthy young male subjects, a gradual reduction of food energy intake to levels about a third below what they would have consumed resulted in the lowering of body weight and basal metabolism per unit of weight, combined with "perhaps a somewhat intangible saving of energy in the

16. Since we are not told anything about the age- and sex-composition of the slave population represented in the sample studied by Fogel and Engerman, we cannot say whether there were proportionately more adult males – whose calorie *requirements* exceed those of women and children – than was the case for the 1879 U.S. population as a whole.

17. In this connection it would be interesting to know what proportion of the slave force (on the large isolated plantations comprising Fogel and Engerman's sample) were house servants, rather than field hands.

18. Cf. the data from Tigerstedt's *Textbook of Physiology* reproduced by Henry C. Sherman, *Chemistry of Food and Nutrition*, 7th Edition (New York: Macmillan, 1946), p. 190.

muscular activities of everyday life."[19] Adoption of more languid movements, perhaps. Taking place under unstressed conditions, these organic adaptations reportedly "seemed to involve no mental or physical cost except for *a somewhat vague lowering of animal spirits*." At the risk of belaboring the point, it may be suggested that the "optimum" dietary standard for slaves which the rational southern planter is supposed to have sought to establish, would not be determined solely by considering the fuel *needs* of "the human engine." His slaves were also men, and setting their rations with a view to achieving some "lowering of animal spirits" could have effected a saving of supervisory and police costs – without entailing much loss in routine work performance.

These comparisons in terms of nutritional equivalents may be contrasted with Fogel and Engerman's comparison of the value of slave consumption with the value of free farm income. The difference is a substantive one, and we must be reminded that calories and welfare are only loosely related. It is well known that a nutritionally adequate diet can be secured today for far less than most of us spend on food. The extra expenses, we assume, are for satisfactions beyond calories and vitamins. Slaves, even if they were getting a nutritionally balanced diet, were not able to indulge these other food-related desires as were free men. Sweet potatoes and "pot-likker" may have been healthy, but were they the preferred diet of free men? More formally, free men allocated their food expenditures in accordance with their tastes. Since slaves were not able to reallocate their expenditures to the extent that free men could, the slave welfare represented by a calorie of food was less than welfare represented by a calorie in a free man's diet. One might well have asked: At what (low) levels of real income does the preponderance of carbohydrates and fats in diets of free men approach that found in the average diet of southern Negro slaves?

Using the value of consumption rather than nutritional equivalents does not completely remove this problem. But the ranking of foods reflected in market prices undoubtedly was closer to the tastes of slaves than the nutritional ranking, and the use of values gets closer to the question of slave welfare. Among the "Paradoxes of Forced Labor" presented by the final chapter of *Time on the Cross*, there appears the following puzzle:

> Odd as it may seem, the optimal combination [from the slaveholder's viewpoint] of force and pecuniary income was one that left slaves on large plantations with *more* pecuniary income per capita than they would have earned if they had been free small farmers. (Vol. I, p. 239)

19. Sherman, *Chemistry of Food and Nutrition*, pp. 195–196, reporting on the findings of G. F. Benedict and his co-investigators.

To support this, Fogel and Engerman immediately refer readers

> to appendix B, where it is shown that the average pecuniary income actually received by a *prime field hand* was roughly 15 percent greater than the income he would have received for his labor as a free agricultural worker. (*Loc. cit.*, emphasis added)

Appendix B however, says something else: "In other words, the labor income of the slave *family* was 15 percent larger than the labor income of the corresponding free *family*" (Vol. II, p. 158, emphasis added). What are we to make of the discrepancy?

What the authors have done is to construct a slave family of the same size (6.48 persons) and demographic structure as the typical free southern cotton belt farm represented in the Parker–Gallman sample drawn from the 1860 manuscript census. The estimated total slave income (basic maintenance and extra earnings from the produce of slave "patches") which a group of this size and composition would receive was then computed[20] and compared with the estimated *labor* income of the typical free southern farm in the cotton belt.

Now, it is generally acknowledged that the rates of labor force participation and the length of the hours worked per year were significantly greater for the women and children of the slave population than for corresponding members of free farm households. From this it follows that the income earned *by a (male) prime field slave* was certainly *not* greater than the labor income of his free counterpart by as much as fifteen percent – if indeed it exceeded the latter at all.[21] Moreover, the labor income of the free southern farm family to which Fogel and Engerman refer represents only 58 percent of the total income of their farm. The other 42 percent is imputed as a return to farm capital.[22] Yet, the dominant part of the free farm's capital represented the fruits of the past labor of its owners in activities such as land clearing, fencing, house- and barn-raising. Fogel and Engerman's imputation seriously

20. Cf. Vol. II, pp. 159–160. Using "Atwater's weights" (we presume), the authors have adjusted their ($42.99) figure for per capita slave income slightly upward, to allow for the difference between the age–sex composition of the constructed family group and that of the representative plantation population – to which the average maintenance and extra income allowances refer. "Atwater's weights," to which cryptic reference is made by the section (4.11.1) we have quoted from Appendix B above, receive more explicit attention below.

21. See below for discussion of the differences in hours worked by the free and slave labor force. We reckon that a *minimum* adjustment on this account would indicate that the slave work force put in 16 to 22 percent more male equivalent manhours *per worker* than the free southern agricultural labor force. In addition to this one must consider the higher proportion of the women and children in the rural slave population that were part of the work force.

22. This imputation is based on the results of estimating a cross section Cobb–Douglas production function (for all southern farms and plantations in the Parker–Gallman sample) in which there turned out to have been some significant scale economies. Cf. Vol. II, p. 133, 143.

understates the actual share of average gross income which a farm family might expect to derive from the acquisition and improvement of land.

The resolution of this "paradox of forced labor" is thus simple. When free southern farm folk refrained from volunteering for slavery, they were *not* sacrificing pecuniary income in order to avoid the unpleasantries of "gang labor," as the authors would have us believe. The puzzle which seemed to require the latter style of explanation is wholly of their own manufacture. For, Fogel and Engerman's textual representation of the situation implicitly assumes that the women and children of free farm families were putting in the same labor effort as was exacted from their enslaved counterparts, and further supposes that under freedom it would not be possible for a man to acquire property by retaining the fruits of his labor – or to reap windfall capital gains on lands wrested at little non-labor cost from the American wilderness. True, racism and economic power relations in the Reconstruction South militated against the full participation of black freemen in this process. But that is a *different* tragedy. It provides no reason to implicitly depict the free (white) farm folk of the antebellum era as a landless agrarian proletariat whose pecuniary compensation was on average exceeded by that of slaves fortunate enough to find themselves working on large plantations.

We turn now to the ratio between slave consumption and slave production. This is discussed in terms of its complement, "the rate of expropriation" which is treated as a part of the total "exploitation" of slaves in the first volume (Vol. I, pp. 5, 153) but is labelled "the rate of exploitation" in Appendix B (Vol. II, p. 124). The way this concept is used can be seen from the ninth, and perhaps the most counter-intuitive, of the revisionist conclusions listed in the Prologue to the text. We quote it in full:

> 9. Slaves were exploited in the sense that part of the income which they produced was expropriated by their owners. However, the rate of expropriation was much lower than has generally been presumed. Over the course of his lifetime, the typical slave field hand received about 90 percent of the income he produced. (Vol. I, pp. 5–6)

The phrasing rather startlingly suggests that only 10 percent (actually, 12 percent) of all the revenues that the typical slave produced would be taken by his master. This, however, is not the case.

Chapter 4, where this "finding" is discussed in more detail, introduces the concept of the "expected present value" (alternatively called the "average accumulated value") of the income expropriated. What is being taken by the master appears in this context to be the value at the time of the slave's birth of the anticipated future revenues that he will produce, less the anticipated future cost of his maintenance. It is this amount, represented as a fraction of the present value of the anticipated future revenues, which yields the 10 to 12 percent "rate of exploitation." (Cf. Vol. I, p. 153 and Vol. II, p. 124.)

The quantities involved in the comparison, then, are less than the simple totals of the slave revenue and maintenance costs, because a dollar of income produced or expended in the future is worth less than that at present. The higher is the rate of interest (which might be earned) on any principle invested in the present, and the further removed into the future is the anticipated dollar or receipts of disbursements, the smaller will be its present value. Thus, a dollar taken from a slave during his youth must count for more in the present value of all such expropriations than does a dollar taken still later in his life.

For the first decade or so of a slave's life, however, the costs of caring for him exceeded the value of the revenue he produced; only thereafter would he yield a positive net revenue. In reckoning the present value of net revenues anticipated at the time of birth, each dollar of *negative* net revenue (as it is incurred during the slave's childhood) counts more heavily than each dollar of the positive net revenue taken in his adulthood. The importance of this discounting scheme may be gauged from the following fact, gleaned from Appendix B: Corresponding to the 10 to 12 percent exploitation rate referred to in Fogel and Engerman's text, the ratio of the simple (*un*discounted) sum of expected net revenues to the simple sum of expected total revenues is reported as 49 percent.[23]

Let us, for the moment, defer consideration of which of these two ratios is conceptually the more appropriate measure of the degree to which the typical slave was economically "exploited." It seems, both from the foregoing and from Fogel and Engerman's discussion, that before they could get to the stage of choosing whether or not to discount the net revenues, they first had to assemble historical estimates of the typical revenue and consumption expenditure streams throughout the full life cycle of a slave, and then appropriately reduce the net revenue at every age by the (declining) portion of a representative cohort of newborn slaves who could be expected to survive to each age. This, however, is not the case.

23. Cf. Vol. II, p. 125 (sect. 4.11.6.2). The 49 percent figure in question appears to be correct, despite the fact that the algebraic formula for it is confusingly given (incorrectly) as: $B/\Sigma\lambda_t R_{gt}$, where λ_t is the average survival rate to the tth year, R_{gt} is the gross revenue in the t-th year and B is the "birthright." Instead of B, elsewhere defined as a *discounted* magnitude $[B = \Sigma\lambda_t(R_{gt} - M_t)/(1 + i)^t]$, in this context Fogel and Engerman obviously meant to refer to $B^{\circ} \equiv \Sigma\lambda_t(R_{gt} - M_t)$. Notice that, like the discounting factor $(1 + i)^{-t}$, the survival frequency (λ_t) declines with increasing t and therefore it too accords heaviest weight to the (early) negative entries in the net revenue stream. We return to this point later in the text, following explanation of the way Fogel and Engerman have estimated the net revenues, $(R_g - M)_t$.

Instead, the authors argue that in a competitive market for slaves the equilibrium price of a newborn slave (which they call the "value of a birthright") could not be substantially different from the sum of discounted expected net revenues over his lifetime. (Cf. Vol. II, pp. 58–59, 83.) Thus, if we are prepared to grant their unverified assumption that the market for slaves was in competitive equilibrium, Fogel and Engerman have ingeniously managed to finesse a formidable research task by using the average market price of a newborn slave instead of *calculating* the numerator of their ratio expression for the "exploitation" rate.[24] But two distinct qualifications must be noted.

In the first place, the estimate of the value of a birthright does not derive from *market* prices at which actual transactions in newborn infant slaves were concluded. It was, instead, obtained by extrapolation from a large body of information about the *appraisal* values placed on older (male) slaves. Although the text (cf. Vol. I, p. 73 and Figure 15) describes an age distribution of some 5,000 slave valuations simply as "prices of male slaves in the Old South," Appendix B (Vol. II, p. 79) speaks of the "age–price profile" in question as having been "developed from data in the probate records" without elaborating on the nature of that data. The precise geographical and temporal make-up of the sample of probated estates is not disclosed, nor is one told the number and size distribution of the estates involved. The latter might indicate that the number of independent *sets* of age-specific relative valuations lay well below 5,000, since it is likely that large slaveholding units (upwards of 50) were disproportionately represented among the estates probated. Still more remarkable is the authors' total silence about the relationship between appraisal values and market prices of slaves.[25]

24. The method of calculation outlined here (i.e., replacing the present value of the expected net revenue stream by the value of the birthright) is not the one described in the relevant portions of Appendix B, specifically Vol. II, pp. 119–120, including section 4.11.1 quoted above and the sections referred to therein. The method Fogel and Engerman *describe* is incorrect, but we have verified in private conversation with the authors that they followed the different procedure outlined here.

25. Some students of the southern probate records casually assert that slave appraisals were usually low in relation to actual market prices. Cf., e.g., W. D. Postell, *The Health of Slaves in Southern Plantations* (Baton Rouge: Louisiana State University Press, 1951), p. 52. However, the important question here, which remains unanswered, is whether there were significant disparities between the relative age-specific appraisal values and the relative age-specific transaction prices.

More generally it is most plausible to think that the appraisers worked with conventional valuations which were both less subject than market prices to regional variations, and less sensitive to changing expectations about the future course of market values. Perhaps this is why the dispersion of relative values drawn from estates in a region as large as the Old South is not greater than it appears to be from Fogel and Engerman's Figure 15, in Vol. I, p. 72. And

On the assumption that Fogel and Engerman have not been misled by substituting relative appraisal values for relative market prices, it is important to add a brief word about the derivation of the age profile of slave "prices." Their procedure was to average the relative values observed in the probate data for each age, and then fit a curve to the averages. This use of averages does not generate accurate statistical estimates of the margin of error surrounding the fitted age-profile. In view of the importance the authors attach to the intercept of this curve (the value at zero age), the absence of a proper estimate of the standard error of this intercept is a serious omission in their quantitative work.[26]

Momentarily suspending these doubts, suppose that somehow the authors have come up with the right figure for the market price of a newborn infant slave. It remains to consider the theoretical legitimacy of their intended finesse. This brings us to the second necessary qualification. Rather surprisingly, the technical discussion of the purchase market for slaves (Appendix B, sect. 2.1.3) abstracts completely from the most elementary considerations of the modern theory of asset-pricing under uncertainty. When the yield of an asset is subject to random variation, only an individual who is utterly indifferent to risk ("risk neutral") would find the asset just worth buying when the present value of its *expected* yields (that is, the expected stream of net revenues) was infinitesimally greater than the purchase price. Thus, Fogel and Engerman's approach would be justifiable only if those on the buying side of the (perfectly competitive) slave market treated the prospective returns on their investments as if these were foreseen with certainty.

This is a rather strong assumption to have left unstated. Most of the theoretical and applied economic analysis of decision-making under uncertainty proceeds on the different hypothesis that risk *aversion* is the dominant mode of behavior. For risk averse individuals the positive valuation placed upon a dollar of income (unexpectedly) gained is less than the negative valuation associated with a dollar of income (unexpectedly) lost.[27] Comparing the two net income streams, one whose

perhaps, too, this is why they are able to report that an "age-price profile" for male slaves computed from the probate data during a period of rapidly falling market prices of slaves (1838–1843) "was quite similar to" the corresponding profile computed from data for the period 1850–1860, when slave prices were rapidly rising. Fogel and Engerman (Vol. II, p. 79) note this counter-theoretic "similarity," describing it as a puzzle for which no explanation has yet been suggested.

26. According to Appendix B (Vol. II, p. 80) the relative "price" observations for each age were first averaged, and a sixth-order polynomial (in age) was then fitted, by least squares regression, to the sample midpoint observations thus obtained. The estimated equation, however, is not reported.

27. This is tantamount to saying that the risk averse individual is one for whom the marginal utility derived from income (or wealth) is diminishing. The measures of risk aversion proposed

present value was known with certainty, and a second whose present value remained uncertain but *on the average* was identical to that of the first, risk averse individuals would always offer less for the right to receive the uncertain net income stream. Moreover, the greater the range of variation around any given average (or expected) present value, the less the asset would be worth to a risk averter: the prospect of an outcome very far above the expected present value would be correspondingly more than counterbalanced by the prospect of an outcome equally far below it.

Consider, then, the stream of net revenue from the ownership of a slave. Clearly it could not be known with certainty, and therefore the prevalence of risk aversion among those on the buying side of the market would imply that the competitive market price would always be a *lower bound* estimate of the sum of discounted expected net revenues. This is to say that – even in the best of circumstances, in which the market value of the birthright had not been understated – Fogel and Engerman's figure of 10–12 [percent] would represent a *lower bound* measure of "the rate of exploitation" that they wish us to consider.

The extent of downward bias deriving from the substitution of asset prices for expected present values in this connection is comparatively large when the asset in question is a very young slave, rather than an adult. In the case of a newborn infant there is a particularly wide dispersion in the a priori distribution of future physical and intellectual capacities, as well as of personality traits. In addition, the shape of the a priori distribution of survival rates would change with age and the accumulation of information about the individual's physical constitution and medical history. On balance there seems to be good reason to suppose that the variance of the a priori distribution of future net revenues would *diminish* as a male slave passed from infancy to youth, and would continue to do so as he entered the prime of adulthood.[28]

by Arrow and Pratt make use of this property of the usual bounded form of utility index, and thus incorporate the hypothesis that risk aversion increases with the level of income (or wealth). Cf. e.g., K. J. Arrow, *Aspects of the Theory of Risk-Bearing*, Yrjo Jahnsson Lectures, Helsinki, 1965, Ch. 2.

28. What happens thereafter is considerably less clear, since the declining variance of the individual slave's survival may be offset by increased variance in the various dimensions of "performance" with the onset of senescence. The situation for females passing from adolescence into their reproductive years is more complex than that for males: decreased variance of the a priori distribution of fertility can be offset by increased "risk" due to childbearing. In the present state of knowledge all these statements must be regarded as conjectural, but they equally serve to suggest the implausibility of assuming that the variance of the future net revenue stream is independent of the slave's age. We are indebted to Professor Warren C. Sanderson for impressing upon us the fact that it is upon just this implausible assumption that Fogel and Engerman must rely in order to infer an age profile of average net revenues from their age

Part of the rise in the "age–price profile" of male slaves (to an apparent peak around age 27) therefore reflected progressively smaller asset-price discounts on account of risk.

Because Fogel and Engerman ignore the influence of attitudes toward risk upon the prices of assets, the complicated method they have devised for utilizing the information contained in their "age–price profiles" must lead them to draw erroneous inferences about the shape of the (unobserved) age-profile of average net earnings yielded by male and female slaves in the Old South.[29] Supposing risk aversion to have been the predominant investor attitude, the net revenues inferred by Fogel and Engerman for the years before the slave's peak level of net revenue will tend to be low *by comparison* with the peak net revenue. As there is no strong basis for supposing that their net earnings profile is too high (relative to the peak) in the subsequent portion of the life cycle, the simple undiscounted sum of inferred net revenues up to and beyond the apparent peak earnings period of the slave's live will have been *understated* if Fogel and Engerman have managed to set the absolute peak level of net earning for males at a correct dollar amount by using independent data on the hire rates of prime-age males (cf. Vol. II, pp. 81–82).[30] The full significance of this particular bias will shortly become clear.

Let us return to the question whether we should be interested in the discounted version of the "rate of exploitation" or in the undiscounted

profile of slave prices and expected survival rates. Unless, of course, they attempt to defend their whole approach by maintaining that slaveholders gave no consideration whatsoever to risk.

29. Cf., Vol. I, pp. 73–78, 82–83, for these inferences. The estimation method, discussed in Vol. II, pp. 80–81, involves using relative prices for adjoining ages and year-to-year survival frequencies to infer an underlying age profile in net revenues. The authors employ an iterative procedure in order to jointly find the uniform discount rate required to set the present value of the inferred remaining stream of average anticipated (i.e., survival adjusted) net revenues equal to the price of a slave at any given age. This internal rate is found to be 10 percent, or so we have reason to believe from the figure cited – in a different connection – in Vol. II, p. 78.

30. The argument developed here extends to their inferences about females' earnings as well. Fogel and Engerman state (Vol. I, p. 83) that "on average, net income from childbearing was only about 10 percent of the total net income earned by women during their childbearing years." They go on to argue from this that manipulation of the sexual lives of slaves in order to *further* raise fertility could not have substantially affected the overall net income derived from the ownership of females. But inasmuch as the derivation of these net income (revenue) figures abstracts from the differentially greater risk associated with the yield via the (sale of) birthrights of the offspring – compared with the risk associated with net revenues from participation in field work – the 10 percent figure cited is clearly a *lower* bound estimate of the magnitude in question. Whether or not the latter is relevant for the slaveholder's decision-making, as the authors' discussion would suggest, and whether or not their argument on this point is germane to the thesis that there was little interference by masters in the sexual lives of the slaves because it would not have been very profitable to do this, are important questions. But they raise issues quite distinct from those being considered in this review.

version which, by Fogel and Engerman's own reckoning, is five times larger. This problem is not addressed in the text of *Time on the Cross*, but a line in Appendix B acknowledges that the choice between the two is "a moral rather than an economic question." The issue posed is whether the owner of human capital is entitled to receive interest on his investment, or whether a man is entitled to the fruits of his own labor.[31] Nevertheless, the authors proceed immediately to justify giving their exclusive attention to the *discounted* sum of expected net revenues on account of its power to explain an historical *curiosum*, namely, the alleged difference between the behavior of Jamaican and mainland planters in regard to slave child rearing. Fogel and Engerman assert that if child rearing was discouraged in Jamaica – a "fact" about whose validity they previously expressed some serious doubts – this was because "the accumulated expropriation" of Jamaican slaves "never becomes positive."[32] Since the accumulated expropriations expected over an average life is simply another expression for "the value of a birthright," this statement (on their reasoning) says no more than that the average price of a newborn slave in Jamaica was negative. People cannot be expected to encourage the production of commodities (slaves) with negative prices.

The question then is what one gains by articulating this proposition in terms of expropriation rather than slave prices. According to Fogel and Engerman's way of putting things, the negative price for newborn infants meant that Jamaican slaves were exploiting their owners! They did so because their mortality rate was so high that the slaveowners incurred the costs of rearing children who were so inconsiderate as to die before earning enough to yield an overall 11 percent (opportunity cost) rate of return on the slaveholder's investment. Had American Negro slaves been placed in a regime in which they too died younger, would we find it instructive to say that their rate of expropriation was lower? No more than we would think it illuminating to say that they were "exploited less" had they happened to be transferred into the hands of an especially risk averse class of planters whose behavior in the purchase market would tend to establish a lower price (birthright value) on an asset that might well perish long before average experience suggested it

31. Cf. Vol. II, p. 125. The (discounted) measure corresponding to the first "moral" position is termed a "Robinsonian" measure (Vol. II, p. 87) to distinguish it from the second, "Marxian," measure of exploitation – although there appears to be no precedent in either of the early or the recent writings of Joan Robinson to support the ethical propriety of considering *only the present value* of an expected future difference between the marginal productivity of labor and the real wage.

32. Vol. II, p. 120. Cf. Section 4.11.2.1 (pp. 120–122) for Fogel and Engerman's skeptical questions about the "traditional interpretation" of the slave experience in Jamaica, and elsewhere in the Caribbean and South America.

should. One may rightly wonder whether "exploitation" and "expropriation" – ethically loaded terms referring to the unjust use of another man's labor – are really the appropriate words to employ as labels for a quantitative measure which looks at "justice" entirely from a slaveowner's vantage point. The same doubt extends to the authors' preference for the discounted version of the exploitation rate.

For the benefit of the general reader, Fogel and Engerman (Vol. I, pp. 155–156) explain their finding of a low rate of exploitation in just these terms: "a substantial part of the income taken from those slaves who survived into the later years was not an act of expropriation, but a payment required to cover the expenses" of rearing children who failed to live until they could amortize themselves. To these "just" expenses, which include the interest foregone, the authors' measure of expropriation would also add the interest cost (at 10 percent per annum) on the child rearing "loan" extended to those slaves who did survive. After all, free men, as *Time on the Cross* (Vol. I, p. 155) tells us, "must also bear the cost of rearing the young, including those who fail to survive, as well as of supporting the sick and the aged."

Free people, however, ordinarily are not required to borrow money for the expenses of their childhood. They are supported by their parents and more generally by their parents' generation. And when they become adults they do not repay their parents with compound interest for the pecuniary cost of their own early years – much less for the upbringing of brothers and sisters prematurely deceased. In turn, they support children of their own. Thus, the way such intergenerational transfers of income are effected among the members of free societies does not confront individuals with the costs of raising children and supporting elderly dependents when they themselves are children, but rather allows them to assume these burdens contemporaneously with the income they earn in their adulthood. Consequently, the undiscounted version of the rate of exploitation constitutes the conceptually closer analogue to the proportion of income which parents must devote to the maintenance of children (and elderly dependents) in a free society.[33]

The undiscounted version of the rate of exploitation, it may be recalled, is put at 49 percent in Fogel and Engerman's Appendix B. Yet even this under-represents the truth. We have already noticed that the numerator of this ratio is calculated as the undiscounted sum of expropriations, that is, of expected future net revenues for a newborn infant, and have concluded that the authors' estimates understate this sum because they have ignored the effect of risk aversion on the prices of

33. It is closer because a dollar spent on childrearing is weighted the same as a dollar of earnings. In any discounted sum, *contemporaneous* expenses and earnings would also be weighted equally.

slaves. What of the denominator of the (undiscounted) exploitation rate? It is defined as the sum of undiscounted expected future *gross* revenues, and thus is calculated as the undiscounted sum of expropriations *plus* the undiscounted sum of expected future maintenance cost over the slave's life. Consequently, if the latter sum has not been understated by Fogel and Engerman, we may unequivocally conclude that their 49 percent rate of exploitation is an underestimate.[34]

Now the facts of the matter suggest that if there is anything wrong with Fogel and Engerman's estimate of the average undiscounted value of lifetime maintenance expenditures on a slave, the error is one of *overstatement* rather than under-representation. In order to obtain an age-profile of the value of a typical slave's consumption stream, the authors first adjusted upward the familiar figures (based on plantation records) of average maintenance costs per slave. Then, as the illustrative passage from Appendix B (sect. 4.11.1) quoted earlier tells us, "Atwater's weights" were used to convert the average adjusted maintenance figure "into age and sex specific values." By consulting the source referred to in the U.S. Department of Agriculture publication cited (as [366]) by Fogel and Engerman, one learns that "Atwater's weights" are a set of "relative quantities of potential energy," that is, *calories* "in nutrients required" by persons of varying ages.[35]

We may put aside the (unmentioned) fact that the data underlying the "required calories" estimates W. O. Atwater published in 1886 were the "standard rations" then being assumed by the Munich School of physiological chemists and have nothing whatsoever to do with the actual calorie consumption of Negro slaves in the American South, or with the actual or required consumption of other Americans for that matter. The simple point to be noted is that satisfying the relatively high calorie requirements of infants and children does not necessarily entail a commensurate relative expense. There is no reason to think that food (let alone other) expenditures would be proportional to calorie content over the course of human life cycle, and some substantial basis for thinking that calories are provided in relatively inexpensive forms during childhood. Breast-feeding is an exemplary practice in this regard. On these and still other grounds[36] it appears that the use of "Atwater's

34. The undiscounted rate of exploitation, E_x^o, is calculated as $\hat{E}_x^o = [B^o]/[B^o + \Sigma\lambda_t M_t]$. $\hat{E}_x^o$ is understated unless $\Sigma\lambda_t M_t$ has been understated by the same proportional amount as is B^o (where λ_t is the probability of a slave living in age t, M_t is the maintenance cost of a slave of age t, and B^o is the birthright calculated in the absence of discounting).

35. Cf. *Massachusetts Bureau of Statistics of Labor, 17th Annual Report* (March 1886), Part III, "Food Consumption," esp. pp. 262–267.

36. It appears that Fogel and Engerman use Atwater's estimates of the calorie requirements of children and youths relative to requirements for adults doing moderate work, rather than

weights" has led Fogel and Engerman to use too high a relative level for slave maintenance costs during the early years. And even in computing the undiscounted sum of planters' expected maintenance expenditures, the application of a declining survival rate to each successive age-specific expenditure estimate places heaviest weight upon the (overstated) initial portion of the lifetime "maintenance cost profile." Thus there are two quite distinct bases for regarding the 49 percent figure supplied by Fogel and Engerman's second volume as a *lower bound* estimate of the conceptually appropriate undiscounted "exploitation rate," just as the startlingly low 12 percent figure presented by their primary volume must be treated as a *lower bound* proportion for the sum of the discounted appropriations.

Since the circumstances of being enslaved denied the Negro people access to the interest-free mode of intergenerational financing commonly arranged by free men, it seems to us appropriate to worry most about the understatement of the undiscounted exploitation rate. For only the latter measure counts the entailed financing burdens as part of the economic expropriation to which their slavery rendered them subject. To omit this consideration, as Fogel and Engerman chose to do in treating the interest foregone as a "just" expense incurred by the slaveholders who had to undertake the financing of the intergenerational transfers among "their people," implicitly drags the discussion around to looking at slavery once again as Phillips did – from the paternal planters' viewpoint.

Time on the Cross concludes the text discussion (Vol. I, p. 156) of the "exploitation" issue by pointing out that "the 12 percent rate of expropriation falls well within the modern tax rates on workers," even those whose incomes are at the "poverty" level. Fogel and Engerman do not disabuse the casual reader of the distinct impression he has received that the slaves were in some sense less heavily "taxed" than are some free persons in America today, but they do point out that the contemporary poor receive offsetting transfer payments and governmental services. Having thus acknowledged that taxation in modern society is not an act of expropriation but a payment for public goods and services, they ask whether the slaves did not also receive some services "which offset the [modest amount of] income expropriated from them?" In response the authors point out that the slaves "shared in the benefits" of the large scale purchases of clothing made by the planter. More importantly, through their master's intervention slaves were "in effect, able to borrow at prime rates," thereby making considerable "savings on interest

expressing them as (smaller) fractions of the estimated calories required by adults engaged in vigorous labor.

charges." The suggested parallel with modern arrangements is unmistakable. But we cannot think that Fogel and Engerman seriously mean to rehabilitate slavery as a kind of antebellum credit union, when free people had no need of the sort of "credit facilities" that were being extended to the slaves.

Taking the evidence on the material treatment of slaves together, a distinct pattern can be seen. The slave diet was compared with an inappropriate standard which makes it look better than might appear on deeper consideration. The value of slave consumption was compared with the value of free farm income under a set of historically unrealistic assumptions which again represent the slaves to have been in a more favorable position than was the case. And the relationship between slave production and consumption is treated in a manner which both under-represents the revenues accruing to the slaveowners and implicitly adopts the masters' point of view on the justice of exacting compensation for the (socially unnecessary) interest costs entailed in rearing a slave from infancy. All quantitative studies are subject to error in some degree. But the description of the comparative material conditions of American Negro slavery which emerges from *Time on the Cross* contains a preponderance of errors that run in one direction, imparting an upward bias of undetermined magnitude. In the instance of the rate of exploitation or expropriation, the distortion has been seen to be so large as to negate the usefulness of Fogel and Engerman's published "findings."

Evidence and methods on the relative efficiency of slave agriculture

Fogel and Engerman's discussion of the system of agriculture based on Negro slavery contains two analytically distinct classes of assertions about productive efficiency. One has to do with the comparative resource utilization typical of different agrarian production organizations; the other concerns the comparative performance of the workers associated with those organizations.

The authors begin (Vol. I, pp. 191–193) with statements about "the relative efficiency of slave agriculture," defining efficiency operationally as "the ratio of output to the average amount of the inputs" of labor, land and capital. Slave agriculture is discussed as an archetypal production organization to be compared with free family farming, thus: "southern slave farms were 28 percent more efficient than southern free farms," and "compared with northern farms . . . slave farms were 40 percent more efficient" (Vol. I, p. 192). It would be of interest to know whether these reported differences in the average level of measured efficiency are statistically significant, but neither the text nor the relevant sections of

Appendix B (Vol. II, pp. 126–142) presents the measures of farm-to-farm and plantation-to-plantation variance that would be needed in carrying out such significance tests. In all likelihood, however, this is not the proper way to interpret the authors' actual "findings."[37] Rather than taking their statements about the efficiency differences between slave and free farms literally, as statistical assertions about the representative individual production units, we should read them as relating to comparisons of the ratios of output to inputs for different collections, or *aggregations* of farms and plantations. It is at least clear that such an aggregate productivity comparison underlies their statement that "southern agriculture *as a whole* was about 35 percent more efficient than northern agriculture in 1860."[38]

From this aggregative empirical foundation, Fogel and Engerman (Vol. I, pp. 209–210) go on to identify "the special quality of plantation labor" as being the source of the superior efficiency of slave agriculture, and to elaborate upon their basic contention that the typical black field-hand, far from being lazy, inept, or uncooperative, "was harder-working and *more efficient* than his white counterpart" (Vol. I, p. 5, emphasis

37. Appendix B (Vol. II, p. 139, Tables B.23 and B.24) discloses wide variation in the relative efficiency indexes which are presented as *averages* for slave plantations belonging to different regions and different broad size-classes. For example, the measured total factor productivity of plantations holding 16–50 slaves in the New South is 70.5 percent greater than that of "plantations" in the 1–15 slave category in the Old South. Thus, within the group of slave farms the difference from the mid-point to the extreme of this range is at least 35 percent, which is just as large as the relative productivity advantage that Fogel and Engerman report for their comparison of "all slave farms" and "northern farms." This suggests that the latter productivity differential in favor of the slave mode of farming is not statistically significant.

38. Vol. I, p. 192, emphasis added. Unfortunately, the text immediately goes on to restate this in the following way: "that is, on average, a southern farm using a given amount of labor, land, and capital could produce about 35 percent more output than a northern farm, or groups of farms, using the same quantities of these inputs." This is a formally correct restatement if we take the qualifying "on average" to refer to *weighted* averages of all the individual southern and northern farms, the weights corresponding to their contributions to the respective aggregate agricultural outputs of the two regions. Appendix B, Tables B.21 and B.22 (cf. Vol. II, pp. 135–137), and the accompanying discussion make it clear that the relative efficiency index derives from an aggregate total factor productivity calculation for southern and northern agriculture. But in describing the derivation of parallel average productivity measures for the farms in different regions and size classes *within* the South (Vol. II, pp. 138–140) Fogel and Engerman do not explicitly say whether the averages are weighted or unweighted. And as their southern production in this case comes not from the full Census of Agriculture for 1860, but instead from the Parker–Gallman sample, it also remains unclear whether the weighting – if weighting was implicitly or explicitly employed – followed the representation of farm types in all southern agriculture, or just in the 5,230 farm sample drawn from counties that produced at least 1,000 bales of cotton in 1860. For further details of this sample, cf. William N. Parker, ed., *The Structure of the Cotton Economy of the Antebellum South* (Washington: Agricultural History Society, 1970), esp. the articles by Gallman, Foust and Swan, and Wright.

added). Superior "efficiency" is thus said to have characterized the work performance of the individual slaves, as well as the class of production organizations that utilized them.

While they are analytically distinct, it is important to notice that the two types of statements involving comparisons of efficiency are not empirically unconnected. Fogel and Engerman have not developed any independent quantitative support for their propositions regarding the comparative personal efficiencies of the typical slave and free worker in agriculture.[39] Instead, they have arrived at these conclusions essentially by the process of eliminating some other conceivable explanations for the measured factor productivity advantage of slave-using agriculture – such as differential economies of scale, technical knowledge or managerial ability.

For example, their cross-section analysis of the variation of factor productivity with changes in the size of the slave workforce employed on southern farms in 1860 leads them to conclude that although positive scale effects were significant, these do not completely account for the efficiency advantage of the slave-using sector as a whole. Moreover, it is pointed out that such economies of scale "were achieved only with slave labor" – presumably because "at the crux of the superior efficiency of large-scale operations on plantations" lay the organization of field slaves into "highly disciplined, interdependent teams capable of maintaining a steady and intense rhythm of work" (Vol. I, pp. 193, 204). In much the same vein, Fogel and Engerman argue that if the managers of plantations possessed any superior technological knowledge and entrepreneurial skills, these consisted primarily of the organizational know-how required in creating "a highly disciplined, highly specialized, and well-coordinated labor force" (cf. Vol. I, pp. 199–203).

This line of argument does not, however, lead *Time on the Cross* into full agreement with studies of modern plantation agriculture which give

39. It already has been noted above that Fogel and Engerman reject as tainted by racism all contemporary statements, and more recent historical interpretations, which would suggest that slaves were less competent, and less diligent workers than free northern farm laborers. The fact that the slaves were black and the free workers were white obviously complicates the question, but the race issue should not be allowed to completely obliterate more general predispositions to regard slaves as inferior workers. As David B. Davis (*The Problem of Slavery in Western Culture* [Ithaca: Cornell University Press, 1966], pp. 59–60) points out: "The white slaves of antiquity and the Middle Ages were often described in terms that fit the later stereotype of the Negro. Throughout history it has been said that slaves, though occasionally as loyal and faithful as good dogs, were for the most part lazy, irresponsible, cunning, rebellious, untrustworthy and sexually promiscuous." Moreover, it is one thing to argue against a presumption of inferior work performance by black slaves, but it is quite another to establish their superiority. Discounting the contrary qualitative evidence will not suffice for the latter purpose.

most emphasis to the role that organization and managerial ability play in ensuring success in competition with independent family farming.[40] Instead, the authors insist that what counted in the antebellum South was the *combination* of superior management and the "superior quality" of black labor. The latter, unlike free white labor, would be "driven" in gang work. On further consideration, Fogel and Engerman suggest that the fruits of this special combination of capabilities might just as well be entirely inputed to labor as to management: "In a certain sense, all, or nearly all, of the advantage is attributable to the high quality of slave labor, for the main thrust of management was directed at improving the quality of labor" (Vol. I, p. 210). But even putting it that way, the extent to which this effort succeeded because of the "responsiveness" of the plantation workers is left unclear.

Were it not for the need to explain the apparent superior productivity showing of plantations, there would be less reason to view the allegedly greater capacity of Negro slaves for being "driven" in gang labor as indicative of some general superiority of the quality of the labor services they provided. An overall quality advantage ought to mean that black slave workers would also perform more effectively than free workers (white or black) when employed within the regime of independent family farming. Yet, when Fogel and Engerman speak of "the superiority of slave labor in the plantation context" (Vol. I, p. 205), it is the specific context that matters. They are referring to the advantages slaveowners derived from the special way black workers responded to the non-pecuniary motivation set up by the "rhythm" of a repetitive gross motor activity such as hoeing, and to the rivalrous interaction of the hoe gang and plough gang.[41] And surely there is a legitimate question to be faced here: was this particular "quality" of the antebellum Afro-American

40. In the essay on "Plantations" in *The International Encyclopaedia of the Social Sciences*, W. O. Jones maintains that such economic advantage as the modern plantation possesses derives from "its ability to mobilize unskilled labor"; the plantation succeeds by substituting supervisory and administrative skills for skilled, adaptive labor, making most of the availability of a labor force whose principal skill is "to follow orders."

41. One should not be tempted into speaking of "the superiority of black labor in the context of slavery," for slavery clearly was neither a sufficient nor a necessary condition for eliciting a response to the intrinsic motivation of group competition and work rhythm. Both phenomena have been remarked upon by ethnographers and students of work organization among *free* non-industrial peoples. Rhythm is sometimes reported explicity as an "incentive" in tillage labor, where a line of workers may reap or hoe in unison; in the Dahomean *dokpwe*, and the Haitian *combite*, we are told, special drummers and songs are used. Gang competition as a work "incentive" is more widely observed and certainly not restricted to peoples of African stock. In rice planting among the Betsileo, for example, the women attempt to plant shoots faster than the men can prepare the field ahead of them. Cf. Stanley H. Udy, Jr., *Organization of Work* (New Haven: HRAF Press, 1959), pp. 114–115.

labor force not specific to hoe culture and organizationally similar production tasks? Can it then support more general inferences about the comparative personal efficiency of individual slave workers in the multiplicity of non-repetitive, discretionary farm chores called for by the regime of the family farm? Doubts on this score would become stronger if there were no reason to believe southern plantation agriculture was productively more efficient than northern farming.

Similarly dependent upon the "finding" that slave agriculture exhibited a pronounced physical efficiency advantage is Fogel and Engerman's assertion that blacks must share in any of the credit awarded to management because key supervisory and managerial functions were performed by *slave* overseers on the majority of the large plantations in the cotton belt (Vol. I, pp. 210–212). This intriguing conclusion is an inference based on the absence of an identifiable white overseer on 70 percent of the cotton belt plantations holding over 100 slaves, coupled with the absence on 75 percent of these overseer-less plantations of a white adult male other than the owner who might have performed the duties of an overseer. But quite obviously, there are two unstated premises underlying the inference that the authors draw from these census observations: (1) they assume a large plantation could not be properly run without an overseer in addition to the resident owner, and (2) they suppose the large plantations must have been well run – because they were so efficient. Once the latter presumption is withdrawn, however, this piece of inference unravels along with the rest of the fabric of Fogel and Engerman's argument.

It now should be evident that a great deal hinges on the validity of the relative indexes of aggregate factor productivity which the authors have developed for slave and free farming operations. This makes it necessary to look more skeptically into the details of their construction – as described by Appendix B. For it appears that in as many as three different respects the procedures followed give rise to a systematic overstatement of the relative efficiency of production on southern slave farms – at least in the usual sense in which "efficiency" has been used in the present discussion. In adumbrating these suspicions we concentrate on the simplest of the factor productivity comparisons, that between southern and northern agriculture as a whole; but the exercise will serve to indicate the nature of the problems that also arise in regard to the productivity comparisons made among the different segments of the agricultural industry of the antebellum southern cotton belt.

The estimated relative factor productivity standing of southern agriculture will be biased upward to the extent that the ratio of southern factor inputs to northern factor inputs is understated. Inasmuch as this appears to be the case with respect to both the measures of labor and land, we take up these two major points in turn, considering first a number of deficiencies in the comparative treatment of the labor inputs. The third problem with Fogel and Engerman's measurement of relative productivity involves the definition of productivity itself.

In reckoning the amount of labor services deployed by northern and southern agriculture, respectively, Fogel and Engerman count a southern man-year as equal to a northern man-year. This neglects the greater length of time which the climate of the more southerly latitudes afforded for field work. Most northern farming c. 1860 was carried on in a region having 160 to 180 frost-free days, whereas the center of the southern farming region lay in a zone having 220 to 240, or roughly 60 *additional* frost-free days. This, however, substantially exaggerates the proportional difference between the duration of the southern and northern farm work year.[42] A rather conservative estimate would suggest that on account of the difference in latitude alone the annual number of hours put in by a farm worker in the south was 10 percent greater than that worked by his counterpart in the north. The latter, modest figure makes allowance for the following considerations: (1) the days of field work "lost" in the north occur around the winter solstice, when daylight hours are shortest, (2) outside the "lost" winter months the greater average duration of daylight per day allows northern farmers more time for field work – particularly at the period of the grain harvest, and (3) during the slack winter quarter antebellum northern farm workers in wheat and corn regions may have put in as much as a daily average of four and one-half hours on livestock care and chores, compared with one hour per day spent on chores in the eastern and delta cotton regions.[43]

42. Cf. Edward Higbee, *American Agriculture: Geography, Resources, Conservation* (New York: Wiley and Sons, 1958), p. 27, for maps of frost-free periods based on the records for the years 1899–1938. According to the discussion of farm hours by J. H. Blodgett ("Wages of Farm Labor in the United States," U.S. Department of Agriculture Bureau of Statistics, *Miscellaneous Series-Bulletin No. 26* [Washington, 1903], pp. 23–24), however, 3 to 4 months were lost for field work in the North, whereas perhaps 2 months were lost in the South – typically 6 weeks in the hot months when cultivation ceased as corn and cotton crops mature during the lull from active growth, and 2 more weeks in winter. (It is noted that the traditional week of freedom afforded slaves at Christmas coincided with the winter suspension of field work.) Putting the difference between the time lost in the north and in the south at 6 weeks, and taking the 6 day week as normal for slaves in the antebellum period, we can think of latitude putting 36 extra field work days at the disposal of the southern plantation. No extra allowance is considered for differences in field work time due to suspensions of activity enforced by rain, etc.

43. The 10 percent extra southern labor input figure is based upon the estimate of 36 extra field days discussed in the previous footnote. It was developed in the following steps: (1) The 36 extra field work days was translated into 367.2 hours, using 10.2 hours per day. The latter is the average amount of daylight in the latitude of Charleston, S.C. during the December–January period when the net loss of time occurs for the North (Cf. *American Almanac*, 1888). (2) Outside the winter months the length of the northern period of daylight is greater. In

A second oversight in reckoning the ratio of southern to northern labor services is rather more substantial. Fogel and Engerman neglect to consider that over the course of the whole year *slave* laborers put in more hours of work than did (southern or northern) free farm workers.[44] A rough and rather conservative indication of the quantitative dimension of this omission is provided by considering the difference between the number of hours worked annually by *black* members of the southern agricultural labor force when they were in bondage, c. 1860, and when they were free men, c. 1870. For this purpose we may make use of the estimates assembled by Roger Ransom and Richard Sutch, which count an hour of female or child labor effort as fractions of an hour of male labor effort.[45] On this basis the proportional increment in annual (male

Jume–August, when the difference is greatest, farms in the latitude of New York City had approximately 54 extra hours of daylight compared with farms in the latitude of Charleston, S.C. – according to the sunrise–sunset intervals published in the *American Almanac* for 1888. (3) According to the W.P.A. National Research Project field survey conducted in 1936, average daily chore hours per worker in northern wheat- and corn-region farms exceeded those on southern Eastern and Delta cotton-region farms by 3.5 hours during the winter quarter. We add 1 hour of chores to the assumed 10.2 hours per day of field work, bringing the southern work day to 11.2 hours for the winter quarter. It is therefore appropriate to subtract [3.5 × 36 =] 126 hours of chore work from the 313 [= 367 – 54] net additional hours afforded southern farms by the latitude difference. This gives a remainder of 187 extra hours, which represents 9 percent of the 2,163 hours estimated as the annual per man input of labor in Northern corn regions by the National Research Project Survey for 1936. Cf. John A. Hopkins, *Changing Technology and Employment in Agriculture* (U.S. Department of Agriculture, Bureau of Agriculture Economics, Washington, D.C., May 1941), pp. 23–27. An alternative procedure, using the figures supplied by Hopkins and assuming that due to differences in *weather* as well as in climate (associated with latitude) the South enjoyed 60 extra days of field work, yields a 14.8 percent adjustment in the per worker input of labor time for the South relative to the North. On the strength of this we round the previous, conservative 9 percent figure upward, to 10 percent.

44. Their text says that plantations' comparative ability to fully utilize potential labor arose, "not because slaves worked more hours per day or more days per week than free farmers. The best available evidence is that both slaves and free farmers averaged approximately 70–75 hours of work per week during the peak labor periods of planting, cultivating, and harvesting. Nor does it appear that slaves worked more days per year" (Vol. I, p. 208). We are unable to find any citations supporting these assertions in the Appendix B Notes to Chapter 6. Moreover the statement about length of the average work day carried the significant qualifying phrase: "during the peak labor periods." For evidence and arguments contradicting Fogel and Engerman on this point, see below.
45. Cf. R. Ransom and R. Sutch, "The Impact of the Civil War and of Emancipation on Southern Agriculture," Table A, p. A.5. We are grateful to Professors Ransom and Sutch for permission to use the data presented in this unpublished paper in computing the per worker male equivalent hours figures cited here. The fractional weighting of women's and children's labor-time differences gives a particularly conservative measure in this case, because the proportional decline in the hours worked by secondary family workers in the transition from slavery to freedom was more pronounced than the proportional decline in the case of males. For all members of the black work force the absolute reduction in estimated annual labor time runs in

equivalent) hours per worker that corresponded to the difference between the condition of freedom and the condition of slavery can be put in the neighborhood of 16 to 22 percent. It is possible that this difference might overstate the size of the permanent reduction of effort which freedom brought to black agricultural workers. In 1870 the transient effects of the first "taste of freedom" to allocate one's time and the postwar disruption of southern agricultural organization had perhaps not disappeared completely. On the other hand, there are good grounds for thinking that confining attention to black workers' transition between slavery and freedom must understate the proportional difference between the annual labor input of slaves compared with free white members of the (northern or southern) antebellum farm labor force. Modern studies of family labor supply indicate that leisure is a *superior* good, particularly the leisure of secondary workers (women and youths); relative to the demand for other commodities, the family demand for leisure increases with increases in wealth. On average, in 1860 free farming families had greater non-human wealth than did the newly freed blacks of 1870. Therefore it is to be expected that, *ceteris paribus*, the labor time supplied by the free antebellum farm family worker would be less than that estimated to have been supplied by black freedmen during the era of Reconstruction.

By multiplicatively combining the two "correction factors" just considered, one may arrive at a rough assessment of the effect of these omissions on the overall ratio of southern slave labor inputs to northern free labor inputs. The upshot is that the relative labor input index for slave agriculture should be 28 to 34 percent higher than Fogel and Engerman say it is, which alone would raise the *relative* total factor input index for slave agriculture by 15 to 18 percent.[46] Consequently, the

the range of 500–600 hours. These estimates are consistent with Charles Seagrave's estimates of declines of between 9 and 74 days worked per year by Louisiana class 1 field hands in the immediate post-emancipation period 1864–1867. Cf. C. E. Seagrave, "The Southern Negro Agricultural Worker: 1850–1870," Unpublished Ph.D. dissertation, Stanford University, 1971, pp. 71–72.

46. The calculation is made as follows: Relative to free northern farming the southern slave farm sector labor input index is to be raised by (1.10)(1.16) = 1.28 or (1.10)(1.22) = 1.34. Fogel and Engerman (Vol. II, pp. 126–127) adopt the Cobb–Douglas form of aggregate production function and therefore compute the index of total factor inputs as a weighted *geometric* average of the labor, land and capital input indexes. Their weight for labor – as previously noted above – is 0.58, so the adjustment factor by which the relative total input index for slave agriculture (vis-à-vis northern agriculture) should be multiplied is $(1.28)^{.58} = 1.154$, or $(1.34)^{.58} = 1.185$. These ratios, divided into the ratio of southern slave factor productivity to northern agricultural factor productivity (which Fogel and Engerman report as 1.40), yield the partially "corrected" versions of the latter relative productivity ratios which are mentioned in the text below: 1.40/1.185 = 1.18, and 1.40/1.154 = 1.21.

estimate of the total factor productivity differential for the southern slave farm sector compared with northern agriculture should be on this account cut from the 40 percent reported by Fogel and Engerman to something more like 18 to 21 percent.

This, however, probably does not exhaust the downward adjustment that would be necessary simply to rectify the net tendency of the errors they have introduced in measuring the relative inputs of labor. That is not to say that all the measurement errors operate in one direction. The authors point out in Appendix B (Vol. II, p. 138) that because they have followed nineteenth-century Census practice in ignoring labor force participation by women on free family farms, their estimates of the labor input for northern agriculture (and for the southern free farm sector) must on this account be too low, relative to the figures for southern farming (and slave agriculture) as a whole. They suggest that on this account their total factor productivity estimates under-represent the efficiency advantage held by slave-using farms. But Fogel and Engerman do not notice that still another procedure of theirs for "refining" the southern labor input measure introduces what is probably a more than offsetting downward bias in the relative labor input index for southern agriculture vis-à-vis northern agriculture.[47] The aggregate southern labor force estimate appears to have been recalculated so that it is expressed in terms of equivalent (prime-age adult male) worker units, using for this purpose the age-profiles of relative gross earning which Fogel and Engerman inferred from the "age–price" profiles for slaves. But the same adjustment could not at the time be carried out for the northern agricultural labor force. Thus the "refinement" must substantially reduce the level of the southern labor input relative to that measured for northern agriculture: quite apart from the accuracy of the "equivalent worker" weights, their effect is to count members of the southern labor force who were either younger than or older than the inferred age of peak gross earnings as being less than a full worker. Unfortunately we cannot determine by how much this further contributes to inflating the reported relative factor productivity standing of southern agriculture.

The second major source of upward bias in Fogel and Engerman's relative efficiency estimates for southern agriculture is their use of average

47. After these two procedures are described, at the beginning of the second paragraph in Vol. II, p. 138, there follows this statement: "This adjustment in the southern labor input without a corresponding adjustment in the northern labor input biases the relative advantage of the South downward." On careful reading it becomes clear that this applies *only* to their adjustment for labor force participation by women and children in southern agriculture, and not to the "equivalent worker" adjustments.

land values to adjust acreage figures in reckoning the relative inputs of the services of land. This adjustment has the effect of raising the relative total factor productivity index for southern (vs. northern) agriculture by 25.6 percent.[48] In other words, it accounts for more than the apparent southern efficiency advantage remaining after the (preceding) attempts made here to partially correct for the bias introduced by Fogel and Engerman's treatment of the relative labor inputs.

Some weighting of the relative acreage figures clearly is needed to allow for the greater resource inputs represented by improved lands in comparison with unimproved lands, and perhaps also for natural variations in average soil fertility between the regions. But the authors' use of the simple ratio of the aggregate value of agricultural land in the south to that in the north, based on the 1860 census, deserves fuller discussion than it receives in Appendix B (Vol. II, p. 136). Implicitly, the theory of rent has been invoked to justify the supposition that greater soil fertility would merely permit landowners to extract the market value of the extra crop yield per acre as an incremental rent. It is further tacitly supposed that all such expected future rental earnings would be capitalized into the prices of the land – at a uniform discount rate – so that the latter would vary in strict proportion to the former. We have already had occasion to point out that this gambit, in effect, ignores the possible intervening influence of attitudes towards risk in determining the market value of the assets (lands) in question. But in the case at hand the authors' procedure also requires one to stipulate the existence of a perfectly competitive capital market (establishing a uniform *national* rate of discount), a perfectly competitive national land market, and perfect markets for all of the agricultural products that might be raised on northern and southern lands. It is a tall order.

Even if the lattermost of this string of implicit assumptions were warranted, it might reasonably be argued that the others collectively abstract from the existence of a set of historical circumstances that may well have caused the relative average prices of farm land in the antebellum South to understate their relative average crop yields, in comparison to the farm lands of the North.[49]

48. Cf. Vol. II, pp. 132, 135, and Tables B.20 and B.21. The ratio of southern to northern land inputs is reduced by a factor of 0.40 (from 1.257 to .503) by the value-weighting of acreage. Since land gets a .25 weight in the geometric averaging of all inputs, the latter index is only reduced by the factor ($.40^{.25}$ =) 0.796 on this account. The effect on measured total input productivity is calculated as 1/(.796) = 1.256.

49. Thus, were resident southern landowners preponderant in the market for southern rural land because they had better access to information than non-residents, and were they more risk-averse as a class than northern rural landowners (because those having access to mortgage finance tended to be the larger, wealthier planters, and the degree of risk aversion increases

Moreover, the assumption that uniform national prices were received by all agricultural producers in 1860 is patently at variance with well known facts. To see what comes of tacitly ignoring this aspect of historical reality, we may proceed by way of a heuristic example. Suppose that everywhere land was of the same physical quality in terms of crop yield per acre – given that the amounts of capital and labor applied per acre also were everywhere identical. Imagine, further, that in a part of this hypothetical territory – call it the North – the state subsidized the transportation of crops to market. Then, for any level of final market prices, the on-farm price received by the growers would be higher in the subsidized region. Under the other assumptions Fogel and Engerman have freely invoked, landowners in the North would be extracting a rent equal to the transport subsidy on the (standard per acre) crop yield, leaving farm operators there no worse off than those in the rest of the country. The resulting higher average value of northern farm lands – reflecting the capitalization of these differential rents – would be accepted by Fogel and Engerman as indicative of higher land "quality," and so would raise the per acre index of total factor inputs calculated for the North in comparison with the index they would calculate for the South. But because crop yields per acre were taken at the outset to be everywhere identical, the index of physical output per unit of total factor input *as measured* would then turn out to be lower in the (northern) region. This "finding" would not reflect anything regarding the relative physical efficiency of resource utilization within agriculture per se, but rather the existence of an external condition represented in the example by the arbitrary northern transportation subsidy.

At the close of the antebellum era the pattern of North–South differences in the local prices of agricultural commodities – largely reflecting the effects of regional differences in transportation costs – was not so far removed from the circumstances just imagined. There are several alternative adjustments that might have been attempted to prevent this situation from imparting an upward bias to the relative factor productivity measures computed for agriculture in the (higher transport cost) South. But as long as one continues to use local average land value as an index of land input "quality," an obvious thing to do is to symmetrically weight the physical outputs so that a given quantity of

with wealth), it would follow that the market price established for the same future expected stream of land rental yields would be *lower* in the South than in the North. Note that higher southern mortgage rates, and/or shorter time horizons on the part of investors in southern land, would have parallel effects biasing Fogel and Engerman's index of the relative "quality" of southern land inputs in a downward direction. We are not prepared to assert that all these awkward conditions obtained, but the authors have neither discussed the possibility nor adduced any evidence to suggest that such was not the case historically.

production counts for less if high transport costs – or other regional-specific conditions extrinsic to agriculture – cause farmers to be paid less for it.[50] Fogel and Engerman unfortunately have omitted making any such correction of their output measures; in justification they cite Richard Easterlin's computations for 1840 as showing "about the same relative agricultural output for the South vis-à-vis the North using either nationally uniform prices or regional prices applied to regional physical production" (Vol. II, p. 134).

From the same study by Easterlin, however, it appears that in comparing aggregate agricultural production in the South Atlantic states with production in the Middle Atlantic and New England states for 1840, the effect of switching from national price-weights to regional price-weights lowers the relative output measure for the southern region by a factor of 0.899.[51] Had just this correction factor been applied by

50. As an alternative to the strategy considered in the text discussion, Fogel and Engerman might have attempted to apply a common *national* set of relative average prices in weighting improved and unimproved acreage in the two regions. In the same spirit, it would be possible to compute two separate indexes of relative unit values for all the improved lands within each region, and then set the median values of the two indexes equal.

It should be clear that the procedures sketched here would, and probably should be employed to remove biases in the measurement of land inputs due to the effect of varying transportation conditions on land price levels *within* the South – and not only between the South and the North. It remains unclear to what extent the apparent factor productivity advantage reported for free and slave farms of all sizes in the New South, vis-à-vis corresponding farms in the Old South, actually derives from the lower level of land prices associated with inferior transport conditions in the former region. Cf. Vol. II, p. 139, Table B.23, for these comparisons. Fogel and Engerman's text discussion of intra-South factor productivity differences (Vol. I, pp. 192–195) does not mention their finding that these extend to free farms as well, but the latter suggests that the greater relative efficiency of New South plantations compared with those of the Old South cannot properly be taken as solely reflecting regional differences in slave plantation characteristics and management.

51. Cf. R. A. Easterlin, "Farm Production and Income in Old and New Areas at Mid-Century" (unpublished manuscript, 1973), forthcoming in *The Old Northwest: Essays in Economic History*, D. C. Klingaman and R. K. Vedder, eds. The comparison cited by Fogel and Engerman (Vol. II, p. 134) is for the entire South against the entire North in 1840. This yields a (.938) correction factor which would not have quite as large an effect in reducing the relative southern output. (Still, 7 percent represents a fifth of the 35 percent relative efficiency advantage they find for all southern agriculture.) In 1840, however, the transport conditions in the Old Northwest and the trans-Mississippi west were much inferior to those prevailing in the southern Gulf Plains and Delta regions, and correspondingly the general level of local prices was higher in the latter than it was in the North Central census region. By 1860, on the other hand, these conditions had been dramatically transformed by the building of railroads and the fuller development of the northern water routes leading to the eastern seaboard. (Cf., e.g., Albert Fishlow, "Antebellum Interregional Trade Reconsidered," in R. L. Andreano, ed., *New Views on American Economic Development* [Cambridge: Schenkman Publishing Company, 1965], pp. 187–200.) For this reason we think the comparison of northern and southern price structures in 1840 based on conditions prevailing along the eastern seaboard – which we have

Fogel and Engerman, it would have canceled out almost half of the substantial (26 percent) upward effect which their dubious land value adjustment imparts to the relative level of factor productivity presented for southern agriculture in comparison with northern farming as a whole.

The third major problem raised by Fogel and Engerman's procedures basically is a conceptual one: it concerns the proper interpretation of their measures of agricultural output in the South relative to that in the North, and hence of their relative efficiency findings. Throughout the preceding discussion the concept of total input efficiency has been used in the same way that the authors employ it – a usage carrying strong *physical* or technical connotations. Indeed, it is precisely this physical interpretation upon which Fogel and Engerman rely in arguing that they can infer something about the "task" efficiency of slaves compared with free laborers on the basis of measures of the comparative rate at which a given bundle of labor, land and capital inputs could be transformed into agricultural "output" by slave and free farms.

The products of northern and southern farming were not, however, physically identical. Wheat, corn and hogs, for example, were raised in the regions above and below the Mason-Dixon line, but in different proportions. Moreover, the North grew neither cotton, nor rice, nor cane sugar. To form an aggregate measure of agricultural output for the two regions it is necessary somehow to render these physically disparate commodities commensurable, and for this purpose Fogel and Engerman adopt the economist's conventional method of weighting the items in the set of output quantities by standard (or uniform) relative prices. This means that the measures of relative aggregate output for northern and southern agriculture depend upon a relative set of exchange values of the various crops prevailing in 1860 and hence reflect *inter alia* the relative commodity preferences of the consumers who participated in the markets where these prices were established. In this aggregation process the initial concept of physical efficiency necessarily undergoes a subtle transmutation: "efficiency" comes to mean using less resources to produce a unit of whatever some standard group of consumers happens to *want*. There is an ineluctable element of arbitrariness about this – which economists recognize by referring to the measurement effects of using one set of price-weights, rather than some other, as "the index number problem." The problem arises in comparing two bundles of commodities which are not identical in composition, that is, in the relative quantities of the various goods they contain. Placing relatively high valuations on

referred to in the text – is more apposite for the purpose of adjusting the 1860 regional agricultural output ratio.

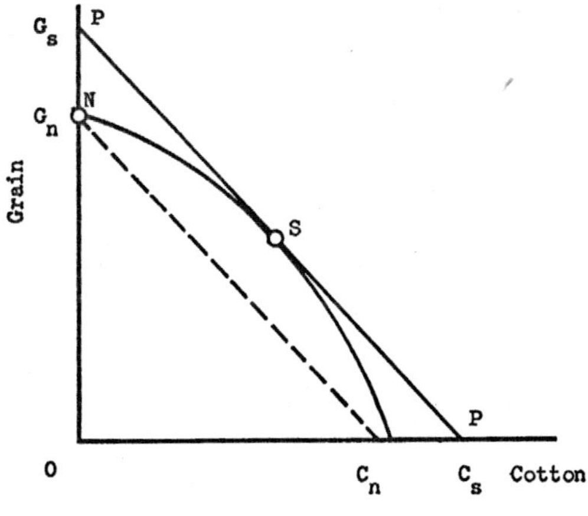

Figure 1

goods which are more amply represented in one bundle (than in the other) makes the aggregate size of that particular bundle appear larger in comparison.

An extreme manifestation of this general problem occurs when one output bundle contains a collection of commodities that is totally missing from some other bundle to which the first is being compared. The easiest way to see what this implies for Fogel and Engerman's "findings" will be to suppose that we were considering two modes of agricultural production that were equally efficient in the physical or "technical" sense. This can be represented by stipulating that, given the same bundle of costly resources, the northern mode and the southern mode would both have the technical capacity to produce the full array of the combinations of "grain" and "cotton" described by the concave transformation locus in Figure 1.

For the moment assume that northern and southern agriculturalists faced the same relative prices for cotton and grain, indicated by the slope of the line *PP*. Were they free to adjust the composition of their output, both should produce the mix of cotton and grain indicated by the point *S* in Figure 1, as that will bring in the maximum *revenue* (price-weighted output) attainable along the common transformation curve. When both are at *S*, their respective aggregate products are identical, whether we measure both in terms of "grain equivalent" units along one axis or in terms of "cotton equivalent" units along the other axis. By assumption, the amount of resource input required to produce along the common transformation curve also is the same for northern- and southern-style agriculture; so the ratio between measured total output and measured total input for the South just matches the corresponding "efficiency" measure for the North.

But now suppose that northern agriculturalists in reality were debarred by extraneous (climatic) conditions from raising any "cotton." Having to specialize in "grain" at point N, their output (evaluated at the prevailing commodity price ratio indicated by the dashed line parallel to PP) would be necessarily smaller than the output recorded for southern agriculture as C_s, or alternatively as G_s. In this extreme situation, which happens to mirror the historically relevant case, the supposed index of relative *technical* efficiency is subject to an upward bias of undetermined magnitude.[52] The cause is the index number problem created by the absence from the northern output set of a class of commodities that figure importantly among the outputs of southern agriculture. Rather than telling us about relative technical efficiency, Fogel and Engerman's findings really report on relative "revenue-getting efficiency" (which is to say, on relative profitability) under a particular set of product- and factor-price conditions. And the relative *revenue* efficiency of the sector which can freely adjust its output mix so as to maximize revenues must in general overstate its relative *technical* efficiency, in comparison with a sector that is confined to producing only some portion of the commodity array.

In the foregoing exposition the effect of climate might have been likened to that of a prohibitive tax levied on the marketing of cotton, sugar and rice grown in the North, or, equivalently, to a subsidy paid the growers of those crops in the South. From our earlier consideration of the question of regional differences in land values, however, we should be prepared for the argument that competition among "cotton" growers would bid up the rental price of any inelastically supplied factor that was required to produce the (subsidized) crop. If one takes southern land as the sole region-specific input, it would then appear – always assuming perfectly competitive market conditions – that southern rents, and hence land values, would automatically incorporate an appropriate upward adjustment which would prevent the difference between the regions' climatic endowments from reflecting itself in a misleadingly high relative measure of southern efficiency. On this line of reasoning – which the authors do not advance – it would seem that by using relative land *values* Fogel and Engerman actually have managed to allow for the

52. Note that if a higher relative price for cotton ruled than that indicated by the slope of PP in Figure 1, S-producers would move towards greater specialization in growing cotton and the comparison of aggregate outputs evaluated at the new (steeper sloped) price-line would show an even greater advantage for southern agriculture. It should be apparent from the text discussion that Fogel and Engerman's "efficiency" measures for different regions and farm-types *within* the South are subject to the same distorting influences caused by crop-mix variations.

awkward problem of region-specific crops in the southern agricultural output-mix.

But this is not the case. In the antebellum South there was a factor of production in still more inelastic supply than land, and equally specific to the region: black slave labor. Would not the prices bid for the latter asset reflect the higher revenue which the South's climate made it possible to derive from crops produced with slave labor on a given acre of land, crops that always could be produced more profitably in the South using slaves than using free workers? Elsewhere in *Time on the Cross* it is maintained that such was indeed the case; the presumption that (expected) movements in the price of cotton should have been reflected in the movements of slave prices lies at the roots of Fogel and Engerman's entire discussion of the rational capitalistic character of antebellum slavery.[53] It cannot be abandoned lightly. But to the extent that the rent-creating effects of increases in the price of region-specific southern staples were reflected in the market for *slaves* rather than the land market, the use of average land values in computing the relative measure of land inputs cannot have captured the general effect of latitude on the length of the growing season and the differential ability of the South to raise crops which brought comparatively high revenues per acre.

The conclusion seems inescapable: Fogel and Engerman's factor productivity measures at best can speak to the issue of the comparative "revenue-getting efficiency" of the southern agricultural system, not the comparison between the technical or "standard physical task" efficiency of agriculture using slaves and free family farming. Furthermore, as has been seen from the preceding discussion of the methods used to measure the land and labor inputs, their "findings" lean heavily toward exaggerating even the relative *revenue*-efficiency of southern agriculture. Their inferences about the relative personal efficiency of slave workers, correspondingly are overdrawn.

On welfare-efficiency and the morality of slavery

Some broader patterns begin to emerge from the welter of details sampled for discussion in the foregoing, admittedly incomplete methodological appraisal of *Time on the Cross*.

53. Cf. Vol. I, pp. 95–96 especially, where they refer to an equation (eq. 3.10 in Appendix B, Vol. II, p. 62) for predicting the course of slave prices on the basis of cotton prices and other information. The justification for this specification clearly has to be that there was enough land in crops other than cotton, in the short-run, and enough land clearable at constant costs per acre, in the long-run, to warrant supposing that slave prices would reflect expected (and actual) cotton price changes. Otherwise the latter would tend to be capitalized into movements in southern land prices.

Although the authors present their empirical "findings" as objective economic statements uncontaminated by any judgments about the "morality" of slavery, their cliometric investigations have been conducted within a conceptual framework whose ethical perspective seems peculiarly one-sided. The authors consider the diet of slaves as given and assess its caloric worth without asking whether blacks under freedom would have chosen to work hard enough to require so much food energy, or whether the intake allowed them was adequate for *their* actual energy needs. The authors do not inquire how poor a free man – say, a freed black in the Reconstruction period – might have to have been before he chose to obtain such a level of food energy in the carbohydrate-intensive way the slaves were compelled to obtain theirs. Nor do the authors ask how impoverished a free family would have to have been in the nineteenth century before the husband, wife and children "chose" to toil the number of hours expected of slave families. In reckoning what was being "expropriated" by the masters the authors start by accepting the fact that blacks as slaves were not financially responsible for their own offspring; thus they tacitly suppose that each generation would in any event have had to finance its own upbringing, paying interest charges for loans obtained against future earnings. And, finally, in measuring the comparative "efficiency" of the agricultural system based on slavery, the authors have in effect accepted the contemporary market valuations as measuring the social welfare benefits derived from the specific goods produced by slave labor – while failing to count the longer average hours worked, that is, the additional leisure lost by slaves, as among the social resource costs incurred for that worthwhile "output."

Thus, in quantifying the economic dimensions of the experience of slavery, Fogel and Engerman recurringly slip into a tacit acceptance of the status quo of black bondage as the appropriate point of departure for making their evaluations. The resulting work looks at the "economic performance" for the system of slavery mainly from the perspectives of the owners of the human capital and the consumers of the commodities that it produced; the condition of freedom is not correspondingly adopted as an alternative which might be systematically employed in quantifying the economic welfare burdens imposed upon the slave population.

In a brief, concluding exercise (cf. Vol. I, p. 244) Fogel and Engerman do present a measure of welfare costs to the blacks of the "non-pecuniary disadvantages" of laboring under the slave plantation's gang system: $75 per head, annually. But this estimate is conceptually inadequate and empirically unfounded. To derive it they argue that the difference between the post-Emancipation earnings of freedmen employed on labor gangs and the earnings of black sharecroppers provides a pecuniary measure of the blacks' distaste for the system in which they were compelled to work under slavery.[54] But beyond Fogel and Engerman's factual misconstruction of C. E. Seagrave's evidence on this point, it hardly seems adequate to represent the "non-pecuniary" disadvantages of being "driven" by *slave*-drivers as measureable in terms of the difference between the earnings obtained under two alternative systems of *free* labor. And to cap it off, the authors have reckoned the net economic burden imposed on the slaves by deducting – from this inappropriate measure of the gross burden – an allowance for the fictitious pecuniary advantage which slaves allegedly enjoyed in comparison with free agricultural workers. (Cf. Vol. I, pp. 244–245, particularly Table 3.)

For reasons such as these it is unfortunately not possible to accept the sanguine belief that the quantitative methods applied in writing *Time on the Cross* truly have fulfilled the authors' expectations by providing "a more *accurate and complete* portrayal of slavery than was previously available."[55]

That the tacit ethical orientation of Fogel and Engerman's "cliometric" contributions should have defeated this aspiration to completeness as well as to accuracy, really is not so surprising. In an important respect the slant of their quantitative work reflects the economist's professional habits of mind, and the methodological pull of the tradition established by Conrad and Meyer's studiously *de-personalized* approach to the issue of slavery's profitability. Those two pioneers of the "new economic history" stressed that the analytical problems of determining the profitability of holding slaves were not different from those met in determining the returns from investments in machines or cattle. Trouble comes, however, from adhering to this bent when venturing beyond the quantification of profitability – a dimension of the institution's performance which certainly was of more immediate interest from the vantage point of some

54. Despite gang wages 2.11 to 2.42 times as large as the earnings of sharecroppers (on 4 Louisiana plantations during 1865–1866, say Fogel and Engerman, "planters found it impossible to maintain the gang system once they were deprived of the right to apply force," and sharecropping became the predominant mode through which southern Negro labor was mobilized. (Cf. Vol. I, pp. 238–239; Vol. II, p. 160.) Yet, as the source they cite for these Louisiana earnings differentials makes clear, during the two years in question the weather was miserable and the sharecroppers took a particularly bad financial beating. Moreover, it is noted there that the high wages set in these Louisiana parishes by the Freedmen's Bureau *did succeed in recruiting black gang labor*: in May, 1866 only 21 percent of the Negroes under the supervision of the Bureau in Louisiana were sharecroppers instead of working under various types of wage contracts. This "anomalous" preponderance of the system of paying wages for gang labor seems to have persisted in the Louisiana sugar-growing regions. Cf. C. E. Seagrave, "The Southern Negro Agricultural Worker: 1850–1870" (unpublished Ph.D. dissertation, Stanford University, April, 1971), pp. 41–42, 53–54.

55. Vol. II, p. 19, emphasis added. Undoubtedly Fogel and Engerman are right in identifying the validity of this methodological claim as "the real question."

members of antebellum society (the masters) than from that of others (the slaves). In defining what is meant by the *social* "optimality" of resource allocation, or in devising criteria for comparing the allocative "efficiency" of different economic systems, the natural predisposition of economists is to consider how affairs appear to the human agents who are capable of acting so as to better satisfy their wants. Modern economic welfare theory simply does not encourage one to view life also from the standpoint of the lathes and the livestock.

Certainly *Time on the Cross* makes it perfectly clear that it is *not* any insensitivity on the authors' part to the moral evil of slavery which has led them to re-evaluate the economic performance of the institution by reference to standards that tend to embrace the viewpoint of the owners of productive assets, rather than that of the assets in question. The immorality of slavery for Fogel and Engerman is unquestionable; it is a fundamental ethical precept which can be, and is, asserted categorically – regardless of their supposed exoneration of slavery from the "economic indictments" falsely brought against it by abolitionist propaganda. "Even if slavery did produce, on the average, better material conditions than obtained for free Negro laborers, or white laborers for that matter, the *moral* indictment of slavery still prevails" (Vol. II, p. 222). Indeed, we are warned that the historian of slavery who persists in the neoabolitionist penchant for "continually linking the issue of morality with physical cruelty, with sexual abuses, or with mistreatment in respect to food, clothing and shelter," runs the grave risk of having "obfuscated rather than clarified the profound immorality of the *system*."[56]

What is one to make of this effort to separate "economics" from "morality?"[57] A dichotomy works two ways: the author's insistence that economic matters should not be permitted to becloud issues of "pure morality" also suggests that no prior ethical judgments have conta-

56. Vol. II, p. 222. Kenneth Stampp is charged with having thus "inadvertently obfuscated" the true immorality of slavery, and with having failed "to stress that proof of good treatment was insufficient to remove the moral brand" from the institution.

57. It is the thesis of Fogel and Engerman's Ch. 5 ("The Origins of the Economic Indictment of Slavery," Vol. I, esp., pp. 158–161) that the "moral purity" of the eighteenth-century radical Quaker position against slavery subsequently was diluted by the addition of an "economic indictment" constructed to meet the propaganda needs of nineteenth-century abolitionists. But as an essay in intellectual history this seems quite incorrect. Cf. D. B. Davis, *The Problem of Slavery*, pp. 291–309, 316–317, on the elements of rational analysis in Quaker theology, reflected in a willingness to examine Biblical texts in the light of reason and human standards of justice, as well as for the inclusion in early Quaker tracts of arguments concerning slavery's social and economic consequences. Davis (p. 317) explicitly cites an American Quaker pamphlet of 1713 as anticipating Hinton Rowan Helper's (1857) warning that Negro bondage would promote economic divergences and political conflicts between rich slaveholders and poor whites.

minated the "purely economic" findings upon which *Time on the Cross* is based. But do the methods of welfare economics enable one to carry through an ethically neutral re-examination of the comparative social efficiency of the system of slavery? Is it possible to conduct the sort of "value-free" inquiry which Fogel and Engerman appear to envisage as establishing the economic facts concerning the consequences of this particular institutional arrangement, the objective historical truths about which moral judgments subsequently may be made?

The brief answer is that modern welfare theory is quite incapable of supporting such an undertaking. Not only does the central analytical concept of the "welfare efficiency" of a specific pattern of resource allocation have a distinct ethical content, but the ethical premises upon which it rests makes this a peculiarly inappropriate framework within which to comprehend systems based on varying degrees of personal involition.

The notion that questions concerning the allocative efficiency of alternative economic arrangements can be usefully separated from concerns with other aspects of those arrangements, such as the distribution of wealth, income, and ultimately of the human happiness that may be derived from them, is fundamental in modern economic welfare theory. But this notion rests on the idea that maximization is good; that states of the world in which more of an inherently desired thing is available to be (potentially) shared by all are "better" – in some widely shared sense of the word – than states in which there is less. By moving to such a state at least some individual could be given more of what he desired (made "better off") without necessarily rendering anyone worse off. To such a change reasonable men freely would assent. Economists describe states where any individual's further gain must come at someone else's expense to be welfare-efficient, or Pareto-efficient, and a move toward such a position is said to be "Pareto-safe."

Pareto efficiency, then, is not an ethically neutral concept. It rests on the premise that each individual's desires (preferences among goods, and between goods and leisure, and goods today vs. goods tomorrow) should be allowed to count. Thus Pareto-safe moves are only ethically safe for the "scientific" economist to recommend because maintaining the new position presumably would require no coercion. Indeed it is because one presumes that all commodities "consumed" are voluntarily chosen, and all efforts and sacrifices made for the production of commodities are freely rendered, that the commodities ethically can be called "goods." But, once the presupposition of autonomous individual preferences is seriously questioned, it becomes unclear how truly voluntary "choice" is. The serious possibility that what individuals seem to want may be systematically shaped by what they have been allowed to have therefore undermines the ethical foundations of normative welfare analysis. If people who had been long enslaved eventually "chose" to continue in the security of their chains, should we unhesitatingly say that this test revealed bondage to be a "better" condition than freedom?

Welfare analysis based on the search for Pareto optimality not only subscribes to the complex ethical character of the criterion, but "counts" individual preferences only as these can be expressed through market behavior. Recommendations of Pareto-safe changes in the pattern of resource allocation therefore must implicitly accept the past and the existing distribution of income and wealth, the institutional working rules, and the larger social and political power structure. The criterion applies to consensual, "no injury" changes from whatever status quo has come to prevail as a result of the past economic and non-economic processes.

But because the prior specification of property rights can, and usually does, exercise a powerful role in determining whether a particular change is deemed Pareto-safe, the rule of unanimity itself carries a strong bias in favor of the status quo. A slave set free might not be able, given his prior lack of training, to earn sufficient income to both compensate his master for the loss of his services and improve his own economic welfare. The two parties could not agree on manumission. Yet if a prospective master were obliged to fully compensate a free man for the welfare loss entailed in entering perpetual bondage, it is unlikely that the two could agree to that change either. So in determining which, between slavery and freedom, is the more welfare-efficient economic system, the thing that may well matter most is whether the new economic historian will start from an ethical presumption of the human right to freedom, or accept a factual status quo which finds a people already "stolen" and held in bondage.

Modern welfare economics is grounded on the supposition that all market and non-market transactions of interest between individual actors are voluntary. Involuntary transactions, in which goods are wrested from unwilling "sellers" or forced upon unwilling "buyers," amount to theft and extortion, respectively. Such a theory is not helpful for deriving any precise statements about the welfare consequences of changes which entail the introduction or further extension of involuntary transactions of the sort essential to slavery. As the ethical premise that each individual's preferences must count underlies the notion that the only "Pareto-safe" (welfare-efficiency justified) changes are those to which there would be unanimous assent, it is difficult to use this apparatus to assess the *comparative* economic welfare efficiency of slave and free societies. For in imagining the change from one to the other one must acknowledge that the entailed redistribution of property rights violates the ethical premises for making formally justifiable statements about the resulting change in social welfare. When people are enslaved, *welfare necessarily is transferred* to their masters, and there is no ethically neutral way to compare the welfare efficiency of the resulting institution with the set of outcomes characterizing an alternative institution under which that particular interpersonal welfare transfer need not take place. Any such comparison would require weighing the slaves' losses against the masters' gains.

There would be no difficulty conducting an analysis of economic welfare efficiency that treated slaves as objects, mere instruments of production whose condition was excluded from the purview of welfare considerations except insofar as it impinged on the well-being of the actors whose preferences *did* count. Economic theory is thus well set up to guide us in making coherent statements about the welfare efficiency of slavery from the standpoint of everyone but the slaves. If this were what *Time on the Cross* had set out to do, it would be both a less arresting and a less misleading book.

7

Explaining the relative efficiency of slave agriculture in the antebellum South

ROBERT W. FOGEL and STANLEY L. ENGERMAN*

In 1968 we undertook to measure and explain the relative technical efficiency of input utilization in the agricultural sectors of the North and South in 1860. The principal instrument that we employed for this task was the geometric index of the relative total factor productivity, which is defined by equation (1) (symbols are defined in Table 1):

$$G_s/G_n = \frac{Q_s/Q_n}{(L_s/L_n)^{\alpha L}(K_s/K_n)^{\alpha K}(T_s/T_n)^{\alpha T}} \tag{1}$$

This index[1] was originally computed from published census data and the results were reported in 1971, both with and without adjustments for differences in the quality of outputs and inputs. The ratio of G_s/G_n yielded by the unadjusted computation was 109.2.[2] Crude adjustments for differences between the weights of northern and southern livestock, for land quality, for the proportion of women and children in the labor

Source: Robert W. Fogel and Stanley L. Engerman, "Explaining the Relative Efficiency of Slave Agriculture in the Antebellum South," *American Economic Review* (June 1977), 275–296. Reprinted with permission of the authors and the American Economic Association.

* Professor of economics and history, Harvard University, professor of American history and institutions, University of Cambridge; professor of economics and history, University of Rochester, respectively. Research on this paper was supported by National Science Foundation grants GS-3262, GS-27262, SOC 76002; and a grant from Harvard University. Earlier versions were presented to faculty colloquia and seminars at the London School of Economics and the universities of Cambridge, Aberdeen, Uppsala, Oslo, Glasgow, Texas A&M, Oxford, Cologne, Berlin (The Free University), Moscow, Edinburgh, Jerusalem, and Tel Aviv. We benefited from the discussions following these presentations as well as from comments and criticisms by D. G. Champernowne, Michael Edelstein, Ephim Fogel, Michael Fogel, Robert Gallman, Zvi Griliches, Mark Hopkins, Laurence Kotlikoff, David Landes, Donald McCloskey, W. B. Reddaway, Joseph Reid, Jr., Richard Rosett, Allan Sanderson, Richard Sylla, James Trussell, and G. Nicholas von Tunzelmann.

1. In the computations that follow, this index is multiplied by 100 to put it in percentage form. Hereafter we refer to G_s/G_n as the geometric index of total factor productivity, or the productivity index, or the index of efficiency. See the authors (1974a) (hereinafter referred to as *TOTC*), II, pp. 126–131.
2. See Table 1 for brief descriptions of the way in which Q, L, K, and T were measured in the various computations. For further details see the authors (1971) and *TOTC*, II, pp. 131–136.

force, and for other factors, did not reduce this ratio as we thought they would, but increased it to 138.9.[3]

All differences between the northern and southern indexes of total factor productivity are, in a certain sense, errors of measurement. If output was correctly measured, and if all the inputs and conditions of production were fully specified and correctly measured, the ratio G_s/G_n would be equal to 100. To explain why G_s/G_n deviates from 100, then, is a process of accounting for such errors of measurement as omitted inputs, failure to adjust for differences in the quality of inputs, neglect of economies of scale or of improvements in the organization of production, omitted outputs, disequilibria in markets, and differences in product mixes.[4]

In order to measure the effect of slavery on the process of production, it is therefore necessary to distinguish those mismeasurements that represent specific features of the slave system from those that are due merely to imperfections in the data, imperfections in methods of aggregation, or other mismeasurements that have no particular bearing on the operation of the slave system. In other words, we wish to obtain a residual measure of efficiency limited exclusively to measurement errors

3. Because of differences in the values of the α_i, the values of G_s/G_n presented in Tables B.20 and B.21 of *TOTC*, II, were 106.4 and 140.8. In the 1971 article the factor shares were $\alpha_L = 0.60$, $\alpha_K = 0.20$, and $\alpha_T = 0.20$. In *TOTC* the corresponding factor shares, which were derived from a production function for the cotton South by dividing the output elasticities by $1 + \sigma$, were 0.58, 0.17, and 0.25. See fn. 8, below.

4. To restate the point more formally, equation (1) assumes that the production function in the *i*th region is $Q_i = f(L_i, K_i, T_i)$ rather than $Q_i = f(L_iA_{iL}, K_iA_{iK}, T_iA_{iT})$, where A_{iL}, A_{iK}, A_{iT} are the factor-augmenting coefficients in the *i*th region needed to transform the inputs of labor, capital, and land into "efficiency units." Note that in the augmenting formulation, differences in rainfall or sunshine between regions do not necessarily imply different regional production functions. As long as the output elasticities are the same for both regions, and there are no problems in aggregating output, the production functions will be the same even though the factor-augmenting coefficients differ. However, to the extent that the greater rainfall and sunshine of the South raises A_{sT} relative to A_{nT}, the failure to convert the land input in both regions into units of equal efficiency, as is the case when equation (1) is employed, raises G_s relative to G_n even when the production functions are identical.

When the output elasticities, and hence the factor shares, in the North and the South differ, an index number problem arises, since the same factor shares must be applied to the North and the South in order to prevent the unit of measurement from affecting the result. If the factor shares of the two regions do not differ greatly, the index number problem will be minor. As we pointed out in our 1971 article, the value of G_s/G_n is robust to plausible alternative estimates of the factor shares. Had we reduced the labor share from 0.58 to 0.5, and raised the capital and land shares proportionately so that they summed to 0.5, the partially adjusted index of G_s/G_n would have risen from 138.9 to 147.6. Had we made the labor share 0.7, while reducing the capital and land shares proportionately, the value of G_s/G_n would have declined from 138.9 to 132.2. The issues posed by differences between the northern and southern product mixes are discussed in Section IV, below.

called "specific features of slavery." We then have the further task of identifying which specific features of slavery account for what parts of the aggregate value of the residual.

In our 1971 paper we stressed that a higher productivity index for the South than for the North did not necessarily imply that the southern advantage was due to special features of the slave system. We thought it was possible that slave-using plantations were less efficient than those using free labor, but that for some still undisclosed reason free southern farms were extraordinarily efficient. The high value of the southern productivity index would then be the consequence of averaging over a high index for free farms and a low index for slave plantations. Another possibility was that both slave and free farms that engaged in diversified agriculture were about as efficient as free farms in the North but plantations specializing in the export staples were highly efficient. In that case the relative productivity of the South might be due not to slavery per se, but merely to an unusually favorable market situation in 1860 for those export staples that happened to be produced by slave labor.

While we did not at that time rule out these alternatives, evidence in the 1860 Census indicated that the large slave plantations produced not only more cotton per capita but also more food per capita than small free farms in the South. It therefore seemed likely that the relative efficiency of southern agriculture was probably related to certain special features of the slave system. We conjectured that two features of slavery were particularly important. The first is that labor, and perhaps other inputs, were employed more intensively under the system of slavery than under the system of farming with free labor. There is much testimony for the proposition that slaves worked more days per year and, perhaps, more hours per day than free farmers. Since our efficiency indexes measured the labor input not in man-hours but in man-years, the more intensive utilization of labor shows up not as greater labor input but as a higher level of productivity. In 1971 we were inclined to believe that our failure to take account of the greater number of hours worked per year by slaves than by free men explained all, or nearly all, of our index of the superior efficiency of slavery. We also considered the much-debated possibility that there were economies of scale in the slave sector of agriculture. Even scholars who thought that slave labor was less efficient than free labor had suggested that the lower quality of labor might have been offset by the superior entrepreneurship associated with large-scale plantations.

To test these hypotheses we launched a search for additional data. A sample of 5,700 estates containing information on the price, age, sex, skills, and handicaps of slaves was retrieved from the probate records of

Table 1. *Definitions of symbols used in equations and tables*

Q = output. For unadjusted G_s and G_n, both Q_s and Q_n were based on the quantities reported in the 1860 Census of agriculture. The factors for seed and feed as well as the ratios for converting the stock of livestock into annual production were obtained from Towne and Rasmussen. Uniform national prices of 1860, again taken from Towne and Rasmussen, were used to aggregate the quantities produced in each region into Q_s and Q_n. In partially adjusted and more fully adjusted G_s, the output of animal products was reduced to take account of the low slaughter weights prevailing in the South relative to northern slaughter weights.

L = input of labor. *Free Labor in the North:* In unadjusted G_n, L_n was taken to be equal to the census count of farmers and other agricultural occupations listed in the 1860 Census plus 17 percent of males aged 10–15. Thus children under 10 and females were excluded from the labor force. Those included were counted as equivalent full hands. In partially adjusted G_n, females and children under 10 continued to be excluded and males 60 or over were also excluded. Males between 10 and 59 were converted into equivalent full hands, using the weights applied to male slaves in partially adjusted G_s. *Free Labor in the South:* In unadjusted and partially adjusted G_s, the procedures were those employed in the corresponding northern indexes. In more fully adjusted G_s, free males age 15 or over were given the age-specific weights derived from the age-earning profiles of male slaves. On farms with 0–5 slaves, free females age 10 or over were given one half the corresponding age-specific weight for female slaves, and free boys aged 10–14 were given the same age-specific weight as male slaves of that age category. The weights applied to free females and children on plantations with over 5 slaves were reduced linearly as plantation size increased, reaching zero for plantations with 50 or more slaves. *Slaves:* In unadjusted G_s, 83 percent of all slaves aged 10 or over were assumed to be in the labor force and all were counted as equivalent full hands. In partially adjusted G_s, a deduction was made for rural slaves employed as domestics rather than in agricultural production. Rough estimates of age- and sex-specific weights based on reports of various authorities were used to convert males and females into equivalent full hands. The weights employed for males were: ages 10–14, 0.40; ages 15–19, 0.88; ages 20–54, 1.0; ages 55–59, 0.75; ages 60 or over, 0. Weights for females at each age ranged between 70 and 78 percent of the corresponding weights for males. In more fully adjusted G_s, the weights used to convert males and females into equivalent full hands were based on age-earnings profiles reported in *(TOTC) Time on the Cross* for slaves of each sex. No adjustment was made for females engaged in domestic service. However, a deduction was made for males who were engaged in activities, primarily artisan crafts, not covered by the output measure.

K = input of capital. In unadjusted and partially adjusted G_s and G_n, K was measured as the annual rental value of livestock, implements and machinery, and buildings. This was taken to be equal to the value of these items multiplied by the rate of return on farm capital (10 percent) plus average annual rates of depreciation of 2 percent for buildings and 10 percent for implements and machinery In more fully adjusted G_s, K was measured by the value of implements and machinery, and a corresponding adjustment was made in G_n for purposes of comparison with more fully adjusted G_s.

T = input for land. In unadjusted G_s and G_n, T was measured by total acres in farms. In partially adjusted G_s and G_n, T was measured by the value of land plus improvements. In more fully adjusted G_s, T was measured by the value of land plus improvements and buildings, and a corresponding adjustment was made in G_n for purposes of comparison with more fully adjusted G_s.

$\alpha_L, \alpha_K, \alpha_T$ = shares in value of output of labor, capital, and land

α_i = output elasticities of the inputs
A = the intercept of the production function
G = geometric index of total factor productivity
σ = the scale factor $(\alpha_1 + \alpha_2 + \alpha_3 - 1)$
Y = the age of land (years of land settlement)
V = the value of land plus improvements
δ = the rate of land depletion
i = the rate of interest

I = number of improved acres
U = number of unimproved acres
γ_1 = price per acre of I
γ_2 = price per acre of U
s = a subscript denoting the South
n = a subscript denoting the North
$\hat{}$ = a "hat" over a variable denotes the logarithm of that variable

Table 2. *Indexes of total factor productivity on southern farms, by subregion and size of farm (G_n = 100)*

Size of Farm as Measured by the Number of Slaves Per Farm	Slave Exporting States (Old South)	Slave Importing States (New South)	All States in Parker-Gallman Sample (Cotton South)
0	98.4	112.7	109.3
1-15	103.3	127.2	117.7
16-50	124.9	176.1	158.2
51 or more	135.1	154.7	145.9
All slave farms	118.9	153.1	140.4
All farms (slave and nonslave) in the subregion	116.2	144.7	134.7

Source: TOTC, II, p. 139. The slave-exporting (Old South) states are Georgia, North Carolina, South Carolina, and Virginia; the slave-importing (New South) states are Alabama, Arkansas, Florida, Louisiana, Mississippi, Tennessee, and Texas.

southern courts. Southern archives yielded a sample of the business records of roughly 100 large plantations containing either detailed information on the organization of production, including the daily activities of each slave in the labor force, or demographic information needed to adjust the labor input of women.[5] The data in these sources, combined with the data in the Parker–Gallman sample of over 5,000 southern farms listed in the manuscript schedules of the 1860 Census,[6] made it possible to refine the input and output measures of G_s. The net effect of these refinements was to reduce G_s/G_n to 134.7.[7] The new data

5. A further description of these two samples, as well as of 21 additional samples containing evidence relevant to the analysis of the slave economy, is contained in the authors (1975), Table 2, pp. 6–8. The appendix of the same source (pp. 137–139) contains a state and county distribution of the 77,000 slaves in the probate sample, by plantation size. It also contains more extended description of 6 of the other 22 samples.

6. James Foust gives a detailed description of the design of the Parker–Gallman sample and of the information contained in it. He also tests various statistics computed from the sample against the aggregate 1860 Census to assess the representativeness of the sample.

7. The evidence collected between 1971 and 1973 indicated that our previous belief that slaves worked more hours per year than free farmers was incorrect. We continued, therefore, to measure the labor input of slaves and free men in man-years, presenting only a brief and, in retrospect, inadequate justification for this procedure (see *TOTC*, I, pp. 207–208). The question is discussed more fully in Section III of this paper.

Paul David and Peter Temin (p. 277) have argued that the interim weights that we applied to labor in the North biased the productivity comparison in favor of the South rather than in favor of the North. However, the ratio of equivalent peak-productive hands to persons on farms in the North yielded by our partially adjusted procedure is 0.273. If we had applied the same age- and sex-specific weights in the North that we did for the free farmers in the South under

Table 3. *The relationship between total factor productivity and farm size in each region (index of free farms in each region = 100)*

Number of Slaves Per Farm	Slave Exporting States (Old South)	Slave Importing States (New South)	All States in Parker-Gallman Sample (Cotton South)
0	100.0	100.0	100.0
1–15	105.0	112.9	107.7
16–50	126.9	156.3	144.7
51 or more	137.3	137.3	133.5
All slave farms	120.8	135.8	128.5

Source: TOTC, II, p. 139.

also permitted the computation of total factor productivity indexes by farm size and subregion. Tables 2 and 3 show that the superior efficiency of southern agriculture was not due primarily to the high performance of the free farms of the South. Free farms of the Old South fell below the efficiency of northern farms by 2 percent, while free farms in the New South exceeded the efficiency of northern farms by 13 percent. Thus only 4 percent of the efficiency advantage of southern over northern agriculture was due to the superior performance of the free sector. Slave farms accounted for 96 percent of the southern advantage.

Table 3 shows that within each region efficiency increased with farm size, except that in the New South the efficiency index is higher for medium than for large plantations.[8] While we considered the possibility that in the West this intermediate category of slave plantations was

the more fully adjusted procedure, the ratio of equivalent peak-productive hands to persons on farms would have been 0.389. In other words, if we had used the procedure proposed by David and Temin, the labor input of northern farms would have increased by 42.5 percent. As a consequence the ratio G_s/G_n would have been not 134.7, but 165.4.

8. Table 3 suggests economies of scale. To test for this possibility we fitted

$$\hat{Q} = \hat{A} + \alpha_2(\hat{K} - \hat{L}) + \alpha_3(\hat{T} - \hat{L}) + (1 + \sigma)\hat{L}$$

to measures of the inputs and outputs derived from the Parker–Gallman sample. The resulting regression was

$$\hat{Q} = 2.898 + \underset{(0.0113)}{0.1815}(\hat{K} - \hat{L}) + \underset{(0.0125)}{0.2606}(\hat{T} - \hat{L}) + \underset{(0.0124)}{1.0645}\hat{L}$$

(figures in parentheses are standard errors). The scale factor (σ = 0.0645) is significant at well beyond the 0.001 level. Similar regressions, fitted to data for various regions, indicate that the scale factor was larger in the New South than in the Old South. A more complete discussion of these regional regressions will be presented in the authors' forthcoming book.

actually more efficient than large plantations, we believed that the reversal was probably due to measurement errors. One was a failure to adjust adequately for the locational component of land values, which might have accounted for a much larger share of total land value on slave plantations with 51 or more slaves, especially in the New South, than on slave plantations in the 16–50 category. Another was the inadequacy of our adjustment for omitted products. Large slave farms, especially in the West, probably engaged much more heavily in home manufacture than did small ones. Large slave farms also appear to have devoted a larger share of the labor force to domestic services than did small plantations. We did not think that when these adjustments were made the entire differential in efficiency between the Old and New South would disappear. The continuous flow of labor from the Old South to the New South suggests that the long-run equilibrium between the two regions had not been attained by 1860. Hence one would expect to find some efficiency advantage in the newer area.

The criticism of our efficiency computation have largely followed the lines of analysis set forth in both our 1971 essay and in *Time on the Cross*. The important and widely cited critique of our productivity measures by Paul David and Peter Temin, for example, is largely a restatement of the caveats that we incorporated in the presentation of our findings, except that in virtually every place where we said that the measurement bias was negligible or went against the South, David and Temin sought to make the case that it was large or went in favor of the South. In this effort, the critics did not present new bodies of evidence that we overlooked but either conjectured upon the possibility that missing evidence could be found that would overturn our findings or else dwelt upon what they considered to be internal inconsistencies in our analysis or between various parts of the evidential corpus. The debate over efficiency has thus focused on a set of issues that both sides view as the agenda for a new round of research.[9] The balance of this paper reports on our progress in working through that agenda.

I. The use of 1860 price relatives and cotton output

In chapter 3 of *Time on the Cross* we presented evidence indicating that the 1850's were a boom period for cotton planters, with the demand for cotton increasing rapidly and cotton prices generally well above their long-run trend. These findings led Thomas Haskell, David and Temin, Gavin Wright, Harold Woodman, and a number of others to argue that

9. Other important critiques of our efficiency measures include Lance Davis, Thomas Haskell (1974, 1975), Harold Woodman, and Gavin Wright (1974, 1975).

Table 4. *The ratio of the prices of the principal products of northern farms to the price of cotton*

	1860 (1)	1850 (2)	(3)[a]
Corn/cotton	4.0	3.4	118
Wheat/cotton	8.9	6.8	131
Hogs/cotton	42.5	27.5	155
Cattle/cotton	33.4	24.3	137

Source: Computed from data in Marvin Towne and Wayne Rasmussen, pp. 283, 284, 294, 297, 308. Cotton is in dollars per pound, hogs and cattle in dollars per hundredweight, corn and wheat in dollars per bushel.

[a]Columns (1) ÷ (2) × 100.

the high relative efficiency of southern agriculture indicated by the ratio G_s/G_n is merely an artifact of the temporarily inflated price of cotton in 1860 – of our decision to use 1860 price relatives instead of those of a more normal year in computing the aggregate output of both the North and the South.

Even if this argument about the direction of the bias were correct, there would still be the question of the magnitude of the bias. Between 1857 and 1860 there was a very substantial supply response on the part of cotton producers, which led to a fall in prices from the 1857 peak. By 1860, cotton prices had declined to within 8 percent of their long-run trend, or equilibrium, value. If, in aggregating southern output, we reduced the price applied to cotton by 7.5 percent $[1 - (1/1.08) \approx 0.075]$, the ratio G_s/G_n would decline from 134.7 to 131.8.[10]

What has been overlooked by Haskell and others is that 1860 was a boom year for all of agriculture and not merely cotton. Consequently, the direction of the bias introduced by using 1860 prices to aggregate output does not turn on whether cotton was high relative to its price in other years, but whether it was higher than normal relative to other agricultural prices, particularly to those of the principal northern agricultural products. Table 4 shows that the prices of the principal northern products relative to cotton were *higher* in 1860 than in 1850 (the only other year in which the data are sufficiently complete to permit the type of inter- and intraregional efficiency comparisons that we require). Had we chosen the 1850 set of price relatives or computed our efficiency

10. The cotton share of southern farm output (0.284) was computed from data underlying the computations described in *TOTC*, II, pp. 131–138.

Table 5. *The ratio of an index of all farm product prices to the price of cotton (ratio for 1811–20 = 100)*

1860	135
Average for the Half Century	
1811-60	114
Decade Averages	
1811-20	100
1821-30	96
1831-40	115
1841-50	136
1851-60	143

Source: Computed from U.S. Bureau of the Census, 1960, pp. 115, 124. For each time period the average value of the index of all farm product prices was divided by the average price of cotton. The resulting ratios were then expressed as a percentage of the ratio for 1811-20.

indexes for 1850, as some have advocated, we would have increased (not reduced) the measured efficiency of slave agriculture relative to that of free agriculture as well as the advantage of large plantations relative to small farms.

Is it possible that both 1850 and 1860 are rare exceptions and that the price relatives of most other years would in fact support the case of the critics? Table 5 provides an answer to that question. It shows that the ratio of all farm product prices to that of cotton was 18 percent higher in 1860 than it was on average over the entire half century from 1811 to 1860. Thus in choosing the price relatives of 1860 to construct the output indexes, we chose a set of prices less favorable to the South than those that prevailed in 34 of the 49 years preceding 1860.

Wright (1975) argued that the choice of 1860 biased the productivity computation in favor of the South for still another reason. He believes that the South was the beneficiary of "random fluctuations in yields around their normal levels" (pp. 449–450) that made the cotton crop of 1860 unusually large. This fortunate event, he conjectured, caused cotton production in the New South to be between 35.2 and 43.5 percent above its predicted, or normal, level (p. 444). Wright presented no actual evidence on yields to support this conjecture. Since the U.S. Department of Agriculture (*USDA*) did not begin collecting data on cotton acreage until after the Civil War, there is no basis for systematic estimates of annual cotton yields per acre harvested during the antebellum years.

Over the years 1867–1900, for which data on cotton yields are available, the average annual yield per acre is 177.1 pounds and the standard deviation is 20.10.[11] Thus a chance deviation in yields of between 35 and 44 percent above the mean (between 3.1 and 3.8 standard deviations) is an event so rare (less than one in a thousand) that one would expect it to have occasioned great comment among planters and in the agricultural publications of the time. Yet while much was said about the large size of the 1860 crop, the available commentaries are devoid of references to an extraordinarily high yield (see, for example, U.S. Bureau of the Census, 1862, p. 84; Lewis Cecil Gray, chs. 30 and 37; James Watkins, p. 10).

Wright based his conjecture on a supply curve for cotton that he has estimated, in which the output of cotton in a given year is made a function of the price of cotton (lagged one year) and the cumulative sales of public land (lagged two years) in four states of the New South and Florida (Wright 1971, pp. 111, 114). When Wright argues that the 1860 production of cotton in these states was above the predicted level, he means that observed output was above the level predicted by a model in which only cumulated past sales of public land can shift the supply curve of cotton. He arbitrarily assigns the entire residual for 1860 to cotton yields, although at least some part, if not all of it, is merely the artifact of an equation that failed to take account of such other determinants of supply as the proportion of privately held land that was in farms, the proportion of land in farms that was improved, the proportion of improved land sown in cotton, and the labor to land ratio. Rather than being fixed during the decade of the 1850s, as Wright assumed, these ratios were changing in such a manner as to increase the supply of cotton more rapidly than the cumulative total of public land sales. Between 1850 and 1860 the amount of improved land in the farms of the four states of the New South singled out by Wright increased by 59 percent, which was 1.6 times more rapid than corn production, 8.4 times more rapid than sweet potato production, and 20 times more rapid than the stock of hogs (U.S. Bureau of the Census 1862, pp. 196–236). This suggests that cotton was getting an increasing share of improved land at the expense of the principal food and feed crops.[12] In

11. Computed from *USDA*, 1955, p. 5. The observation for 1866 was dropped because yields in that year were abnormally low as a result of the postwar disorganization of southern agriculture. But its inclusion would not affect the argument.

12. Regressions relating yield per acre of cotton and yield per acre of corn in the cotton states estimated for the period 1867–1900 indicate that the elasticity of corn yields with respect to cotton yields was 1.1. It follows that if weather caused the cotton yield of these states to be 35 percent above normal, one would expect corn yields to be 38 percent above their normal level. Since Wright argues that yields in 1850 were below normal, if the acreage devoted to corn had

several cases, including oats and rice, output not only failed to keep pace with rate of growth of improved land but declined absolutely. Public land sales are, of course, irrelevant to the supply of cotton in states that accounted for over a quarter of the crop of 1860, since they were not public-land states. In South Carolina, for example, cotton production increased by 17 percent between 1850 and 1860, although land in farms decreased slightly (see U.S. Bureau of the Census 1862, pp. 196–209).

What then explains the big increase in the output of cotton between 1850 and 1860? A complete answer to this question is beyond reach, but factors explaining about 91 percent of the increase can be identified. While we do not know what *annual* cotton yields were prior to the Civil War, in 1868 the U.S. commissioner of agriculture asked his corps of crop reporters to ascertain the normal cotton yields, as well as the normal share of tilled land sown in cotton, that had prevailed in 1860 and the years immediately preceding it. The figures obtained by this survey (pp. 414–415) indicate that the shift in the geographic locus of cotton production from the Old to the New South explains about 8 percent of the increase in output between 1850 and 1860. Assuming that within each state cotton just maintained its share of improved land, the increase in improved land explains 41 percent of the growth in the cotton crop. The amount of land switched within states from other crops to cotton cannot be known with certainty. But if we assume that the entire shift was confined to corn, the failure of corn production to keep pace with the increase in improved land implies that within-state reallocations of improved acreage explain another 42 percent of the growth in the cotton crop. These estimates leave a residual of 9 percent to be explained by all other factors including increases in the use of fertilizers, increases in the labor to land ratio, and random fluctuations in yields.[13]

been held constant, one would expect the random fluctuation of yields hypothesized by Wright to have made the 1860 output of corn at least 38 percent greater than in 1850. That corn output actually increased by only 19 percent, therefore leads to the improbable conclusion that there was not only a proportionate decline but an absolute decline of 16 percent in the acreage devoted to corn between the two dates.

13. The increase in output due to interstate shifts has two components: that due to the increase in the Southwide proportion of land in cotton and that due to the increase in the Southwide average yield per acre. Data for estimating both components were obtained from U.S. Bureau of the Census, 1895, pp. 92, 100; and *USDA*, 1868, pp. 414–415. The reallocation of corn land to cotton within states was computed by subtracting the actual 1860 production of corn in each of the 10 cotton states from the crop that would have been observed in each state if the growth of output had kept pace with the increase of improved land. The sum of these differences divided by 13.350 bushels, the average corn yield per harvested acre in these states between 1867 and 1900 (*USDA*, 1954), gives the number of acres switched from corn to cotton (there was no trend in corn yields between 1867 and 1900). The 1860 output of cotton divided by 177.1 pounds, the average per acre yield of cotton between 1867 and 1900, gives the number of acres in cotton in 1860. The last figure divided into the acreage that would have

But even if one grants so fortunate an event in 1859–1860 as cotton yields that were 1.65 standard deviations above the mean (an event expected only once in 20 years), and assuming that northern farmers shared none of the benefits of the favorable weather that supposedly visited the South during 1859–1860, the appropriate adjustment would just reduce G_s/G_n from 134.7 to 128.7. If we grant both fortuitously high cotton yields and inappropriately high price relatives, the ratio G_s/G_n declines to 126.3.[14]

II. Problems in measuring the land input

We turn now to the two principal criticisms of our measure of the land input. In our quality adjustment of the land input we used land values (V) rather than the rental value of land $[(i + \delta)V]$, which contains a term for land depletion. It has been argued that land was depleted in the South, especially in the slave-selling states, much more rapidly than in the North.[15] To test this hypothesis we examined the relationship of land yields to the length of settlement in the selling states.[16] The effect of the length of settlement on land yields was estimated from equation (2):

$$\hat{Q} - \hat{T} = \beta_0 + \beta_1(\hat{L} - \hat{T}) + \beta_2(\hat{K} - \hat{T}) + \beta_3 Y \tag{2}$$

The equation was fitted to output and input measures constructed from the Parker–Gallman sample. When T was measured by total acres, the resulting regression was

$$\begin{aligned} \hat{Q} - \hat{T} = 3.988 &+ \underset{(0.0243)}{0.6070}(\hat{L} - \hat{T}) \\ &+ \underset{(0.0174)}{0.2682}(\hat{K} - \hat{T}) - \underset{(0.00077)}{0.00570}Y \end{aligned} \tag{3}$$

$$R^2 = 0.5045; \quad N = 1{,}539$$

been in cotton if corn land had not been switched to cotton, represents the percentage increase in the output of cotton due to the within-state shift of land into cotton. This computation assumes that none of the increase in corn production between 1850 and 1860 is due to random fluctuations in yields. As fn. 12 indicates, such a fluctuation implies a greater reallocation of corn land to cotton than we have allowed. The distribution of interaction terms was resolved by converting the calculation to annual rates of change.

14. The reduction in price, of course, only applies to the output of cotton reduced by 15.8 percent, the reduction which corresponds to 1.65 standard deviations. To grant a random increase in yields of 1.65 standard deviations above the mean is to attribute more than 175 percent of the unexplained increase in the cotton crop to good fortune.
15. See Cairnes, pp. 52–53; Phillips, pp. 332, 336; Gray, pp. 447–448; Genovese, pp. 85–105.
16. See Wright (1969), ch. 4, for an earlier attempt to test this hypothesis. Wright did not, however, construct an aggregate index of output or adjust for differences in the quality of the inputs of labor.

When T was measured by improved acres, the resulting regression was

$$(4) \qquad \hat{Q} - \hat{T} = 3.336 + \underset{(0.0242)}{0.3736}(\hat{L} - \hat{T}) + \underset{(0.0167)}{0.1786}(\hat{K} - \hat{T}) - \underset{(0.00071)}{0.00558}Y$$

$$R^2 = 0.2589; \quad N = 1{,}539$$

In both regressions, β_3, which we interpret as the rate at which land yields changed with the length of settlement, is statistically significant, negative, but small. Whether this rate of decline, barely 1/2 of 1 percent per annum, was more or less than in the North remains to be determined. However, even if one assumes that the northern depletion rate was zero, an adjustment for depletion in the South would raise that region's input of land by less than 6 percent. This rise, in turn, would reduce G_s/G_n from 134.7 to 132.9. Combining the adjustment for depletion with those for high cotton prices and fortunate yields, reduces G_s/G_n to 124.5.

David and Temin centered their criticism of our adjustment for differences in land quality on our failure to remove the locational component of land values. This omission created a more serious problem than the neglect of depletion, especially for the intra-South efficiency comparisons. The problem would not arise if farm-gate prices had been used in constructing the output index. For then farms located far from markets would receive lower prices for their products and also have lower values per acre of land than farms close to markets. Since uniform national prices were employed in constructing the output index, we implicitly assumed that all farms used the same average amount of transport service. If, as is frequently asserted, large slave plantations were generally better located than small farms, the assumption would introduce a bias against large plantations in the productivity comparisons. To test this hypothesis we estimated equation (5), on farms of various sizes, both by state and for the South as a whole.[17]

$$(5) \qquad V = \gamma_1 I + \gamma_2 U$$

The preliminary results of the analysis are summarized in Table 6, which shows that the locational component of land (estimated as γ_2 per acre) for the South as a whole was an average of 44 percent of land values. Thus 56 percent of so-called land values were due to investment

17. See Wright (1969), p. 95. Wright's regressions were fitted to the counties in the various soil categories that were constructed by Gray. Wright did not attempt to produce state or Southwide estimates of γ_1 and γ_2 by farm size but he did point out that it was γ_1 that explained most of the value of farmland and improvements.

Table 6. *The share of improvements in the total value of land plus improvements, by farm size*

Number of Slaves per Farm:	0	1-15	16-50	51+	All Farms in Cotton South
(1) Improved acres per farm (I)	46.85	121.25	349.76	930.24	141.94
(2) Unimproved acres per farm (U)	140.41	315.69	653.37	1,710.85	320.72
(3) Price per acre of I in \$ (γ_1)	13.138	20.243	23.294	30.949	22.30
(4) Price per acre of U in \$ (γ_2)	2.572	2.533	2.931	12.613	4.288
(5) $\gamma_1 - \gamma_2$ (\$)	10.566	17.710	20.363	18.336	18.012
(6) $\gamma_2(I + U)$ (\$)	481.63	1,106.77	2,940.17	33,312.07	1,983.89
(7) $(\gamma_1 - \gamma_2)I$ (\$)	495.02	2,147.34	7,122.16	17,056.88	2,556.62
(8) Total value of land and improvements per farm (Row 6 + Row 7 in \$)	976.65	3,254.11	10,062.33	50,368.95	4,540.51
(9) Improvements as a share of total value of land and improvements (Row 7/Row 8, percent)	50.69	65.99	70.78	33.86	56.31
(10) Location as a share of total value of land and improvements (100 − Row 9, percent)	49.31	34.01	29.22	66.14	43.69

Source: Computed from data in the Parker-Gallman sample, using the values of γ_1 and γ_2 estimated from the Southwide regressions run on equation (7) for each size class. Values of γ_1 and γ_2 were, in all cases, significant at the 0.001 level. The entries in rows 1-4 of the all-farms column are weighted averages of the corresponding entries for columns 1-4. The weights in rows 1 and 2 are the proportion of farms. The weights in rows 3 and 4 are the proportion of improved and unimproved acres, respectively.

in the land, and not, as is so often argued, to locational rents. Plantations with 51 or more slaves, however, were an exception. These large plantations, it turns out, were much better located than small ones. The average locational rent per acre on large plantations was more than four times that on smaller-sized farms, whether slave or free.[18] Consequently,

18. It might be argued that better (more fertile) land was brought into production first. In that case $\gamma_1 - \gamma_2$ would measure not only the average investment per improved acre but also the superior quality of the land on which the improvement had been made. Even if this were the case all of $\gamma_1 - \gamma_2$ belongs in the quality adjustment, since whether this amount is due entirely to improvements or reflects some superior virgin quality, it is "more" land in an economic sense. We can test the hypothesis that more fertile land was improved first by making use of Martin Primack's estimates of labor required to improve an acre (pp. 154–155, 233–243), and annual wage rates on southern farms (*USDA* 1868, p. 416). These indicate that the average value of improvements per acre was \$20.05. Since $\gamma_1 - \gamma_2 =$ \$18.01, Primack's data suggest that all of $\gamma_1 - \gamma_2$ is investment. Probably ease of land clearing rather than natural fertility was the principal factor determining which land was improved first.

It might also be argued that the land belonging to plantations with 51 or more slaves was more fertile than the land of smaller farms. If so, some part of γ_2 for this class would represent not locational advantage but the superior fertility of land yet to be brought into production, and the subtraction of all of γ_2 from γ_1 would underestimate the quantity of quality-adjusted

Table 7. *The effect of correcting for the locational component of land values on the relative values of the indexes of total factor productivity (index of free southern farms = 100)*

Number of Slaves per Farm	Index Before Correction, All States in Parker-Gallman Sample	Index After Correction, All States in Parker-Gallman Sample
0	100.0	100.0
1-15	107.7	100.8
16-50	144.7	133.1
51 or more	133.5	147.7

even though investment per improved acre on large plantations exceeded the cotton-South average, investment accounted for only 34 percent of land values.[19]

It follows that the previous failure to correct for locational rents biased the efficiency index for plantations with 51 or more slaves down-

land plus improvements that must be included in the land input of this class. Alternative assumptions regarding the distribution of γ_2 between locational advantage and superior fertility led to variations in the index of total factor productivity for this class of farms ranging from 147.7 to 132.8 (see Table 7, col. 3). Two aspects of this result should be stressed. First, even if we assumed that the locational advantage of farms with 51 or more slaves was no greater than that of farms with 16–50 slaves, none of the arguments in the balance of this paper would be altered. Second, the principal effect of variations in the distribution of γ_2 is on the assessment of the comparative efficiency of intermediate and large plantations. Assuming that plantations in the 51-or-more class had greater locational advantage than those in the 16–50 class leads to the conclusion that they were more productive than those in the 16–50 class. If we assumed that locational advantages were identical, then both classes would have roughly the same indexes of total factor productivity.

19. For the North γ_2 is just $1.80 per acre. Thus the locational component per acre was lower in the North than in the South. The result is surprising only if considered in a partial rather than a general equilibrium context. Between 1840 and 1860 over 15,000 miles of railroad track were built in the North, bringing millions of acres close to a rail route. This massive increase in supramarginal land brought about by railroad construction probably lowered rather than raised the average locational rent (see Fogel, 1964, p. 223, n. 10). According to Haskell (1975) our assumption that "an acre of northern farmland was an average of 2.5 times better in quality than southern farmland" is "extraordinary" (p. 38). But an "average" acre of northern farmland was superior to an "average" southern acre in 1860, not primarily because of its natural qualities, as Haskell appears to believe, but because more capital had been invested in its improvement. Over 54 percent of northern farmland had been improved by 1860 but for the South the corresponding figure is only 30 percent. Consequently, even if land in both

ward, while the indexes for plantations with 1–15 and 16–50 slaves were biased upward. Table 7 shows that after correction for locational rents, total factor productivity on slave farms increases continuously with farm size, but small slave farms have no productivity advantage over free farms.

III. The length of the work year

One of the most important results of the work over the past two years is the finding by Jacob Metzer and John Olson that slaves worked fewer hours per year than free farmers. This directly contradicts the hypothesis of our 1971 paper that the measurement of the labor input in man-years rather than man-hours was the principal reason that G_s exceeded G_n. The belief that slaves worked more days per year than free men is not only widely held but was recently reasserted by David and Temin (pp. 768–771) who attributed the phenomenon to the fact that there were more frost-free days in the South than in the North. They put the average length of the work year of northern farmers at 2,163 hours. Noting that there are between 220 and 240 frost-free days in the South but only between 160 and 180 such days in the North, David and Temin argued that it was reasonable to assume that slaves worked 10 percent more days per year than free northern farmers. Moreover, since the days during the winter were both longer and warmer in the South than in the North, they also reasoned that slaves probably averaged more hours per day than northern farmers.

Systematic data bearing on the average number of days worked per year and per season during antebellum times are available only for the South. Such averages have been computed by Metzer and Olson from the daily work records that were kept by the owners or overseers of slave plantations.[20] Processing of most of these is still in progress, and the computations employed in this paper are based on a subsample of 7 cotton plantations that are displayed in Table 8.

regions had been of equal quality in the natural state and if expenditures per improved acre had been the same in both regions, the average northern acre would have been 1.8 times better than the average southern acre. But northerners invested about 30 percent more on each of their improved acres than did southerners. Thus about 90 percent of the "superior" quality of northern land represented investment. (Computed from data in Primack, pp. 154–155, 233–243; U.S. Bureau of the Census, 1895, pp. 84–100; Clarence Danhof, p. 77; and *USDA*, 1868, p. 416).

20. The periods covered by these records range from a single season to several years. The detail contained is uneven, but it is possible to determine the daily work records of fieldhands and sometimes also that of artisans, servants, and others engaged in nonagricultural labor. It is also possible to determine holidays and days lost due to rain or illness.

Table 8. *Days worked per season for a sample of southern cotton plantations*

	Spring	Summer	Fall	Winter	Total
Prudhomme-Bermuda (LA)	71.6	72.1	65.6	61.9	271.2
Flinn-Green River (MS)	70.3	72.6	71.9	67.0	281.8
Monette-Hope and Pleasant Hill (LA)	73.9	74.5	67.1	65.6	281.1
Le Blanc (LA)	75.7	68.1	67.2	70.7	281.7
Pre Aux Cleres (LA)	73.5	69.5	68.6	68.2	279.8
El Destino (FL)	72.6	68.9	70.2	67.7	279.4
Average of six short-staple plantations (equal weights)	72.9	71.0	68.4	66.8	279.1
Kollock-Ossabow Island (GA)	77.6	73.5	70.9	70.7	292.7
Average of seven plantations (equal weights)	73.6	71.3	68.8	67.4	281.1

Source: Olson.

This table shows that there was relatively little variation in the number of days worked per season, although the number of work days during the spring planting and cultivating period was about 7 percent greater than during the peak harvest months of the fall. The average number of days worked per year within the sample ranged from 271 to 293. The average number of days worked per year in the sample of 6 short-staple plantations is 279. Adding the long-staple Kollock plantation raises the average to 281 days.

Thus the number of days in the work year of slaves appears to have fallen short of the potential by about 23 percent. This result is explained primarily by the almost total absence of Sunday work.[21] Occasionally, a few hands were used on Sundays for special tasks. But such incidents were rare. This nearly total absence of Sunday work is a unique feature of the large slave plantations, and it bears on the special nature of the slave-labor system.

Unfortunately, information on the length of the agricultural workday for the antebellum era is fragmentary, although a recurrent theme is that the day extended from sunrise to sunset. The earliest systematic studies of regional and seasonal variation in the length of the workday carried out by the *USDA* pertain to the first third of the twentieth century. Olson points out that these studies yield seasonal estimates of the length of the workday that are quite similar to those obtained by subtracting standard time allowances for meals during antebellum times from the interval between sunrise and sunset in each region and season. Combining the information on the number of workdays presented in Table 8 with these seasonal estimates of the average length of the workday, Olson

21. The balance of the shortfall is explained by other holidays and half-days on Saturdays (6 days), by illness (11 days), and by rain and inclement weather (15 days).

Table 9. *Hours worked per season and per year for a sample of slave cotton plantations*

	Spring	Summer	Fall	Winter	Average per Season	Total
Prudhomme-Bermuda	759	771	702	477	677	2,709
Flinn-Green River	745	777	769	516	702	2,807
Monette-Hope and Pleasant Hill	783	797	718	505	701	2,803
Le Blanc	802	729	719	544	698	2,794
Pre Aux Cleres	779	744	734	525	696	2,782
El Destino	770	737	751	521	695	2,779
Average of six short-staple farms	773	760	732	514	695	2,779
Kollock (long staple) Ossabow Island	823	786	759	544	728	2,912
Average of seven cotton farms	780	763	736	519	700	2,798

Source: Olson.

produced Table 9, which presents the number of hours in the slave work year for the sample of 7 cotton plantations. The total hours worked per year within the sample ranged from a low of 2,709 to a high of 2,912. The average for the entire sample is 2,798 hours.[22] Since the last figure is 29 percent *greater* than the 2,163 hours that David and Temin hold was typical on northern farms, and 18 percent greater than their estimate of the length of the slave work year, this finding might seem to substantiate the proposition that the slave work year exceeded the free one.

But such a conclusion is warranted only if one accepts the contention that the average work year of antebellum farmers in the North was just 2,163 hours. David and Temin cite a *USDA* report by John Hopkins on changing conditions of agricultural labor and technology between World War I and 1936 as the source for this figure. But Hopkins put the length of the northern work year during this period at between 2,800 and 3,370 hours (pp. 23, 27). Combining the samples reported by Hopkins with those of several other *USDA* studies, Olson computed the average length of the agricultural work year in the various subregions of the North. Although there was a fair degree of variation from sample to sample, as well as by the principal subregions, the average of every sample exceeded the 2,163 hours asserted by David and Temin by at least 31 percent. The lowest subregional average of 3,006 hours was found in the corn and general farming belt; the highest was 3,365 hours in the western dairy region. The average for the overall sample of 1,605 northern farms was 3,130 hours.

22. Ralph Anderson, using a different sample of plantations and working independently of Olson, produced an estimate of the length of the slave work year that is quite similar to Olson's.

Comparison of these figures with Table 9 reveals that slaves worked approximately 10 percent fewer hours than northern farmers.[23] The contention that the number of frost-free days (or the length of the growing season) was the principal factor determining the length of the work year is, thus, incorrect. While the number of frost-free days determines which plants can be raised in a particular region, there is little relationship between the length of the growing season and the duration of the period from seedtime to harvest for particular crops. The growing season in South Dakota, for example, is about 150 days but the period from seedtime to harvest is 310 days for winter wheat and only 115 days for spring wheat (see James Covert pp. 35, 36, 43, 44).[24]

The length of the work year was determined not only by the duration of the planting, cultivating, and harvest seasons of a particular mix of crops but also by the mix between field crops and animal products (including dairy products). Olson stresses that the length of the northern work year was positively correlated with the degree of specialization in livestock and dairying. The implications of the labor-intensive methods of rearing livestock (which was already characteristic of the North by 1860)[25] and of dairying are revealed by a *USDA* study showing that the

23. This conclusion, of course, rests on the assumption that the northern work year was not shorter in antebellum times than during the first third of the twentieth century. The assumption is consistent with available fragmentary data. See Olson and the sources cited there. The discussion of the length of the northern work year involves two issues. First, since David and Temin turned to *USDA* data on hours worked by farmers during the first third of the twentieth century, there is the question of the average length of the work year indicated by this body of evidence. The second issue is whether or not an average derived from data for the early twentieth century may be applied to the antebellum period, given the changes that occurred in income and in the technology of feeding, milking, planting, and harvesting. Gallman has pointed to factors which suggest that hours worked in northern agriculture may have been longer in the early twentieth century than in the mid-nineteenth. These are discussed in some detail by Olson. Clearly, a continued search for evidence in antebellum sources bearing on this question is called for. But even if we granted the contention that the slave work year was 10 percent longer than the northern work year G_s/G_n would fall from 134.7 to 127.5. Combining this adjustment with the previous ones for high cotton prices, fortunate yields, and land depletion, reduces G_s/G_n to 117.9. So even if these conjectured corrections of southern inputs and outputs advanced by the critics were all correct, the efficiency of southern agriculture would still exceed that of northern agriculture by 18 percent. There is, of course, also the adjustment to the input of northern labor proposed by David and Temin. But as we pointed out in fn. 7, the direction of this adjustment is opposite to that conjectured by the critics. If we made it, G_s/G_n would rise from 117.9 to 144.8, thus wiping out the effect of the proposed adjustments to southern inputs and outputs.

24. The relationship between the growing period, the growing season, and the period between seedtime and harvest are clarified by Covert, p. 14.

25. See Fogel (1965), p. 216. Corn consumption per equivalent hog more than doubled in the North between 1840 and 1860 but remained relatively constant in the South. See Percy Wells Bidwell and John Falconer (pp. 393, 437), Gray (pp. 842–845), and Gates (pp. 199, 218).

average duration of the workday increased by over an hour on both weekdays and Sundays in counties that switched from general farming to dairying (see Olson; Hopkins, pp. 26–27). The principal reason for the longer work year in the North than on slave plantations is that the North specialized in dairy and livestock while slave plantations did not. Olson estimates that about 38 percent of the product of northern farms in 1860, as measured by value-added, originated in livestock and dairying. The corresponding figure for the cotton South is just 9 percent; for large plantations it is hardly 5 percent.

The finding that the slave work year was shorter than the free work year does not contradict the proposition that slave labor was more intensely exploited than free labor, but only the proposition that such exploitation took the form of more hours per year. What had been insufficiently emphasized is the possibility that slaves worked more intensively per hour than did free men.

IV. The problem of differences in product mix

There is still the problem of the regional differences in the mix of products. Because the output mixes of northern and southern agriculture differed, the attempt to compare G_s and G_n poses an index number problem. This is an issue which, of course, plagues all productivity comparisons, whether over space or time. David and Temin argue that in our case the problem is insuperable because cotton could be grown only in the South, not in the North. Fortunately, the problem is not quite so intractable.

The influence of product mix can be tackled by taking advantage of the fact that there was a class of free farms that could, and did, produce cotton. While it is true that free southern farms were slightly more efficient than northern farms, this edge explained only 4 percent of the ratio $(G_s - G_n)/G_n$. Thus nearly all of the southern productivity advantage is explained by the extent to which the productivity of medium and large slave plantations exceeded the efficiency of small free farms, whether these small farms were located in the North (where they could not produce cotton) or in the South (where they did produce cotton).

To put the issue somewhat differently, while both the large slave and small free farms of the South produced cotton, the large slave plantations were 48 percent more efficient than small free farms (see Table 7). Of course, the cotton share of output on these small farms (29 percent) was less than that of large slave plantations (61 percent). But since there was no climatic obstacle that prevented the free southern farms of the cotton belt from choosing exactly the same mix of products that was selected by large slave plantations, it may be assumed that they chose the product mix that was most efficient for them. Presumably a product mix with a larger cotton share would have decreased, or at least not increased, their efficiency. In other words, it appears that it was the manner in which cotton was produced, rather than the mere capacity to produce cotton, that is the principal factor accounting for the superior efficiency of large plantations. This interpretation is supported by the finding that small slave plantations, those with 1–15 slaves, were not more efficient than free southern farms (see Table 7) even though their cotton share (39 percent) was a third greater than that of free farms.

The last point needs elaboration, since Gavin Wright (1974, 1975) has argued that free farmers in the cotton belt were just as efficient in the production of cotton as large plantations but that they chose to produce less cotton in order to reduce riskiness. The basic propositions of his argument are that both small free and large slave farms were equally efficient in the production of cotton, that both were equally efficient in producing other commodities, and that the difference in mix between cotton and other commodities alone explains the differences in the indexes of total factor productivity by farm size. If Wright's conjectures are correct, the overall efficiency index of farms of each size class would be given by geometric averages of the indexes for cotton and other commodities, with the weights on each invariant commodity index being the share of that commodity in total output – the shares varying with size classes (see Evsey Domar).

If we let A_c equal the efficiency index for cotton and A_0 equal the efficiency index for all other commodities, the relationship of the overall efficiency index in each size class to A_c and A_0 is given by the following four equations:

(6a) $$A_c^{0.29}A_0^{0.71} = 1.00$$ (0 slaves)

(6b) $$A_c^{0.39}A_0^{0.61} = 1.01$$ (1–15 slaves)

(6c) $$A_c^{0.53}A_0^{0.47} = 1.33$$ (16–50 slaves)

(6d) $$A_c^{0.61}A_0^{0.39} = 1.48$$ (51+ slaves)

Since there are only two unknowns, only two equations are needed for a solution. If A_c and A_0 were invariant with size class, or approximately so, the ratio between A_c and A_0 should be approximately the same, regardless of which two equations are used to solve for A_c and A_0. However, as the following classification shows, this is not the case. The ratio A_c/A_0 varies from 1.1 to 7.1.

Equations used to solve for A_c and A_0	Ratio of A_c to A_0
(6a) and (6b)	1.1
(6a) and (6c)	3.3
(6a) and (6d)	3.4
(6c) and (6d)	3.8
(6b) and (6d)	5.7
(6b) and (6c)	7.1

In other words, it was not the mere difference in product mix but the manner in which cotton was produced that made large slave plantations more efficient than either small free farms or small slave farms. The threshold size for the efficiency of the gang system appears to be above 15 slaves.[26]

There is another aspect to Wright's argument. That is the contention that small free farms chose the observed mix in order to reduce riskiness – to reduce the variance of their income. In order to explore the implications of this suggestion, let us for the moment accept Wright's assumption that both large slave and small free farms were equally efficient in producing cotton. In that case, as we have seen, the income yield per average unit of input was more than three times as large in the production of cotton as in other products on farms of both sizes.[27] Consequently, by increasing the cotton share of their output from 29 to 61 percent (the share on large slave plantations), small farmers could have increased their mean income by 48 percent.

Wright's conjecture implies, therefore, that farmers were willing to forgo close to half of their mean income in order to gain some unspecified reduction in the variance of that income. Not only is this an extraordinary price to pay for insurance, but there is no evidence to show that within the relevant range (cotton shares between 29 and 61 percent of gross farm product) the relative variance of income was positively correlated with the share of income originating in cotton. The absence of a positive correlation between cotton shares and the relative variance is indicated by the facts that yields in cotton were no more variable than those of other farm products and that the price of corn, which Wright argues was

26. This is not to say that the level of the overall efficiency index of each size class was independent of the share of cotton in total output. Quite the contrary, farms that were more efficient in cotton production should have been more heavily specialized in that crop. In other words, the optimum share of cotton in total output was a function not only of relative prices but of a farm's comparative advantage in that crop. Moreover, the mix of crops was a major determinant of the degree to which the labor force was utilized (see Section V, below).

27. This result is obtained by solving equations (6a) and (6d) for A_c and A_0.

the principal substitute for cotton, was actually more variable than the price of cotton.[28] Nor do the benefits of a more mixed "portfolio" seem to have been potent enough to have provided less variation in price than that associated with cotton. Over the years 1831–60, Thomas Senior Berry's index (p. 564) of the average price of 20 or more agricultural products "identified" with the North (i.e., excluding cotton, sugar, and rice) has a coefficient of variation (0.23) that is quite similar to that for cotton alone (0.25).[29]

Wright has also argued that the objective of small farms may have been not the minimization of the variance of their income but "safety first." The exact meaning of safety first is never clearly defined, but Wright appears to equate it with the guaranteeing of the food supply. Thus before turning to the market with all its risks to obtain products that they did not produce, free farmers first sought to ensure that they would not starve. However, as we showed in our analysis of the slave diet (1974b), free southern farmers could have guaranteed a nutritious diet, not only high in protein but exceeding all other nutrient requirements, out of their own production for less than six cents per capita per day. Thus it took less than one-third of the average annual product of a free farm to insure an adequate diet for all those living on such farms. If the free farms of the cotton belt were as efficient in cotton production as were the large plantations, they could have had both an ensured food supply and a 48 percent increase in their mean income by raising the cotton share of their output from 29 to 61 percent.[30]

28. The relative variance of incomes on free and slave farms in 1860 was computed from the Parker–Gallman sample by weighting outputs on farms of all sizes by uniform national prices. The coefficient of variation was between 30 and 40 percent larger on free farms (with an average cotton share of 29 percent) than on slave farms (with average cotton shares ranging between 39 and 61 percent). Over the years from 1867 to 1900 the coefficient of variation in corn yields fell below that of cotton yields by just 0.02 (*USDA*, 1954, 1955). The relative variance of the price of corn in New Orleans over the years 1840–60 was 25 percent greater than the relative variance of cotton prices over the same period (computed from Cole).

29. For the period 1831–1846 there are 20 commodities in Berry's index for northern agriculture. For the period 1846–1860, the number of commodities is 29. Cotton prices are from U.S. Bureau of the Census, 1960, p. 124.

30. To farmers in debt, safety-first could well have meant guaranteeing a high enough cash income to meet mortgage and other debt calls. The point at issue is not whether the food supply mattered to antebellum farmers but whether they perceived it as the most binding constraint in the determination of their economic decisions. Illiquidity could well have appeared as a more serious menace than an inadequate food supply. Wright does not explore this issue, although it is widely suggested in the traditional literature on nineteenth-century agriculture. Moreover, if A_c exceeded A_0 by 3.4 times, and if farmers sought to ensure some minimum absolute level of income, then given the relative variances of income from cotton and corn, the much higher mean income associated with specialization in cotton indicates that the choice of the higher cotton share would have reduced rather than increased the likelihood of falling below that minimum.

V. Sources of efficiency on large plantations

The finding that large slave plantations were 48 percent more productive than the small free farms of the South poses a new problem: What feature, or features, of the organization and operation of large slave plantations gave them such a marked advantage? Examination of the managerial records of these plantations suggests that part of the answer lies in the persistence with which planters sought to exploit complementarities and interdependencies made possible by concentration in the production of one or the other of the four principal slave crops: cotton, sugar, rice, and tobacco.

The central focus of planters was the organization of the labor force into highly coordinated and precisely functioning gangs characterized by intensity of effort. "A plantation might be considered as a piece of machinery," said Bennet H. Barrow (Edwin Adams Davis, p. 409) in his Highland Plantation rules. "To operate successfully, all its parts should be uniform and exact, and its impelling force regular and steady." "Driving," the establishment of a rigid gang discipline, was considered the crux of a successful operation. Observers, such as Robert Russell, said that the discipline of plantation life was "almost as strict as that of our military system" (p. 180). Frederick Law Olmsted described one instance in which he observed two very large hoe gangs "moving across the field in parallel lines, with a considerable degree of precision." He reported that he repeatedly rode through their lines at a canter with other horsemen, "often coming upon them suddenly, without producing the smallest change or interruption in the dogged action of the labourers" (p. 452).

Each work gang was based on an internal division of labor that not only assigned every member of the gang to a precise task but simultaneously made his or her performance dependent on the actions of the others. On the McDuffie plantation, the planting gang was divided into three classes which were described in the following way (as quoted by Metzer):

> 1st, the best hands, embracing those of good judgment and quick motion. 2nd, those of the weakest and most inefficient class. 3rd, the second class of hoe hands. Thus classified, the first class will run ahead and open a small hole about seven to ten inches apart, into which the second class drop from four to five cotton seed, and the third class follow and cover with a rake. [p. 135]

Interdependence and tension were also promoted between gangs, especially during the period of cultivation when the field labor force was divided into plow gangs and hoe gangs. The hoe hands chopped out the weeds that surrounded the cotton plants as well as excessive sprouts. The plow gangs followed behind, stirring the soil near the rows of cotton plants and tossing it back around the plants. Thus the hoe and plow gangs each put the other under an assembly-line type of pressure. The hoeing had to be completed in time to permit the plow hands to carry out their tasks. At the same time the progress of the hoeing, which entailed lighter labor than plowing, set a pace for the plow gang. The drivers or overseers moved back and forth between the two gangs, exhorting and prodding each to keep up with the pace of the other, as well as inspecting the quality of the work. In operations such as cotton picking, which did not lend themselves as naturally to interdependence as planting and cultivating, planters sought to promote intensity of effort by dividing hands into competing gangs and offering bonuses on a daily and weekly basis to the gang that picked the most. They also made extensive use of the so-called "task" methods. These were, literally, time–motion studies on the basis of which a daily quota for each hand was established.

In addition to the use of assembly-line methods and time–motion studies to insure maximum intensity of effort in a particular operation, planters sought to allocate their slaves among jobs in such a manner as to achieve "full capacity" utilization of each person. In this connection slaves were given "hand" ratings – generally ranging from one-eighth to a full hand – according to their age, sex, and physical ability. The strongest hands were put into field work, with the ablest of these given tasks that would set the pace for the others. Plow gangs were composed primarily of men in their twenties or early thirties. Less sturdy men and boys, as well as prime-aged women, were in the hoe gangs. Older women were occupied in such domestic duties as house servants and nurses; older men worked as gardeners, servants, and stock-minders. Metzer's analysis (p. 134) of the records of the Kollock plantations indicates that the "hand"-to-slave ratio was 0.9 in field work but only 0.6 in nonfield work. Metzer points out that in allocating slaves among jobs, planters pursued the principle of comparative, rather than absolute, advantage. Thus during the harvest period, most of the labor of picking cotton was provided by women, even though women had lower daily cotton-picking rates than men. On the Pleasant Hill plantation, for example, women provided 31 percent more labor time in cotton picking than did men.

Data on the cotton-picking rates of pregnant women and nursing mothers provide still another illustration of the degree to which planters succeeded in utilizing all those in the labor force. Estimates derived from Metzer's regression of the daily cotton-picking rates of women by age, and by weeks before and after childbirth, are summarized in Table 10. This table shows that down to the last week before birth, pregnant women picked three-quarters or more of the amount that was normal for

Table 10. *Cotton-picking rates of pregnant women and nursing mothers as a percentage of the cotton-picking rates of women the same age who were neither pregnant nor nursing*

Weeks Before (−) or After (+) Childbirth	Age			
	20	25	30	35
−12 to −9	82.3	83.3	84.1	84.8
−8 to −5	77.4	78.8	79.8	80.6
−4 to −1	74.8	76.3	77.4	78.3
+2 to +3	3.9	9.8	14.1	17.4
+4 to +7	64.9	67.1	68.6	69.8
+8 to +11	91.3	91.8	92.2	92.5

women of corresponding ages who were neither pregnant nor nursing. Only during the month following childbirth was there a sharp reduction in the amount of cotton picked. Some mothers started to return to field work during the second or third week after birth. By the second month after birth, picking rates reached two-thirds of the level for nonnursing mothers. By the third month, the level rose to over 90 percent.

Another way in which planters sought to achieve full capacity utilization of labor was in the selection of the product mix. Labor requirements in cotton production had a very marked seasonal pattern, with one peak reached in the late spring and a second in October, Consequently, secondary crops were chosen so that their peak labor requirements were complementary to those of cotton (see Metzer, Figure 1). Corn was an excellent match. It could be planted before cotton and could be harvested either early or late, depending on other pressures, because the kernels, protected in the ears, did not suffer if harvesting was delayed beyond maturation.

VI. Some issues of interpretation

It should not be assumed that slave labor was more efficient than free labor in all occupations. There is no evidence that the productivity of slave labor exceeded that of free labor in urban industries. As Claudia Goldin (pp. 104–105) points out, the much higher elasticity of demand for slave labor in the cities than in rural areas (the ratio is more than 10 to 1) indicates that whatever advantage there was in slave labor was specific to agriculture.

Preliminary analysis also suggests that within *U.S.* agriculture, the slave system of labor raised productivity only for slave farms that specialized in one of four principal products: sugar, cotton, rice, and tobacco. Economies of scale seem to have been greatest in sugar, since nearly 100 percent of all cane sugar in the United States was produced on large slave plantations. The slave system seems to have been less productive in tobacco than in cotton. The scale factor in the Old South (where tobacco was a relatively important crop), while statistically significant, was only a third as large as the scale factor for the New South. Although the issue is now under investigation, there appears to have been no productivity advantage to slave labor in general farming and relatively few large slave plantations engaged in general farming.

The available evidence indicates that greater intensity of labor per hour, not more hours of labor per day nor more days of labor per year, is the reason why the index of total factor productivity is 48 percent higher for slave plantations than for free farms. There is no evidence that land was used more intensively in the South than in the North, but even if it was, the depletion rate of southern land yields was so low (0.6 percent per annum) that this can, at most, account for 5 percent of the value of $(G_s - G_n)/G_n$. The interim estimates thus indicate that slaves employed on medium and large plantations worked about 72 percent more intensively per hour than free farmers. In other words, on average, a slave on these plantations produced as much output in roughly 35 minutes as a free farmer did in a full hour.

Once it is recognized that the fundamental form of the exploitation of slave labor was through speed-up (increased intensity per hour) rather than through an increase in the number of clock-time hours per year, certain paradoxes resolve themselves. The longer rest breaks during the work day, and the greater time off on Sundays, for slaves than for free men appear not as boons that slave-owners granted to their chattel but as conditions for achieving the desired level of intensity. The finding that slaves earned 15 percent more income per clock-time hour is less surprising when it is realized that their pay per equal-efficiency hour was 33 percent less than that of free farmers.

David and Temin argue (pp. 778–783) that while the index of total factor productivity may be acceptable in comparing the relative efficiency of free countries it cannot be applied to a comparison of the free North and the slave South – that in this instance a morally weighted index of efficiency is required. However, the issue of the relative efficiency of slave labor did not originate with *Time on the Cross*. It is an issue with a long history that traces back to such commentators on slavery as Adam Smith, Alexis de Tocqueville, Cassius Marcellus Clay, Hinton Rowan Helper, Frederick Law Olmsted, and John Cairnes. Is the geometric index of total factor productivity appropriate to the resolution of the question of the efficiency of slave labor as that question actually evolved in historical literature?

Much of chapters 5 and 6 of *Time on the Cross* was devoted to reviewing both the pre- and post–Civil War debates on the inefficiency of slave agriculture and slave labor. From this review it is clear that what the critics of slavery meant was: other inputs held constant, but substituting slave for free labor and slave managers for free managers, the output of slave farms would be much less than the output of free farms. About this "fact" Clay, Helper, Olmsted, and most other antislavery critics had no doubt. This confidence stemmed from the conviction that slavery "degraded" labor, that slavery turned plantation owners into "idlers," that "comparing man with man," slave laborers were less than half as productive as whites, that Africans were "far less adapted for steady, uninterrupted labor than we are," and that "white laborers of equal intelligence and under equal stimulus will cut twice as much wood, split twice as many rails, and hoe a third more corn a day than Negroes." (See Clay, p. 204 and Olmsted, pp. 91, 467–468.)

Nor does the geometric index of total factor productivity do violence to the issue of efficiency as it was perceived and discussed by the principal scholars who preceded us. Certainly neither Ulrich Bonnell Phillips, nor Gray, nor Ralph Betts Flanders, nor Robert R. Russell, nor Kenneth M. Stampp were talking about a morally weighted measure of productivity, but of the comparative efficiency of slave and free labor, in just the manner that the issue was raised by the antebellum critics of slavery.

To the extent that the argument for moral weighting is really an objection to using observed prices for aggregating southern output, one needs to assess the effect of slavery on the observed prices. On all agricultural commodities except slave-produced staples, the South was a price taker. Since the South contributed about three-quarters of the world's supply of cotton, its behavior did affect the world price of cotton. In the absence of slavery, however, the supply of cotton would presumably have shifted to the left. This implies that the observed price of cotton was lower, not higher, than it would have been if slaves had been free to make their own choices about the provision of their labor. Consequently, the use of observed prices to aggregate output yields a lower value of G_s/G_n than would be obtained by aggregation based on the counter-factual price of cotton.

Of course, the fact that blacks who toiled on large plantations were more efficient than free workers does not imply that blacks were inherently superior to whites as workers. It was the system that forced men to work at the pace of an assembly line (called the gang) that made slave laborers more efficient than free laborers. Moreover, the gang system, as already noted, appears to have raised productivity only on farms that specialized in certain crops.[31] It should, of course, be emphasized that greater efficiency does not mean greater good. As we attempted to demonstrate in *Time on the Cross*, freedom has value and the loss of freedom by slaves was greater than the gain in measured output to free persons.

References

Anderson, R. V., "Labor Utilization and Productivity, Diversification and Self Sufficiency, Southern Plantations, 1800–1840," unpublished doctoral dissertation, Univ. No. Carolina 1974.

Thomas S. Berry, *Western Prices Before 1861*, Cambridge, Mass. 1943.

Percy W. Bidwell and John I. Falconer, *History of Agriculture in the Northern United States, 1620–1860*, Washington 1925.

John E. Cairnes, *The Slave Power: Its Character, Career, and Probable Designs: Being an Attempt to Explain the Real Issues Involved in the American Contest*, introduction by Harold D. Woodman, New York 1969.

Cassius M. Clay, *The Writings of Cassius Marcellus Clay: Including Speeches and Addresses*, New York 1848.

Arthur H. Cole, *Wholesale Commodity Prices in the United States, Statistical Supplement*, Cambridge, Mass. 1938.

Covert, J. R., *Seedtime and Harvest*, U.S.D.A. Bur. Statist., Bull. 85, Washington 1912.

Clarence H. Danhof, *Change in Agriculture: The Northern United States, 1820–1870*, Cambridge, Mass. 1969.

David, P. A. and Temin, P., "Slavery: The Progressive Institution?" *J. Econ. Hist.*, September 1974, *34*, 739–83.

Edwin A. Davis, *Plantation Life in the Florida Parishes of Louisiana 1836–1844, as Reflected in the Diary of Bennet H. Barrow*, New York 1943.

Davis, L. E., "One Potato, Two Potato, Sweet Potato Pie: Clio Looks at Slavery and the South," paper presented to the MSSB–Univ. Rochester conference on *Time on the Cross*, 1974.

Domar, E. D., "On the Measurement of Technological Change," *Econ. J.*, December 1961, *71*, 709–29.

Ralph B. Flanders, *Plantation Slavery in Georgia*, Chapel Hill 1933.

Robert W. Fogel, *Railroads and American Economic Growth: Essays in Econometric History*, Baltimore 1964.

———, "American Interregional Trade in the Nineteenth Century," In Ralph Andreano,

31. It is important to distinguish between the technological characteristics of the production process and the manner in which the labor employed in that process was obtained. While it was force, not volunteerism, that ultimately permitted gang labor to exist, it does not follow that force alone would have led to high levels of productivity, if that potential was not inherent in the production process. If force alone created high levels of productivity, small plantations with 1–15 slaves should have been more efficient than free farms, even though they did not utilize the gang system. Similarly, the argument that some mix of coercion and volunteerism may have been necessary in the initial creation of a factory labor force does not rule out economies of scale or other technological efficiencies as features of the factory system.

ed., *New Views on American Economic Development: A Selective Anthology of Recent Work*, Cambridge, Mass. 1965.

——— and Engerman, S. L. "The Relative Efficiency of Slavery: A Comparison of Northern and Southern Agriculture in 1860," *Explor. Econ. Hist.*, Spring 1971, *8*, 353–367.

——— and ———, (1974a) *Time on the Cross*, Vols. I, II, Boston 1974.

——— and ———, (1974b) "Further Evidence on the Nutritional Adequacy of the Slave Diet," Univ. Rochester 1974.

——— and ———, "The Relative Efficiency of Slave and Free Agriculture in 1860 and 1850," Harvard Univ. 1975.

——— and ———, *Further Evidence on the Economics of American Negro Slavery*, forthcoming.

Foust, J. D., "The Yeoman Farmer and Westward Expansion of U.S. Cotton Production," unpublished doctoral dissertation. Univ. No. Carolina 1967.

Gallman, R. E., "The Agricultural Sector and the Pace of Economic Growth: U.S. Experience in the Nineteenth Century," in David C. Klingaman and Richard K. Vedder, eds., *Essays in Nineteenth Century Economic History: The Old Northwest*, Athens, Ohio 1975.

Paul W. Gates, *The Farmer's Age: Agriculture 1815–1860*, New York 1960.

Eugene D. Genovese, *The Political Economy of Slavery: Studies in the Economy and Society of the Slave South*, New York 1965.

Claudia D. Goldin, *Urban Slavery in the American South, 1820–1860: A Quantitative History*, Chicago 1976.

Lewis C. Gray, *History of Agriculture in the Southern United States to 1860*, 2 vols., Washington 1933.

Haskell, T. H., "Were Slaves More Efficient: Some Doubts About *Time on the Cross*," *New York Rev. of Books*, September 19, 1974, 38–42.

———, "The True and Tragical History of *Time on the Cross*," *New York Rev. of Books*, October 2, 1975, 33–39.

Hinton R. Helper, *The Impending Crisis of the South: How to Meet It*, Cambridge, Mass. 1968.

Hopkins, J. A., *Changing Technology and Employment in Agriculture*, U.S. Bur. Agr. Econ., Washington 1941.

Lebergott, S., "Labor Force and Employment, 1800–1960," in Dorothy S. Brady, ed., *Output, Employment, and Productivity in the United States After 1800*, Nat. Bur. Econ. Res., *Stud. in Income and Wealth*, Vol. 30, New York 1966.

Metzer, J., "Rational Management, Modern Business Practices, and Economies of Scale in the Ante-Bellum Southern Plantations," *Explor, Econ. Hist.*, Apr. 1975, *12*, 123–50.

Frederick L. Olmsted, *The Cotton Kingdom*, New York 1953.

Olson, J. R., "Clock-Time vs. Real-Time: A Comparison of the Lengths of the Northern and Southern Agricultural Work-Years," mimeo., Univ. Conn, 1976.

Ulrich B. Phillips, *American Negro Slavery: A Survey of the Supply, Employment and Control of Negro Labor as Determined by the Plantation Regime*, New York 1918.

Primack, M. L., "Farm Formed Capital in American Agriculture: 1850 to 1910," unpublished doctoral dissertation, Univ. No. Carolina 1962.

Russel, R. R., "The General Effects of Slavery upon Southern Economic Progress," *J. Southern Hist.*, Feb. 1938, *4*, 34–54.

Russell, Robert *North America: Its Agriculture and Climate*, Edinburgh 1857.

Kenneth M. Stampp, *The Peculiar Institution: Slavery in the Ante-Bellum South*. New York 1956.

Towne, N. W. and Rasmussen, W. D., "Farm Gross Product and Gross Investment in the Nineteenth Century," in *Trends in the American Economy in the Nineteenth Century*, Nat. Bur. Econ. Res., *Stud. in Income and Wealth*, Vol. 24, Princeton 1960.

Watkins, J. L., *Production and Price of Cotton for One Hundred Years*, USDA Misc. Series, Bull. No. 9, Washington 1895.

Woodman, H., "The Old South and the New History," paper presented to the MSSB–Univ. Rochester conference on *Time on the Cross*, 1974.

Wright, G., "The Economics of Cotton in the Antebellum South," unpublished doctoral dissertation, Yale Univ. 1969.

———, "An Econometric Study of Cotton Production and Trade, 1830–1860," *Rev. Econ. Statist.*, May 1971, *53*, 111–20.

———, "The Economic Analysis of *Time on the Cross*," paper presented to the MSSB–Univ. Rochester conference on *Time on the Cross*, 1974.

———, "Slavery and the Cotton Boom," *Explor. Econ. Hist.*, October 1975, *12*, 439–51.

U.S. Bureau of the Census, *Preliminary Report of the Eighth Census, 1860*, Washington 1862.

———, *Eleventh Census of the United States: 1890; Report on the Statistics of Agriculture in the United States*, Washington 1895.

———, *Historical Statistics of the United States, Colonial Times to 1957*, Washington 1960.

U.S. Department of Agriculture, *Report of the Commissioner of Agriculture, 1867*, Washington 1868.

———, Agr. Marketing Service, *Corn: Acreage, Yield, and Production, 1866–1943*, Washington 1954.

———, Agr. Marketing Service, *Cotton and Cottonseed*, Statist. Bull. 164, Washington 1955.

IV

The South since the Civil War

"The trap of debt peonage"

by Roger L. Ransom and Richard Sutch

At the end of the Civil War, the southern economy was in disarray. With the abolition of slavery, large-scale agriculture was no longer profitable. Former slaves sought to control their own lives and preferred to work their own farms. By 1868, arrangements arose whereby much of the plantation land was divided into single-family plots to be farmed by tenants. By 1880 about 80 percent of black farm operators in the Cotton South were tenants, and over two-thirds of these tenants were sharecroppers. In addition, about one-quarter of white farm operators were sharecroppers (Ransom and Sutch, 1977, 84). Under the system of sharecropping, the landowner provided almost all materials of production, housing, and land in exchange for one-half of the tenant's output. This approach provided access to land and capital and an opportunity for individual initiative for poor farmers.

Many sharecroppers could not afford to purchase food and other supplies before they harvested their crops. To solve the problem, they borrowed against their future share of the crop at a nearby country store. This arrangement arose, in part, because the Civil War had destroyed much of the South's banking and financial institutions. This left rural areas without complete financial services. Rural merchants, then, became a major source of credit, providing tenant farmers with food, clothing, and other essentials until their crops could be harvested.

The roles of sharecropping and merchant lending in the postbellum southern economy have generated much controversy. Roger Ransom and Richard Sutch, in *One Kind of Freedom: The Economic Consequences of Emancipation* (1977), examine financial reconstruction, arguing that local merchant credit monopolies were widespread in the rural South. This, they contend, contributed to economic stagnation. Their chapter "The Trap of Debt Peonage," from *One Kind of Freedom*, explains how merchant creditors exploited their customers, cunningly springing the trap of debt peonage on their borrowers. An outline of the chapter will show how each piece of Ransom and Sutch's argument is carefully fitted together, how evidence is mustered to bolster each of the premises of the model. Do you think they have proven their case? Did merchant monopolists trap borrowers in debt peonage?

Like *Time on the Cross*, *One Kind of Freedom* is a controversial book and has generated an outpouring of criticism. In 1978, a symposium on Ransom and Sutch's findings was held (see *Explorations in Economic History*, January 1979). Most of the participants questioned Ransom and Sutch's contention that the merchant lender "forced" the majority of tenant farmers to specialize in cotton and kept them trapped in debt peonage. How prevalent were merchant monopolies? Although 54 percent of all rural locations in Ransom and Sutch's sample had just one store, only 20 percent of all stores were in locations where there were no competitors. Did the region's high interest rates yield competitive or monopoly profits? What is the evidence that debt peonage was widespread? There was a high degree of geographical mobility among sharecroppers. Around the turn of the century, over half of the black share tenants in the South had been at their current location for one year or less (Wright, 1986, 93). There is also evidence of upward economic mobility among sharecroppers, some of whom climbed the "agricultural ladder" to farm ownership. How many emerged from the "magic embrace" of merchant credit? All agree that some indebtedness existed; the debate is over its pervasiveness and the strength of its grip.

Other critics question the internal consistency of Ransom and Sutch's model. They contend that the tenants did not overproduce cotton, which was to the South's comparative advantage. Even wealthier farmers, who were not in debt to merchant lenders, voluntarily specialized in cotton. Could merchant monopolists have done better by not impoverishing their customer and not requiring cotton production?

As you read this essay, consider the questions mentioned above and ponder the following:

- What is the relationship between lack of "self-sufficiency" and the need for credit?
- Was there an active labor market in the postbellum rural South?
- How much information did merchant monopolists need to trap a sharecropper in debt peonage?
- For what reasons did southerners increase cotton production? Is evidence on prices conclusive?
- What is the implication about monopoly power of *increased* specialization in cotton over time? Was merchant monopoly power increasing, decreasing, or remaining the same?

As Ransom and Sutch (1979, 86) note, it is important to ask critical questions of any work of scholarship. The debate surrounding their book has helped to sharpen arguments on all sides.

Additional Reading

Stephen DeCanio, "Cotton 'Overproduction' in Late Nineteenth-Century Agriculture," *Journal of Economic History*, 33 (September 1973), 608–33.

Price Fishback, "Debt Peonage in Postbellum Georgia," *Explorations in Economic History*, 26 (April 1989), 219–36.

Claudia Goldin, "'N' Kinds of Freedom: An Introduction to the Issues," *Explorations in Economic History*, 16 (January 1979), 8–30.

Robert Higgs, *Competition and Coercion: Blacks in the American Economy, 1865–1914*, Chicago: University of Chicago Press, 1980.

Robert Margo, "Accumulation of Property by Southern Blacks: Comment and Further Evidence," *American Economic Review*, 74 (September 1984), 768–76.

Roger Ransom and Richard Sutch, *One Kind of Freedom: The Economic Consequences of Emancipation*, New York: Cambridge University Press, 1977.

Roger Ransom and Richard Sutch, "Credit Merchandising in the Post-Emancipation South: Structure, Conduct, Performance," *Explorations in Economic History*, 16 (January 1979), 64–89.

Joseph D, Reid, Jr., "White Land, Black Labor, and Agricultural Stagnation: The Causes and Effects of Sharecropping in the Postbellum South," *Explorations in Economic History*, 16 (January 1979), 31–55.

Peter Temin, "Freedom and Coercion: Notes on the Analysis of Debt Peonage in *One Kind of Freedom*," *Explorations in Economic History*, 16 (January 1979), 56–63.

Gavin Wright, *Old South, New South: Revolutions in the Southern Economy since the Civil War*, New York: Basic Books, 1986.

8

The trap of debt peonage

ROGER L. RANSOM and RICHARD SUTCH

More evils have come to the farmers of the State on account of the mortgage and lien bond system than from any other, and indeed from every other source. It has proved a worse curse to North Carolina than drouths, floods, cyclones, storms, rust, caterpillars, and every other evil that attends the farmer.

W. N. Jones, Commissioner, Bureau of Labor Statistics, North Carolina, First Annual Report of the Bureau of Labor Statistics (Raleigh: Josephus Daniels, 1887), p. 76.

Contemporary critics insisted that the monopoly power of the merchant was used not only to exploit southern farmers but to control southern agriculture. The specific charge was made that the merchant forced the farmer into excessive production of cotton by refusing credit to those who sought to diversify production. Charles Otken, one of the most strident critics of the South's merchandising system, insisted that:

For years a class of merchants encouraged their credit customers to raise cotton exclusively, or very largely. They reasoned very naturally and very logically, that, the more goods sold to farmers, the greater their sales and the greater their aggregate profits. . . . The debts of the farmer bound him to cotton. He was powerless.[1]

Otken quoted Henry Grady, who, writing in 1889, had bluntly described how this was done: "When he [the farmer] saw the wisdom of raising his own corn, bacon, grasses, and stock, he was NOTIFIED that reducing his cotton acreage was reducing *his line of credit*."[2]

Otken and Grady were journalists. George K. Holmes, an economist employed by the U.S. Department of Agriculture, made the same

Source: Roger L. Ransom and Richard Sutch, "The Trap of Debt Peonage," in *One Kind of Freedom: The Economic Consequences of Emancipation* (1977). Reprinted with permission of the authors.

1. Charles H. Otken, *The Ills of the South* (New York: G. P. Putnam's Sons, 1894), p. 57.
2. Otken, *Ills of the South*, p. 57. Emphasis in the original. Quoted from the *New York Ledger* (1889).

charge in an address delivered to the American Academy of Political and Social Science in 1893:

> The merchants then took the helm. Such crops as they could most readily market must be produced under their orders, regardless of the fact that they might not be the ones most advantageous to their debtors. The kind of crop that best accorded with this requirement in the cotton regions was cotton.[3]

The ultimate damage wrought by reducing the farmer's right to choose his own crops was even more severe than this passage suggests. The merchant's "cry for cotton and more cotton" was viewed with alarm by southern critics of the system.[4] To them, more was at stake than the farmer's right to cultivate as he saw fit. Ending the South's dependence upon the single crop, cotton, was seen as an indispensable step in securing a prosperous future for the region. Therefore, they feared that the merchants' insistence upon cotton would doom the South to economic backwardness. Even before the Civil War, editorialist James D. B. De Bow saw the South's dependence upon cotton as a curse on southern development. He perceived that economic growth in the long run would have to be based upon a balanced expansion of industry, commerce, and agriculture. The single-minded concentration upon cotton, to his mind, was shortsighted and kept the South dependent upon the northern and European economies. De Bow wrote of the Cotton South:

> No mind can look back upon the history of this region for the last twenty years, and not feel convinced that the labor bestowed in cotton growing during that period has been a total loss to this part of the country. It is true that some of the neighboring states have been benefited to some extent, and [the cotton trade] has served to swell the general commerce of the nation . . . but the country of its production has gained nothing, and lost much.[5]

The South's defeat in the Civil War and the end of slavery were viewed by these economic critics as offering an opportunity for the South to rebuild itself upon a new and sounder foundation fashioned from diversified agriculture and industrial enterprise. De Bow, writing on the future of the South in the first issue of his *Review* to appear after the

3. George K. Holmes, "The Peons of the South," *Annals of the American Academy of Political and Social Science* 4 (September 1893), p. 66.
4. Holmes, "Peons of the South," p. 67.
5. James D. B. De Bow, *The Industrial Resources, Statistics, &c. of the United States, and More Particularly of the Southern and Western States*, 3rd ed. 2 vols. (New York: A. M. Kelly, 1966), 2, p. 114, first edition published in 1852. For an excellent summary of similar complaints, and the attempts at correcting the South's "dependence" upon the North, see Harold D. Woodman, *King Cotton and His Retainers* (Lexington: University of Kentucky Press, 1967), pp. 139–153.

war, struck a note of optimism and resumed his call for economic diversification:

The climates and soils of the vast region, which stretched from the Potomac to the Rio Grande, are favorable to every product upon which industry and capital are expended in any country. The vast mineral resources which geological surveys have divulged, which no hand of industry has yet attempted to develop; and the infinite number of manufacturing sites, all present the most tempting baits to enterprise, and will open up results for it, which nothing in the history of the times has equaled, dazzling and magnificent as have been its past achievements.[6]

Cotton might still play a prominent role, De Bow conceded, but "'King' he may not be, in the sense in which many of us formerly recognized him."[7]

In the years immediately following the war, the tendency for farmers to purchase rather than to grow their own provisions was not considered unwise. High cotton prices were an obvious inducement to concentrate on cotton, and, as the *Southern Cultivator* noted in 1873, it was not uncommon for "men in other avocations" to purchase their supplies and provisions "and yet prosper."[8] However, when cotton prices returned to their normal level and the farmers continued to buy provisions on credit at premium prices, observers began to advocate that the farmer grow his own supplies. "The South must prepare to raise her own provisions, compost her fertilizers, cure her own hay, and breed her own stock," claimed Henry Grady, editor of the *Atlanta Constitution*. "The farmers who prosper at the South are the 'corn raisers,' *i.e.*, the men who raise their own supplies, and make cotton their surplus crop."[9] Similar views were propounded on a monthly basis by editors of farm journals and local newspapers.[10] When farmers did not respond to what seemed a significant incentive to home production, these writers began to suspect that the merchant, through his insistence upon cotton, must be responsible for the farmer's dependence upon purchased supplies.

The decline in the production of food in the South

There is no question that the production of food and grain crops per capita fell dramatically in the southern states following the Civil War.

6. James D. B. De Bow, "The Future of the South," *De Bow's Review* 1 (January 1866), pp. 8–9.
7. De Bow, "Future of the South," p. 9.
8. *Southern Cultivator* 31 (September 1873), p. 343.
9. Henry W. Grady, "Cotton and Its Kingdom," *Harper's New Monthly Magazine* 63 (October 1881), pp. 723–724.
10. To illustrate the concern of periodicals, consider the following citations from four years of the *Rural Carolinian*, all of which urge more diversified farming: *Rural Carolinian* 1 (1869), pp. 11–12, 114, 182; idem, 1 (1870), pp. 376, 398–399; idem, 2 (1871), pp. 265–267,

Table 1. *Per capita production of food, Five Cotton States: 1850–1890*

Food	1850	1860	1870	1880	1890
Grains (corn-equivalent bushels)					
Corn	31.1	29.6	14.7	15.6	16.3
Other food crops[a]	6.7	6.3	2.6	3.9	2.7
Total grains	37.7	35.8	17.3	19.5	18.9
Livestock (number of head)					
Swine	2.11	1.64	0.73	0.88	0.73
Other cattle	0.73	0.51	0.29	0.31	0.30
Sheep	0.47	0.31	0.26	0.24	0.22

[a] Food crops, in addition to corn, were wheat, rye, rice, oats, cowpeas, beans, Irish potatoes, sweet potatoes, buckwheat, and barley.

Sources: Production of agricultural products: 1850: U.S. Census Office, Seventh Census [1850], *The Seventh Census of the United States* (Washington: Robert Armstrong, 1853), pp. 345–348, 377–384, 429–433, 456–460, 482–486. *1860:* U.S. Census Office, Eight Census [1860], *Agriculture in the United States in 1860* (Washington: GPO, 1864), pp. 2–5, 26–29, 66–69, 84–87, 128–131. *1870:* U.S. Census Office, Ninth Census [1870], *The Statistics of the Wealth and Industry of the United States* (Washington: GPO, 1872), pp. 81–85. *1880:* U.S. Census Office, Tenth Census [1880], *Report on the Production of Agriculture* (Washington: GPO, 1883), pp. 3–10. *1890:* U.S. Census Office, Eleventh Census [1890], *Reports on the Statistics of Agriculture* (Washington: GPO, 1895), pp. 74–83. Also see the historical summary in ibid., pp. 84–115. *Population for all years:* U.S. Bureau of the Census, *Historical Statistics of the United States* (Washington: GPO, 1960), Series A-155, A-156, A-161, A-162, A-165, pp. 12–13.

We need only note the production statistics in 1870 to see that outputs of grains and meat sharply declined in the South after 1860.[11] Nor was this decline a temporary change. Table 1 summarizes the per capita production of food in the Five Cotton States from 1850 to 1890, and Figure 1 illustrates the enormous fall in food available from crops and swine. The per capita production of corn, by far the most important food crop, fell to one-half its prewar level in 1870, and did not appreciably improve thereafter. The loss in corn supply was not replaced by other crops. Table 1 shows that per capita outputs of ten other crops fell even more dramatically than did corn output. The total output of grains, expressed in units nutritionally equivalent to a bushel of corn, averaged one-half the prewar level in the thirty years following the Civil War.

388–389, 489–493; idem, 3 (1871), pp. 13–14; idem, 3 (1872), pp. 286–287, 377, 627–628; and idem, 4 (1872), p. 171.

11. We can make use of the 1870 data in this context despite the underenumeration in that year . . . since we have reason to believe that both population and production were underreported by roughly the same proportion.

The number of swine per capita similarly declined without subsequent recovery. Our examination of nineteenth-century animal husbandry suggests that neither the slaughter weight nor the ratio of animal slaughters to the stock of hogs in the South changed dramatically in the postbellum period.[12] Therefore, the amount of pork produced from a given swine population would not be substantially greater after the war. The implication of Table 1 must be that the available pork per capita declined by about one-half. Since roughly the same proportional decline occurred in per capita stocks of cattle and sheep, there could have been no marked increase in meat from these animals that would have offset the loss of pork after 1860. Of the remaining foodstuffs enumerated by the censuses, only the production of butter, which fell dramatically in 1870, showed a tendency to recover its prewar level of per capita production in the following years.[13]

The decline in food output was nearly 50 percent. It is conceivable that a portion of this decline could be explained by the reduced food requirements of the black population. Slaves required abundant calories to sustain their work effort. Following emancipation there was a reduction of work effort on the part of the black population that we have estimated to have been between 28 and 37 percent. It follows that a reduction of food intake would accompany this reduction in work effort. However, the reduction in food requirements would be significantly less

12. There is an extensive debate concerning the slaughter weights of hogs on antebellum plantations. The consensus that seems to be emerging is that the median dressed weight was in the neighborhood of 140 pounds, and the live weight approximately 185 pounds. Robert E. Gallman, "Self-Sufficiency in the Cotton Economy of the Antebellum South," *Agricultural History* 44 (January 1970), pp. 15–16; Eugene D. Genovese, *The Political Economy of Slavery: Studies in The Economy and Society of the Slave South* (New York: Pantheon, 1965), pp. 115, 122–123; Sam Bowers Hilliard, *Hog Meat and Hoecake: Food Supply in the Old South, 1840–1860* (Carbondale: Southern Illinois University Press, 1972), pp. 102, 261; and Richard Sutch, "The Treatment Received by American Slaves: A Critical Review of the Evidence Presented in *Time on the Cross*," *Exploration in Economic History* 12 (October 1975), pp. 367–369. Our survey of the production statistics for slaughterhouses available in the manuscript returns to the Census of Manufacturing for all eleven southern states in 1880 revealed that the average live weight in that year was 185 pounds. There is also evidence to suggest that hogs slaughtered by commercial slaughterhouses weighed on average more than those slaughtered on the farm. A study by Sutch of the slaughter ratio, which surveyed sources for both the pre- and postwar periods, concluded that killings as a ratio to the June inventory held constant at approximately 80 percent throughout the period in question (Sutch, "Treatment," pp. 369–370).

13. Outside the Five Cotton States, the decline in beef production was less marked. Nevertheless, even in Texas, which was the state where cattle production was most pronounced, the per capita stock of "other cattle" declined. The average output of butter per capita in 1860 was 5 pounds; in 1870 it dropped to 2.7 pounds; by 1880 it was back to 4.6 pounds. See the sources for Table 8.1.

than the decline in the number of hours worked per capita. We estimate that for the population as a whole, the number of calories per capita required could not have fallen by more than 9.0 to 11.5 percent.[14] In fact, the fall in consumption of food should have been much less than this calculation of the decline in energy requirements. Free people opted for a diet with a greater proportion of meat than that provided by slave masters. To provide a given number of calories through meat would require more corn to be produced than if the calories were consumed in the form of cornmeal. Therefore, the shift in diet should have limited the decline in production of grains to something smaller than the fall in calories required. We conclude that the reduction in work effort might, at most, account for one-fifth of the decline in food output. The fall in production left unexplained is still enormous.

The increased concentration upon cotton

The fall in food output seems to be associated with an equally dramatic shift in the composition of agricultural output. Figure 2 presents the ratio of cotton output to grain output for each census year from 1850 to

14. There is some disagreement concerning the diet of slaves. At one extreme, the standard daily slave ration of 0.5 pound of pork and 2 pounds of cornmeal for an adult field hand implies a caloric intake of 4,056 per day, and is probably a minimum. At the other extreme is the suggestion by Robert William Fogel and Stanley L. Engerman that supplements to the pork and corn ration raised the daily caloric consumption of adult field hands to 5,357 calories (*Time on the Cross*, 2 vols. [Boston: Little, Brown & Co., 1974] 2, p. 97). As Richard Sutch argued, this figure exaggerates the true diet because of biases and errors involved with Fogel and Engerman's estimating procedure ("Treatment," pp. 394–396; also see Sutch for the sources and procedures used to estimate the caloric content of these diets). A plausible estimate of energy requirements for a typical adult suggests that 1,200 calories would be expended merely in sleeping, resting, and light personal activity, such as dressing and eating (ibid, p. 385; J. V. G. A. Durnin and R. Passmore, *Energy, Work and Leisure* [London: Heinemann Educational Books, 1967], pp. 31, 39, 46). A slave restricted to 4,056 calories per day could then be expected to work at a rate requiring approximately 4.8 calories per minute over a ten-hour period. Slaves provided 5,357 calories could be expected to work at tasks requiring 7 calories per minute. Assuming the maximum reduction in work effort was 37 percent, the implied decrease in the calorie requirements for adults who expended 4.8 calories per minute at work would be 17.9 percent; for adults expending 7 calories per minute at work, the reduction implies a 22.7 percent decline. Since approximately half the population was black, the net reduction in energy requirements that could be explained by the reduction of black work effort could not have exceeded 9 to 11.5 percent. There are a number of reasons for believing that the actual decline was less than this. First, it is not obvious that the fall in energy requirements for children would parallel that for adults, as implicitly assumed in the above calculations. Second, our estimates assume that the time released by the reduction in adult work effort was spent in sleep or rest. Had the released time instead been spent in recreation, housekeeping, or child care, the energy requirements of free blacks would have been higher.

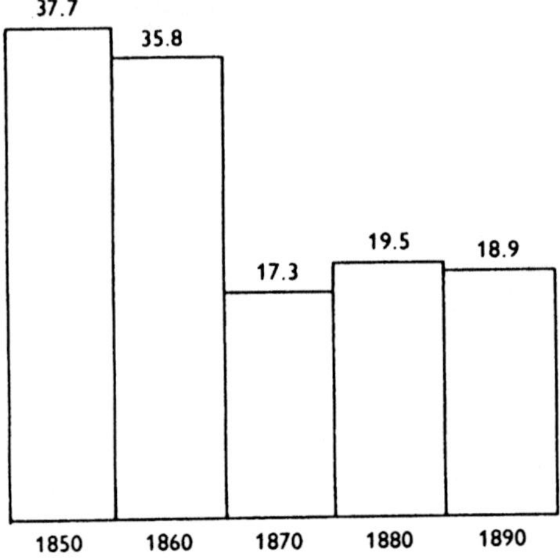

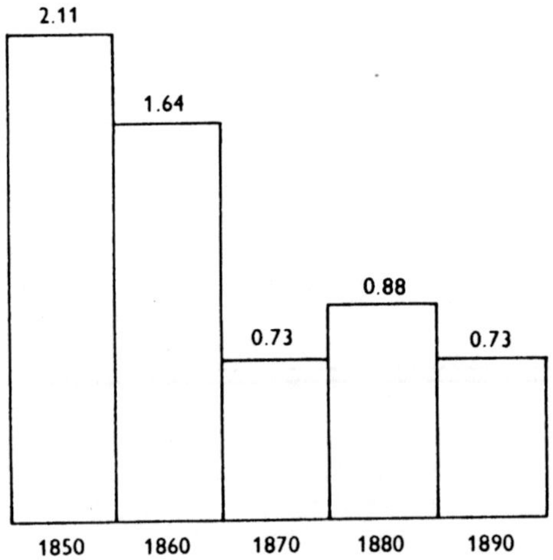

Figure 1. Production of food in the five cotton states: 1850, 1860, 1870, 1880, and 1890. (*Source*: Table 1.)

1890. Over the years, a shift toward cotton and away from grain is apparent.

This change cannot be adequately explained as a reaction to a shift in relative prices. Such prewar price data as are available suggest that the farmer received six to eight times the price of a pound of cotton for a

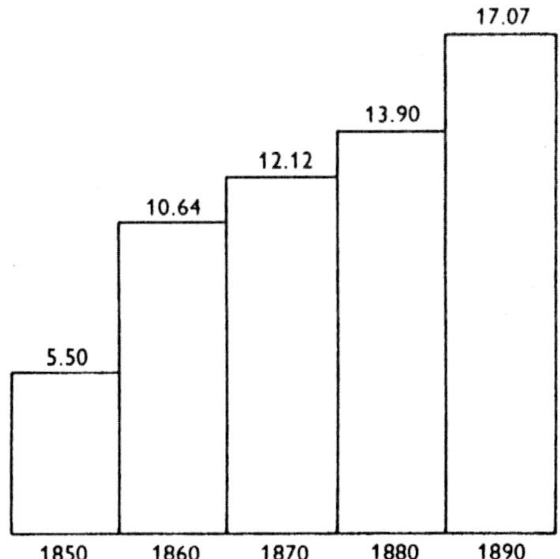

Figure 2. The number of pounds of cotton produced for each bushel of grain grown, Five Cotton States: 1850, 1860, 1870, 1880, and 1890. (*Source*: For grain production in corn-equivalent units, see sources to Table 1.)

bushel of corn.[15] Figure 3 displays the trends in the ratio of farmgate corn prices to cotton prices from 1869 to 1890. The cotton famine that accompanied the wartime disruption meant that corn prices were low relative to cotton prices, and this may have induced a shift of production into cotton. The ratio of corn prices to cotton prices was close to 5.5 in 1869, the first year for which we have farmgate prices of cotton.[16] By the mid-1870s, however, the ratio returned to its prewar level, and the

15. Wholesale cotton prices are available from Lewis Cecil Gray, *History of Agriculture in the Southern United States to 1860*, 2 vols. (Washington: Carnegie Institution, 1933), 2, p. 1027. We adjusted Gray's figures downward by 0.75 cent per pound to reflect Alfred Conrad and John Meyer's estimate of the cost of transportation and marketing ("The Economics of Slavery in the Ante Bellum South," *Journal of Political Economy* 66 [April 1958], p. 105). Prices received by farmers for corn in Virginia are available from Arthur G. Peterson, "Historical Study of Prices Received by Producers of Farm Products in Virginia, 1801–1927," Virginia Agricultural Experiment Station, *Technical Bulletin* 37 (Blacksburg: Virginia Polytechnic Institute, 1929), pp. 168–169. Gray (*History of Agriculture*) presents wholesale prices for corn in New Orleans comparable to those he collected for cotton. Farmgate prices of corn by state for 1848 can be found in U.S. Patent Office, *Annual Report of the Commissioner of Patents, for the Year 1848* (Washington: Wendell & Van Benthuysen, 1849), p. 653. The corn prices per bushel ranged from 5.1 to 9.2 times the cotton price per pound; ten years later the same ratio ranged from 6.4 to 8.4.

16. The average ratio for all five states, displayed in Figure 3, is a weighted average, computed by weighting the ratio of prices for each state by the total value of corn and cotton production for that state in 1879.

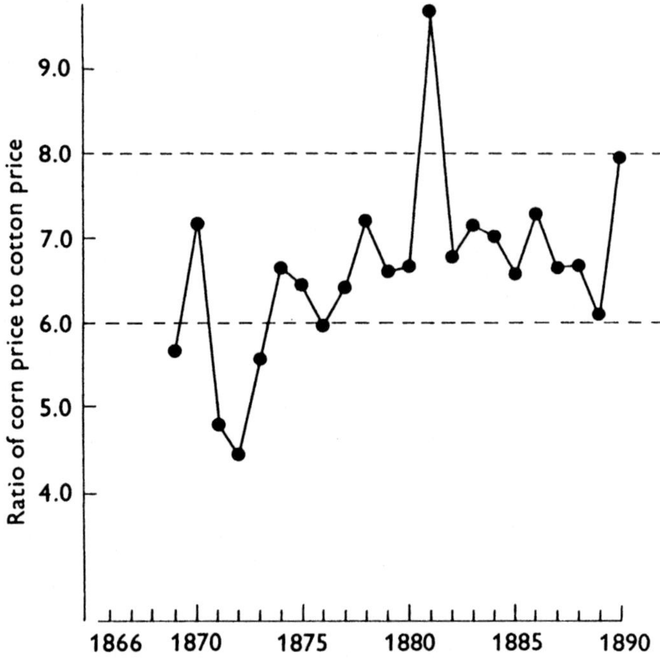

Figure 3. The ratio of the price of corn per bushel to the price of cotton per pound, Five Cotton States: 1869 to 1890. (*Source*: Note 16.)

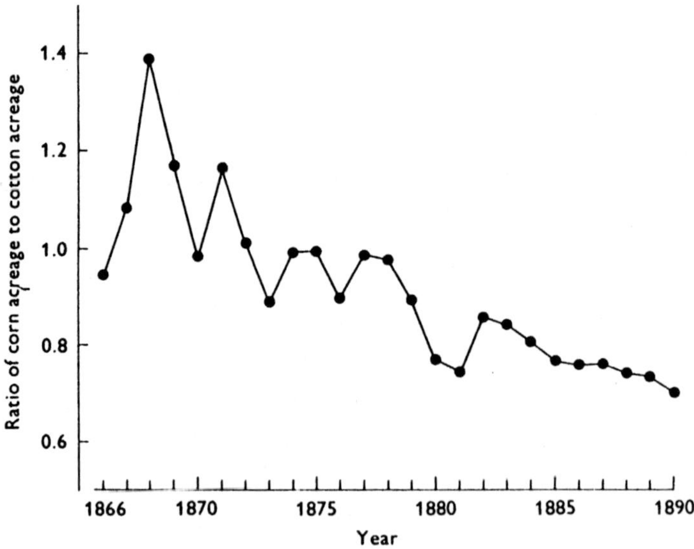

Figure 4. The ratio of corn acreage to cotton acreage. Five Cotton States: 1866 to 1890. (*Source*: Note 17.)

value of a bushel of corn remained about six to eight times that of a pound of cotton for the next fifteen years. Since the prices displayed in Figure 3 represent the prices received by farmers who sold cotton or corn, they greatly understate the return to corn production for farmers who would otherwise have had to purchase corn at the credit prices charged by merchants.

If a sharp rise in cotton prices associated with the war is taken to be an explanation for the initial shift of acreage into cotton, the rapid return of relative prices to their prewar levels should have induced a rapid shift back to corn. As Figure 4 shows, there was a considerable shift of acreage from cotton to corn between 1866 and 1868. Thereafter, the trend was sharply reversed. There is no indication that a change in agricultural productivity took place that might explain an increased attention to cotton. Data on the yields per acre in corn achieved in the Five Cotton States show that, relative to cotton yields, corn yields actually rose from 1869 to 1876. An improvement in the relative yield of corn, if anything, should have encouraged a relative increase in the acreage devoted to that crop.[17] In fact, as we have already noted, Figure 4 reveals that exactly the opposite took place. Corn acreage as a fraction of cotton acreage fell steadily from 1868 to 1890. Southern farmers were increasingly devoting their land to the staple crop, not foodstuffs.

The increasing concentration upon cotton appears even more puzzling when considered in light of the postwar labor shortage. The relative decline in labor could plausibly explain a shift toward land-intensive crops and away from those with high labor requirements. But there is no question that cotton was considerably *more* labor-intensive than were grain crops. It was commonly observed that twice as much labor was required to cultivate an acre of cotton as to cultivate an acre of corn. This being so, the labor shortage should have induced a shift toward corn, not cotton.[18]

17. The discussions in the text concerning cotton and corn yields and acreage are based on data reported in U.S. Department of Agriculture, Agricultural Marketing Service, "Corn: Acreage, Yield, and Production of All Corn . . . 1866–1943," *USDA Statistical Bulletin*, Number 56 (Washington: GPO, 1954), pp. 9, 10, 13, 14, 16; and U.S. Department of Agriculture, Agricultural Marketing Service, "Cotton and Cottonseed: Acreage, Yield, Production, Disposition, Price, Value, by States, 1866–1952," *USDA Statistical Bulletin*, Number 164 (Washington: GPO, 1955), pp. 17, 18, 20–22. Our conclusion takes into consideration the fact that corn prices did not fall relative to cotton prices during the period when relative yields were shifting.

18. We fail to see the force in the argument, advanced by Gavin Wright and Howard Kunreuther, which relates the shift toward cotton to a "land constraint" ("Cotton, Corn and Risk in the Nineteenth Century," *Journal of Economic History* 35 [September 1975], pp. 538, 549–550). It seems to us that they erroneously interpret the microeconomic effect of the landlords' use

The disappearance of self-sufficiency following the war

Before the enormous fall in food production, documented in Table 1, the South, particularly the Cotton South, produced very nearly enough food to meet all its needs. Sam Hilliard, in his comprehensive study of southern self-sufficiency before the war, cautiously concluded that the South as a whole was "largely feeding itself," but he noted that those areas of the South "in which commercial crops were important were also low in one or more of the basic commodities."[19] Other studies have supported this conclusion. They suggest that cotton producers were largely meeting their food needs.[20] On the other hand, the southern states, particularly in the Southeast, probably imported some food toward the end of the antebellum period to meet the needs of their urban populations and to fill deficits in the rice and sugar regions.[21]

of acreage restriction to control sharecroppers as a macroeconomic "land shortage." Since renters of small farms devoted a larger fraction (58.1 percent) of their acreage reported in crops to cotton than did sharecroppers (53.6 percent), the acreage restrictions imposed upon sharecroppers do not seem to have biased their crop mix toward cotton (see Table 8.2).

19. Hilliard, *Hog Meat and Hoecake*, pp. 235, 234.
20. See Gallman, "Self-Sufficiency"; and William K. Hutchinson and Samuel H. Williamson, "The Self-Sufficiency of the Antebellum South: Estimates of the Food Supply," *Journal of Economic History* 31 (September 1971).
21. The theme of a South importing foodstuffs from the North and West is an old one. Guy S. Callender ("The Early Transportation and Banking Enterprises of the States in Relation to the Growth of the Corporation," *Quarterly Journal of Economics* 17 [November 1902]) argued this case. Louis B. Schmidt ("Internal Commerce and the Development of a National Economy before 1860," *Journal of Political Economy* 47 [December 1939]) and Douglass C. North (*The Economic Growth of the United States, 1790–1860* [Englewood Cliffs: Prentice-Hall, 1961], Chapter 9) based their model of national economic development on the importance of an interregional trade of foodstuffs. Albert Fishlow, on the other hand, disputed the Schmidt-North thesis that southern food imports played a leading role in western development, though he conceded that the South received some imports of meats and grains from the West ("Antebellum Interregional Trade Reconsidered," *American Economic Review* 54 [May 1964]; idem, *American Railroads and the Transformation of the Ante-Bellum Economy* [Cambridge: Harvard University Press, 1965], Chapter 7). More recently, Stanley Engerman computed self-sufficiency estimates for the South in 1840, 1850, and 1860 and found that the South Atlantic area and the four-state area comprising Alabama, Arkansas, Louisiana, and Mississippi were deficit regions in grain and meat in 1860; but he noted that his calculations were based upon very generous estimates of food requirements ("The Antebellum South: What Probably Was and What Should Have Been," *Agricultural History* 44 [January 1970]. Table 1, pp. 134–136). The analysis of trade patterns in the 1850s by Robert W. Fogel emphasizes the growing rail traffic to the southeastern states in that decade ("American Interregional Trade in the Nineteenth Century" and "A Provisional View of the 'New Economic History,'" both in Ralph L. Andreano, ed., *New Views on American Economic Development* [Cambridge: Schenkman, 1965]). Diane Lindstrom has suggested that the cotton areas largely fed themselves; the food imports mainly provisioned the cities and the rice and sugar regions ("Southern Dependence upon Interregional Grain Supplies: A Review of the Trade Flows, 1840–1860," *Agricultural History* 44 [January 1970]).

If the South were only barely self-sufficient in food production before the war, the dramatic decline in per capita outputs of grain and pork can only imply that the South was unable to provision its own population in the postbellum period. Whatever the degree of dependence upon food supplied by the West or North before the war, there is little doubt that the South was a substantial net importer of food following the war.

The disappearance of self-sufficiency seems puzzling given the considerable change in the size distribution of farms. As Gavin Wright and Howard Kunreuther have demonstrated using the Parker–Gallman sample of farms, small farms before the Civil War had more swine per capita than large farms and devoted a relatively larger fraction of their acreage to corn production than to cotton production. If these patterns reflected a characteristic tendency for small farms to devote a greater fraction of their resources to food production, then, if anything, the switch to small-scale farms after the war should have resulted in an increased emphasis on food production, rather than the shift toward cotton that is observed.[22]

By 1880 the farms in the Cotton South were devoting 50 percent of their acreage to cotton. Table 2 shows that, as was the case before the Civil War, small farms planted a smaller fraction of their land in cotton than did the largest farms. Nevertheless, the lack of crop diversification among small farms is striking. Only 7.8 percent of the acreage on these farms was devoted to crops other than cotton and corn, while large farms reported 12.4 percent of their land in other crops. The table also reveals the greater number of crops reported by large farms compared with small farms. This lack of diversification was certainly puzzling to contemporaries. "It is a strange juncture of circumstances in which the great market staple of the State is selling at the cost of production, while everything else raised on the farm sells at a handsome profit," mused Thomas Janes, Georgia's commissioner of agriculture.[23] Janes condemned the increasing reliance on purchased foodstuffs, writing that he was "profoundly convinced that the greatest draw-backs to the prosperity of Georgia farming, is the mistaken policy of trying to make money with which to buy provisions, instead of raising provisions, not only for a support, but to make money."[24]

22. Wright and Kunreuther, "Cotton, Corn and Risk," pp. 526–529. As Wright and Kunreuther point out, William Brown and Morgan Reynolds ("Debt Peonage Re-examined," *Journal of Economic History* 33 [December 1973]) are incorrect to infer from the Gallman study that small farms were less diversified than large farms before the Civil War (Wright and Kunreuther, pp. 528–529, note 6).

23. Thomas P. Janes, Georgia Department of Agriculture, *Annual Report . . . for the Year 1875* (Atlanta: J. H. Estill, 1876), pp. 54–55.

24. Janes, *Annual Report*, p. 90.

Table 2. *Percent of reported acres in crops devoted to cotton and to crops other than cotton and corn, and average number of different crops reported on farms, by tenure and farm type, Cotton South: 1880*

Farm size,[a] form of tenure	Percent of acreage in cotton[b]	Percent of reported acreage in crops other than cotton and corn[b]	Average number of different crops reported
Small farms	50.9	7.8	4.2
Owned	45.7	11.8	4.8
Rented	58.1	3.9	3.7
Sharecropped	53.6	5.2	3.8
Medium-scale farms	46.2	13.0	5.4
Owned	43.1	15.1	5.7
Rented	56.1	7.9	4.7
Sharecropped	50.0	4.5	5.1
Large farms	52.4	12.4	5.6
Owned	51.6	13.0	5.6
Rented	58.4	6.2	6.0
Sharecropped	57.1	10.4	5.2
All farms	50.2	8.9	4.5
Owned	45.7	12.6	5.0
Rented	57.8	4.6	3.9
Sharecropped	53.2	5.7	4.0

[a] Small farms reported 50 acres or less in crops, medium-scale farms reported more than 50 but 100 acres or less, large farms reported 100 acres or more.
[b] For cotton farms only.
Source: A sample of Cotton South farms drawn from the 1880 Census of Agriculture.

The advocates of self-sufficiency were not blind to the obvious economic advantage the South enjoyed in the cultivation of cotton. What they attacked was the practice of relying upon cotton to the exclusion of homegrown food. "Instead of cotton fields, and patches of grain, let us have fields of grain, and patches of cotton," was the advice of a Georgian quoted with approval by the *Southern Cultivator*.[25] James De Bow felt it was a "plain maxim of common sense" that a farmer should "make on the plantation everything that can be made suitable for man or beast."[26] The advice that filled the agricultural journals was to resist the "lure" of the staple crop and remain free from a dependence on others for supplies.[27]

25. *Southern Cultivator* 28 (November 1870), p. 379.
26. *De Bow's Review* 3 (April–May 1867), p. 365.
27. Frequent reference to the "profitability" of cotton in the South can be found in the journals we cite, and many observers were quite sanguine (though often incorrect) about the prospect of favorable cotton prices in the future. However, support for growing *some* cotton should not be

Farmers were not unaware of these arguments, and some struggled to resist the trend toward increasing reliance upon cotton. "It should be the first object to raise all of the food necessary for man or beast," insisted a farmer's "study with a moral" that appeared in an 1871 issue of the *Rural Carolinian*.[28] Another article reasoned that "no planter can be in a bad condition, financially, with his barns filled with corn and his smoke-house filled with bacon."[29] A South Carolina farmer who signed himself "Panola" noted the advantages of cotton when a farmer took care to "feed himself and put his cotton crop in his pocket." In that way, he pointed out, "his surplus of grain will feed his family, and his cotton crop will allow them an occasional frolic."[30]

Despite these expressions of a desire for independence, southern farmers nevertheless were dependent on purchased, rather than farm-grown foodstuffs. To demonstrate just how great this reliance was, we have constructed estimates of the food remaining to farm families for consumption on farms in the Cotton South in 1879. Our estimating procedure, follows that of Robert Gallman and our own earlier estimates of southern self-sufficiency after the war.[31] For each farm in our 1880 sample, the outputs of food crops were converted to corn-equivalent units and then aggregated to determine the total food production. Allowances for seed were then subtracted, along with the corn-equivalent food needs for work stock and for hired labor. What remained was our estimate of grain available to the family either directly in the form of grain or indirectly as meat from animals slaughtered.[32] We report this residual in Table 3 as a per capita figure.

taken as refuting or disavowing advice favoring diversified farming for individual farmers. Stephen J. DeCanio is surely mistaken when he suggests that there was about equal sentiment for and against diversified farming in the postbellum literature (*Agriculture in the Postbellum South: The Economics of Production and Supply* [Cambridge: MIT Press, 1974], pp. 94–118). He has, we think, seriously misinterpreted the viewpoints of writers who, while strongly favoring production of home supplies, concede the obvious advantage of raising some cotton. It is difficult to reconcile DeCanio's characterization of Henry Grady's endorsement of diversification as "half-hearted" (p. 104) with Grady's original comment (Grady, "Cotton and Its Kingdom," pp. 723–724).

28. "A Lesson for Cotton Planters," *Rural Carolinian* 3 (December 1871), pp. 125–126; reprinted from *The Plantation*.
29. *Rural Carolinian* 2 (April 1871), p. 397.
30. *Southern Cultivator* 29 (March 1871), p. 97.
31. Gallman, "Self Sufficiency"; Roger Ransom and Richard Sutch, "Debt Peonage in the Cotton South After the Civil War," *Journal of Economic History* 32 (September 1972), pp. 659–664.
32. The crops included in our calculation were corn, rice, barley, buckwheat, oats, rye, wheat, cowpeas, dried beans, and Irish and sweet potatoes. The animals included as feed-consuming units on the farm were horses, oxen, mules, milch cows, and sheep. Since we express all food available to the family – including meat – as corn-equivalent grain, we allocate no food to the swine on the farm. This assumes that the farmer had the option of consuming his "surplus" either directly as grain or indirectly as slaughtered hogs fed from the surplus food available.

Table 3. *Per capita grain available to household members on farms, Cotton South: 1879*

Type of farm[a]	Bushels of grain per household member available as food	Percent of farms reporting deficits when consumption requirement per capita is		
		No bushels of corn	10 bushels of corn	15 bushels of corn
Small family farms	9.7	24.3	59.7	71.8
Other small farms	6.1	39.2	61.6	66.5
Medium-scale farms	34.5	16.1	28.5	37.0
Large farms	93.0	19.5	22.3	24.3
All farms	17.9	23.9	52.7	63.1

[a] See Chapter 4, Table 3 for definition of farm type.

The estimates of Table 3 are based on what we consider to be conservative approximations of feeding and planting practices on southern farms.[33] We therefore expect that our estimates of residual food exaggerate the amount of food remaining for family members. The implication of the figures is immediately clear: small farms in the Cotton South did *not* produce enough grain to meet their food requirements. Small family farms reported an average of only 9.7 bushels of grain per capita above the needs of the farm's work stock. Other small farms fared worse, producing only 6.1 bushels of corn per capita in residual grain production. One out of every four small farms was found to have a deficit of grain even if no allowance was made for human consumption.

At the very least, an average of 10 bushels of corn per year would be required to provide the minimal needs of each family member; a more plausible estimate would be 15 bushels per household member.[34] Figure 5 illustrates that almost 70 percent of the small farms produced

33. Gallman, in his study of antebellum self-sufficiency, employed estimates that he believed *over*stated actual feed and seed practices ("Self-Sufficiency," p. 19). We employed feed estimates in our earlier paper that, we felt, *under*stated the actual needs of the farm (Ransom and Sutch, "Debt Peonage," pp. 660–662). For our purposes here, we have revised our earlier estimate to reflect more realistic standards for the South around 1880. Nevertheless, we have kept our estimates conservative.

34. We estimate in Appendix E that an average working adult would require at least 20 bushels of corn per year to meet direct and indirect food needs; a child would need about half that amount. Considering that children constituted approximately one-half of the population, an average of 15 bushels of corn per capita would provide adequate food for the typical farm family. Hired farm labor, if any, was assumed to require 20 bushels of corn-equivalent grain per capita as board annually.

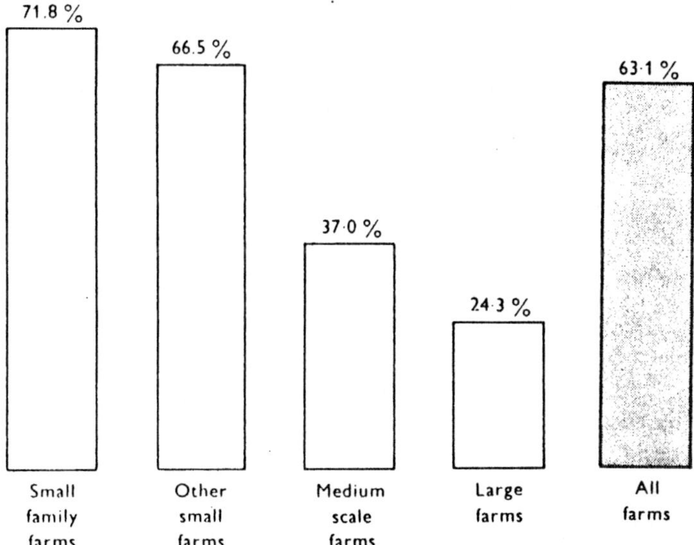

Figure 5. Percentage of farms reporting food deficits when per capita consumption of corn equivalents is 15 bushels: 1879. (*Source*: Table 3.)

insufficient grain to meet this standard. Our estimates confirm what many writers claimed at the time: the great majority of southern farmers had to purchase supplies. Indeed, even if we reduce the allowance for family consumption by one-third, 60 percent of the small farms would have produced inadequate supplies of corn and other grains.[35]

The impact of the cotton lien

The magnitude and pervasiveness of these food deficits throughout the Cotton South require explanation. What was the "lure" that made cotton so irresistible? The response given at the time by those farmers who were asked this question was invariably the same: cotton was required to secure a loan needed to finance the farm's operation.

Any lender requires collateral to secure the loans he makes. In the case of most tenants, what little personal property they possessed was

35. It should not be assumed from the fact that the "all farms" category averaged 17.9 bushels of grain per household member that the South, or even the rural South, was self-sufficient, since family members living in separate dwelling units were not included in the farm household population, nor were the family members of hired laborers. For the same reasons, we suspect that the food requirements of the largest farms have been understated relative to the small farms.

typically insufficient to cover their credit needs. Additional security was required by the rural merchant in the form of a lien on the future crop output of the farm. In the view of the merchant, cotton afforded greater security for such loans than food crops. Cotton was a cash crop that could readily be sold in a well-organized market; it was not perishable; it was easily stored; and because its yield per acre and future price were more predictable, cotton entailed less risk than food crops.[36] For these reasons, the merchant frequently stipulated that a certain quantity of cotton be planted to further enhance the security of his loan.

This stipulation was not typically spelled out as part of the legal language of the crop lien contract, an omission that has led some historians to conclude that contemporary allegations that merchants refused credit to diversified farming operations were exaggerated.[37] But, of course, it was not necessary for this requirement to be a part of the contract. The lien was arranged and signed only after the merchant had assured himself that the stipulated crops had already been selected and that the work was well underway.[38] It was the universal complaint of the farmers that the rural merchant predicated his willingness to negotiate credit on the condition that sufficient cotton to serve as collateral had been planted.

It was obvious to the farmer that the merchant's requirements that he plant cotton had a less subtle motivation as well. The merchant's insistence on cotton had the convenient effect of driving the farmer into increased dependence upon *purchased* supplies. The more cotton the farmer had to grow, the fewer resources remained to produce food. Farmers perceived that a cotton lien enhanced the merchant's lucrative

36. Our sample of farms illustrates the greater predictability of cotton yields per acre across farms in the year 1879. In each of the counties sampled, the proportional variance in the physical yields per acre was higher for corn than for cotton. Throughout the period 1867 to 1890, farmgate prices for corn fluctuated far more widely than did farmgate prices for cotton. The total effect was to make raising corn for sale a more risky prospect in the view of the merchant. This does not mean, however, that from the perspective of the farmer who was purchasing corn the risks would be viewed the same. As Wright and Kunreuther have pointed out, in that case the farmer must sell cotton at an uncertain future price and use the proceeds to purchase corn at an uncertain future price. The combination of these market uncertainties with the usual risks in growing crops made growing cotton to purchase corn appear more risky than corn production (Wright and Kunreuther, "Cotton, Corn and Risk," Table 5, p. 537).

37. Thomas D. Clark, "The Furnishing and Supply System in Southern Agriculture since 1865," *Journal of Southern History* 12 (February 1946), pp. 36–37; Jacqueline P. Bull, "The General Merchant in the Economic History of the New South," *Journal of Southern History* 18 (February 1952), pp. 41–42.

38. Crops were pitched in January or February. See *Rural Carolinian* 4 (January 1870), p. 247; *Southern Cultivator* 30 (February 1872), p. 41. Note that the crop lien contract reproduced in Chapter 6 as Figure 6.2 does not stipulate the amount of cotton to be grown. The contract is dated February 29, 1876; yet the preparation of the cotton land was usually begun in January.

business of selling supplies at exorbitant credit prices, but they could do little about it. "We ought to plant less [cotton and tobacco] and more of grain and grasses," claimed a correspondent from Montgomery County, North Carolina, in 1887, "but how are we to do it; the man who furnishes us rations at 50 per cent. interest won't let us; he wants money crop planted."[39] This is not an isolated example. Other responses to a North Carolina survey confirm that farmers felt strong pressure to plant cotton at the expense of food crops:

> The landlord and merchants who furnish supplies on time won't let [the tenants] sow much grain – they want cotton; and having to buy on time, they have to do as the merchant or landlord says, and the result is, they do not often pay out, and when they do they have nothing left.
>
> We shall soon be swallowed up by the commission merchants and guano men. It is cotton! cotton! cotton! Buy everything and make cotton pay for it.
>
> As a rule, tenants are forced to make a certain amount of cotton in order to get their supplies furnished them, and they cannot, therefore, pay the attention to making their bread and meat that they ought. . . . He is bound to feed his family, and not having anything, he is bound to buy on time. To do this he must promise the merchant to plant a certain amount of cotton.
>
> We are obliged to buy on time and pay 50 or more per cent., hence are compelled to make money crop mostly to pay with.[40]

There is little question that the practice of merchants asking for crop liens from their customers was common throughout the South and that cotton was generally a requirement for extending such a lien.[41]

The monopolistic pricing system employed by merchants throughout the Cotton South would, by itself, allow merchants to exploit their customers. Any farmer lacking sufficient cash to buy all his supplies was forced to pay the exploitive credit prices. The additional insistence by the merchant that the farmer forgo self-sufficiency obviously increased the farmer's dependence on credit and served to inflate the merchant's profits. The exploitation was thus compounded.

39. North Carolina, Bureau of Labor Statistics, *First Annual Report . . . for the Year 1887* (Raleigh: Josephus Daniels, 1887), pp. 131–132.

40. Ibid., pp. 88–89, 92, 111, 129.

41. Additional testimony to the fact that merchants insisted upon cotton to secure their liens can be found in Mathew B. Hammond, *The Cotton Industry* (New York: American Economic Association and Macmillan Co., 1897), pp. 150–152; Eugene W. Hilgard, U.S. Census Office, Tenth Census [1880], *Report on Cotton Production in the United States*, 2 vols. (Washington: GPO, 1884), 1, p. 357; 2, p. 251; Otken, *Ills of the South*, pp. 54–64; and A. B. Hurt, U.S. Department of Agriculture, "Mississippi: Its Climate, Soil, Productions, and Agricultural Capabilities," *USDA Miscellaneous Special Report*, Number 3 (Washington: GPO, 1883).

Critics of southern merchants never tired of explaining the gains of being free from dependence on supplies sold at monopolistic prices. The formula for independence seemed simple enough, and the logic was compelling. As Mr. Hill of Jonesboro, Georgia, exhorted listeners at the county fair in August of 1873:

> Make cotton your surplus crop! . . . Make your own fertilizers. . . . Thus you become independent of the Guano merchants. Raise your own provisions. Thus you become independent of the provision merchants. Your cheapest and safest line of transportation runs from your own fields and hog-pens to your own barn and meathouses! With no debts for your supplies, you will need no accommodation credits at two percent per month. Thus you can become independent of brokers, cotton factors and lien merchants. You can then sell your cotton at your own time, to your own chosen buyers, and will get your own money.[42]

It is important to realize that farmers who were initially paying monopolistic prices, and who then took this advice to become self-sufficient, would nevertheless have been adversely affected by the presence of the credit monopoly even though they might escape direct exploitation. Farmers who were being exploited by merchants' usurious interest rates had been initially forced into this position by their need for credit. Presumably, a comparison of the farmgate price of cotton with a cash farmgate selling price for corn had led them to prefer a crop mix that concentrated upon cotton and that therefore necessitated the purchase of food. It was this food deficit that produced a need for credit. By becoming self-sufficient, a farmer could avoid this necessity. But self-sufficiency would require a crop mix different from the one that would have maximized the farmer's income in the absence of a credit monopoly.

The existence of the monopoly of credit, coupled with the farmer's need for credit, invariably led to one of two outcomes. Either the farmer paid an exploitive price for supplies and was forced to grow even more cotton than he would have wished, or he chose self-sufficiency and grew less cotton than he would have wished. Either way, he would be unable to escape the adverse effects of the merchant's control of credit.[43] Of the two alternatives, the advice of Mr. Hill and many of his contemporaries was for farmers to choose the latter.[44]

42. B. H. Hill, "The True Policy of the Southern Planter," *Rural Carolinian* 5 (April 1874), p. 398.
43. For a more rigorous development of the argument presented in the text, see Roger Ransom and Richard Sutch, "The 'Lock-in' Mechanism and Overproduction of Cotton in the Postbellum South," *Agricultural History* 49 (April 1975).
44. We recognize that self-sufficiency would not invariably be superior to exploitation by the merchant. However, as we shall elaborate later in this chapter, there is reason to expect that the merchant would pursue his advantage to a point where self-sufficiency would be the farmer's preferred alternative. We interpret the advice of Mr. Hill and his contemporaries as evidence that the merchant's monopoly was, in fact, fully exploited.

The evidence is that southern farmers did not follow this advice. The advice went unheeded, but not because it was impossible to grow home supplies. Surely southern agricultural productivity on postbellum farms was high enough to provide amply for their needs and produce some cotton as a surplus crop as well. Farmers in the South had done so before the war, and they could do so after. The explanation for the persistent concentration upon cotton after 1865 is that cotton farmers were effectively prevented from practicing self-sufficiency as a means of escaping the merchant's power. They were locked in to cotton production.

The lock-in and persistence of cotton overproduction

In order to take the advice to provision his own farm and sever the relationship with the provisioning merchant, a farmer would have to alter his crop mix. The crop decisions could be made only at the beginning of a new season. If he had not produced sufficient food in the previous season to meet the needs of the farm for a full year, the typical farmer would not have sufficient stocks of foodstuffs to supply his farm over the coming season. Unless he had these stocks, or the cash to purchase them, he would be forced to borrow to cover the first year of his program of self-sufficiency. But this need for credit inexorably drove him back to the very merchant he sought to escape.[45]

The merchant had an obvious incentive to thwart the farmer's quest for independence. Moreover, he had the means to do so. The merchant simply refused to grant credit to a farmer who was not willing to accept a requirement that cotton be made the principal crop. Despite his desire to escape, the farmer was still locked into the production of cotton. His lack of self-sufficiency, of necessity, forced him to seek credit year after year, and the merchant's conditions for a loan ensured that the farm could not become self-sufficient. A farmer from Swain County, North Carolina, observed the plight of the cultivator. "The mortgage system," he wrote in 1887, "is working its deadly way into this county, and making sad havoc where its tempting offers are once entered into. Alas! one never gets out from its magic embrace until he dies out or is sold out."[46]

45. In fact, a move to self-sufficiency might not be enough to free the farmer completely from the grips of the merchant. If the discussion is extended to include the farm's needs for supplies in addition to foodstuffs, then the farmer must clear enough cash from the sale of cotton to pay off his debt due on the past season's purchases and to purchase all the supplies required for the coming season. In other words, the cotton crop must finance two years of food deficits and purchased supplies if the farmer is to escape the merchant's control.

46. North Carolina Bureau of Labor Statistics, *Annual Report . . . 1887*, p. 135.

The farmer, faced with the prospect of continual seasonal indebtedness, might still hope eventually to save enough over several successive seasons to accumulate the cash necessary to purchase a year's supplies. But even this hope would be dashed. The low net income of the one-family farm severely limited the farm operator's ability to save, and misfortune or crop failure might wipe out his savings in a single season. Even if luck were with him, the merchant could eliminate the farmer's ability to save at any time. He could demand so much cotton that the cost of food at monopolistic prices would reduce the farmer's surplus income literally to a negative value. In this situation the farmer would end the year with insufficient output to pay his debt to the merchant. If the farmer's savings could not make up the difference, the merchant would have legal claim to part of the *next* crop, and the farmer would be required to sign a new lien contract for the coming year.

In most cases the storekeeper would not need to drive the farmer to this point. The merchant's territorial monopoly was effective enough that the need for credit on the part of a farmer was itself sufficient to guarantee his business for another year. The need for the extra insurance of an end-of-the-year debt would appear only if competition from nearby merchants threatened to lure the farmer away. In any case, the merchant would avoid driving the farmer so far into debt at the end of a season that he would become discouraged and work inefficiently or attempt to abscond without paying his debts. The merchant was compelled to provide for the needs of a farm, and once he had expropriated all the remaining income, there was no gain to creating additional debts that could never be repaid. An illustration of the merchants' cognizance of the dangers of accumulating debt is provided by the comment of the editor of the *Rural Carolinian* in regard to a merchant's reaction to some "unlucky" farmer confronted with serious losses: "Immediately [the farmer] is offered several cents a pound for his cotton more than it is worth. . . . [The merchant] offers this bonus to induce the rascally inclined customer to pay his debts."[47] In other words, if the occasion required, the merchant could simply adjust the price of cotton – and the farmer's income – to whatever level would keep the farmer at his job, but never free of the merchant's control. This ultimate trap of debt peonage, where the farmer ended the season still in debt to the merchant, was an extreme, probably resorted to in only a fraction of cases. But the lock-in mechanism, which held income sufficiently low to prevent an escape to self-sufficiency, undoubtedly kept a majority of small farmers in a perpetual cycle of cotton overproduction and short-term debt.

Contemporaries alleged that the lock-in was universal throughout the

47. *Rural Carolinian* 7 (April 1876), p. 178.

South. Charles Otken referred to it as the "vast credit system whose tremendous evils and exorbitant exactions have brought poverty and bankruptcy to thousands of families, . . . crushed out all independence and reduced its victims to a coarse species of servile slavery."[48] Agriculturalists, who employed less rhetoric and relied upon more careful observation, reached the same conclusion. Thomas Janes, commissioner of agriculture for Georgia during this period, conducted surveys which revealed that approximately 75 percent of the state's farmers were buying on credit.[49] Janes warned farmers against entering "the whirlpool of credit and debt which has engulfed so many, and from which so few have escaped unscathed."[50] Years later, a committee of the U.S. Congress reported on the "condition of the cotton growers." They concluded:

> That generally the financial condition of the farmers is bad, a very large percentage insolvent, and that very few indeed are substantially increasing in the possession of property. That the few who are actually solvent and making some increase in their estates are those who raise their own supplies, meat, corn, plow stock, producing cotton only as a surplus.[51]

From production statistics alone it is impossible to identify the farms which, by our definition, were gripped in the merchant's trap. But we can identify a large body of farms that must have been easy prey for the coercion of the credit monopolist. We know that at least three-fourths of all farms in Georgia purchased some fraction of their supplies on credit in the 1870s, and less precise reports elsewhere suggest that this figure was typical throughout the Cotton South. It seems likely that virtually every small farm required some credit. Those small farms that were unable to produce enough grains even to meet the needs of animals on their farms could hardly avoid seeking credit. Probably most of the farms that failed to produce 15 bushels of corn per family member (63.1 percent of all farms) were exploited through exorbitant credit prices and were susceptible to manipulations of the merchant. Even if *no* farms other than small farms with grain deficits were caught by the merchant,

48. Otken, *Ills of the South*, p. 11.

49. Georgia, Department of Agriculture, "Consolidation of the Reports of Crops, &c." (August 15, 1875), p. 9; and idem, "Consolidation of the Reports of Crops, etc., for the Month of August, 1876," p. 2; both in *Publications of the Georgia State Department of Agriculture from September, 1874 to January, 1878* (Atlanta: J. P. Harrison & Co., 1878), volumes 1, 2.

50. Thomas P. Janes, "Report of the Commissioner," in Georgia, Department of Agriculture, *Annual Report . . . 1875*, p. 54.

51. U.S. Congress, Senate, Committee on Agriculture and Forestry, "Present Condition of Cotton-Growers of the United States Compared with Previous Years," *Report of the Committee . . . (February 23, 1895)*, Senate, Report Number 986, 53rd Congress, 3rd Session, 2 vols. (Washington: GPO, 1895), 1, p. iii.

our self-sufficiency estimates suggest that 56 percent of all farms in the Cotton South would have been locked in. Over 300,000 farms and families paid homage to the merchant's power.[52]

The genesis of debt peonage

Our analysis of debt peonage and the power of the merchant to force farmers into overproduction of cotton has considerable appeal as an explanation of the persistent dependency on outside sources of foodstuffs displayed by the South throughout the latter part of the nineteenth century. The paradox of why free farmers in the New South ignored the widely publicized incentives to turn to self-sufficiency is easily resolved by an explanation that argues farmers were not, in fact, "free." Farmers grew cotton rather than food because the will of the merchant prevailed over the interests of the farmer.

Another aspect of the appeal of the lock-in argument is that the origins of this system and its emphasis on cotton are easily explained in terms of events immediately following the Civil War. The spectacularly high prices for cotton that followed the famine of the wartime period made farmers eager to plant as many acres of cotton as their labor allowed. In those halcyon days, there was no conflict between the farmer's interest and his supplier's interest on the question of growing cotton. The lure of cotton profits was so enormous that, despite a shortage of supplies and the collapse of southern banking and factorage systems, ways were found to finance the crops. To the small farmer, as we have seen, this invariably meant a crop lien from a local merchant or a wealthy planter. However, the famine prices were short-lived. By 1868 the trend in prices had already begun to favor a shift of production back to corn. Yet, for many small farms, the trap had by this time already been sprung. The collapse of the cotton prices made crop liens worth less than had been anticipated. Bad crops in 1866 and 1868 added to the difficulties. Saddled with debts incurred because of losses, farmers had no alternative but to accede to the merchants' demand that they grow cotton to repay their debts. Farmers soon found that this practice locked them into the continued need for credit to begin each new season. The merchant had been quick to seize an opportunity to prevent a shift to greater grain production.

52. There were 546,332 farms in the Cotton South in 1880. The estimate that 56 percent of these farms were locked in was obtained by multiplying the fraction of farms under 50 acres (0.782) times the fraction of small farms which had grain deficits assuming a human requirement of 15 bushels per capita (0.713). See Figure 5 in this chapter.

The "profitability" of cotton

Economists are usually skeptical of arguments that seem so clearly to deny the power of competitive behavior. A simpler, more direct, reason for the southern farmer's perference for cotton could be posited: perhaps conditions following the war had changed to make it profitable to specialize in the cash crop and purchase supplies. Two critics of the debt-peonage argument have summarized this view:

> Farmers in Kansas grow wheat, not because local merchants force them, but because it is wealth-increasing to do so. The proceeds from wheat sales permit farmers to buy more food and other things (cotton goods) than "growing their own." Presumably the same mechanism operated in the South, but economic conditions were appropriate for cotton, not wheat.[53]

This argument apparently convinced these critics without any additional consideration. Yet the argument does not demonstrate that southern farmers were actually better off producing cotton rather than food or that they were free to grow food if they wished. To presume, as these economists have, all the necessary conditions for a competitive world begs the fundamental issue in question: did or did not the southern economy work in an efficient and nonexploitive way?

Whether or not economic conditions in the South "were appropriate for cotton" was a question contemporaries struggled to resolve without success. The editor of the *Rural Carolinian* expressed his puzzlement over this issue in 1874:

> Figures do not lie, it is said. Well, perhaps they don't; but they sometimes tell the truth in such a way that it is more deceptive than a downright lie. Figures are made to say that cotton planting is the most profitable branch of agriculture. This is true, no doubt; but, then, these same figures are made to show that cotton planting is a losing business, and all the planters, or at the best, most of them, are becoming bankrupt. There is a good deal of truth in this too, we fear.[54]

The editor's confusion is easily understood in light of the serious obstacles to accurate estimation of the returns from various crops even on those farms that kept careful records of their costs and receipts.

The key to the problem lies in accurately establishing how many additional bushels of corn the farmer could expect to produce by shifting to corn raising the labor currently required to produce a given quantity

53. Brown and Reynolds, "Debt Peonage Re-examined," p. 868. Others emphasizing pecuniary motives to specialize are Robert Higgs, *Competition and Coercion: Blacks in the American Economy 1865–1914* (New York: Cambridge University Press, 1977), and Stephen DeCanio, "Cotton 'Overproduction' in Late Nineteenth-Century Southern Agriculture," *Journal of Economic History* 33 (September 1973), pp. 611–615; idem, *Agriculture in the Postbellum South*, pp. 12–15, 261.
54. *Rural Carolinian* 5 (April 1874), p. 353.

of cotton. The answer to this question cannot be obtained from the census, since the census did not report the amount of labor expended upon each crop. A search of the agricultural literature makes it clear that cotton required considerably more labor and animal power per acre of land throughout the year than did the cultivation of corn:

The number of days' work needed upon an acre of cotton, from the first to the last, is greater than upon any other crop, and the other expenses bestowed upon it greater.[55]

Cotton culture requires more labor, more mules, more ploughs, and more expensive machinery (as gins and screws) than the growing of corn, oats, wheat, peas, clover and grasses.[56]

"Every observing farmer knows," remarked one contributor to the *Southern Cultivator*, "that for each additional acre of land planted in cotton, two must be deducted from the number in corn."[57] This rule of thumb is consistent with the statements of other contemporaries. Another writer in the *Southern Cultivator* presented statistics that imply that 3 acres of corn could be produced by giving up 1 acre of cotton.[58] He was criticized by a third correspondent of the agricultural journal who set the ratio at 1.67 acres of corn per acre of cotton forgone.[59] It does not seem unreasonable on the basis of these observations to assume that 1 acre of cotton would release sufficient labor and capital to cultivate between 1.67 and 2 acres of corn.

In 1879 the small-scale family-operated farms in our sample from the Cotton South averaged 178 pounds of cotton per acre. The same farms produced 11.3 bushels of corn per acre. Hypothesizing that the labor and other resources devoted to a parcel of average cotton land were diverted to corn production, we can calculate that the typical operator of a small family farm would obtain between 10.6 and 12.7 bushels of corn for every 100 pounds of cotton forgone.[60] We can ignore the production

55. *Southern Cultivator* 33 (February 1875), p. 54.
56. *Southern Cultivator* 33 (December 1875), p. 462.
57. *Southern Cultivator* 28 (March 1870), p. 82.
58. *Southern Cultivator* 28 (September 1870), p. 292. The correspondent discusses a hypothetical farm of 200 acres. A switch from all cotton to one-half cotton and one-half corn reduced the labor requirements from fifteen hands to ten hands.
59. *Southern Cultivator* 28 (November 1870), pp. 374–376.
60. We assume that the average yield of corn and cotton per acre is achieved with the resources shifted between crops. Actually a farmer would choose to shift those resources that would maximize the yield difference. Since the marginal yield differential would be equal to or greater than the average differential, our assumption minimizes the gain expected from such a shift. Wright and Kunreuther have suggested that our calculation of the trade-off between cotton and corn is "inappropriate because it ignores the land constraint" ("Cotton, Corn and Risk," footnote 26, p. 538). In note 18 of this chapter we point out what seems to be an error in their argument that there was a macroeconomic land constraint. In any case, in this instance we fail

of cotton seed, since the seed would be used to pay for the ginning and bailing of cotton.[61] However, in addition to the output of grain, the corn crop yielded fodder.[62] The value of the corn fodder was equivalent to between 10 and 18 percent of the value of the grain.[63] We shall take the lower estimate of the fodder yield for the purposes of our calculation. This adjustment raises the corn–cotton trade-off to between 11.7 and

to see the force of Wright and Kunreuther's objection, since our calculation is made for the hypothetical shift of a *marginal* amount of land, labor, and work stock from one crop to another in a *microeconomic* context. Our purpose is merely to demonstrate that a move towards self-sufficiency, if possible, would have been desirable.

61. *Southern Cultivator* 29 (November 1871), p. 410; *Rural Carolinian* 6 (February 1875), p. 231. The cotton prices given below are for cotton ginned and baled.

62. It was common southern practice, not employed elsewhere, to strip the green leaf blades from the growing cornstalks around August to be used as fodder. This practice was "well nigh universal in the leading cotton states" (R. J. Redding, "Culture Experiments on Corn," *Georgia Agricultural Experiment Station Bulletin*, Number 10 [December 1890], p. 140). According to experiments run at a number of the southern Agricultural Experiment Stations, this practice reduced corn yields between 10 and 18 percent. Nevertheless, the pulling of fodder was practiced apparently because of the shortage of animal feed and the relative amount of free labor time available in August (*Southern Cultivator* 29 [August 1871], p. 283). Moreover, according to the calculations of the Experiment Stations, the value of the fodder collected more than made up for the loss in corn yield. See R. J. Redding, "Culture Experiments," pp. 140–141; idem, "Culture Experiments on Corn," *Georgia Agricultural Experiment Station Bulletin*, Number 15 (December 1891), p. 105; idem, "Fertilizer, Culture and Variety Experiments on Corn," *Georgia Agricultural Experiment Station Bulletin*, Number 23 (December 1893), p. 82; idem, "Fertilizer, Culture & Variety Experiments on Corn," *Georgia Agricultural Experiment Station Bulletin*, Number 27 (December 1894), p. 191; William C. Stubbs, "Report," *North Louisiana Experiment Station Bulletin*, Number 22 (January 1889), p. 310; S. M. Tracy and E. R. Lloyd, "Corn," *Mississippi Agricultural and Mechanical College Experiment Station Bulletin*, Number 33 (March 1895), p. 64.

63. As a southern rule of thumb, each bushel of shelled corn produced as a by-product approximately 10 to 14 pounds of pulled fodder. Numerous citations suggest that the market value of 100 pounds of pulled fodder equaled or exceeded the price of a bushel of corn. Therefore, each bushel of corn produced was accompanied by 10 to 14 percent of a bushel of corn equivalents in the form of fodder (see *Southern Cultivator* 28 [March 1870], p. 82; [September 1870], p. 292; 29 [July 1871], p. 249; [November 1871], p. 409; *Rural Carolinian* 6 [February 1875], p. 232; R. J. Redding, "Corn Culture," *Georgia Agricultural Experiment Station Bulletin*, Number 30 (November 1895), pp. 373–374; idem, *Georgia Agricultural Experiment Station Bulletin*, Number 10 [December 1890], p. 142; Number 15 [December 1891], p. 105; Number 23 [December 1893], p. 82; Number 27 [December 1894], p. 191). This ratio reflects the relative value of fodder as an animal feed relative to corn (Redding, *Georgia Agricultural Experiment Station Bulletin*, Number 30, p. 378; W. A. Henry, *Feeds and Feeding* [Madison: W. A. Henry, 1898], pp. 631–633). The yield of fodder would be considerably increased if the stover were harvested or if livestock were pastured in the cornfield after the harvest. The value of the tops and tassels of the cornstalk was placed at 8 percent of the value of the grain by Redding (*Bulletin*, Number 30, p. 378). This brings the value of the by-products to over 18 percent of the corn. A correspondent of the *Rural Carolinian* noted that the value of blades and shucks was 17.7 percent of the value of the corn grown (6 [February 1875], pp. 232–233).

14.0 bushels of corn equivalents for every 100 pounds of cotton, or 12.85 bushels if we take the midpoint.

Given this physical trade-off between crops, we can ask whether the farmer who was buying corn at credit prices should have attempted to grow more corn. The value of the cotton he must forgo is easily estimated, since cotton prices were fairly uniform throughout the South, and frequent surveys by the U.S. Department of Agriculture provide reliable testimony concerning the farmgate price. Over the three crops of 1878, 1879, and 1880, the average December 1 farmgate price for cotton in the Cotton South was 9.5 cents per pound.[64] If the farmer were purchasing corn, as we assume, the relevant price for evaluating the additional corn output would be the purchase price rather than the selling price. The price the typical farmer paid for corn is less certain. The surveys taken in Georgia during these years suggest that the credit prices for corn charged by merchants were 53 percent above the farmgate prices farmers received when they sold corn the previous December. There is no reason to believe that the statistics for Georgia exaggerate the situation throughout the South. We have therefore applied this markup to the average farmgate price of corn that prevailed in the Cotton South from 1878 through 1880 – 62.3 cents per bushel.[65] Our estimated credit price was therefore 95.3 cents per bushel. The answer to our question is thus clear. A farmer who could have traded between 11.7 and 14.0 bushels of corn worth $11.15 to $13.34, for 100 pounds of cotton worth $9.50 would have been well advised to do so. The fact that many did not is testimony to the coercive power of the merchant.

The farmer who paid credit prices for corn could have increased his income at the margin by approximately 29 percent simply by shifting resources from cotton to corn. This does not mean that the farmer who could obtain corn at the *cash* price was unwise to depend on purchased corn. Using the same procedure employed in the calculation above to estimate the trade-off when valued at cash prices, we find that 12.9 bushels of corn would be worth $9.45.[66] This amount almost exactly

64. Cotton prices for each state in the Cotton South are available from U.S. Department of Agriculture, Bureau of Agricultural Economics, "Prices of Farm Products Received by Producers," Volume 3, "South Atlantic and South Central States," *USDA Statistical Bulletin*, Number 16 (Washington: GPO, 1927). The prices for each state included in our definition of the Cotton South were weighted by the number of farms in the state.

65. The farmgate prices of corn for each state in the Cotton South were taken from U.S. Department of Agriculture, "Prices of Farm Products," and were weighted by the number of farms in that state.

66. The Georgia data suggest that cash prices for corn sold by merchants were 18 percent above the farmgate price from the previous December. Applying this factor to the established farmgate

equals the value of the 100 pounds of cotton that could be produced from the same labor. As one would expect, the retail price of corn and cotton reflected the relative productivity of labor in producing these two crops.[67]

These figures make clear the source of the confusion that troubled the editor of the *Rural Carolinian.* Calculated at cash prices, the farmer's dependence on cotton would not seem unwise. But in practice, the farmer who sought to produce cotton at the sacrifice of self-sufficiency was required to pay much higher prices for corn and was prevented from increasing his own corn production in response. As a result, he might very well have entered a losing business.

The burden of monopoly

The rural merchant of the Cotton South was a monopolist who held a local, territorial monopoly over credit. As a monopolist he exploited his customers by charging exorbitant prices. In the traditional economic analysis, a monopolist is condemned not merely for overcharging but also for underselling, since the quantity of the good demanded is typically lower as a consequence of its higher price. In this particular instance, however, the furnishing merchant was able to prevent the farmers' demand for credit from contracting in response to the exorbitant interest rates charged. The merchant compelled the farmer to plant and cultivate more cotton and less foodstuffs than he would have freely chosen to do given the high price of credit. Apparently the merchant used his control over the farmers' crop decisions not merely to maintain the balance between cotton and corn production that had existed before the appearance of the credit monopoly, but to push significantly beyond that point toward specialization in cotton. As we have seen, there was an otherwise inexplicable shift away from grain crops and animal husbandry and toward cotton in the Cotton States following the Civil War. The monopolist in this case both overcharged and oversold his product.

Every farmer in the Cotton South was harmed as a consequence of the merchants' coercion. Those who entirely avoided the need for credit by achieving self-sufficiency in grain and pork were making crop decisions that were less than optimal. In a free market they might well have

price (62.3 cents) gives a cash price of 73.5 cents, making 11.7 to 14.0 bushels of corn worth between $8.60 and $10.29. The midpoint yield of 12.85 bushels would have been worth $9.45.

67. The figures presented in this section to support our conclusions are revised from earlier estimates presented in Roger Ransom and Richard Sutch, "The 'Lock-in' Mechanism and Overproduction of Cotton in the Postbellum South," *Agricultural History* 49 (April 1975), pp. 423–424. The adjustments are quantitatively small and do not change the conclusions.

chosen a crop mix that required the purchase of some corn. Their self-sufficiency in foodstuffs would represent, therefore, a self-imposed reduction in economic efficiency designed solely to evade exploitation by a monopolist. The farmers who avoided the credit system by accumulating sufficient cash to finance all their grain purchases without asking for credit were forgoing the interest such cash assets might have earned had they been productively invested.[68]

It would be presumptuous to attempt to quantify these economic losses. To do so would require more knowledge than we have about the nature of the demand for cotton, the efficiency of crop production, the productivity of alternative investments, and the numbers of farmers who were directly and indirectly affected by the system. One point is clear, however: the magnitude of the losses borne by the farmers exceeded the gains achieved by the merchants. The losses did not arise solely from the transfer of income from producers to the providers of credit. In particular, the crop mix chosen by most farmers was economically inefficient and therefore southern agriculture was less productive than it might have been. While we cannot measure the extent to which regional income was reduced in the aggregate by this imposed inefficiency, we can obtain a feeling for what the merchants' exploitation may have meant to the tenant farmers who were trapped within the system.

There were three direct effects of the credit monopoly: it reduced the farmer's income, it reduced the security of the farmer's livelihood, and it reduced the farmer's independence. The most obvious impact of the monopoly was to lower the real income of the farmer. One crude measure of the magnitude of this reduction can be gained by calculating the real income of black tenants operating family farms in 1879–1880. In Chapter 1 we calculated that the material income of black tenant-farm operators was about 29 percent above the consumption standard of slaves, or approximately $41.39 per year per capita in 1859–1860 prices. That calculation, however, assumed that there was no exploitation of farmers in the postwar era. In Appendix A an alternative cost-of-living index is presented for 1879–1880 on the assumption that 60 percent of the farm family's purchases were made on credit. When we use that index to recalculate the material income of black tenant families, the figure falls to $35.82 per capita, or 13.5 percent less than when we assumed all purchases were made for cash. Although a number

68. In addition to the microeconomic losses discussed in this chapter, there were macroeconomic losses that fell upon the southern economy as a whole. As we shall discuss in Chapter 9, the increased production of cotton induced by the credit system lowered world cotton prices sufficiently that the additional output of cotton forced upon each farmer did not contribute to his total revenue.

of assumptions are required to make such a calculation, we believe our estimate provides an order of magnitude for the proportion of agricultural output that was diverted to the merchants.

A 13.5 percent rate of exploitation would be, of course, considerably less than the rate of exploitation of slave labor, which we have estimated at approximately 55 percent. According to our estimates, the material income of tenants who were exploited by merchants was nearly 12 percent above the consumption of slaves who were exploited by their masters. The fact that blacks were materially better off as freedmen than as slaves does not, of course, excuse the merchants' exploitation. Nor can a reduction in real income of 13.5 percent be dismissed as trivial, particularly when it is remembered how low were agricultural outputs per capita in the first place. In considering the fraction of output that was left to the farmer, it is also significant that the rate of exploitation could be adjusted by the merchant. In good years the tenant lost proportionately more than in years of poor harvests. The merchant not only impoverished his customers, he stifled their hopes and reduced their incentive as well.

The farmer caught up in this system also was compelled to take greater risks. Forced to plant cotton that would be sold after the harvest at a yet unknown price to finance the season's purchases of corn at prices also yet to be established, the farmer fulfilled his corn requirements on terms that embodied not only the risk attendant upon an uncertain crop yield but the risk inherent in the fluctuations of the relative price of corn and cotton as well. A glance at Figure 3 suggests that the year-to-year changes in the ratio of the price of corn to the price of cotton were not insignificant. Had the farmer grown his own corn, he would have faced only the crop risk of an uncertain corn yield.[69] The farmer had to be compelled by the merchant to assume the increased risks involved in the exchange of cotton for corn since he was not compensated for assuming this added burden by expectations of higher income.

The southern tenant was neither owner of his land nor manager of his business. Caught between requirements imposed by the landlord and those imposed by the merchant, his independent decision making was limited to the mundane and menial aspects of farming. The larger decisions – concerning land use, investments in the farm's productivity,

69. Wright and Kunreuther have emphasized the increased risk imposed upon the farmer who was forced to exchange cotton for corn. They go on to argue that this increase in riskiness may have induced some farmers to plant even more cotton than required by the merchant in a hope that a good crop would be sufficiently remunerative to allow them to escape the cycle of annual debt in the future. This suggestion is intriguing. However, at present very little evidence exists that a significantly large class of "gambler farmers" actually arose. See Wright and Kunreuther, "Cotton, Corn and Risk."

the choice of technology, and the scale of operation – were all made for him. Undoubtedly, as a consequence, his pride, his ambition, and his efficiency as a tiller of the soil were reduced. The magnitude of these losses cannot, of course, be measured; but neither should such implications be ignored.

"The economic revolution in the American South"

by Gavin Wright

Regional differences in the patterns of development are an important part of American economic history. As a new region was settled, migration and economic development were usually accompanied by convergence of per capita income of the region with the national average. However, with the Civil War and the abolition of slavery, incomes in the South fell dramatically behind those in the rest of the nation. "Poverty and stagnation seemed rooted in Southern culture." Its standard of living refused to converge to the national mean.

In "The Economic Revolution in the American South," Gavin Wright explores this region's growth process for the period between the Civil War and the 1980s. Economic theory predicts a long-run convergence of wages and income due to labor, capital, product, and technology flows. Wright admits that this approach has much legitimacy but that it fails to explain the initial divergence or the forces that dampened the process of convergence for so long. He identifies institutional factors in the South that blocked the natural convergence and explains how these impediments were removed.

Wright's plot is complex, with a number of interacting elements. As you read this essay, be sure you understand how these elements fit together. Critics of Wright accept his major premises but disagree with his emphasis on the importance of government policy during the New Deal. For example, how would Wright's story have been different if the federal government had not imposed minimum wages on industry? Lee Alston (1987) argues that without minimum wages, southern wages may not have converged as rapidly but the end result may have been preferable because minimum wage laws have penalized the young and minorities. Without the New Deal, the South would still have caught up to the rest of the nation, but with less pain, displacement, and outmigration, according to Alston.

Economic history is a laboratory for the impact of public policy. Wright argues that the Southern economy was absorbed into the national economy by flows of labor and capital that destroyed the South's regionalism. However, it would have been difficult to predict the impact of key public policies that triggered this absorption. Many of the same institutional changes and flows of products, labor, and capital have emerged with the freeing of trade between the United States and Mexico. Does the South provide a lesson here? Can we expect a regional integration of the Mexican economy with that of the United States?

Additional Reading

Lee Alston, "The Wright Interpretation of Southern U.S. Economic Development: A Review Essay of *Old South, New South* by Gavin Wright," *Agricultural History*, 61 (Fall 1987), 52–67.

Richard Easterlin, "Interregional Differences in per Capita Income, Population, and Total Income, 1840–1950," in *Trends in the American Economy in the Nineteenth Century*, Princeton, NJ: Princeton University Press, 1960, 73–140.

Robert Margo, *Race and Schooling in the American South, 1880–1950: An Economic History*, Chicago: University of Chicago Press, 1990.

Gavin Wright, *Old South, New South: Revolutions in the Southern Economy since the Civil War*, New York: Basic Books, 1986.

9

The economic revolution in the American South

GAVIN WRIGHT

As recently as twenty-five years ago, regional economic backwardness in the states of the traditional American South was considered an intractable problem of continuing national concern. Poverty and economic stagnation seemed rooted in Southern culture, the same culture which maintained segregation and traditional race relations. The eminent historian of the South, C. Vann Woodward, wrote in 1961: "The modern South rests on these very foundations and is continuous in its economic, political, and racial institutions and doctrines with the order established in 1877. . . . In racial policy, political institutions and industrial philosophy, there has been no break with the founding fathers of the New South" (Woodward, 1961, p. E3).

Obviously, much has changed since then. But as the attention of economists has been taken up by new sets of concerns, like energy, inflation, and the competitive position of American manufacturing centers in the Northeast and Midwest, not many have stopped to look back and ask why the perception and reality of the Southern economy has changed so drastically in such a short time. Those who do look back over a longer period often imply that the rise of the South was essentially a long-term process of national convergence in factor prices and per capita incomes; that is, a gradual but reasonably steady reflection of basic economic forces which are relatively well understood by economists.[1]

This article draws on research first published in *Old South, New South: Revolutions in the Southern Economy Since the Civil War* (New York: Basic Books, 1986). The author is grateful to Basic Books for permission to reprint material. For valuable comments on an earlier draft, thanks are due to Gary Saxonhouse, Robert Staiger, and the editors of this journal.

Source: Gavin Wright, "The Economic Revolution in the American South," *Journal of Economic Perspectives* (Summer 1987), 161–78. Reprinted with permission of the author and the American Economic Association.

1. For example, the U.S. Advisory Commission on Intergovernmental Relations wrote in 1980: "Since the turn of the century, regional manufacturing wage rates have generally been converging, largely as a result of a slow but steady relative increase in wages in the southeast"

Even on its own terms, this level of understanding is unsatisfactory. If regions have converged in recent years, why did they diverge initially? If divergence happened in the past, why should it not happen again in the future? In other words, comprehending the forces of equilibration also means knowing what held these forces at bay for so many years. And a close look at the historical record will show that convergence for the South was not nearly as persistent and unidirectional as modern writers imply.

This analysis of Southern economic history is built around the proposition that the region's distinctive culture and economic life were rooted in the regionalization of the labor market. The modern period of equilibration only began in earnest when the institutional foundations of that regional labor market were undermined, largely by federal farm and labor legislation dating from the 1930s. Ironically, the resurgence of the South came in the wake of policies which threatened to cripple the region's industrialization, by forcing up labor costs in low-wage sectors. This apparent paradox calls for a closer look at initial conditions as well as at the regional growth process over the last 50 years. Though it may be the case that Southern wages and incomes were bound to converge to national levels eventually, the path actually taken was a choice of one among several alternative paths to that result.

Was there a Southern economy?

The urban specialist Jane Jacobs, in her lively recent polemic *Cities and the Wealth of Nations*, indicts the economics profession for persisting in "the idea that national economies are useful and salient entities for understanding how economic life works and what its structure may be" (Jacobs, 1984, pp. 29–36). This complaint is, of course, a very old one in the history of economics. But Jacobs means more than the simple observation that factor mobility within countries is imperfect. She holds that the true "salient entities" in economic life are metropolitan centers, which share not only factor supplies but information, techniques, innovations and incremental adaptations of all kinds; cities are, in short, the communities of interactive problem-solving which underlie the fundamental process of economic development. Indeed, Jacobs is equally critical of the famous "New South" advocate Henry Grady for thinking in terms of "large, amorphous regional economies" rather than urban centers.

Jacobs has identified a crucial set of considerations; nevertheless, the

(1980, p. 5). See also Weinstein, Gross, and Rees (1985, p. 53), whose per capita income graph creates a striking visual impression of continuous convergence.

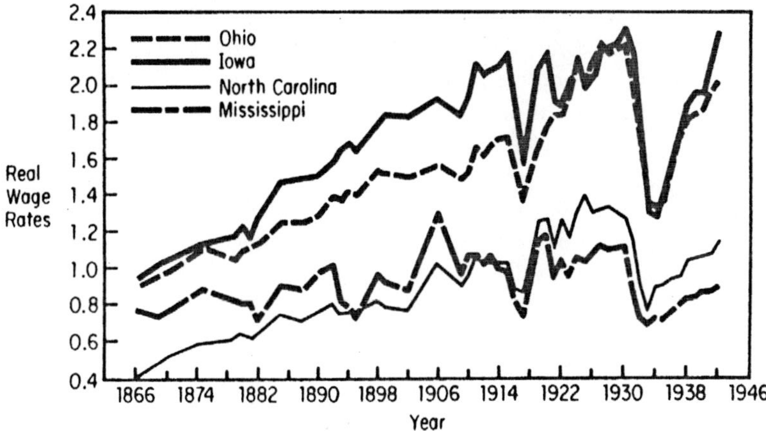

Figure 1. Farm labor wage rates per day in selected states, 1866–1942 (deflated by wholesale price index).

historical record shows that there have been regional and national economies, in both the simple and the more sophisticated senses of the term. In the simpler sense, regionalism in the unskilled labor market is quite evident. Flows of labor were overwhelmingly in an east-west direction, the South remaining isolated from all other regions of the country. During the heyday of European immigration to the United States before World War I, the South was almost untouched; less than 2 percent of the Southern population was foreign-born in 1910. Wage indicators confirm this separation. A convenient measure of a market-determined price of raw labor is the farm wage, which shows no tendency toward convergence before World War II (Figure 1). Both the absolute and relative differentials were higher in the 1920s than at any time since the Civil War. This gap was neither strictly agricultural nor strictly racial. The wages of black and white farm laborers were virtually identical; and the farm labor wage was closely linked to wages in sawmills and textiles, the two largest Southern industries. Textile manufacture in particular employed white labor almost exclusively until the 1960s.

It was not just that North–South labor market adjustments were slow; adjustments occurred with reasonable speed, but in different directions. East and West converged within the North and South, but North and South did not converge toward each other. These patterns were genuinely regional, not mere aggregations of numerous independent local phenomena. In such basic eco-demographic indicators as average farm size and land-labor ratios, for example, *every single Southern state* moved in the same direction in *every single decade* between 1880 and 1930 – toward smaller farm size and fewer acres per person – trends which were contrary to those prevailing throughout the rest of the country.[2]

Evidently, Northern and Southern regional labor markets were subject to the same sorts of centripetal forces that characterize physical processes like river drainage and locational processes like the emergence of metropolitan centers. The labor market can be considered a network, and the presence of loyalties among members of kinship, ethnic, and cultural groups gives rise to "network externalities" of the sort that theorists have now begun to analyze (Katz and Shapiro, 1985). Since the cost of using a communication network like a labor market declines as the number of participants rises, this process is an example of increasing returns to scale, in which initial conditions matter even in the long run.[3]

If this conception is accurate, then the logical place to look for the "causes" of such regionalization is not in overt barriers to mobility at a point in time, but in history. Richard Steckel (1983) has shown that the East–West lines of migration go back to the early nineteenth century and were rooted in certain geo-agricultural continuities, such as familiarity with seeds, crops, livestock, and climate. This "natural" regional separation was ratified and institutionalized by slavery, which served to insulate the South from outside labor flows after 1807, when importation of African slaves ended. Then the region was consumed by the turbulence of war and Reconstruction at the very time when a truly national (non-Southern) labor market was developing elsewhere, lubricated by mass immigration from abroad. Such elements of timing are important because much of the actual flow of information in long-distance industrial labor markets operates though informal channels, such as letters from relatives and word-of-mouth communications within ethnic groups. Statistical studies confirm that the existence of a first wave of migrants from a country is the most important single factor in generating the second wave (Dunleavy 1983). Thus, labor market flows and linkages tend to persist, once begun. Rather than thinking of kinship, ethnic, and linguistic loyalties as market "imperfections," these forces are better considered as part of the way the market functions and

2. There is actually one exception at the state level: Texas, where farm acreage per person increased between 1870 and 1890. There figures reflect the rise of the cattle kingdom in western Texas, not really part of the Southern region by any reasonable historical or economic definition.

3. The theoretical implications of increasing returns for technological choices are analyzed by Arthur (1983) and for international trade by Helpman and Krugman (1985). The path-dependent character of increasing-returns processes has been emphasized by David (1975, 1986) as a way of underscoring the crucial role of history in economic life.

Table 1. *Nonagricultural wealth owned by state residents as a percentage of total nonagricultural wealth, 1880–1920*

	1880	*1900*	*1920*
New England	105	114	122
Middle Atlantic	118	121	125
East north central	90	92	92
West north central	74	66	59
Mountain	44	54	60
Pacific	104	108	112
South	90	84	82
South (excl. Texas)	91	80	73
Alabama	82	72	62
Arkansas	73	67	59
Georgia	88	81	72
Louisiana	114	101	85
Mississippi	84	63	42
North Carolina	94	75	54
South Carolina	87	75	58
Tennessee	90	75	59
Texas	81	107	126
Virginia	97	83	68

Source: Lee, Everett S., *et al.*, *Population Redistribution and Economic Growth: United States, 1870–1950*. Vol. 1. Philadelphia: American Philosophical Society, 1957, 729–33. The regional aggregates are weighted averages of state figures.

expands in particular directions. These directions were in turn reinforced by the recruiting strategies of employers, who found it much cheaper to utilize existing channels or expand them incrementally than to lay out the large fixed cost that would have been required to redirect the established lines of the market.

The persistence of a Southern regional labor market is thus both a reflection of and a cause of the persistence of the distinctive Southern regional culture documented by sociologists such as Reed (1983). The South was a quasi nation. Regionalism in the labor market, however, is analytically separable from the persistence of regional wage differentials. International trade theory has long maintained that factor prices can be equalized by commodity flows between nations as well as by migration of the factors themselves. But this effect did not prevail between the South and the rest of the country for two reasons. First, factor-price equalization through commodity flows requires that endowments of trading partners are reasonably similar, so that each one produces some of each major commodity (Helpman and Krugman, 1985, chapter 1). But the South's factor endowment differed from the rest of the United States, especially in the importance of exotic commodities (such as cotton) which could not be grown in the North. The second reason is closely related: Southern resource allocation was determined mainly by *international* demand. There was no more reason for interregional trade to pull Southern wages up to U.S. national norms than for international trade to pull Southern wages down to the levels of countries like India and Egypt.

The looming threat of an internal factor-price equalization effect did, however, become increasingly important in American political life after World War I. That development is taken up in a later section.

Was the South a colonial economy?

Like many less developed countries, the post–Civil War South had natural resources and labor, but was short on skills and capital. Aspiring Southern producers usually needed outside help, and over time an ever-growing fraction of the nonagricultural wealth of the region came to be owned by "outsiders." This trend, too, was unique among large American regions (Table 1). What set the South apart was not that capital flowed in, but that capital was not quickly followed by flows of people and/or indigenous accumulation, as in the North Central, Mountain, and Pacific regions.

Southern industries tended to produce a narrow range of cheap, standardized, low-skill commodities, which added relatively little value to the region's raw material. Being subject to outside ownership, and having to go north to buy complex goods made with Southern cloth or lumber or iron, it is understandable that many Southerners came to feel that they were part of a "colonial economy." But those who used this phrase meant more than mere description; they meant that Southern growth was actively suppressed. As one historian wrote: "Profits that might have been re-invested in southern enterprise or helped to stimulate the local economy were drained off to the North. More important, decisions affecting the economic health of the region were made by men in northern boardrooms who had a vested interest in maintaining it in its colonial status" (Hackney, 1972, p. 195).[4]

Economists who have looked into the subject have found almost no merit in this analysis. The intensive use of natural resources and unskilled labor was, after all, a logical reflection of the region's comparative advantage. The idea that an anti-Southern conspiracy could have been maintained among business interests across the entire rest of the country is implausible on its face; and the idea that increased inflows of outside capital would damage Southern growth seems utterly fallacious.

4. The classic exposition of this interpretation is Woodward (1951, Ch. 11).

In the case of the textiles industry, the active encouragement, technical assistance, and financial supplements from the Northern-based textile machinery industry helped undermine the competitive position of New England textiles in the national economy. Most economists, therefore, have felt that the "colonial economy" idea confused symptoms with causes, and had little to do with the real reasons for Southern backwardness (Danhof, 1964).

A partial exception is the case of the Birmingham steel industry, where slow progress after 1990 has often been attributed to the dominance of U.S. Steel and its notorious "Pittsburgh Plus" pricing formula, whereby the price of steel was based on the distance from the company's Pittsburgh headquarters. As late as the 1950s, these and other related corporate policies were considered major causes of regional stagnation by many southerners, including the economist George W. Stocking (1954).

But even in this instance the colonialism argument does not work. Whatever U.S. Steel's motives may have been, corporate suppression was not the main reason for slow growth of the Southern iron and steel industry. Indeed, elsewhere in the country the same pricing policies were given credit for *encouraging* the geographic dispersion of steel production (Warren, 1973, p. 131). After all, local firms have no reason to charge less than the import price; in Pennsylvania, Ohio, Illinois, and Michigan, the "price umbrella" provided by the Pittsburgh-plus formula allowed old firms to survive and expand, and new firms to appear and grow. If U.S. Steel had been intent on stifling incipient competition, it would have been better advised to "dump" cheap steel in the relevant areas, as the German steel cartel did in many countries. Instead, their conservatism offered opportunities for competitors, but few responded in the South.

The experience of U.S. Steel in Birmingham does, however, illustrate some of the ways in which Southern producers faced problems different than producers in every other part of the country. The company poured $23.5 million into improvements and expansion at its Birmingham branch between 1907 and 1913, but encountered a continuing series of problems in labor costs, product quality, and marketing. The labor was inexperienced in industry, and turnover and absenteeism were high; these problems were serious enough to induce U.S. Steel to undertake, begining in 1915, an ambitious program of "welfare capitalism" in an effort to stabilize and improve the work force. Extraction costs were high for iron ore and coal because the mines were underground rather than open-pit, and the terrain irregular and full of seams. Most important, Alabama red hematite ore is relatively low in iron content and unusually high in phosphorus, qualities that raised costs and presented special problems in the technological adaptation (Chapman, 1953, chapters 5 and 6).

In other words, the distinctive resource base of the South required adaptations in technology, but the South lacked a strong indigenous community of engineers and mechanics devoted to these tasks. Here is the element of truth in the "colonial economy" thesis, and it is no small matter. From the time of the great innovations of Bessemer and Kelly in the 1850s, the evolution of steel-making technology involved an interactive process of adapting techniques to the peculiarities of national and regional iron ores. The early success of Bessemer (unbeknownst to the inventor) depended on an iron ore unusually low in phosphorus. British, French, German and Belgian ores all shared the high-phosphorus problem, and the efforts at solution led to the Basic Bessemer process by the late 1870s. By perverse fate, the new process required an ore *higher* in phosphorus content than Birmingham ore. Only the Basic Open Hearth process allowed successful steel-making at the Ensley plant in 1898; even then, economical use required more iron and steel scrap than Birmingham could command. The introduction of the duplex process (an amalgamation of Bessemer and open-hearth principles) in 1906 solved the scale problem, but by that time steel-making in the North had been established for nearly forty years. At every step, the South had to wait for a new technology to emerge somewhere else in the world.

U.S. Steel gave Birmingham access to capital and technological expertise, but Birmingham was only one part of a large corporate portfolio of holdings and interests, and not a very typical part at that. U.S. Steel did not have to suppress incipient Southern industrial expansion, but the company may not have appreciated the full potential of its Southern properties. It did not undertake tinplate production there until a three-year engineering study in the 1930s demonstrated that this omission was costing the company $1 million per year! G. W. Stocking suggested that U.S. Steel had been "blinded . . . to the profit potentialities of its Birmingham properties," and that "out of concern for its northern plants carried the principle so far as to defeat its ends" (Stocking, 1954, pp. 104–111). In effect he conceded that U.S. Steel had no strong economic interest in stifling the South; the company's real crime was not suppression but neglect.

These episodes illustrate features of the development process often stressed in economic history. Historical studies emphasize that technological progress is usually incremental and cumulative, and that progress is often specific to the currently adopted technology (David, 1974; Rosenberg, 1976). In the pre–World War II era, incremental progress had strong location-specific elements. Americans do not fully appreciate the extent to which our country's rise to world leadership in steel after

1870 depended on the unusually rich iron ore fields of the Mesabi range (Allen, 1977). The United States did more than passively live off the rents from these resources, but this unique resource base served as the foundation for an advanced national technology and applied science oriented towards this particular bundle of resources. The South was part of the nation, but not really part of the common resource environment. In agriculture, for example, the Southern soil, climate, and disease environment was sufficiently distinctive that producers had difficulty absorbing the benefits of the increasingly sophisticated American agricultural research establishment (Rubin, 1975).

In many ways, generating an advanced technology is itself a network activity with increasing returns to scale. At least prior to the modern era, significant aspects of technology were location-specific. Such an interpretation helps to explain why the South had such difficulty developing its own technology for its own environment. The scale economies involved were very large, at the level of entire industries or even entire economies.

But the fundamental problem was not the small size of the Southern economy; rather, it was the historic absence of an indigenous technological community and the high set-up costs required to establish one. When a group of Georgians set out in the 1880s to establish a state school of technology, they had to rely on northern models, and the model chosen was the "shop culture" approach: highly practical "trade school" training, producing "graduates who could work as machinists or as shop foremen, but who were not well prepared for engineering analysis or original research" (McMath, 1985, p. 9). The choice may have been the only one feasible at that time.

Regional wage or income differentials for skilled and professional jobs were substantially lower than for the unskilled, presumably because these individuals relied less on informal channels of communication.[5] The fact that the probability of out-migration increased with education must have discouraged those employers and local officials who hoped to capture for the regional economy some of the returns to investments in higher education.[6]

5. This pattern is consistent with much other evidence, including a recent analysis of "local labor markets" which finds that "local market effects on wages are substantially smaller among more educated workers, indicating that their wages are determined in broader geographic markets" (Topel, 1986, p. S142).

6. This interpretation resembles a model presented by Helpman and Krugman (1985, Ch. 10), in which nontradeable goods are subject to increasing returns to scale. In that case, factor owners who are able to take their factors with them have an unambiguous incentive to migrate to the larger economy, even if factor prices are equalized (p. 197).

Southernization: The road not taken

The primary respect in which Southern factor endowments differed from those of the rest of the nation, however, was labor. The decisive step in America's surge to world economic prominence in the 19th century was an emerging "American system" of technology, manifested in a specialized machine tool industry producing almost exclusively for the U.S. market. This development was genuinely national, not in the sense that it was the object of explicit public policy, but in the sense (as Jane Jacobs writes of urban centers) that the nation was a "technological community" sharing a communication network and a common market environment. Economic historians still debate what the precise factor-saving properties of the American system were (Temin, 1971; David, 1975; Field, 1983; James and Skinner, 1985). The important point is that this distinctive national technology was well-adapted to the labor market setting which prevalied more or less everywhere in the country except in the South.

Conventional American thinking about technology virtually equates "technological progress" with "mechanization" and "labor-saving" change, but this perception shows a cultural bias. A good illustration is the contrast between historical patterns of change in the United States and Japan. The United States was the world leader in large scale mechanization, with a farm implements industry as an integral component of the machine-tools sector. Japanese agriculture, in contrast, developed through biological-chemical technology, including seed improvements with large applications of fertilizer (Hayami and Ruttan, 1970; Kawagoe, Otsuka, and Hayami, 1986).

The comparative history of the textile industries in Japan and in the South is still more instructive.[7] In many ways the parallels were remarkable, two examples of low-wage competitors gradually overtaking the older centers of production through a combination of learning, investment, and the cumulation of experience. The labor systems were entirely different, but both followed "foreign models": the South followed Samuel Slater's mill village system, while Japan consciously reproduced the all-girl dormitories of Lowell, Massachusetts. In both cases improvements in high-speed ring spinning facilitated progress by requiring less skill than the older mule technology which still predominated in England. In both cases the first installations were imported – Japan's primarily from Platt Brothers of Oldham, the South's from Saco-Lowell and other machine shops in New England.

7. This paragraph draws on Saxonhouse (1979) and Saxonhouse and Wright (1984a, 1984b).

At this point, however, the parallels diverge in a crucial respect. While the South continued to rely on outside machinery and expertise, Japan began to create a distinctive technology. Even the move to ring-spinning in Japan violated established rules of thumb, which called for the use of the mule where local cottons were extremely short-staple. The Japanese industry pulled off this trick by perfecting a labor intensive cotton mixing process, which allowed foreign cottons to be blended cost-effectively within the technological range of the ring. Over time, the Japanese industry pioneered labor intensive innovations which allowed them to economize on materials and make "cheap goods" which were nonetheless serviceable. These product characteristics contributed to Japan's ability to expand markets even during the Great Depression. By the 1920s Japan was making her own textile machinery. These developments stand in strong contrast to the relative technical passivity of the Southern industry. The textile machinery industry did not move South until the 1960s, when the United States lost its claim to world leadership in this technology (U.S. Textile Mills Product Industry, 1983, pp. 2–15a, 3–22).

Here we have a central reason for persistent Southern backwardness. In the absence of an advanced labor-using technology, Southern firms had to choose between mechanized labor-saving approaches from the North and retaining older techniques. In lumber and iron-making, Southern producers of the 1920s were using hand methods that had been phased out decades earlier elsewhere. Small wonder that the South concentrated on producing simple low-skill commodities. Of course, over time the South might have gradually built up an indigenous technological community specializing in some of those areas where Southern output dominated national totals. In textiles, for example, a "Southernization" process of sorts was underway. Georgia Institute of Technology opened its school of textile engineering in 1899. A graduate of this program, I. H. Hardeman, was an early pioneer in applying air conditioning and humidity control to Southern mills (Arsenault 1984, p. 602). In the 1920s Georgia Tech established a ceramics department in response to appeals from local businesses for a method of processing Georgia's deposits of kaolin and other clays. Even a half-century later elements of Southern-specific technological development appear in Georgia Tech's research on solar and biomass conversion technologies, utilizing the abundant local resources of sunshine and trees (McMath, 1985, pp. 166, 441).

But for the most part – and almost completely as far as the labor market was concerned – Southernization was the path not taken. There were two reasons why not. First, as a low-wage region in a high-wage country, the South had difficulty investing in education without encouraging out-migration. Southern families may have demanded little education because of poverty, ignorance, and opportunities to employ child labor on farms or in cotton mills. But the planters and employers who dominated regional politics were well aware that education greatly increased the probability that a young person would leave both the home county and ultimately the entire region (Lieberson, 1978). Planters and other employers often expressed the view that schooling would "spoil" blacks for work in farms, mines, or sawmills. Cotton mill managers knew that a high school diploma was as good as a ticket to leave the mill village. In this situation, the gains to schooling were not just inappropriable by employers but were actually negative because of induced out-migration. The structure of the situation led many Southern employers to be suspicious and hostile toward "outsiders" and outside influence.

If local monopsony power had been the only interest behind these policies and attitudes, they would have been transitory. But even in state and regional coalitions, Southern employers were not poised to benefit from increased education levels, and stood to lose from the opening of a North–South flow of information, people, and ideas. The politics of the New Deal years provides the clearest indication of Southern priorities. Southern Democrats were extremely powerful in Congress during the 1930s, but they did not use their power to bring home federal money for work relief or other projects; although the South was the poorest region in the country, it stood *last* among regions in per capita federal expenditure between 1933 and 1939 (Wright, 1986, p. 260). Southern Congressmen often obstructed the application of federal programs to their region, and on many issues (such as the coverage of Social Security in agriculture, and local allocation of welfare benefits) they were successful (Alston and Ferrie, 1985).

In fact, they had good reason to be suspicious of outside influence, because national political forces were increasingly intent on eliminating the low-wage economy of the South. These forces were the second and ultimately the decisive reason why Southernization was the road not taken.

What became of the Southern economy?

There were many motives for the effort to impose national wage norms and labor standards on the South. Many outsiders sympathized with Southern workers and viewed institutions like the mill village and plantation sharecropping as barbaric. Also, the argument that low wages were themselves the cause of low productivity and poverty (an idea that has a long history in economics and is currently undergoing a revival in economic theory) was prominent in the political rhetoric of the day. But economic motives were surely present as well. The fear of low-wage Southern competition united Northern workers and Northern employers. The Southern textiles industry felt outside pressures on its labor costs very early, in decisions of the War Labor Board during World War I, in Northern support for strikes in the late 1920s, in national reform campaigns against child labor and night work (Shiells and Wright, 1983). The most far-reaching changes for textiles and many other Southern industries came with the labor controls of the National Industrial Recovery Act of 1933 and subsequently the Fair Labor Standards Act of 1938. All these measures had their major economic effects in the South. The thirty-two and one-half cent minimum wage law which went into effect in October 1939 affected 44 percent of textile workers in the South, but only 6 percent in the North. The wage policies of federal work-relief programs like the Work Project Administration also served to raise Southern wages, and by the end of the 1930s this policy goal had become explicit. Nor did these pressures end with the New Deal. Wartime wage decisions closed the gap even further, and expansions of minimum wage coverage during the 1950s and 1960s created many wage distributions like that displayed in Figure 2, where the great majority of workers earned precisely the federal minimum. National labor unions with branches in the South also pushed for quick elimination of regional differentials.

A much larger number of workers were affected by events in agriculture, especially blacks. That story is rather separate, although it has certain parallels to the industrial situation. In brief, acreage reduction and the incentives created by the federal farm programs of the 1930s led to widespread demotion and displacement of tenants (Whatley, 1983). Reform efforts to protect the status of tenants encouraged further displacement through mechanization. Displacement was only partial so long as the harvest bottleneck remained. But the development of a successful mechanical harvester by 1950, coupled with cutbacks in cotton acreage in the older producing states, generated a decline of *one million* farm operators between 1950 and 1959 and an unknown but also sizable decline in the number of farm laborers. In agriculture as in industry, reduced employment through mechanization was not the simple result of autonomous technological changes, but represented as well the effects of government policy (Whatley, 1985). The important point in the present context, however, is that the decline in agricultural employment did not have to imply large scale regional out-migration. It might instead have provided the manpower for an emerging labor-intensive Southern industrial development, but that path was blocked by the industrial labor policies just reviewed. As a result, the majority of

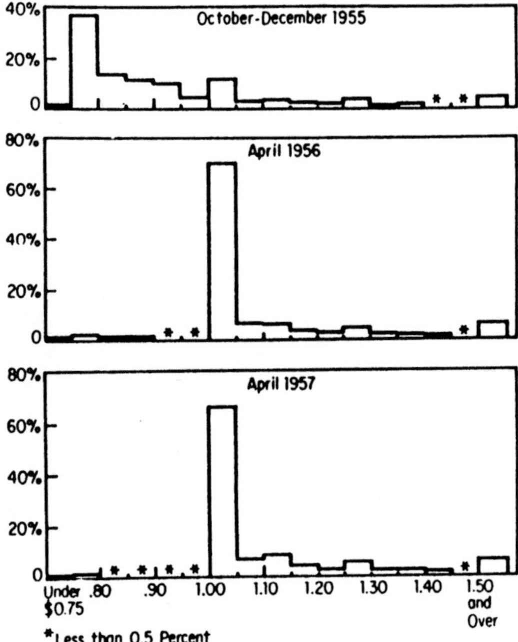

Figure 2. Percent wage distribution of nonsupervisory workers in Southern sawmills, 1955–1957.

the departing farm population had few options other than leaving the South.[8]

What then were the overall effects of these policies? In the 1940s and 1950s, Southern economists like John Van Sickle (1943) argued that national wage standards would stifle regional industrial growth, as indeed they were intended to do.[9] The argument was eminently logical,

8. The experience of the North Carolina tobacco belt offers a glimpse of an alternative scenario. Tobacco mechanization was delayed until the 1970s, partly by technical constraints but partly also by barriers to consolidation of farms, barriers that have gradually been relaxed since the 1960s. The small farm owners who have dominated tobacco have had much more control over the timing of their departure from agriculture. In contrast to the sharecroppers of the cotton belt, displaced tobacco farmers have been able to find jobs in local industry with relatively little increase in unemployment or out-migration (Johnson, 1984).

9. Unlike many writers on both sides of these issues, Van Sickle acknowledged explicitly that his position rested both on economic assumptions about regional factor mobility and on value judgments about the authenticity of Southern regional culture. He wrote that the South was held together by "those emotional loyalties which more than any other force, make the concept of regionalism a reality" (p. 39), and asked of the Fair Labor Standards Act: "Does it promise to promote or retard the legitimate aspirations of the Southern Region?" (p. 184). In the tradition of economics, however, Van Sickle treated the evolution of technology as entirely exogenous.

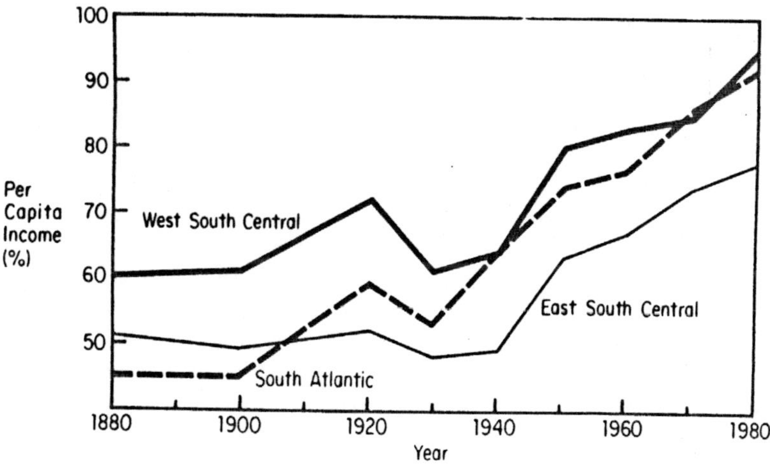

Figure 3. Per capita income of Southern regions, as percentage of U.S. average, 1880–1985.

yet looking at the record of Southern growth since the 1930s, it is hard to detect a stifling effect (Figure 3). Every part of the South made sustained progress toward the national per capita income norm, with the most dramatic gains made during World War II and the trend continuing through the widely fluctuating national economic circumstances of the 1950s, 1960s, and 1970s. This regional growth had many components: defense spending, the attraction of the sunbelt, oil and natural gas, the weaknesses of unions and state regulations on business. But when all the "exogenous" developments point in the same direction at the same time, it generally indicates some common background element. The abolition of the low-wage sectors seemed to lift an economic incubus which had held the South down.

This simple picture has an element of illusion. In part, convergence in per capita income was simply the effect of low income people moving from South to North. Through the 1950s, the median educational level of black migrants was only 6.6 years. By contrast, migrants into the South were highly educated by Southern standards. (By 1960, more than 35 percent of white males in the South with five or more years of college had been born outside the region.) In terms of employment opportunities, it is not clear that predictions of adverse consequences were wrong. In textiles, for example, employment never returned to its peak of the 1930s. Alternatively, from the standpoint of output, the robustness of Southern industry in the face of higher labor costs reflects the fact that at that historical point the South had a well-developed set of high-wage technologies readily available.

To the economic historian taking a view of the South and its political economy in the broadest sense, it appears that a more fundamental transformation was underway, a basic change in the priorities of the region's economic interest groups. One new factor common to the post-war South was the all-out effort to attract business through tax breaks, municipal bonds for plant construction, industrial development corporations, research parks, and expenditures on publicity far beyond other regions. Historian James C. Cobb (1982) called it *The Selling of the South*. Abolishing the low-wage sectors eliminated the vested interest in isolation; once the doors were flung open, the rush of absorption into the national economy was breath-taking. Another Southern historian has written recently: "In 1940 the raison d'être of Southern state governments was the protection of white supremacy and social stability; thirty years later their central purpose was the promotion of business and industrial development" (Bartley, 1982, p. 160).

Though the transformation may have lowered the priority level of white supremacy for the South, the economic costs were concentrated on blacks. The preponderance of black laborers in agriculture made this inevitable. But blacks also suffered in other industries. Tobacco manufacturing had long made extensive use of black workers, and the wage increases had dramatic effects. Beginning in the 1930s, the industry began to mechanize the leaf-handling processes which had long been the preserve of black workers, and black employment fell precipitously. In 1930 the industry labor force was 67.9 percent black; by 1960 the share was down to 26.8 percent (Northrup, 1970, pp. 29, 31). Perhaps the single best indicator of the unequal racial impact of the changes in the labor market is the pattern of out-migration (Table 2). During World War I more Southern whites than blacks left the region, but during World War II black out-migration was twice as great. The effects continued through the 1950s, as black teenage employment in lumber and sawmills declined by 74 percent, in the wake of extensions in level and coverage of the federal minimum wage (Cogan, 1982).

The overall effect of this history on black Americans is complex, mixed, and ironic. Displacement and suffering were severe. Yet in abolishing the low-wage South, the federal government also destroyed the nation's most powerful bastion of racism and white supremacy. The civil rights movement of the 1960s was able to use the South's hunger for capital inflows as an effective weapon in forcing desegregation.[10] Similarly, migration to the North allowed dramatic increases in incomes

10. This thesis is argued most comprehensively in Jacoway and Colburn (1982).

Table 2. *Net migration from the South, 1870–1880 to 1940–1950*

Decade	*Native White*	*Black*
	(In thousands)	
1870–1880	91	−68
1880–1890	−271	88
1890–1900	−30	−185
1900–1910	−69	−194
1910–1920	−663	−555
1920–1930	−704	−903
1930–1940	−558	−408
1940–1950	−865	−1581
1950–1960	−234	−1202
1960–1970	1807	−1380
1970–1980	3556	206
1980–1985	1810	87

Source: Eldridge, H. T., and D. S. Thomas, *Population Redistribution and Economic Growth*, Vol. III. Philadelphia: American Philosophical Society, 1964, p. 90; Bureau of the Census, *Historical Statistics of the United States to 1970*. Washington, DC, pp. 94–95; Kasaida, J. D., M. D. Irwin, and H. L. Hughes, "The South is Still Rising". American Demographics, June 1986, p. 35; Isaac Robinson, "Blacks Move Back to the South," *ibid.*, p. 43.

and educational opportunities for many blacks; yet the same migration channeled other blacks into the high-unemployment ghettos which if anything have worsened with the passage of time.

Implications

It would overstate the case to conclude that imposing national labor standards on the South was "the cause" of the economic revolution which has occurred in the region since World War II. Clearly many other long-term developments have had a bearing on these events: transport costs and communications, the mobility of individuals and corporations, the raw material and energy requirements of industrial production, and doubtless other factors. But federal labor policy did not retard or discourage economic progress in the South, and indeed appears in retrospect to have been one of the key triggering mechanisms behind the region's participation in these global economic trends. Obviously, policy effects of this sort cannot be utilized repeatedly and may not be predictable with any precision. But those who take the historical view believe that economic life is full of such historically specific equilibra and unique transitions, so that economists who ignore them do so only at their own peril.

The particular episode recounted here does have lasting relevance for contemporary issues. Perhaps the most direct connection is to the ongoing discussions of black economic progress. Before accepting sweeping indictments of black culture and family values, economists should at least be aware that the circumstances under which blacks entered American urban life were different from those of every other ethnic or minority group. It has been pointed out frequently that many other groups faced prejudice, discrimination, and hostility, and yet were successful. But virtually every other group came to American cities because of job opportunities. By contrast, Southern blacks came into cities which already had double-digit black unemployment; where unemployment rates for migrants were in excess of 20, 30 or even 40 percent; and where entry-level jobs for unskilled and uneducated workers had virtually been abolished as a matter of policy. To know this historical background is not the same as knowing what would be right or effective as policy. But the perspective is helpful just the same.

The broader set of implications is for the scope of our domain as economists in considering the development process. Factor prices and per capita incomes may well tend to converge among regions and nations. But there is a big difference between convergence via absorption into another economy, with massive flows of labor and capital in both directions, and convergence via the establishment of new growth centers with distinct technologies and organizations adapted to local circumstances. Japan is an example of a new growth center, as was the United States in the 19th century; the postwar U.S. South is an example of absorption. Southern history is not a case study in economic development; it is a case of a region being forced from one growth trajectory to another. The new growth path has largely destroyed the South's regionhood. But this effect was not an inevitable by-product of growth itself, but a result of the particular path taken; in effect, a policy decision.

Economists tend to think of regional and national loyalties either as pure consumption goods, or as the propaganda of special interest groups looking for subsidies or trying to hold onto a labor supply. From that standpoint, national boundaries or internal divisions appear as market imperfections, barriers to full equilibrium in product and factor markets. Nationhood certainly has this character, but national institutions are also the embodiments of basic community loyalties and values by which people live, and national economies have historically been the carriers of economic progress and the shapers of technology and economic organization. Whether or not capitalist firms are patriotic, their location, property interests and legal/political support made the nation or quasi nation a logical horizon for cost calculations.

So which is better, absorption or the establishment of an independent growth center? Is it better to move toward a unified world environment, in which technological adaptation comes to be unrelated to local resource endowments, or is it better to have a multiplicity of overlapping geographic horizons, reflecting in part the historic national traditions, cultures and loyalties that exist in the world? Clearly, the answer does not lie in a static efficiency calculation at a point in time. And although no general answer may exist at all, clearly the assessment in particular cases cannot be independent of an evaluation of an economy's political legitimacy and culture. Applying such a test, absorption of the South into the national economy was right in this non-Southerner's view, because Southern regional policy was not democratic and denied access to the political process and other fundamental human rights to large portions of its population. This judgment is made easier by the fact that the South was historically part of the country; other cases around the world pose much harder dilemmas. But if reorienting regional and national loyalty is the indirect effect of economic policy, then economists ought to give such matters more explicit attention, even if it means surrendering the fiction that a rigorous efficiency criterion undergirds our advice.

References

Allen, Robert, "The Peculiar Productivity History of American Blast Furnaces, 1840–1913," *Journal of Economic History*, September 1977, *37*, 605–33.

Alston, Lee J. and Joseph T. Ferrie, "Labor Cost, Paternalism, and Loyalty in Southern Agriculture: A Constraint on the Growth of the Welfare State," *Journal of Economic History*, March 1985, *45*, 95–117.

Arsenault, Raymond, "The End of the Long Hot Summer: The Air Conditioner and Southern Culture," *Journal of Southern History*, 1984, *50*, 597–628.

Arthur, Brian, "Competing Technologies and Lock-in by Historical Small Events: The Dynamics of Allocation Under Increasing Returns," Center for Economic Policy Research Publication No. 43, Stanford University, 1983.

Bartley, Numan, "In Search of the New South: Southern Politics After Reconstruction." In Kutler, Stanley T. and Stanley N. Katz, eds., *The Promise of American History*. Baltimore: The Johns Hopkins University Press, 1982.

Chapman, H. H. et al., *The Iron and Steel Industries of the South*. University, Alabama: The University of Alabama Press, 1953.

Cobb, James C., *The Selling of the South: The Southern Crusade for Industrial Development, 1936–1980*. Baton Rouge: Louisiana State University Press, 1982.

Cogan, John, "The Decline in Black Teenage Employment: 1950–1970," *American Economic Review*, 1982, *72*, 621–38.

Danhof, Clarence, "Four Decades of Thought on the South's Economic Problems." In Greenhut, Melvin L. and W. Tate Whitman, eds., *Essays in Southern Economic Development*. Chapel Hill: University of North Carolina Press, 1964.

David, Paul, *Technical Choice, Innovation, and Economic Growth*. New York: Cambridge University Press, 1975.

David, Paul, "Understanding the Economics of QWERTY: The Necessity of History." In Parker, William N., ed., *History and the Modern Economist*. New York: Basil Blackwell, 1986.

Dunleavy, James A., "Regional Preferences and Migrant Settlement," *Research in Economic History*, 1983, *8*, 217–52.

Field, Alexander, "Land Abundance, Interest/Profit Rates, and Nineteenth-Century American and British Technology," *Journal of Economic History*, June 1983, *43*, 405–459.

Hackney, Sheldon, "Origins of the New South in Retrospect," *Journal of Southern History*, 1972, *38*, 191–216.

Hayami, Yujiro, and Vernon W. Ruttan, "Factor Prices and Technical Change in Agriculture Development: The United States and Japan, 1880–1960," *Journal of Political Economy*, September 1970, *78*, 115–41.

Helpman, Elhanan and Paul R. Krugman, *Market Structure and Foreign Trade*. Cambridge: MIT Press, 1985.

Jacobs, Jane, *Cities and the Wealth of Nations*. New York: Random House, 1984.

Jacoway, Elizabeth and David R. Colburn, eds., *Southern Businessmen and Desegregation*. Baton Rouge: Louisiana State University Press, 1982.

James, John and Jonathan Skinner, "The Resolution of the Labor-Scarcity Paradox," *Journal of Economic History*, September 1985, *45*, 513–40.

Johnson, Paul R., *The Economics of the Tobacco Industry*. New York: Praeger, 1984.

Katz, Michael L. and Carl Shapiro, "Network Externalities, Competition, and Compatibility," *American Economic Review*, June 1985, *75*, 424–40.

Kawagoe, Toshihiko, Keijiro Otsuka and Yujiro Hayami, "Induced Bias of Technical Change in Agriculture: The United States and Japan, 1880–1980," *Journal of Political Economy*, June 1986, *94*, 523–44.

Lieberson, Stanley, "Selective Black Migration from the South: A Historical View." In Bean, Frank D. and W. Packer Fresbie, eds., *The Demography of Racial and Ethnic Groups*. New York: Academic Press, 1978.

McMath, Robert *et al.*, *Engineering the New South: Georgia Tech. 1885–1985*. Athens, GA: The University of Georgia Press, 1985.

Northrup, Herbert R. "The Negro in the Tobacco Industry." In Northrup, Herbert R. and Richard L. Rowan, eds., *Negro Employment in Southern Industry*. Philadelphia: Wharton School of Finance and Commerce, 1970.

Reed, John Shelton, *Southerners: The Social Psychology of Sectionalism*. Chapel Hill: University of North Carolina Press, 1983.

Rosenberg, Nathan, *Perspectives on Technology*. Cambridge: Cambridge University Press, 1976.

Rubin, Julius, "The Limits of Agricultural Progress in the Nineteenth Century South," *Agricultural History*, 1975, *49*, 385–402.

Saxonhouse, Gary, "Technology Choice, Adaptation and the Quality Dimension in the Japanese Cotton Textile Industry." In Ohkawa, K. and Y. Hayami, eds., *The Comparative Analysis of Japan and Less Developed Countries*. Tokyo: The International Development Center of Japan, 1979.

Saxonhouse, Gary and Gavin Wright, "Two Forms of Cheap Labor in Textile History." In Saxonhouse, Gary, and Gavin Wright, eds., *Technique, Spirit, and Form in the Making of the Modern Economies: Essays in Honor of William N. Parker*. Greenwich, CT: JAI Press, 1984a.

Saxonhouse, Gary and Gavin Wright, "Rings and Mules Around the World." In Saxonhouse, Gary and Gavin Wright, eds., *Technique, Spirit, and Form in the Making of the Modern Economies: Essays in Honor of William N. Parker*. Greenwich, CT: JAI Press, 1984b.

Shiells, Martha and Gavin Wright, "Nightwork as a Labor Market Phenomenon: Southern Textiles in the Interwar Years," *Explorations in Economic History*, 1983, *20*, 331–50.

Steckel, Richard H., "The Economic Foundations of East-West Migration during the 19th Century," *Explorations in Economic History*, 1983, *20*, 14–36.

Stocking, George W., *Basing Point Pricing and Regional Development: A Case Study of the Iron and Steel Industry*. Chapel Hill: University of North Carolina Press, 1954.

Temin, Peter, "Labor Scarcity and the Problem of American Industrial Efficiency in the 1850s," *Journal of Economic History*, September 1966, *26*, 277–98.

Topel, Robert H., "Local Labor Markets," *Journal of Political Economy*, June 1986, *94*, S111–S143.

United States Advisory Commission on Intergovernmental Relations, *Regional Growth: Historical Perspective*. Washington, D.C.: U.S. Government Printing Office, 1980.

The United States Textile Mill Products Industry. Columbia, S.C.: University of South Carolina Press, 1983.

Van Sickle, John V., *Planning for the South: An Inquiry into the Economics of Regionalism*. Nashville: Vanderbilt University Press, 1943.

Warren, Kenneth, *The American Steel Industry 1850–1970*: A *Geographical Interpretation*. Oxford: Clarendon Press, 1973.

Weinstein, Bernard L., Harold T. Gross and John Rees, *Regional Growth and Decline in the United States*. New York: Praeger, 1985.

Whatley, Warren, "Labor for the Picking: the New Deal in the South," *Journal of Economic History*, December 1983, *43*, 905–29.

Whatley, Warren, "A History of Mechanization in the Cotton South: The Institutional Hypothesis," *Quarterly Journal of Economics*, November 1985, *100*, 1191–1215.

Woodward, C. Vann, *Origins of the New South, 1877–1913*. Baton Rouge: Louisiana State University Press, 1951.

Woodward, C. Vann, "New South Fraud is Papered by Old South Myth," *Washington Post*, July 9, 1961.

Wright, Gavin, *Old South, New South: Revolutions in the Southern Economy Since the Civil War*. New York: Basic Books, 1986.

V

The rise of American industrial might

"The railroads: The first modern business enterprises, 1850s–1860s"

by Alfred D. Chandler, Jr.

Alfred Chandler's writings have "established the framework in which most scholars now understand the history of big business" (Porter, 1992, 125). This essay is part of Chandler's Pulitzer and Bancroft Prize-winning volume *The Visible Hand: The Managerial Revolution in American Business* (1977). In *The Visible Hand*, Chandler first describes traditional enterprise, under which most economic coordination is implicitly carried out by the "invisible hand" of the market. He then delineates the advantages of the "visible hand" of management in creating economies of scale within large firms and chronicles the rise of big business, beginning with the railroads.

According to Chandler, a modern business enterprise has many distinct operating units and is managed by a hierarchy of salaried managers. He advances seven propositions about the development of modern business enterprises (pp. 6–10):

1. They replaced small traditional enterprise when administrative coordination permitted greater productivity, lower costs, and higher profits than coordination by market mechanisms.
2. The advantages of internalizing the activities of many business units within a single enterprise could not be realized until a managerial hierarchy had been created.
3. Modern business enterprises arose when the volume of economic activities reached a level that made administrative coordination more efficient and profitable than market coordination.
4. Once a managerial hierarchy had been successfully established, the hierarchy itself became a source of permanence, power, and continued growth.
5. The careers of the salaried managers who directed these enterprises became increasingly technical and professional.
6. As the enterprise grew and as its managers became more professional, management became separated from ownership.
7. In their decisions, career managers favored long-term stability and growth rather than maximizing current profits.

In this reading, Chandler argues that the railroads were the first modern business enterprises, and that running a big railroad required the creation of a sizable hierarchical administrative organization.

- What would have happened (to profits, to efficiency) if none of the railroads had developed these hierarchies?
- Many railroad executives were willing to share their new forms of organization, potentially "trade secrets," with other railroads. Is this consistent with profit maximization?

Economists traditionally assume that companies know what their cost curves are. Chandler describes the process whereby railroads actually discovered their cost curves. He notes that most railroads initially found that there were diseconomies of scale and that managerial reorganization, rather than technological change alone, converted these into economies of scale. Thus, modern business enterprise also reshaped the cost curves.

- Many of the cost accounting procedures of the railroads measured financial efficiency rather than economic efficiency (rate of return). Which measure would the owner prefer?

The later chapters of *The Visible Hand* focus on distribution and production, especially in the modern industrial corporation. Chandler's later works are even broader and include more of the international context. In *Scale and Scope* (1990), Chandler compares and contrasts the histories of modern corporations around the world, focusing on those in the United States, Britain, and Germany.

Additional Reading

Alfred D. Chandler, Jr., *Strategy and Structure: Chapters in the History of the Industrial Enterprise*, Cambridge, MA: MIT Press, 1962.

Alfred D. Chandler, Jr., *The Visible Hand: The Managerial Revolution in American Business*, Cambridge, MA: Harvard University Press, 1977.

Alfred D. Chandler, Jr., *Scale and Scope: The Dynamics of Industrial Capitalism*, Cambridge, MA: Harvard University Press, 1990.

Alexander J. Field, "Modern Business Enterprise as a Capital-Saving Innovation" *Journal of Economic History*, 47 (June 1987), 473–85.

Glenn Porter, *The Rise of Big Business, 1860–1920*, second edition, Arlington Heights, IL: Harlan Davidson, 1992.

10

The railroads

The first modern business enterprises, 1850s–1860s

ALFRED D. CHANDLER, JR.

Innovation in technology and organization

Modern business enterprises came to operate the railroad and telegraph networks for both technological and organizational reasons. Railroad companies were the first transportation firms to build and to own rights-of-way and at the same time to operate the common carriers using those rights-of-way. Telegraph companies also both built the lines and ran the messages through them. The enterprises, both public and private, that constructed and maintained the canals and turnpikes rarely operated the canal boat companies, stage lines, or mail routes that used them.[1] Even when they did, their rights-of-way were used by many other independent transportation companies.

On the railroad, however, the movements of carriers had to be carefully coordinated and controlled if the goods and passengers were to be moved in safety and with a modicum of efficiency. The first railroads – those using horses for motive power – were often able to allow common carriers operated by other individuals and companies to use their rails.[2] But as soon as the much faster steam locomotive began to

1. For example, as Walter S. Sanderlin, the historian of the Chesapeake and Ohio pointed out, the directors of the canal "refused to have any connection with the business of transportation." *The Greater National Project: A History of the Chesapeake and Ohio Canal* (Baltimore 1946), p. 190. The Middlesex Canal had a fleet of six to nine boats in commission from 1808 to 1818 when they were sold. Christopher Roberts, *The Middlesex Canal, 1783–1860* (Cambridge, Mass. 1938), pp. 137–138. The important exceptions to this generalization were the anthracite coal companies of eastern Pennsylvania.
2. These developments can be followed in Edward C. Kirkland, *Men, Cities and Transportation* (Cambridge, Mass., 1948), I, chap. 4; and in Julius Rubin, "Canal or Railroad?" *Transactions of the American Philosophical Society*, n.s., vol. 51, part 7 (November 1961). Rubin stresses that the railroad was a serious alternative to the canal for overland transportation, even before the steam locomotive had been proved practical. One reason that the Pennsylvania legislators decided in 1825 to build a state system of canals rather than railroads was "insufficient experience with the

replace the horse-drawn vehicles, operations had to be controlled from a single headquarters if only to prevent accidents. Considerations of safety were particularly compelling in the United States, where nearly all railroads relied on a single line of track. For a time railroad managers experimented in hauling cars owned by local merchants and freight forwarders. However, the coordination of the movement of cars and the handling of charges and payment proved exceedingly difficult. By 1840 the railroad managers found it easier to own and control all cars using their roads. Later, express companies and other large shippers operating on a national scale came to own their own cars; but only after the railroads had devised complex organizational arrangements to handle the movement of and charges for such "foreign" cars.

Because they operated common carriers, railroads, unlike the major canal systems, became privately rather than publicly owned enterprises. In the early years of the Republic, American merchants and shippers gave strong support to government construction and operation of costly rights-of-way.[3] On the other hand, these businessmen rarely, if ever, proposed that the government operate the common carriers. Only a small number of American railroads were initially operated by the state, and by 1850 with very few exceptions these had been turned over to private business enterprises. These same merchants and shippers who distrusted government ownership were also fearful of private monopoly. Therefore, the charters of the early roads generally provided for close legislative oversight of these new transportation enterprises.

The railroads did not begin to have a significant impact on American business institutions until the nation's first railroad boom which began in the late 1840s and 1850s. Before that time railroad construction did not fundamentally alter existing routes or modes of transportation, since the first roads were built in the 1830s and 1840s to connect existing commercial centers and to supplement existing water transportation. The lines from Boston to nearby towns (Lowell, Newburyport, Providence, and Worcester); from Camden to Amboy in New Jersey (the rail link between New York and Philadelphia); from Philadelphia to Reading, Philadelphia to Baltimore, and Baltimore to Washington, were all short, rarely more than fifty miles.

This was also true of those lines connecting the several towns along the Erie Canal. In the south and west, railroads were longer because distances between towns were greater, but they carried fewer passengers and smaller amounts of freight. Until the 1850s, none of the great lines

general-purpose railroad to justify a large-scale project." It was a "risky step into the unknown" (p. 56). Also some legislators expressed concern at the possibility of having the state operate common carriers.

3. George Rogers Taylor, *The Transportation Revolution* (New York, 1951), pp. 24–26, 48–52.

planned to connect the east with the west were even close to completion. Before 1850 only one road, the Western, which ran from Worcester to Albany, connected one major regional section of the country with another. Except for the Western, no railroad was long enough or busy enough to create complex operating problems.

During the 1840s the technology of railroad transportation was rapidly perfected. Uniform methods of construction, grading, tunneling, and bridging were developed. The iron T rail came into common use. By the late 1840s the locomotive had its cams, sandbox, driver wheels, swivel or bogie truck, and equalizing beams. Passenger coaches had become "long cars," carrying sixty passengers on reversible seats. Boxcars, cattle cars, lumber cars, and other freight cars were smaller but otherwise little different from those used on American railroads a century later.[4]

As technology improved, railroads became the favored means of overland transportation. They not only quickly captured the passenger and light-weight and high-value freight traffic from the canals and turnpikes but also began soon to compete successfully as carriers of textiles, cotton, grain, coal, and other more bulky products. Indeed, some of the first roads in the north, such as the Boston and Lowell and the Reading, were built by textile manufacturers and anthracite coal mine owners to replace canals they had already constructed to carry their products to market; while railroads in the south and west were constructed specifically to carry cotton and grain.[5] In the decade of the 1840s, only 400 miles of canals were built to make the nation's total mileage at the end of the decade just under 4,000. In that same decade, over 6,000 miles of railroads went into operation providing a total of 9,000 miles of track by 1850.[6]

As the country pulled out of the long economic depression of the late 1830s and early 1840s, railroad building began in earnest. The railroad boom came in the mid-1840s in New England and then in the late 1840s in the south and west. In the decade of the 1850s, when more canals were abandoned than built, over 21,000 more miles of railroad were constructed, laying down the basic overland transportation network east of the Mississippi River. As dramatic was the almost simultaneous

4. Particularly useful on the railroad technology of this period is Kirkland, *Men, Cities and Transportation*, I, 284–313.

5. For example, Patrick Tracy Jackson, one of the founders of the mill complex at Lowell, estimated that the time and cost saved by rail over canal transportation were equivalent to moving Lowell within ten miles of Boston. George S. Gibb, *The Saco-Lowell Shops* (Cambridge, Mass., 1950), p. 74.

6. U.S. Bureau of the Census, *Historical Statistics of the United States, Colonial Times to 1957* (Washington, D.C., 1960), pp. 427–429; Taylor, *Transportation Revolution*, p. 32.

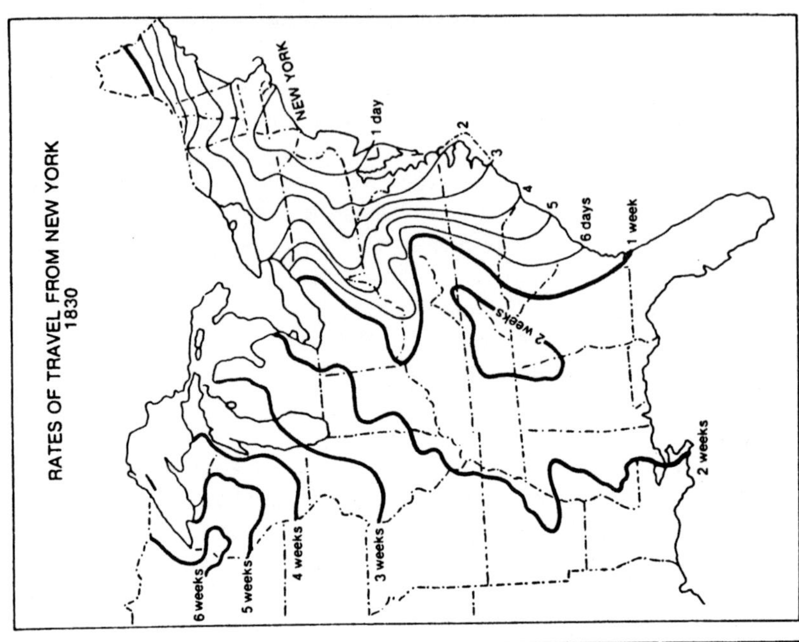

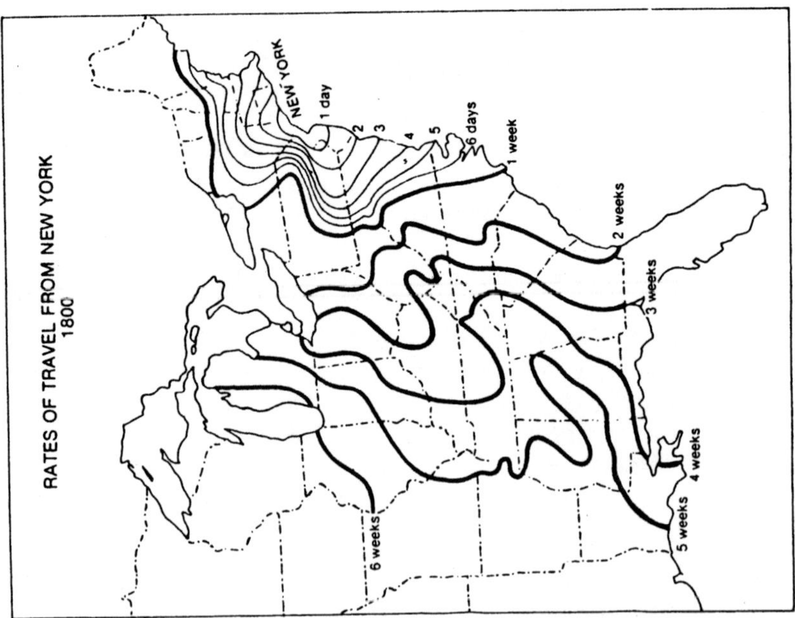

Rates of travel, 1800, 1830, 1857. Adapted from Charles O. Paullin, *Atlas of the Historical Geography of the United States* (Washinton, D.C.: Carnegie Institute and American Geographical Society, 1932), plate 138A, B. C.

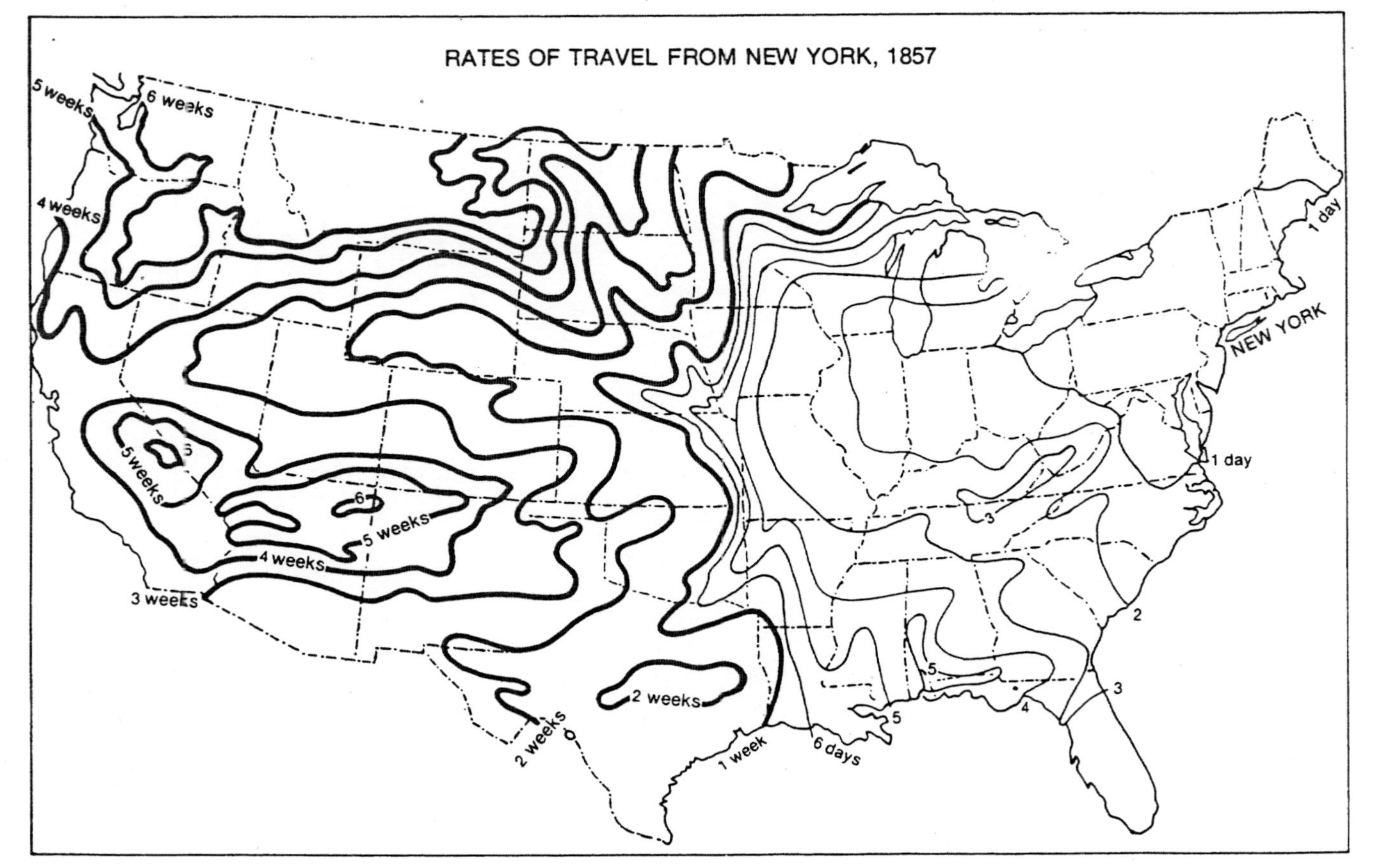
RATES OF TRAVEL FROM NEW YORK, 1857
5 weeks
6 weeks
4 weeks
5 weeks
6
6
5 weeks
4 weeks
3 weeks
2 weeks
2 weeks
1 week
6 days
5
5
4
3
2
3
1 day
NEW YORK
1 day

completion between 1851 and 1854 of the great intersectional trunk lines connecting east and west (the Erie, the Baltimore and Ohio, the Pennsylvania, and the New York Central) and the building of a whole new transportation network in the old northwest. In 1849 the five states of the old northwest, a region endowed with a superb river and lake system, had only 600 miles of track. By 1860 the 9,000 miles of railroad covering the area had replaced rivers, lakes, and canals as the primary means of transportation for all but bulky, low-value commodities.

The reason for the swift commercial success of the railroads over canals and other inland waterways is obvious enough. The railroad provided more direct communication than did the river, lake, or coastal routes. While construction costs of canals on level ground were somewhat less than for railroads, the railroad was cheaper to build in rugged terrain.[7] Moreover, because a railroad route did not, like that of a canal, require a substantial water supply, it could go more directly between two towns. In addition, railroads were less expensive to maintain per ton-mile than canals. They were, of course, faster. For the first time in history, freight and passengers could be carried overland at a speed faster than that of a horse. The maps emphasize how the railroad revolutionized the speed of travel. A traveler who used to spend three weeks going from New York to Chicago, could by 1857 make the trip in three days. The railroad's fundamental advantage, however, was not in the speed it carried passengers and mail but its ability to provide a shipper with dependable, precisely scheduled, all-weather transportation of goods. Railroads were far less affected by droughts, freshets, and floods than were waterways. They were not shut down by freshets in the spring or dry spells in the summer and fall. Most important of all, they remained open during the winter months.

The steam locomotive not only provided fast, regular, dependable, all-weather transportation but also lowered the unit cost of moving goods by permitting a more intensive use of available transportation facilities. A railroad car could make several trips over a route in the same period of time it took a canal boat to complete one. By 1840, when the new mode of transportation had only begun to be technologically perfected, its speed and regularity permitted a steam railway the potential to carry annually per mile more than fifty times the freight

7. Taylor, *Transportation Revolution*, p. 53, indicates that canals cost somewhat less than railroads on moderate terrain. Rubin, "Railroads and Canals," p. 30, notes that contemporaries emphasized how much railroad transportation shortened distances between towns. All accounts of canals stress high maintenance costs, particularly with the reoccurrence of freshets; for example, Sanderlin, *The Great National Project*, pp. 191–193.

carried by a canal. Even at that early date, Stanley Lebergott writes, "railroads could provide at least three times as much freight service as canals *for an equivalent resource cost* – and probably more nearly five times as much."[8]

The history of competition on specific routes supports these estimates. For twenty years, the trip from Boston to Concord, New Hampshire, by way of the Middlesex Canal, the Merrimack River, and ancillary canals, took five days upstream and four down. When the extension of the Boston and Lowell reached Concord in 1842, the travel time was cut to four hours one way.[9] A freight car on the new railroad made four round trips by the time a canal boat had made only one. To handle the same amount of traffic, a canal would have to have had approximately four times the carrying space of the railroad and, because of ice, even this equipment would have had to remain idle four months a year.

With the completion of the railroad to Concord, the historian of the Middlesex Canal points out "the waterway is immediately marked for defeat; in 1843 the expenses of the canal were greater than its receipts. The end has come."[10] The end came almost as quickly to the great state works of Pennsylvania and Ohio. For example, the net revenues of Ohio canals which were $278,525 in 1849, were only $93,421 in 1855; they dropped to a deficit of $107,761 in 1860.[11] For a time the Erie and

8. Stanley Legerbott, "United States Transport and Externalities," *Journal of Economic History*, 26:444–446 (December 1966); italics added. Robert William Fogel, in his pioneering work, *Railroads and American Economic Growth: An Econometric History* (Baltimore, 1964), argues that the railroads were not indispensable for economic growth. By 1890 the social savings "attributed to the railroad for all commodities . . . is well below 5 per cent gross national product" (p. 223). Fogel's findings have been strongly challenged by new economic historians in such articles as that of Legerbott given above; Peter D. McClelland, "Railroads, American Growth and the New Economic History: A Critique," *Journal of Economic History*, 28:102–123 (March 1968); and Paul David, "Transportation and Economic Growth: Professor Fogel On and Off the Rails," *Economic History Review*, 20:507–525 (December 1969). Fogel concentrates almost wholly on estimating the differences between rail and canal transportation in the seasonal movement of crops and on the impact of railroads on the demand for iron. In estimating the cost differences between rail and water he develops only the grossest estimates of cargo losses in transit, transshipment costs, costs resulting from time lost in slow movement, the closing down of waterways in the winter months, and capital costs. Fogel's handling of inventory costs is particularly disconcerting. David points out that to maintain inventory at Union Stock Yards in Chicago in 1890 would have required 10,000 acres, or a half of all privately utilized land in Chicago in that year (p. 512). Fogel has little analysis of the barriers to the expansion of factory production created by the need to maintain costly inventories and an idle working force during winter months.
9. Kirkland, *Men, Cities and Transportation*, pp. 161, 162.
10. Roberts, *Middlesex Canal*, p. 160.
11. Harry N, Scheiber, *Ohio Canal Era* (Athens, Ohio, 1969) pp. 302, 304. Scheiber's chap. 11 has an excellent analysis of the swift railroad victory in the 1850s. Hartz indicates a comparable failure of the Pennsylvania Canal system in his *Economic Policy and Democratic Thought*, pp.

the Chesapeake and Ohio canals continued to carry bulky products – lumber, coal, and grain – primarily from west to east. By the 1870s they had even lost to the railroad on the grain trade. And in the 1850s river boat lines lost much of the rapidly expanding trade of the Mississippi to the railroads.[12] Never before had one form of transportation so quickly replaced another.

The swift victory of the railway over the waterway resulted from organizational as well as technological innovation. Technology made possible fast, all-weather transportation; but safe, regular, reliable movement of goods and passengers, as well as the continuing maintenance and repair of locomotives, rolling stock, and track, roadbed, stations, roundhouses, and other equipment, required the creation of a sizable administrative organization. It meant the employment of a set of managers to supervise these functional activities over an extensive geographical area; and the appointment of an administrative command of middle and top executives to monitor, evaluate, and coordinate the work of managers responsible for the day-to-day operations. It meant, too, the formulation of brand new types of internal administrative procedures and accounting and statistical controls. Hence, the operational requirements of the railroads demanded the creation of the first administrative hierarchies in American business.

The men who managed these enterprises became the first group of modern business administrators in the United States. Ownership and management soon separated. The capital required to build a railroad was far more than that required to purchase a plantation, a textile mill, or even a fleet of ships. Therefore, a single enterpreneur, family, or small group of associates was rarely able to own a railroad. Nor could the many stockholders or their representatives manage it. The administrative tasks were too numerous, too varied, and too complex. They required special skills and training which could only be commanded by a full-time salaried manager. Only in the raising and allocating of capital, in the setting of financial policies, and in the selection of top managers did the owners or their representatives have a real say in railroad management. On the other hand, few managers had the financial resources to own even a small percent of the capital stock of the roads they managed.

Because of the special skills and training required and the existence of an administrative hierarchy, the railroad managers came to look on their work as much more of a lifetime career than did the plantation overseer

161–180. U.S. Bureau of the Census, *Historical Statistics*, p. 455, gives the freight carried on the Erie. See also Sanderlin, *The Great National Project*, chaps. 11, 12.

12. Louis C. Hunter describes the way that the railroads took over trade from the steamboats in the 1850s in *Steamboats on the Western Rivers* (Cambridge, Mass., 1949), chap. 12.

or the textile mill agent. Most railroad managers soon expected to spend their life working up the administrative ladder, if not on the road with which they started, then on another. This career orientation and the specialized nature of tasks gave the railroad managers an increasingly professional outlook on their work. And because they had far greater personal, if not financial, commitment to the continuing health of their enterprise, they came in time to have almost as much say about financial policies and the allocation of resources for future operations as did the owners and their representatives. The members of the administrative bureaucracy essential to the operation of the railroad began to take control of their own destinies.

The construction of the nation's new transportation network and the evolution of the nation's first modern business enterprise – as well as the first modern managerial class – fall into two distinct chronological periods. External changes in each period had a significant impact on internal organizational and managerial development. The first period extended from the beginning of the railroad boom in the late 1840s to the coming of the economic depression of the 1870s. It was a period of almost continuous growth of the network (except of course during the Civil War) and a period of impressive organizational innovation. By the start of the depression of the 1870s, the 70,000 miles of track in operation provided the nation with the basic overland transportation network that would serve until the coming of the automobile and airplane in the twentieth century. By the 1870s the large railroads of over 500 miles in length had perfected complex and intricate mechanisms to coordinate and control the work of thousands of employees, the operations of tens of millions of dollars' worth of roadbed and equipment, and the movement of hundreds of millions of dollars' worth of goods. By that time, too, the railroad had worked out complicated intercompany arrangements so that a carload of goods or produce could be moved from almost any sizable town in the country to another distant commercial center without a single transshipment. In other words, goods placed in a car did not have to be reloaded until they reached their destination.

The second period of American railroad history, extending from the depression of the 1870s to the prosperous first years of the new century, was one of competition and consolidation, although railroad building continued apace. By 1900 close to 200,000 miles of line were in operation. Except along the disappearing frontier in the west, this new mileage filled in the existing network. Indeed, much of the construction was not needed to meet the existing demand for rail transportation. This overbuilding was one consequence of the creation of the giant consolidated systems, the managers' response to increasing competition. These managers adopted the strategy of consolidation because they wanted to have their own tracks into all the major commercial centers of the areas they served. They were unwilling to rely on potential competitors to provide outlets for the freight and passenger traffic they carried. By the beginning of the new century not only had the American railroad network been virtually completed but the boundaries of the major railroad systems had also become fixed. The systems would continue to operate in much the same areas and in much the same ways until the second half of the twentieth century, when the automobile, truck, and airplane had reoriented American transportation. For several decades the consolidated railroad systems remained the largest business enterprise in the world.

The early history of the business enterprises created to operate the telegraph and then the telephone was quite similar to that of the railroads. As the railroads marched across the continent, so too did the telegraph. Invented in 1844, it began to be used commercially in 1847. Railroad managers quickly found the telegraph an invaluable aid in assuring the safe and efficient operation of trains; and telegraph promoters realized that the railroads provided the only convenient rights-of-way. Because the telegraph was easier and cheaper to build than the railroad, it reached the Pacific first, in 1861. By the beginning of that decade 50,000 miles of wire were in operation. Two decades later, according to the census of 1880, 31,703,000 messages had been sent per year over 291,000 miles of wire.[13]

The telephone, commercialized in the 1880s, at first only supplemented the telegraph. It was used initially almost wholly for local conversations. Then with the development of the "long lines" in the 1890s the telephone became increasingly employed for long-distance calls. Thus, where the railroad improved communication by speeding the movement of mail, the telegraph and then the telephone permitted even faster – indeed almost instantaneous – communication in nearly every part of the nation.

The enterprises that built, owned, and operated these new instruments of communication soon governed a large number of units scattered over a wide geographical area. The coordination of a large number of messages to all parts of the country called for even tighter internal control than did the movement of railroad transportation traffic. Not surprisingly, the nation's telegraph network was by 1866 dominated by a single enterprise, Western Union. Nor is it surprising that its administrative and accounting procedures were very similar to those of

13. U.S. Bureau of the Census, *Historical Statistics*, p. 484. The story of the telegraph and telephone is given in more detail in Chapter 6.

the railroads. As the telephone network began to expand in the 1890s, the pioneering group – the Bell interests – maintained its control of the industry "through traffic" by means of the American Telephone and Telegraph Company, which built and operated through or long-distance facilities. In modern communication, as in modern transportation, the requirements of high-volume, high-speed operations brought the large-scale managerial enterprise and with it oligopoly or monopoly.

The impact of the railroads on construction and finance

Any detailed analysis of the history of modern business enterprise in the United States must, therefore, pay particular attention to the 1850s. There was some preliminary activity in the 1840s. Not until the 1850s, however, did the processes of production and distribution start to respond in strength to the swift expansion of the new forms of transportation and communication and the increasing availability of a new source of energy – coal. During the 1850s, railroad and telegraph enterprises began to devise the organizational structures and accounting procedures so central to the operation of the modern firm. In that decade, too, the demands of railroad building led to a fundamental change in the nation's financial and construction industries. Before considering the broader impact of the railroad and telegraph on transportation, communication, production, and distribution, it seems well to indicate how the railroads helped to centralize the American capital market in New York City and at the same time revolutionize the construction industry.

The demands of the railroads during the 1850s on American financial intermediaries and on construction contractors were unprecedented. Railroads required far larger amounts of capital to build than did canals. The total expenditures for canals between 1815 and 1860 reached $188 million, of which 73 percent was supplied by state and local governments with funds raised through sales of state and municipal bonds.[14] By 1859 the investment in the securities of private railroad corporations had passed the $1,100 million mark; and of this amount close to $700 million had been raised in the previous ten years. In that decade many large railroads were being constructed simultaneously. Before 1850 the largest railroad enterprise, the Western Railroad between Worcester and Albany, had cost $8 million to build. In the short period between 1849

14. Carter Goodrich, *Government Promotion of American Railways and Canals, 1800–1890* (New York, 1960), p. 270. The railroad figures come from Henry Varnum Poor's carefully compiled stock and bond list in Alfred D. Chandler, Jr., *Henry Varnum Poor, Business Editor, Analyst and Reformer* (Cambridge, Mass., 1956), pp. 207–210. See, for example, *American Railroad Journal*, 32:784 (December 3, 1859).

and 1854 more than thirty large railroads were completed. Many cost more than the Western. The great east–west trunk lines – the Erie, the Pennsylvania, the Baltimore and Ohio, and the New York Central – were capitalized at from $17 to $35 million.[15] Major roads in the west – the Michigan Central, the Michigan Southern, and the Illinois Central – cost from $10 to $17 million. Other roads in the west and those in the south that went through less populated territory rarely required less than $2 million and often more than $5 million. By comparison, during the same decade of the 1850s, only a few of the largest textile mills or ironmaking and metalworking factories were capitalized at over $1 million. In fact, during the 1850s there were only forty-one textile companies capitalized at $250,000 or more; and these mills had been financed over a thirty-year period.[16]

The railroads were the first private business enterprises in the United States to acquire large amounts of capital from outside their own regions. The textile mills of New England, and the iron and other metalmaking enterprises of Pennsylvania, had been financed locally or in Boston or Philadelphia. The state and municipal bonds used to finance canals were sold abroad through large mercantile houses, through the Second Bank of the United States, and by personal visits of canal commissioners to Europe.

With the coming of the railroad boom of the late 1840s, capital required for railroad construction could no longer be raised, as it had been earlier, from farmers, merchants, and manufacturers living along the line of the road or by having the railroad president go to European money markets. This was particularly true in the transallegheny west, where much of the territory had only recently been opened to settlement. Funds for the simultaneous construction of so many large railroads had to come from the older commercial centers of the east. Soon only the largest financial communities of Europe could provide the vast amount of capital required.

Those seeking funds for the new roads in the late 1840s came increasingly to New York City. After the demise of the Second Bank in 1836, Boston replaced Philadelphia as the major source of capital for the modest railroad construction of that time. During the 1840s Boston capital supplied funds to build New England roads, the first roads in the west, and even those in the Philadelphia area. By 1847, however, Boston merchants had little more surplus to invest. As a result, money

15. Alfred D. Chandler, Jr., ed., *The Railroads: The Nation's First Big Business* (New York, 1965), p. 16.

16. Evelyn H. Knowlton, *Pepperell's Progress: A History of a Catton Textile Company* (Cambridge, Mass., 1948) p. 32.

rates were higher in Boston than in New York. By the early 1850s even the largest and most prosperous Massachusetts roads were relying on New York for capital for new construction.[17]

At the same time Europeans, troubled by the political unrest which culminated in the Revolution of 1848, began for the first time since the depression of the late 1830s to look for investment opportunities in the United States. First they purchased United States government bonds – those issued to finance the Mexican War. Next they began to buy state bonds. Then finally in 1851 and 1852 the Germans and the French, and a little later the British, began to purchase American railroad securities in quantity. To meet the needs of American railroads seeking funds and those of Europeans looking for investments, a number of importing and exporting firms located in New York, particularly those concentrating on the buying and selling of foreign exchange, began to specialize in handling railroad securities. By the mid-fifties such partnerships as Winslow, Lanier; Duncan, Sherman; Meyer and Stucken; De Coppet and Company; Cammann and Whitehouse; De Launay, Islin and Clark; and De Rham and Moore were on their way to becoming the nation's first specialized investment banking firms. As agents for a railroad they sold its securities for a straight fee or on commission, acted as its transfer agent in New York, and advised their railroad client on financial matters. Occasionally they even purchased rails, locomotives, and other equipment. At the same time, they became agents for larger European investors who had purchased or were planning to buy American railroad stocks and bonds.

As soon as the American capital market became centralized and institutionalized in New York City, all the present-day instruments of finance were perfected; so too were nearly all the techniques of modern securities marketing and speculation. Bonds became the primary instrument to finance railroad construction. The promoters of the American roads and those initial investors who lived along their lines preferred to maintain control over their investment by owning stock; the eastern and European money men, however, believed that bonds assured a safer and more regular income. Railroad builders inevitably underestimated the cost of construction, causing first mortgage bonds to be followed by second and third mortgage bonds. Then came income and debenture bonds. At the same time, to attract a somewhat different set of

17. The triumph of New York over Philadelphia and Boston in becoming the nation's financial center is reviewed in Alfred D. Chandler, Jr., "Patterns of Railroad Finance, 1830–1850," *Business History Review*, 28:248–263 (September 1954). The resulting institutionalizing of the national capital market is told in more detail in Chandler, *Poor*, chap. 4. Dorothy R. Adler, *British Investments in American Railways* (Charlottesville, Va., 1970), chaps. 1–3, has additional information on the return of the British investors to the American market.

customers, bonds which could be converted into stock appeared, as did a variety of preferred stocks.

The great increase in railroad securities brought trading and speculation on the New York Stock Exchange in its modern form. Before the railroads the volume of stocks in banks, insurance companies, and state and federal bonds was tiny. One day in March 1830 only thirty-one shares were traded on the New York Stock Exchange.[18] By the mid-1850s the securities of railroads, banks, and also municipalities from all parts of the United States were being traded in New York. Where earlier hundreds of shares had been traded weekly, hundreds of thousands of shares changed hands weekly in the 1850s. In a four-week period in the 1850s transactions totaled close to a million shares.

The new volume of business brought modern speculative techniques to the buying and selling of securities. Traders sold "long" and "short" for future delivery. The use of puts and calls was perfected. Trading came to be done on margin. Indeed, the modern call loan market began in the 1850s, as New York banks began to loan to speculators on call in order to provide funds to cover the interest they were beginning to pay on their deposit accounts. In the 1850s skillful securities manipulators were becoming nationally known figures. Jacob Barker, Daniel Drew, Jim Fiske, and Jay Gould, all made their dubious reputations by dealing in railroad securities.

By the outbreak of the Civil War, the New York financial district, by responding to the needs of railroad financing, had become one of the largest and most sophisticated capital markets in the world. The only significant innovations after the Civil War were the coming of the telegraphic stock ticker to record sales and the development of the cooperative syndicate of several investment bankers to market large blocks of securities. For more than a generation this market was used almost wholly by the railroads and allied enterprises, such as the telegraph, express, and sleeping car companies. As soon as American manufacturers had comparable needs for funds, they too began to rely on the New York markets. However, except for the makers of electrical equipment, few manufacturers felt such a need until the 1890s. When they did begin to seek outside funds, the institutions to provide such capital were fully developed. No further innovation was needed. New York provided an even more efficient national market for industrials than it did for railroads. In American industry the lack of a well-organized national capital market cannot be considered a constraint on the rise of modern business enterprise.

18. Herman E. Krooss and Martin R. Blyn, *A History of Financial Intermediaries* (New York, 1971), pp. 56–57, 86–87.

The simultaneous construction of many large railroads during the 1850s modernized the construction trade as much as it did the business of finance. Before the railroad boom of that period, construction companies were still small partnerships. The earlier railroads, built in much the same manner as turnpikes and canals, were largely constructed by local part-time contractors: usually farmers, merchants, or even professional men who lived along the line of the road. Each contracted to build a small section, working under the supervision of the road's chief engineer. By the 1840s more full-time professional contractors began to make a career of railroad and canal construction. Their enterprises, however, remained small. They continued to rely on local labor and materials. The building of one road required the services of many small firms.

The railroad boom created new needs and opportunities. On the large roads it became increasingly difficult for the engineer and his assistants to oversee the work of many small contractors. Labor and equipment often became hard to find at the time they were most critically needed. As a result, in the late 1840s and early 1850s engineers like Horatio C. Seymour (the former state engineer of New York), Alvah C. Morton of Maine, and Joseph Sheffield and Henry Farnum from Connecticut formed companies to build railroads.[19] These great contractors handled all aspects of construction and were often engaged in building more than one road. They supplied all necessary equipment, including rails and even locomotives and rolling stock. They recruited labor and often subcontracted parts of the construction. They did all this for a flat fee, either on a per mile or total cost basis, receiving at least part of their payment in railroad stocks or bonds. One contractor, Horatio Seymour, on his premature death in 1853, was reported to have on hand more than $30 million worth of business.[20] Such contractors thus became heavily involved in railroad finance. Some railroad promoters used the contracting firm as a way to make higher profits than they might by

19. For the appearance of the large contractor see Chandler, *Poor*, pp. 112–113, 313, and Thomas C. Cochran, *Railroad Leaders, 1843–1899* (Cambridge, Mass., 1953), pp. 99–100, 111–114. For specific contractors see John B. Jervis, *Railway Property* (New York, 1861), chap. 4; Henry W. Farnum, *Henry Farnum* (New York, ca. 1889), esp. pp. 41–45, 54–55.

20. *American Railroad Journal*, 26:488 (July 30, 1853). Seymour and Morton had formed a construction company shortly before the former's death. In 1855 and 1856 the firm advertised in the pages of the *American Railroad Journal* that it was "prepared to contract for the construction and equipment of railroads in any part of the country; also to furnish Corps Engineers and contractors; Locomotive Engines, Cars; Railroad Iron, Chairs; Spikes, Switch-Irons, etc." The firm would also "sell and negotiate loans on all kinds of railroad securities . . . [and] dispose at private sales, in amounts to suit persons desirous of investing, a large amount of valuable Railroad and other Securities." *ARJ*, 28:509 (August 11, 1855). The firm listed regularly in the *Journal* the securities of the roads which it was constructing and had for sale.

simply operating the road. These large contractors relied increasingly on immigrant labor. Even though the Irish and German famines had brought a flood of immigrants into the United States in the late 1840s and early 1850s, these firms soon had agents overseas recruiting workers in Britain and western Europe.

The new labor supply and the railroad experience brought the large contracting company quickly into urban construction. After the 1840s, mayors and councils in the growing American cities let out contracts similar to those of the railroads (though usually smaller) for the paving of streets, the building of schools, and the construction of water and sewage systems. By the Civil War the letting of such contracts had become a valuable piece of political patronage, and urban contractors were becoming ever more closely tied to city politics.

In these ways, then, the nation's first railroad boom provided a basic impetus to the rise of the large-scale construction firm and the modern investment banking house. However, these firms created no new problems of internal management in their operation. Neither the construction company nor the investment banking house built a large geographically extended administrative network of operating units. They were not yet full-fledged modern business enterprises. Although the investment banking houses had partners and occasionally salaried managers in other American cities and European financial centers, most of their day-to-day buying and selling activities were handled in a small office near or on Wall Street. And although construction companies carried out a number of multimillion dollar jobs in different parts of the country, each project was managed locally by a handful of managers. None was permanent. When the road was completed that contracting unit moved on to another job in another place. Only the home office had a permanent staff. There the senior partner of the firm with one or two associates negotiated contracts and provided general supervision of operations from a single office. That office too was normally located in New York City. The management of such enterprises did not require the constant, almost minute-to-minute supervision that operation of the railroads demanded.

Structural innovation

Such constant coordination and control were, however, fundamental to the management of the railroads. Once a large road was financed, constructed, and in operation, the next challenge was that of management. Without the building of a managerial staff, without the design of internal administrative structures and procedures, and without communicating internal information, a high volume of traffic could not be carried safely and efficiently. Obtaining the full potential of the new technology called for unprecedented organizational efforts. No other business enterprise, or for that matter few other nonbusiness institutions, had ever required the coordination and control of so many different types of units carrying out so great a variety of tasks that demanded such close scheduling. None handled so many different types of goods or required the recording of so many different financial accounts.

The men who faced these challenges were a new type of businessman. It is worth emphasizing again that they were salaried employees with little or no financial interest in the companies they served. Moreover, most had had specialized training. The pioneers of modern management – George W. Whistler of the Western, Benjamin Latrobe of the Baltimore & Ohio, Daniel C. McCallum of the Erie, Herman Haupt and J. Edgar Thomson of the Pennsylvania, John B. Jervis of the Michigan Southern, and George B. McClellan of the Illinois Central – were all trained civil engineers with experience in railroad construction and bridge building before they took over the management of their roads.[21] Because they worked for a salary and not a share of the profits, because they had professional training and had developed professional expertise, their way of life was much closer to that of the modern manager than to that of the merchants and manufacturers who owned and operated business enterprises before the coming of the railroads.

To meet these unprecedented challenges these engineers had little to go on. The operation of the early canals and turnpikes provided few clues. The first railroads with their small size and light traffic developed only a modicum of useful experience. Nor did the managers of the first large roads borrow directly from the practices and procedures of military or other nonbusiness bureaucracies. Of the pioneers in the new managerial methods, only two – Whistler and McClellan – had military experience, and they were the least innovative of the lot.

The military model may, however, have had an indirect impact on the beginnings of modern business management. Because the United States Military Academy provided the best formal training in civil engineering in this country until the 1860s, a number of West Point graduates came to build and manage railroads. Some of these West Point trained engineers had served in or had an acquaintance with the Ordnance Department or the Corps of Engineers, two of the very few professionally manned, hierarchical organizations in antebellum America.

21. Brief backgrounds (and sources of information) on Latrobe, McCallum and Thomson are given in Alfred D. Chandler, Jr., "The Railroads: Pioneers in Modern Corporate Management," *Business History Review*, 39:16–40 (Spring 1965); and on Haupt, Jervis, McClellan, and Whistler, in Dumas Malone, ed., *Dictionary of American Biography* (New York, 1946), VII, 400, XI, 59–60, 581–582, XIX, 72.

Yet even for such officers, engineering training was probably more important than an acquaintance with bureaucratic procedures. There is little evidence that railroad managers copied military procedures. Instead all evidence indicates that their answers came in response to immediate and pressing operational problems requiring the organization of men and machinery. They responded to these in much the same rational, analytical way as they solved the mechanical problems of building a bridge or laying down a railroad.

These administrative challenges first appeared in the 1850s when the railroads grew large enough to require the coordination of the activities of several geographically contiguous operating divisions. The operations of the early small roads remained relatively simple, although even the earliest railroads required the management of more varied activities than did a contemporary textile mill or armory. An early road from thirty to fifty miles in length with relatively heavy traffic employed about fifty workers and was administered by a superintendent who had under him a manager responsible for each of the road's major functional activities: transportation and traffic, maintenance of way, and maintenance of locomotives and rolling stock. On lightly traveled roads the superintendent himself often supervised the functional activities and arranged for and maintained train schedules.

On these early roads personal management was easy; the superintendent and his functional assistants worked out of the same office. As in a New England textile mill, the superintendent conferred weekly with the treasurer or president, and occasionally with the board of directors. The treasurer maintained the books which were, in the words of the Boston & Worcester directors, "kept in a strictly mercantile style, according to the Italian method of book keeping by double entry."[22]

The coordination of the movements of trains and the flow of traffic did not yet raise complex scheduling problems. For example, on the busy forty-four-mile Boston & Worcester Railroad, passenger trains left each terminal at precisely the same time – 6:00 A.M., 12:00 noon, and 4:00 P.M.[23] One daily freight train departed immediately after the morning passenger train. The trains would meet at the mid-point,

22. Quoted in Kirkland, *Men, Cities and Transportation*, I, 338. The operations of many early roads are described in detail in J. Knight and Benjamin H. Latrobe, *Report on the Locomotives and the Police and Management of Several of the Principal Railroads in the Northern and Middle States* (Baltimore, 1838), pp. 4, 13–19. Knight and Latrobe point out that the Boston & Worcester employed fifty-one operating workers (that is, those not involved in construction work).

23. Stephen, Salsbury, *The State, the Investor, and the Railroad: Boston & Albany, 1825–1867* (Cambridge, Mass., 1967), pp. 182–184. The succeeding pages in chap. 9, "The Western Railroad in Crisis: An Operating Man's Nightmare," cover the crisis and the organizational response to it.

Framingham. Neither train would move on to its destination until the other had pulled into the station. On the longer but more lightly traveled roads to the south, trains ran one way one day and the other way the next. Except for the Western, which in 1840 became the first intersectional railroad in the country by connecting Worcester and Albany, no road before 1850 demanded a complicated operating structure.

As the Western neared completion, the inadequacies of the traditional, personal methods of management became clear. That road, which was just over 150 miles in length, had been built in three different sections or divisions. As each came into operation, each became a separate operating division with its own set of functional managers. Because of the road's length, the morning passenger train that started from Worcester at 9:30 A.M. did not reach the western terminal on the Hudson River until late that afternoon. As the company ran three trains a day each way (two passenger trains and one freight), the trains moving in opposite directions met twelve times daily. Since they ran on a single track, without the benefit of telegraphic signals, through mountainous terrain, such scheduling threatened tragedy. It came quickly. Even before the road had reached the Hudson River, the Western suffered a series of serious accidents, culminating in a head-on collision of passenger trains on October 5, 1841, killing a conductor and a passenger and injuring seventeen others.

The resulting outcry helped bring into being the first modern, carefully defined, internal organizational structure used by an American business enterprise. After the accident, the Massachusetts legislature launched an intensive investigation into the operations of the Western. *The American Railroad Journal and Mechanics Magazine* called for administrative reform. The company's directors, fully agreeing appointed a committee of three directors (two Boston businessmen and a physician) and the engineer in charge of construction, Major George W. Whistler, to find a remedy.

The solution outlined in the committee's "Report on Avoiding Collisions and Governing the Employees" was, in the words of the road's historian, to fix "definite responsibilities for each phase of the company's business, drawing solid lines of authority and communication for the railroad's administration, maintenance, and operation."[24] The new organizational structure called for a comparable set of functional managers on each of the three geographically contiguous operating divisions and then the creation of a headquarters at Springfield to monitor and coordinate the activities of the three sets of managers. Each

24. Salsbury, *Boston & Albany*, pp. 186–187.

division had its assistant master of transportation (later called division superintendent), its roadmaster, and its senior mechanic or foreman in charge of roundhouses and shops.

On each division the assistant masters of transportation were responsible for the movement of trains and of freight and passenger traffic, the roadmasters for the maintenance of way, and the mechanics for the repair and maintenance of locomotives and rolling stock. The assistant masters of transportation reported to the master of transportation at Springfield headquarters, the mechanics to the master mechanic, who headed the main shops in Springfield and who also reported to the master of transportation. The roadmasters, on the other hand, reported directly to the superintendent and not to the master of transportation as did those in the other functional departments. The superintendent (soon to be the general superintendent) was responsible to the president and directors for the operation of the road. All managers were to make regular reports based on the information received from their subordinates: station agents, conductors, locomotive engineers, the shop foreman, and the foreman of repair gangs. To prevent accidents, precise timetables were determined by the division superintendents working with the master of transportation and the general superintendent. These were given to the conductor who had "sole charge of the train," and who was given detailed instruction about how to handle delays or breakdowns.[25] No changes could be made in the schedules without written permission from the master of transportation and then only after consultation with his three division managers.

The need to assure safety of passengers and employees on the new, high-speed mode of transportation made the Western Railroad the first American business enterprise to operate through a formal administrative structure manned by full-time salaried managers. This embryonic modern business enterprise included two middle managers – the master of transportation and the master mechanic – and two top managers – the super-intendent and the president. The latter, who became in 1852 a full-time officer, was the link between the full-time salaried managers and the part-time representatives of the owners elected to the board of directors.[26]

When other long and heavily traveled lines came into operation in the early 1850s, the most important of these being the lines that connected the east and the west and the first major lines in the west, they began to create organizational structures similar to that of the Western Railroad. By then it was the volume and velocity of traffic rather than the need for

25. Ibid., p. 187.
26. Ibid., p. 157.

safety that demanded better organization. The coming of the telegraph in the late 1840s, as well as the perfection of procedures first developed on the Western, helped to make rail travel relatively safe. But the great increase in the volume of the railroad's business made a smooth and efficient coordination of the flow of trains and traffic increasingly difficult. Where the Western as late as 1850 ran freight trains for a total that year of 453,000 miles, the Erie in 1855 ran a total of 1,676,000 miles; and where the Western carried 261,000 tons of freight in 1850, the Erie moved 842,000 in 1855. By 1855 the Erie was operating 200 locomotives, 2,770 freight, and 170 passenger and mail cars.[27] Freight had become a more important source of income than passengers or mail for all the large roads.

Rising costs of moving freight underlined the problems of operating these longer lines efficiently. To their surprise, the managers and the directors of the larger roads quickly realized that their per mile operating costs were greater than were comparable costs on smaller roads. The basic reason, argued Daniel C. McCallum, general superintendent of the New York and Erie, was the lack of proper internal organization:

> A Superintendent of a road fifty miles in length can give its business his personal attention, and may be constantly on the line engaged in the direction of its details; each employee is familiarly known to him, and all questions in relation to its business are at once presented and acted upon; and any system, however imperfect, may under such circumstances prove comparatively successful.
>
> In the government of a road five hundred miles in length a very different state exists. Any system which might be applicable to the business and extent of a short road, would be found entirely inadequate to the wants of a long one; and I am fully convinced that in the want of system perfect in its details, properly adapted and vigilantly enforced, lies the true secret of their [the large roads] failure; and that this disparity of cost per mile in operating long and short roads, is not produced by a *difference in length*, but is in proportion to the perfection of the system adopted.[28]

In perfecting such a system the senior managers on three of the four east–west trunk lines, none of whom had had military experience, made significant innovations in the management of modern, multiunit business enterprise. Benjamin Latrobe of the Baltimore & Ohio concentrated on the needs of financial accounting as well as operational precision. McCallum of the Erie articulated the principles of management for this new type of business enterprise; while J. Edgar Thomson of

27. The comparisons of the two roads and the sources of information are given in Chandler, *Poor*, p. 320; also Edward H. Mott, *Between the Ocean and the Lakes: The Story of the Erie* (New York, 1899), p. 483.

28. Daniel C. McCallum, "Superintendent's Report," in *Annual Report of the New York and Erie Railroad Company for 1855* (New York, 1856), quoted in Chandler, *The Railroads*, p. 101, where much of McCallum's report is reprinted.

the Pennsylvania worked out the line-and-staff concept as a means of integrating more effectively the functional activities of several regionally defined operating units. The fourth trunk line, the New York Central, which had not been constructed like the others as a single work, but formed by a consolidation of many small lines, continued to be operated by merchants and financiers rather than by engineers. That road contributed almost nothing to the development of modern management.

The Baltimore & Ohio first reshaped its organization when it began to complete earlier plans to cross the mountains and reach the Ohio at Wheeling. In 1846 its president, Louis McLane, and its chief engineer, Latrobe, decided that the rapid growth of traffic, particularly from the newly opened coal mines, "the great augmentation of power and machinery demanded by the increasing business," as well as the anticipated further expansion of traffic when the Ohio was reached, demanded "a new system of management."[29] Assisted by a committee of the board, Latrobe outlined a new set of regulations "after diligent investigation, with the aid of the experience of other roads in New England and elsewhere." The objectives of the new plan were clearly defined:

> [They] consisted in confining the general supervision and superintendence of all the departments nearer to their duties, and, by a judicious subdivision of labor, to insure a proper adaptation and daily application of the supervisory power to the objects under its immediate charge; in the multiplication of checks, and to effecting a strict responsibility in the collection and disbursement of money; in confining the company's mechanical operations in their shops to the purposes of repairs, rather than of construction; in promoting the economical purchase and application of materials and other articles needed in every class of the service; and in affecting a strict and more perfect responsibility in the accounting department generally.[30]

The plan itself as set forth in a printed manual, *Organization of the Service of the Baltimore & Ohio Railroad*, began by departmentalizing the road's functions into two basic activities: "First, the working of the road. Second – the collection and disbursement of revenues."[31] The second task was far more complicated than it had been in the early factories where only the mill agent or his clerk handled money, or on a canal where toll masters and senior engineers did the same. On a large

29. *Organization of the Service of the Baltimore & Ohio R. Road, under the Proposed New System of Management* (Baltimore 1847), p. 3; and the *Twentieth Annual Report of the President and Directors to the Stockholders of the Baltimore & Ohio Rail-Road Company* (Baltimore, Md., 1846), pp. 11–14. Much of the following on the creation of the first management structures on railroads appeared in Alfred D. Chandler, Jr., "The Railroads: Pioneers in Modern Corporate Management," *Business History Review*, 39:16–40 (Spring 1965).
30. *Twenty First (1847) Annual Report* of the Baltimore & Ohio, p. 13.
31. This and the following quotation are from the *Organization of the Service of the Baltimore & Ohio Rail-Road, 1847*.

railroad, scores of individuals – conductors, station agents, freight and passenger agents, purchasing agents, managers and foremen in charge of shops and roundhouses and of the repair of track and roadbed – all had sizable sums of money pass through their hands each day.

Under the new system of management on the Baltimore & Ohio, financial responsibility was centralized in the company's treasurer, who not only supervised internal transactions but also handled external financing, including making the routine arrangements for assigning shares of stocks and bonds to the merchants and bankers who had agreed to market them, assuring the proper recording of sales and other transfers of securities, and sending out dividends and interest payments. Directly subordinate to the treasurer was the secretary who was wholly concerned with internal transactions. (In a short time the secretary's duties became those of the comptroller.) He inspected all passenger and freight accounts and supervised those who routinely handled the company's monies. Under the secretary was the chief clerk, into whose office in Baltimore flowed receipts and reports from all agents and conductors who received or disbursed funds along the road line. The chief clerk's office not only compiled and audited these accounts but also began to issue "daily comparisons of the work done by the road and its earnings with the monies received therefore." Daily figures were in turn summarized into monthly reports. These data thus became tools of the management as well as checks on the honesty and the competence of railroad employees. The reports remained, however, only records of financial transactions. Though detailed and numerous, they were not yet consolidated and reorganized to permit a realistic analysis of the costs involved in operating the road.

In organizing the operating department, Latrobe set up a structure similar to that of the Western to integrate the three major types of functional activities in the two (and when the road reached Wheeling, three) geographical divisions.[32] He reshaped the lines of responsibility for operation "by confining the departments of transportation, of construction and repairs of the road, and of repairs of machinery to a separate superintendency, each being subject to the immediate supervision of a professional engineer, under the direction of the President."[33] The heads of these departments were responsible for carrying out their carefully defined duties and for appointing subordinate managers and employees, usually with the "concurrence of the General Superintendent and the President." The functional managers of the Baltimore & Ohio

32. *Twenty-First (1847) Annual Report of the Baltimore & Ohio Rail-Road*, p. 13.

33. This and the following quotations are from the *Organization of the Service of the Baltimore and Ohio Rail-Road, 1847*.

then reported directly to their superiors in the central headquarters. As on the Western, the managers in the transportation department became responsible for the movement of traffic as well as the movement of trains.

The general superintendent was the key administrator. The organizational manual described this manager as "an officer of general duty . . . who besides duties peculiar to himself is charged with the supervision and control of the whole system, subject to the President and Directors." Into his office flowed a series of reports. Each of the operating departments forwarded weekly and monthly statements. The master of machinery, for example, was to report on "the condition and performance during the week of each locomotive and engine in service or under repair – the condition of the cars, and also the stationary machinery and workshops – and will present a monthly estimate of the probable expenses of their repair during the ensuing month." Besides reading reports, the senior operating executive maintained constant communication with department heads regarding problems and policies, inspected the road's facilities, and conferred with the president and the road's financial officers.

Daniel C. McCallum of the Erie further shaped the organizational form developed on the Western and the Baltimore & Ohio. After its completion in 1851 the Erie had been plagued by high operating costs. These threatened to become intolerable when, in the spring of 1853, the short lines along the Erie Canal consolidated to form a single enterprise, the New York Central, and so make that route a much more effective competitor for through traffic. That autumn Erie's board sought to reorganize its administrative structure in order to ensure a more precise accountability and control over expenses and a more effective appraisal of men and managers. The directors hoped to achieve this objective by making available "comparisons of the expenses of the various operations with those of similar roads, with the several divisions of the road itself; and the expense of different conductors engine-men, etc. with each other."[34]

To carry out this task the directors promoted McCallum from superintendent of one of the road's five operating divisions to general superintendent. When McCallum took office, the Erie had already adopted a structure similar to that of the Western and the Baltimore & Ohio.[35] Although he did define more precisely the lines of authority and responsibility, McCallum's major contribution consisted, first, of enun-

34. *Report of the Directors of the New York and Erie Railroad Company to the Stockholders in November 1853* (New York, 1853), pp. 47–48.

35. It included five divisions and two short branches of just under twenty miles apiece.

ciating "general principles" of administration and, second, of perfecting the flow of internal information so essential for top and middle management to coordinate complex widespread activities and to monitor and evaluate the performance of the large number of managers handling them. McCallum emphasized that a definition of "general principles" was particularly necessary because "we cannot avail ourselves to any great extent of the plan of organization of shorter lines in framing one for this, nor have we any precedent or experience on which we can fully rely in doing so."[36] For McCallum the six basic principles of general administration were these:

(1) A proper division of responsibilities.
(2) Sufficient power conferred to enable the same to be fully carried out, that such responsibilities may be real in their character [that is, authority to be commensurate with responsibility].
(3) The means of knowing whether such responsibilities are faithfully executed.
(4) Great promptness in the report of all derelictions of duty, the evils may be at once corrected.
(5) Such information, to be obtained through a system of daily reports and checks, that will not embarrass principal officers nor lessen their influence with their subordinates.
(6) The adoption of a system, as a whole, which will not only enable the General Superintendent to detect errors immediately, but will also point out the delinquent.

In putting these principles into practice, McCallum gave the superintendents in charge of geographical divisions the power to carry out their responsibilities for the day-to-day movement of trains and traffic by an express delegation of authority. These regional officers were to be:

> held responsible for the successful working of their respective Divisions, and for the maintenance of proper discipline and conduct of all persons employed thereon, except such as are in the employment of other officers acting under the directions from this office, as hereinafter stated. They possess all the powers delegated by the organization to the General Superintendent, except in matters pertaining to the duties of General Ticket Agent, General Freight Agent, General Wood Agent, Telegraph Management, and Engine and Car Repairs.

This power included control over the hiring and firing of subordinates, subject to the veto of top management. In McCallum's words, each officer had "the authority with the approval of the President and General

36. This and the following quotations are from McCallum, "Superintendent's Report" in the *Erie Annual Report (1855)* reprinted in Chandler, *The Railroads*, pp. 102–105.

Superintendent to appoint all persons for whose acts he is held responsible, and may dismiss any subordinate when, in his judgment, the interest of the company will be promoted thereby." The Erie's general superintendent stressed the value of adhering to explicit lines of authority and communication. "All subordinates should be accountable to and be directed *by their immediate superiors only*; as obedience cannot be enforced where the foreman in immediate charge is interfered with by a superior officer giving orders directly to his subordinates."

McCallum, nevertheless, failed to define precisely the relationship between the geographical division superintendent and the other functional managers of the division who reported to the general superintendent. He saw the problem clearly enough, pointing out that there were "some exceptions" to the rule that subordinates can communicate only through their senior officers. For example, "Conductors and station agents report, daily, their operations directly to the General Superintendent," and not to their division superintendents. He thought that the general superintendent would have the time and information needed to coordinate these activities. To illustrate more clearly these lines of authority, McCallum drew up a detailed chart – certainly one of the earliest organization charts in an American business enterprise.[37]

McCallum stressed that channels of authority and responsibility were also channels of communication. He paid close attention to improving the accuracy of the information and the regularity and speed with which it flowed through these channels. Hourly, daily, and monthly reports were more detailed than those called for on the Baltimore & Ohio. The hourly reports, primarily operational and sent by telegraph, gave the location of trains and reasons for any delays or mishaps. "The information being edited as fast as received, on convenient tabular forms, shows, at a glance, the position and progress of trains, in both directions on every Division of the Road." Just as important, the information generated on these tabular forms was filed away to provide an excellent source of operational information which, among other things, was useful in determining and eliminating "causes of delay." McCallum's use of the telegraph brought universal praise from the railroad world both in this country and abroad. What impressed other railroad managers was that McCallum saw at once that the telegraph was more than merely a means to make train movements safe. It was a device to assure more effective coordination and evaluation of the operating units under his command.

Daily reports, the real basis of the system, were required from conductors, agents, and engineers. These were then consolidated into monthly statements. Reports on each locomotive, for example, included

37. Chandler, *Poor*, pp. 147–148.

miles run, operating expenses, cost of repairs, and work done. Such data, flowing regularly from the division superintendents and other operating officers to the general superintendent, were supplemented by further detailed information provided both by the divisional managers and the heads of the functional departments. This information, so essential for regular and economical flow of trains and traffic, also made possible the comparison of work of the several operating units with one another and with those of other railroads. It provided the comparative statistics that the directors had asked for in the 1853 report. In order to have a constant and impersonal evaluation of the performance of the road's operating managers, "it is very important," McCallum insisted, "that principal officers should be in full possession of all information necessary to enable them to judge correctly as to the industry and efficiency of subordinates of every grade." In order to permit a more effective evaluation McCallum called for each of the five operating divisions to have its own separate and detailed set of accounts.

Central to coordinating flows and evaluating performance, these statistical data were also, McCallum pointed out, essential in understanding and controlling costs and in setting rates. The Erie and other roads had recently raised their rates, which they had found to be "unremunerative," only to discover that in so doing higher rates had threatened to "destroy this business."[38] By cutting traffic they had reduced net revenue. "To guard against such a result, and to establish the mean, between such rates as are unremunerative and such as are prohibitory, requires an accurate knowledge of the cost of transport of the various products, both for long and short distances." Important too was an understanding of the traffic flows along the line, for prices should be "fixed with reference to securing, as far as possible, such a balance of traffic in both directions as to reduce the proportion of 'dead weight' carried." Unused or excess capacity on a return trip warranted lowering prices for goods going that way. McCallum's concern, however, was almost wholly with operating costs and revenues. He said little about what costs should be allocated to construction or capital accounts. Nor did he consider ways to account for long-term depreciation of engines, rolling stock, rails, and other equipment.

McCallum's organizational innovations received wide attention. Henry Varnum Poor, the editor of the *American Railroad Journal*, was particularly impressed by his achievements and devoted much space to them. For example, Poor noted in 1854 that McCallum was already increasing

38. This and the following quotations are from McCallum's "Superintendent's Report" in *Erie Annual Report (1855)*, p. 79.

the Erie's efficiency at the same time he reduced the size of its work force. Moreover, he continued:

> By an arrangement now perfected, the superintendent can tell at any hour in the day, the precise location of every car and engine on the line of the road, and the duty it is performing. Formerly, the utmost confusion prevailed in this department, so much so, that in the greatest press of business, cars in perfect order have stood for months upon switches without being put to the least service, and without its being known where they were. All these reforms are being steadily carried out as fast as the ground gained can be held.[39]

Poor had McCallum's organization chart lithographed and offered copies for sale at $1 apiece. Douglas Galton, one of Britain's leading railroad experts, described McCallum's work in a parliamentary report printed in 1857. So too did the New York State Railroad Commissioners in their annual reports. Even the *Atlantic Monthly* carried an article in 1858 praising McCallum's ideas on railroad management.[40]

McCallum's principles and procedures of management, like his organization chart, were new in American business. No earlier American businessman had ever had the need to develop ways to use internally generated data as instruments of management. None had shown a comparable concern for the theory and principles of organization. The writings of Montgomery and the orders of plantation owners to their overseers talked about the control and discipline of workers, not the control, discipline, and evaluation of other managers. Nor does Sidney Pollard in his *Genesis of Modern Management* note any discussion about the nature of major principles of organization occurring in Great Britain before the 1830s, the data at which he stops his analysis.[41]

McCallum's methods and concepts of administration were tested and further rationalized on the Pennsylvania rather than on the Erie. Before the end of the 1850s the Erie had fallen into the hands of unscrupulous financiers who, like its notorious treasurer Daniel Drew, cared little about efficient administration. McCallum soon left the road to develop a profitable bridge-building business. On the Pennsylvania, however,

39. Quoted in Chandler, *Poor*, p. 147, from *American Railroad Journal*, 27:549 (September 2, 1854).

40. Chandler, *Poor*, pp. 148, 153; *American Railroad Journal*, 29:280 (May 3, 1856); *Atlantic Monthly*, 2:641, 651–654 (November 1858).

41. Sidney Pollard, *The Genesis of Modern Management* (Cambridge, Mass., 1963), chap. 7, and "The Genesis of the Managerial Profession: The Experience of the Industrial Revolution in Great Britain," *Studies in Romanticism*, 4:57–80 (Winter 1965). Pollard, by stopping his analysis at 1830, does not consider the impact of the operation of railroads on management in Great Britain. *Genesis of Modern Management*, p. 132.

engineers rather than financiers continued to run the road. J. Edgar Thomson, the builder and first superintendent of the Georgia Railroad, had come to the Pennsylvania in 1849 to take charge of its construction. In 1852, he became its president and controlled its destinies until his death in 1874. When Thomson took command, he modified the centralized administrative structure set up by Herman Haupt, a highly successful civil engineer who had been the general superintendent of the road since 1849. Thomson's first move was to follow the example of his competitors and to separate the road's financial and operating departments.[42] The modified organization remained quite adequate until 1857.

Then increasing traffic plus rising costs and the onslaught of a business depression brought a major reorganization. Thomson enlarged his central office, this time separating the accounting from the treasury department and creating a secretary's office and a legal department.[43] The legal department was similar to one Latrobe had set up on the Baltimore & Ohio. The two were among the first such departments to be established in an American business firm and handled the ever-increasing legal work involved with contracts, claims, and charters. Thomson appointed a new middle manager "controller and auditor" as the head of the new accounting department and placed under him two "assistant auditors" and several senior clerks. At the same time, Thomson set up a purchasing department to handle the centralized buying of supplies for the company as a whole. Finally he greatly expanded the staff of the general freight agent. Both the new purchasing and the enlarged freight office were placed in the transportation department.

Thomson's major achievement was to clarify relations between the functional offices of the division and those of the central office. In so doing he relied heavily on the Erie model. The organization manual which Thomson signed in December 1857 included many of McCallum's words and phrases. Thomson's plan, however, differed from McCallum's because he centralized the authority, as well as the responsibility for the moving of trains and traffic, and put this authority in the hands of the division superintendents in charge of transportation. They were explicitly delegated the authority to give orders to men and managers in the other functional departments. In the words of the 1857 manual:

42. *Fifth Annual Report of the Pennsylvania Rail-Road* (1851), pp. 42–85, and James A. Ward, "Herman Haupt and the Development of the Pennsylvania Railroad," *Pennsylvania Magazine of History*, 95:73–97 (January 1971), esp. 78, 86.

43. The activities of these departments are described in *Pennsylvania Rail-Road Company: Organization for Conducting the Business of the Road, Adopted December 26, 1857* (Philadelphia, 1858), pp. 9–16.

The Division Superintendent shall, *on their respective Divisions* (subject to the directions and approval of the General Superintendent), exercise all the powers delegated by the organization to the General Superintendent, for the control and the use of the road, its branches and connections, for the transportation of Freight and Passengers, including the movement of Motive Power employed thereon, whether engaged in the transportation of Freight and Passengers, or in the construction and repairing of the road, or the supply of fuel and materials. They shall also have general charge of all employees connected with Motive Power and Transportation on their respective divisions, and see that they perform the duties assigned them, and shall render such assistance to the Master of Machinery in preserving discipline, in the arrangement of the Locomotives to their particular service, in securing the services of competent engine men, and other responsible persons for the Motive Power, as the General Superintendent and the best interests of the company may require. They shall be furnished with copies of all rules and regulations, and orders to foremen of shops, and others holding positions of responsibility and trust connected with the Motive Power or Transportation of the company, and shall enforce their observance.

Thus the division superintendent was on the direct line of authority from the president through the general superintendent. All orders concerning the movement of trains and traffic went out of the division superintendent's office to workers in the motive power, maintenance of way, and transportation departments. The master of machinery set rules and standards for "the discipline and economy of conducting the business of the shops," and he or his divisional assistants hired, fired, and promoted people in their departments. But even in these activities, they were to have, as the new organizational manual emphasized, the "assistance" of the division superintendents.[44] In a short time the same became true for the chief engineer and his subordinate engineers responsible for the maintenance of way.[45] This line-and-staff concept, by which the managers on the line of authority were responsible for ordering men involved with the basic function of the enterprise, and other functional managers (the staff executives) were responsible for setting standards, was first enunciated in American business by the Pennsylvania Railroad in December 1857.

The decentralized line-and-staff divisional form of organization initially put into operation on the Pennsylvania became, in the years after the Civil War, widely used, though often in a modified form, by other large American railroads, including the Michigan Central, the

44. *Pennsylvania Rail-Road Company: Organization . . . 1857*, p. 7. In addition, the manual defined the relations between the financial and operating departments. "Orders issued by the Accounting Department to Officers or Agent of the Transportation Department will be sent to the General Superintendent, and by him immediately distributed and enforced" (p. 11).

45. For example, *By-Laws and Organization for Conducting the Business of the Pennsylvania Rail-Road Company, to Take Effect June 1, 1873* (Philadelphia, 1873), pp. 20, 25–26. When construction was completed, the chief engineer at the head of the department of maintenance of way became explicitly a staff officer to "act as a consulting engineer."

Michigan Southern, and the Chicago, Burlington & Quincy.[46] On these and other roads the division engineers (responsible for maintenance of way) reported at first to the chief engineers who remained primarily responsible for completing the construction of the road. Once the road was built the chief engineer joined the staff of the general superintendent as a "consulting engineer" and the division engineers reported directly to their division superintendent. Once construction was completed, large American railroads had two major departments: one for operations and one for finance. Only in the 1870s did they add a third – the traffic department. Figure 2 is an organization chart showing the line-and-staff structure on a large railroad in the 1870s. By then full-time vice presidents headed the major functional departments. (The largest roads might have as many as nine divisions and three general superintendents.)

Not all railroads adopted this decentralized divisionalized structure. Indeed, a more "natural" form of organization was generally used by the British and European railroads.[47] In what became known as the "departmental" structure, the president and general superintendent did not delegate their authority. Instead, the functional managers on the geographical divisions – transportation, motive power, maintenance of way, passenger, freight, and accounting – reported directly to their functional superiors at the central office. This was true of the New York Central and a number of other American roads, particularly those where managers gave little attention to the problems of organization.[48] In time, however, nearly all the railroads in the United States carrying heavy traffic over long distances came to use the divisional line-and-staff type of organization.

By the coming of the Civil War the modern American business enterprise had appeared among American railroads. The needs of safety and then efficiency had led to the creation of a managerial hierarchy, whose duties were carefully defined in organizational manuals and charts. Middle and top managers supervised, coordinated, and evaluated the work of lower level managers who were directly responsible for the day-to-day operations. In the 1850s large roads were already employing from forty to sixty full-time salaried managers, of whom at least a dozen

46. The information on the operating structure of these roads comes from their annual reports in the 1850s. There is very useful information, including an organization chart, in David Lee Lightner, "Labor on the Illinois Central Railroad, 1852–1880," Ph.D. diss., Cornell University, 1969, pp. 68–73.

47. The departmental organization of the British railroads is described in detail in Ray Morris, *Railroad Administration* (New York, 1920), chap. 6.

48. A description of the more informal departmental structure of the New York Central, a road created by consolidation of several small roads and headed by merchants and financiers, is given in Chandler, "The Railroads: Pioneers in Modern Corporate Management," pp. 38–39.

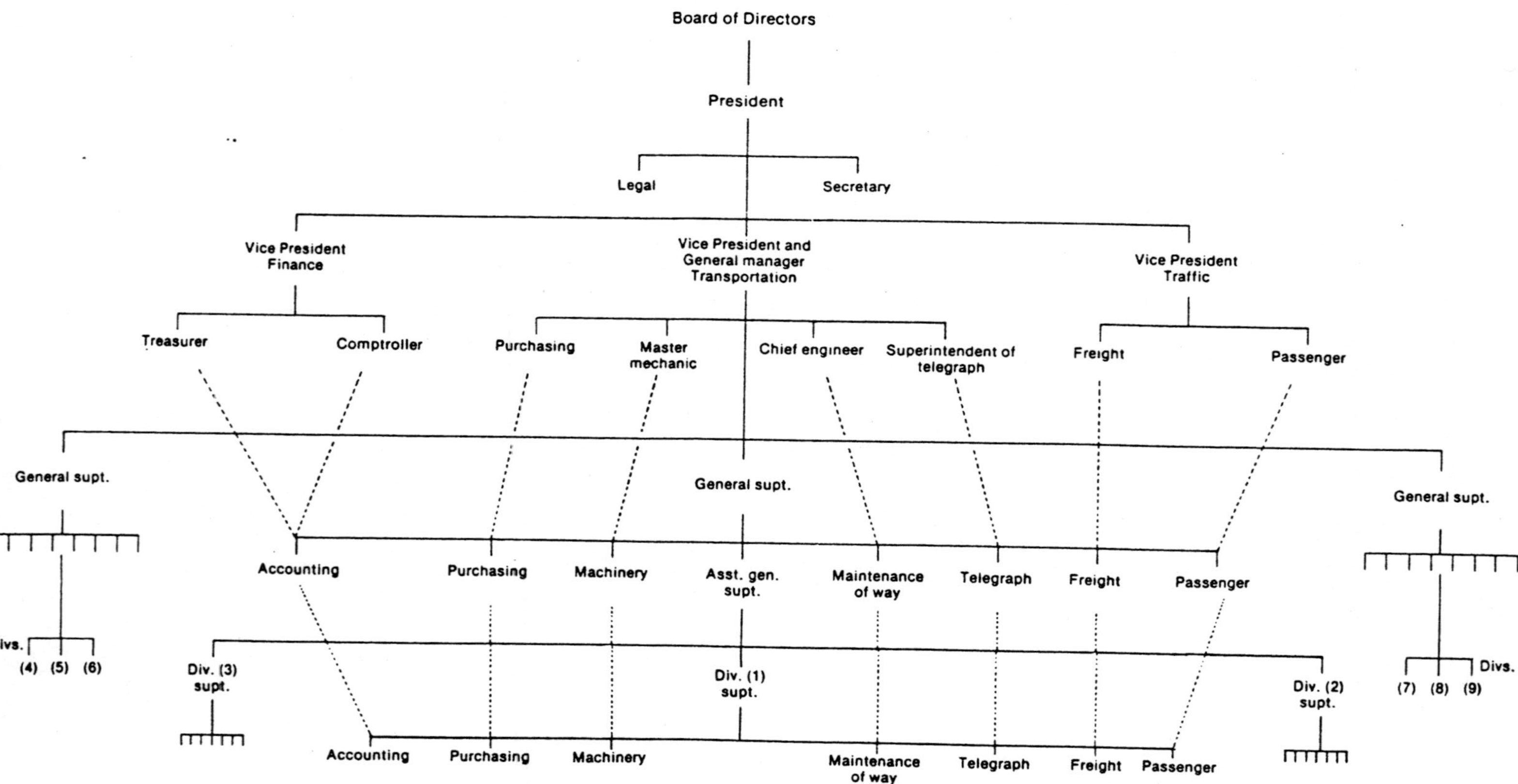

Figure 2. Simplified organization chart of a large railroad, 1870s.

and often more were middle or top management.[49] In the 1850s top management included the president, the general superintendent, and the treasurer. By the 1870s it also included the executive in charge of the traffic department and a general manager who supervised the work of two or three general superintendents. By then middle management included the general superintendents, their assistants, and the heads of the machinery (motive power and rolling stock), maintenance of way, telegraph, freight, passenger, and purchasing offices within the transportation department; the controller and his assistants and the treasurer's assistants within the financial department; and the heads of the legal department and secretary's office. In addition, on the roads still being built, there were the chief engineer and his assistants who had charge of construction. No private business enterprise with as many managers or with as complex an internal organization existed in the United States – nor, except for railroads in Britain and western Europe, in any other part of the world.

Accounting and statistical innovation

As Latrobe, McCallum, and Thomson so clearly understood, a constant flow of information was essential to the efficient operation of these new large business domains. For the middle and top managers, control through statistics quickly became both a science and an art. This need for accurate information led to the divising of improved methods for collecting, collating, and analyzing a wide variety of data generated by the day-to-day operations of the enterprise. Of even more importance it brought a revolution in accounting; more precisely, it contributed substantially to the emergence of accounting out of bookkeeping. The techniques of Italian double-entry bookkeeping generated the data needed, but these data, required in far larger quantities and in more systematic form, were then subjected to types of analysis that were new. In sum, to meet the needs of managing the first modern business enterprise, managers of large American railroads during the 1850s and 1860s invented nearly all of the basic techniques of modern accounting.

Of all the organizational innovators, J. Edgar Thomson and his associates on the Pennsylvania Railroad made the most significant con-

49. For example, in 1856 the Illinois Central had 44 officers and 3,501 employees (about 800 of which were involved in new construction). Lightner, "Labor on the Illinois Central Railroad," p. 72. In 1852, before its western division had been fully opened for operations, the Baltimore & Ohio already had 63 managers, 4 in top management (the president, general superintendent, treasurer, and chief engineer), 9 in middle management, and 50 in the lower levels, including foreman of shops and repair gangs and full-time freight and passenger agents. These data were compiled by Harold W. Geisel for an honors thesis at Johns Hopkins University in 1967.

tributions to accounting. Their work and that of other managers received much public attention. Investors, shippers, and railroad directors were as much concerned about the accuracy and value of the new procedures as were the managers themselves. Railroad trade journals, particularly Henry Varnum Poor's *American Railroad Journal*, and the new financial journals (first the *Banker's Magazine*, and then the *Commercial and Financial Chronicle*) carried articles, editorials, and letters about the subject. Comparable public discussion of accounting methods had never occurred before in the United States; and it would be another thirty or forty years before similar accounting discussions took place in manufacturing and marketing.

The new accounting practices fell into three categories: financial, capital, and cost accounting. Financial accounting involved the recording, compiling, collating, and auditing of the hundreds of financial transactions carried out daily on the large roads. It also required the synthesizing of these data to provide the information needed for compiling the roads' balance sheets and for evaluating the company's financial performance. Where the largest of the textile mills had four or five sets of accounts to process and review, the Pennsylvania Railroad had, by 1857 (the year Thomson reorganized his accounting office), 144 basic sets of accounting records.[50] Of these accounts, the passenger department had 33, the freight department 25, motive power 26, maintenance of cars 9, and maintenance of way 22. Eight more were listed under general expenses, while construction and equipment had 21. Moreover, where the textile company's accounts were compiled only semiannually, those of the Pennsylvania were summarized and tabulated monthly, and were forwarded in printed form by the comptroller to the board of directors by the fifteenth of the following month. The totals of the monthly reports were then consolidated in the road's annual report.

In the preparation of these reports the accounting office collected, summarized, and printed detailed operating as well as financial data. As early as 1851 the Pennsylvania's annual report showed for each month the number of passengers entered at each station, as well as the tonnage on local and through freight to Pittsburgh and Philadelphia and from each of the way stations. By 1855 traffic data of over two hundred major products were listed.[51] This mass of printed information on expenses and receipts, and on passengers and products moved, remains a magnificent and little-used source for the flows and costs of American transportation at mid-century.

50. *Pennsylvania Railroad Company: Organization . . . 1857*, p. 11. The accounts are itemized on pp. 21–23.

51. The *Fourth (1851)*, the *Fifth (1851), the Seventh (1853)*, and the *Tenth (1856) Annual Report(s) of the Pennsylvania Rail-Road*, pp. 60–61, 103–104, 74–76, respectively.

The processing and analyzing of these data required the Pennsylvania and other large railroads to build extensive comptrollers' departments and to hire full-time internal auditors. By 1860 the railroads probably employed more accountants and auditors than the federal or any state government. In any case, after 1850 the railroad was central in the development of the accounting profession in the United States.

In reviewing the balance sheets and other condensed information provided by the new comptrollers' department, railroad managers, directors, and investors quickly employed these data to evaluate and compare the performance of the different roads. In addition to the balance sheets themselves, they began in the late 1850s to use the "operating ratio" as a standard way to judge a road's financial results. Profit and loss were not enough. Earnings had to be related to the volume of business. A better test was the ratio between a road's operating revenues and its expenditures or, more precisely, the percentage of gross revenue that had been needed to meet operating costs.[52] Such ratios had never before been used by American businessmen. They remain today a basic standard for judging the performance of American business enterprise.

In drawing up their balance sheets, the railroads were the first American businesses to pay close and systematic attention to capital accounting. Again the problem was unprecedented. No other type of private business enterprise had ever made such huge investments in capital, plant, and equipment. In discussing capital accounting in the 1850s, railroad managers, stockholders, and journalists at first gave the most attention to defining clearly the distinction between the construction or capital account and the operating account.[53] On the one hand, by charging operating expenses to construction accounts, promoters and managers could give the appearance of making profits that were not really earned. This they did to improve their chances of raising funds for completing or continuing construction.

On the other hand, by charging construction costs to operating costs, the investors in the road benefited at the expense of its users. Railroad reformers, such as Henry Varnum Poor in the 1850s and Charles Francis Adams, the chairman of the Massachusetts Railroad Commission, in the 1860s and 1870s, repeatedly urged the railroad officials to delineate clearly these two sets of accounts. To see that they were properly

52. See Chandler, *Poor*, p. 139, for use of the operating ratio in the 1850s, and William J. Ripley, *Railroads: Finance and Organization* (New York, 1915), pp. 112–115, for its use well into the twentieth century.

53. Kirkland, *Men, Cities and Transportation*, I, 340–344, II, 332–335. One of Poor's earliest editorial campaigns in 1849 urged roads to set aside funds for renewal and replacement. Chandler, *Poor*, p. 50.

differentiated, the reformers proposed that outsiders – either groups of investors or railroad or legislative commissions – have the opportunity to review a railroad's books.

Once a road was completed and the construction account closed, its total amount was recorded on the asset side of the consolidated balance sheet as a capital or property account. The problem then arose as to how to account for depreciation and even obsolescence of the road's capital assets. For not only were such capital assets of far greater value than those of the factory, but they depreciated at a more rapid rate. The early roads, such as the Boston & Worcester, began by following the textile mill procedures. They put money aside in contingency funds or in their profit and loss or their surplus accounts, in order to have it available for expensive repairs or the purchase of new equipment. Every now and then, usually in good years, the financial officers wrote down the value of their plant and equipment. During the 1850s, however, the managers on the new large roads began to find it easier to consider depreciation as an operating cost and did so by charging repairs and renewals to the operating accounts.

The directors of the Pennsylvania Railroad explained these new concepts of renewal accounting in their annual report of 1855. By charging repairs and renewals to operating expenses, the property accounts would continue to reflect the true value of the capital assets. "The practice of the Company in relation to its running equipment is to preserve the number of cars and locomotives charged to construction account, in complete efficiency; thus, if a car or locomotive is destroyed, or has become old and worthless, a new one is substituted in its place, and its cost charged to the expense account."[54] The same was true for rails, cross ties, and bridges.

Such a procedure neatly avoided the complex problem of determining depreciation, but it did not assure the availability of funds for extensive renewal and repairs. The company estimated that the charge for "the annual decay" of the roadbed was $110,000 and the "depreciation" on "running machinery" was $40,000. "If the Company had been declaring dividends from its profits, it would be prudent to carry a portion of the year to a reserved fund." After balancing receipts with expenditures, the company deducted for taxes, interest, and other expenses; then it set dividends at 6 percent. The balance or surplus went into a "contingent fund," part of which was used to invest in bonds of connecting roads.[55]

54. This and the following quotations are from the *Ninth Annual Report of the Pennsylvania Rail-Road (1855)*, p. 15.

55. This phrase and the following quote are in the *Tenth Annual Report of the Pennsylvania Rail-Road (1856)*, p. 12.

The funds in these contingency accounts, as those in sinking funds set up for the payment of bonds, were to be placed in "safe" investments. These accounts, however, quickly became mere bookkeeping devices with funds "loaned" out to other accounts of the road itself. After the Civil War, even the Pennsylvania dropped the use of separate contingency accounts, and merely kept the surplus account high enough to meet anticipated demands for repair and renewal of rails and equipment.

By the 1870s this type of renewal accounting had become the standard form of capital accounting used by American railroads. Repair and renewals were charged to operating expenses and not to the capital or the property accounts. These two accounts – one for construction and the other for equipment – were to be altered only when new facilities were added or existing ones dropped. A convention of state railroad commissioners meeting in June 1879 to set up uniform accounting methods for American railroads defined the procedure in this manner: "No expenditure shall be charged to the property accounts, except it be for actual increase in construction, equipment, and property, unless it be made on old work in such a way as to clearly increase the value of the property over and above the cost of renewing the original structures, etc. In such cases only the amount of increased cost shall be charged, and the amount allowed on account of old work shall be stated."[56] In the model financial statement proposed by the commissioners (Table 1) such additions (or subtractions) were to be listed under a separate heading "Charges and Credits to Property During the Year." Under that heading was also listed changes in the value of real estate and other property held by the company.

By charging repairs and renewals to operating expenses, the value of the property was theoretically maintained at its original value. The method of renewal accounting meant the profit would continue to be considered, as it always had been in American business, as the difference between operating income and expenses but not as the rate of return on investment on actual capital assets. In fact, the use of renewal accounting made it impossible to know how much capital had been invested in roadbed, plant, and equipment since so much of the cost of capital equipment had been absorbed as operating expense. Such accounting methods thus, of necessity, made the operating ratio, rather than the rate of return, the basic tool for analyzing the financial performance of

56. "Proceedings of the Convention of Railroad Commissioners Held at Saratoga Springs, New York, June 10, 1879," Appendix 21, a pamphlet in Baker Library, Harvard University. For background of the movement for uniform accounting that led to this meeting, see Kirkland, *Men, Cities and Transportation*, II, 335–339.

Table 1. *Form of accounts recommended by the convention of railroad commissioners held at Saratoga Springs, New York, June 10, 1879*

General Exhibit
Total income
Total expense, including taxes
Net income
Interest on funded debt
Interest on unfunded debt
Rentals
Balance applicable to dividends
Dividends declared (percent)
Balance for the year
Balance (profit and loss) last year
Add or deduct various entries made during the year not included above (specifying same)
Balance (profit and loss) carried forward to next year
CHARGES AND CREDITS TO PROPERTY DURING YEAR
Construction and equipment (specifying same)
Other charges(specifying same)
Total charges
Property sold or reduced in value (specifying same)
Net addition (or reduction) for the year
ANALYSIS OF EARNINGS AND EXPENSES
Earnings:
From local passengers
Through passengers
Express and extra baggage
Mails
Other sources, passenger department
Total earnings passenger department
Local freight
Through freight
Other sources, freight department
Total earnings freight department
Total transportation earnings
Rents for use of road
Income from other sources (specifying same)
Total income from all sources
Expenses:
Salaries, general officers and clerks
Law expenses
Insurance
Stationery and printing

Outside agencies and advertising
Contingencies
Repairs, bridges (including culverts and cattle guards)
Repairs, buildings
Repairs, fences, road crossings, and signs
Renewal rails
Renewal ties
Repairs, roadway and track
Repairs, locomotives
Fuel for locomotives
Water supply
Oil and waste
Locomotive service
Repairs, passenger cars
Passenger-train service
Passenger-train supplies
Mileage, passenger-cars (debit balance)
Repairs, freight cars
Freight-train service
Freight-train supplies
Mileage, freight cars (debit balance)
Telegraph expenses (maintenance and operating)
Damage and loss of freight and baggage
Damage to property and cattle
Personal injuries
Agents and station service
Station supplies
    Total operating expenses
    Taxes
    Total operating expenses and taxes

ASSETS AND LIABILITIES

Assets:

Construction account
Equipment account
Other investments (specifying same)
Cash items:
  Cash
  Bills receivable
  Due from agents and companies
Other assets:
  Materials and supplies
  Sinking funds
  Debit balances
    Total assets

Table 1. *(continued)*

Liabilities:
Capital stock
Funded debt
Unfunded debt, as follows:
Interest unpaid
Dividends unpaid
Notes payable
Vouchers and accounts
Other liabilities
Profit and loss or income accounts
Total liabilities
PRESENT OR CONTINGENT LIABILITIES NOT INCLUDED IN BALANCE-SHEET
Bonds guaranteed by this company or a lien on its roads (specifying same)
Overdue interest on same
Other liabilities (specifying same)

Source: *Proceedings of the Convention of Railroad Commissioners Held at Saratoga Springs, New York, June 10, 1879* (New York, 1879), Appendix IX, no. 21.

railroad enterprises. Finally, this method of defining depreciation also meant that American railroad accounting overstated operating costs and understated capital consumption.[57]

The basic innovations in financial and capital accounting appeared in the 1850s in response to specific needs and were perfected in the years after the Civil War. Innovations in a third type of accounting – cost accounting – came more slowly. In making his recommendations for detailed divisional accounts, McCallum had emphasized the need to develop comparative cost data for each of the operating divisions on a large road. "This comparison [of division accounts] will show," McCallum wrote in 1855, "the officers who conduct their business with

57. As one accounting historian has emphasized: "Over time, replacement accounting understates capital consumption." Richard P. Brief, "Nineteenth-Century Accounting Era," *Journal of Accounting Research*, 3:21 (Spring 1968). Brief gives an excellent analysis of replacement accounting in this article which can be supplemented by his "The Evolution of Asset Accounting," *Business History Review*, 40:1–23 (Spring 1966). Useful too is L. E. Andrade, "Accounting Thought in the United States, 1815–1860," in J. Van Fenstermacher, ed., *Papers Presented at the Annual Business History Conference, February 26–27, 1965* (Kent, Ohio, 1965), pp. 113–120.

the greatest economy, and will indicate, in a manner not to be mistaken, the relative ability and fitness of each for the position he occupies. It will be valuable in pointing out the particulars of excess in the cost of management of one Division with another, by comparison of details; will direct attention to those matters in which sufficient economy is not practiced; and it is believed, will have the effect of exciting an honorable spirit of emulation to excell."[58] Not until the late 1860s, however, did cost accounting become a basic tool for railroad management.

The railroad manager who most effectively developed McCallum's proposals for cost accounting and control was Albert Fink, a civil engineer and bridge builder. Fink, after receiving his training on the Baltimore & Ohio, joined the managerial staff of the Louisville & Nashville, becoming its general superintendent in 1865 and the senior vice president in 1869.[59] Fink's aim was to determine with much more precision the basic measure of unit cost, the ton mile. His first step in obtaining accurate cost of carrying one ton for one mile in each of his divisions was to reorder the financial and statistical data compiled by his accounting and transportation departments.[60] He consolidated some of the existing accounts and subdivided others. Most important of all, he recategorized existing accounts according to the nature of their costs rather than according to the departments in which the functions were being carried out.

Table 2 shows how Fink reordered his accounts into four fundamental categories. One included those costs which, within limits, did not vary with the volume of traffic. Here he placed twenty-seven accounts involving primarily the maintenance of roadway and buildings and "general superintendence" or overhead. A second category included nine sets of accounts that varied with the volume of freight but not with the length of road or train-miles run. These were largely station expenses "incurred at stations in keeping up an organized force of agents, laborers, etc. for the purposes of receiving and delivering freight, selling tickets,

58. McCallum, "Superintendent's Report," in the New York and Erie's *Annual Report (1855)*, reprinted in Chandler, *The Railroads*, p. 107.

59. *Dictionary of American Biography*, VI, 387–388.

60. See especially Albert Fink, *Cost of Railroad Transportation, Railroad Accounts and Government Regulation of Railroad Tariffs* (Louisville, Ky., 1875), reprinted in Chandler, *The Railroads*, pp. 108–117. See also Fink, *Investigation into Cost of Transportation on American Railroads, with Deductions for its Cheapening* (Louisville, 1874), and his *Cost of Railroad Transportation, Railroad Accounts, and Governmental Regulation of Railroads* (Louisville, 1875). Charles Ellet, another competent engineer, had made a detailed analysis of railroad costs in the early 1840s which he published in the *American Railroad Journal*. His work appears to have had much less impact than that of McCallum or Fink, possibly because he had much less practical experience than the other two and because he wrote before American railroads had developed large operating units with extensive traffic. Chandler, *Poor*, pp. 38, 296.

Table 2. *Albert Fink: classification of operating expenses and computation of unit costs*

Headings of Accounts

MAINTENANCE OF ROADWAY AND GENERAL SUPERINTENDENCE

Road repairs per mile of road—

1. Adjustment of track
2. Ballast
3. Ditching
4. Culverts and cattle-guards
5. Extraordinary repairs—slides, etc.
6. Repairs of hand and dump-cars
7. Repairs of road tools
8. Road watchmen
9. General expense of road department
10. Total
11. Cross-ties replaced—value
12. Cross-ties, labor replacing
13. Cross-ties, train expenses hauling
14. Total cost of cross-ties per mile of road
15. Bridge superstructure repairs
16. Bridge watchmen
17. Shop-building repairs
18. Water-station repairs
19. Section-house repairs
20. Total cost of bridge and building repairs per mile of road
21. General superintendence and general expense of operating department
22. Advertising and soliciting passengers and freight
23. Insurance and taxes
24. Rent account
25. Total per mile of road
26. Salaries of general officers
27. Insurance and taxes and general expense
28. Total per mile of road
29. *Total cost per mile of road for maintenance of roadway and buildings*

29½. Total cost per train mile for maintenance of roadway and buildings

STATION EXPENSES PER TRAIN MILE

30. Labor loading and unloading freight
31. Agents and clerks
32. General expense of stations—lights, fuel, etc.
33. Watchmen and switchmen
34. *Expense of switching—*
    - Engine repairs
    - Engineers and firemen's wages
    - Expense in engine-house
    - Supervision and general expense
    - Oil and waste
    - Water supply
    - Fuel
35. Total per train mile
36. Stationery and printing
37. Telegraph expenses
38. Depot repairs
39. Total per train mile
40. *Total station expenses per train mile*

MOVEMENT EXPENSES PER TRAIN MILE

41. Adjustment of track
42. Cost of renewal of rails—value
43. Labor replacing rails
44. Train expenses hauling rails
45. Joint fastenings
46. Switches
47. Total cost of adjustment of track and replacing rails per train mile
48. Locomotive repairs
49. Oil and waste used on locomotives
50. Watching and cleaning
51. Fuel used in engine-house
52. Supervision and general expense in engine-house
53. Engineers and firemen's wages
54. Total engine expenses per train mile
55. Conductors and brakemen
56. Passenger-car repairs

57. Sleeping-car repairs
58. Freight-car repairs
59. Oil and waste used by cars
60. Labor oiling and inspecting cars
61. Train expenses
62. Total car expenses per train mile
63. Fuel used by locomotives
64. Water supply
65. Total fuel and water expense per train mile
66. Damage to freight, and lost baggage
67. Damage to stock
68. Wrecking account
69. Damage to persons
70. Gratuity to employees
71. Fencing burned
72. Law expenses
73. Total per train mile
74. *Total movement expenses per train mile*
75. GRAND TOTAL for maintenance and movement per train mile.

Formula for Ascertaining the Cost of Railroad Transportation per Ton-Mile

$$\text{Movement expenses per ton-mile} = \frac{\text{Movement expenses per train mile (items 41 to 74)}}{\text{average number of tons of freight in each train}} = a$$

$$\text{Station expenses per ton-mile} = \frac{\text{Cost of handling freight (items 30 to 40) at forwarding station + at delivery station}}{\text{length of haul}} = b$$

$$\text{Maintenance of road per ton-mile} = \frac{\text{Cost of maintenance of road per mile per year (items 1 to 29)} \times \dfrac{\text{total miles run by freight-trains per year}}{\text{total revenue trains, pass. and freight, per year}}}{\text{average number of tons of freight transported over one mile of road per year}} = c$$

$$\text{Interest per ton-mile} = \frac{\text{Cost of road per mile} \times \dfrac{\text{rate of interest per annum}}{100} \times \dfrac{\text{number of freight-train miles per year}}{\text{number of revenue-train miles, freight and pass., per year}}}{\text{average number of tons of freight transported over one mile of road per year}} = d$$

Total cost per ton-mile $= a + b + c + d$.

In order to make use of this formula it is necessary to know fifty-eight items of expense [above], all of which vary on different roads, and enter into different combinations with each other. Some of the items of movement expenses (41 to 74) change with the weight of trains, and have to be ascertained in each individual case. The average cost for the year can be made the basis of the estimate. Besides the items shown [above], the following other items enter into the calculation: the average number of tons of freight in train per mile of the round trip of the train, the average length of haul, the number of miles run over the road with freight and passenger-trains per annum, the cost of the road, the rate of interest, and the total number of tons of freight carried during a year over one mile of road. Without these data it is impossible to make a correct estimate of the cost of transportation on railroads.

Source: Albert Fink, *Cost of Railroad Transportation, Railroad Accounts, and Government Regulation of Railroad Tariffs* (Louisville, 1875), pp. 47–48.

etc." A third class of thirty-two sets of items, "movement expenses," varied with the number of trains run. But, as Fink pointed out, since the trains rarely ran fully loaded, the expenditures did not vary precisely with the volume of business. The accounts in these categories were determined for each division on a per-train-mile run basis. In addition to these operating expenses Fink had a fourth category, the interest charges that, of course, had no relation to traffic carried or trains run. Interest charges increased only when expanding business called for new construction and an enlarged debt. Table 2 gives the complex formula Fink used to convert these sixty-eight sets of accounts into costs per ton-mile. A comparison of these internal accounts (and the methods devised to use them to ascertain and control costs) with those employed in the textile mills, armories, shipping, and merchant enterprises, emphasized dramatically how much more complex railroads were to manage than any other contemporary business enterprise.

Fink stressed how costs varied on the different divisions or "branches," as they were then called, on the Louisville & Nashville. Movement expenses, for example, went from a high of 41.3 percent of total expenses on the main stem to a low of only 17.6 percent on the less-traveled Richmond branch. Station expenses ran from only 4.3 percent of all expenses on the Knoxville branch to 18.1 percent on the main stem, maintenance of road from 9.3 percent on the Glascow branch to 22.5 percent on the Bardstown branch, and the interest account from 26 percent on the main stem to 59.2 percent on the Richmond branch. By developing a time series on the costs of the different divisions and by knowing the division's physical and economic characteristics, the general superintendent was able to identify with some precision the reasons for the differences in costs. Such historical data and constant reviewing of current financial and operating data permitted him to evaluate performance of different divisions and their operating executives.

In addition, Fink emphasized that such cost analysis was fundamental to ratemaking. The "mere knowledge of average costs per ton mile of all expenditures" was of "no value," for "no freight is ever transported under the average condition." If rates are to be based on costs, then "we must classify freight according to conditions affecting the cost of transportation, and ascertain the cost of each class separately."[61] And Fink knew, as did every railroad manager, that costs were only one factor in the complex calculus that determined rates.

Cost per ton-mile rather than earnings, net income, or the operating ratio thus became the criterion by which the railroad managers controlled

61. Quoted in Chandler, *The Railroads*, p. 115. The percentages of expenses on the different divisions are given on pp. 110–111.

and judged the work of their subordinates. One reason was that revenues, particularly those from through traffic, could not be easily allocated to separate divisions. Also, many factors completely out of the division superintendent's control affected the amount of revenues his jurisdiction produced. Thus while financial and capital accounts remained primarily the concern of the financial officers, cost accounting became increasingly the province of the transportation department and came to be used as an operational rather than a financial control.

The volume of financial transactions handled by a large railroad, as well as the volume of traffic and passengers carried, encouraged, indeed forced, railroad managers to pioneer a modern business accounting. This sharp increase in the business activity of the firm thus revolutionized accounting practices. The new methods, devised in the 1850s and perfected in the following years, were quickly adopted by the first large industrial enterprises when they appeared in the 1880s. They remained the basic accounting techniques used by American business enterprise until well into the twentieth century. Only in cost accounting did the large industrial enterprises modify and adjust the methods initially devised by the railroads in the mid-nineteenth century, and this because the operations being costed were so different from those in transportation.

Organizational innovation evaluated

The railroads were, then, the first modern business enterprises. They were the first to require a large number of salaried managers; the first to have a central office operated by middle managers and commanded by top managers who reported to a board of directors. They were the first American business enterprise to build a large internal organizational structure with carefully defined lines of responsibility, authority, and communication between the central office, departmental headquarters, and field units; and they were the first to develop financial and statistical flows to control and evaluate the work of the many managers.

In all this they were the first because they had to be. No other business enterprise up to that time had had to govern a large number of men and offices scattered over wide geographical areas. Management of such enterprises had to have many salaried managers and had to be organized into functional departments and had to have a continuing flow of internal information if it was to operate at all.

Nevertheless, the innovations made by the early large intersectional roads in organization, accounting, and control went beyond mere necessity. The railroads could have operated well enough with only rudimentary organizational structures, without the line and staff distinction, without an internal auditing staff, and without the development of the more sophisticated financial, capital, and cost accounting procedures devised by McCallum, Thomson, and Fink. Indeed, many roads continued to operate for many years in an ad hoc informal way. Lines of authority and communication remained unclear, and operational and accounting information imprecise and unsystematically collated and analyzed. This was particularly true on the shorter roads, on those with relatively light traffic, and even on the larger and more traveled ones where senior managers paid little explicit attention to organizational matters. In fact, on some roads the quality of the management and the attention paid to internal organization regressed. A dramatic example was the Erie, when speculators, whose interests were to manipulate securities rather than to provide transportation, took control of the road.

By the 1880s, however, the innovations of the 1850s and 1860s had become standard operating procedures on all large American railroads. Expanding traffic and the growth and size of the roads forced the senior railroad managers to pay attention to their administrative and informational procedures. Moreover, as railroad managers became more professional, information about these methods became disseminated more systematically. By the 1870s organization and accounting were topics for discussion at formal meetings of railroad managers. They were reviewed in such periodicals as the *Railroad Gazette*, and the *Railroad Journal* and such books as Marshall Kirkman's *Railroad Revenue: A Treatise on the Organization of Railroads and the Collection of Railroad Receipts*.[62]

The innovations of the 1850s and 1860s, which became standard practice in the 1870s and 1880s, increased the efficiency and productivity of transportation provided by the individual routes. Improved organization and statistical accounting procedures permitted a more intensive use of available equipment and more speedy delivery of goods by providing a more effective continuous control over all the operations of the road. These innovations also made possible the fuller exploitation of a steadily improving technology which included larger and heavier engines, larger cars, heavier rails, more effective signals, automatic couplers, air brakes, and the like. These improvements permitted the roads to carry a much heavier volume of traffic at higher speeds.

The organizational innovations described in this chapter, however, affected only the productivity and performance of the individual railroads and not necessarily the railroad system as a whole. The creation of an efficient national overland transportation network required close cooperation between railroad companies so that traffic might move easily

62. Published in New York in 1879. Kirkman also published such books as *Railway Disbursement* (New York, 1877); *Railroad Revenue and Its Collection* (New York, 1877, revised 1887); and *Railroad Service: Trains and Services* (New York, 1878).

from one road to another. As the railroad network grew, as it became more interconnected, through traffic passing from one line to the next was increasingly important to the profits of the individual railroad companies. In the years after the Civil War, external relations were becoming as critical to the successful operation of the new large railroads as were the development of internal organization and controls before the war.

"Notes on the social saving controversy"

by Robert W. Fogel

The transportation revolution that occurred in the nineteenth century played a major role in American economic development. Improvements in roads, the construction of canals, and the development of steamboats all made the movement of people and goods more efficient. The most celebrated improvement of the century, however, was the railroad. Shipping by rail was fast, flexible, and inexpensive. By 1860, more than 30,000 miles of track linked all of the country's major cities. At century's end, over 200,000 mile of track crossed the country.

The noted economist Joseph Schumpeter emphasized the immense importance of railroads in causing modern economic growth. Walt Rostow (1960) supported this idea, arguing that the railroads "triggered" the American "take-off" into "self-sustained growth." Without a doubt, the railroad did have important consequences for the American economy. These include regional population growth, economic specialization and interdependence, the rise of mass markets, and the reduction of many products' prices. Such accomplishments prompted many historians to consider railroads indispensable to American economic growth.

Robert Fogel (1964) challenged this "axiom of indispensability" in *Railroads and American Economic Growth*. Another important work, *American Railroads and the Transformation of the Antebellum Economy*, by Albert Fishlow followed a year later and generally concurred with Fogel. These two books spawned a new round of debates on the importance of the railroad. "Notes on the Social Saving Controversy" is Fogel's attempt to describe the debate that ensued, rebut the criticisms, and raise additional questions.

In his investigation of the incremental contribution of railroads to economic growth, Fogel focuses on their "social savings." "The social savings of railroads in any given year" is "the difference between the actual cost of shipping goods in that year and the alternative cost of shipping exactly the same bundle of goods between exactly the same points without the railroad." Fogel's estimates of the social savings of railroads imply that railroads did not save nineteenth-century American society very much resources. The United States economy would not have been drastically smaller without them.

Fogel's calculation was considered suspect by many critics because the social savings rate was found to be so low and, more important, because he had posed such an enormous "counterfactual." Fogel did not only seek to retell history, he also asked what an alternative history would have been. This struck many historians as sacrilegious, but this sort of exercise is central to all economic analysis. Demand-and-supply analysis is implicitly counterfactual. The counterfactual approach is carried out every day when we ask questions about changes in current public policy. For example," "If we cut tax rates, what would be the new tax revenue?" "If we deregulated airlines, what would be the new market structure and prices?"

As Donald McCloskey noted (p. 18), the numerous assumptions, measurements, and calculations of the essay have been devoted to producing just one number. This parallels the efforts by Fogel and Engerman to measure relative slave efficiency with a single number. The calculations in this essay are simpler than they appear at first glance, requiring elementary algebra and geometry. Rudimentary tools of micro-economics are applied to complex issues. The debaters get considerable mileage out of concepts learned in an introductory economics course, such as elasticity of demand, cross-price elasticity, elasticity of substitution, and the shape of the marginal cost curve.

It is ironic that great energy is expended on measurement because, in the end, precision does not matter. Why will approximations of the "upper bound" suffice?

The debate about transportation flourished in the 1960s and 1970s. However, as many of the questions have been resolved, economic historians have now turned their attention to other questions.

Additional Reading

Paul David, "Transport Innovation and Economic Growth: Professor Fogel On and Off the Rails," *Economic History Review*, 22 (December 1969), 506–25.

Albert Fishlow, *Railroads and the Transformation of the Antebellum Economy*, Cambridge, MA: Harvard University Press, 1965.

Robert Fogel, *Railroads and American Economic Growth: Essays in Econometric History*, Baltimore: Johns Hopkins University Press, 1964.

Peter McClelland, "Social Rates of Return on American Railroads in the Nineteenth Century," *Economic History Review*, 25 (August 1972), 471–88.

Lloyd Mercer, "Building Ahead of Demand: Some Evidence for the Land Grant Railroads," *Journal of Economic History* 34 (June 1974), 492–500.

W. W. Rostow, *The Stages of Economic Growth: A Non-Communist Manifesto*, New York: Cambridge University Press, 1960.

11

Notes on the social saving controversy

ROBERT W. FOGEL

This paper explores a number of the unresolved issues posed by the debate on the social saving of railroads. The final section includes a brief summary of the main findings of the new economic history of transportation.

It is now more than 17 years since the first discussion of the social saving of railroads at a meeting of economic historians[1] and more than 16 years since the first publication of a paper dealing with this question.[2] The ensuing train of research has been substantial. Applications of the social saving approach and critiques of these applications have been set forth in at least a dozen books and in several score of journal articles and reviews. The debate, as Patrick O'Brien recently observed, has been both exciting and illuminating.[3] Because of the rich interaction between the

Source: Robert W. Fogel, "Notes on the Social Saving Controversy," *Journal of Economic History* (March 1979), 1–54. Reprinted with permission of the author and the Economic History Association.

The author is Professor of Economics and History at Harvard University, Since this paper is based on class lecture notes, his first debt is to students in more than a dozen classes whose insightful comments and criticisms shaped these notes. He also benefited from seminar discussions of earlier versions of this paper at the London School of Economics, Essex, Glasgow, Cornell, Westfälische Wilhelms-Universität, the Catholic University of Louvain, Washington (Seattle), Berkeley, Monash, Australian National University, the Kyoto Summer Seminar (Doshisha University), Stanford, Johns Hopkins, Northwestern, Uppsala, and Oslo. Robert Margo, Charles Kahn, Harry Holzer, Kenneth Sokoloff, and Georgia Villaflor provided insightful assistance during the final phases of the research. John Coatsworth. Stanley L. Engerman, David H. Fischer, Albert Fishlow, Roderick Floud, Ephim Fogel, David Galenson, Knick Harley, Gary Hawke, Bradley Lewis, Peter McClelland, Donald McCloskey, Jacob Metzer, Patrick O'Brien, and G. N. von Tunzelmann commented on drafts. Jeffrey G. Williamson provided data needed to replicate his simulations.

1. The discussion was held at the first annual Cliometrics Conference, Purdue University, December, 1960.
2. In this Journal, 22 (June 1962), 163–197.
3. Much of the social saving literature is cited in the bibliography to Patrick O'Brien, *The New Economic History of Railways* (London, 1977). To this listing one should add: John Coatsworth, "Growth Against Development: The Economic Impact of Railroads in Porfirian Mexico," mimeo 1976, which is a translation and revision of *Crecimento contra desarrollo: El impacto economico de los*

investigators and the critics, important aspects of the transportation revolution of the nineteenth century have been clarified.

In this paper I seek to explore a number of still unresolved issues that have been posed by the debate. The comments that follow are divided into four parts. The first part deals with the nature of the social saving model and the limits of its usefulness for historical analysis. The next part takes up an array of practical and conceptual issues that have been raised about the data and procedures actually employed by myself and other researchers in our various estimates of the social saving. The third part focuses on the difficulties of attempting to pass from a social saving calculation to warranted statements about the impact of railroads on the long-term pattern of a nation's economic growth. The final part includes a brief summary of the main findings of the new economic history of transportation and emphasizes that, in retrospect, the line of continuity between the newer and older research is stronger than it at first appeared.

ferrocarriles en el porfiriato, 2 vols., Sepsetentas No. 271–272 (Mexico City, 1976). Jeffrey G. Williamson, *Late Nineteenth-Century American Development: A General Equilibrium History* (Cambridge, 1974), especially ch. 9.; Jeffrey G. Williamson, "The Railroads and Midwestern Development, 1870–1890: A General Equilibrium History," in David C. Klingaman and Richard K. Vedder, *Essays in Nineteenth Century Economic History* (Athens, Ohio, 1975), ch. 11; G. N. von Tunzelmann, *Steam Power and British Industrialization to 1860* (Oxford, 1978), chs. 3, 6, and 11; Wray Vamplew, "Nihilistic Impressions of British Railway History," in Donald N. McCloskey, ed., *Essays on a Mature Economy: Britain after 1840* (Princeton, 1971), ch. 10; Jan de Vries, "Barges and Capitalism: Passenger Transportation in the Dutch Economy, 1632–1839," *A. A. G. Bijdragen*, 21 (1978), ch. 8; Donald N. McCloskey, "New Model History," *Times Literary Supplement*, December 12, 1975; Peter Temin, *Causal Factors in American Economic Growth in the Nineteenth Century* (London, 1975), ch. 5; C. H. Lee, *The Quantitative Approach to Economic History* (London, 1977), ch. 4; and Jon Elster, *Logic and Society: Contradictions and Possible Worlds* (Chichester, 1978), ch. 6. This supplement to O'Brien's list is far from exhaustive. In addition to other relevant works that are cited below, there are numerous interesting reviews and brief commentaries, especially in essays analyzing the methodology of the New Economic History. Some of these are listed in Peter D. McClelland, *Causal Explanation and Model Building in History, Economics, and the New Economic History* (Ithaca, 1975).

Social saving calculations did not originate with present-day economists and economic historians. Such calculations were carried out by legislators and men of affairs who were involved in the decision processes on government aid for internal improvements during the nineteenth century, not only in America, but also in Europe. Albert Fishlow cites two early social saving estimates in *American Railroads and the Transformation of the Antebellum Economy* (Cambridge, 1965). Richard H. Tilly called my attention to an essay by Ernst Engel (the Prussian statistician identified with "Engel's Law") which presents a calculation of the social saving attributable to German railroads during 1840–1880. Ernst Engel, "Das Zeitalter des Dampfes in technisch-statistischer Beleuchtung". *Zeitschrift des Königlichen Preussischen Statistischen Bureaus*, (Berlin, 1880). Richard Hodne in his *An Economic History of Norway 1815–1970* (Tapir, 1975), p. 221, cites a study of the social saving of railroads in Norway by E. O. J. Savanøe that appeared in *Statsøkonomisk Tidsskrift* in 1887.

The nature and limitations of the social saving model

I defined the social saving of railroads in any given year as the difference between the actual cost of shipping goods in that year and the alternative cost of shipping exactly the same bundle of goods between exactly the same points without the railroad. The second and third chapters of *Railroads and American Economic Growth* dealt with the estimation of this cost differential in the transportation of agricultural products for 1890. Because my formulation of the social saving model was verbal rather than algebraic, there has been some confusion regarding certain aspects of the model. The deficiency can be remedied by specifying a two-sector model in which the activities of one of the sectors, transportation, can be carried out under either of two production function.[4] Thus,

$$Q_A = a(L_a, K_a, Q_{Ta}) \tag{1}$$

$$Q_T = w(L_w, K_w) \tag{2}$$

$$Q_T = r(L_r, K_r). \tag{3}$$

(See Table 1 for the definitions of symbols.)

The r process is superior to w so that the fixed quantity of transportation, Q_T, can be produced under r with less labor and capital than under w. In other words,

$$L_w = L_r + \Delta L \tag{4}$$

$$K_w = K_r + \Delta K. \tag{5}$$

Now, national income under the r function is $Q_A + Q_{Tc}$ where Q_{Tc} (which equals $Q_T - Q_{Ta}$) is assumed fixed, as is Q_{Ta}. Substitution of the w for the r function, keeping Q_T constant, will require the transfer of ΔL and ΔK from the production of all other things. Then national income (Y) will be

$$Y = Q'_A + Q_{Tc}, \quad \text{where} \tag{6}$$

$$Q'_A = a(L_a - \Delta L, K_a - \Delta K, Q_{Ta}). \tag{7}$$

It follows that the social saving is also the loss in national income caused by the substitution of an inferior for a superior transportation technology (or the gain in going from the inferior to the superior technology), which is given by

$$(Q_A + Q_{Tc}) - (Q'_A + Q_{Tc}) = Q_A - Q'_A \approx \frac{\partial Q_A}{\partial L}\Delta L + \frac{\partial Q_A}{\partial K}\Delta K, \tag{8}$$

4. The model which follows differs from that presented in Robert W. Fogel and Stanley L. Engerman, eds., *The Reinterpretation of American Economic History* (New York, 1971), p. 101, by allowing part of the output of the transportation sector to be purchased for use in the production of other output.

Table 1. *Definitions of principal symbols in equations and diagrams*

Q_T = output of transportation
Q_{Ta} = the part of Q_T used to produce Q_a
$Q_{Tc} = Q_T - Q_{Ta}$ = transportation purchased as a final product
Q_A = output of the all-other-things sector
L = labor
K = capital
ΔL, ΔK = labor and capital shifted from the all-other-things sector
a = the all-other-things function and inputs into it
w = the inferior transportation function and inputs into it
r = the superior transportation function and inputs into it
Y = national income
P_A = price of Q_A in the terminal period (that is, with railroads)
D = intercept of the demand function for transportation
P = price of transportation
ϵ = elasticity of demand
S_t = social saving estimated on the true value of ϵ
S_o = social saving estimated on the assumption $\epsilon = 0$
P_w = price of transportation in a non-railroad world, if price = marginal cost
P_w' = price of transportation in a non-railroad world, if price > marginal cost
P_r = price of transportation in a railroad world
$\phi = P_w/P_r$
B = bias in the social saving caused by setting $\epsilon = 0$
i = social rate of return on the investment in railroads
_d = distance in (statute miles) or pence, depending on the context
R_w = steamboat rate per ton-mile on wheat on the upper Mississippi
MR = marginal revenue
MC = marginal cost
Q_r = output of transportation in a railroad world
Q_w = output of transportation in a non-railroad world, if price = marginal cost
Q_w' = output of transportation in a non-railroad world, if price > marginal cost
C_c = construction cost of a canal (book value in 1889)
C_o = annual operating cost of a canal in constant dollars
X_p = cross-section of a canal prism in square feet
X_l = length of a canal in statute miles
X_r = total rise and fall of a canal in feet
X_f = annual tonnage of freight carried by a canal
X_{tm} = annual ton-miles of freight on the New York canals
X_d = average distance of a haul on the New York canals during a year
X_{cw} = a dummy representing the Civil War years
Q_g = quantity of eastbound wheat, corn, and oats shipped by lake from Chicago, in tons
M = quantity of wheat, corn, and oats produced nationally (in tons); a market-size variable
R_r = Chicago to Buffalo rate on wheat by railroad, in constant dollars
R_w = Chicago to Buffalo rate on wheat by lake (including Buffalo elevating changes) in constant dollars
B_l = an index of the average size of grain-carrying lake vessels
N = annual length of the season of navigation
K_b = an index of the capital stock of grain-carrying lake vessels
Q_i = the output of an industry benefiting from railroad-induced economies of scale in year i
C_i = the cost of producing Q_i
P_j = a vector of the prices of the inputs used to produce Q_i
x = the scale coefficient (the sum of the output elasticities in the industry-wide production function) for an industry benefiting from railroad-induced economies of scale
$\hat{}$ = a "cap" over a variable designates the natural logarithm of that variable

and which may be expressed in value terms as

$$\left(\frac{\partial Q_A}{\partial L}\Delta L + \frac{\partial Q_A}{\partial K}\Delta K\right)P_A \approx (Q_A - Q'_A)P_A. \tag{9}$$

Interpretation of the model

Several points should be noted about this model. First, the model does not purport to be, and is not, a complete or literal description of either the American or any other late nineteenth-century economy. It is a model designed to set an upper bound on the resource saving brought about by an improvement in transportation technology. The model produces an upper bound by setting the elasticity of demand (ϵ) at zero and thereby fixing the volume of transportation at the level observed with the superior (cheaper) form of transportation. If the elasticity of demand is allowed to be greater than zero, the rise in the cost of transportation would reduce the quantity of transportation purchased and hence also reduce the diversion of resources from the all-other-things sector to the transportation sector (that is, it would reduce ΔL and ΔK).

Second, the increase in the cost of transportation is identically equal to the decrease in national income. This identity is brought about by the assumptions that the demand for transportation is perfectly inelastic, and that ΔL and ΔK come from resources previously employed in the production of Q_A rather than from previously unemployed resources.

Third, the model is not designed to deal with other important issues such as the effect of transportation improvements on the spatial location of economic activity, induced changes in the industrial mix of products within the all-other-things sector, induced changes in the aggregate savings rate, and possible effects on either the rate of technological change in various industries or on the overall supplies of inputs. In order to take up such issues the model would have to be expanded considerably. The elasticities of demand and supply in each sector would have to be specified and estimated, and the number of sectors would have to be increased to permit analysis of the effect of transport changes on the geographic location of production and the redistribution of inputs among industries. A savings function would have to be specified, estimated, and so on. These are worthy enterprises, but they are also difficult. So far, only Jeffrey G. Williamson and Bradley G. Lewis have responded to the challenge in a substantial way.[5]

5. The Williamson model is discussed in the third section of this paper. Lewis, in a dissertation under way at the University of Chicago, is investigating the effect of railroads on the location of economic activity and other consequences stemming from the impact of railroads on relative prices.

It should be clear, then, that the social saving is not a description of what actually happened but an answer to a hypothetical problem, a problem similar in nature to those that engineers must solve successfully to build bridges and to those that manufacturers must confront in choosing between alternative machine designs. This answer rests on a detailed examination of actual economic and technological characteristics of the alternative modes of transportation in historical context. The solution of the problem illuminates actual history not only because it provides a measure of the primary (cost-reducing or resource-saving) effect of railroads in the provision of a specified volume of transportation service, but also because it brings together a great deal of relevant information regarding actual experience and systematically assesses the implications of this information. To carry out his computation of the social saving of U.S. railroads in 1859, Albert Fishlow, for example, not only had to delve into the differential cost of transportation provided by railroads, waterways, and wagons for both passengers and freight but also had to determine how these differentials varied for specific categories of freight and passengers over a variety of routes and at different points in time. His analysis indicated that by 1859 railroad passenger transportation yielded direct benefits that were less than half of those yielded by the carrying of freight. Even more surprising and informative was his discovery that the great trunk lines accounted for just 8 percent of the social saving of railroads. Fishlow's analysis showed that the trunk lines were constructed along routes where waterways were rather good substitutes for railroads. It was in the interior of the country where wagons or coaches were often the most feasible substitutes that the social saving of railroads was greatest, accounting in Fishlow's calculation for nearly two thirds of the total.[6]

The social saving model defines the *r* function on the basis of the railroad technology at its most efficient aggregate level during the period under study, that is, by the aggregate technology prevailing at the end of the period. There is, however, no specification of how the *w* function should be defined. Fishlow defined the *w* function on the aggregate level of waterway and wagon technology actually in operation at the end of the period. In my book, I defined three plausible *w* functions and carried out social saving calculations for each. The first calculation was based on canals that had actually been constructed by 1890; the second allowed for an additional 5,000 miles of canals that very likely would have been constructed in the absence of railroads; the third adjusted the social saving for plausible improvements in wagon roads (such as surfacing).[7]

6. Albert Fishlow, *American Railroads*. p. 93.

7. Robert W. Fogel, *Railroads and American Economic Growth: Essays in Econometric History* (Baltimore, 1964). ch. 3.

It should be noted that these successive characterizations of the *w* function do not purport to represent actual shifts in that function over time but are merely a set of plausible alternative characterizations of the production function for transportation in the absence of railroads.

Which is the "right" specification of the *w* function? There is no single "right" specification, but rather a fairly large set of alternative specifications for which a social saving calculation can usefully be performed. The more detailed the set of specifications, the brighter the light that will be shed on the economic potential of alternatives to railroads, alternatives that were thwarted by the investment in railroads. These alternatives provide fine tuning on the magnitude of the incremental benefits of railroads as well as a means of decomposing the overall figure. Alternative specifications also permit the historian, with his advantage of hindsight, to be able to identify errors made by planners and investors in the past because certain of their assumptions regarding future technological or market developments turned out to be wrong. For example, the set of decisions that led to a 94 percent increase in the density of the U.S. railroad networks between 1890 and 1914 were based, to an extent that has yet to be evaluated, on a failure to take adequate account of the rate of improvement in motor vehicles. If the speed of advance in motor transportation had been known, some of the extensions of railroads would not have taken place. Economic historians can now engage in categories of project evaluation that the engineers and planners of the 1890s could not entertain. Historical hindsight makes it possible to determine which part of the increment to the railroad network after 1890 (or even before that date) should not have been built, as well as the extent to which the rate of improvement in common roads should have been accelerated.

Fishlow's calculation of the social saving was not made more realistic, as some have argued, by his assumption that in the absence of railroads waterways would have been limited to those actually in use in 1860. That is the least plausible of all possibilities. There can be little doubt that the relatively high prices of agricultural products in the North Atlantic states and in Europe would have made the extension of the canal system into the North Central states a highly profitable investment.[8] But given the high cost of investigating this possibility,

8. Cf. Fogel, *Railroads*, pp. 92–107. David has pointed out that the reduction in the β estimate of the social saving due to the extension by 5,000 miles of the canal system implies a social rate of return on the investment in excess of 50 percent per annum. Paul A. David, "Transportation Innovations and Economic Growth: Professor Fogel On and Off the Rails," *Economic History Review*, 2nd Ser., 22 (Dec. 1969), 506–525, rpt. as ch. 6 of Paul A. David, *Technical Choice, Innovation, and Economic Growth* (Cambridge, 1975), pp. 291–314.

and considering the other issues to which he gave priority, Fishlow's decision not to pursue this matter made sense. Although his assumption yielded, not a least upper bound for the social saving but a relatively high upper bound, such a bound was quite adequate for the analytical issues he set out to address. The choice as to how far one ought to pursue calculations of the social saving on plausible alternative characterizations of the w function depends not only on the quality of the available data and on the cost of the investigation, but also on the research priorities that an investigator assigns to the array of issues that might be pursued.

That the authors of the major studies of the social saving of railroads often struck out in widely different directions should cause neither surprise nor consternation. We are richer, not poorer, because Fishlow tested the Schumpeter hypothesis of construction ahead of demand, because Jacob Metzer investigated the impact of railroads on the national unification of the Russian grain market, because Gary R. Hawke probed so insightfully into railway pricing policy, and because John Coatsworth demonstrated the intimate connection between railroad construction and the concentration of land ownership in Mexico.

A technological definition of the social saving

One of the most interesting questions related to the social saving model was raised by Stanley Lebergott, who focused not on the w function but on the r function. Lebergott argued that the social saving calculation should not be based on the observed railroad rate at the end of the period under investigation, or even on that rate adjusted for monopoly profit, but on the rate that would have prevailed if the railroad system had operated at the minimum point of its long-run supply function.

Figure 1 depicts the long-run supply function suggested by Lebergott. The quantity of freight service supplied is measured by tons of freight carried per mile of railroad track. Lebergott's argument rests on the quite plausible assumption that the supply price dropped continuously with the intensity of track utilization, up to some point, and then rose. Although Lebergott did not know at what intensity of track utilization this minimum was reached, he suggested that for the antebellum era it could probably be represented by the data of the Philadelphia and Reading Rail road. During the 1850s this company hauled about 25,000 tons per mile of track per year. Lebergott estimated that at such intensities of road utilization the rate would be just 0.24 cents per ton-mile. This rate is less than one tenth the average rate that Fishlow

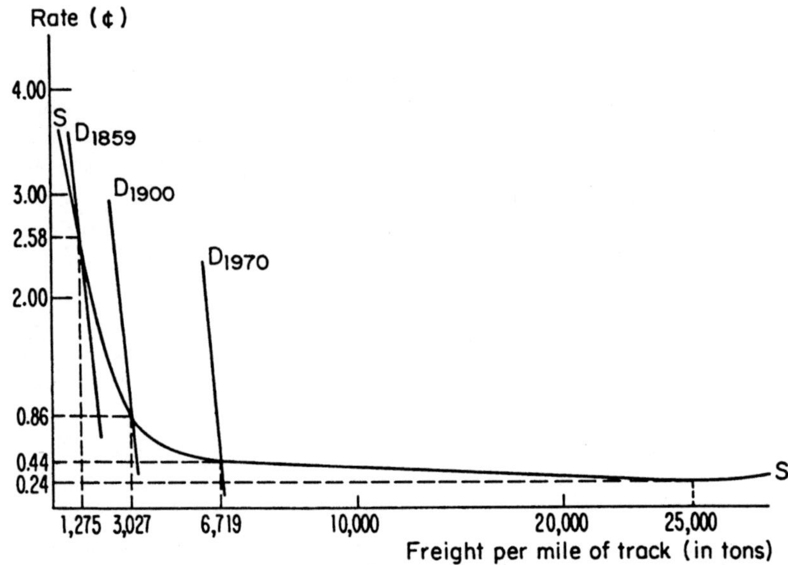

Figure 1. Technologically possible vs. economically attainable freight rates (rates in 1859 cents).

Source: U.S. Bureau of the Census, *Historical Statistics of the United States, Colonial Times to 1970* (Washington, D.C., 1975), pp. 199, 201, 728, 731, 733; Fishlow, *American Railroads*, p. 337; Lebergott, "United States Transportation," pp. 445, 453–454, 460; Poor, "History," pp. 484–485; Edwin Frickey, *Production in the United States, 1860–1914* (Cambridge, Mass., 1947), p. 100.

DISCUSSION

The *SS* curve is the long-run supply of railroad transportation, with the y-axis representing the rate per ton-mile and the *x*-axis representing the tons of freight transported per mile of track. The *SS* curve reaches a minimum at the price and intensity of track utilization that Lebergott suggested for the antebellum era. The curves designated as D_{1859}, D_{1900}, and D_{1970} represent the demand for transportation, measured in tons of freight transported per mile of track. The price and output points at which the D_i curves and the *SS* curve interesect represent the actual average rates and tonnages transported per mile of track in the designated years. The assumption that the observed points all lie on the SS curve implies not only that these were years of long-run equilibrium but that increases in locomotive power, car capacity, and rail capacity did not shift the *SS* curve from its antebellum position, and particularly that the minimum point of this curve was not shifted downward and outward (cf. footnote 10). Under these assumptions it is clear that the demand for transportation, from the inception of railroads down to the present, has fallen far short of the level required to realize this antebellum potential.

estimated was actually charged by railroads in 1859.[9] Lebergott thus appears to suggest that Fishlow and others who used actual end-period railroad prices have grossly underestimated the social saving.

Lebergott's approach demonstrates that railroad systems in 1859 operated at a level that was very far from the minimum cost that was *technologically* feasible. Of course, a level of operation that is technologically feasible is not necessarily *economically* feasible. Whether or not the railroad system as a whole could have achieved an average freight rate as low as that achieved by the Philadelphia and Reading Railroad depends on the nature of the demand for railroad services, both on the Philadelphia and Reading and on the system as a whole. Figure 1 indicates the systemwide average number of tons carried per mile of track per year during 1859, 1900, and 1970, which were 1,275, 3,027 and 6,719, respectively. Quite clearly the system never came close to the intensity of track utilization achieved by the Philadelphia and Reading during the 1840s and 1850s. In other words, the technological condition for Lebergott's longterm minimum cost was never economically feasible for the railroad system as a whole.[10] Indeed, that technological minimum could have been achieved for the system only if all markets (or virtually all markets) demanded railroad service for the sole purpose (or virtually the sole purpose) of carrying a steady flow of minerals and ore in unit trains between fixed points.[11] In reality most markets sent commodities of a highly varied nature to a large number of locations; most trains were made up of cars bound for a wide variety of points; and there were sharp daily, weekly, monthly, and seasonal variations in volume. Consequently, unit trains, and the low costs attendant upon them, were not

9. Stanley Lebergott, "United States Transportation Advance and Externalities," this Journal 26 (Dec. 1966), 443, 445. Lebergott puts the ton-miles of freight carried per dollar of cost at 413; the reciprocal yields a rate of 0.24 cents per ton-mile. Over the period from 1852 to 1857, the freight carried by the Philadelphia and Reading averaged 25,226 tons per mile of road per a annum. Henry V. Poor, *History of the Railroads and Canals of the United States of America* (New York, 1860), pp. 484–485. Fishlow, *American Railroads*, p. 337, put the average railroad freight rate in 1859 at 2.58 cents per ton-mile.

10. I have located the price and output points for 1859, 1900, and 1970 on the same curve. This, of course, stretches the argument very much in Lebergott's direction since it implies that all of the decrease in railroad rates was due to a movement along a fixed long-run supply curve, allowing naught to downward shifts in the supply curve. However, Fishlow has shown that at least 50 percent of the increase in total factor productivity between 1830 and 1910 can be attributed to various technological improvements in rails, cars, locomotives, and other equipment. Cf. Albert Fishlow, "Productivity and Technological Change in the Railroad Sector," in Conference on Research in Income and Wealth, *Output Employment and Productivity in the United States After 1800*, Vol. 30 of Studies in Income and Wealth (New York, 1966), pp. 583–646.

11. Coal accounted for about three quarters of the total freight hauled by the Philadelphia and Reading Railroad during 1852–1857. Poor, *History*, p. 485.

economically feasible for the system as a whole and so are not relevant to a measurement of the economically feasible social saving.

Bias due to the assumption that $\epsilon = 0$

J. Hayden Boyd and Gary M. Walton have questioned the advisability of computing the social saving on the assumption that the demand for transportation was completely inelastic. They believe that at least for pasenger transportation enough is known about the elasticity of demand to transform the passenger social saving from an upper bound estimate to a reasonably accurate one. Their survey of econometric estimates of the demand elasticity for passenger transportation during the post–World War II era led them to conclude that $\epsilon = 1$ was the most reasonable estimate.[12] My aim here is not to pin down the passenger and freight elasticities with precision but rather to consider the plausible range on the upward bias that might have been introduced into some of the social saving estimates because of the assumption that $\epsilon = 0$.

If the demand for transportation is described by a long-linear function of the form

$$Q = DP^{-\epsilon}, \tag{10}$$

the ratio of the "true" social saving (S_t) to the social saving computed on the assumption that $\epsilon = 0$ is given by

$$\frac{S_t}{S_0} = \frac{\phi^{1-\epsilon} - 1}{(1 - \epsilon)(\phi - 1)} \quad \text{(for } \epsilon \neq 1) \tag{11}$$

and

$$\frac{S_t}{S_0} = \frac{\ln \phi}{\phi - 1} \quad \text{(for } \epsilon = 1), \tag{12}$$

where ϕ is the ratio P_w/P_r. Alternatively, the bias (B) caused by setting ϵ at 0, expressed as a percentage of the "true" social savings, is:

$$B = \left[\frac{(1 - \epsilon)(\phi - 1)}{\phi^{1-\epsilon} - 1} - 1\right]100 \quad \text{(for } \epsilon \neq 1) \tag{13}$$

$$B = \left(\frac{\phi - 1}{\ln \phi} - 1\right)100 \quad \text{(for } \epsilon = 1). \tag{14}$$

It follows from equations (11) through (14) that the magnitude of the bias depends not only on the elasticity of demand but also on the proportional increase in the transportation rate [that is, ϕ and $(\phi - 1)$] caused by the absence of the railroad.

12. J. Hayden Boyd and Gary M. Walton, "The Social Saving from Nineteenth-Century Rail Passenger Services," *Explorations in Economic History*, 9 (Spring 1972), 247–248, 253–254.

Table 2. *Estimates of the potential upward bias (B) in the social saving estimates of Fogel, Fishlow, and Hawke as a function of ϵ (bias in percent)*

	1 Fogel's Agricultural Social Saving	2 Fishlow's Freight Social Saving	3 Hawke's Freight Social Saving	4 Fishlow's Passenger Social Saving	5 Hawke's Passenger Social Saving with an Infinite Elasticity of Demand for Comfort	6 Hawke's Passenger Social Saving with a Zero Elasticity of Demand for Comfort
$\epsilon \backslash \quad \phi$	1.87	3.33	2.64	2.52	2.39	4.82
0.0	0	0	0	0	0	0
0.4	15	32	24	23	21	46
0.75	28	66	49	46	43	98
1.0	39	94	69	64	60	143
1.5	62	158	113	105	97	251
2.0	87	233	164	152	139	382

Note: The entries for B are computed from equations (13) and (14) in the text. The sources of the data from which the values of ϕ were calculated are: Col. 1, Fogel, *Railroads*, pp. 42, 47, 84–87, 110; Table 3. Cols. 2 and 4, Fishlow, *American Railroads*, pp. 93, 337; cols. 3, 5, and 6, Hawke, *Railways*, pp. 48, 88, 141, and 188. It will be noticed that holding ϵ constant, the greater the value of ϕ, the larger the upward bias in the estimated social saving.

Table 2 shows that even with a quite inelastic demand curve for freight and passenger transportation ($\epsilon = 0.4$), calculations based on the assumption of zero elasticity may bias the social saving estimates upward by as much as 46 percent. If the appropriate estimate of ϵ is as much as one, which seems likely for passenger transportation, the upward bias would range up to 143 percent. Another point worth noting about Table 2 is that the potential upward biases vary quite widely from estimate to estimate. For this reason casual comparisons of different social saving estimates may be quite misleading. Fishlow argued that he could project safely his 1859 social saving to 1890 by using the ratio of railroad receipts in the two years as a blow-up factor. As I have pointed out elsewhere, this is a frail procedure and cannot be a substitute for detailed and considered calculations of the type that Fishlow constructed for the antebellum U.S., Hawke for England, Coatsworth for Mexico, and Metzer for Russia. Other, more plausible but equally frail, blow-up procedures yield projections less than a third of that computed by Fishlow.[13] Table 2 suggests still another reason for caution. If the elasticities of demand for freight and passengers are 0.4 and 1.0

13. Fogel, *Railroads*, pp. 219–234: Robert W. Fogel, "Railroads as an Analogy to the Space Effort," *Economic Journal*, 76 (Mar. 1966), 16–43.

respectively, Fishlow's estimated social saving in 1859 is, for this reason alone, too high by 39 percent.

So it seems to me that Boyd and Walton were right in urging that we go beyond calculations based on the assumption that $\epsilon = 0$. It is time to move from guesses about the relevant elasticities to estimation of them. Toward that end, a number of regression estimates of demand, supply, and cost curves are presented later in this paper. Although based on the limited data available in published sources, these regressions do suggest that much progress can be made toward producing reasonably tight estimates of critical parameters, especially if the abundant data in government and private archives are used.

Relationship between the social saving and the social rate of return

Marc Nerlove and Fishlow have questioned the relevance of the social saving (whether calculated absolutely or as a percentage of GNP) as a measure of the impact of railroads on the economy's capacity to produce, even when the analysis is limited only to the resource-saving effect of railroads. They argue that the social rate of return on the capital invested in railroads is more appropriate.[14] Although the social rate of return is a very useful measure for certain purposes, it does not supersede either the absolute or relative social saving measures. This can be shown by letting

$$i = f(K) \tag{15}$$

be the function that relates the marginal social rate of return to the quantity of capital invested in railroads. Then the gain in national income can be represented by

$$\Delta Y = \int_0^{K_0} f(K)dK - i_0 K_0, \tag{16}$$

where K_0 is the stock of capital invested in railroads at the relevant time period and i_0 is the social rate of interest, which here, in order to simplify the expositions, is assumed to be independent of the investment in railroads.[15] Nerlove's position assumes that, when comparing any two projects, if

$$g(K_j) > f(K_0), \tag{17}$$

14. Marc Nerlove, "Railroads and American Economic Growth," this Journal, 26 (Mar. 1966), 11–15; Fishlow, *American Railroads*, pp. 52–54.

15. If the social rate of interest was a function of the level of investment in railroads, equation (16) would become

$$\Delta Y = \int_0^{K_0} f(K)dk - \int_0^{K_0} h(K)dk,$$

where $h(K)$ is the function for the social rate of interest.

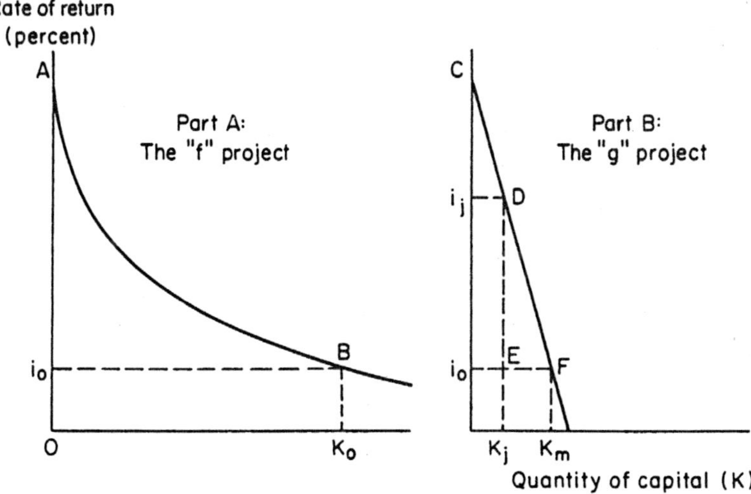

Figure 2. The relationship between the social saving and the social rate of return.

DISCUSSION

The rate of return on railroads in 1890 is represented by the "f" project. Here the investment in railroads (K_0) has expanded to the point where the marginal social rate of return on railroad capital (i_0) is equal to the social rate of return. The "g" project is new, with only K_j capital invested so far. Consequently, the marginal rate of return i_j is well above i_0. The social saving from the investment in "g" is given by the areas $CDEi_0$. This area is considerably samller than the areas ABi_0, which represents the social saving of railroads. As the "g" project matures, the capital invested in it will increase to K_m. Then the marginal rates of return on the two projects will be equal and the social saving on the "g" project will be represented by the area CFi_0, which is smaller than the social saving of the "f" project.

then the g project must have made a greater contribution to national income than the f project. But this need not be true. Even when (17) holds, it is also possible for

$$\int_0^{K_0} f(K)dK > \int_0^{K_j} g(K)dK \tag{18}$$

to hold (see Figure 2). Relationship (17) implies that if another dollar were to be invested, it would earn a higher return in g than f. It carries no implication as to which project contributed more to national income over the entire range of the investment in each project. To answer the question one needs relation (18).

Equation (16) is, of course, the social saving. Consequently, it is not the marginal social rate of return, which is merely a point on $f(K)$, but the area under $f(K)$ up to i_0K_0, or up to $h(K)$ (see note 15), that measures the resource saving effected by the cumulated investment in railroads.[16]

Problems of measurement

The preceding discussion indicated that social saving computations based on the assumption that $\epsilon = 0$ are inherently upward biased. Nevertheless, it is possible that the execution of a computation will be based on data so defective and on statistical procedures so ill suited to the task that the inherent upward bias will be overwhelmed and the resulting computation will seriously underestimate the resource saving of railroads. This is, in fact, the argument of various critics. They hold that the railroad rates employed in the several computations have been too high, that the water and wagon rates have been too low, and that major components of the social saving have been omitted altogether because of such conceptional errors in the design of the computation as the failure to take account of economies of scale in the all-other-things sector. The balance of the second part presents evidence relevant to the assessment of these contentions.

The representativeness of the water rates

Perhaps the most widespread criticism of the various social saving computations is that the water rates employed were unrepresentative and far too low. Peter McClelland and Harry Scheiber have focused on the water rates employed in my calculation of the interregional social saving, contending that my use of grain rates on the Chicago to New York route biased that estimate sharply downward. McClelland based his criticism on the fact that the New York-to-Chicago rate was much lower than either the Buffalo-to-New York rate, which he placed at 0.35 cents per ton-mile, or the St. Louis-to-New Orleans rate, which he placed at either 0.27 or 0.19 cents per ton-mile, depending on whether one employed the "less-than-carload" or the "bulk" rate. Scheiber's criticism was based on the average rate prevailing on Ohio canals during the late antebellum years, which he put at 1.4 cents per ton-mile.[17]

The rates cited by McClelland and Scheiber were for distances substantially shorter than the average distance of an interregional haul in the non-railroad case. This fact is of critical importance because both

16. Quite similar points were made by David, "Transportation Innovations," p. 521, and by G. R. Hawke, *Railways and Economic Growth in England and Wales 1840–1870* (Oxford, 1970), pp. 10–12.

17. Peter McClelland, "Railroads, American Growth and the New Economic History," this Journal, 28 (Mar. 1968), 106; Harry N. Scheiber, "On the New Economic History – and Its Limitations," *Agricultural History*, 41 (Oct. 1967), 387.

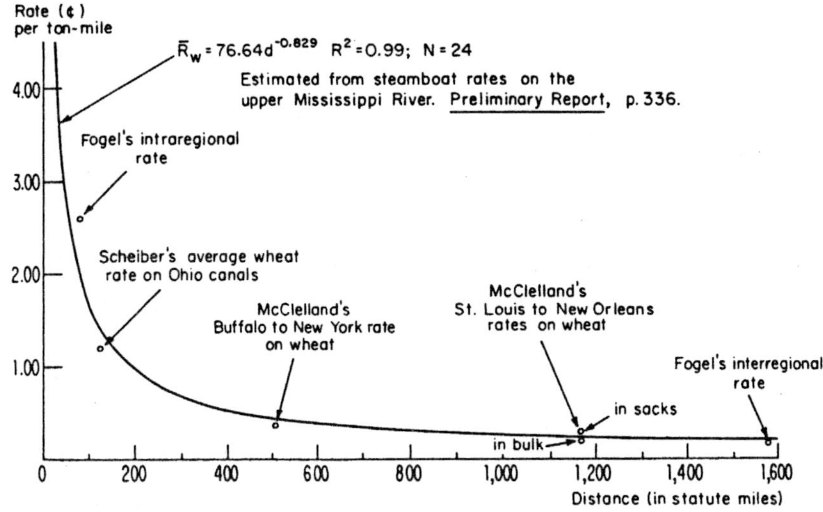

Figure 3. The relationship between water rates and distance.
Sources: Fogel, *Railroads*, pp. 38, 77; McClelland, "Railroads," p. 106. Scheiber, "On the New Economic History," p. 387. Scheiber did not give the average distance of a wheat haul over Ohio canals in the 1850s. But data compiled by Roger Ransom ["Government Investment in Canals: A Study of the Ohio Canal, 1825–1860," (unpublished Ph.D. thesis, University of Washington, 1963), pp. 123–128] for 1849–1850, 1851, and 1854–1856 indicate that the average length of a haul on wheat and corn varied between 90 and 148 miles. Scheiber (p. 394) put the average haul on all commodities carried on Ohio canals at 150 miles.

water and rail rates were negatively correlated with distance. Figure 3 presents a regression relating distances and rates estimated from rates prevailing on the upper Mississippi. Superimposed on this diagram are my rates for both the interregional and intraregional shipments, the three rates cited by McClelland, and Scheiber's rate for Ohio canals. Note that these rates cluster rather tightly around the regression curve. Note also that the average rate employed in my intraregional computation was 18 times larger than the one employed for the interregional computation and far higher than the rates McClelland and Scheiber cited. My average intraregional rate was high because the average distance of an intraregional haul was short (just 81 miles in the North Atlantic region), but the average length of an interregional haul was 1,574 miles. What is needed for the computation of the interregional social saving is a rate appropriate to that long distance rather than the rates for the shorter distances cited by McClelland and Scheiber.

If I had substituted the "carload" water and rail rates between St. Louis and New Orleans for rates that I actually employed, the interregional social saving would have changed only slightly.[18] This is because railroad rates per ton-mile over the St. Louis-to-New Orleans route were also higher than those on the Chicago-to-New York route. As I pointed out in my book, it is the difference between the water and rail rates that counts.[19]

When he turned to my intraregional computation, McClelland dropped the suggestion that the Buffalo-to-New York or St. Louis-to-New Orleans rates were more appropriate than the ones I employed. Although he made no statement about the direction of bias, he contended that my intraregional water rates were unrepresentative because they were based on regressions that covered only 12 of 29 commodities. Yet as I pointed out in *Railroads*, pp. 70–71, "These 12 commodities represented 77 percent of the tonnage shipped from counties." Moreover, "The rates on the remaining items were made proportional to some [comparable] commodity for which a regression equation existed. The proportions were calculated from a scattering of water tariffs that contained both a rate on the commodity in question and on the commodity for which the regression equation existed." Even if one assumes an improbably large downward bias in the rates calculated from proportions (and there is no reason to suspect a systematic bias), the small share of these commodities in the total originated tonnage as well as the small share of water costs in the total of intraregional shipping charges would make the estimate of the intraregional social saving insensitive to such errors. Thus, if there were a 50 percent downward error in these water rates, the correction would increase the first approximation of the intraregional social saving by only 3.5 percent – that is, it would raise the first approximation from 2.5 to 2.6 percent of GNP.

Both McClelland and Paul A. David present still another reason for believing that the water rates were biased downward. They contend that government subsidies for the construction of canals and for the improvement of natural waterways were overlooked. However, I allowed an annual rental charge of $18 million for uncompensated capital costs.[20]

18. Only the third digit is changed. The interregional social saving would have risen from 0.61 to 0.64 percent of GNP and the overall social saving on agricultural products would have been raised from 1.78 to 1.81 percent of GNP. "Less-than-carload" rates are irrelevant since virtually all interregional shipments went at "carload" rates.

19. The railroad rate from St. Louis to New Orleans was 0.572 cents per ton-mile. This is based on a railroad rate of 20 cents per hundred pounds and a rail distance of 699 miles. See U.S. Inland Waterways Commission, *Preliminary Report of the Inland Waterways Commission*, U.S. Senate, Doc. 325, 60th Cong., 1st Sess. (1908), pp. 344–345 (hereinafter referred to as *Preliminary Report*): U.S. Pay Department (War Department). *Official Table of Distances* (Washington, D.C., 1906), p. 427.

20. McClelland, "Railroads," pp. 111–113; David, "Transportation Innovation," p. 513; Fogel, *Railroads*, pp. 46–47, 87–88.

Lebergott recognized that the calculation included such an adjustment but held that it was not large enough. To demonstrate his point he multiplied the cumulated construction costs of the New York State canals to 1882 by 0.06 and divided the product by the ton-miles of transportation provided by that system in 1882. The resulting figure is 0.53 cents per ton-mile, which he compared to a figure implicit in my computation of 0.07 cents per ton-mile.[21] There are several difficulties with Lebergott's calculation. One is that it rests on the incorrect assumption that all capital costs of canals were uncompensated.[22] More important is the absence of an adjustment for the fact that over 90 percent of water-borne freight service in 1890 took place on the Great Lakes, the coastal routes, and the western rivers where uncompensated capital charges per ton-mile were far less than they were on such artificial waterways as the New York State canals. If all federal expenditures on rivers and harbors between 1822 and 1890 are attributed exclusively to vessels engaged in the coastal and inland trade, the annual charge for uncompensated capital employed with waterborne freight,

21. Lebergott, "United States Transportation," p. 440.

22. In 1889 state and private canals had net earnings equal to 1.3 percent of the cost of construction (at book value). U.S. Bureau of the Census, *Eleventh Census of the United States: 1890, Report on Transportation Business in the United States*, Vol. 14, Part II, pp. 475, 480 (hereinafter referred to as *Census of Transportation 1890*).

Discounting the stream of annual expenditures on construction and operation, as well as the annual net earnings of the New York canals at 6 percent, it appears that over 90 percent of the capital cost had been paid by 1882. The computation is based on data in New York State, *Annual Financial Report of the Auditor of the Canal Department: 1884*, "Statement of Receipts and Payments in Each Year on Account of All the State Canals." Revenues were obtained by adding "Tolls" and "Rent on Surplus Water." The annual sum of capital and operating costs was estimated by adding the following annual payments: "Canal Commissioners and Superintendent of Public Works," "Repairs of Canals," "Expenses of Collectors and Inspectors," "Weighmasters," and 70 percent of "Miscellaneous Expenses." It was estimated that approximately 30 percent of 'Miscellaneous Expenses" was unrelated to the operation of the canals. This procedure of obtaining the combined capital and operating expenditures was adopted because direct information on annual capital expenditures was not available before 1875, but the cumulated sum of capital expenditures for the period 1817–1874 is available, as are the annual construction costs for 1875–1892 (see New York State, *Annual Report of the State Engineer and Surveyor: 1893*, pp. 47–57). Of course if "Miscellaneous Expenditures" had been disaggregated, the desired annual combined cost series would have been directly available. It was possible to test the assumption that 70 percent of "Miscellaneous Expenditures" was canal costs. If the annual operating costs in the *Annual Financial Report* (p. 63) are subtracted from the total costs computed from "Statement of Receipts," one obtains a series of estimated annual construction costs. The cumulated sum of this estimated series for the period 1817–1874 comes to within 1.06 percent of matching the cumulated sum of actual construction costs for the same period reported in the *Annual Report of the State Engineer*. For the period 1875–1882, when both annual construction and operating costs are directly available, the indirect procedure yields annual totals that are within 4.0 percent of the actual annual totals of operating and construction costs.

outside of canals, is just 0.02 cents per ton-mile. Consequently, even if one were to accept Lebergott's figure for canals, uncompensated capital costs over the entire waterway system would average less than 0.04 cents per ton-mile. This figure is still too high since in the absence of railroads water-borne freight service would have increased greatly, and it is likely that most of the increase would have come on the Great Lakes, the western rivers, and the coastal routes.[23]

The foregoing comments indicate that further research into water and rail costs in 1890 and in other years is warranted not merely because it would provide a tighter estimate of the social saving but because it would deepen our knowledge of the performance characteristics of alternative transportation systems over a wide range of technological improvements, products, geography, and other economic circumstances. Work on these issues to date should be considered only a start in the right direction.

Demonstration that the water rates employed in the social saving calculation were reasonably representative of the water rates actually prevailing in 1890, or at the end of whatever period might be relevant, does not rule out the possibility that these rates introduced an upward bias into the social saving calculation. One must still deal with the question of what the water rates would have been in the absence of railroads. I assumed that the long-run cost curve of water transportation was either constant or, more likely, declining.[24] The same assumption was made by some but not all of the others who computed a social saving. No elaborate econometric justification for the assumption of a fall in water rates with the size of vessels and canals seemed needed since that assumption is embedded deeply in the engineering and transportation literature of the nineteenth and twentieth centuries and buttressed by much evidence for both the United States and Europe.[25] I argued

23. Cumulated federal expenditures on rivers and harbors during 1822–1890 were $180.4 million. Ton-miles of transportation in 1889 were 1.4 billion by canal and 48.3 billion by all other domestic contiguous waterways. See Appendix, Section A, for a discussion of the method of computing ton-miles of water transportation and the average water haul. Harold Barger, *The Transportation Industries 1889–1946* (New York, 1951), pp. 254–255; *Census of Transportation 1890*, Part II, pp. xi–xiii, and *passim*; U.S. Bureau of the Census, *Historical Statistics of the United States, Colonial Times to 1970* (Washington, D.C., 1975), p. 765 (hereinafter referred to as *Historical Statistics*); New York State, Committee on Canals, *Report of the Committee on the New York Canals, 1899–1900*, pp. 181–184 (hereinafter referred to as *New York Canals*); George G. Tunnell, "Statistics of Lake Commerce," U.S. House of Representatives, Doc. No. 277, 55th Cong. 2d Sess., *passim*.

24. By "long-run" I mean that capital is fully variable, so that the size of canal locks, prisms, and vessels on all the relevant waterways (actual or potential) could be increased as warranted by the increased traffic.

25. This evidence is discussed below.

that in the American case the long-run cost curve appeared to be downward sloping, so that the use of observed 1890 water rates, after including an adjustment for state subsidization of water transportation, would bias the computed social saving upward.

This proposition has been challenged by Lebergott, McClelland, David, Meghnad Desai, Donald Wellington, Colin M. White, and G. N. von Tunzelmann.[26] They have raised two principal objections to the use of observed water rates in 1890 or, more generally, at the end of the period under study. One rests on the assumption that canal transportation was inherently monopolistic and that the competition of railroads was necessary to prevent water rates from being raised to monopolistic levels. Hence it is argued that even if the long-run cost curve were constant or declining, monopolistic practices would have led to a rise in water rates in the absence of railroads.[27] The second objection is to the proporsition that the long-run marginal cost curve of water transportation was downward sloping. A variety of arguments, mainly of an *a priori* nature, have been set forth to support the counter proposition that the long-run marginal cost curve was rising.

The effect of monopoly pricing by waterways

McClelland and the others who have raised the monopoly issue have not confined themselves to the question of the direction of the effect, but have also suggested that the magnitude is so large as to render the social saving computation worthless. Yet it can be shown that even if the conjecture about the direction of the bias were correct, the magnitude would be moderate, at least in the American case. This is because canals would have provided only a relatively small fraction of the transportation service required in the absence of railroads. The point is illustrated by Table 3, which shows the approximate distribution of the payments required to move agricultural products from farms to secondary markets on the assumptions that $\epsilon = 0$ and canals charged long-run marginal costs. Suppose that in the absence of railroads, canal owners doubled the charge for using canals. Then, if we continue to assume that $\epsilon = 0$, which is the assumption that maximizes the impact of the monopolistic practice, the extra cost of shipping would be $39 million (see Table 3), which if added to my estimate of the social saving before adjustment for

26. Meghnad Desai, "Some Issues in Econometric History," *Economic History Review*, 2nd Ser., 21 (1968), 1–16; Donald Wellington, "The Case of the Superfluous Railroads," *Economic and Business Bulletin*, 22 (Fall 1969), 33–38; Colin M. White, "The Concept of the Social Saving in Theory and Practice," *Economic History Review*, 2nd Ser., 24 (1976), 82–100.

27. Much of the discussion has failed to distinguish between the equity and efficiency effects of monopoly pricing. As will be shown below, to the extent that canals used monopoly power to set rates above marginal costs, the increased revenue was mainly an income transfer.

Table 3. *Approximate cost of moving agricultural products from the farms to the secondary markets of the U.S. in the non-railroad case, assuming that canals charged long-run marginal cost, that $\epsilon = 0$, and allowing no extension of canals or improvement of common roads*

Category of Service	1 *Ton-miles of Service (millions)*	2 *Rate (dollars)*	3 *Cost of Service (million dollars) (Col. 1 × Col. 2)*	4 *Percentage Distribution of Total Cost among Services*
1. Wagons	3,107	0.165	513	65
2. Canals	3,505	0.011	39	5
3. Other waterways	26,805	0.0050	134	17
4. Waterway-associated services (insurance, transshipping, storage)			107	13
5. Totals	33,417		793	100

Notes: Column 1, line 1: Approximately 36.8 million tons shipped an average of 62.7 miles to waterways. An additional 23.5 million tons shipped an average of about 28 miles from farms to local purchasers. An additional 142 million ton-miles were allowed for the wagon portion of shipments going by waterways to secondary markets. Fogel, *Railroads*, pp. 42, 46, 76, 86, 87; cf. Winifred Rothenberg, "The Marketing Perimeters of Massachusetts Farmers, 1750–1855" (mimeo, Brandeis University, 1978). Line 2: Approximately 10 percent of intraregional railroad shipments sent an average of 150 miles; approximately 75 percent of interregional shipments sent an average of 250 miles. Fogel, *Railroads*, 42. 84–87. Line 3: Approximately 90 percent of intraregional rail shipments sent an average of 150 miles; approximately 75 percent of interregional shipments sent an average of 1324 miles; approximately 25 percent of interregional shipments sent an average of 1574 miles; *ibid.*

Column 2, line 1: Fogel, *Railroads*, pp. 84, 86. Lines 2 and 3: Average interregional rate (Fogel, *Railroads*, p. 42), adjusted to consider distances indicated in notes to column 1, lines 2 and 3, and weighted by corresponding ton-miles. U.S. Inland Waterways Commission *Preliminary Report*, U.S. Sentate, Doc. 325, 60th Cong. 1st Sess., 1908, p. 336. Allowance for neglected capital costs (Fogel, *Railroads*, p. 47) distributed according to ton-miles.

Column 3, line 4. Fogel, *Railroads*, pp. 47, 92.

limited technological adaptation would raise that estimate from 3.4 to 3.7 percent of GNP. Even if warranted, this correction is not so large that it alters the basic analysis of the resource-saving effect of railroads.[28]

28. In this connection it should be noted that my estimate of the effect of an extension of the canal system on the social saving (cf. Fogel. *Railroads*, pp. 94–98) is also robust with respect to a plausible range of error in the estimate of construction costs. Assuming that the combined annual interest and depreciation rates were 0.07, the annual rental cost of the canal extensions would be $11.3 million. Consequently, if construction costs were twice that indicated by the regression, my estimate of the agricultural social saving would rise from 1.8 to 1.9 percent of GNP.

The same point holds with respect to the argument that some of the rivers designated as navigable by the Army Engineers were too shallow to handle the volume of traffic that would have been diverted to these waterways in the absence of railroads. Such a contingency could have been handled by canalizing these rivers or building parallel canals along the necessary portions of the rivers in question. If we suppose that the increased traffic would have required

This correction is not warranted, however, and should not be made. Contrary to the assumptions of those who raised the monopoly issue, monopoly in water transportation implies that there was an upward rather than a downward bias in the estimated social saving. Two points are involved here: one historical, the other analytical. The historical issue bears on the way in which the monopoly would have been exercised. Lebergott, McClelland, and the others assumed that monopoly power would have been exercised to raise water rates. This is quite a reasonable assumption for the English case where most canals were privately owned and where there is considerable evidence that canal tolls charged before the coming of the railroad were in excess of marginal costs. For this reason Hawke, after an examination of the pre-railroad pricing policy of canals, assumed that monopoly power was used to inflate tolls on average by 150 percent. In addition to the toll, there was a payment to the owners of the boats that carried the freight. Both in England and the United States the boat owners were numerous and operated competitively.[29] Taking both the toll and the boat charge into account, Hawke estimated that in the absence of railroads the canal shipping rate would have increased by approximately one third.[30]

The American case is entirely different. More than 80 percent of the tonnage shipped via canal in 1890 was borne on canals owned not by private firms but by state governments or the federal government.[31] These governments used their monopoly power to lower tolls below marginal costs rather than to raise them above marginal costs.[32] The

parallel canals along 5,000 miles of such rivers (this is considerably greater than the mileage of the navigable rivers thus far contested), the additional construction costs would once again raise the social saving by just one tenth of 1 percent of GNP. Cf. Gilbert Fite, review in *Agricultural History*, 40 (Apr. 1966), 147–149; John A. Shaw, "Railroads, Irrigation, and Economic Growth: The San Joaquin Valley of California," *Explorations in Economic History*, 24 (Winter 1973), 211–227.

29. *New York State, Annual Finanical Report of the Comptroller, Relating to Canals: 1884* Assembly, Vol. 1, No. 4, p. 17, commented on the devastating effects of the business cycle recession that began in 1882 on canal operators. Their difficulties, the report said, were due to their failure to combine and act monopolistically:

> On the 1st of January, 1883, there were 4,749 boats of all classes registered as navigating the State canals. . . . If the canals with their equipments were owned by a corporation, or even if the equipments only were under one management, they would represent a single harmonious system competing with the railways in the transportation of freight. As they are now operated and managed, the equipments are furnished by almost as many individual owners as there are boats, and representing as many conflicting interests. These owners are without organization. . . .

30. Hawke, *Railways*, pp. 80–86.
31. *Census of Transportation 1890*, Part II, pp. 469–479; cf. *Preliminary Report* (1908), pp. 188–209.
32. As pointed out in footnote 22, state and private canals reported combined net earnings in 1889 that amounted to just 1.3 percent of their cost of construction. *Census of Transportation 1890*,

policy of subsidizing canal transportation was not due to the competitive pressure of the railroads but to political pressure put on government officials by the users of transportation. Roger Ransom, who studied the Ohio Canal, estimated that even in the 1830s and 1840s, before railroad competition became significant in that state, tolls were not set high enough to cover long-run marginal costs.[33] In the American case, parties on all sides of the transportation debates of the nineteenth century agreed that it was the competitive pressure of waterways that kept railroad rates low, rather than the competitive pressure of railroads that kept waterway rates low. "Railroad companies," said Albert Fink, Commissioner of the Trunkline Executive Committee, "fully recognize the potent influence of water competition and are not afraid of it, but on the contrary, they have met it and must meet it wherever they find it, without complaint and as one of the inevitable conditions under which they have to struggle for existence."[34] Since there is no historical basis for the proposition that U.S. canals, in the absence of railroads, would have pushed tolls above marginal costs, the question of whether an upward adjustment of the observed rates should be made on this account need not be pursued further.

The issue does have to be pursued in the English case, where Hawke estimated that canal shipping rates, in the absence of railroad competition, would have exceeded marginal cost by about one third. Contrary to some current arguments, however, the appropriate adjustment for this monopoly power will reduce rather than increase Hawke's estimated social saving. If this result seems paradoxical, it is because so much attention has been directed to demonstrating that the counterfactual water rates would have been higher than observed water rates. Consequently, another and quantitatively far larger effect going in the opposite direction has been overlooked. This is the bias due to the assumption that $\epsilon = 0$. If canal owners were, in the absence of railroads, monopolists maximizing profits by setting prices in such a way as to equate marginal revenues and marginal costs, then they must have been operating in the elastic portions of their demand curves. Indeed, we can

Part II, pp. 475, 480. See the section, *The Representativeness of the Water Rates* for a discussion of my upward adjustment in water rates to compensate for the subsidy of the capital employed in water transportation.

33. Roger L. Ransom, "Government Investment in Canals: A Study of the Ohio Canal, 1825–1860," unpublished Ph.D. dissertation, University of Washington, 1963, pp. 135–136. The tolls represent the receipts of the canal but not the entire benefit of the canal. When external benefits were added to the canal receipts, Ransom obtained a social rate of return for the 1840s that exceeds the market rate of return.

34. Cited in Lewis M. Haupt, "Canals and their Economic Relation to Transportation," *Papers of the American Economic Association*, Series I, Vol. 5, No. 3 (1890), p. 67.

infer the relevant elasticity of demand by inserting Hawke's estimates of the ratio of canal rates to marginal costs into the well-known equation relating price, marginal revenue, and the elasticity of demand, which may be written as:

$$\epsilon = \frac{1}{\frac{P}{MR} - 1}. \tag{19}$$

Since profit is maximized when marginal cost equals marginal revenue, (19) becomes

$$\epsilon = \frac{1}{\frac{P}{MC} - 1}. \tag{20}$$

It follows from equation (20) that if the price of canal transportation exceeded marginal cost by about a third ($P/MC \approx 1.32$), then the elasticity of the demand for canal transportation was in the neighborhood of 3. Even if we take the case of the Leeds and Liverpool Canal, where the discrepancy between price and marginal cost was substantially greater than Hawke (p. 84) thought was typical, the implied value of ϵ is 1.1. In either case, it follows from Table 2 that Hawke's assumption that $\epsilon = 0$ introduced a substantial upward bias into his estimate of the freight social saving, a bias that is much larger than the downward bias due to his neglect of the misallocation of resources associated with monopoly pricing.

Both biases are measured and shown in Figure 4 and Table 4. In Part A of Figure 4, the demand curve XX has an elasticity of 1.1. The social saving of £26.6 million, as calculated by Hawke, is represented by the area $(P_w - P_r) \cdot Q_r$. But if $\epsilon = 1.1$, the quantity of transportation demanded at the rate of P_w is Q_w, and that is just one third of the ton-miles provided in the railroad case. Consequently, the social saving is reduced to £15.0 million, which is represented by the area P_wCEP_r. It follows that the upward bias in Hawke's estimate of the social saving before allowing for the possibility of monopoly pricing by canals is £11.5 million – which is represented by the area CDE. What then is the downward bias due to the neglect of the misallocation of resources attributable to the use of canal monopoly power, which would have raised the non-rail rate from P_w to P'_w? That is represented by the area ABC and amounts to just £0.4 million. The area $(P'_w - P_w) \cdot Q'_w$, which comes to £2.5 million, is not a reduction in real income but, as Hawke pointed out, an income transfer. Thus the downward bias in Hawke's social saving calculation due to misallocations attributable to canal

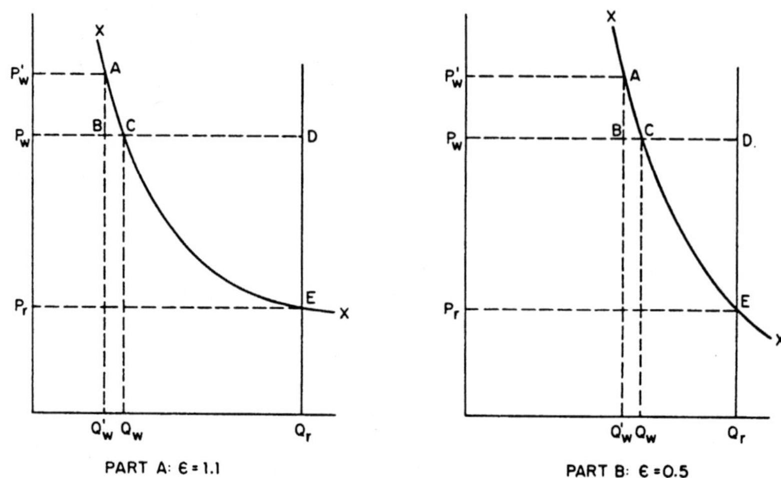

Figure 4. Diagram showing the upward and downward biases in Hawke's freight social saving estimate due to monopoly pricing by canals and the assumption that $\epsilon = 0$.

Notes: This diagram should be considered in conjunction with Table 4, which gives the values of the variables and areas displayed here.

monopoly pricing is hardly 3 percent of the upward bias due to the assumption that $\epsilon = 0$.

The last finding does not rest on the assumption that the elasticity of demand for transportion was greater than one. Part B of Figure 4 and column 2 of Table 4 give similar results for the case in which $\epsilon = 0.5$. Even with this rather inelastic curve, the ratio of the downward to the upward bias is just 4 percent, and Hawke's net overestimate of the "true" social saving is 30 percent.

The shape of the long-run marginal cost curves of waterways

Analysis of the long-run marginal cost curves of waterways did not begin with the debate over the social saving of railroads. It originated with the engineers who had charge of building canals or boats, and with nineteenth-century transportation economists. The results of their investigations led repeatedly to the conclusion that the unit cost of water transportation decreased as boat size, tonnage carried, and distance increased. The finding soon gained the status of a self-evident proposition and is now deeply embedded in the literature of transportation

Table 4. *The calculation of the biases in Hawke's freight social saving estimate due to the monopoly pricing by canals and the assumption that* $\epsilon = 0$

Variables and Areas Shown in Figure 4	*Values of Variables and Areas When* $\epsilon = 1.1$	$\epsilon = 0.5$
1. P_r	1.23 d	1.23 d
2. P_w	3.24 d	3.24 d
3. P_w'	3.93 d	3.93 d
4. Q_r (in ton-miles)	$3,175 \times 10^6$	$3,175 \times 10^6$
5. Q_w (in ton-miles)	$1,060 \times 10^6$	$1,956 \times 10^6$
6. Q_w' (in ton-miles)	857×10^6	$1,776 \times 10^6$
7. $P_r \cdot Q_r$	£16.27×10^6	£16.27×10^6
8. $P_w \cdot Q_r$	£42.86×10^6	£42.86×10^6
9. $P_w \cdot Q_w$	£14.31×10^6	£26.41×10^6
10. $P_w' \cdot Q_w'$	£14.03×10^6	£29.08×10^6
11. $(P_w - P_r) \cdot Q_r$	£26.59×10^6	£26.59×10^6
12. P_wCEP_r	£15.03×10^6	£20.27×10^6
13. CDE	£11.56×10^6	£6.32×10^6
14. ABC	£0.36×10^6	£0.24×10^6
15. $(P_w' - P_w) \cdot Q_w'$	£2.46×10^6	£5.11×10^6

Sources and Notes: Line 1: P_r exceeds the figure of 1.21*d* given by Hawke for 1865 (Hawke, p. 62) because of the addition of 55×10^6 ton-miles for livestock not included in Hawke's figure of $3,119.6 \times 10^6$ ton-miles and the addition of £0.5×10^6 livestock (Hawke, p. 141) to the figure for railroad revenues that Hawke gives for 1865 on p. 88. Line 2: Computed by multiplying 1.23*d* by $P_w \cdot Q_r \div P_r \cdot Q_r$. Line 3: Computed by multiplying 1.23*d* by the sum of $P_w \cdot Q_r$ and Hawke's estimate of the difference between the saving of charges and the social saving for 1865 (p. 89) and then dividing by $P_r \cdot Q_r$ [$1.23(42.9 + 9.1) \div 16.27 = 3.931$]. Line 4: Hawke's figure of $3,120 \times 10^6$ (p. 62) plus an allowance of 55×10^6 ton-miles for livestock. This allowance was computed from the data in Hawke, pp. 140–141, on the assumption that the average weights of cattle, swine, and sheep were 1,000 lbs., 200 lbs., and 150 lbs., respectively. Hawke's figure of 309×10^6 livestock miles was inflated by the ratio of total livestock receipts to the livestock receipts covered by the ten roads in his Table V.03. Lines 5 and 6: Computed from $Q = DP^{-\epsilon}$. Line 12: Computed from $D\int_{1.23}^{3.24} P^{-\epsilon}dp$. Line 13: $CDE = (P_w - P_r) \cdot Q_r - P_wCEP_r$. Line 14: Computed from $D\int_{3.24}^{3.93} P^{-\epsilon}dp$ less $(P_w' - P_w) \cdot Q_{w'}$.

engineering and economics. "In the case of waterways," wrote Kirkaldy and Evans, authors of a British textbook on transportation economics of World War I vintage, "the extra wear and tear arising from increased traffic is practically negligible; and the actual working experience of some of the canal companies, such as the Manchester Ship Canal, proves that this is so; that a very substantial increase of traffic can be accommodated on a waterway without anything like an equivalent increase in the cost of maintenance." Otto Franzius, author of a leading treatise on waterway engineering, presented evidence drawn from the experience of German inland waterways. He reported that with a 58 percent increase in the carrying capacity of boats, construction costs per gross ton declined by 9 percent and the ship maintenance and crew costs per delivered ton declined between 2 and 16 percent. Engineers consulted by the U.S. Senate Select Committee on Transportation Routes to the Seaboard (Windom Committee) in the early 1870s concluded that "the enlargement of the New York canals so as to pass boats of 600 to 1,000 tons, will reduce the cost of transportation on that part of the line 50 per cent."[35]

David questioned my assumption that the long-run marginal cost curve of waterways was downward sloping because "only one page is devoted to supporting this assertion," and he found it to be "not a very satisfactory page."[36] Even though it is now obvious that my discussion was too brief, the fact remains that the issues that most concerned David, such as the adequacy of the water supply, were investigated in detail by engineers appointed by various federal, state, and private agencies. Their findings, which are set forth in published documents as well as in secondary sources, were not only that the water supply was plentiful but that the enlarged canals would have reduced per ton-mile costs.[37]

Desai and von Tunzelmann argued that because water transportation was a shrinking industry only the most efficient carriers would have survived. From this *a priori* statement they drew two conclusions: one is that the long-run supply curve was upward sloping; the other is that use of the waterway rates of 1890 imparted a downward bias to the social saving calculation.[38] Suppose it were true that water transportation was

35. Adam W. Kirkaldy and Alfred Dudley Evans, *The History and Economics of Transport* (London, 1915), p. 221; Otto Franzius, *Waterway Engineering* (Cambridge, 1936), pp. 433–435; U.S. Senate, *Select Committee on Transportation Routes to the Seaboard*, Report No. 307, 43d Cong., 1st Sess., Vol. 1, p. 247. Cf. also J. Stephen Jeans, *Waterways and Water Transport* (London, 1890), ch. 27; Edwin F. Johnson, *The Navigation of the Lakes and Navigable Communications Therefrom to the Seaboard, and to the Mississippi River* (Hartford, 1966); John R. Meyer, Merton J. Peck, John Stenason, Charles Zwick, *The Economics of Competition in the Transportation Industries* (Cambridge, Mass., 1959), pp. 111–113; J. E. Palmer, *British Canals: Problems and Possibilities* (London, 1910). ch. 3. See also the sources cited in William Pierson Judson, *History of the Various Projects, Reports, Discussions, and Estimates for Reaching the Great Lakes from Tide-Water, 1768–1901*, Oswego Historical Society, Pub. No. 2. (Oswego, N.Y., 1901). *The Index to the Reports of the Chief of Engineers, U.S. Army, 1866–1912*, U.S. House of Representatives, Doc. No. 740, 63d Cong., 2d Sess., 2 vols., lists many reports investigating the relationship between waterway costs and vessel size, prism size, distance, and so forth.

36. David, "Transportation Innovation," p. 511.

37. See the sources cited in footnote 35.

38. Desai, "Some Issues,' p. 10; von Tunzelmann, *Steam Power*, pp. 39–41.

a shrinking industry. In order to proceed from this proposition to the conclusion that the long-run cost curve is upward sloping, it is necessary to consider the characteristics of both the enterprises that went out of business and those that survived. The boatmen who continued to operate owned larger vessels than those who retired, and the canals that survived could accommodate larger vessels than those that were abandoned.[39] The fact that it was the larger boats and canals that tended to survive and the smaller ones that tended to fail is *prima facie* evidence of economies of scale and hence quite in keeping with the engineers and transportation economists who held that the long-run cost curve was downward sloping. Moreover, although it is true that the traffic on most canals was shrinking, the traffic on the waterway *system* was not. The traffic on the Great Lakes, the coastal routes, and the Mississippi system was growing at a fairly high rate, although not as rapidly as railroad freight. The registered tonnage of sailing and steam vessels on the Great Lakes increased at an annual rate of 3.3 percent between 1868 and 1890. Consequently, waterways still accounted for over a third of all non-wagon freight ton-miles in 1889.[40] Nor should one exaggerate the decline of business on the canals. On the New York State canals traffic in 1890 was virtually at the average level of the previous two decades, and well above the pre–Civil War average.[41]

It is possible to test the judgment of the engineers and transportation economists by estimating waterway cost functions. Equation (21), which relates the construction cost of a canal to the cross section of its prism (X_p), the length of the canal (X_l), and its total lockage (X_r), is estimated from data compiled by H. Jerome Cranmer. His data set covers 44 canals that accounted for 79 percent of total canal investment prior to 1860.[42]

$$\begin{aligned} \hat{C}_c &= \underset{(1.0894)}{-0.5883} + \underset{(0.2069)}{0.5103\hat{X}_p} + \underset{(0.1308)}{0.6851\hat{X}_l} + \underset{(0.1139)}{0.0550\hat{X}_r} \qquad (21) \\ \bar{R}^2 &= 0.82; \quad N = 44 \end{aligned}$$

Since this equation is log-linear, the coefficients are elasticities, and each coefficient, minus 1, yields the relevant elasticity of marginal cost. It is

39. *New York Canals*, p. 171; U.S. Bureau of Statistics (Treasury Dept.), "The Grain Trade of the United States," *Monthly Summary of Commerce and Finance*, No. 7, Series 1899 1900 (Jan. 1900), p. 1972; *Preliminary Report*, pp. 193–209; H. Jerome Cranmer, "Canal Investment, 1815–1860," in Conference on Research in Income and Wealth, *Trends in the American Economy in the Nineteenth Century*, Vol. 24 of Studies in Income and Wealth (Princeton, 1960), p. 564; *Census of Transportation 1890*, Part II, pp. 474–477; Tunnell, "Statistics," pp. 3, 4, 26.

40. Barger, *The Transportation Industries*, p. 184, and the Appendix, Section A, below.

41. *New York Canals*, pp. 181–183.

42. Cranmer, "Canal Investment," pp. 547–564. Figures in parentheses are standard errors.

evident that the marginal cost of canal construction declined with increases in all of the variables, although the effect on cost of a canal's rise and fall (X_r) was slight.

Equation (22) relates the annual operating costs of canals to capacity (as measured by prism size) and total freight carried (X_f). It is estimated for 1889 from a cross-sectional regression on 13 canals.[43]

$$\hat{C}_0 = \underset{(2.4032)}{5.6857} - \underset{(0.5385)}{1.0905}\hat{X}_p + \underset{(0.0996)}{0.9230}\hat{X}_f \qquad (22)$$

$$\bar{R}^2 = 0.90; \quad N = 13$$

It is evident from equation (22) that the marginal cost of canal operations with respect to total tonnage carried is declining. Moreover, since this equation was estimated over canals with prisms of varying sizes, it permits one to determine how canal operating costs vary when the size (X_p) of the canal itself may vary. If canal size (X_p) is held constant, and given the range within which these canals were operating, which was far below capacity, a 100 percent increase in the tonnage carried would have increased operating costs by just 90 percent. Thus if canals could only expand traffic within the limits of the existing system, they would have experienced moderately declining marginal costs up to the bottleneck point.

If an increase in freight brought canals beyond the bottleneck point, then it would have paid to enlarge the canals to accommodate the increased traffic. Suppose, for example, that canal traffic would have increased threefold in the absence of railroads. This would have pushed most canals past their bottleneck points, thus requiring enlargements. If canals responded by doubling capacity, then it follows from equation (22) that total operating costs would have increased by 29 percent ($2^{-1.0905}3^{0.9230} = 1.29$). Operating costs per ton, however, would have declined by 57 percent [$1 - (1.29 \div 3) = 0.57$]. The construction costs of the enlarged canals would have been greater than the costs of those they replaced. It follows from equation (21) that doubling the capacity (X_p) of the canals would have made the new canals 42 percent more expensive than the old ones ($2^{0.51} = 1.42$). Assuming unchanged interest and depreciation schedules, the annual capital charge would have risen by 42 percent, but capital charges *per ton* would have declined by 53 percent [$1 - (1.42 \div 3) = 0.53$]. Since capital charges were on the order of 80 percent of the annual long-run cost of canals, overall canal charges per ton would have declined by a little over 53 percent.[44]

43. The data for this regression are from *Census of Transportation 1890*, Part II, pp. 475–483, 484.

44. Assuming that the depreciation and interest rates summed to 0.07, the annual rental value on the construction costs (book value) of state and private canals in operation in 1889 is $10.5

There is still the question of the long-run curve of the vessels that accounted for about half the cost of shipping by canal and virtually all of the cost of shipping on the Great Lakes, the coastal routes, and the rivers. Unfortunately, the data needed to run regressions that relate the marginal cost of boats on these routes to tonnage are not readily available. This task should be undertaken in the future, but not because the tenets of the engineers are really in doubt. That both construction costs and manning costs per gross ton fell with the volume of the ship is quite well established. Such regressions would be useful because they would give a much more precise picture of the nature of specific water alternatives and would permit a reduction of the upward bias in current social saving estimates.

McClelland presented a table and chart showing that freight rates for flour carried on the Erie Canal varied sharply during the navigation season. These data reveal that in each of the five years from 1859 through 1863, rates reached a peak in November, during which time they were 37 to 138 percent higher than the rates of the preharvest months of May and June. McClelland contends that these data undermine Fishlow's assumption of constant or declining long-run marginal cost and invalidate his use of 1859 waterway rates as measures of marginal cost.[45] But monthly data have little bearing on the question of long-run costs. With the stock of boats virtually fixed over any given navigation season, all rates were quasi-rents that may have been above or below long-run marginal costs. Normally the rates would have been below long-run marginal cost in the preharvest months and above long-run marginal cost during the months immediately following the harvest. If the revenue of vessels over the entire season equaled their annual long-run marginal cost, the industry would be in long-run equilibrium, even though rates in any given month were either above or below the long-run equilibrium rate. The response to long-run disequilibrium rates would have been spread out over a number of years by boat owners who would either have added to the stock of vessels or have failed to replace vessels that were retired.

McClelland's point is useful as a caution against inadvertently choosing a rate, such as the May or June rate, that was far below long-run marginal costs. But his criticism of Fishlow was misdirected, since 1859 and 1860 were fairly normal years and Fishlow used annual average rates and not the rates of a particular month. McClelland was also in error in suggesting that the transitory rise in average annual rates during the

million. The operating expenses of the same canals in 1889 were $2.1 million. *Census of Transportation 1890*, Part II, pp. 475, 480.

45. McClelland, "Railroads," pp. 115–120.

Civil War surge of traffic implied that the Erie Canal was operating in the zone of increasing marginal costs. Equation (23) relates the real annual operating costs of the New York canals over the years 1853–1880 to the average length of a haul (X_d), total tons shipped (X_f), and a dummy variable representing the Civil War years (X_{cw}).[46]

$$\hat{C}_0 = \underset{(3.8241)}{13.4337} + \underset{(0.2621)}{0.4220}\hat{X}_f - \underset{(0.6547)}{1.2133}\hat{X}_d - \underset{(0.1536)}{0.1449}X_{cw} \quad (23)$$

$$\bar{R}^2 = 0.26; \quad N = 28; \quad D.W. = 1.34$$

Since the coefficient on X_f is less than 1, it is quite clear that on the New York State canals, as on other canals, marginal cost declined as the tonnage shipped increased. Moreover, since the coefficient on distance (X_d) is negative, and since the effect of the Civil War was to increase the proportion of long hauls in grain shipments, this factor would have led to a decline in marginal costs.[47] That the dummy variable (X_{cw}) for the Civil War years is negative (although not statistically significant) after account is taken of tonnage and distance, suggests the existence of other war-related factors that served to reduce canal operating costs. Consequently, the Civil War experience of the New York canals tends to confirm rather than refute the proposition that the long-run marginal cost of canal shipping declined as the tonnage transported increased. The transitory rise in overall rates (payments to boats plus tolls) between 1860 and 1863 thus appears to have been due to a lagged response in the supply of boats and either deliberate setting of tolls above costs by

46. The data for this regression are from New York State, *Annual Financial Report of the Comptroller Relating to Canals: 1884*, p. 63; *New York Canals*, pp. 156–157, 181. C_o was deflated by the Warren–Pearson price index.

47. Since operating costs were less than 20 percent of the annual long-run cost of the New York canals, one cannot rule out *a priori* the negative coefficient on $\hat{X}_d$. On the other hand, it is possible that the mix of commodities transported was changing over time in such a way that an appropriate measure of this mix would be positively correlated with distance and negatively correlated with costs (or vice versa), when total tonnage shipped is held constant. Then the negative coefficient of $\hat{X}_d$ would be due to the omission of a mix variable. Tests of such an hypothesis were unsuccessful because of difficulties in constructing an appropriate index of commodity mix from published data, although all the regressions attempted yielded a negative coefficient on the Civil War dummy. An alternative approach is to regress total costs on the logarithm of ton-miles and a Civil War dummy; this is equivalent to imposing the constraint that the coefficients on tons and on distance are the same.
The results of this regression were as follows:

$$\hat{C}_o = \underset{(4.035)}{12.7608} + \underset{(0.1967)}{0.04998}\hat{X}_{tm} - \underset{(0.1259)}{0.3404}X_{cw}$$

$$\bar{R}^2 = 0.17; \quad N = 28; \quad D.W. = 1.17$$

the canal authorities (perhaps prompted by wartime exigencies) or errors on their part in anticipating the prices of their inputs.[48]

The elasticity of substitution and the cross elasticity of demand

In *Railroads and American Economic Growth*, I pointed out that arguments which inferred the indispensability of railroads from their victory over waterways in the competition for the carriage of the nation's freight involved the implicit assumption that the elasticity of substitution between these two forms of transportation was quite low. But suppose the elasticity of substitution was moderately high. Then the shift to railroads could have been induced by a relatively small cost differential between railroads and waterways, and the resource saving attributable to railroads would be relatively low. I argued that the issue could only be settled by measuring the cost advantage of railroads, and so proceeded to compute the social saving on the transportation of agricultural products.

A number of investigators have taken up the point on the elasticity of substitution and pushed it in a direction that is both novel and surprising. The first to do so was Lebergott, who argued that since canals and railways were sellers of equivalent transportation services and since they competed vigorously with each other, in long-term equilibrium they had to charge identical prices; otherwise the more expensive service would have been driven out. He concluded, therefore, that a positive social saving was merely "a measure of estimating error."[49]

The difficulty with this argument becomes apparent when it is extended to wagons. Wagons and railroads co-existed, offered alternative means of performing the same service, and competed vigorously with each other. Hence wagon and railroad costs must have been equal;

48. The same basic point was made by Fishlow, who noted that "McClelland's . . . own data show that a doubling of canal traffic between 1859 and 1863 left canal freight rates virtually unchanged! Over the interim, they had temporarily risen owing to adjustment problems, to be sure, but that is totally irrelevant to the long-run question under consideration." See Albert Fishlow, "Internal Transportation," in Lance Davis *et al.*, *American Economic Growth: An Economist's History of the United States* (New York, 1972), p. 516. It might be added that it is unlikely that the supply of canal boats had reached long-term equilibrium by 1863.

49. Lebergott, "United States Transportation," p. 439. Cf. David, "Transportation Innovation," p. 513; McClelland, "Railroads," p. 114; Peter D. McClelland, "Social Rates of Return on American Railroads in the Nineteenth Century," *Economic History Review*, 2nd Ser., 22 (Aug. 1972). 477–478; White, "The Concept," p. 85; Colin M. White, "Railroads and Rigor," *Journal of European Economic History*, 4 (Spring 1975), 194. The preceding writers held that I failed to recognize that railroads and waterways provided a homogeneous product. Desai ("Some Issues," p. 10), on the other hand, held that I assumed perfect subsitutability. He contended that it was the heterogeneity of railroad and waterway services that undermined my analysis.

otherwise the more expensive form of transportation would have been driven out. Since we know that wagon rates, in the American case, were an average of 10 to 20 times higher than railroad rates, this argument obviously is fallacious. The point, of course, is that wagons, railroads, and waterways co-existed even though they charged different rates because they were not perfect substitutes for each other. All three co-existed because each had an advantage over the others in the functions in which it specialized. Down to the end of the nineteenth century wagons, with average hauls of less than 20 miles, dominated short-haul transportation and could, despite their high average rate, usually deliver goods over very short distances more cheaply than could either waterways or railroads. American railroads, with average hauls in 1890 of about 250 miles, had their greatest advantage in short-to-medium distances. The advantage of waterways, with average hauls in 1889 of about 650 miles, was in medium-to-long distances, especially with bulky, low-value items such as grain, lumber, coal, and ore.[50]

Given the specialized characteristics of each medium and the variety of requirements of shippers, one would hardly expect the elasticity of substitution between the waterway and railroad *systems* to be infinite. Hawke recognized this difficulty and sought to refine the argument by limiting its application only to waterways and railways that directly confronted each other (as in the competition of the railroad trunk lines with the vessels of the Great Lakes and Erie Canal) and that carried "the same freight . . . between the same points." In such cases, he said, the "difference in costs and charges," including "hidden costs," must "be precisely zero." Turning to the case of wagons, Hawke said that the situation was quite different since wagons were "not required to perform the same services as railways" and canals but were used "for transport to and from railway stations" and canals.[51] Thus, directly competing waterways and railroads had infinite elasticities of substitution (or cross elasticities of demand), whereas wagons and waterways or wagons and railroads were complementary and so had negative cross elasticities of demand.

Even if one granted that directly competing lines, such as the Great Lakes or Erie and the trunk lines, were perfect substitutes for each other, it does not follow that the elimination of measurement error would reduce the social saving to zero. The most that could be said is that one or another railroad line could have been removed without increasing the social cost of transportation. Indeed, if we focus on particular railroad

50. The average haul of railroads in 1899, was 247 miles (*Historical Statistics*, p. 733). The method of estimating the average distance of a water haul in 1889 is given in the Appendix, Section A.

51. Hawke, *Railways*, pp. 20–21.

lines, it is possible to make the social saving negative, since some railroads were economic failures that could not cover out-of-pocket costs, let alone long-run costs. The social saving for the railroad system as a whole, however, must be positive because in its absence waterways and wagons, in combination, would have to have provided service in areas and for commodities that could have been serviced more cheaply by railroads. Either waterways would have had to carry large quantities of freight over short-to-medium distances where their services were relatively costly (see Figure 3), or wagons, with decreasing but nevertheless much higher marginal costs (with respect to distance) than railroads, would have had to extend substantially the average length of their hauls.

As I stressed in *Railroads and American Economic Growth* (cf. pp. 23–25, 46–47, 51, 73, 212–214), about 85 percent of the agricultural social saving is due to the savings on the extra wagon transportation charges that would have been required in the absence of railroads. That a large part of the social saving was due to the reduction of wagon charges is also a major finding of Fishlow's study of antebellum railroads, of Metzer's study of Russian railroads, and of Coatsworth's study of Mexican railroads. The Mexican case is particularly instructive because in that country waterways were not a feasible substitute for railways. In the Mexican case, the social saving of railroads was, therefore, in the neighborhood of 30 percent of GNP.[52] The lesson, as John Meyer recently emphasized, is that the provision of substitutes for wagon transportation was the crux of the transportation revolution.[53] The best substitute (prior to the coming of motor vehicles, pipe lines, and so forth) was a combination of waterways and railroads, but in the United States, England, and Russia either waterways alone or railroads alone would have achieved most of the cost saving over wagons achieved by the combination of low-cost services. Railroads were indispensable only where waterways were not a practical alternative, as in Mexico, for example.

The hypothesis of an infinite elasticity of substitution is inappropriate even when applied to such directly competing transportation modes as the Great Lakes and the trunk-line railroads. The ratio of railroad to waterway rates for wheat and other grains shipped interregionally fluctuated sharply from year to year, partly because of the intense rate wars that periodically engulfed the trunk lines. If the elasticity of substitution was infinite, these sharp fluctuations in relative rates should have led to complete shifts of the grain traffic from waterways to

52. Coatsworth, "Growth Against Development," chs. 3 and 4.

53. See his "Review of *The New Economic History of Railways*," *Journal of Business History* (forthcoming).

railroads and back again, as the ratio of rates swung in favor of one or the other transportation mode. Although there was a certain amount of shifting in traffic with shifts in relative rates, examination of the data reveals that these shifts were too moderate to sustain the hypothesis of an infinite or nearly infinite elasticity of substitution. Between 1878 and 1879, for example, the ratio of rail to water rates for wheat over the Chicago to Buffalo route fell by 49 percent and the ratio of the quantities of grain carried by water to those carried by rail fell by 50 percent, which suggests an elasticity of substitution of about 1. Similarly, between 1881 and 1882 the ratio of rail to water rates rose by 16 percent and the ratio of water to rail quantities rose by 22 percent, which suggests a substitution elasticity of 1.4.[54]

A more reliable measure of the degree of substitutability between the Great Lakes and the railroads may be obtained by using regression analysis to estimate the cross elasticity of the demand for waterway transportation with respect to the price of railroad transportation. Equations (24) and (25) represent the demand and supply equations for grain transportation between Chicago and Buffalo, estimated by two-stage least squares from data covering the years from 1868 through 1898.[55]

54. *New York Canals*, pp. 190, 208. Cf. footnote 55.

55. Data for these regressions were derived as follows: R_w for 1868–1895, from Tunnell, "Statistics of Lake Commerce," p. 29; R_w for 1896–1898, from *New York Canals*, p. 190, col. 4; all values were deflated by the Warren–Pearson price index. M, from *Historical Statistics*, p. 512 (converted to tons). R_r, from *New York Canals*, p. 190, col. 1 minus col. 5. The years 1868 through 1878 were years in which a premium existed on greenbacks, but the values of R_r in Tunnell were given in gold. To obtain a consistent currency series, the rates for these years were multiplied by an implicit deflator (A/B, where A is the currency values of lake freight rates from Tunnell, p. 29; and B is the undeflated lake freight rate from *New York Canals*, p. 109, col. 4). The entire series was then deflated by the Warren–Pearson price index. Q_g is from U.S. Bureau of Statistics, "The Grain Trade," pp. 1964–1965 (converted to tons). N is calculated from the number of days between the opening of the lake at Buffalo and the closing of the Welland Canal. For the years in which the closing date of the Welland Canal was missing, the average difference between the closing dates of the Welland Canal and of the port of Buffalo (over the entire period) was added to the closing date at Buffalo (see the *Annual Report of the Buffalo Merchants' Exchange, Including Statistics of the Trade and Commerce at Buffalo: 1884*, pp. 37–38; 1891, pp. 95–96; 1899, pp. 88–89; see also Buffalo Chamber of Commerce, *Statistics of the Trade and Commerce of Buffalo, 1875*, p. 66). B_l: since average sizes of grain-carrying vessels were not available, the index was calculated from a weighted average of the average sizes of sailing vessels (B_r) and steam vessels (B_s). B_r was obtained from *New York Canals*, p. 198, col. 2 ÷ col. 1; B_s from col. 4 ÷ col. 3. The respective weights were the estimated proportions of grain-carrying vessels which were sailing and steam vessels. The estimated number of sailing vessels carrying grain was $0.5 \times K_r/B_r$, where K_r is the total tonnage of sailing vessels (from *New York Canals*, p. 198, col. 2). The estimated number of steam vessels carrying grain was $(K_s/144117)^{0.27428} \times (48049/B_s)$, where K_s is the total tonnage of steam vessels (from *New York Canals*, p. 198, col. 4); 144117 is the value of K_s in

$$\hat{Q}_g = 4.725 + 0.7383\hat{M} + 0.9484\hat{R}_r - 0.5514\hat{R}_w \quad (24)$$
$$(2.76) \quad (0.2181) \quad (0.3024) \quad (0.2938)$$
$$\bar{R}^2 = 0.47; \quad N = 31; \quad D.W. = 1.27$$

$$\hat{Q}_g = 1.562 + 1.7972\hat{B}_1 + 0.8234\hat{N} + 0.7654\hat{K}_b + 0.6679\hat{R}_w \quad (25)$$
$$(7.90) \quad (0.7245) \quad (0.4979) \quad (0.7874) \quad (0.2228)$$
$$\bar{R}^2 = 0.84; \quad N = 31; \quad D.W. = 1.63$$

Equation (24) shows that the cross elasticity of the demand for waterway transportation with respect to railroad rates (the coefficient of $\hat{R}_r$) was very nearly 1.[56] Thus, it appears that neither the arguments that implied zero cross elasticities nor those that presumed infinite cross elasticities are correct. Directly competing waterways and railroads were good but not perfect substitutes for each other. Nor should this finding be very surprising. The large number of grain traders differed widely in their assessments of the cost of time as well as in the significance they

year 1868, the first observation; 48049 is one third of the steam tonnage in 1868; and 0.27428 is the elasticity of Q_g with respect to K_s, obtained from a previous regression. The weight in each case was therefore the number of sailing vessels carrying grain and the number of steam vessels carrying grain, each divided by the sum of the two. K_b: since the capital stock of grain-carrying vessels in tons was not available, the index was calculated from a weighted average of K_r and K_s (defined above). The respective weights were 0.7904 and 0.2096. These were obtained by dividing the elasticities of Q_g with respect to K_r and to K_s by the sum of the two elasticities.

56. The coefficient on R_r was quite robust to various alternative data series and specifications of the demand and supply functions, varying between a low of 0.95 and a high of 1.12.

It should be noted that I have treated R_r as an exogenous variable. During the period covered by the regression, railroad rates on wheat were set by a cartel. The cartel did not allow rates to vary from day to day, as dictated by supply and demand. To the extent that the cartel took market conditions into account in setting rates, it did so with a lag. Moreover, the rates set were frequently the outcome of a political process that subordinated profit maximization to external pressures as well as to the internal compromises needed to maintain the cartel. When the cartel was successful, the rates it set tended to persist for relatively long periods of time, unlike the water rates, which fluctuated from day to day. When the cartel broke down and rate wars ensued, prices also deviated from the levels dictated by supply and demand, but were determined by the exigencies of the struggle between the cartel and the "cheaters." Thus a coefficient of variation (computed as the standard error around a time trend, divided by the mid-period trend value of rail charges on wheat between Chicago and Buffalo) was less than 40 percent of that of the corresponding coefficient of variation of water rates. Cf. D. T. Gilchrist, "Albert Fink and the Pooling System," *Business History Review*, 24 (Spring 1960), 24–29; Edward C. Kirkland, *Industry Comes of Age: Business, Labor, and Public Policy 1860–1897*, Vol. 6 of *The Economic History of the United States*, Henry David, *et al.*, eds. (New York, 1961), 85–93; Paul W. MacAvoy, *The Economic Effects of Regulation: The Trunk-Line Railroad Cartels and the Interstate Commerce Commission Before 1900* (Cambridge, Mass., 1965), chs. 3–5; Alfred D. Chandler, Jr., *The Visible Hand: The Managerial Revolution in American Business* (Cambridge, Mass., 1977), pp. 137–143.

The sources of the data for the computation are cited in footnote 55, under variables R_w, R_r, Q_g.

attached to various advantages or disadvantages of railroads and waterways. A dealer selling corn abroad, for example, might prefer the all-water route from Chicago to New York at most of the observed water and rail rates because corn arriving by barge in New York harbor was placed directly on ocean vessels, thus avoiding elevator and other transfer charges that would have been incurred with a rail shipment. On the other hand, a dealer whose ultimate customer was some miles inland from the harbor might find that savings in transshipping and wagon costs made rail transportation far cheaper than water at any of the observed ratios of water to rail rates. A whole array of similar, detailed cost considerations affected the choices made by individuals between the alternative modes and thus produced an *aggregate* cross elasticity of demand that was neither zero nor infinity but fairly close to 1.[57]

It is difficult to assess Hawke's interesting suggestion that wagon transportation was a net complement to both waterways and railroads because the available data relevant to this issue are still so scanty. Wagons served not only as complements to railroads and waterways for freight shipped over long distances but as substitutes for these carriers over short distances. Since a transshipping cost was incurred when transferring freight from wagons to railroads, there was a perimeter surrounding each market within which direct shipment by wagon cost less than shipment by a combination of wagons and railroads, even if the railroad rate had been zero. Just how far away from the designated market this perimeter might be located depends on the ratio of the transshipping cost to the wagon rate as well as on the ratio of the rail rate to the wagon rate. Consequently, a rise in the rail rate would have the effect of both pushing outward the perimeter that bounds the area in which direct wagon shipment was cheaper (the substitution effect) and reducing the quantity shipped to market per square mile in the area beyond that perimeter (the complementary effect). Whether wagons and railroads were net complements or net substitutes thus depends on whether the substitution or complementary effect was stronger. About all that can be said at present is that it is more likely that the complementary effect would exceed the substitution effect in the post-bellum United States than in England. This is because the ratio of either railroad or waterway to wagon rates was less than 0.1 in the United

57. The word aggregate was emphasized because some of the arguments made for an infinite cross elasticity really apply to individual shippers. Even if each individual shipper had an infinite cross elasticity of demand, the cross elasticity of the aggregate demand curve could still be in the neighborhood of 1 because of differences among individuals in the slopes of the linear portions of their isoquants as well as in the range over which linearity prevailed.

States. In Hawke's case, however, the ratio of railroad to wagon rates is 0.27 and the waterway to wagon ratio is between 0.42 and 0.56.[58]

The ratios are relatively high in the English case partly because average English wagon rates were a bit lower than U.S. wagon rates but mainly because the average British railroad and waterway rates were considerably higher than those of the late nineteenth-century United States. A variety of factors contributed to the relatively high English waterway and rail rates. One reason frequently mentioned for the high cost of water transport is the small prisms of English canals that kept the vessels narrow and hence thwarted the reduction of freight rates that could have been achieved through increases in the capacity of barges. Another point that deserves emphasis is the short average distance of the English haul, which c. 1865 was just 33 miles by rail and about 40 miles by canal. But as I have already noted, U.S. rail and waterway hauls in 1890 were from seven to over ten times as long. Consequently, the small physical size of England and the pattern of its internal trade prevented the English from exploiting the potential of the water and rail modes of transportation, which exhibited rapidly declining average costs with respect to distance (cf. Figure 3), to the same extent as was possible over the American expanses.[59]

Railroad rates and wagon rates

Although most of the criticisms of the social saving computations have dealt with waterway rates, some attention has been devoted to railroad rates. O'Brien argued that, because of monopolistic practices in both England and the United States, the observed railroad rates exceeded marginal cost, so that use of these rates biased downward the social saving computations. Lebergott suggested that the monopolistic pricing policies and profits of American railroads were cloaked by the fact that railroad construction was financed with bonds sold at discounts and hence had high yields to maturity. The thrust of this argument is that if adjustments were made for inflated bond rates it would be found that the profit on U.S. railroad operations in 1890 was well above competitive levels (which implies that rates exceeded marginal costs). The extent of the excess profits is not specified in these critiques, but the suggestion is that it is substantial enough to invalidate the attempts of

58. Fogel *Railroads*, pp. 71, 107–109; *Historical Statistics*, p. 733; Hawke, *Railways*, pp. 62, 86, 180.

59. Hawke, *Railways*, pp. 61, 86. Cf. the discussion of Figure 1.

Fishlow and Hawke to calculate social rates of return and to throw into doubt the relevance of the various social saving calculations.[60]

The validity of these propositions for U.S. railroads in 1890 can be assessed by computing the ratio of the net earnings of railroads to the reproduction cost of the capital embodied in them, and then comparing this ratio to various alternative yields. By using reproduction costs rather than book value, the possibility of inflated capital cost is circumvented. By using net earnings before payment of interest, all returns to capital are covered, including dividends, retained earnings, and interest.

Data collected by the Interstate Commerce Commission indicate that the net operating income of railroads in 1890 (operating revenue less operating expenses, including depreciation, and tax accruals) was $330 million.[61] Melville J. Ulmer estimated that the value of the reproducible capital employed in railroad operations in 1890 (value of land and value of capital in such non-railroad operations as hotels were excluded) was $5,827 million, which implies a rate of return of 5.7 percent (330 ÷ 5,827 = 0.057).[62] Fishlow's series on the real net capital stock of railroads indicates a figure for 1890, when converted into dollars of 1890, of $5,446 million.[63] Use of Fishlow's data thus implies an 1890 rate of return of 6.1 percent (330 ÷ 5,446 = 0.061). Although it may be appropriate to exclude land values from capital formation and efficiency estimates, it is inappropriate to do so for profit calculations because competitive firms need to earn the market rate of return on all of their earning assets, including land. Adding $1,495 million for land to the estimates of the reproducible capital derived from Ulmer and Fishlow yields rates of return of 4.5 and 4.8 percent, respectively.[64] Since the last two figures are below the 1890 yield on industrial common stocks (5.07 percent), the 1890 yield on the stock of utilities (6.03 percent), and the 1890 interest rate on commercial paper (5.62 percent), there seems to be little ground for believing that railroads were reaping monopoly profits in that year.[65]

60. O'Brien, *The New Economic History*, pp. 40–45; Lebergott, "United States Transportation," pp. 439–440. Cf. McClelland, "Social Rates," *passim*.

61. *Historical Statistics*, p. 737.

62. Melville J. Ulmer, *Capital in Transportation, Communications and Public Utilities: Its Formation and Financing* (Princeton, 1960), p. 256.

63. Fishlow, "Productivity," p. 606. The 1890 value for real net capital stock was obtained by interpolating between Fishlow's 1889 and 1899 figures. The interpolated figure was then converted into dollars of 1890 with the Warren–Pearson price index in U.S. Bureau of the Census, *Historical Statistics of the United States, 1789–1945*. (Washington, D.C., 1949), p. 231.

64. Simon Kuznets, *National Product Since 1869* (New York, 1946), p. 201.

65. *Historical Statistics*, p. 1003; Sidney Homer, *A History of Interest Rates* (New Brunswick, N.J., 1963), p. 320.

Suppose, however, that only the reproducible capital stock (as derived from Fishlow) should form the basis for the calculation of the railroad rate of return, and that 5.1 percent (the yield on common stocks) is accepted as the competitive rate of return. By how much would the adjustment for monopoly profits increase the estimated social saving of railroads? At a rate of 5.1 percent, the competitive profit of railroads should have been $278 million (0.051 × 5,446 = 278) instead of $330 million, which yields $52 million as the monopoly component of profit. Since gross operating revenues in 1890 were $1,052 million, the elimination of the monopoly component of profits would have reduced these revenues to $1,000 million, or 95.1 percent of the observed level.[66] In other words, the elimination of monopoly profit would have reduced freight and passenger rates by an average of 4.9 percent. If the rail freight rates employed in my calculation were reduced by 4.9 percent, the interregional social saving would rise by $4.3 million and the intraregional social saving by $4.8 million.[67] Thus the assumption that one sixth of railroad profits was due to monopoly pricing implies a downward bias in the social saving of $9.1 million. Elimination of this presumed bias would raise the agricultural social saving from 1.78 percent to 1.86 percent of GNP.[68] For reasons I have already indicated, however, even this small adjustment is inappropriate.

McClelland objected to Fishlow's use of a wagon rate of 15 cents per ton-mile. "Fishlow's only justification for using that number," he wrote, "is a reference to Taylor's *Transportation Revolution*." After tracking down Taylor's sources, McClelland concluded that the 15-cent figure "does not inspire confidence." He suggested that 20 cents per ton-mile might be more reasonable, and estimated that such an upward revision would increase Fishlow's freight social saving by $50 million or 48 percent.[69]

Although it is useful to call attention to the need for further research into antebellum wagon rates, it does not follow that Taylor's estimate is wrong merely because it was based on a few citations. Moreover, it is unlikely that the true figure for 1859 would be as high as 20 cents. Some light can be cast on this issue by making use of the 1906 USDA

66. *Historical Statistics*, p. 737.

67. Fogel, *Railroads*, pp. 42, 72, 86–87; cf. note 50 on pp. 84–85.

68. This calculation gives the order of magnitude of a possible divergence between rates and marginal costs on a fixed quantity of railroad transportation. One could also compute the effect on the estimated social saving of allowing the quantity transported to respond to the lower rate. If we assume that the elasticity of demand was 1, and that the marginal cost of transportation was approximately constant over the range of increase in transportation service, then the combined effect of a reduction in rates and in quantities carried would be to raise the agricultural social saving from 1.78 to 1.93 percent of GNP.

69. McClelland, "Railroads," pp. 108–109.

survey of rural wagon transportation in 1,894 counties, which indicated that the average rate per ton-mile (when team, wagon, and driver were hired from commercial haulers) was 20.5 cents.[70] Since input prices were 53 percent higher in 1906 than they had been in 1859, McClelland's conjecture implies that the productivity of wagon transportation increased by 49 percent between the two dates.[71] So large a productivity increase seems unlikely in light of the fact that 93 percent of all country roads were still unimproved in 1904. Taylor's wagon rate, which implies a 12 percent gain in productivity, is more plausible.[72]

The issue of antebellum wagon transportation should not be left in such a highly conjectural and unsatisfactory state. Much can be learned about this important but almost wholly unknown aspect of the nineteenth-century transportation system by turning, as Winifred B. Rothenberg has, to primary sources. Her study of the account books of Massachusetts farmers reveals perimeters of marketing by wagon between 1750 and 1855 that are wider than has hitherto been presumed. She has also discovered information on wagon rates that indicates a rise between these dates in the real cost of rural wagon transportation.[73] Nor are farm records the only possible sources of information on wagon transportation. Much can also be learned from the records of gristmills, blast furnaces, railroads, and other non-agricultural enterprises that purchased wagon services from farmers.

The uncertainty that surrounds the average wagon rate for 1859 does

70. Fogel, *Railroads*, p. 56.

71. The total factor productivity index was constructed from the price dual, in the rate-of-change form. The rate of change in wagon rates implied by McClelland's conjecture is obtained by solving $20.5 = 20e^{x47}$. A divisia index of the rates of change in input prices between 1859 or 1860 and 1906 was constructed using wages of farm labor from *Historical Statistics*, p. 163, and prices of horses and mules from Marvin W. Towne and Wayne D. Rasmussen, "Farm Gross Product and Gross Investment in the Nineteenth Century," in Conference on Research in Income and Wealth, *Trends*, p. 286. It was assumed that the price of wagons moved with the wholesale price index (*Historical Statistics*, pp. 200, 201). The weights applied were: labor, 0.44; teams, 0.40; wagons, 0.16. Cf. Fogel, *Railroads*, p. 72.

If the 1906 wagon rates are projected backward to 1859 on the basis of the index of input prices, we obtain an 1859 wagon rate of 13.4 cents. Even this figure may be too high since the USDA rates were based on the assumption of zero backhauls and because very few farmers hired commerical service but used their own wagons, teams, and labor. Highway engineers argued that the cost of wagon transportation to farmers was less than half the commerical rate. An investigation of rates paid to farmers for hauling in central Illinois c. 1906 revealed rates in the neighborhood of 10 cents per ton-mile. The last figure projected back to 1859 by the index of input prices yields a figure of 6.5 cents. Cf. Fogel, *Railroads*, pp. 107–109.

72. The procedure followed was described in footnote 71. Taylor's figure implies that wagon rates rose at an annual rate of 0.7 percent.

73. Winifred Rothenberg, "The Marketing Perimeters of Massachusetts Farmers, 1750–1855," mimeo, Brandeis University., 1978.

not really imperil Fishlow's contention that his estimate of the freight social saving represents an upper bound. If one simultaneously increases the wagon rate by a third, as McClelland suggests, and shifts from the assumption that $\epsilon = 0$ to $\epsilon = 0.4$, Fishlow's estimate of the freight social saving would fall by one percent. In this case the upward bias due to the assumption that $\epsilon = 0$ is slightly greater than the downward bias that McClelland would attribute to a low wagon rate. But $\epsilon = 0.4$ is probably a lower bound on the long-run elasticity of the aggregate transportation demand.[74] If, as Fishlow argued, $\epsilon = 1$ is a more appropriate figure for the elasticity during the antebellum era, then the upward bias would exceed the potential downward bias by nearly 300 percent.[75]

The impact of railroads on long-term economic growth

Even if the resource saving of U.S. railroads were relatively small, derived (or indirect) effects of the railroads could still be large enough to sustain the view that railroads were indispensible to American economic growth during the nineteenth century, or at least were much more important than is suggested by the social saving calculations. It is useful to divide the derived effects of railroads into two categories. *Disembodied* effects are those that followed from the saving in transportation costs per se and which would have been induced by any innovation that lowered transportation costs by approximately the amount attributable to railroads. *Embodied* effects are those attributable to the specific form in which railroads provided cheap transportation services. Much effort has been devoted to the investigation of the proposition that the specific inputs required for railroad construction and operation induced the rise of industries, productive techniques, and management and labor skills that were essential to economic growth. To review this rich literature adequately would require a separate paper.[76] Consequently, this section

74. In the long run a rise in the price of transportation would lead to a shift away from transportation-intensive goods as well as to a change in the locus of economic activity. As pointed out below, the Williamson model implies that with increases in the price of transportation of the magnitude indicated by Fishlow's social saving, all transportation of agricultural goods from the Midwest to the East could have halted and the United States could have become a net importer of foodstuffs.

75. The data required for these computations come from Fishlow, *American Railroads*, p. 51, and from McClelland's one-third increase in the wagon rate.

76. This work includes, in addition to studies previously cited in connection with the social saving controversy, Stefano Fenoaltea, "Railroads and Industrial Growth, 1861–1913," *Explorations in Economic History*, 9 (Summer 1972), 325–351; Wray Vamplew, "The Railways and the Iron Industry: A Study of Their Relationship in Scotland," in M. C. Reed, ed., *Railways in the*

is limited to a consideration of several attempts to identify substantial disembodied effects of railroads that were not covered by the social saving calculations.

Railroad-induced economies of scale

One of the most interesting arguments along this line was set forth by Paul David. He called attention to the possibility that social saving calculations failed to measure the increases in income made possible by long-run declining marginal costs in the transportation-using industries. In the absence of railroads, the scale of operation of such industries would have been lower than it actually was, so that a part of the benefit of railroads was the output gain attributable to a higher scale of operation. This gain, David pointed out, was not originally included in the social saving calculations. He supported his argument with a diagram that showed a gain from economies of scale in the transportation-using industry that was more than ten times as great as the social saving. David did not identify the transportation-using industries to which this diagram might apply, but maintained that such scale effects "remain unexplored, and cannot be ruled out."[77]

Although further exploration along the lines that David suggests would certainly be useful, it is not likely that adjustments for unmeasured scale effects would significantly alter present estimates of the social saving. This is certainly the case for U.S. agriculture during the nineteenth century since, with the exception of slave plantations, there is no evidence of economies of scale. Suppose, however, that late

Victorian Economy (Newton Abbot, 1969), pp. 33–75; Rainer Fremdling, "Railroads and German Economic Growth: A Leading Sector Analysis with a Comparison to the United States and Great Britain," this Journal, 37 (Sept. 1977), 583–604; and Chandler, *The Visible Hand*.

77. Quotations of David in this section are from his "Transportation Innovation," pp. 515–519. His diagram, which is reproduced as Part A of Figure 5, makes the "total indirect social benefit" from economies of scale equal to about 97 percent of the f.o.b. value of the end-period output of the transportation-using industry. My estimate of the agricultural social saving equals 6.9 percent of the gross farm product of agriculture in 1890. Cf. footnote 79 and Part A of Figure 5.

In a paper published three years after *Railroads and American Economic Growth*, I noted that the best case for demand-induced economies of scale attributable to railroads was in the Bessemer steel industry. In the absence of the railroad's demand for this type of metal, it is possible that only open-hearth steel would have been available. During the late nineteenth century, open-hearth firms were small scale and produced a more expensive product than Bessemer firms, which were large scale. Taking into account the difference in the cost of production in the two types of firms, the estimated maximum gain in income not already covered by the social saving due to economics of scale in Bessemer production was just $7.0 million or 0.06 percent of GNP in 1890. See Fogel, "Railroads as an Analogy," pp. 27–30.

nineteenth-century agriculture experienced economies of scale similar to those which Engerman and I found for the slave South.[78] Suppose also that the entire social saving on agricultural freight was charged against the agricultural sector. Then the absence of railroads would have led to a shift of 6.9 percent of inputs from agriculture to transportation ($214 \div 3{,}107 = 0.069$).[79] Given a scale coefficient of 1.07, the reduction of the scale of agricultural activities to 0.931 of the level actually attained in 1890 ($1 - 0.069 = 0.931$) would have reduced agricultural output by 7.4 percent ($0.931^{1.07} = 0.926$; $1 - 0.926 = 0.074$). In other words, the unmeasured social saving due to the reduction in the scale of agricultural production is, in this case, \$16 million [$(0.074 - 0.069) \times 3107 = 16$]. When expressed as a percentage of GNP, the adjustment for the loss attributable to a lower scale of operation in the transportation-using sector raises the agricultural social saving from 1.8 to 1.9 percent of GNP.

Even this small adjustment is inappropriate for two reasons. First, as already mentioned, econometric evidence suggests that there were no scale economies in free agriculture until some time after World War I. Second, scale economies, both in slave South and in post–World War I agriculture, were at the level of the firm and therefore would have been captured even in the absence of railroads.[80] When scale economies are internal to the firm, increases in the scale of firms are independent of the scale of the industry. Consequently, the relatively small reduction in the scale of agriculture occasioned by the absence of railroads would have taken the form of a reduction in the number of firms rather than in the scale of each firm.

What explains the discrepancy between David's suggestion that neglected scale effects in transportation-using industries might be ten times as great as the social saving and the preceding demonstration that such effects are a tenth or less of the estimated social saving? David did not base his diagram on known features of the agricultural,

78. The scale coefficient is 1.0645. See Robert W. Fogel and Stanley L. Engerman, *Time on the Cross: The Economics of American Negro Slavery* (Boston, 1974), Vol. 2, p. 143. Cf. Gavin Wright, *The Political Economy of the Cotton South* (New York, 1978), who argues against a scale effect in slave agriculture.

79. My estimate of the agricultural social saving of railroads in 1890 is \$214 million. Towne and Rasmussen put farm gross product in the same year at \$3,107 million. Consequently, if \$214 million of resources had been shifted from agriculture to transportation, the scale of agriculture would have been reduced to 93.1 percent of its actual 1890 level. Fogel, *Railroads*, pp. 47, 110, 220; Towne and Rasmussen, "Farm Gross Product," pp. 255–312.

80. Cf. Robert W. Fogel and Stanley L. Engerman, "Explaining the Relative Efficiency of Slave Agriculture in the Antebellum South," *American Economic Review*, 67 (June 1977), 275–296: Ralph A. Loomis and Glen T. Bartin, *Productivity of Agriculture: United States 1870–1958*, U.S. Dept. of Agriculture, *Technical Bull.* No. 1238 (Washington, D.C., 1961), pp. 24–25.

manufacturing, or service sectors in the United States, Great Britain, or any of the other nations for which social savings estimates have been computed. Rather than being applicable to these economies, David's diagram incorporates certain empirically unrealistic assumptions. Chief among these is the assumption that a doubling of output would have led to a 41 percent decline in unit costs. This implies a scale coefficient in the transportation-using sector of about 4.2, which is far in excess not only of prevailing scale coefficients in U.S. agriculture, but also of scale coefficients for manufacturing (which rarely range above 1.2), and of Denison's estimate of the scale coefficient of 1.1 for the U.S. economy as a whole during 1929–1957.[81] Even Denison's estimate would be too high a figure to apply to the social saving computations of Fishlow, Coatsworth, and Hawke because not all scale economies in the United States during 1929–1957 were external to the firm and because scale effects were probably confined to a smaller sector of the economy in the antebellum United States and in nineteenth-century Mexico and Russia than in twentieth-century America.

The magnitude of the induced social saving in David's diagram is influenced by several additional assumptions that have the effect of shifting the equilibrium level of output in the absence of railroads far to the left. Among these assumptions are the following: The share of transportation in the c.i.f. price increased sharply between the early railroad era and 1890; learning-by-doing led to about a 40 percent rise in the productive efficiency of transportation-using industries and none of this gain would have been achieved in a non-railroad world; the elasticity of demand for transportables (for the output of transportation-using industries) was around 9 during the early railroad era but declined to about 1 near the end of the nineteenth century.[82]

Recent work by new economic historians has shed light on some of these issues. In his penetrating study of the American textile industry David pointed out that the efficiency gains attributable to learning-by-doing were independent of the scale of the industry and that virtually all of these gains would have been achieved and diffused through the textile

81. See the Appendix, Section B, for a discussion of the procedure used in inferring the scale coefficient implicit in David's f.o.b. cost curve. Griliches's estimation of production functions in U.S. manufacturing on data for 1954, 1957, and 1958 yielded scale coefficients that varied between 1.043 and 1.127. According to Denison, "most economists believe that in the United States the number can hardly be higher than, say, 20 percent [that is, a scale coefficient of 1.2] at the outside." Zvi Griliches, "Production Functions in Manufacturing: Some Preliminary Results," in Conference on Research in Income and Wealth, *The Theory and Empirical Analysis of Production*, Vol. 31 of Studies in Income and Wealth (New York, 1967), pp. 304–308; Edward F. Dension, *Why Growth Rates Differ* (Washington, D.C., 1967), p. 227.

82. These elasticities were estimated by geometric procedures from David's diagram.

industry even if the number of firms (and total output) was originally a small fraction of the number brought into being by the protective tariff. Recent estimates of late antebellum demand elasticities for such transportables as raw cotton, cotton textiles, and pig iron have yielded figures well below 9. Nor was it reasonable to assume that the elasticity of demand for transportables declined by more than 80 percent during the last two thirds of the nineteenth century. In the case of cereal crops and livestock it is likely that elasticities increased as the century wore on. The progressively greater share of the output of these commodities sold abroad probably tended to make the total demands more rather than less elastic. In the case of cotton, econometric estimates indicate that the elasticity of demand was about 50 percent higher after the Civil War than before.[83]

The point, of course, is that David's diagram should be redrawn to accord with existing empirical information. In Part B of Figure 5, the implied scale coefficient is reduced to 1.1, the level of demand is not fixed but increasing, the elasticity of demand remains constant, and the share of transportation in the c.i.f. price is nearly constant in the non-railroad case and declining in the railroad case. Figure 5 shows that when these changes are made, the unmeasured gain in income due to an increase of scale in the transportation-using industry is quite small relative both to the measured social saving and to the output of the transportation-using industry. It follows that the magnitude of the "indirect social benefit" that David inferred from his diagram turned not on general theoretical considerations but on specific empirical assumptions implicitly incorporated into that diagram, assumptions that exaggerated the relative magnitude of the unmeasured social saving. So, although David's diagram served the useful purpose of directing attention to the neglected question of railroad-induced scale effects in transportation-using industries, it also gave a misleading impression of the magnitude of this effect.

Railroad-induced structural changes

The social saving model is an effective tool in the analysis of the comparative efficiency of transportation systems. When the social saving

83. Paul A. David, "Learning by Doing and Tariff Protection: A Reconsideration of the Case of the Ante-Bellum United States Cotton Textile Industry," this Journal 30 (Sept. 1970), 521–601; Robert Brooke Zevin, "The Growth of Cotton Textile Production After 1815," in Fogel and Engerman, *The Reinterpretation*, pp. 122–147; Robert W. Fogel and Stanley Engerman, "A Model for the Explanation of Industrial Expansion During the Nineteenth Century: With an Application to the American Iron Industry," *Journal of Political Economy*, 77 (May/June 1969), 306–328; Gavin Wright, "Cotton Competition and the Post-Bellum Recovery of the American South," this Journal, 34 (Sept. 1974), 610–635.

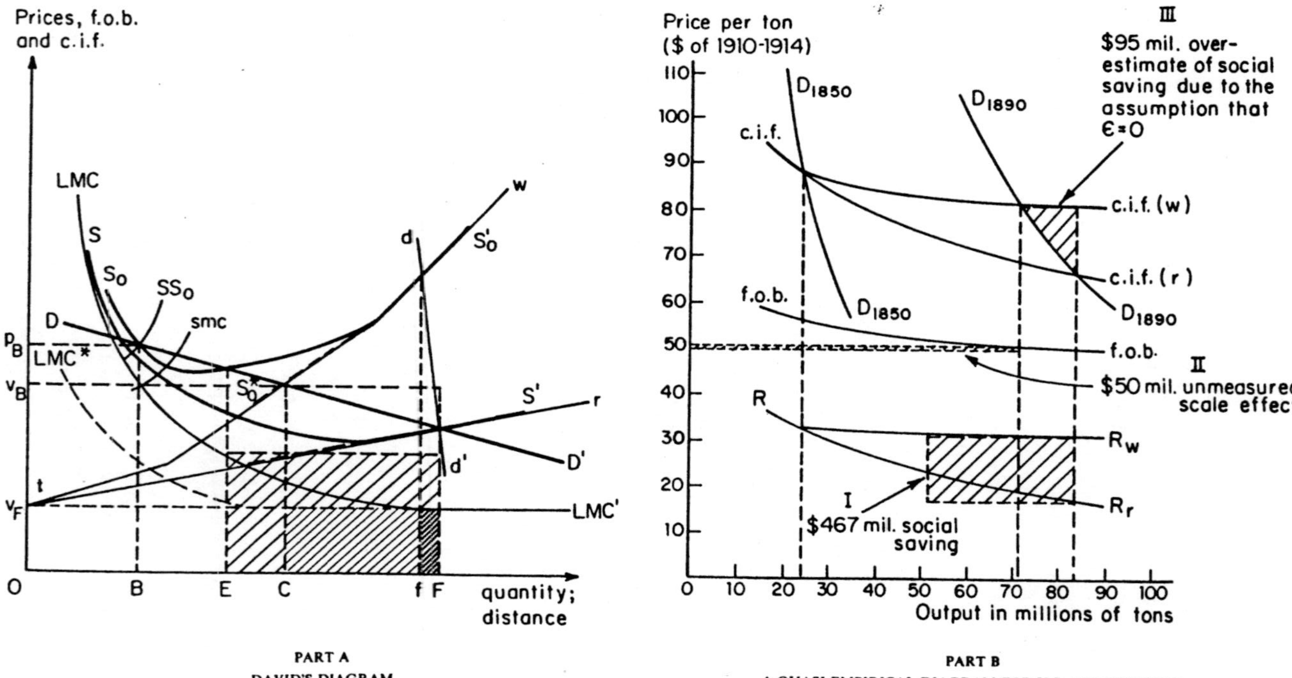

PART A
DAVID'S DIAGRAM

PART B
A QUASI-EMPIRICAL DIAGRAM FOR U.S. AGRICULTURE

Figure 5. Two diagrams on the relative magnitude of railroad-induced scale effects in transportation-using industries.

DISCUSSION OF PART A OF FIG. 5

The curve labelled *MXC-LMC'* is the f.o.b. supply curve of the transportation-using industry. It is downward sloping because of economies of scale, which must be external to the firm. The slope of *LMC-LMC'* to the left of *E* implies that the scale coefficient of the underlying industry production function is 4.2 (cf. the discussion in the Appendix, Section B). David assumes that learning-by-doing will shift *LMC-LMC'* to *LMC*-LMC'* but that such a shift will occur only in a railroad world.

The curve *tw* gives the cost of delivering a unit of output in a non-railroad world and *tr* gives the cost of delivering a unit of output in a railroad world.

The curves $S_0S'_0$ is the c.i.f. supply curve in a non-railroad world and is obtained by summing *LMC-LMC'* and *tw* vertically. The curve *SS'* is the c.i.f. supply curve in a railroad world and is obtained by summing *LMC-LMC'* and *tr* vertically. Note that David has subtracted v_f from *tw* and *tr* before making the addition of the relevant curves.

The curve *DD'* is the long-run market demand curve for transportables (that is, for the output of the transportation-using industry). David argues that in a non-railroad world output would not have expanded beyond *OE*, whereas in a railroad world output would have expanded to *OF*. Consequently, he argues that the entire shaded area above *EF* is "the measure of the total indirect social benefit accruing from the introduction of the 'railroad' *qua* transportation technique." David compares the shaded area over *EF* with the area $fF \cdot v_f$. "Fogel's actual estimate," he writes, "is over-represented in the figure by the insignificant area $fF \cdot v_f$, since he takes the long-run demand for transportables to have been even less price-elastic than the schedule labelled *dd'* allows." Note that the shaded area over *EF* is virtually equal to the area designating the f.o.b. value of the output of transportables in the end period ($v_f \cdot OF$).

DISCUSSION OF PART B OF FIG. 5

I have called this diagram "quasi-empirical" because although it is based on observed U.S. prices, outputs, and transportation rates, it retains a number of unrealistic assumptions that are necessary to allow for a direct comparison with David's diagram. The most important of these hypothetical assumptions is that the scale coefficient in nineteenth-century agriculture between 1850 and 1890 was 1.1. A scale coefficient of 1.1 implies that more than 50 percent of the gain in total factor productivity that Gallman has estimated for this period [cf. Robert E. Gallman, "Changes in Total U.S. Agricultural Factor Productivity in the Nineteenth Century," *Agricultural History*, 46 (Jan. 1972), 207], is attributed here to an increase in scale.

The f.o.b. supply curve can then be derived directly from the price and output measures of crops and livestock set forth in Towne and Rasmussen, "Farm Gross Product" by following the procedure outlined in Appendix, Section B. In order to keep the f.o.b. curve from shifting (again for convenience of comparison with David's diagram), it is necessary to assume no changes in total factor productivity other than those attributable to scale and to keep input prices constant. Then the observed price and output point for 1850 ($55.4 and 24.2 million tons) and the assumed scale coefficient locate the f.o.b. curve. The observed output in 1890 (83.2 million tons) and the f.o.b. curve yields the assumed actual price of $49.2 in 1890. The price per ton for 1850 was obtained by dividing the value of crops and livestock by the tonnage. Only crops and livestock entering farm gross product are included. Forest products were excluded from both the numerator and denominator. The prices are in constant dollars of 1910–1914.

The curve marked R-R_r gives the estimated average actual dollar value of transportation required to deliver a ton of agricultural output from the f.o.b. point to the c.i.f. destination. The 1850 point was estimated by assuming that the ratio of the observed average annual price of corn in Cincinnati to the corresponding price in New York measured the ratio of the f.o.b. to c.i.f. prices [computed from Arthur Harrison Cole, *Wholesale Commodity Prices in the United States 1700–1861, Statistical Supplement* (Cambridge, Mass., 1938), p. 314]. The 1890 point as estimated in a similar manner using the ratio of the Wisconsin and New York prices of wheat as reported in Williamson, *Late Nineteenth-Century*, p. 259. The remainder of the curve was interpolated log-linearly. Such interpolation does not necessarily imply that increases in the productivity of railroads were a function of the scale of agriculture; an incidental temporal correlation between agricultural output and railroad productivity is sufficient.

The curve marked R-R_w gives the price of delivering a ton of agricultural output from the f.o.b. point to the c.i.f. destination in a non-railroad world. The 1890 point was obtained by multiplying the 1890 price in a railroad world by 1.87 (see Table 2 above). It was assumed that the 1850 prices of transporting a ton of agricultural output were identical in the railroad and in a non-railroad world, since over 90 percent of the transportation of agricultural commodities in that year went by means other than railroads (cf. Fogel, *Railroads*, pp. 4–5; Fishlow, *American Railroads*, pp. 18–19). However, choosing a point slightly above $32.4 for 1850 would have little effect on the analysis. The remainder of the R_w curve was interpolated log-linearly between the 1850 and 1890 points.

The curve marked *c.i.f.-c.i.f.(r)* is obtained by the vertical addition of the *f.o.b.* and R-R_r curves. Similarly, the c.i.f.-c.i.f.(w) curve is the result of the vertical addition of the *f.o.b.* and R-R_w curves.

The constant elasticity demand curves for 1850 and 1890 are located by the outputs and c.i.f. prices for the respective years and the assumed elasticities, which in both cases were put at 0.8.

Three shaded areas are shown in the diagram. The rectangle marked *I* is the estimated social saving and is given by the 1890 difference between the R_w and R_r curves ($14.51) and the amount of output (32.2 million tons) shipped by railroad. Note that only about 39 percent of farm gross product was shipped by rail (cf. Fogel, *Railroads*, pp. 74, 76). The rectangle marked *II* is the scale effect induced in agriculture by the railroad. It is the additional cost of producing 71 million tons of output because of the reduced scale of production (71.0 × $0.71 = $50). The traingle marked III is the overestimate of the social saving due to the assumption that $\epsilon = 0$.

Thus, the scale effect is about 11 percent of the measured social saving or about 1.2 percent of gross farm product. Its omission is more than offset by the upward biases due to the assumption that $\epsilon = 0$.

It is worth noting that an increase in the elasticity of demand will have effects that go in opposite directions. The greater ϵ, the greater the upward bias in the social saving estimate due to assuming that $\epsilon = 0$. But the greater ϵ, the greater the downward bias in the social saving due to neglect of the scale effect. Given the magnitude of the scale effect, however, increasing ϵ cannot reverse the finding that the upward bias exceeds the downward bias.

Note also that this diagram does not allow for the substantial decline in the long-run cost of waterway transportation associated with the increased volume of output that was indicated in the second part of this paper.

estimate is built up road by road, as Fishlow did, or commodity by commodity, as Hawke and Metzer did, it is possible to obtain a fairly fine-grained picture of the relative advantages of different carriers under a variety of circumstances. On the other hand, the social saving model is poorly adapted to the analysis of the impact of railroads on the structure of economic activity. It is, for example, possible that "even a social saving as small as one fourth of 1 percent of national income would have ended all or most" production of agricultural surpluses in the North Central states.[84] The social saving model contains no mechanism for assessing either this possibility, or the possibility that a small social saving could have led to dramatic shifts in the balance between agriculture and manufacturing or between investment goods and consumer goods. The social saving model cannot answer these and other structural questions because it has only one sector besides transportation.

The Williamson model transcends this limitation by allowing, in addition to transportation, two production sectors in the Midwest and one in the East.[85] It also contains mechanisms through which one could analyze the influence of railroads on the pattern of interregional trade as well as on the sectoral allocations of labor and capital. Charles Kahn has been investigating the properties of the Williamson model and it was my original intention to present his findings as an appendix to this paper. Kahn's investigation, however, has opened up so many interesting issues that it has burst the bounds of an appendix and deserves to be elaborated in a separate paper. Meanwhile, I would like to offer some brief observations on the Williamson model that draw heavily from Kahn's preliminary findings and also from some unpublished notes that Claudia Goldin has generously made available to me.[86]

Although Williamson attributes the social saving computed from his model to railroads, it is actually the social saving due to *all improvements in transportation and distribution* between 1870 and 1890. He did not measure the cost of railroad transportation from farms to eastern markets directly but instead used the difference in the spot prices of wheat in Iowa and New York as a proxy. Throughout the period from 1870 and 1890, however, most of the wheat shipped eastward from Chicago, Minneapolis, Duluth-Superior, and Milwaukee went by Great Lakes vessels.[87] Consequently, the price differential used by Williamson as a measure of the decline in rail transport costs was quite heavily influenced by the rapid fall in grain transportation rates on the Great Lakes and, to

84. Fogel, *Railroads*, p. 21.
85. See Williamson, *Late Nineteenth-Century American Development*, ch. 9.
86. Several of the points which follow were also raised in McCloskey, "New Model History."
87. U.S. Bureau of Statistics, *Monthly Survey*, pp. 1964–1967; Tunnell, "Statistics," pp. 30–59.

a significant degree, by the decline in grain rates on the Erie Canal, and by the decline in elevator charges, drayage charges, insurance charges, and other marketing costs. The differential in spot prices also, of course, was influenced by short-term disequilibria in both the New York and Iowa markets. Since the spread between the "gold points," or more properly the "wheat points," was quite a high percentage of the Iowa farm price, the disequilibrium component of the observed prices could be quite large. Since Iowa was on the outermost fringes of the wheat belt in 1870, it is likely that its spot price was subject to much greater year-to-year variance at the beginning of the period than was that of farms near the center of wheat production, and that the rate of decrease in the Iowa–New York differential would be much greater than that in the differential between New York and a more central location. The switch from a "railroad" social saving to a social saving due to all increases in transportation and distribution productivity between 1870 and 1890 is not an error but a rather interesting innovation.

It appears that there were errors either in the original computation (perhaps in the program) or in the data sets and simulation results reported by Williamson in his appendices, and that these errors led to an overstatement of the 1890 social saving by about 60 percent. Kahn's efforts to replicate Williamson's results yielded an 1890 social saving not of 21 percent but of 12.8 percent, which is still, of course, a relatively large figure. The estimated social saving also turns out to be substantially influenced by a number of unrealistic assumptions built into the model. One of these is the assumption that it was possible to more than double the amount of service provided by the transportation sector without any diversion of inputs from other sectors. In other words, increases in the ouput of transportation result in a net increase in GNP by the same amount, since there is either no alternative cost for the extra resources required to increase transportation output, or because no additional resources are required. When Kahn amends the model to allow for the alternative cost of the increases in transportation services, the 1890 social saving declines from 12.8 to 6.7 percent of GNP.

The social saving in 1890 generated by Williamson's model poses a difficult index number problem, since the magnitude of the estimate relative to GNP varies considerably with the selection of the prices in which to evaluate real GNP and sectoral output (1870, current-year, or counterfactual current-year). The magnitude of the social saving in particular years is also affected by whether or not one smoothes the series of spot wheat prices to eliminate variations in the inferred cost of transportation that are due to local disequilibria. This exercise suggests that a substantial proportion of the remaining social saving is due to unusual conditions in the extreme years. It would be quite premature, however, to draw the conclusion that appropriate revisions of the Williamson model will necessarily result in a rather small social saving attributable to productivity changes in the transportation sector. Not all of the plausible adjustments are in the direction of reducing the social saving. If, for example, one permits greater flexibility in the intersectoral movement of labor and capital than Williamson allowed, the social saving increases somewhat.

Perhaps the two most interesting of Kahn's preliminary findings are that "dynamic" or time-path effects may be a considerable part of the social saving, and that a small social saving could result in large changes in the patterns of trade. To determine what part of the social saving in 1890 was due to markups in that year and what part was due to the social saving in previous years, Kahn re-ran the simulation under the constraint that transportation costs (Williamson's Z_A and Z_I) did not increase to counterfactual levels until 1890. This run yielded a social saving of 3.7 percent of GNP instead of the 6.7 percent figure obtained when the social saving is allowed to rise continuously (and after an adjustment for the fact that transportation had an alternative cost). It thus appears that the dynamic considerations could account for close to half of the social saving.[88]

The sensitivity of trading patterns to small social savings turns up in both the original Williamson model and in Kahn's various alternative simulations. In all of the models there are years in which the United States is a net importer of grains. Similarly, exports and imports between the East and the West sometimes reverse directions. From the strictly modeling viewpoint, this result poses the question of how to deal with prices that are sometimes exogenous and sometimes endogenous (Williamson assumed that grain prices in the East were fixed in Liverpool).[89] The more intriguing question opened up by this finding is

88. This result obtains when, following Williamson, the social saving is computed in 1870 prices. If 1890 prices are used, the dynamic effects are nearly wiped out. The sensitivity of the dynamic effects to the prices employed serves to re-emphasize the seriousness of the index number problem alluded to above.

89. Some aspects of this problem are addressed by Frank Lewis ("Explaining the Shift of Labor from Agriculture to Industry in the United States: 1869 to 1899," unpublished Ph.D. dissertation, University of Rochester, 1976), who stressed the unrealism of models in which the United States can import agricultural goods at the same price at which it exports them. Lewis uses a simpler framework than Williamson's, allowing him to have separate international buying and selling prices for wheat (the difference being the trans-Atlantic shipping costs). For intermediate prices, demand is the inelastic domestic demand rather than the elastic international demand. Including this international transportation wedge reverses many conclusions about the effects of changes in agricultural productivity. In Williamson's model, declining domestic transportation costs act in many respects like increases in agricultural productivity. Thus, allowing a Lewis-like refinement in the Williamson model could well increase the transportation social saving.

the possibility that regional trading patterns, economic alliances, and political alliances may have been affected profoundly by processes that had only a small impact on the level of GNP.

The exciting new lines of research opened up by the Williamson model clearly deserve to be followed up. But such a pursuit should not be counterposed to further analyses based on the social saving model. The social saving model is, as I have suggested, quite a useful device for analyzing the relative importance of various applications of a given innovation, or the incremental gain in the productivity attained by substituting one innovation for another when such substitution appears possible. Von Tunzelmann's considered and inventive application of the social saving model to the evaluation of the resource saving of steam engines shows that this model has a much wider range of applications than have so far been undertaken. As useful as the Williamson model is for tracing the impact of transportation on some aspects of the structure of production, the practical problems of focusing on these issues forced Williamson, as we have seen, to settle for a rather crude depiction of the transportation sector.

The influence of railroads on economic growth is too complicated to be encompassed by one or even a few models. The models thus far employed in the new economic history of railroads have been quite diverse, and, more often than not, were designed to illuminate quite specific issues. This was the case in Fishlow's analysis of internal migration patterns, in Metzer's study of the unification of the Russian grain market, and in the studies by Fishlow, Hawke, Fenoaltea, Vamplew, and Fremdling of the impact of railroads on the growth of manufacturing industries. Moreover, it is likely that some of the most important aspects of the connection between railroads and economic growth will not yield to formal modeling and will be better served by more traditional historiographic approaches.

The role of controversy

It is in the nature of debates that points of disagreement and discontinuity are exaggerated, while the points of agreement and continuity are slighted. This statement certainly fits early reactions to estimates of the social saving of railroads. Many scholars were jarred when they learned of computations that yielded figures far below the level that then seemed appropriate. Now, more than a decade and a half later, much of the original shock has dissipated. In recent years I have often been asked why anyone should have expected a large social saving.

Still, passions remain fairly high by scholarly standards, and it is probably premature to attempt an assessment of the relationship between the newer and older research. Nevertheless, I wish to report that when, in preparation for the writing of this paper, I reviewed both the old and new literature, I was struck more by the elements of continuity than by those of discontinuity. Certainly the new economic history has done little to change our perception of the sequence of events that constitute the history of modern transportation. Nor has it eroded the proposition that the *collective* impact of advances in transportation technology during the nineteenth century was of such a magnitude as to warrant the title of a "transportation revolution." Nor has it contradicted the belief that this transportation revolution accounts for a considerable part of the growth in per capita income during the nineteenth century.

The contribution of the new work has been to provide a more detailed and somewhat more precise analysis of the nature of that revolution. Much effort has been aimed at measuring the contribution of particular systems and devices to the more or less continuous decrease in unit transportation costs during the nineteenth century.[90] The design of appropriate measures of productivity and the explanation of changes in productivity have required a detailed analysis of the performance characteristic of the large array of devices employed in each of the modes of transportation. The demands of measurement have also required a search for bodies of data not previously assembled by transportation historians as well as a careful reconsideration of the reliability and relevance of those series that had been assembled and utilized in earlier studies.

Much time was devoted to such tedious tasks as the determination of equivalences between various weights and measures, assessment of the homogeneity or non-homogeneity of commodities and services to which particular price series pertained, assessment of the completeness of coverage in various data sources, and construction of new time series from underlying company records, trade association reports, and censuses.

It would be surprising if the many thousands of hours of work spent on such tasks did not produce new insights. In this paper I have alluded to a number of these. Here I wish to summarize briefly the most important findings:

1. It is a misleading oversimplification to identify wagons, waterways, and railroads with a sequence of temporal stages in which each was predominant or to suggest that railroads replaced waterways because waterways had reached the limit of their technological capacity. Nor is it correct to describe waterways as more efficient carriers than wagons, and railroads as more efficient than waterways. The transportation system

90. As Fishlow ("Productivity," pp. 642–644) has pointed out, the social saving can be interpreted as a measure of total factor productivity. Cf. Fogel and Engerman, *The Reinterpretation*, p. 102.

that evolved during the nineteenth century embraced all three modes. The quantities of service delivered by each mode increased throughout the nineteenth century, although at unequal rates. Each mode was more productive than the other two in some domain, and this pattern of specialized pre-eminence continued to the end of the nineteenth century.[91]

2. Nineteenth-century innovations in transportation techniques served to reduce unit transportation costs mainly over medium and long distances. Unit transportation costs of freight were usually as high (or higher) over short distances by railroads and waterways as they were by wagon. Spectacular reductions in short-haul transportation had to await the perfection of motor vehicles.

3. Waterways and railroads were good, but not perfect, substitutes for each other. Waterways generally had an advantage over railroads in the carrying of bulky, low-value items over long distances. Railroads had an advantage in carrying high-value items over both medium and long distances, and in carrying bulky, low-value items over medium distances. For most categories of freight, however, these edges were much smaller than the edge that either waterways or railroads enjoyed over wagons for hauls of medium and long distances.

4. The crux of the transportation revolution of the nineteenth century was the substitution of low-cost water and railroad transportation for high-cost wagon transportation. This substitution was made possible by a dense network of waterways and railroads. Whereas the combination of waterways and railroads provided the most efficient substitute, in most cases so far studied either by itself would have provided most of the resource saving effected by the combination. Railroads were indispensable, however, in regions where waterways were not a feasible alternative.

5. There is no uniform answer to the question of whether the resource gain brought about by railroads or by waterways was the greater. The answer varies with country or region and time period. In mountainous countries, such as Mexico, railroads were the only effective substitutes for wagons. In the United States before 1850 the contribution of waterways may have exceeded that of railroads. After 1860 or 1870 the railroad contribution was probably greater, not because the waterway potential for increased productivity had run its course, but because the marginal cost of transportation with respect to the *density* of the network was higher for waterways than for railroads.

91. The specialized pre-eminence of waterways during the last half of the nineteenth century has been neglected by economic historians because of a preoccupation with canals, which were, in many cases, superseded by railroads, and which only provided a small share of total waterway transportation. Cf. the Appendix, Section A.

6. Productivity advanced at a brisk pace for both waterways and railroads throughout the nineteenth century. Douglass C. North estimated that total factor productivity on ocean freight increased at an annual rate of 3.3 percent over the period from 1814 to 1860. C. K. Harley's analysis of ocean vessels over the period from 1873 to 1890 indicated annual rates of productivity growth of 2.2 percent for sailing vessels and 3.1 percent for steamships.[92] In the case of inland waterways, Erik F. Haites, James Mak, and Gary Walton found that the annual rate of increase in the total factor productivity of Mississippi steamboats was 6.5 percent between 1815 and 1830 and 2.4 percent between 1830 and 1860. We are still without a study of total factor productivity on U.S. inland waterways during the last third of the nineteenth century. The course of freight rates on the Great Lakes, however, suggests a rapid increase in productivity on that waterway. The freight on wheat between Chicago and Buffalo (in constant dollars) declined at an annual rate of 2.6 percent between 1868 and 1898. Since real wages (the main cost component of both waterway services and the construction of vessels) were rising, it is probable that total factor productivity increased more rapidly on the Greal Lakes during this period than on railroads.[93] In the case of railroads, Fishlow's estimates show that total factor productivity gained at annual rates of 5.7 percent between 1839 and 1859, and 2.6 percent between 1859 and 1910.[94] The productivity studies of the past decade, then, suggest that the technological advances of waterway carriers of freight – on the Mississipi at least up to 1860, and on the Great Lakes and ocean routes throughout the century – were quite rapid, even if they did not always match railroad advances.

7. The capacity of various nations and regions to exploit technological possibilities of waterways and railroads depended on the nature of their demand for transportation. Average railroad and waterway rates

92. Douglass C. North, "Sources of Productivity Change in Ocean Shipping," *Journal of Political Economy*, 76 (Sept./Oct. 1968), 965. Charles K. Harley, "The Shift from Sailing Ships to Steamships, 1850–1890: A Study in Technological Change and Its Diffusion," in Donald N. McCloskey, ed., *Essays on a Mature Economy* (London, 1971), p. 228. The rate of growth in total factor productivity for freight transported by sailing ships can be computed from Harley's essay. The rate of productivity growth for freight carried by steamships, however, requires information on the growth of productivity in the building of steamships, which was not reported. I am grateful to Professor Harley for supplying the needed information.

93. Erik F. Haites, James Mak, and Gary M. Walton, *Western River Transportation: The Era of Early Internal Development, 1810–1860* (Baltimore, 1975), pp. 183–184. Interestingly enough, Haites, Mak, and Walton found that the total factor productivity of flatboats increased at an annual rate of 3.8 to 4.4 percent between 1815 and 1860 (ibid., p. 76). Fishlow ("Productivity," p. 626) indicates that railroad total factor productivity rose at an annual rate of 2.3 percent between 1870 and 1900.

94. Fishlow, "Productivity," p. 626.

were higher in England than in the United States because the English economy required hauls mainly of short-to-medium distances, whereas the U.S. hauls were mainly medium-to-long distances.

It is worth noting that although some of these points were developed in the original social-saving studies, not all of them were. And some points vaguely adumbrated in the original studies emerged clearly only in the course of the subsequent debate. I stress this point, because some observers of the debate have misunderstood it. They have interpreted the sharp disagreements among the cliometricians as evidence of the failure of social science methodology, and particularly of quantitative methods, in history.

There is in this view a confusion between artistic and scientific processes. A painting, a concerto, a novel, and even certain types of histories can be the perfect creation of a single individual during a relatively brief period of intense activity. Such artistic works normally have a highly personal quality. Scientific creations, however, are usually protracted over long periods, approach perfection quite gradually, and involve the efforts of a large number of investigators. The social saving controversy has demonstrated the great complexity of the analysis of the developmental impact of railroads, the wide range of issues that need to be pursued, the large amounts of data that must be retrieved, and the many pitfalls that may be encountered in the analysis of these data. Such problems are resolved through collective effort, one aspect of which is the intense debate over the significance and validity of successive contributions.

The various criticisms of the social saving computations served to identify areas in which the initial results were either incorrect, incomplete, or inadequately supported. Quite often the objections were of a conjectural nature, even though they were expressed in a rhetoric that suggested a high degree of certitude. Whatever the rhetoric, the list of criticisms constituted the agenda for subsequent rounds of research. The results of the interaction between the investigators and the critics have been a gradual deepening of the analysis, an improvement of estimating procedures, and the searching out of additional, or more reliable, bodies of evidence bearing on the points at issue. Rather than being a sign of the failure of the cliometric method, the controversy is a sign that the method is working.

Appendix

A. *The method of estimating ton-miles of water transportation and the average length of a water haul in 1889*

I have employed Barger's estimates of the total ton-miles and average distances of hauls in 1889 of the coastwise and intercoastal routes. The corresponding estimates for the Great Lakes and for other inland routes, however, are too low. For the Great Lakes, Barger assumed an average haul of 578 miles, which is well below the estimates of C. H. Keep, secretary of the Lake Carriers' Association, and other experts on water shipping who wrote on the subject in the 1890s. Based on statistics for the Detroit River (through which over three quarters of all the Great Lakes traffic passed in 1889) or the Soo Canal, they put the average length of a haul between 700 and 750 miles (Tunnell, "Statistics," p. 12; *New York Canals*, p. 197).

Barger apparently misinterpreted the data in *Census of Tronsportation 1890*, Part II, pp. 395–465, which deals with transportation on the Mississippi River system. The 2.6 billion ton-miles that he attributed to the system's total movement of coal and lumber refer only to 4.0 million tons of coal shipped from five cities (*ibid.*, p. 408), which means that the average haul on these coal shipments was 658 miles. Since more than half of all lumber shipments on the Mississippi originated in northern Wisconsin or Minnesota, and since 17 percent of all lumber originating on the upper Mississippi (as defined by the census) was destined for the lower Mississippi (*ibid.*, p. 440; cf. pp. 408–409), it appears likely that the average hauls on lumber and coal were about the same.

Barger put the average haul of all other commodities on the Mississippi, as well as all other rivers and canals, at 40 miles. He took this last figure from data obtained from the Army Engineers for the 1920s. But between 1889 and the 1920s, the pattern of traffic on rivers and canals had changed drastically, with much of the long-distance haulage having been abandoned. During the 1890s the Mississippi steamboat packets engaged in the long-distance transportation of agricultural products went out of business. After the turn of the century, long-distance towing of barges carrying agricultural products between St. Louis or Cincinnati and New Orleans was also abandoned. By the time of World War I, only local traffic in agricultural products on the Mississippi system could compete successfully with railroads. See U.S. Department of Agriculture, *Bulletin* No. 71, "Inland Boat Service." by Frank Andrews, (December 19, 1914), pp. 7–9; cf. U.S. Engineer Dept., Board of Engineers for Rivers and Harbors (War Dept.), *Transportation in the Mississippi and Ohio Valleys*, Transportation Series No. 2 (Washington, D.C., 1929), Ch. 3.

In developing his estimate of ton-miles for the other-inland-routes category, Barger did not include an adjustment for the double counting of tonnage which occurs when freight is carried on more than one waterway (for example, on the Great Lakes and on the St. Mary Falls Canal). Such duplication is not a problem if one merely desires to measure ton-miles. It is a problem, however, if one also needs to estimate tons originated (tons not having had a previous line-haul on a

Appendix Table 1. *Estimated ton-miles of water transportation, tons originated, and average length of a haul in 1889*

System	1 *Tons Originated* (10^6)	2 *Average Haul (miles)*	3 *Ton-miles* (10^9)
1. Coastwise	11.9	1,226	14.6
2. Intercoastal	0.307	6,185	1.9
3. Great Lakes (domestic)	25.3	700	17.7
4. Mississippi system	29.4	478	14.1
5. Canals	9.54	143	1.4
6. Totals	76.5		49.7
7. Average haul per ton originated		49,700 ÷ 76.5 = 650 miles	

Sources and Notes: Lines 1 and 2: Barger, *Transportation Industries*, pp. 254–55. Line 3: Col. 1. *ibid.*; col. 2 Tunnell, "Statistics," p. 12; *New York Canals*, p. 197. Line 4: Col 1, Barger, *Transportation Industries*, pp. 254–55; col. 2, computed from data in Census of Transportation 1890, pp. 408, 439-40 on the assumption that lumber had the same average haul as coal, and that the average haul on all commodities except coal and lumber was 200 miles. Line 5: Cols. 1 and 2, *Census of Transportation* 1890, Part II, pp. 474-79. Tonnage on ship canals and on canalized rivers were excluded. Since such canals were connecting links between other waterways (such as between Lake Superior and Lake Michigan), this tonnage has already been attributed to some other waterway. The exclusion of the ton-miles of these canals from col. 3, however, imparts a downward bias into the average haul. About 60 percent of the tonnage and 70 percent of the ton-miles entered in line 5 are attributable to the New York State canals, the data for which are reported in *New York Canals*, pp. 181–83. For the other canals, I assumed that the ratio of the average length of a haul to the "averaging working length" for the New York canals (0.686) also prevailed on other canals. "Averaging working length" of the New York canals was defined as the length of each canal in the system, weighted by that canal's share in the total tonnage. An analogous definition was used for the other canals. Thus 0.686 times the "average working length" of the other canals yielded the estimated average haul on these canals. It should be noted that about half of the tonnage on the New York canals originated elsewhere, so that the sum of col. 1 tends to overstate tons originated. This will impart a downward bias on the estimated average haul (in line 7), but this double counting does not bias the average haul on canals or the total ton-miles on canals.

connecting waterway) and the average haul of tons originated, as is the case in this paper.

The revised estimates, presented in Appendix Table 1, omit transportation on the rivers that were not part of the Mississippi system, so both the totals for tonnage and ton-miles may be understated, but the likely error is small. The revised estimate of the total ton-miles of contiguous domestic water transportation for 1889 is 49.7 billion, which exceeds Barger's estimate (the sum of the first 4 columns of his Table H-1) by 13.9 billion.

B. *The method of estimating the scale coefficient implicit in David's f.o.b. supply curve*

David's discussion of the diagram is quite terse, and not all of the specifications of his f.o.b. supply curve, which he identifies as *LMC-LMC'*, are stated explicitly. However, for reasons indicated in the text, it is clear that the economies of scale involved here must be external to the firm, so that *LMC-LMC'* must be the *industry-wide* supply curve. Since the *LMC-LMC'* curve is the locus of the long-run equilibrium points of the individual firms summed horizontally, *LMC-LMC'* must also be the locus of the average costs of the individual firms summed horizontally. This is because in the long run (that is, a period long enough for the individual firm to vary its plant size but not the scale of the industry) the individual firms will adjust their plant size so as to produce at the point at which long-run marginal cost and long-run average cost intersect, and this will be true at every industry-wide scale of operation. Since movements along the *LMC-LMC'* curve are due to changes in the scale of the industry, the *LMC-LMC'* curve will be of the form:

$$C_i/Q_i = Q_i^{(1/x)-1} f(p_j)$$

which follows from the total cost curve,

$$C_i = Q_i^{1/x} f(p_j),$$

where C_i is the total cost of the industry-wide output in period i, Q_i is the industry-wide output in period i, x is the scale coefficient (the sum of the output elasticities of the industry-wide production function), and p_j is a vector of the prices of inputs.

Measurements performed on David's diagram indicate that when $Q_2 \div Q_1 = 2$, $(C_2 \div Q_2) \div (C_1 \div Q_1) = 0.59$. Hence we may write:

$$\frac{\dfrac{C_2}{Q_2}}{\dfrac{C_1}{Q_1}} = \frac{C_2}{C_1} \times \frac{Q_1}{Q_2} = \frac{C_2}{C_1} \times 0.5 = 0.59,$$

$$\text{or } \frac{C_2}{C_1} - 1.18.$$

Since the p_j are presumed to remain constant, it follows that:

$$\frac{C_2}{C_1} = \left(\frac{Q_2}{Q_1}\right)^{1/x},$$

or $1.18 = 2^{1/x}$, and $x = 4.2$.

"Industrial structure and the emergence of the modern industrial corporation"

by Jeremy Atack

In his study of the managerial revolution in America, Alfred Chandler (1977) proposes that the modern industrial corporation evolved in response to the technological changes that occurred in the latter half of the nineteenth century. Chandler's argument is that the modern business corporation evolved by taking advantage of continuous production process technologies and advances in transportation. As evidence for his thesis, Chandler surveyed primary and secondary literature, carefully weaving together case studies to draw general conclusions. He noted that power and other mechanical innovations led to higher fixed costs in plant and equipment for many of the modern industries. In addition, the technological revolution in transportation and communication caused by the completion of railroad and telephone networks created a national market for many products. With expanded markets, the potential economies of scale could be exploited, with large firms producing more output at a lower average cost. More output required a more complex system of production and distribution, which contributed to the increase in the size and complexity of the firm.

While Chandler's generalizations have convinced many, he has not attempted to test the hypotheses quantitatively. Jeremy Atack takes up this task in "Industrial Structure and the Emergence of the Modern Industrial Corporation." Atack tests Chandler's key argument about rising economies of scale by measuring the extent to which the average industrial firm at the end of the nineteenth century differed in size from firms prior to the changes in technology and transportation.

Chandler's chapter on railroads emphasized the difficulties businesses had in measuring their own cost curves. Similarly, Atack stresses the problems modern economists have in knowing the curves' shapes. Atack is uncomfortable with standard procedures for analyzing production functions to determine economies of scale. He argues that there is a wide range of efficient scales that production functions often fail to reveal. Instead, because he has the luxury of dealing with the long run, Atack utilizes the economist's version of Darwin's "survival of the fittest" by applying the survivor technique to a large sample of manufacturing plants and revealing differences across industries in the sizes of surviving plants and their ranges.

No method is perfect. Any method raises questions. For example, how can we untangle changes in plant size due to technological change from those occurring because of the working out of long-run equilibrium? What period of time is the "long run?" How can the survivor technique evaluate new products, such as refined petroleum and photographic film, that did not exist in the earliest period?

Additional Reading

Alfred D. Chandler, Jr., *The Visible Hand: The Managerial Revolution in American Business*, Cambridge, MA: Harvard University Press, 1977.

John James, "Structural Change in American Manufacturing, 1850–1890," *Journal of Economic History*, 43 (June 1983), 433–59.

Naomi Lamoreaux, *The Great Merger Movement in American Business, 1895–1904*, New York: Cambridge University Press, 1985.

Anthony O'Brien, "Factory Size, Economies of Scale, and the Great Merger Wave of 1898–1902," *Journal of Economic History*, 48 (September 1988), 639–49.

Oliver Williamson, "The Modern Corporation: Origins, Evolution, Attributes," *Journal of Economic Literature*, 19 (December 1981), 1537–68.

12

Industrial structure and the emergence of the modern industrial corporation

JEREMY ATACK

I. Introduction

Alfred D. Chandler, Jr.'s thesis that the modern U.S. industrial corporation evolved in response to the technological changes in the latter half of the 19th century has been widely acclaimed and has had a profound impact on contemporary thought regarding the business enterprise (Chandler, 1977; Williamson, 1981, 1982). Unfortunately, it has not been subjected to rigorous empirical testing, which reflects not a lack of interest in his ideas but rather the unavailability of appropriate data for the entire period and the difficulties in modeling many of the qualitative factors in the model. Although this paper does not overcome all of these problems, it represents the first systematic attempt to address the core of Chandler's thesis with quantitative evidence.[1]

In the long run, competition, whether pure or tainted by elements of monopoly, tends to drive less efficient producers out of business. Using this observation and counterfactual analysis, I develop an indirect and admittedly incomplete test of Chandler's key argument that the modern business corporation evolved by taking advantage of continuous production process technologies and the opportunities afforded by the railroad and declining transport costs to market a high volume of production nationwide. This is accomplished by measuring the extent to which the average industrial firm at the end of the century (when most of the

Source: Jeremy Atack, "Industrial Structure and the Emergence of the Modern Industrial Corporation," *Explorations in Economic History* (1985), 29–52.

I thank Fred Bateman, Larry Neal, Kenneth Sokoloff, and the anonymous referees of this Journal for their helpful comments and suggestions on earlier drafts of this paper. Any remaining errors and the interpretation are my own.

1. John James' recent important article looks at only one half of Chandler's argument. It examines the role played by technological change in altering the structure of American industry in the latter half of the 19th century. It does not address the issue of the role played by transportation and distribution in the changing market structure. However, despite the differences in scope and methodology, our conclusions are generally mutually consistent. See James (1983).

developments discussed by Chandler had taken place) differed in size from firms that survived the Civil War decade, that is, prior to such changes. In the process, I also develop a quantitative measure of the early spread of factory production in America which extends the analyses by Chandler, Laurie and Schmitz, and Sokoloff (Chandler, 1972; Laurie and Schmitz, 1981; Sokoloff, 1984).

My evidence comes from the various censuses of manufacturing but, although it has a quantitative basis, the results regarding Chandler's thesis are ordinal rather than cardinal. They indicate that few industries, in aggregate, exhibited a radically different industrial structure in 1900 from that which should have evolved from a long-run adjustment to conditions as they had existed in 1870.[2] The typical plant at the turn of the century in most industries was no larger than an efficient plant in 1870 would have been. Industrial structure in 1900 can therefore be interpreted as the long-run equilibrium outcome of the forces put in motion between 1850–1870, rather than the product of new, radically different, influences in the subsequent period. Nevertheless, the thrust of Chandler's thesis is substantiated. In some industries, the average scale of operation in 1900 was much larger than that of an efficient plant of 1870. These were generally those industries identified by Chandler as adopting high-speed, continuous production technologies and embracing the nationwide marketing opportunities afforded by a national transportation system and communications media. At the same time, however, three industries (leather tanning, boots and shoes, and clothing) which were not among those thought by Chandler most likely to be affected by these changes, also experienced dramatic changes in establishment size between 1870 and 1900.[3] Although the changes in these industries were not quite of sufficient magnitude to make the average plant in 1900 larger than the very largest surviving plants of 1870, the relative changes in their average size of plant far exceeded those in the other industries which fall outside Chandler's discussion.

II. Constraints upon the early development of large scale factory production

In the face of scarce labor and capital, most manufacturing enterprises in the first half of the 19th century remained small and large firms emerged

2. This might be construed as inconsistent with James' finding that the direction of technological change after 1880 differed from that before 1880, becoming more biased toward labor augmentation (James, 1983, pp. 441–443). It is not. My argument is in terms solely of plant size and does not imply that the industrial structure in 1900 was unchanged from that in 1870.

3. James (1983, pp. 444, 448) also notes the marked change in relative size of optimal plants in these industries. The changes in the clothing industry are discussed in some detail by Fraser (1983).

only when and where those constraints could be eased. Firms, for example, sought to create a captive labor force. The New England textile mills did this by tapping the pool of unmarried farmers' daughters, offering a supplementary source of income to the impoverished farm sector, and education and strict moral guidance to their charges (Abbott, 1908–1909; Ware, 1931, pp. 198–235). In the South, slaves were often used, especially on the "iron" plantations, or else manufacturers such as William Gregg and Daniel Pratt built model communities to tie labor to the mill.[4] Capitalization remained small so long as the market for equity capital was thin. Businesses were forced to rely upon the personal resources of the owner, relatives, and friends, reinvestment of profits, and the good offices of their suppliers for investment funds (Davis, 1957). Raising capital was made even more difficult by unlimited liability which made investors unwilling to relinquish day-to-day supervision to professional managers, and prevented both the division of labor within, and between, firms (Ware, 1931, pp. 147–157).

Power, too, restricted the firm's growth potential. Where more than human strength was needed, water power was usually substituted (Hunter, 1979; Atack *et al.*, 1980). Yet the power potential of most water rights was quite limited and the water supply was frequently unreliable and seasonal; unusable in winter's ice, spring's freshets, and the drought of summer. The cost burdens of seasonality, however, were not great so long as fixed capital remained small and production was interruptable. More serious at the time was the physical limit to the exploitation of the hydraulic potential of a site. This constrained industrial development and limited urban growth. Extensive industrial development and urbanization based upon waterpower was confined to relatively few sites such as those along the Merrimack River in Massachusetts at Lowell and Lawrence. However, urban growth alone was no panacea. Although it brought the promise of an adequate labor supply and afforded a concentrated market area, it also brought competing demands for the limited water resources as drinking water and for sanitation (Hunter, 1979, pp. 204–291 and pp. 530–535). And at many of the sites where the water supply was more regular and abundant, development potential was handicapped by remote location and the high cost of transportation.

4. For a discussion of the general use of slave labor in the South, see Starobin (1970); for labor in the southern iron industry, see Bradford (1959). The efforts of southern industrialists to keep white labor are described in Gregg (1855). See Mitchell (1928).

III. The emergence of the factory as the dominant production method

These constraints gradually eased, especially after 1840. The adoption of steam power, made feasible and economical by new and cheaper supplies of coal, played a critical role in the developments by freeing firms from waterpower's straitjacket (Chandler, 1972). The impact was revolutionary. Steam-powered plants could be located in towns and cities rather than alongside the nearest feasible water right. Location decisions were simplified. Labor supplies posed less of a problem. A market was to be found at the factory gates and, since the city was often a node on the transportation system, manufacturers also had easier access to more distant consumers.

These changes had a profound impact upon production methods. The factory, characterized by mechanization and the specialization of labor, began to replace artisanal shops by 1850, especially in urban areas. For a while, the small scale shop continued to survive in rural areas where it was shielded by high transport costs from competition with the more efficient urban factory (Sokoloff, 1984), but its days were numbered.

Although a factory as compared to an artisan's shop is recognizable when confronted by the choice, it is less easy to provide a clear-cut operational definition for that complex organizational and institutional form. Sokoloff provides none. However, in their study of Philadelphia's industrial development, Laurie and Schmitz suggest a simple classification of manufacturing enterprises into artisan shops, sweatshops, manufactories, and factories based on clearly defined and measurable principles (Laurie and Schmitz, 1981). They define a factory as any enterprise using an inanimate power source (water or steam, or a combination of the two), while artisan shops, sweatshops, and manufactories were distinguished from one another by the size of their labor force and none used an inanimate power source.[5] Albeit crude, this classification scheme proves extremely useful and, for Philadelphia, their results show a sharp increase in factory employment between 1850 and 1880 across all industries. In Philadelphia's clothing industry, for example, factory employment in 1850 accounted for only 10% of the industry's total, but by 1880, a majority (52%) of clothing industry workers worked in factories (Laurie and Schmitz, 1981, p. 59).

5. Laurie and Schmitz define an artisan shop as an establishment employing six or fewer workers and using no inanimate power. Sweatshops and manufactories likewise used no inanimate power but had larger labor forces, 7–25 employees for sweatshops, and over 25 workers for manufactories. See Laurie and Schmitz (1981, pp. 53–65). They also separately identify "Outwork" establishments, something we cannot do with the data at our disposal.

Table 1. *The percentage of industry value-added produced in artisan shops, sweatshops, manufactories, and factories 1850 and 1870*

Industry SIC	Industry	Method of production							
		Artisans[a]		Sweatshops[b]		Manufactory[c]		Factory[d]	
		1850	1870	1850	1870	1850	1870	1850	1870
2011	Meat packing	32	31	11	0	15	0	41	69
2041	Flour milling	9	5	0	0	0	0	91	95
2057	Bread and other bakery products	86	76	10	9	0	0	4	15
2082	Malt liquors	37	21	25	0	0	0	37	79
2085	Distilled, rectified, and blended liquors	10	4	20	4	0	0	70	93
2100	Tobacco manufacture	24	30	30	33	46	35	0	2
2211	Cotton textiles	0	0	0	0	4	3	96	97
2231	Woolen goods	0	4	0	0	0	12	100	83
2321	Men's, youth's, and boys' clothing	12	16	39	24	49	42	0	18
2351	Millinery	18	10	27	27	53	17	1	47
2421	Sawmills and planing mills	2	1	1	2	0	0	96	97

2431	Millwork	13	3	16	2	0	0	71	95
2511	Wood household furniture	52	18	14	6	4	8	31	68
2700	Printing, publishing, and allied industries	19	25	30	19	0	0	50	56
3111	Leather tanning and finishing	54	20	16	7	0	0	30	73
3131	Boots and shoes	38	33	23	20	39	25	0	23
3199	Saddlery and harness	62	71	18	20	20	8	0	1
3251	Brick and structural tile	16	8	54	61	30	7	0	24
3312	Pig iron	1	0	1	1	34	0	64	99
3321	Gray iron foundries	4	1	5	1	0	40	90	58
3444	Sheet metal work	89	41	5	6	0	27	5	26
3511	Steam engines	5	2	1	3	2	12	92	83
3522	Farm machinery and equipment	23	2	9	5	0	58	67	35
3799	Wagons and carriages	32	33	48	30	16	17	4	21

Source: Calculated from the Bateman–Weiss samples from the manuscript censuses of manufactures.

[a] Artisan shops: No inaminate power; 1–6 employees.

[b] Sweatshops: No inaminate power; 7–25 employees.

[c] Manufactories: No inanimate power; over 25 employees.

[d] Factories: Steam or water power.

A similar pattern emerges for the whole country between 1850 and 1870 across a wide range of industries. Despite there being virtually no change in the proportion of establishments using steam and water power between 1850 and 1870, the fraction of total value-added produced in factories expanded rapidly.[6] Some industries in particular experienced sharp increases in the fraction of factory value-added (Table 1). Whereas in 1850 no boots and shoes or men's clothing had been produced in factories, by 1870, 23 and 18%, respectively, of their industry value-added was accounted for by factory production.[7] And in the millinery industry where only 1% of value-added in 1850 had been produced in mechanized works, 47% came from steam or water-powered mills by 1870. Rapid advances in factory production were also evident in industries such as meat packing, malt liquors, millwork, furniture making, leather tanning, and pig iron which had begun the switch to inanimate power before 1850. By 1870, more than half of the value-added in these industries came from establishments which we have called factories.

In a few industries there was little change in the proportion of factory-produced goods. By 1850, flour, cotton textiles, and lumber were almost exclusively manufactured in plants using steam or water for power. They were the pioneers of the new system.

Even in tobacco manufacture, the handicraft industry par excellence before the introduction of Bonsack's cigarette machine in the 1880s, 2% of industry value-added by 1870 was coming from factories. However, it would be fair to characterize factory production of tobacco products and saddlery and harness as insignificant in 1870. These were the only industries in which factory organization had failed to make an impression.

In four of the industries shown in Table 1 (woolen goods, iron foundaries, steam engines, and agricultural implements), the proportion of industry value-added produced by factories apparently declined. No significance should be attached to this result. It simply reflects an increase in the fraction of plants for which no power source was given in 1870.

6. Although Laurie and Schmitz allow factories to use water or steam power, or a combination of the two, we have not been able to distinguish the latter from establishments using a combination of animate power sources. Our figures therefore represent lowerbound estimates on the use of inanimate power and the spread of the factory system.

7. These results are not directly comparable with those of Laurie and Schmitz because they portray the spread of the factory system by the increasing percentage of the industry's labor force employed in factories. I use the fraction of total industry value-added originating in factories. Furthermore while they give results for 1850 and 1880, I only have data for 1850, 1860, and 1870.

The rise of the factory was usually paralleled by a decline in artisan shops. The percentage of industry value-added produced in artisan shops fell in 18 of 24 industries in Table 1. It rose only in tobacco manufacture, woolen goods, clothing, printing, saddlery and harness, and carriages and wagons. Except for woolens, each of these industries also experienced an increase in factory production. Increases in small-scale production seem quite plausible in these activities. Men's clothing, for example, included tailoring establishments catering to the custom trade and with rising incomes, growing urbanization, and higher valued activities for women, the substitution of professionally tailored men's clothes for domestically produced ones seems eminently plausible. Increasing literacy too likely created new markets for printing shops and newspaper offices.

Sweatshops in six industries made marginal gains in their share of total industry value-added. None seems particularly dramatic, and, given the sample sizes involved, the changes are probably well within the margin of error. Some dramatic gains, however, were registered by the largest of the nonmechanized enterprises, the manufactories. Some of their increased importance might be attributed to extensive growth but the data do not permit us to quantify this. Artisan's shops grew and became sweatshops: sweatshops grew and became manufactories. A number of industries, which in 1850 had no manufactories, saw quite significant fractions of their output produced by such enterprises by 1870. In farm machinery, for example, manufactory value-added rose from zero in 1850 to 58% in 1870. Given the nature of the product, it seems unlikely that those businesses were producing plows, reapers, seed drills and so on, from scratch. More likely, they were assembly plants but the census data do not permit such a determination.

IV. Economies of scale and the survivor technique

Although the factory became the dominant mode of production in most industries, its adoption did not necessarily imply large-scale operation; the technology of the day was not one that demanded high rates of output to realize lowered production costs. Efficiency came from the form rather than the size of the organization. Sokoloff argues that much of this gain in efficiency stemmed from better utilization of the labor input, particularly entrepreneurial labor (Sokoloff, 1984), while the "maximum speed of cutting or shaping wood, cloth, or textile products by machinery was quickly reached. Nor did the spinning and weaving of natural fibers or the tanning of natural leather lend itself to massive increase of throughput by a greater application of energy" (Chandler, 1977, p. 242). Indeed, what evidence we have confirms that the potential economies of scale were often realizeable by relatively small plants (Atack, 1976, 1977; Sokoloff, 1984).

Scale economies are usually estimated by the ordinary least-squares fit of a homogeneous production function. That approach, however, disguises the rapid exhaustion of scale economies in the 19th century manufacturing data because it implies a linear cost function and scale economies that are independent of plant size. A number of alternative production function forms have been developed overcoming the problem,[8] but the basic approach remains flawed within the context of Chandler's thesis. His emphasis upon both forces internal to the firm (the technology of continuous production) and external (falling transport costs and the widening market) makes production function analysis inappropriate as a test of his hypothesis.

What in needed is a methodology incorporating factors internal to the firm and its production technology and externalities that is capable of dealing with dynamic adjustments. Such a technique exists. It is called the "survivor technique."[9]

The survivor technique uses the economic theory of long-run equilibrium adjustment to identify those size classes of plant that not only survived the rigors of market competition and the test of time, but also succeeded in increasing their share of total industry value-added. Competitive pressures guarantee that in the long run only the efficient firms survive. And survival is the ultimate "market test" of efficiency.

A number of assumptions are implicit in the technique. These have been discussed in detail by others, notably by William Shepherd, but there still appears to be some confusion about them (Saving, 1961; Shepherd, 1967). Shepherd, for example, argues that "survivor estimates for firm sizes are likely to be more valid for atomistic industries . . . than for highly concentrated ones," because the assumptions of atomistic competition ensure that, in the long run, market pressures force all surviving plants to operate at minimum long and short-run average cost (Shepherd, 1967, p. 115). Unfortunately, survivorship is perhaps least readily identified under conditions of perfect competition for, whereas demand shifts under conditions of atomistic competition affect only the number of firms in the industry, such changes under other market structures permanently alter the market solution, including the optimum plant size. What evidence we have suggests that American industry,

8. See, for example, the variable scale elasticity production functions developed by Ringstad (1974); Soskice (1968); and Zellner and Revankar (1969). There is also the translog production function, which under certain conditions is nonhomogeneous. See Griliches and Ringstad (1971, p. 10). For a discussion of the merits and disadvantages of each see Atack (1976, Chapter 2).

9. The fundamental idea of the survivor technique may be traced back to John Stuart Mill and Willard Thorp, but it owes its modern revival to Stigler (1950, 1958).

even before the Civil War, was not characterized by perfect competition, but rather by local monopolies protected from competition with each other by high transportation costs (Bateman and Weiss, 1975a,b).

Profit-maximizing behavior, however, still ensures the survival of lower cost plants even under conditions of imperfect competition, monopolistic competition, or oligopoly. Survivorship under these conditions no longer carries the implication of cost minimization. To avoid confusion between survivorship and the economic concept of optimum firm size, Leonard Weiss coined the phrase "minimum efficient scale" (MES) to characterize the smallest range of surviving firms (Weiss, 1964, 1965). This terminology is appropriate regardless of market structure and we will also use this convention.

Atomistic competition also presupposes no technological change and yet the movement toward a deterministic surviving plant size may be most pronounced when technological change is greatest. Under these same conditions, production function estimates are unreliable and biased as they assume technological homogeneity between observations. Although the pre–Civil War period was not one of exceptionally rapid and profound technological change, there was some, most notably the steam engine. Its adoption was usually essential for the development of continuous production processes. Water power, even where large expenditures had been made on storage such as in the headwaters of the Merrimack, remained dependent upon the seasons and random events such as showers of rain. It was inconsistent with round-the-clock, all-year-long production. Shorter working hours per day, fewer hours per year, and the limited potential development determined by nature are all reflected in the relative output levels of steam and water-powered plants. Steam-driven plants in almost every industry were, on average, larger than water-powered plants. For example, steam-driven saw mills produced an average of $5,400 (1860 dollars) value-added in 1870 compared with only $1,400 for water-powered mills. Simiarly, iron blast furnaces and rolling mills had mean values-added of $56,700 and $4,700, respectively, for steam- and water-powered plants.[10] These differentials were to be found in every region, including New England.

Since production delays represented ever increasing opportunity cost and capital losses, steam gradually replaced water even in those areas which still had fairly abundant water power. Whereas in 1850, among those enterprises reporting a source of motive power, steam was used by

10. Data from the Bateman–Weiss samples from the manuscript censuses. Prices were adjusted by the rise (or fall) in the Warren–Pearson price index back to 1860 dollars. See U.S. Department of Commerce (1975, Series E52–63).

only 8% and water by 35%, by 1870 steam was used by 21% and the fraction of water-powered plants had declined to 25%.[11]

Externalities, such as higher population and transport densities, a more skilled labor force, more sophisticated capital markets, and a superior supply of ancillary and support services, also came to play a more important role in determining relative costs between establishments over time. Such factors could well have placed plants in different locations on separate families of cost curves quite independently of the technology which they used. The large manufacturer, for example, may have been able to exercise some monopsony power to purchase inputs at lower prices than his smaller competitors. Certainly the large New England textile firms had access to the imperfect capital markets of the time at preferential rates (Davis, 1957; Ware, 1931, pp 146–157; McGouldrick, 1968, pp. 21–28, 121–138). This would, per force, affect their choice of technique and shift their cost curves. It would also influence their ability to survive.

Much of the foregoing discussion has suggested reasons why costs should have fallen for larger firms, but a strong case can also be made for decreasing returns to scale in the very largest plants arising from the traditional source, managerial inefficiency. The tools to manage effectively (cost accounting, organizational forms, etc.) were only developed slowly, beginning at first in the railroads and then spreading to other industries, but their impact was not very great until after the Civil War (Chandler, 1977, pp. 81–121, 377ff.).

V. Plant survivorship, 1850–1870

Applying the survivor technique to the Bateman–Weiss manufacturing samples reveals marked differences across industries in the sizes of surviving plants and their ranges (Table 2). The results generally reveal a wide range of surviving plants in almost every industry and suggest that a considerable portion of the long-run average cost curve may have been flat or almost so. This finding is consistent with the 20th century cost function studies reported in Walters (1963), the survivor technique results reported by Saving (1961), and production function estimates for the 19th century (Atack, 1976, 1977; James, 1983; Sokoloff, 1984). A wide range of plants of different sizes thus seem to have been cost competitive with one another. In five industries (flour milling, bread

11. The percentage of plants using steam or water power as a fraction of those reporting a power source rose from 43% in 1850 to 57% in 1860 and dropped to 46% in 1870. Changes in the definition of an establishment may account for the decline between 1860 and 1870. During this same period the switch from water to steam also slowed. See Atack *et al.* (1980).

and bakery products, tobacco manufacture, saw and planing mills, and brick works), however, the range of surviving plants was relatively narrow, embracing less than \$16,000 value-added. These products were typically locally produced and consumed. Plants producing them supplied markets limited by product perishability, by localized brand loyalties, or by a low value-to-weight ratio in the presence of high transport costs.

Comparing my estimates of the range of optimal plant sizes generated by the survivor technique using the Bateman and Weiss samples from the manuscript censuses of manufactures with those reported by James derived from translog production function estimates on aggregate census data shows little overlap between them. Part of this may be due to differences between our data sets and estimation techniques for production function estimates which I have made using the Bateman–Weiss data showed a much higher degree of overlap between the ranges.[12] Nevertheless, surviving plants were generally equal to or larger than the optimal (i.e., constant returns to scale) plant size implied by production function estimates even in my estimates, suggesting the existence of positive externalities which further reduced unit costs for larger firms.

Estimates of the minimum efficient scale of operation are also given in Table 2. The minimum efficient scale of plant was the smallest size of plant which increased its share of total industry value-added over the period. In industries suspected of not being perfectly competitive, this measure is to be preferred to the range of optimal plant sizes because long-run equilibrium is reached at some output less than that which minimizes long-run average cost if the market is other than perfectly competitive. The minimum efficient scale in many industries was often quite small. In flour milling, for example, firms producing as little as \$100 (1860 dollars) value-added in 1870 could still be efficient. At the opposite end of the scale, the minimum efficient scale in cotton textiles was apparently \$128,000.[13] Small textile mills could not, apparently, survive but small flour mills could.

The ratio of the percentage of value-added in 1870 produced in optimally sized plants to the percentage produced in those plants in 1850 is an attempt to measure the extent of the adjustment toward optimally sized plants over the period. The larger this number the greater the proportionate adjustment toward optimality between 1850 and 1870. In most cases, the increase in the proportion of output

12. My production function estimates were made using a variable scale elasticity production function formulation after Zellner and Revankar (1969) rather than the translog formulation used by James and the estimates used cross-sectional data rather than pooled cross-section/time series.

13. In 1850, the cost-minimizing size for a cotton textile mill was less than half this amount, \$54,000. See Sokoloff (1984).

Table 2. *Plant survival in the United States by industry, 1850–1870[a] (1860 dollars)[b]*

Industry SIC	Industry	MES[c] ($000)	Range of optimal plant sizes ($000)[d]	Ratio of 1870 optimal value added to that in 1850	% of Industry value-added from optimal plants, 1870
2011	Meat packing	32	32–64	3.8	69
2041	Flour milling	0.1	0.1–8	1.5	54
2057	Bread and other bakery products	0.5	0.5–16	1.8	87
2082	Malt liquors	32	32–128	Inf.[e]	44
2085	Distilled, rectified, and blended liquors	32	32–128	2.4	52
2100	Tobacco manufacture	2	2–16	1.6	49
2211	Cotton textiles	128	128–*	Inf.	63
2231	Woolen goods	32	32–256	2.5	87
2321	Men's, youth's, and boys' clothing	16	16–256	1.6	59
2351	Millinery	64	64–128	Inf.	40
2421	Sawmills and planing mills	0.5	0.5–16	1.5	50
2431	Millwork	2	2–64	1.4	75
2511	Wood household furniture	32	32–128	2.7	44

2700	Printing, publishing, and allied industries	2	2–64	1.9	99
3111	Leather tanning and finishing	8	8–128	1.8	68
3131	Boots and shoes	16	16–256	1.4	53
3199	Saddlery and harness	0.5	0.5–64	1.2	100
3251	Brick and structural tile	1	1–8	1.1	40
3312	Pig iron	64	64–256	2.0	68
3321	Gray iron foundries	4	4–128	1.1	96
3444	Sheet metal work	2	2–32	1.1	49
3511	Steam engines	8	8–128	1.9	88
3522	Farm machinery and equipment	32	32–*	Inf.	66
3799	Wagons and carriages	32	32–128	4.3	23

[a] The following plants sizes (measured in terms of value-added) were used: \$0–249, \$250–499, \$500–999, \$1000–1999, \$2000–3999, \$4000–7999, \$8000–15,999, \$16,000–31,999, \$32,000–63,999, \$64,000–127,999, \$128,000–255,999, \$256,000 and over.

[b] The values of inputs and outputs were adjusted by the appropriate price index for the product from the Warren–Pearson price index. See U.S. Department of Commerce (1975), Series E52–63. (1860 = 100).

[c] MES = Minimum Efficient Scale, that is the smallest size class of plant increasing its share of total industry value-added, 1850–1870. See Weiss (1964).

[d] Range of size classes of plant increasing their share of total industry value-added.

[e] Inf. = infinite.

[f] * = Upper bound is open ended.

produced in optimally sized plants was quite large; in 17 of the 24 cases, there was better than a 50% increase. Moreover, in all but seven cases (malt liquor, tobacco, millinery, furniture, brick, sheet metal, and wagons and carriages) more than half of 1870 value-added originated in optimally sized plants. In some cases the increase was exceptionally dramatic. Whereas in 1850 no farm machinery manufacturer produced more than $32,000 value-added, by 1870 two-thirds of industry output was produced by plants larger than that. Among them would be firms such as McCormick ($407,000 (1860 dollars) value-added in 1870) and Case ($283,000 value-added). However, as the data in Table 1 indicate, there is little relationship per se between the growth of factory production and the concentration of industry value-added in plants of optimal size. Factory production did not guarantee survival, nor did survival necessarily imply factory production.

VI. 1870 optimal plants and industrial structure, 1870–1900

We have used the range of optimal plant sizes from Table 2 as the basis for estimating the number of optimal plants which industry value-added could have sustained with no changes in technology, externalities, or the costs of transport between 1870 and 1900. These estimates are shown in Table 3.[14] The figures indicate the number of plants that would have been in the industry if all plants had been the same size as either (a) the minimum efficient scale of plant in 1870 (the larger number), or (b) the largest surviving plants in 1870 (the smaller number).

In 1870, the number of plants in just over half of the selected industries (meat packing, flour milling, bread and bakery products, tobacco, lumber milling, millwork, printing and publishing, saddlery and harness, brick, pig iron, iron castings, sheet metal, and steam engines) fell within the range defined by the surviving plants. The distribution of plants could, therefore, be consistent with the majority of plants having adjusted their scale of operation into the optimal range. However, a glance at Table 2, which shows the percentage of value-added originating in optimal plants in 1870, shows that this was not necessarily the case; a combination of plants that were "too small" and "too large" could produce a total value-added and number of plants consistent with an optimal range.

In the remaining 11 industries (malt and distilled liquors, cotton and wool textiles, clothing, millinery, wooden furniture, leather tanning, boots and shoes, farm machinery, and carriages and wagons) the actual

14. See James (1983, p. 444) for estimates of optimal plant size based upon the actual supply and demand conditions facing firms between 1850 and 1890.

number of establishments in 1870 was greater than the number of minimum efficient scale plants, suggesting that relatively few establishments in those industries had achieved an efficient scale in 1870 despite the marked increases in factory production from 1850 (Table 1). Except for textiles, these industries in 1870 were still dominated by small-scale artisanal shops. Most agricultural implements manufacturers, for example, were little more than village blacksmiths, and handmade shoes still had not been displaced by the mass-produced factory product.

By 1900, the number of establishments and their characteristics were radically different in many industries. In only three industries (millinery, wooden household furniture, and wagons and carriages) was the actual number of establishments in an industry greater than the predicted range. These were the only industries in which a majority of plants had not apparently expanded their scale of operation to at least that of a minimally efficient plant circa 1870. Why small, inefficient plants should survive is difficult to explain if we assume perfect knowledge and zero transport costs. But neither condition existed then, nor does it now. The persistence of plants smaller than the minimum efficient scale of operation may reflect nothing more than continued turnover of enterprises at the entry level, akin to that today among small, specialized, retail establishments in shopping malls. Successive entrepreneurs each think they can succeed where others failed. Or, it may reflect the difficulties in bringing extensive mechanization to these industries and the localized markets which they served. The "efficient" producers may simply have been those located in the larger markets. The less efficient were located in the smaller markets protected from competition by positive transport costs. Sokoloff has found some evidence of this. "Competing" leather tanneries were rarely located in the same town as one another so competition was limited to the transportation margin (Sokoloff, 1984).

There were fewer establishments in four industries than predicted. In these cases, the long-run changes in plant size led to establishments that were generally considerably larger than the very largest surviving plant of 1870. Three of these were ones in which there had been rapid technological change: Meat packing, tobacco, and blast furnaces. The other industry, brickmaking, is something of a puzzle. Although its product had one of the lowest value-to-weight ratios and, hence, was a good for which cheaper transportation might have had a large impact on the feasible market area, brickmaking is, even today, classified as a local industry. Perhaps it reflects nothing more than a change in tastes favoring brick for housing, paving, and so on.

The nature, timing, and extent of technological change influences how the hypothetical number of 1870 optimal plants compared with the

Table 3. *Number of optimal 1870 plants that industry value-added could support, 1870 and 1900*[a]

Industry SIC	Industry	1870		1900	
		Number of potential 1870 optimal plants	Actual number of establishments[b]	Number of potential 1870 optimal plants	Actual number of establishments[c]
2011	Meat packing	106–212	206	3,041–6,082	1,134
2041	Flour milling	6,689–424,124	22,573	19,975–1,597,908	25,258
2057	Bread and other bakery products	633–20,270	3,550	10,209–326,503	14,917
2082	Malt liquors	63–254	1,972	833–3,335	1,509
2085	Distilled, rectified, and blended liquors	38–151	719	367–1,467	967
2100	Tobacco manufacture	1,599–12,795	5,204	20,117–160,935	14,976
2211	Cotton textiles	41–324	819	359–2,837	1,055
2231	Woolen goods	151–1,206	1,938	416–3,327	1,035
2321	Men's, youth's, boys' clothing	160–2,564	7,838	1,897–30,352	5,880
2351	Millinery	16–33	1,668	584–1,168	16,151

2421	Sawmills and planing mills	4,847–155,099	26,930	21,982–703,440	33,035
2431	Millwork	192–6,143	1,605	1,511–48,337	4,204
2511	Wood household furniture	202–809	5,423	1,669–6,678	7,972
2700	Printing, publishing, and allied industries	499–15,980	2,159	3,906–124,997	22,312
3111	Leather tanning and finishing	144–2,310	4,237	797–12,760	1,306
3131	Boots and shoes	275–4,403	23,428	737–11,798	1,600
3199	Saddlery and harness	208–26,627	7,607	960–122,829	12,934
3251	Brick and structural tile	1,743–13,945	3,114	7,081–56,649	5,423
3312	Pig iron	129–516	396	1,673–6,689	668
3321	Gray iron foundries	217–6,954	2,328	4,260–136,317	9,324
3444	Sheet metal work	503–8,048	6,646	2,377–38,025	12,466
3511	Steam engines	313–5,009	2,400	NA	NA
3522	Farm machinery and equipment	46–713	2,076	170–2,721	715
3799	Wagons and carriages	254–1,016	11,847	487–1,947	7,632

[a] Number of potential 1870 optimal plants = (value-added [1860 dollars] at time t)/MES(1870) or max(survivor 1870). See Table 2 for Minimum Efficient Scale of plant in 1870 and the largest surviving plant in each industry.

[b] From U.S. Census Office (1873).

[c] From U.S. Census Office (1902).

number of plants actually in an industry at the decadal intervals at which they were measured by the Census Bureau. Consider the case of meat packing. In 1870 and 1880, the number of plants in the industry lay within the range of the numbers of optimal 1870 plants. By 1890, however, there were fewer plants in the industry than predicted. This is precisely when the packing industry was revolutionized by the introduction of the refrigerator car making possible a nationwide distribution network and the conversion of meat packing to a high volume, continuous disassembly, process that made full use of by-products. Firms such as Swift and Company, P. D. Armour, and the Cudahy Packing Company drove smaller firms out of business as they integrated vertically and spread out horizontally into cities beyond their home bases of Chicago, in the cases of Swift and Armour, and Omaha for Cudahy (Yeager, 1981).

A similar story can be told for the tobacco industry which was revolutionized by Duke's adoption of Bonsack's continuous-process cigarette-making machine in 1885 and his successful national advertising campaign to promote the product. As a result, by 1890, the number of tobacco plants was closer to the lower-bound number of optimally sized 1870 plants than had been the case in 1880. And by 1900, with the American Tobacco Company dominating the industry through merger and predatory practices, the industry had been transformed into one with fewer plants than we would have predicted had those changes not taken place since 1870 (Burns, 1983).

Similarly, continuous production processes lent themselves well to the production of pig iron and steel. During the 1880s and the 1890s the American iron and steel industry switched to open-hearth production and the integration of all functions from the smelting of the raw iron ore to the rolling of finished products in a single mill (Temin, 1964).

In most industries, however, it is impossible to reject the notion that establishment size in 1900 was little different from the scale required of an efficient plant in 1870. Whatever the changes taking place in the latter half of the 19th century, they did not result in a different structure of industry from that which should have come about through the long-run adjustment process to the forces already evident in 1870. Factory production was already well established in most industries by that date and the dramatic impact of technological changes emphasizing high-speed, continuous production processes, and of lowered transport costs was quite narrowly confined.

Although the typical establishment in 1900 was little different in size from an efficient 1870 plant in that industry, size did change over time. In virtually every industry (except for printing and publishing), the ratio of the actual number of establishments in an industry to the minimum number of optimal 1870 plants declined each decade from 1870. The increasing size is consistent with a widening of market opportunities permitted by cheaper transportation and the existence of modest economies of scale which could be both internal and external. At the same time, the failure of most industries in 1900 to exhibit a radically different industrial structure from that which had its genesis in the 1860s, is evidence of the absence of dramatic technological change forcing a break with historical evolutionary patterns.

To restate the Chandler thesis, it is his contention that the modern business enterprise, as exemplified by American Tobacco, Carnegie Steel, or Armour and Company, emerged as a response to two combined forces, continuous production process technology and the transportation revolution of the declining railroad freight rates. The most direct test of this hypothesis given the data at our disposal is to order our industries by the impact of technology and of transportation. This appears in Table 4. The rate of technological progress is crudely categorized as "high" or "low." and the impact of transport costs reductions on the feasible market range is similarly classified. Our assignment of industries between the various cells is inevitably somewhat subjective as the categories are so broadly drawn but they are defensible. The new technology not only was continuous process or large batch, it also required intensive energy use; energy that often could only come from steam power. Writes Chandler:

> "The application of continuous process machinery and nearly continuous-process factories to the production of tobacco, grain products, canned foodstuffs, soap, and film greatly increased the volume of output and sharply decreased the labor force required in processing. . . . The furnace and foundry and the distilling and refining industries lent themselves more readily to mass production than did the mechanical industries. In those industries where the processes of production required the application of heat and involved chemical rather than mechanical methods, improved technology, a more intensified use of energy, and improved organization greatly expanded the speed of throughput and reduced the number of workers needed to produce a unit of output. Enlarged stills, superheated steam, and cracking techniques all brought high volume, large-batch, or continuous-process production of products made from petroleum, sugar, animal and vegetable fats, and some chemicals, and in the distilling of alcohol and spirits and in the brewing of malt liquors. In the furnace industries . . . better furnaces, converters, and rolling and finishing equipment, all of which required a more intensive use of energy, did much the same thing." (Chandler, 1977, p. 243).

To this list of industries, I have added boots and shoes, clothing, and leather tanning. In boots and shoes and clothing, the widespread use of the sewing machine and the adoption of standard sizes revolutionized production although not quite in the manner described by Chandler. Leather tanning became more concentrated as a result of changes in the

Table 4. *Technological change, transportation, and the adjustment to 1870 optimal plant sizes, 1900*[a]

	Pace of technological progress	
Impact of transportation	High	Low
High	Meat packing Flour milling Malt liquor Leather tanning Pig iron	Sawmills and planing mills Millwork Wood furniture Bricks Gray iron foundries Sheet metal
Low	Distilled liquor Tobacco manufacture Clothing Boots and shoes	Bread and baked goods Cotton textiles Wool textiles Millinery Printing and publishing Saddlery and harness Farm machinery Wagons and carriages

Steam engines are not included in this table as the 1900 Census does not separately identify this industry. If included, I would have placed it in cell (2, 1) = High Technology–Low Transport.

meat packing industry, objections to the offensive and polluting nature of the production process, and the chemical revolution which allowed the substitution of chemical tanning agents for the natural ones formerly used. The balance of the industries were categorized as experiencing only slow technological change. Thus, the cotton textile industry which began to switch from throstles to ring spinning during this period is classified as one experiencing slow technological progress because ring spinning did not fundamentally alter the nature and organization of the production process.

The categorization of the impact of transportation is derived from Nelson's study on the great merger movement at the end of the century, except that we have also allocated those industries, such as brick making, or lumber, whose markets were predominently local (Nelson, 1959, pp. 158, 159, Table C-3). Even though their potential feasible market area was fairly small because of the low value-to-weight ratio and the ubiquity of the raw materials, a sharp decline in transport costs could result in a large percentage increase in the feasible market area and bring new competitive forces to bear in the local marketplace.

The cell assignments in Table 4 provide fairly strong support for

Chandler's hypothesis. If we compute the cell mean ratios of the actual number of plants in an industry as a fraction of the minimum number of optimal 1870 plants in 1900 (see Table 3) which is a measure of establishment size in 1900 relative to that of the largest surviving plants in 1870, the ratio for the cell where the impact of technology and transportation are both high is the smallest, and it is largest where the impact of each was least.[15] The second lowest ratio is for industries in the cell experiencing a dramatic change in technological progress but producing products with a high value-to-weight ratio such as tobacco and distilled liquor. Declining transport costs had relatively little impact on the geographic market area for such products. The value for the Low Technology–High Transport cell was about one-third larger than that for the High Technology–Low Transport cell which was about double that of the High Technology–High Transport cell. The Low Technology–Low Transport cell ratio was more than three times as large. Minor cell reassignments of industries whose cell assignment might be questionable (such as leather tanning, boots and shoes, and clothing) only serves to reinforce these results.

The ratio for the High Technology–High Transport cell, 1.1, indicates that by 1900 the average establishment in those industries was almost as large as the very largest surviving plant of 1870. Indeed, if leather tanning is removed from this cell the ratio is less than one, indicating that under conditions as they existed in 1870, an average plant of 1900 could not have survived. On the other hand, plants in the industries in the Low Technology–Low Transport cell were little, if any different, in 1900 from those which had emerged from the Civil War decade. For them we cannot reject the notion that things had not changed during the era of massive industrialization in the United States.

VII. Conclusion

Although in aggregate terms few industries showed a dramatically different structure in 1900 than had been present in 1870, those which did are precisely those upon which Chandler focuses. High-speed, continuous production processes and the railroads of the late 19th century so changed conditions in meat packing, flour milling, liquor, tobacco, and pig iron production that they evolved a different structure by 1900 from that which emerged from the Civil War decade. In these industries the average 1900 establishment was at or beyond the upper size limit for

15. The average ratio of the number of 1900 plants to the number of 1870 plants of the largest optimal size that would have been needed to produce the 1900 value-added (in 1860 dollars) by cell (row,column) were (1,1), 1.1; (2,1), 2.1; (1,2), 2.9; (2,2), 9.2.

plants able to survive in 1870. Their transition from a structure that was consistent with long-run adjustment to pre-1870 conditions to one that was incompatible with plant survival under those same circumstances also agrees with the dating provided by Chandler.

In most industries, however, the industrial structure which had emerged by 1900 was one which could have resulted from the long-run equilibrium adjustment of plants to conditions which had existed in 1870. The changes which took place after that date had little or no effect except perhaps to reinforce the trend. The principal force behind that long-term adjustment appears to have been the switch to factory production and the adoption of inanimate power sources, particularly steam. For them, the scale effects of technological change internal to the plant and improved transportation external to it were minimal.

Our results do, however, suggest that Chandler may have been overgeneralizing in his assertion that industries such as leather tanning, boots and shoes, and clothing were unaffected by the changes taking place in the latter quarter of the century. On the contrary, my results show that in these industries some very large enterprises had emerged by 1900, the like of which would not have been predicted by conditions as they existed in 1870. The reasons for their emergence and successful survival require a separate study, but I believe that the answer lies in declining transport costs which permitted firms taking advantage of wider market opportunities to realize substantial scale economies in their marketing operations.

References

Abbott, E. (1908–1909), "History of the Employment of Women in the American Cotton Mill", *Journal of Political Economy*, *16* (November 1908), 602–621; (December 1908), 680–692; and *17* (January 1909), 19–35.

Atack, J. (1976), "Estimation of Economies of Scale in Nineteenth Century United States Manufacturing and the Form of the Production Function," unpublished Ph.D. thesis, Indiana University.

Atack, J. (1977), "Returns to Scale in Antebellum United States Manufacturing," *Explorations in Economic History*, *14*, 337–359.

Atack, J., Bateman, F. and Weiss, T. J. (1980), "The Regional Diffusion and Adoption of the Steam Engine," *Journal of Economic History*, *40*, 281–308.

Bateman, F. and Weiss, T. J. (1975a), "Comparative Regional Development in Antebellum Manufacturing," *Journal of Economic History*, *35*, 182–208.

Bateman, F. and Weiss, T. J. (1975b), "Market Structure before the Age of Big Business: Concentration and Profit in Early Southern Manufacturing," *The Business History Review*, *49*, 312–336.

Bradford, S. S. (1959), "The Negro Ironworkers in Antebellum Virginia," *Journal of Southern History*, *25*, 194–206.

Burns, M. R. (1983), "Economies of Scale in Tobacco Manufacture, 1897–1910," *Journal of Economic History*, *43*, 461–474.

Chandler, A. D., Jr. (1972), "Anthracite Coal and the Beginnings of the Industrial Revolution in the United States," *The Business History Review*, *46*, 141–181.

Chandler, A. D., Jr. (1977), *The Visible Hand: The Managerial Revolution in American Business*, Cambridge, Mass.: Harvard Univ. Press.

Davis, L. E. (1957), "Sources of Industrial Finance: The American Textile Industry, A Case Study," *Explorations in Entrepreneurial History*, *9*, 189–203.

Fraser, S. (1983), "Combined and Uneven Development in the Men's Clothing Industry," *The Business History Review*, *57*, 522–547.

Gregg, W. (1855), "Practical Results of Southern Manufacturers," *De Bow's Review*, *18*, 777–790.

Griliches, Z. and Ringstad, V. (1971), *Economies of Scale and the Form of the Production Function*, Amsterdam: North Holland.

Hunter, L. C. (1979), *A History of Industrial Power in the United States, Volume 1: Waterpower in the Century of the Steam Engine*, Charlottesville: Univ. Press of Virginia.

James, J. A. (1983), "Structural Change in American Manufacturing, 1850–1890," *Journal of Economic History*, *43*, 433–460.

Laurie, B. and Schmitz, M. (1981), "Manufacture and Productivity: The Making of an Industrial Base, Philadelphia, 1850–1880," pp. 43–92. In T. Hershberg (Ed.), *Philadelphia: Work, Space, Family, and Group Experience in the Nineteenth Century*, New York: Oxford Univ. Press.

McGouldrick, P. F. (1968), *New England Textiles in the Nineteenth Century*, Cambridge, Mass.: Harvard Univ. Press.

Mitchell, B. (1928), *William Gregg, Factory Master of the Old South*, Chapel Hill: Univ. of North Carolina Press.

Nelson, R. (1959), *Merger Movements in American Industry 1895–1956*, Princeton, N.J.: Princeton Univ. Press for the NBER.

Ringstad, V. (1974), "Some Empirical Evidence on the Decreasing Scale Elasticity," *Econometrica*, *42*, 87–102.

Saving, T. R. (1961), "Estimation of Optimum Plant Size by the Survivor Techniqe." *Quarterly Journal of Economics*, *75*, 569–607.

Shepherd, W. A. (1967), "What Does the Survivor Technique Show about Economies of Scale," *Southern Economic Journal*, *34*, 113–122.

Sokoloff, K. (1984), "Was the Transition from the Artisanal Shop to the Non-Mechanized Factory Associated with Gains in Efficiency?; Evidence from the U.S. Manufacturing Censuses of 1820 and 1850," *Explorations in Economic History*, *20*, 351–382.

Soskice, D. (1968), "A Modification of the CES Production Function to Allow for Changing Returns to Scale Over the Function," *Review of Economics and Statistics*, *50*, 446–448.

Starobin, R. (1970), *Industrial Slavery in the Old South*, New York: Oxford Univ. Press.

Stigler, G. (1950), "Monopoly and Oligopoly by Merger," *American Economic Review*, *40*, 23–34.

Stigler, G. (1958), "The Economies of Scale," *Journal of Law and Economics*, *1*, 54–71.

Temin, P. (1964), *Iron and Steel in Nineteenth Century America*, Cambridge, Mass.: MIT.

U.S. Census Office (1873), *Ninth Census*, Washington, D.C.: U.S. Govt. Printing Office.

U.S. Census Office (1902), *Twelfth Census*, Washington, D.C.: U.S. Govt. Printing Office.

U.S. Department of Commerce (1975), *Historical Statistics of the United States from Colonial Times to 1970*. Washington, D.C.: U.S. Govt. Printing Office.

Walters, A. A. (1963), "Production and Cost Functions," *Econometrica*, *31*, 1–66.

Ware, C. F. (1931), *The Early New England Cotton Manufactures*, Boston: Houghton Mifflin.

Weiss, L. W. (1964), "The Survival Technique and the Extent of Suboptimal Capacity," *The Journal of Political Economy*, *72*, 246–261.

Weiss, L. W. (1965), "The Extent of Suboptimal Capacity: A Correction," *Journal of Political Economy*, *73*, 300–301.

Williamson, O. E. (1981), "The Modern Corporation: Origins, Evolution, Attributes," *Journal of Economic Literature*, *19*, 1537–1568.

Williamson, O. E. (1982), "Microanalytic Business History," *Business and Economic History*, Papers and Proceedings of the Business History Conference, Second Series, *11*, 106–115.

Yeager, M. (1981), *Competition and Regulation*, Greenwich, Conn.: JAI Press.

Zellner, A. and Revankar, N. S. (1969), "Generalized Production Functions," *Review of Economic Studies*, *36*, 241–250.

"The origins of American industrial success, 1879–1940"

by Gavin Wright

Since the founding of the American colonies in the seventeenth century, the economic growth of what is now the United States has been phenomenal. By 1900, the standard of living in America was about the best in the world and per capita incomes were still rising. A number of attempts have been made to explain this economic success story. One explanation states that abundant and varied natural resources form the foundation of economic development and points out that the United States possesses fertile soil, forests, fuels, and metals, plus geographic features that either encourage their use or impose much lower barriers to their employment than other regions face.

"The Origins of American Industrial Success, 1879–1940," by Gavin Wright, shows the centrality of natural resources in our industrial growth but simultaneously challenges the resource endowment theory. Wright agrees that the known range of mineral resources in the United States was far wider than in any other country. However, he points out the endogeneity of the rate of discovery and exploitation of mineral resources. After all, the resources had been there for eons, just as the oil fields of Saudi Arabia have been. Economic growth is not simple or automatic. Other important factors existed. "Industrial success requires an uncountable number of mutually interdependent elements."

One of the most important features of Wright's argument lies in the integration of international mineral markets. Market integration is a key to economic development and is, therefore, a focus of several of the essays in this reader. Rothenberg focused on product market integration, Wright's earlier essay highlighted southern labor market integration, and Sylla's essay (yet to come) deals with capital market integration.

Make sure to address these questions as you read the essay:

- What institutions drove American industrial success?
- How did the resource "endowment" depend on other factors?
- The essay tells us that by 1940 the United States had become a net importer of raw materials. Did we run out of raw materials? Is the world running out? How do price and quantity measures answer these questions.

Additional Reading

Moses Abramovitz, "Catching Up, Forging Ahead, and Falling Behind," *Journal of Economic History*, 46 (June 1986), 385–406.

Moses Abramovitz, "The Catch-Up Factor in Postwar Economic Growth," *Economic Inquiry*, 28 (January 1990), 1–18.

John James and Jonathan Skinner, "The Resolution of the Labor-Scarcity Paradox," *Journal of Economic History*, 45 (September 1985), 513–540.

Simon Kuznets, "Notes on the Pattern of U.S. Growth," in Robert Fogel and Stanley Engerman, editors, *The Reinterpretation of American Economic History*, New York: Harper and Row, 1971, 17–24.

Richard Nelson and Gavin Wright, "The Rise and Fall of American Technological Leadership," *Journal of Economic Literature*, 30 (December 1992), 1931–1964.

13

The origins of American industrial success, 1879–1940

GAVIN WRIGHT*

The United States became the world's preeminent manufacturing nation at the turn of the twentieth century. This study considers the bases for this success by examining the factor content of trade in manufactured goods. Surprisingly, the most distinctive characteristic of U.S. manufacturing exports was intensity in nonreproducible natural resources; furthermore, this relative intensity was increasing between 1880 and 1920. The study then asks whether resource abundance reflected geological endowment or greater exploitation of geological potential. It was mainly the latter. (JEL 042)

Recent thinking about American economic performance has been marked by alarm over the country's loss of its "competitive edge." Most of this discussion is not rooted in an understanding of the historical origins of the economic leadership now thought to be in jeopardy. Modern economists tend to assume that the American advantage has been technological and dates from the remote recesses of history, about as far back as anyone really cares to go. In a volume on U.S. competitiveness, Harvey Brooks writes: "Both our firms and our government, *long accustomed to being the technological leaders in almost every field*, have until recently measured their performance against domestic rather than foreign competitors" (Bruce R. Scott and George C. Lodge, 1985, p. 331; emphasis added). For one country to maintain a technologically based advantage over others for long historical periods is anomalous, and surely calls for explanation. Indeed, it is difficult to see how policies can respond appropriately to "what we have lost" without knowledge of

Source: Gavin Wright, "The Origins of American Industrial Success, 1879–1940," *American Economic Review* (September 1990), 651–668. Reprinted with permission of the author and the American Economic Association.

* Department of Economics, Stanford University, Stanford, CA 94305. This research was supported by the Center for Economic Policy Research at Stanford, and the paper was written while in residence at the Institute for Advanced Study in Princeton, NJ. Those who have offered useful advice are too numerous to list, but the author is particularly grateful to Paul David for suggesting and encouraging the project, and to Stanley Engerman, Alex Field, Albert Hirschman, Nate Rosenberg, Gary Saxonhouse, and Robert Staiger for specific suggestions. Research assistance by David Green and Jeff Sundberg was much appreciated.

what it was that we had and how we got it. It would be an understatement, however, to say that the subject has been understudied. This paper makes a modest beginning by analyzing American trade in manufactured goods between 1879 and 1940. The competitive success of American manufacturing exports in foreign markets is by no means a comprehensive measure of "success." But because the turn of the century marked the emergence of the United States to a position of world economic preeminence, we may hope to learn something about the broader questions by studying the characteristics of the country's trade with the rest of the world during that key era.

The results are surprising. They suggest that the single most robust characteristic of American manufacturing exports was intensity in nonreproducible natural resources. In fact, their relative resource intensity was *increasing* over the half-century prior to the Great Depression. This does not mean that there was no American technological leadership, in the broad sense of that term. Abundant resources were themselves in many ways a reflection of the advanced state of American technology. But the distinctively American industrial innovations were in many respects specific to the pre-World War II U.S. resource environment and national market, both of which were unique among the countries of the world. Since then, relative American resource abundance has greatly diminished, not primarily from depletion of national reserves but because of the integration of world markets for minerals and other commodities. Twentieth-century patterns of resource discovery and production suggest that the historic basis for U.S. mineral abundance was much more a matter of early "development" than of geological "endowment."

I. The ascendance of American industry on a global scale

Americans have enjoyed high material living standards since the eighteenth century if not earlier, and the acceleration to modern rates of per capita growth occurred during the first half of the nineteenth century. Broadly based American *industrial* leadership on a worldwide basis, however, can only be dated from the very end of the nineteenth century. According to Paul Bairoch (1982), the U.S. share of total world manufacturing output passed Great Britain's between 1880 and 1900 (Chart 1). In per capita levels of industrial output, the United States was a weak fourth among the nations of the world in 1880, and surpassed Britain only after 1900 (Chart 2). Contemporary testimony suggests that American technology and manufactured goods began to play a qualitatively different role in the world as of the 1890s or shortly thereafter. The first wave of alarmist European books on "Americanization" dates from 1901 and 1902, with titles and themes (*The American Invaders*,

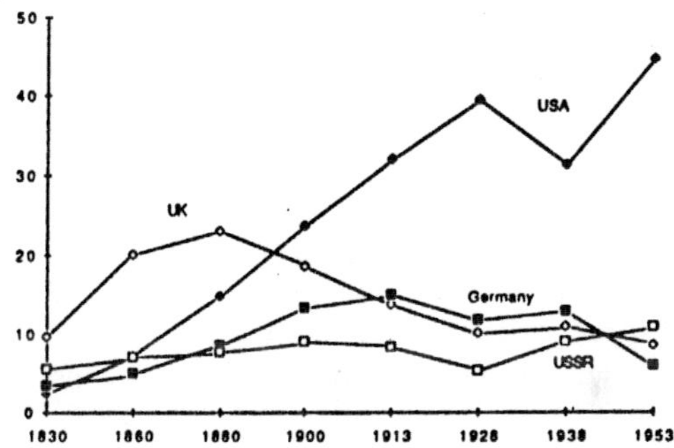

Chart 1. Shares of world industrial output, 1830–1953.

Source: Bairoch (1982, pp. 296, 304).

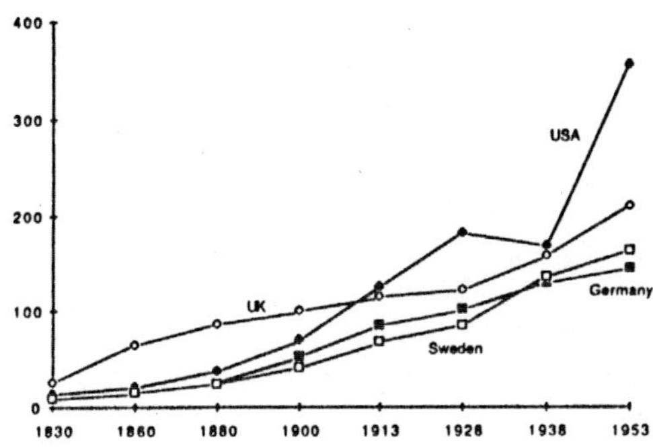

Chart 2. Industrial output per capita.

Source: Bairoch (1982, pp. 294, 302).

1901; *The Americanization of the World*, 1901; *The American Invasion*, 1902) that would again become familiar in the 1920s and 1960s (William Woodruff, 1975, p. 123). Rapid inflows of standardized, machine-made American shoes after 1894 (said to be more comfortable and more stylish than the traditional types) caused consternation in the British boot-and-shoe industry and forced a drastic technological overhaul (R. A. Church, 1968). Equally dramatic was the burst of American exports of machine tools and other engineering goods after 1895, not only to Britain but to the Continent and other parts of the world (Roderick C. Floud, 1974, pp. 60–62; 1976, pp. 72–82). Though the suddenness of the American "invasion" after 1895 may be attributable to temporary factors, it seems clear that a crossover point of some sort was reached at that time.[1]

Industry studies seem to confirm this timing. Robert Allen has shown that prior to the 1890s American blast furnaces had no distinctive world-class status in either labor productivity or fuel efficiency (Allen, 1977, pp. 608–609). By 1900, after key breakthroughs in adapting the technology to the new Mesabi iron ore, the U.S. industry was the world leader by both of these indicators. Pig iron was an input in the production of steel, which was in turn crucial for railroads, construction, and a wide range of machinery and manufactured goods. According to Allen, before the 1890s American steel rails would not have been competitive in the domestic market without tariff protection (Allen, 1981). Advances in steel were in turn complementary to progress in other industries. U.S. rubber-tire makers, for example, were well behind the French during the bicycle craze of the 1890s, and only gained a productivity advantage in conjunction with mass production of automobiles shortly before World War I (M. J. French, 1987, p. 66). None of this denies that twentieth-century U.S. technology emerged from an evolutionary learning process over a much longer period, as economic historians have long stressed (Paul David, 1975; Nathan Rosenberg, 1976; David Hounshell, 1984). But the qualitative changes in industrial America's place in the world after 1890 justify a closer look at this period.

The timing of U.S. industrial performance corresponds closely to the more comprehensive finding of U.S. world leadership by Angus Maddison, based on estimates of Gross Domestic Product per man-hour (Maddison, 1982, p. 212; compare also Moses Abramovitz, 1986). But Maddison seems to assume that U.S. leadership in *productivity* corresponded closely to a position of "world leadership" in *technology*. This is surely not the only possibility. In terms of conventional growth-accounting, the U.S. edge could equally well have been attributable to capital or natural resources. Interestingly, Maddison's figures actually show that the world leader in GDP per man-hour prior to World War I was not the United States but Australia. His explanation is confined to a footnote: "In defining productivity leadership, I have ignored the special case of Australia, whose impressive achievements before the First World War were due largely to natural resource advantages rather than to technical achievements and the stock of man-made capital" (p. 258). Can we be certain that the United States was not also a "special case" whose performance depended on "natural resource advantages"?

1. S. J. Nicholas (1980) argues that the apparent decline in the price of American "engineering goods" mainly tracks the prices of iron and steel products, and that the sudden "invasion" of U.S. goods reflected temporary delivery lags by British firms during 1895–1900. As argued below, both of these elements reflected more lasting features of American industrial success.

Contrary to expectations of increasing resource scarcity, post–Civil War American Development featured *declining* relative costs of materials (Louis P. Cain and Donald G. Paterson, 1981, pp. 358–360). Major new metals discoveries continued until World War I, while the rate of discovery of new oil fields accelerated after 1900 (U.S. National Resources Committee, 1937, p. 149). The timing of leadership in industrial production coincides remarkably with American world leadership in coal production (after 1900), and that margin also grew over time. The United States was also the world's leading producer of copper, petroleum, iron ore, zinc, phosphate, molybdenum, lead, tungsten, and many other minerals. At the same time, continuing advances in internal transportation reduced the real costs to manufacturers, creating what historical geographers call the "minerals-dominant economy" of the late nineteenth century (Harvey S. Perloff and Lowden Wingo Jr., 1961, pp. 193–197). The improvements were often qualitative as well as quantitative, most strikingly perhaps in the iron ore from the rich Mesabi range, which began to arrive in the steel mills of the lower Great Lakes in the 1890s. Allen's estimates of total-factor-productivity in iron and steel as of 1907–1909 put the United States at a par with Germany (15 percent ahead of Britain), but the ratio of horsepower to worker was twice as large in America as in either of the other two contenders (Allen, 1979, p. 919). If we were to adopt the conventional view that resource abundance is an *alternative* to technologically based manufacturing, we might well be led to question the authenticity of America's leadership position before World War II. But as argued below, this is not the only choice available to us.

II. Hypotheses from the international trade literature

A number of hypotheses bearing on American industrial history emerge from the literature on the bases for international trade. According to the Heckscher–Ohlin model, the composition of a country's trade reflects the relative abundance of factors in that country's endowment. Simple two-factor versions of this theory have frequently been rejected, beginning with the "Leontief Paradox," which revealed that in 1947 U.S. exports were more capital-intensive than were competitive imports (Wassily Leontief, 1953). Attempts to rationalize this result, however, have generated more refined propositions. According to the "neo-factor-proportions" approach, American exports have actually been intensive in skills or human capital. This interpretation was suggested by Leontief himself, and has been supported by an empirical regularity first identified by Irving B. Kravis (1956a), that average wage levels in American export industries have been persistently higher than wage levels in import-competing industries. It has become a standard convention in empirical trade studies to take the relative industry wage as a proxy for skill requirements, and on this basis the skill intensity of American exports has been claimed as a pattern as far back as 1899 if not earlier (Helen Waehrer, 1968). Studies for more recent periods have supported this view with detailed evidence on the occupational structure of the labor force (Donald B. Keesing, 1968).

An alternative "third factor" interpretation for the paradox is that capital is complementary to natural resources, and that the United States had moved into a position of resource scarcity by 1947 (Kravis, 1956b). This possibility is supported by Jaroslav Vanek's important study of the natural resource content of U.S. foreign trade, 1870–1955 (Vanek, 1963), which showed that the country had moved from a net export to a net import position in natural resources over that period. This finding raises the possibility that U.S. comparative advantage may have had a different basis at an earlier time.

A different (though not necessarily mutually exclusive) intellectual strategy is taken by the "neo-technology" approach. The concept of a "technological gap" between the United States and the rest of the world was a commonplace in discussions of trade and direct investment during the 1950s and 1960s (Atlantic Institute, 1970). Though theory makes a sharp distinction between "factor proportions" and "technology" effects, in practice the two ideas are often similar. Employment of skilled professional and scientific personnel is correlated with investment in research, often called "R&D intensity" or simply the "technology factor" (Raymond Vernon, 1970). Similarly, American "technology" has often been linked as much with managerial performance as with science-based production methods. Since the vertically integrated modern business corporation developed earlier and diffused more widely in the United States than elsewhere (Alfred D. Chandler and Herman Daems, 1980), the conceptual correlations among technology, organization, and personnel are likely to be high.

A more difficult conceptual challenge is technological leadership manifest in the form of new products, exported from the United States because they were unavailable elsewhere (Kravis, 1956b). Because exports were small as a percentage of output for almost all American industries, the U.S. case would seem to be a likely example of the historical process described by Staffan Burenstam Linder (1961) whereby new products originally designed for the domestic market begin to enter foreign trade as production expands: "International trade is really nothing but an extension across national frontiers of a country's own web of economic activity" (p. 88). Vernon's "product-cycle" model is perhaps the best-known version: *New products* tended to appear first in the United States because they were responsive to *high-income wants*, and because they were associated with an environment of *high labor costs*. As processes became more mature and routine, trade would be displaced by production abroad, but the volume of U.S. exports was maintained by a continuing flow of new innovations (Vernon, 1966).

There is an ever-present danger of anachronism in applying such concepts historically. The United States did not invent the firearm, the shoe, the bicycle, the camera, or the automobile, and the American versions of these goods were not regarded in European countries as well suited to "high-income wants" (which were better served by the English of French). The size and character of the U.S. domestic market were certainly crucial, but the bulk of the new American exports were producers goods, whose "novelty" lay not so much in consumer taste as in technical specifications or quality. The approach taken here therefore concentrates on the supply side, by analysis of the changing factor content of manufacturing trade over the era of American ascendancy. Though we cannot claim to measure or establish the nature of American "technological leadership" in a rigorous sense, we can illuminate that subject by finding the characteristics of those U.S. products that had the greatest impact on world markets.

This has been the approach of earlier historical work.[2] Using the standard methodology of empirical trade studies, N. F. R. Crafts and Mark Thomas present an analysis of comparative advantage in British manufacturing trade between 1910 and 1935, which they contrast unfavorably with that of the United States (Crafts and Thomas, 1986). They find that Britain continued to export products intensive in capital and unskilled labor and to import goods intensive in human capital (as reflected in the average industry wage). A similar regression for the United States in 1909 shows a reverse result. They conclude: "The U.S. appears already to be following the 'advanced country' pattern of exporting human capital intensive goods and importing unskilled labor-intensive goods in 1909" (p. 637). The next section considers whether this impression should be modified on the basis of a richer data set.

2. An extensive literature on the so-called "labor-scarcity paradox" takes a similar tack, assessing U.S. performance indirectly by measuring the factor-saving bias of U.S. technology relative to British. The suggestion by H. J. Habakkuk (1962) that American technology was capital-intensive and labor-saving has given way to a more complex picture: American methods were more intensive in the use of raw materials and fuel and were characterized by a faster pace and more intensive utilization of capital (David, 1975; Field, 1983). The provocative early successes of the "American system" were limited to a small subset of industries in the 1850s (John James and Jonathan Skinner, 1985). This work concentrates on the mid-nineteenth century, giving little attention to change over time or to the overall scope of U.S. industrial performance.

III. New evidence on American trade in manufactures

A. *Average factor intensities*

One of the reasons that American manufacturing trade has been understudied is that the Commerce Department trade data are entirely separate from the censuses of manufactures, which have no information about foreign markets. It is not a simple task to match these two sources. Fortunately, a Stanford dissertation by Mary Locke Eysenbach estimated production coefficients for 165 industries according to the system used in Leontief's 1947 interindustry study, and matched these to export and import data for 1879, 1899, and 1914 (Eysenbach, 1976). The present research has replicated her procedures and extended the data set to 1909, 1928, and 1940.[3] For most sample years there are just over 100 usable observations, providing a level of detail roughly comparable to three-digit SITC categories.

To explore the factor intensity of manufacturing trade, I have used Eysenbach's production coefficients to trace relative changes over the entire period of observation. Her capital and labor coefficients are primarily from the census of 1899, while the natural resource coefficients were taken from Vanek (1963) and hence originate in the input-input table for 1947. Thus, this is primarily a study of compositional changes in manufacturing trade over time rather than the actual implicit factor flows in each year. As a sensitivity check, however, estimated coefficients for alternative years have been used wherever possible. Since all of the coefficients are U.S.-based, the question of whether the factor content of imports accurately corresponds to foreign production techniques is not addressed.Despite these limitations, the procedures follow the spirit of much of the literature on these subjects, and the results (shown in Tables 1 through 3) are suggestive.

Table 1 does confirm that American manufacturing exports were more capital-intensive than American imports from 1879 to 1928. But in terms of contemporary coefficients, the country's surge to world industrial supremacy was not marked by a shift toward capital-intensive manufacturing exports, nor by an increasing tendency to trade capital-intensive for labor-intensive manufactures with the rest of the world. (It is interesting that the relative capital intensity of exports *in terms of 1947 coefficients* did rise until 1914, after which it declined.) Movement in the direction of the Leontief Paradox within manufacturing is detectable, at least after World War I.

It should be noted that the figures in Table 1 omit refined sugar, an industry that if included would single-handedly generate a Leontief

3. David Green deserves most of the credit for the detective work that this task entailed.

Table 1. *Capital-labor ratios for manufactured goods, 1879–1940 ($000 per employee in 1909 dollars)*

	1879	1899	1909	1914	1928	1940
A. 1899 Coefficients						
Exports	4.186	4.059	4.052	3.961	3.946	3.374
Imports	2.608	2.886	2.785	2.850	2.907	3.221
Exports/Imports	1.61	1.41	1.46	1.39	1.36	1.05
B. 1909 Coefficients						
Exports	5.405	4.877	4.967	4.811	4.959	4.193
Imports	2.999	3.079	3.020	3.073	3.486	4.444
Exports/Imports	1.80	1.58	1.64	1.57	1.42	0.94
C. 1947 Coefficients						
Exports	4.725	5.170	6.350	6.790	6.330	5.265
Imports	2.910	3.440	3.420	3.690	4.325	5.850
Exports/Imports	1.62	1.50	1.86	1.84	1.46	0.90

Sources: 1899 coefficients from Mary Locke Eysenbach. *American Manufactured Exports*, 1897–1914, New York: Arno Press, 1976, pp. 302–306; 1909 coefficients from U.S. Census of Manufactures; 1947 coefficients from Wassily Leontief, "Factor Proportions and the Structure of American Trade," *Review of Economics and Statistics*, November 1956, *38*, 403–407.

Trade Figures: for 1879, 1899, 1914 from Eysenbach, pp. 271–275; 1909, 1928, 1940 from U.S. Commerce Department, *Foreign Commerce and Navigation of the United States*. Exact industry groupings available on request.

Table 2. *Measures of skill intensity of manufactured goods, 1879–1940*

	1879	1899	1909	1914	1928	1940
A. Percentage Earning More than $12/Week in 1890						
Exports	52.3	48.7	48.2	45.9	46.6	42.9
Imports	48.5	45.7	47.1	44.1	42.3	41.3
Exports/Imports	1.08	1.07	1.02	1.04	1.10	1.04
B. Average Wage (1909)						
Exports	0.467	0.482	0.487	0.502	0.504	0.541
Imports	0.431	0.433	0.460	0.426	0.463	0.471
Exports/Imports	1.09	1.11	1.06	1.18	1.09	1.15
C. Percentage Women and Child Labor (1909)						
Exports	10.1	10.7	9.9	11.0	11.2	10.4
Imports	30.6	29.0	30.2	27.8	24.2	21.1
Exports/Imports	0.33	0.37	0.33	0.40	0.46	0.49

Sources: Percent $ / week from Eysenbach, pp. 307–311; average wage from 1909 Census of Manufactures (wage bill divided by labor force); women and child labor from 1909 Census of Manufactures (females aged 16 and over, under 16, and males under 16, divided by labor force).

Paradox for manufacturing in every sample year. If classified as a manufactured good (following Eysenbach), refined sugar would account for nearly one-quarter of manufacturing imports before 1900, and sugar refining (in the United States, at any rate) had a capital–labor ratio five times as high as the average for manufacturing. It is open to question whether sugar refining techniques outside the United States were really this capital-intensive. Because the industry is exceptional and because we are not in any case trying to account for all international flows, it seems

Table 3. *Nonrenewable natural resource coefficients in manufacturing goods, 1879–1940 (1947 coefficients)*

	1879	1899	1909	1914	1928	1940
A. Direct Use						
Exports	0.0742	0.0677	0.0918	0.0988	0.09984	0.0564
Imports	0.0131	0.0194	0.0170	0.0133	0.0290	0.0369
Exports/Imports	5.66	3.49	5.40	7.43	3.39	1.53
B. Direct and Indirect Use						
Exports	0.1107	0.1239	0.1647	0.1800	0.1635	0.1240
Imports	0.0565	0.0747	0.0766	0.0749	0.0934	0.1127
Exports/Imports	1.96	1.66	2.15	2.40	1.75	1.10

Sources: Coefficients from Eysenbach, pp. 297–301; trade figures, see Table 1.

more informative to leave it out. Though extreme, sugar refining does illustrate one of the compositional reasons for the trend shown in the first two panels of Table 1, namely, the high capital intensity of many agricultural processing industries, which were declining in relative prominence among U.S. exports. Two of the largest contributors to the decline in relative capital intensity of exports were grain mill products, and meat packing and wholesale poultry.

Table 2 displays two indices of skill intensity: (1) following Eysenbach, the percentage of the labor force earning more than $12 per week in 1890, and (2) the average industry wage in 1909.[4] By both measures, there is some tendency for export industries to pay higher wages than import-competing industries. But there is little sign of a trend in the relative skill intensity of exports and imports. As measured by the 1890 "high-wage" index, the skill content of exports went steadily downward. As measured by the 1909 average wage, however, the skill content of exports had an upward trend. There was also an upward trend, however, in the skill content of imports by the same measure (excepting 1914). One of the reasons for this puzzling pattern is suggested by the third panel of Table 2, which reaveals a much more dramatic contrast between exports and imports in the percentage of the labor force who are women and children (under the age of 16). It is perhaps not surprising to see that imports are far more women-and-child-intensive than exports, since these workers are associated with "low-wage" and labor-intensive processes (but it is interesting that this direct measure of labor-force composition is a clearer separator than capital-intensity or wage levels, which one might take to be more fundamental). What is striking is the decline over time in this relative

4. Several other skill indices were proposed by Eysenbach, all based on 1890 data. They give results similar to those presented here.

intensity, entirely concentrated on the import side. Here we have another likely contributor to the trend toward the Leontief Paradox. Employment of women and child workers in American manufacturing was concentrated in only a handful of industries: canning, preserving, and freezing on the one hand, and textiles and apparel on the other. The first remained a strong net export category, but in the second, the growth of imports was increasingly stifled by tariff barriers, particularly after the 1922 Fordney–McCumber tariff.

Easily the largest factor-intensity differentials were in nonreproducible natural resources, as shown in Table 3. Recall that these are weighted averages for manufactured goods alone and exclude entirely exports of agricultural goods and crude materials. We still find not only that U.S. exports had far higher natural resource content than imports but that this trend was growing both absolutely and relatively over *precisely the historical period when the country was moving into a position of world industrial preeminence.* Using the more inclusive index of direct and indirect use, the resource intensity of manufacturing exports grew by 64 percent to its peak, and even after a slight decline, the 1928 level was still nearly 50 percent higher than that of 1879. The figures confirm a little-noticed analysis by Robert E. Lipsey (1963): "The composition of manufacturing exports has been changing ceaselessly since 1879 in a fairly consistent direction – *away from products of animal or vegetable origin and toward those of mineral origin*" (p. 59; emphasis added).

Table 3 also clearly shows that the resource intensity of imports was growing as well, and that signs of a reversal in the relative balance are detectable even in 1928. By 1940, the historic U.S. specialization had virtually disappeared. This is the modern trend identified first and most clearly by Vanek (1963), of no small importance for interpreting recent American industrial history. But because of his choice of dates and coverage, Vanek missed the fact that the declining phase had been preceded by a long epoch of rising natural resource intensity, of no less importance in interpreting the country's place in the industrial world.

B. *Regression analysis*

Simple factor-intensity comparison between exports and imports is not conclusive in the presence of more than two factors (Edward Leamer, 1980). An apparent pattern of specialization may merely represent the effect of a third factor, acting as a complement or substitute for one of the other two. This section therefore follows the general format of Crafts and Thomas (1986) and earlier studies in the international trade literature by regressing the net trade balance for each industry against measures of factor intensity. On no account should the coefficients be

Table 4. *Regressions for manufactured net exports of the United States, 1879–1940*

	Constant	Capital/ Labor	Natural Resource Coefficient	Average Wage	Percent Women and Children	R^2
1879	−3127	2092**	−10830	−1853		0.079
	(0.68)	(2.24)	(0.74)	(0.27)		
	−228	1725*	−12690		−156	0.103
	(0.06)	(1.77)	(0.83)		(1.53)	
1899	−4068	3729*	−4324	−802		0.075
	(0.66)	(1.73)	(0.11)	(0.07)		
	1735	3140	−8727		−255**	0.093
	(0.28)	(1.46)	(0.21)		(2.02)	
1909	−8965	2648	46950	959		0.146
	(0.92)	(1.17)	(1.17)	(0.06)		
	260	1810	44154		−380**	0.193
	(0.04)	(0.75)	(0.99)		(2.25)	
1914	−21041**	1600	103103*	28468**		0.261
	(2.56)	(0.53)	(1.71)	(2.12)		
	216	1038	98271*		−329*	0.275
	(0.02)	(0.33)	(1.55)		(1.93)	
1928	−21067	5040	112264**	18856		0.143
	(1.20)	(0.83)	(2.19)	(0.52)		
	−4342	4413	107406**		−333	0.149
	(0.17)	(0.67)	(2.01)		(0.87)	
1940	−31898	−1862	126449**	85642		0.085
	(1.13)	(0.42)	(2.22)	(1.38)		
	23714	−2750	117138**		−629*	0.077
	(1.24)	(0.58)	(2.11)		(1.79)	

Notes: Method of estimation is ordinary least-squares, *t*-ratios (in parentheses) adjusted for heteroskedasticity following procedure of White (1980). *Denotes statistical significance at the 5 percent confidence level; **denotes the 1 percent confidence level. There are 64 nonzero observations in 1879, 83 in 1899, and 96 in the remaining years.

viewed as structural estimates within a Heckscher–Ohlin framework (compare Leamer and Harry P. Bowen, 1981). They are best considered as descriptive summaries of trade patterns in a multifactor setting, a way of pointing out areas of distinctive strength and tracking changes over time. Because the industry or commodity groupings are inevitably arbitrary, R^2 levels by themselves are not particularly meaningful; but *t*-tests on individual coefficients are a reasonable standard for confidence in that factor's contribution, and R^2 comparisons across years should reflect changes in the tightness-of-fit according to factor content. Following Crafts and Thomas, all reported standard errors were recomputed according to the procedure suggested by Hal White (1980) to adjust for heteroskedasticity in the error structure. The effect generally is to reduce the larger *t*-ratios, so that what is reported here is a conservative version of the account that leaps from the data using ordinary-least-squares. The results are robust to changes in precise variable definitions and to transformations of the coefficients into factor shares at various discount rates. Trade values have been deflated by export and import price indices (Lipsey, 1963, pp. 142–143; 1913 = 100) so that coefficients may be compared across years.

The results in Table 4 are broadly consistent with those of the previous section. The capital-labor coefficient is significant in 1879, but it becomes steadily less so in subsequent years and is actually negative by 1940. Thus indications that the Leontief Paradox emerged historically are still present in a multivariate setting. The natural resource coefficient, on the other hand, begins negative and becomes significantly positive after 1909, reaching its peak (in both level and significance) in 1928.

The coefficients of the two labor force variables are also interesting. The coefficient of the average wage is significantly positive in only one year (1914). The coefficient on the percentage of women and child laborers, by contrast, is significantly negative in four of the six years and nearly so in the remaining two. When both variables are included (not shown), the coefficient on the average wage is negative or insignificant in every year. Furthermore, there is an evident inverse relationship between natural resource intensity and the presence of women and children. It appears, therefore, that the concentration of American net exports in "high wage" industries early in the century was attributable to the absence of women and child workers in these "heavy" industries.[5]

An important amendment to this account emerges from Table 5, which uses a new variable created by multiplying the capital–labor ratio and the natural resource coefficient. The results strongly imply that capital and natural resources were complementary factors of production. The coefficient of the new variable is positive through the entire period, growing steadily larger and more significant through 1928. Comparison of R^2 levels between Tables 4 and 5 shows that this new interactive variable is more powerful in accounting for net export performance than the combined effect of its two components, entered separately. The strongest effects are found in 1914 and 1928; in the latter year, for example, the R^2 rises from 0.149 to 0.252 merely by substituting a single variable, the product, for the original two.

This result should caution us against a too-hasty and too-complete rejection of "capital intensity" as a characteristic of American industry. The suggestion is, however, that capital intensity derived not from economy wide abundance of capital per se, but from specialization in an industrial technology in which capital was complementary to natural

5. This does not necessarily mean that the effect is purely compositional, that is, directly explained by the lower wages paid to women and children. Men who worked in these occupational-industrial categories also received lower wages. But these wages did not reflect "skill" levels so much as the ease with which women and children coluld be substituted for men in these industries.

Table 5. *Regressions for manufactured net exports of the U.S., 1879–1940*

	Constant	Capital and Natural Resources/Labor	Average Wage	Percentage Women and Children	R^2
1879	236	2741**	977		0.058
	(0.05)	(2.17)	(0.14)		
	3815	2234		−182*	0.095
	(1.31)	(1.54)		(1.88)	
1899	2495	5650**	4617		0.057
	(0.32)	(2.81)	(0.40)		
	10015*	4677*		−314**	0.088
	(1.98)	(1.95)		(2.58)	
1909	−2974	9312**	6052		0.165
	(0.31)	(3.46)	(0.37)		
	6955*	8045**		−428*	0.229
	(1.93)	(2.68)		(2.67)	
1914	−15799**	13279**	33918**		0.299
	(2.08)	(3.50)	(2.57)		
	7317**	12198**		−386**	0.321
	(2.23)	(3.07)		(2.68)	
1928	−10667	24084**	28310		0.241
	(0.75)	(2.87)	(0.88)		
	9857	22954**		−399	0.252
	(1.09)	(2.61)		(1.40)	
1940	−33084	12118**	86974		0.095
	(1.14)	(2.23)	(1.36)		
	19478**	10590**		−575	0.083
	(2.00)	(1.89)		(1.87)	

Note: See Table 4.

resources. Strictly speaking, these sorts of tests only describe the direction of trade, not the overall "success" of American industry. But the coincidence of timing between resource intensity and American industrial ascendance obliges us to consider the proposition that the abundance of industrial minerals was a deeper cause of American industry's distinctive strength.

IV. Natural resources and American industrial success

Since industrial success like other historical outcomes requires an uncountable number of mutually interdependent elements, do natural resources really deserve special attention? The scope of America's world leadership in natural resources is displayed in Chart 3, which shows U.S. production of 14 major industrial minerals as a percentage of world totals in 1913. The 95 percent of world natural gas and 65 percent of world petroleum were perhaps of somewhat less economic moment in 1913 than they would be at a later date. But copper, coal, zinc, iron ore, lead, and other minerals were at the core of industrial technology for that era, and in every single case the United States was the world's

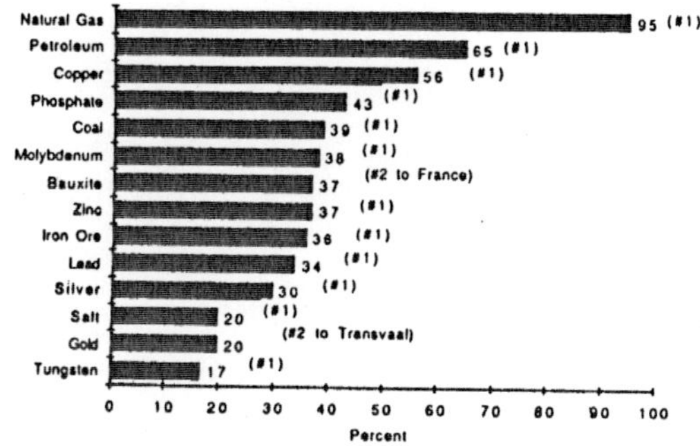

Chart 3. U.S. mineral output, 1913: percentage of world total.
Source: Smith (1919), using data from U.S. Geological Survey (1913).

leading producer by a wide margin. In an era of high transport costs, the country was *uniquely* situated with respect to almost every one of these minerals. Even this understates the matter. Being the number one producer in one or another mineral category is less important than the fact that the *range* of mineral resources abundantly available in the United States was far wider than that in any other country. Surely the link between this geographical status and the world success of American industry is more than incidental. Cain and Paterson (1986) find that between 1850 and 1919, material-using technological biases were significant in nine of twenty American sectors, including those with the strongest export performance, such as petroleum, metals, and machinery.

Resource abundance was a background ingredient in many other distinctively American industrial developments. Continuous-process, mass-production methods, closely associated with modern forms of corporate organization in the analysis of Chandler (1977), were characterized by "high throughput" of fuel and raw materials relative to labor and production facilities (compare Michael Piore and Charles Sabel, 1984). Oliver Williamson (1980) notes that cheap, reliable sources of energy and heat were crucial to this development. Coal was of strategic early importance as a direct source of heat and power, and at a later point as a source of thermal energy for electricity, essential to the efficiency of the moving assembly line and other quasi-flow processes. Alex Field (1987) points out that organizational innovations of this type may be considered "capital-saving" overall, even though firm-level capital requirements were high. In export markets, contemporary comments emphasized non-price competition and particularly the short delivery lags on the part of U.S. suppliers (Nicholas, 1980, pp.

Table 6. *Shares of United States manufacturing exports, 1879–1929 (percent)*

	Iron and Steel Products (except Machinery and Vehicles)	Machinery	Automobiles and Parts	SUM (1,2,3)	Petroleum Products	SUM (1,2,3,5)
1879	2.1	3.4	–	5.5	12.1	17.6
1889	2.4	6.1	–	8.5	13.3	21.8
1899	7.6	10.7	–	18.3	9.2	27.5
1913	10.9	14.5	2.3	27.7	10.1	37.8
1923	8.8	12.4	6.4	27.6	13.1	40.7
1926	5.6	12.9	11.5	30.0	16.8	46.8
1927	5.1	13.9	13.3	32.3	14.7	47.0
1928	5.3	16.4	15.7	37.5	13.9	51.4
1929	5.4	16.4	15.7	37.5	13.9	51.4

Source: 1879–1923 (1963), Tables A-8 and A-12; 1926–1929, U.S. Department of Commerce, *Foreign Commerce and Navigation of the United States for the Calendar Year 1929*, Vol. 1, Tables XII and XXIV.

581–587). Quick delivery is a feature one would expect to see where exports have a "vent-for-surplus" quality, because of the length of a production run on a standardized item. In addition, American producer and consumer goods were often specifically designed for a resource-abundant environment. Some of the adjustment problems of U.S. auto companies in recent years stem from their decades of specialization on large, fuel-using cars. There was a parallel problem facing U.S. locomotive manufacturers in the 1920s, who found their foreign sales handicapped by their design for standard-gauge rails, heavy motive power, and heavy train loads (*Markets of the United States*, p. 71).

The emergence of cheap American steel at the end of the nineteenth century was particularly important. Whereas S. J. Nicholas (1980) suggested that the fall in relative U.S. machinery prices was misleadingly proxied by iron and steel prices, it may be that the world success of American engineering goods was buoyed by exactly that development. Table 6 shows the major role played by iron and steel exports over the half-century under discussion. If we aggregate the three headings under which iron and steel products were listed, we find that their share of U.S. manufacturing exports grew steadily, from 5.5 percent in 1879 to 37.5 percent in 1929. If we add in one other heading in which resource abundance was evidently important, petroleum products, we find that by late 1920s, we have accounted for more than half of all American manufacturing exports. The union of these two sectors is, in essence, the automobile industry. The United States was unquestionably the world's technological leader in automobile production during the 1920s. At the same time, American producers had enormous cost advantages over competitors in raw materials, especially steel. Ford UK faced steel input prices that were higher by 50 percent or more than those paid by the parent company (James Foreman-Peck, 1982, p. 874). It was not accidental that Leontief chose motor vehicles as his most prominently displayed example of the economy as an intricate input-output machine: each million dollars worth of automobiles in 1947 "contained" nearly half that much value in iron and steel, nonferrous metals, and other fabricated metal products (Leontief, 1953, p. 334).

We may also conjecture that there were links between the economy of high throughput and the intensity of the work pace, which also seems to have been a distinctive feature of U.S. industry (Clark, 1987). American firms paid the world's highest real wages and apparently extracted greater effort from the labor force in return. But it is an anachronism to associate "high wages" with "high skill" technologies for the era in which the United States surged to world industrial preeminence. The United States was a well-educated country, but most of the workers in the fast-paced, heavy-industry, mass-production manufacturing in which the country led the world were not well-educated native-born Americans. In 1910 the foreign born and sons of foreign born were more than 60 percent of the machine operatives in the country, and more than two-thirds of the laborers in mining and manufacturing (U.S. Senate, 1911, pp. 332, 334). There is no reason to believe that this labor force was particularly well educated by world standards. Key industries like iron and steel and motor vehicles paid high wages to unskilled workers (who were nonetheless much cheaper than the skilled craft workers used with older technologies), presumably because it was rough, disagreeable, dangerous, demanding work, and because it was vital to have an ample excess labor supply available (compare Daniel Raff, 1988). In the 1930s these industries were central to the movement for industrial unionism, which subsequently provided an alternative mechanism for the continued association between high-wage industries and American industrial success.

V. What became of American resource abundance?

The marked changes in coefficients for 1940 seem to portend the post–World War II pattern, when the United States moved steadily and increasingly into a position of net mineral imports (Chart 4). Beginning mainly in the 1920s, one important mineral after another began to enter the net import column: nonferrous metals, bauxite, lead, zinc, copper, iron ore, and petroleum among others. Without conducting extensive global cost comparisons, it is evident that a country for whom resource prices are determined at the margin by imports is not going to have a major locational advantage in resource costs over its industrial rivals. But what exactly was the process of change in America's resource position? A popular conception is that the country has largely exhausted

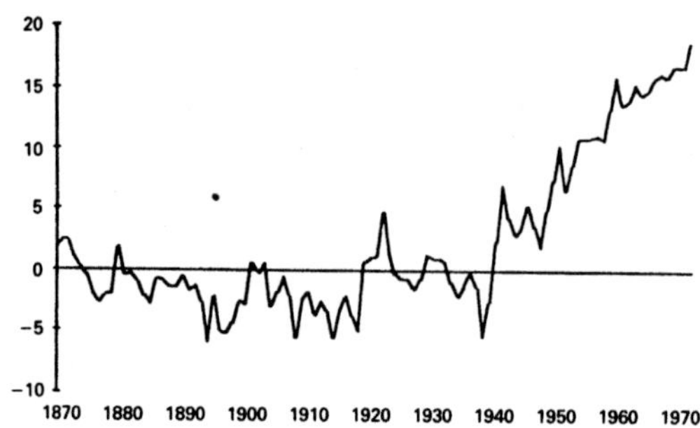

Chart 4. U.S. net mineral imports as a percentage of consumption.
Source: Manthy (1978, Tables MC1 and MC2).

its resource endowment and has had to import so as to avert domestic shortages. Kindleberger has proposed a weaker version of this scenario within the Heckscher–Ohlin framework, in which the more rapid growth of labor and capital relative to resources has turned the country from a net-export to a net-import position with respect to resources (Charles P. Kindleberger, 1960, pp. 347–348). It is doubtful that this account is generally valid. Indeed, a closer look at the trend in world mineral supplies casts a different light on the character of the original position.

In 1919 it could confidently be written that "the United States is more richly endowed with mineral wealth than any other country" (George Otis Smith, 1919, p. 282), and such a statement was consistent with the best geological and industrial knowledge of the day. But the clear pattern of discoveries since that time indicates that there was a systematic historical bias in these perceptions, in that American resources had been much more thoroughly explored and exploited than those of other parts of the world. Chart 5 illustrates this process, by comparing world iron ore "reserves", as indicated by a 1910 survey by the International Geologic Congress, with those reported in a United Nations survey in 1955. Granted that quality differences and extraction and transport costs are neglected in a simple chart, nonetheless the pattern is so clear as to be beyond dispute. Europe and North America had by far the largest reserves in 1910, but their "endowments" (which, to be sure, had increased and not decreased) had grown only slightly in the intervening 45 years. What had been a dominating advantage in 1910 was no more than a respectable presence in 1955.

The case of petroleum is even more extreme (Chart 6). Recall that the United States in 1913 (and for a half-century before) had been the

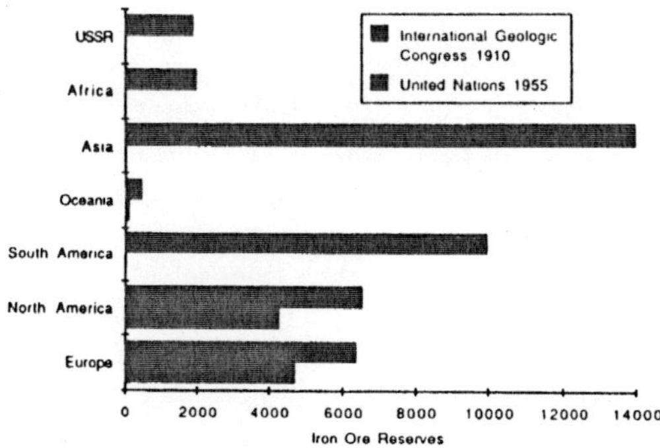

Chart 5. World iron ore reserves, 1910 and 1955.

Sources: International Geologic Congress (1910, pp. 1–56): "Actual Reserves" in millions of tons of metallic iron; United Nations (1955, pp. 19–34): "Reserves" in millions of tons of iron content.

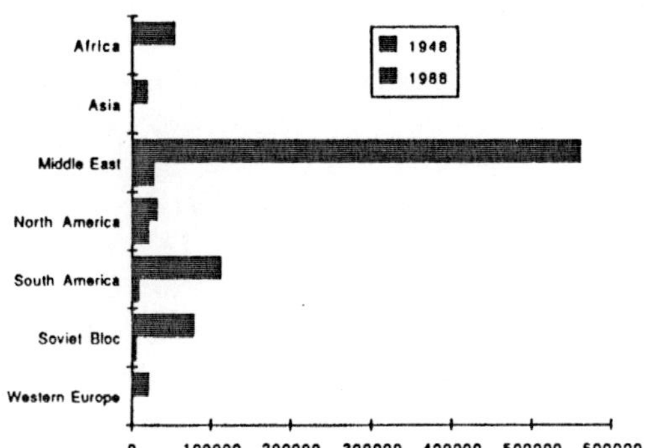

Chart 6. World crude oil reserves, 1948 and 1988.

Source: American Petroleum Institute (1988, Section II, Table 1): "Estimated Proved Reserves of Crude Oil Annually as of January 1 (millions of barrels)."

world's largest petroleum producer and exporter, by a wide margin. As Chart 6 shows, as late as 1948, North American reserves were nearly equal to those of the Middle East. In 1988, though again reserves of all areas had increased, North America was a minor part of the world petroleum picture. It is difficult to avoid the inference that mineral supplies were more a matter of "development" than "endowment."

Where world geological surveys are not available, similar conclusions can be reached by other routes. In the case of bauxite, which takes its name from the French village where it was first developed, the United States and France alternated as first and second in the world until the 1950s. With discoveries in the West Indies in the 1950s, Jamaica quickly moved into first place, at annual production levels larger than those ever achieved in either France or the United States, despite the fact that production levels in those two countries did not decline but continued to grow to levels higher than they themselves had ever achieved. In the late 1960s, Australia replaced Jamaica as number one, again setting new production records without causing an absolute decline in any of the older countries. In both Jamaica and Australia, bauxite production was negligible before World War II. Since the real price of bauxite has declined, it is not the case that domestic reserves have been "exhausted" or that distant supplies have simply been coaxed out along a world supply curve. Rather, early discoveries and mining took place in areas proximate to the early centers of industrial and technological development and within the boundaries of their national jurisdiction.

The last phrase points toward another sense in which resource abundance was historically rather than geologically determined. The United States was the world's largest mineral producing nation, but it was also one of the world's largest countries! Even without Alaska, at 3.5 million square miles, the United States is twice the size of all the countries of eastern and western Europe and Scandinavia combined (excluding Russia). Yet coal and iron ore production in Europe was 30 to 50 percent higher than the U.S. total in the 1910–1913 era. If coal and iron were the imperatives of industrial location ca. 1900, a hypothetical United States of Europe would have rivaled America.

More important than sheer geographic size is economic distance. The United States was a vast free trade area for internal commerce, and the opportunities created by this status provided the incentive for massive investment in transportation infrastructure, including the highly efficient lake transport system that linked Mesabi ore to Pennsylvania coal. In the case of copper, only the combination of national size and efficient internal transportation allow us to say that the "same" economy retained world leadership across the period of American industrial ascendancy, since the early production center in Michigan gave way to remote but larger and richer locations in the Mountain and Southwest regions between 1870 and 1930.

The argument does not stop with national size and efficient transportation. The process of mineral discovery and development was also a prime outlet for creative energies and innovations, often at high levels of technical and organizational sophistication. The United States Geological Survey, formed in 1879 by consolidation of several existing federal surveys, had intimate links with the mining industry. Reports by government geologists in Colorado in the 1880s were crucial in encouraging mining activity and adapting metallurgical knowledge to local requirements (Rodman Wilson Paul, 1960). The American Institute of Mining Engineers became the first speciality group to break away from the American Society of Civil Engineers. Scientifically trained personnel were also important in expanding the range of *uses* for available minerals. An early report by Yale geologist Benjamin Silliman, Jr., foresaw the commercial possibilities of "cracking" petroleum into various compounds, opening up arrays of new uses for what had been considered a useless waste material (Robert V. Bruce, 1987, pp. 140–142). But as Nathan Rosenberg (1985) points out, much of the early use of science by American industry did not deploy new knowledge at the scientific "frontier," but involved repetitive procedures (such as grading and testing materials) for which scientific training was needed but where the learning was specific to the materials at hand. The abundance of mineral resources, in other words, was itself an outgrowth of America's technological progress.

This view of the matter suggests the answer to the question posed above. The country has not become "resource poor" relative to others, but the unification of world commodity markets (through transport cost reductions and elimination of trade barriers) has largely cut the link between domestic resources and domestic industries. American corporations and engineers have been in the forefront of the globalization of the mineral economy. In essence, the process by which the United States became a unified "economy" in the nineteenth century has been extended to the world as a whole. To a degree, natural resources have become commodities rather than part of the "factor endowment" of individual countries.[6] Presumably this is why international economists now distinguish resource-based "Ricardo goods" from others and treat them separately (for example, Robert Stern and Keith E. Maskus, 1981). This procedure may be appropriate for the contemporary world, but it would be hard to do justice to the historic success of American industry within this conception.

VI. Conclusion

Why has the importance of mineral resources in American industrial history been underappreciated? Concern for the future of natural resources is an ancient theme in economics, but most of the attention has been

6. Wilfred J. Ethier and Lars E. O. Svensson (1986) show that in a Heckscher-Ohlin framework with mobility of some factors a country's trade pattern in goods is affected only by its endowment of *nontraded* factors.

channeled into two rather different issues: fear of rising costs from increased resource scarcity and fear of national strategic inadequacy in the event of war. Refuting the first fear has long been the economist's favorite pastime, as it has been easy to show that producers substitute away from relatively scarce resources and that the real prices of "nonrenewable" resources have historically declined. The second fear has always seemed noneconomic in character, if not indeed a cooked-up rationalization for subsidy or protection. Having thus dealt with the "problem" of resource exhaustion, it was easy to overlook a logically distinct aspect of the matter: the contribution of resource location to the competitive potential of a country's industries. Some economic historians, to be sure, have long analyzed national economic histories in terms of world geographical patterns (William N. Parker, 1984). But it is perhaps understandable that Americans have not been inclined to attribute their country's industrial success to what appear to be accidental or fortuitous geographic circumstances. Another reason is that American industrial leadership took on a rather different shape after World War II. Over the course of the twentieth century, the country was able to parlay its resource-based industrial prosperity into a well-educated labor forced, an increasingly sophisticated science-based technology, and world leadership in scientific research itself. In the wake of World War II, there were no serious international rivals in such a wide range of industries that it was easy to lose sight of the resource dimension of industrial performance. After the war, there was a brief period of concern that the nation's resource position had been eroded, culminating in the Paley Commission Report of 1952. But such doubts and fears were largely swept away in the American-led world prosperity of the next 25 years.

To be clear about the argument, there is no iron law associating natural resource abundance with national industrial strength. But the distinctive *American* technologies have, as a matter of history, been relatively resource-using. We have now moved from an era in which the rest of the world adapted to an American technology, with varying degrees of difficulty, to an era in which U.S. firms have had to do the adjusting. The adjustment is not made much easier by the consideration developed in this paper, that historical resource abundance was itself largely an outgrowth of American industrial success.

References

Abramovitz, Moses, "Catching Up, Forging Ahead, and Falling Behind," *Journal of Economic History*, June 1986, 46, 385–406.

Allen, Robert, "The Peculiar Productivity History of American Blast Furnaces, 1840–1913," *Journal of Economic History*, September 1977, 37, 605–633.

———, "International Competition in Iron and Steel, 1850–1913," *Journal of Economic History*, December 1979, *39*, 911–937.

———, "Accounting for Price Changes: American Steel Rails, 1879–1910," *Journal of Political Economy*, June 1981, *89*, 512–528.

American Petroleum Institute, *Basic Petroleum Data Book*, September 1988, *8*.

Atlantic Institute, *The Technology Gap: The United States and Europe*. New York: Praeger, 1970.

Bairoch, Paul, "International Industrialization Levels from 1750 to 1980," *Journal of European Economic History*, Spring 1982, *11*, 269–310.

Bruce, Robert V., *The Launching of Modern American Science 1846–1876*. New York: Knopf, 1987.

Cain, Louis P. and Paterson, Donald G., "Factor Biases and Technical Change in Manufacturing: The American System, 1850–1919," *Journal of Economic History*, June 1981, *41*, 341–360.

——— and ———, "Biased Technical Change, Scale and Factor Substitution in American Industry, 1850–1919," *Journal of Economic History*, March 1986, *46*, 153–164.

Chandler, Alfred D., *The Visible Hand*. Cambridge, MA: Belknap Press, 1977.

——— and Daems, Herman, eds., *Managerial Hierarchies*. Cambridge, MA: Harvard University Press, 1980.

Church, R. A., "The Effect of the American Import Invasion on the British Boot and Shoe Industry, 1885–1914," *Journal of Economic History*, June 1968, *28*, 223–254.

Clark, Gregory, "Why Isn't the Whole World Developed? Lessons from the Cotton Mills," *Journal of Economic History*, March 1987, 47, 141–174.

Crafts, N. F. R. and Thomas, Mark, "Comparative Advantage in U.K. Manufacturing Trade, 1910–1935," *Economic Journal*, September 1986, *96*, 629–645.

David, Paul A., *Technical Choice, Innovation, and Economic Growth*. New York: Cambridge University Press, 1975.

Eckes, Alfred E., *The United States and the Global Struggle for Minerals*. Austin: University of Texas Press, 1979.

Ethier, Wilfred J. and Svensson, Lars E. O., "The Theorems of International Trade with Factor Mobility," *Journal of International Economics*, February 1986, *20*, 21–42.

Eysenbach, Mary Locke, *American Manufactured Exports 1897–1914*. New York: Arno Press, 1976.

Field, Alexander, "Land Abundance, Interest/Profit Rates and Nineteenth-Century American and British Technology," *Journal of Economic History*, June 1983, *42*, 405–431.

———, "Modern Business Enterprise as a Capital-Saving Innovation," *Journal of Economic History*, June 1987, *46*, 473–485.

Floud, Roderick C., "The Adolescence of American Engineering Competition, 1860–1900," *Economic History Review*, February 1974, *28*, 57–71.

———, *The British Machine Tool Industry, 1850–1914*. Cambridge: Cambridge University Press, 1976.

Foreman-Peck, James, "The American Challenge of the Twenties: Multinationals and the European Motor Industry," *Journal of Economic History*, December 1982, *42*, 865–881.

French, M. J., "The Emergence of a U.S. Multinational Enterprise: The Goodyear Tire and Rubber Company, 1910–1939," *Economic History Review*, February 1987, *40*, 64–79.

Habakkuk, H. J., *American and British Technology in the Nineteenth Century*. Cambridge: Cambridge University Press, 1962.

Hounshell, David, *From the American System to Mass Production, 1800–1932*. Baltimore: Johns Hopkins University Press, 1984.
International Geologic Congress, *The Iron-Ore Resources of the World*. Stockholm, 1910.
James, John, and Skinner, Jonathan, "The Resolution of the Labor-Scarcity Paradox," *Journal of Economic History*, September 1985, *45*, 513–540.
Keesing, Donald B., "Labor Skills and the Structure of Trade in Manufactures." In Peter B. Kenen and Roger Lawrence, eds., *The Open Economy*. New York: Columbia University Press, 1968.
Kindleberger, Charles P., "International Trade and the United States Experience, 1870–1955." In Ralph E. Freeman, ed., *Postwar Economic Trends in the United States*. New York: Harper, 1960, pp. 337–373.
Kravis, Irving B. (1956a), "Wages and Foreign Trade," *Review of Economics and Statistics*, February 1956, *38*, 14–30.
——— (1956b), "'Availability' and Other Influences on the Commodity Composition of Trade," *Journal of Political Economy*, April 1956, *64*, 143–155.
Leamer, Edward, "The Leontief Paradox Reconsidered," *Journal of Political Economy*, June 1980, *88*, 495–503.
——— and Bowen, Harry P., "Cross-Section Tests of the Heckscher–Ohlin Theorem: A Comment," *American Economic Review*, December 1981, 71, 1040–1043.
Leontief, Wassily, "Domestic Production and Foreign Trade: The American Capital Position Reexamined," *Proceedings of the American Philosophical Society*, September 1953, 97, 332–349.
———, "Factor Proportions and the Structure of American Trade," *Review of Economics and Statistics*, February 1956, *38*, 386–407.
Linder, Staffan Burenstam, *An Essay on Trade and Transformation*. New York: Wiley & Sons, 1961.
Lipsey, Robert E., *Price and Quantity Trends in the Foreign Trade of the United States*. Princeton, NJ: Princeton University Press, 1963.
Maddison, Angus, *Phases of Capitalist Development*. Oxford: Oxford University Press, 1982.
Manthy, Robert S., *Natural Resource Commodities: A Century of Statistics*. Baltimore: Johns Hopkins University Press, 1978.
Markets of the United States, The Annals, September 1926, *127*.
Nicholas, S. J., "The American Export Invasion of Britain: The Case of the Engineering Industry, 1870–1914," *Technology and Culture*, October 1980, *21*, 570–588.
Parker, William N., *Europe, America, and the Wider World*, Vol. 1. Cambridge: Cambridge University Press, 1984.
Paul, Rodman Wilson, "Colorado as a Pioneer of Science in the Mining West," *Mississippi Valley Historical Review*, June 1969, *47*, 34–50.
Perloff, Harvey S. and Wingo, Lowdon, Jr., "Natural Resource Endowment and Regional Economic Growth." In Joseph Spengler, ed., *Natural Resources and Economic Growth*. Washington: Resources for the Future, 1961.
Piore, Michael and Sabel, Charles F., *The Second Industrial Divide*. New York: Basic Books, 1984.
Raff, Daniel M. G., "Wage Determination Theory and the Five-Dollar Day at Ford," *Journal of Economic History*, June 1988, *48*, 387–399.
Rosenberg, Nathan, *Perspectives on Technology*. New York: Cambridge University Press, 1976.
———, "Why in America?" In Otto Mayr and Pobert Post, eds., *Yankee Enterprise: The Rise of the American System of Manufactures*. Washington: Smithsonian Institution Press, 1981.

———, "The Commercial Exploitation of Science by American Industry." In Kim B. Clark, Robert H. Hayes, and Christopher Lorenz, eds., *The Uneasy Alliance*, Boston: Harvard Business School Press, 1985.

Scott, Bruce R. and Lodge, George C., eds., *United States Competitiveness in the World Economy*. Boston: Harvard Business School Press, 1985.

Simon, Matthew and Novack, David E., "Some Dimensions of the American Commercial Invasion of Europe, 1871–1914," *Journal of Economic History*, December 1964, *24*, 591–605.

Smith, George Otis, ed., *The Strategy of Minerals*. New York: D. Appleton and Company, 1919.

Spengler, Joseph J., ed., *Natural Resources and Economic Growth*. Washington: Resources for the Future, 1961.

Stern, Robert M. and Keith E. Maskus, "Determinants of the Structure of U.S. Foreign Trade, 1958–1976," *Journal of International Economics*, 1981, *11*, 207–224.

United Nations, *Survey of World Iron-Ore Resources*. New York, 1955.

U.S. Department of Commerce, *Foreign Commerce and Navigation of the United States*. Washington: various years.

U.S. Geological Survey, *Mineral Resources of the United States*. Washington: 1913.

U.S. National Resources Committee, *Technological Trends and National Policy*. Washington: 1937.

U.S. Senate, *Report of the Immigration Commission*, Vol. 1. Washington: 1911.

Vanek, Jaroslav, *The Natural Resource Content of United States Foreign Trade 1870–1955*. Cambridge, MA: MIT Press, 1963.

Vernon, Raymond, "International Investment and International Trade in the Product Cycle," *Quarterly Journal of Economics*, May 1966, *80*, 190–207.

———, ed., *The Technology Factor in International Trade*, New York: Columbia University Press, 1970.

Waehrer, Helen, "Wage Rates, Labor Skills, and U.S. Foreign Trade." In Peter Kenen and Roger Lawrence, eds., *The Open Economy*. New York: Columbia University Press, 1968.

White, Hal, "A Heteroskedasticity-Consistent Covariance Matrix Estimator and a Direct Test for Heteroskedasticity," *Econometrica*, May 1980, *48*, 817–838.

Williamson, Oliver, "Emergence of the Visible Hand." In Alfred D. Chandler and Herman Daems, eds., *Managerial Hierarchies*. Cambridge, MA: Harvard University Press, 1980.

Woodruff, William, *America's Impact on the World*. New York: Wiley & Sons, 1975.

"Federal policy, banking market structure, and capital mobilization in the United States, 1863–1913"

by Richard Sylla

America's banking history is full of sensational events. However, episodes such as the "Bank War" between Nicholas Biddle and Andrew Jackson, "wildcat" banking before the Civil War, and especially scenes like the bank runs of the Great Depression, as portrayed in the movie classic *It's a Wonderful Life* or the recent savings and loan debacle, obscure more mundane but potentially more important issues. The central role of a financial system is intermediation. The financial industry is functioning properly when it moves money efficiently from the hands of savers who want to set aside part of their income for later use, but don't want to stuff it under the mattress, to investors who want to use the income to increase the amount of capital devoted to production.

Richard Sylla argues that this mobilization of capital was critical to America's economic rise between the Civil War and World War I. In this essay he explores the effect of bank regulations on patterns of capital movement. He argues that the National Banking Act restrained the growth of banking over large areas of the United States for several decades but also helped link the country's banks together through a reserve system. The first effect left many of the country's bankers in relatively monopolistic positions, thereby allowing these bankers to restrict the local supply of loans and engage in price discrimination. However, the system also promoted an efficient allocation of loanable funds, channeling money from predominantly agricultural to predominantly industrial uses.

Sylla's argument relies on the interpretation of considerable empirical evidence on regional interest rates, bank earnings and profits, loan–asset ratios, and balances. Unlike the other essays, this one contains a fairly elaborate "economic model" that intends to reflect the reality of this period. Sylla then tests the predictions of the model. This explicit model building and testing is an important part of mainstream economics.

Ask yourself these questions as you dissect the essay:

- Is Sylla's argument convincing?
- Are the assumptions of the model realistic? What justifies the shape of the marginal cost curve? The demand curves?
- Are the predictions of the model confirmed?

- Are there alternative models or explanations for the empirical findings? Is it clear that banking regulations are the cause of rural banking monopolies? Are there additional sources? Could banks in rural areas be natural monopolies?
- Are interest rate differentials that exist between country and city banks completely explained? What reasons, other than monopoly, would cause such differentials?
- Are there predictions of the model that are not adequately or fully tested?
- Are the data satisfactory for testing the theory? Is the proxy for interest rates good?
- Sylla argues that the banking system was efficient. Why was it optimal to channel funds from predominantly agricultural to predominantly industrial uses?
- Was the system equitable as well? Were winners and losers created? Was this fair? (Note the discussion of credit monopoly in Chapter 8.)

In a series of papers, John James (1976, 1976) has reexamined these issues. Like Sylla, he finds evidence of local banking monopoly. However, he argues that the National Banking Act's requirements were not very important because of the rapid growth of state banks between 1877 and 1909. The development of deposit and checking accounts made these banks close substitutes for national banks. Marie Sushka and W. Brian Barrett (1984) disagree with both Sylla and James, arguing that monopoly power of local banks declined much earlier, by the mid-1880s, because firms became increasingly sophisticated in their business financing decisions, finding substitutes for local banks. Thus, the rural demand curve was much flatter than pictured in Sylla's Figure 2.

Additional Reading

Lance Davis, "The Investment Market, 1870–1914: The Evolution of a National Market," *Journal of Economic History*, 25 (September 1965), 355–99.

John James, "Banking Market Structure, Risk, and the Pattern of Local Interest Rates in the United States, 1893–1911," *Review of Economics and Statistics*, 58 (November 1976), 453–62.

John James, "The Development of the National Money Market, 1893–1911," *Journal of Economic History*, 36 (December 1976), 878–97.

Richard Keehn, "Market Power and Bank Lending: Some Evidence from Wisconsin, 1870–1900," *Journal of Economic History*, 40 (March 1980), 45–52.

Marie Sushka and W. Brian Barrett, "Banking Structure and the National Capital Market, 1869–1914," *Journal of Economic History*, 44 (June 1984), 463–77.

Richard Sylla, "American Banking and Growth in the Nineteenth Century: A Partial View of the Terrain," *Explorations in Economic History*, 9 (Winter 1971–2), 197–228.

14

Federal policy, banking market structure, and capital mobilization in the United States, 1863–1913

RICHARD SYLLA

The success with which capital funds are mobilized and transferred to industrial and related activities is widely regarded as a critical determinant of both the timing and the pace of industrialization in the modern era. Gerschenkron, for example, has suggested that institutional developments which increased this type of capital mobility played an important role in the varying degrees of industrial progress of nineteenth-century European countries.[1] A functionally similar development, resulting from government intervention at the time of the Civil War, occurred in American banking and provided a powerful capital-supply stimulus for the United States's postbellum industrialization. This study deals with the origins of this banking development, presents an analysis of its potential effects on patterns of capital movement, and tests the hypotheses arrived at in the theoretical analysis using banking data derived primarily from the *Reports* of the Comptroller of the Currency.

The overall argument of the study may be summarized as follows. Two major effects of the Federal government's wartime interventions in banking, which resulted in the National Banking System, were to restrain the growth of banking over large areas of the United States for several decades, and to link the country's banks together through a reserve system that provided a formal, legally sanctioned mechanism for transferring funds between banks. The first effect left many of the country's bankers in relatively monopolistic positions where they could charge high interest rates, restrict loan output in local markets, and

Source: Richard Sylla, "Federal Policy, Banking Market Structure, and Capital Mobilization in the United States, 1863–1913," *Journal of Economic History* (December 1969), 657–686. Reprinted with permission of the author and the Economic History Association.

The author hereby expresses his appreciation to Lance Davis, Stanley Engerman, Donald McCloskey, and the Editor of this *Journal* for valuable suggestions offered to him during the preparation of this article.

1. Alexander Gerschenkron, *Economic Backwardness in Historical Perspective* (Cambridge: Harvard University Press, 1962), especially ch. 1, pp. 5–30 and Postscript, pp. 353–364.

practice price discrimination. The second effect, within this framework of wide variations in the degree of banking competition, promoted an efficient allocation of loanable funds. In practice, this meant a transfer of bank funds from predominantly agricultural to predominantly industrial uses, as well as from the banking system to the country's open capital markets where lumpy investments in railroads and large-scale industry were increasingly financed.

Government policy and the rise of bank entry barriers

To understand fully the restrictive impact of Federal banking legislation on later banking development it is important to recall how unrestricted entry into banking had become in the last antebellum decade. After the Independent Treasury Law of 1846, the Federal government had ceased to concern itself with the country's banks, leaving banking questions entirely in the hands of individual states. In the early 1850s incorporated banking was prohibited in a number of states and territories, either by the laws or by the sentiments of state legislatures. These included Arkansas, California, Florida, Illinois, Iowa, Minnesota, Oregon, Texas, and Wisconsin; and in Indiana and Missouri banking was restricted to state-controlled monopolies.[2] But these laws and sentiments were soon altered. As Bray Hammond notes, "The area from which banking was barred was probably as great in 1852 as at any time; and by 1863, when it was entirely opened up to banking under federal law, all the states but Texas and Oregon had abandoned prohibition, mostly for free banking."[3]

The trend toward free banking, which began in New York and Michigan in the late 1830s, became a major factor in the decline of politically inspired barriers to bank entry. Before free banking, if banking had any legal sanction at all, it was given through specific legislative acts granting charters to individual banks. In states already having incorporated banks, free banking laws were a response to popular revulsion at the frequent corruption involved in older chartering procedures in which politicians accepted bribes or political favors from interested parties in return for allowing the establishment of new banks, and from previously established banks for not doing so. In states without chartered banks, the new laws were more a response to economic needs as reflected in popular opinion. Free banking laws made the chartering of banks an administrative rather than legislative function of state governments.

2. Bray Hammond, *Banks and Politics in America, from the Revolution to the Civil War* (Princeton: Princeton University Press, 1957), p. 605.

3. *Ibid.*, p. 606.

The Federal banking laws of 1863 and 1864 which established the National Banking System were modeled on state free-banking laws, especially the New York law of 1838, and in a nominal sense they represented the extension of free banking to the entire country. This extension, however, was not a major objective of the laws. Congress enacted the legislation primarily to increase the government's borrowing power during the war, by requiring all national banks to invest a portion of their capital in government bonds, and to promote the longer-term objective of giving the country a uniform national banknote currency secured by government bonds. It was thought at the time that existing state banks would aid the government in the achievement of both objectives by simply converting into national banks. Since free banking on a national scale was not a major goal, it is perhaps not surprising that the Federal legislation involved departures from the theory and practice of free banking under earlier state laws. Some of these departures created entry barriers that made the National Banking System incapable of becoming *the* banking system of the United States, a goal that its founders had intended to achieve.

Two entry barriers – minimum capital requirements and loan restrictions – were written directly into the Civil War banking laws. The Banking Act of 1864 provided that a national bank's minimum capital stock was to be $50,000 in towns under 6,000 in population, $100,000 in cities of from 6,000 to 50,000 in population, and $200,000 in cities with more than 50,000 in population.[4] This provision remained in effect until 1900. Capital provisions of the earlier state free banking laws were not so stringent, nor were they enforced as strictly as under the National Banking System.

Table 1 presents information gathered to show why national bank minimum capital requirements constituted a serious barrier to national bank entry in some parts of the country as well as an important reason why the American dual banking pattern of national and non-national banks emerged in the late nineteenth century. The data pertain to 1900, one of the earliest years for which relatively complete American banking data are available. In that year the average capital of non-national banks in the three dominant agricultural areas of the country, the South and the two North Central regions, was actually less than the minimum required capital of national banks. In these three regions non-national banks outnumbered national banks 7,066 to 1,967, while in the more industrially developed northeast (New England and Middle Atlantic States) and the sparsely settled Mountain-Pacific region national banks

4. A. T. Huntington and Robert J. Mawhinney, compilers, *Laws of the United States Concerning Money, Banking and Loans, 1778–1909* (National Monetary Commission publication. Washington: Government Printing Office, 1910), p. 333.

Table 1. *Average capital and capital–deposit ratios of national and non-national commercial banks in the United States, by regions, in 1900*

Region[a]	Average Capital ($ thousand)		Capital-Deposit Ratios	
	National	Non-national	National	Non-national
New England	244	166	0.44	0.11
Middle Atlantic	205	225	0.19	0.16
South	113	39	0.33	0.28
East North Central	152	40	0.24	0.15
West North Central	112	28	0.29	0.24
Mountain-Pacific	137	81	0.19	0.15
United States	167	59	0.25	0.17

[a] The regional groupings of states are: New England (Maine, New Hampshire, Vermont, Massachusetts, Rhode Island, and Connecticut); Middle Atlantic (New York, New Jersey, Pennsylvania, Delaware, Maryland, and District of Columbia); South (Virginia, West Virginia, North Carolina, South Carolina, Georgia, Florida, Alabama, Mississippi, Kentucky, Tennessee, Arkansas, Louisiana, Texas, and Oklahoma); East North Central (Ohio, Indiana, Illinois, Michigan, and Wisconsin); West North Central (Minnesota, Iowa, Missouri, Kansas, Nebraska, South Dakota, and North Dakota); Mountain-Pacific (Montana, Wyoming, Colorado, New Mexico, Arizona, Utah, Nevada, Washington, Oregon, and California).

Source: Calculated from regional sums of individual state data from Board of Governors of the Federal Reserve System, *All Bank Statistics, United States 1896–1955* (Washington: Board of Governors, 1959).

outnumbered non-national 1,764 to 1,630. Overall, in 1900 commercial banks outside the national system outnumbered those in it by 8,696 to 3,731.[5] Obviously the Civil War laws had failed rather strikingly to give the United States a single, unified banking system.

The reason why national bank capital requirements constituted a serious entry barrier was that in many places – especially small, agricultural communities – the amount of deposits a bank could attract was not sufficient to allow the bank to earn a profit on $50,000 of bank capital equal to what could be earned on $50,000 employed in other uses. Deposits are analogous to borrowed capital, introducing an element of leverage into a bank's capital structure, i.e. its capital-deposit ratio.[6] Other things being equal, the bank with the most leverage will earn the highest return on its equity capital. In Table 1 the data showing capital–deposit ratios in 1900 give an indication of why the non-national component of American banking had grown relative to the

5. Data on bank numbers are taken from Board of Governors of the Federal Reserve System, *All Bank Statistics, United States 1896–1955* (Washington: Board of Governors, 1959).
6. See David A. Alhadeff, *Monopoly and Competition in Banking* (Berkeley: University of California Press, 1954), p. 28ff.

national system that had been intended to replace it. Non-national banks in every region in 1900, and most likely in earlier years as well, enjoyed a leverage advantage over national banks. The high minimum capital requirements of national banks were an important cause of this advantage.

The other national bank entry barrier written into the Civil War laws was a provision of the 1864 Act which stated that a national bank could not "hold the possession of any real estate under mortgage, or hold the title and possession of any real estate purchased to secure any debts to it for a longer period than five years."[7] This feature of the law, which remained in effect for more than 50 years, naturally had its greatest effect on national bank entry in agricultural areas where land was the prime asset. Along with restrictive capital requirements, the prohibition of mortgage loans led to the postbellum recovery of non-national banking in rural areas. In contrast with Federal statutes, the most restrictive of antebellum state banking laws, the Louisiana law of 1842, allowed all of a bank's capital to be invested in long-term obligations such as mortgages, and confined only deposited funds and notes issued in excess of capital to short-term loans.[8]

The restriction on real estate lending by national banks, in addition to reviving state banking, promoted a host of substitutes such as mortgage and trust companies, which sometimes shared the same rooms and managements as national banks. It also had the interesting effect – about which more will be said below – of draining bank funds from the countryside, where, judging by interest rates, finance was scarce to the cities where it was more abundant. A Kansas banker in 1908 illustrated this point for the National Monetary Commission:

> It is almost impossible for a bank in a farming community where there are no manufacturing or other interests to absorb loanable funds to avoid entirely all connection with real estate. As it stands at present the country national bank may buy commercial paper in centers, about which it is difficult for the officers to know much, but must turn down the farm mortgage offered at its counter, than which there is no safer investment, and experience has shown none much more available.[9]

Capital requirements and restrictions on loans constituted barriers to entry into national banking in smaller communities and rural areas, but

7. Huntington and Mawhinney, pp. 343–344.
8. Hammond, *Bank and Politics*, p. 681.
9. U.S. National Monetary Commission, Replies to Circular Letter of Inquiry . . . on Suggested Changes in Administrative Features of the National Banking Laws (Washington: Government Printing Office, 1908), p. 135. It is worth noting that in this document a number of bankers and bank examiners raised objections to the real estate loan prohibition even though comments on the prohibition were not solicited.

they do not explain why the growth of non-national banking should have been retarded. In fact, the opposite point is often stressed, namely that non-national banking did expand to offset retardative elements inherent in the national laws. While it is true that non-national banking grew rapidly in the late nineteenth century, its failure to expand even more rapidly is of greater significance than its actual growth. The non-national banks, which included state-chartered and private banks, possessed numerous advantages over the national system. Legal capital requirements were either much lower or nonexistent. Much the same could be said of their regulation by state authorities. Furthermore, they were not prohibited from mortgage lending. In spite of these advantages, it was not until 1906, or more than 40 years after the birth of the National System, that non-national commercial bank assets surpassed the assets of national banks.[10] The factors which induced the expansion of non-national banking are clear; what is puzzling is their delayed and drawn-out impact.

Federal policy dealing with bank note issues, besides adding a further barrier to national bank entry, provides the answer to the question of why non-national banking grew less rapidly than might otherwise have been expected, given the inadequacies of national banking. During the Civil War, when existing state banks were reluctant to join the new National System, Congress decided to speed up conversions to national charters by placing a 10 percent tax on all state bank notes paid out by any bank after July 1, 1866. This tax effectively removed the profitability of state bank note issue and once it was legislated the great majority of state banks did convert. The haste with which state banks took out national charters testifies to the central importance of note issue as a banking function at the time. From then on, until the habit of using checkbook money gradually became widespread, state bank entry was retarded.

Potential national banks faced a similar difficulty. National banks could issue bank notes backed by government bonds, but from 1863 to 1875 ceilings were in effect on total national bank note circulation. From 1863 to 1870 the ceiling was $300 million; most of this had been taken out by existing banks by 1866 when the tax on state issues went into effect and as a consequence few new national banks were formed between 1866 and 1870. The ceiling was then raised to $354 million and the numbers of national banks again began to grow. In 1875 the ceiling was removed, but by that time government bond prices were rising, and national banks, which could issue notes only up to 90 percent of the par value of bonds, found that the profitability of note

10. Board of Governors, *All Bank Statistics*, pp. 39, 43.

issue was rapidly diminishing.[11] In summary, when further national bank note issues had been profitable to the banks they were not possible, and when eventually they became possible they were no longer profitable.

Federal policies regarding bank note issues thus produced another barrier to bank entry, and one which affected both national and non-national banks. This barrier reinforced the differential geographical impact of the national bank capital requirement and loan restriction barriers, for the small towns and rural areas where these barriers were most strongly felt were also the places where the habit of using currency in preference to checkbook money was strongest.

Nothing better illustrates the effectiveness of entry barriers than what happens once they are removed. Such tests are not always possible, but when entry barriers are legal they can be eliminated by the stroke of a pen. In effect this is what was done in 1900 to some of the barriers erected by Civil War banking legislation. Popular dissatisfaction over these barriers found its way into the Gold Standard Act of that year.

The Gold Standard Act amended earlier legislation to allow the formation of national banks with a minimum capital of $25,000 in towns where population did not exceed 3,000.[12] The Act also made significant modifications of the note issue provisions of earlier laws. National banks were allowed to issue notes up to 100 percent of the par value of government bonds deposited as security instead of 90 percent of par as under the old law. The Act further provided for an exchange of outstanding 5, 4, and 3 percent bonds for a new issue of 2 percents, with compensation to reflect the greater market value of the higher coupon issues.[13] These provisions virtually eliminated the major drawback to expansion of national bank circulation, the large spread between 90 percent of the par value of governments and the market prices of the 5, 4, and 3 percent issues which were then selling above par.

The responses to these measures were both rapid and large. From February 1900 to February 1901, national bank circulation rose from $205 to $310 million and expanded further to $675 million by the middle of 1910.[14] In the fall of 1900, moreover, the Comptroller of the Currency reported that in the months since the Gold Standard Act had passed, he had received about one thousand informal applications for the organization of national banks and had approved 509 formal applications,

11. Profitability of note issue is analyzed in detail by Phillip Cagan, *Determinants and Effects of Changes in the Stock of Money, 1875–1960* (New York: National Bureau of Economic Research, 1965), pp. 86–95.

12. Huntington and Mawhinney, *Laws*, p. 446.

13. *Ibid.*, pp. 256, 446–447.

14. *Report of the Comptroller of the Currency, 1913*, pp. 333, 339.

of which 382 were for banks with capitals less than $50,000.[15] In a decade over 4,600 new national banks were established, nearly two-thirds of these with capital less than $50,000, the pre-1900 minimum.[16] Almost 60 percent of the small banks were formed in the South and West North Central regions where entry barriers previously had exerted their greatest impact.

By itself, no one of the legal barriers to bank entry discussed here – national bank capital requirements, loan and note issue restrictions, and the removal of note issue profitability from state banks – would have seriously retarded banking growth. For example, with note issue restricted to national banks, but with lower capital requirements, the countryside would have contained many more national banks, as the response after 1900 indicates. Or, if the high capital requirements of the National System remained in effect but state bank note issues had not been curbed, a similar response would have occurred earlier in the non-national banking sector. Certainly the American banking system was capable of numerous substitutions. But in conjunction with one another the legal entry barriers proved quite effective in restricting such substitutions, and certain regions, as well as small towns and rural areas nearly everywhere, suffered from these restrictions on bank entry.

Entry barriers and bank behavior in theory

In theory, the differential geographical impact of the bank entry barriers discussed in the previous section leads one to expect that banks in smaller towns and rural areas would operate in a less competitive environment than city banks. This would be the expectation within any one region, but also between regions because of different degrees of urbanization and dependence on agriculture. If all country bankers, hypothetically speaking, are monopolists and all city bankers are pure competitors, then if a country banker and a city banker have the same amounts of resources and the same cost curves the former will restrict his output to the point where his marginal costs equal his marginal revenue and charge interest rates greater than his average costs of lending, while the city banker will grant relatively more loans and charge a lower rate of interest, namely that equal to his marginal cost of lending.

A banking structure that allows monopoly in the countryside and pure competition in the cities will violate several economic optimality conditions because some banks will be in a position to engage in monopolistic exploitation of their customers. Allocative neutrality, for

15. *Report of the Comptroller, 1900*, p. xx.

16. Derived from data presented in *Report of the Comptroller, 1910*, p. 20.

example, will be violated because in restricting output and charging high interest rates, country banks will be granting less than an optimal amount of loans, thereby freeing productive resources for use in less profitable employments. Theoretically, with high interest rates in the countryside and low rates in the cities, resource allocation would be improved if loanable funds were transferred from the cities to the countryside and lent there.

The difficulty with applying this analysis to American banking after the Civil War is that the analysis assumes that monopolistic country bankers and competitive city bankers carry on their operations independently of each other. This was not the case because an important feature of the National Banking System was the establishment of a reserve system which institutionalized earlier, less formal, points of contact between country and city banks.

The reserve system enacted in the revised National Bank Act of 1864 delineated three classes of national banks in regard to reserve requirements. New York City was designated the central reserve city of the country and its national banks were required to maintain lawful money reserves equal to 25 percent of their deposits and note circulation.[17] Eighteen other cities were designated reserve cities, which meant that, like New York, they could hold reserves of other national banks.[18] The reserve cities were also required to maintain 25 percent reserves, but only half of this amount had to be held in lawful money. The other half could be held as deposits in New York banks. National banks outside of New York and the reserve cities were required to maintain 15 percent reserves, of which three-fifths, or 9 percent, could be held as deposits in reserve cities including New York.

Under the national banking system reserve city banks continued the antebellum practice of paying interest on bankers' balances deposited with them by other banks. The effect was to create a city demand for the funds of monopolistically situated country banks in addition to the local demand for loans. This placed the country banker in the position of a discriminating monopolist. He faced two demand curves arising from two separate markets and his problem was how to allocate his funds between the two markets in order to maximize profits. Intermarket price discrimination is worthwhile only if the two separate demand curves have different elasticities. This was the case in banking because the city demand curve was perfectly elastic – an individual country banker could

17. Huntington and Mawhinney, *Laws*, pp. 345–346. A later Act of June 20, 1874, repealed the requirement that national banks hold reserves against note circulations. *Ibid.*, p. 418.

18. During the next fifty years Chicago and St. Louis became central reserve cities, and the number of reserve cities increased to 47. See *Report of the Comptroller, 1913*, p. 282.

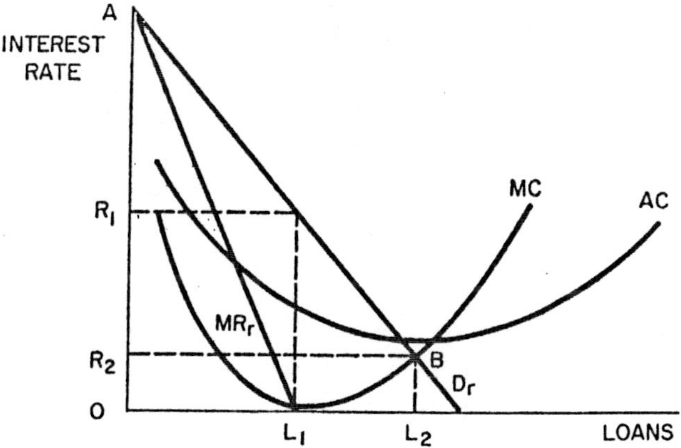

Figure 1. Situation of an isolated country bank monopolist.

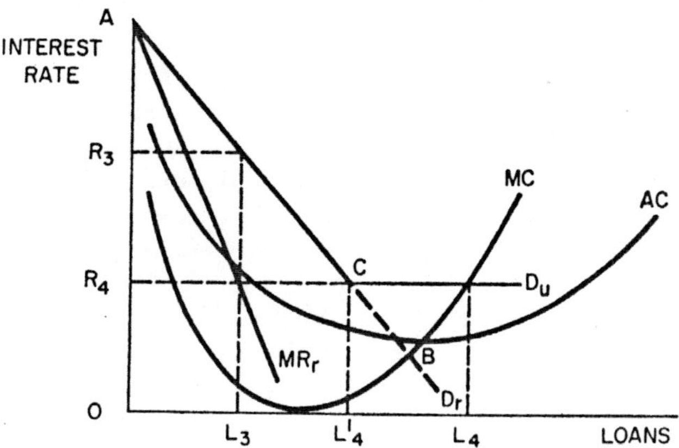

Figure 2. Situation of a country bank monopolist facing a demand for funds from city banks as well as from local borrowers.

not affect the city rate, regardless of how much money he transferred to the cities – while the local demand curve for loans was much less than infinitely elastic.

Several possible situations in which the country banker might have found himself are portrayed in Figures 1 and 2. In Figure 1 we assume the absence of a demand for bank funds from the cities. The banker's demand curve for loans in his (local) market is D_r and the associated marginal revenue curve is MR_r. Given average and marginal cost curves,

AC and *MC*, respectively, the country banker will charge a rate OR_1 and make OL_1 of loans. At this level of loan output marginal cost equals marginal revenue and profits are maximized. Since loan contracts are individually negotiated, however, it is likely that a country bank monopolist will be able to practice some degree of price discrimination *within* his local market. In an extreme situation in which each borrower can be isolated and charged exactly what he is willing to pay for the loan, the banker will maximize profits by granting OL_2 of loans and charging the marginal borrower a rate OR_2. The bank will thereby appropriate to itself the entire amount of surplus that borrowers could obtain if the loan market were purely competitive; this is represented by the area ABR_2 in Figure 1. The average of interest rates charged to all borrowers will then lie between the marginal rate OR_2 and the maximum rate *OA*.

In Figure 2 we add to the situation portrayed in Figure 1 a demand curve D_u, representing the demand for country bank funds on the part of city banks. The country bank's total demand curve for local loans and city balances is now ACD_u. The city demand curve as seen by the country banker is infinitely elastic and it therefore becomes his marginal revenue curve beyond point *C*. If the country banker acts as an ordinary monopolist in his local market, but as a discriminating monopolist between the local and city markets, profits are maximized where *MC* crosses D_u. Marginal revenue in each market is equated to marginal cost, the result being that an amount of loans OL_3 is granted at home at a rate OR_3, and a quantity of funds L_3L_4 is sent off to the city.

Again, however, it is likely that the country banker will be able to practice price discrimination *within* his local market as well as *between* the local and city markets. In this case, OL_4' of loans will be granted at home, the marginal local borower being charged a rate OR_4, and $L_4'L_4$ of funds will be sent to the city where they also earn the rate OR_4. In practice, the marginal country borrower may not be charged exactly the city rate OR_4, for his rate may be marked up to reflect the greater riskiness of a loan to an individual as opposed to the safer city bank. To the extent the country banker is able to discriminate between borrowers in his local market, he will again be able to extract from them a portion of the borrowers' surplus represented in Figure 2 by the area ACR_4. For this reason, and also because of risk premiums, the average of rates he charges to local borrowers will be between OR_4 and *OA*.

Because of the nature of the bank lending process, the last case, in which there is discrimination both among local borrowers and between the local and city markets, probably most nearly represents the situation of country bankers in the late nineteenth century. Several observations can be made about this case. Comparing the situation of the discriminating monopolist of Figure 1 with the last case in Figure 2, it is evident that fewer local loans are granted by the discriminating monopolist in the latter situation (OL'_4 is less than OL_2), but that because of the presence of a demand from city banks, the total amount of bank funds allocated to local and city uses is greater than in the former case (OL_4 is greater than OL_2). Moreover, with allowances for differences in risk premiums and lending costs, *marginal* rates of interest on bank loans in the cities and in the countryside are brought to rough equality, thus making the allocation of loanable funds more efficient. Average lending rates, it is true, are greater in the countryside because entry barriers have led to less competition and more opportunities for price discrimination by country bankers, but average rates are not relevant to the question of resource allocation in this static, partial equilibrium framework.

The point of the analysis can be made clearer by considering a hypothetical example. Suppose that a country banker charges his local borrowers varying rates of interest ranging from, say, 10 percent down to 5 percent. The marginal country borrower pays 5 percent which, because of risks and lending costs, the country banker views as equivalent to the 3 percent, let us say, that he could earn by transferring funds to the cities. When all borrowers who are willing to pay 5 percent or more in the country are accommodated, the remaining loanable funds of the country banker are deposited in city banks at 3 percent. City banks may then lend this money to borrowers who use the funds to finance purchases of stocks on the open market, a common outlet for bankers' balances held by city banks in the nineteenth century. The rate on call loans, a marginal use of bank funds, will be determined in the short run by the supply of and demand for available funds, but more basically by city bankers' costs of lending and the risk premiums they attach to this type of loan, the same factors that determine the marginal loan rates of country bankers. If costs and risks are similar in the cities and the countryside, then the lending rate on call money would approximate the rate paid by the marginal country borrower, which implies an efficient allocation of loanable funds. This result would hold even if the rate paid by the marginal country borrower differed from the call money rate as long as the difference was due to differences in lending costs and in risk premiums attached to the two types of loans by the country and city bankers.

Empirical relationships

The model of bank behavior developed in the preceding section leads to a number of predictions about the price and output behavior of banks in different competitive environments, and also about their profit experience. Given the relevant quantitative information, these predictions can be tested to see whether, and how well, they conform to the banks' historical experience. In what follows two general points are established. The first is that barriers to entry actually did lead to monopolistic behavior and monopoly profits for banks in noncompetitive situations, and the second is that the possibilities opened up by the connection of country banks, through the national bank reserve system, to the demand for funds in the cities led to a flow of bankers' balances from country to city banks well in excess of amounts transferred merely to satisfy reserve requirements.

Monopoly

The theory of monopoly, even when extended as above to include price discrimination practices, predicts that a bank monopolist will charge higher average interest rates, produce less local loan output, and earn higher profits than a competitively situated producer operating under the same cost conditions.[19] Direct information on loan interest rates charged by national banks is too fragmentary to allow a detailed comparison of inter-regional and city-country price variations. A recent study of national bank earnings by Lance Davis does, however, provide extensive indirect information on bank pricing policies.[20]

Using data on national bank net earnings, which were gathered by the Comptroller of the Currency starting in 1869, and gross earnings, which became available in 1888, and calculating bank earnings as a percentage of earning assets, Davis constructed series approximating average annual bank interest rates for six regions of the country similar to the regions used in the present study,[21] and for reserve-city and country banks in each region. The data on earning assets were taken from balance sheets published in the *Annual Reports* of the Comptroller.

19. Pure competition in country banking would rule out price discrimination within the local market. It would also change cost conditions as the competitive banks bid against each other for customers' deposits. In Figure 2 such bidding would tend to raise the level of AC to a point of tangency at its lowest point with D_u. Then both a group of competitive banks and a perfectly discriminating monopolist would grant the same total amount of local loans (OL_4'). The sense in which local loan output is restricted by a monopolistic country bank arises when comparison is made with a city bank having the same cost curves. See fn. 23.

20. Lance E. Davis, "The Investment Market, 1870–1914: The Evolution of a National Market," *The Journal of Economic History*, XXV (Sept. 1965), 355–399.

21. For Davis' regions see notes to Table 2; the regional groupings used in this study are given in the notes to Table 1 above.

Table 2. *Average annual differentials in national bank gross earnings as a percentage of earning assets, 1888–1914 (percentage point units)*

Years	Region[a]					
	I	*II*	*III*	*IV*	*V*	*VI*
	Differential Between Reserve-City Banks in Each Region and New York City Banks					
1888-1900	−0.23	0.79	2.33	1.43	4.44	2.17
1901-1914	0.23	0.33	1.89	0.42	1.89	0.88
	Differential Between Country and Reserve-City Banks in Each Region					
1888-1900	1.15	0.15	1.00	0.45	0.53	2.15
1901-1914	0.11	−0.05	0.03	0.34	1.52	2.80
	Differential Between Country National Banks in Each Region and New York City Banks					
1888-1900	0.92	0.94	3.33	1.88	4.97	4.32
1901-1914	0.34	0.28	1.92	0.76	3.41	3.68

[a] Regions are: I, New England States; II, Middle Atlantic States; III, Southern States; IV, East North Central States plus Minnesota, Iowa, and Missouri; V, North Dakota, South Dakota, Nebraska, Kansas, Montana, Wyoming, Colorado, New Mexico, and Oklahoma; VI, California, Washington, Oregon, Idaho, Utah, Nevada, and Arizona.

Source: Calculated from Lance E. Davis, "The Investment Market, 1870-1914: The Evolution of a National Market," THE JOURNAL OF ECONOMIC HISTORY, XXV (Sept. 1965), Tables 2 and 3, 355-69.

Gross earnings as a percentage of earning assets furnishes a close approximation to average loan interest rates, the major difference lying in the lumping together of loans and security investments in earning assets and investment and loan returns in earnings. Loans, however, were by far the largest component of earning assets at all dates. For this reason, and also because returns from investments – primarily U.S. government bonds – did not vary much between regions, earnings–earning assets ratios adequately reflect geographical differences in loan rates. On the other hand, earning net of bank operating expenses and losses as a percentage of earning assets are a less adequate index of interest rates, but do provide useful information on variations in bank charges between regions for a longer period of time than the series of gross returns.

Table 2 shows the average annual spread between gross earnings of reserve-city banks in each of Davis' six regions and the rate of gross earnings on earning assets of national banks in New York City, the nation's central money market, for two subperiods of the pre–World War I period for which this information is available in the Comptroller's *Reports*. Gross earnings rates in Boston, the only reserve city in New

England (Region I), were near to the New York rate in both subperiods, but reserve-city banks in each of the other five regions earned higher rates of return than the New York City banks, indicating that they charged higher loan rates. Reserve cities in the South (Region III) and the Far West (Regions V and VI) enjoyed the greatest advantage over New York City, which is what I would have expected on the basis of my study of entry barriers. Furthermore, the spreads between the rates earned in the regional reserve cities and the New York rate narrow substantially after the turn of the century. Davis attributed the narrowing of interregional rate differentials to the development of a national market in commercial paper, which increased the degree of competition to which banks in all regions were subjected. To this can be added the reduction of bank entry barriers legislated in the 1900 Gold Standard Act and the ensuing growth of national and state banking, both of which reduced regional variations in banking competition.

Another aspect of spatial differences in interest rates is given in Table 2 which presents, for the same two subperiods of 1888–1914, the spreads between the gross earnings rates of country banks and those of reserve-city banks in each region. Only in the Middle Atlantic states (Region II) were the city and country rates similar in both subperiods. In each of the other five regions the country banks earned higher rates. Country rates in New England, the South, and the Middle West (Regions I, III, and IV) moved closer to the reserve-city rates in these regions after the turn of the century. In the two Far Western regions the city–country differentials did not narrow,[22] but because the reserve city–New York differential for these regions fell sharply during 1901–1914, the spreads between country rates in Regions V and VI and the New York rate did narrow (see table). Again the effect of reduced bank entry barriers is evident, especially in the virtual elimination of city–country rate differentials in New England and the South, but also in the reduced differentials between New York and country banks in every region (see table) after 1900.

Differentials in rates of gross earnings on earning assets, as approximations to interest rate differentials, could, however, reflect nothing more than differences in bank cost functions, and could therefore be unrelated to variations in competition between banks. For the same reason, a narrowing of rate differentials over time might have been caused by reductions in unit costs as more and more small banks grew to a more efficient size of operation. If cost differences explain differences in bank

22. The city–country differential of Region V for 1888–1900 is sharply affected by an extreme value in 1898. If this value is excluded, the average differential for the other 12 years is 1.59 instead of 0.53.

Table 3. *Average annual differentials in national bank net earnings as a percentage of earning assets, 1870–1914 (percentage point units)*

Years	Region[a] I	II	III	IV	V	VI
	Differential Between Reserve-City Banks in Each Region and New York City Banks					
1870-1879	1.04	1.18	2.17	1.37	—	4.08[b]
1880-1889	−0.10	0.24	0.58	0.69	—	2.60
1890-1899	−0.02	0.66	0.54	0.08	−0.47	2.77
1900-1909	−0.50	−0.22	0.75	−0.24	0.21	0.36
1910-1914	−0.26	−0.45	0.52	−0.39	−0.08	−0.04
	Differential Between Country and Reserve-City Banks in Each Region					
1870-1879	1.24	0.39	−0.06	1.13	—	3.88[b]
1880-1889	1.04	0.46	1.23	0.96	—	1.36
1890-1899	0.97	0.26	1.04	0.87	2.10	−0.97
1900-1909	0.60	0.35	0.13	0.42	1.14	0.97
1910-1914	0.07	0.24	−0.03	0.11	0.80	0.75
	Differential Between Country Banks in Each Region and New York City Banks					
1870-1879	2.28	1.57	2.13	2.50	—	7.96[b]
1880-1889	0.94	0.70	1.81	1.65	—	3.96
1890-1899	0.95	0.92	1.58	0.95	1.63	1.80
1900-1909	0.10	0.13	0.88	0.18	1.35	1.33
1910-1914	−0.19	−0.21	0.49	−0.28	0.72	0.71

[a] For states in each region, see Table 2.
[b] 1871-1879.
Source: Calculated from Lance E. Davis, "The Investment Market, 1870-1914: The Evolution of a National Market," THE JOUNRAL OF ECONOMIC HISTORY, XXV (Sept. 1965), Tables 4 and 5. There were no reserve cities in Region V before 1888.

charges, then we would expect *net* returns on earning assets to be more nearly equal between regions and between city and country banks than gross returns. Table 3, which is patterned after Table 2, except for covering a longer period, presents data relevant to this point. Comparing reserve cities with New York we see that during the 1870s cost differences cannot explain interest rate differentials in any of the regions, for the net returns of reserve-city banks everywhere exceeded the New York banks' returns by at least one percentage point. After 1880, Boston (Region I) and New York earned comparable net returns on earning assets, but reserve-city banks in other regions generally earned greater net returns until the end of the century. After 1900, however, net returns in every region but the South fell close to, and by 1910–1914 below, the New York levels. This again is consistent with growing interregional, intercity competition either through a developing commercial paper market, as Davis argued, or directly between banks, as the present analysis implies.

Table 3 indicates that country banks in every region generally earned higher net returns than city banks in the same region, but the earlier-noted tendency for the differentials to narrow over time is again apparent. The same pattern is repeated when we compare the regional country bank net returns with the New York City rate. Not until the turn of the century, and not even then in the South and Far West, did country bank net returns approximate those of the cities. It is clear, therefore, that the higher interest charges of small country banks in the late nineteenth century cannot be explained by their higher costs of operation and failure to realize possible economies of scale; the regional patterns and time trends of average bank loan rates, as approximated by gross and net rates of return on earning assets, appear to be better accounted for by variations in competition due to the differential impact of legal barriers to entry.

In addition to higher prices (interest rates), monopoly theory predicts that a monopolist's output will be held below levels consistent with competitive profit maximization, i.e., where price equals marginal cost. Returning to Figure 2, recall the earlier conclusion that a country bank monopolist who practices price discrimination within his local market and faces an additional demand for funds from the city will make OL_4' of local loans. This level of local loan output is below the competitive level, which for a city bank operating under the same cost conditions would correspond to the level where the marginal cost curve (MC) intersects the demand curve (D_u). Therefore, if country banks were operating in a less competitive framework than their city cousins, we would expect output restriction to show up in a comparison of country and city bank loan–asset ratios.[23]

Table 4 tends to confirm this expectation. If, for any year, we compare the loan asset ratio of non-reserve-city national banks in a given region with the ratio for reserve-city banks in the same region, in a majority of these comparisons (23 of 41) the ratio for the city banks exceeds or equals that of the country banks in its region, indicating that a greater or equivalent percentage of reserve-city bank assets went into loans. In most of the contrary cases, there is little difference between the

23. The output restriction alluded to here corresponds in Figure 2 to the difference between OL_4, the amount of loans which would be made by a city bank, and OL_4', the amount which would be made in the local market by an intramarket discriminating monopolist or, for that matter, by a group of purely competitive country banks. This restriction of output is consistent with efficient fund allocation and should be distinguished from the quantity ($OL_4'-OL_3$), which is the amount output would be restricted by a nondiscriminating-bank monopolist. Empirically, the two types of output restriction are difficult to distinguish.

Table 4. *Loan–asset ratios of reserve-city and non-reserve-city national banks, by region, 1870–1910*

	New England		*Middle Atlantic*		*South*		*East N. Central*		*West N. Central*		*Mountain-Pacific*	
Year	*RC*	*NRC*	*RC*	*NRC*	*RC*	*NRC*	*RC*	*NRC*	*RC*	*NRC*	*RC*	*NRC*
1870	0.53	0.47	0.46	0.47	0.38	0.44	0.48	0.46	0.47	0.43	—	0.28
1875	0.58	0.52	0.50	0.52	0.43	0.43	0.55	0.51	0.54	0.47	0.58	0.46
1880	0.56	0.51	0.51	0.47	0.48	0.44	0.52	0.47	0.54	0.49	0.48	0.41
1885	0.60	0.55	0.53	0.51	0.52	0.55	0.54	0.55	0.58	0.62	0.55	0.53
1890	0.67	0.68	0.64	0.62	0.61	0.64	0.63	0.64	0.60	0.64	0.68	0.60
1900	0.62	0.59	0.53	0.53	0.47	0.53	0.53	0.56	0.52	0.57	0.47	0.43
1910	0.58	0.57	0.51	0.54	0.55	0.60	0.55	0.57	0.56	0.61	0.49	0.53

Note: For indicated years, average of loans reported at each call date was divided by average of assets reported at each call date.
Source: *Reports of the Comptroller of the Currency* for the years indicated.

city–country ratios, the maximum difference being 6 percentage points in the South in 1870. This is all the more striking when we recall that city bank reserve requirements were much more stringent than the requirements to which country banks were subject. The latter had to maintain reserves of 15 percent against deposits (deposits and circulation before 1875), of which only two-fifths (6 percent) had to be held in cash. The reserve-city banks had to hold 25 percent reserves against deposits, *including* net balances due to other banks, of which one-half (12.5 percent) had to be cash. Other things being equal, one would therefore expect the loan–asset ratios of the city banks to be several percentage points below those of the country banks, but in only 8 of the 41 city–country, region–year comparisons did the country bank ratio exceed the city bank ratio by more than three percentage points. Moreover, almost half of the cases (8 of 18) in which the country ratio exceeds the city ratio in a given region lie in the years 1900 and 1910, which lends further support to the argument that declining entry barriers after 1900 increased the degree of banking competition in the countryside. To the evidence of higher interest rates, we can therefore add the evidence of output restriction in building a case for the existence of widespread monopoly in late nineteenth-century country banking.

We are, however, not quite in a position to nail down the argument. For it is still possible that the higher gross and net returns (to which output restriction contributed) realized by country bankers in every region over both New York and regional reserve-city banks until 1910–1914 were necessary in order to make returns on the capital invested in banks equal in the cities and the countryside. For example, because of the minimum capital requirements of national banks, banks formed in smaller communities might not have been able to attract as many dollars of deposits (analogous to borrowed capital) per dollar of equity capital as city banks; in these circumstances country banks would have had to charge higher loan rates and earn greater net returns on earning assets merely to earn a rate of return on equity comparable to that earned by city banks. Profit on equity is the consideration relevant to the question of bank entry, and the consideration which thus provides the acid test of restrictions on competition.[24] If country banks consistently earn higher

24. That is, unless the average cost curves of country banks reached lower levels than those of larger city banks because of real cost differences that could not be competed away. For example, labor costs might have been substantially higher for city banks than for country banks. I deem this unlikely, primarily because studies of bank costs in more recent periods (e.g., Alhadeff, *Monopoly and Competition in Banking*) indicate that average costs decline, or at least do not rise, as bank size increases. Real cost differences remain a possible explanation of differences in bank profit rates but variations in competition due to entry barriers appear to provide an explanation more consistent with the historical circumstances.

rates of return on their equity capital than city banks, in addition to charging higher loan rates and earning higher net returns on earning assets, then it is evident that barriers to entry are preventing competition from carrying out its return-equalizing function at the margin.

These suppositions are supported by the evidence of national bank net earnings as a percentage of capital plus surplus as reported in Table 5. In 43 of 53 region–year comparisons between 1870 and 1910, the country banks of a given region earned greater returns on equity than reserve-city banks in the same region. Bank competition apparently was more effective in the cities. Furthermore, as we move south and west through regions in given years, profit rates in both reserve cities and the countryside tend to rise from levels prevalent in the East, which confirms the differential regional impact of national bank entry barriers.

An argument for the greater monopoly powers of country banks as contrasted with city banks in every region, as well as the greater monopoly power of country and city banks in the South and West in comparison with Eastern banks, would appear to be firmly grounded in quantitative evidence. This evidence relates only to national banks, but the conclusions can be generalized to non-national banks because the more rapid growth of non-national banks in all six regions between the Civil War and 1910 indicates that their profit experience was, if anything, even greater than that of banks in the national system. The more stringent regulation – e.g., higher reserve requirements – of national banks points in the same direction.

Bankers' balances

After monopoly, the second feature of the model to be tested is the predicted behavior of bankers' balances. The monopolistic country banker portrayed in Figure 2 had two outlets for his funds – local loans and bankers' balances held in city banks. Balances held by country national banks with reserve-city banks, and those held by reserve-city banks in central reserve cities, satisfied reserve requirements to the extent of 9 and 12.5 percent of deposits, respectively. But if the model is valid, reserve requirements would play little role in a banker's decision of how much funds to send to the city. This would be decided by extending local loans to the point where the marginal rate of return, adjusted for risk considerations, equaled the rate of return earned on bankers' balances in the cities. This level of local loan output is represented by OL_4' in Figure 2. The remainder of the funds the bank wished to utilize profitably (L_4L_4' in Figure 2), an amount determined by comparing marginal lending costs with the rate earned on city balances, would be sent to the city. Reserve requirements would therefore provide a minimum below

Table 5. *Average profit rates of reserve-city and non-reserve-city national banks, by region, 1870–1910*

	New England		*Middle Atlantic*		*South*		*East N. Central*		*West N. Central*		*Mountain-Pacific*	
Year	*RC*	*NRC*	*RC*	*NRC*	*RC*	*NRC*	*RC*	*NRC*	*RC*	*NRC*	*RC*	*NRC*
1870	10.3	11.5	10.3	11.3	13.3	16.0	11.0	13.7	17.3	15.5	—	21.1
1875	7.9	9.1	8.7	8.9	8.4	9.5	12.0	11.4	6.4	11.6	17.9	20.1
1880	5.6	7.0	5.9	7.6	9.1	7.6	11.5	8.5	6.5	12.7	7.5	18.7
1885	3.0	5.3	5.9	7.2	6.3	9.5	7.4	8.1	7.3	11.7	5.3	14.3
1890	4.3	6.6	7.4	9.2	10.2	11.9	9.3	9.9	9.7	9.1	9.7	14.2
1895	3.1	4.6	6.0	6.6	3.9	7.1	6.8	6.4	1.9	4.4	8.4	3.4
1900	6.9	7.4	9.9	11.3	8.6	12.6	10.8	9.0	7.7	10.5	12.4	12.6
1905	5.4	6.6	8.8	8.8	8.7	12.0	8.2	9.0	7.8	11.1	12.9	16.0
1910	11.9	7.6	7.7	8.0	12.1	10.4	8.3	8.7	11.8	13.2	13.7	15.8

Note: Figures are sums of semiannual unweighted averages of net earnings divided by capital and surplus of national banks in each state and reserve city for the two halves of each year.

Source: Calculated from *Annual Report of the Comptroller of the Currency* for the indicated years, except for 1870, where the data have been taken from the 1873 *Report*.

which city balances could not fall, unless the country banker was willing to forego interest on part of his reserves by holding more than was necessary in cash, but would otherwise be irrelevant to the individual banker's profit-maximizing decision.

These theoretical conclusions are supported by data on bank behavior. A chart published in Margaret Myers, *The New York Money Market*, allows a comparison of cash holdings and bankers' balances with the amounts called for by reserve requirements for country, reserve-city, and New York banks from 1875 to 1914.[25] It shows that country banks held substantial excess reserves in both cash and city balances throughout the period. Cash holdings were far in excess of the required 6 percent of deposits in the early years but declined to a level not far above this by the end of the period. Country bank balances in the cities did not exhibit such a distinctive trend toward the 9 percent level which could be counted as reserves against deposits, but after reaching a peak in the last years of the century they too declined up to 1914. In the reserve cities, where competition between banks was stronger than in the countryside, excess reserves in either cash or balances were never as large in relation to required reserves as in the country. The required amounts were 12.5 percent of deposits for both cash and balances. New York City banks generally stayed close to their minimum required reserves of 25 percent in cash, the major exceptions occurring after financial panics.

It is therefore apparent that country banks sent a great deal more funds to the cities than was called for by reserve requirements. Because any cash reserves above the minimum 6 percent requirement against deposits also applied to the total requirement of 15 percent, the actual excess reserves of country banks held as city balances were much greater than the amount above 9 percent of deposits. To cite an extreme case, on October 1, 1878, the reserve required for the $289.1 million of net deposits held by country national banks was $43.4 million of which two-fifths had to be held in cash while the other three-fifths could be held in the form of reserve-city balances. But on that date the country banks held $39.1 million in cash and $11 million in a fund for the redemption of their bank notes which also counted toward reserve requirements, so that all of the $56 million the country banks had deposited in reserve-city banks on that date were excess reserves which could have been recalled had the banks chosen to lend the funds at home.[26] That they did not indicates that the banks regarded their balances in the cities as at least as profitable, after taking account of the

25. Margaret G. Myers, *The New York Money Market, Origins and Development* (New York: Columbia University Press, 1931), p. 236.

26. Data from *Report of the Comptroller, 1878.*

risks involved, as local loans. Until about 1900 most of the funds country banks had on deposit in the cities were not needed to meet reserve requirements at all, but were mainly held for investment purposes in preference to local loans.

This result can be accounted for by the analysis of Figure 2; short of assuming that country banks were not interested in maximizing profits, it is difficult to account for it in any other way. Moreover, the growth of competition in country banking due to the erosion of entry barriers provides a possible explanation of why excess reserves in both cash and balances began to fall after the last years of the nineteenth century. Increased banking competition would initially have the effect, in Figure 2, of flattening out the *AB* segment of an individual bank's demand curve, thus moving point *B* to the right. The percentage of bank funds sent to the cities would thus decline and loan-asset ratios would be expected to rise. The behavior of cash and bankers' balances in Miss Myers' chart is consistent with this explanation, and Table 4 shows that loan–asset ratios of country banks were generally higher in the latter half of the period 1870–1910 than in the years before 1890.

The regional incidences of the predicted effects of the bankers' balance transfer mechanism are given in Tables 6, 7, and 8. Table 6 shows the *net* amounts of balances due to country banks from other banks–assuredly from city banks since amounts due from and due to other country banks would disappear in the netting process – for a number of years between 1870 and 1910. The figures are given in absolute terms and as a percentage of country bank assets in each region, and they are averaged over the five call dates given for each year in the Comptroller's *Report* in order to eliminate seasonal influences. They are thus indicative of the average net amounts of funds the country banks transferred to the cities. The absolute amounts rise throughout, but the percentage figures reach a peak in 1900 after which they fall off sharply to 1910. This pattern is common to every region. The regional tendencies predicted from variations in bank competition are again apparent, with the percentage of assets transferred out of the countryside rising as we move west. At most dates, however, country banks in the Middle Atlantic and East North Central regions tended to transfer greater percentages of their funds than banks in the adjoining South and West North Central regions, respectively. This might be explained by the presence of more reserve cities, and hence more opportunities for sending off funds, in the former two regions through most of the period.

Tables 7 and 8 show the amounts of funds received by the net recipients under the operation of the transfer mechanism, i.e., by the reserve-city and central-reserve-city banks. Unlike the country banks which transferred smaller percentages of their funds after 1900, the

Table 6. *Net bankers' balances*[a] *of non-reserve-city national banks due from other banks, 1870–1910*

Year	*New England*	*Middle Atlantic*	*South*	*East N. Central*	*West N. Central*	*Mountain-Pacific*
			In Millions of Dollars			
1870	16.4	17.4	2.3	8.8	2.6	0.6
1875	15.2	18.4	5.0	13.5	5.1	1.1
1880	16.4	29.1	6.8	20.6	5.2	3.9
1885	17.4	33.2	7.9	19.0	7.7	4.7
1890	17.3	35.5	14.1	26.5	12.4	11.3
1900	23.9	69.3	32.8	58.9	23.7	28.0
1910	26.1	91.5	57.3	79.2	43.3	50.6
			Above as Percent of National Bank Assets[b] in Non-Reserve Cities			
1870	6.1	6.7	5.1	6.9	9.0	16.7
1875	5.0	6.3	6.0	6.4	8.4	7.6
1880	5.0	9.4	7.6	10.0	8.7	15.4
1885	5.0	9.1	6.1	8.4	6.6	9.1
1890	5.0	8.4	6.2	9.0	6.7	8.2
1900	5.8	11.2	10.1	13.5	10.9	18.3
1910	5.2	6.9	6.1	8.6	7.4	12.7

[a] The dollar values for each region are the sum of "due from national banks," "due from state banks," and "due from reserve agents," less the sum of "due to national banks," "due to state banks," "due to trust companies," and "due to reserve agents," for each state, summed over the states in the region. In order to reduce seasonal influences, the items in quotation marks were averaged arithmetically over the five call dates reported for each year.

[b] Like the net bankers' balances figures, bank assets are annual averages calculated by taking the arithmetic mean of total assets reported at five call dates for each year.

SOURCE: *Report of the Comptroller of the Currency* for each of the indicated years.

percentages of city bank assets received through net transfers from other banks rise throughout the period in most of the regions.[27] This is accounted for by the more rapid growth of bank assets in the countryside than in the cities after 1900, a trend which was partly, but not entirely, offset by the creation of more reserve cities as the newer regions developed. The city banks thus tended to receive an increasing proportion of their funds as net transfers from other banks even as increased banking competition in the countryside after 1900 was leading country banks to keep more of their funds at home. A related factor was the growth of state banks which maintained net balances not only in national bank reserve cities but also in country national banks in their own areas, since these balances counted toward their reserves as well as earning interest.

27. In Table 7, the decline in the percentage received by reserve-city banks in the East North Central region between 1885 and 1890 was primarily a result of the elevation of Chicago to central-reserve-city status.

Table 7. *Net bankers' balances of reserve-city national banks due to other banks, 1870–1910*

Year	*New England*	*Middle Atlantic*	*South*	*East N. Central*	*West N. Central*	*Mountain-Pacific*
			In Millions of Dollars			
1870	4.4	0.5	−0.2	2.8	−0.2	—
1875	8.9	−0.3	0.3	8.6	1.6	0.2
1880	8.1	4.2	1.2	11.5	3.9	0.3
1885	13.5	3.2	1.6	17.1	3.3	−0.1
1890	11.7	5.5	2.9	4.1	8.2	0.5
1900	27.5	38.7	1.9	13.1	21.3	1.7
1910	28.2	133.3	11.1	42.9	72.8	20.0
		Above as Percent of National Bank Assets in Reserve Cities				
1870	3.1	0.3	−2.6	4.3	−1.0	—
1875	5.1	−0.2	1.2	9.1	8.7	2.2
1880	4.3	2.1	4.7	11.1	2.6	7.3
1885	6.7	1.4	4.8	10.9	9.9	−2.9
1890	5.4	2.0	6.9	3.9	13.4	6.3
1900	10.2	7.7	3.0	6.0	15.1	3.8
1910	8.9	14.7	5.1	10.4	18.4	4.4

Note: See notes to Table 6. Unlike the dollar amounts reported in Table 6, the figures of this table and Table 8 are derived by subtracting the "due from . . ." from the "due to . . ." items.
SOURCE: *Report of the Comptroller of the Currency* for each of the indicated years.

Table 8. *Net bankers' balances of central reserve-city banks due to other banks, 1870–1910*

Year	*New York*	*Chicago*	*St. Louis*
	In Millions of Dollars		
1870	65.9		
1875	80.6		
1880	101.8		
1885	113.6		
1890	140.6	28.5	6.6
1900	339.3	60.0	21.2
1910	518.6	152.7	55.6
	Above as Percent of National Bank Assets in Central Reserve Cities		
1870	16.4		
1875	19.3		
1880	22.1		
1885	24.4		
1890	27.1	22.3	16.9
1900	33.7	24.1	23.0
1910	30.6	30.8	25.4

Note: See notes to Tables 6 and 7.
SOURCE: *Report of the Comptroller of the Currency* for each of the indicated years.

The state banks were thus joined to the national bank reserve system, forming another, less formal, layer at the bottom of the reserve pyramid. At the apex of the pyramid were the central-reserve-city banks in New York, Chicago, and St. Louis, which by the first decade of this century, as Table 8 shows, received from a quarter to a third of their total assets as net transfers from other banks, i.e., after amounts due from other banks were deducted from the bankers' deposits they held.

Whether in absolute values or as a percentage of assets, the net amounts of funds transferred out of the countryside were by no means inconsequential. If a not untypical loan–asset ratio of 0.5 is assumed, country banks which transferred 5 to 10 percent of their assets to the cities could have increased their local loans by 10 to 20 percent if the funds had not migrated. Not all of the funds, of course, could have been called back, for reserve requirements before 1914 and the normal course of money flows would have continued to necessitate the holding of some city balances. But contemporaries were well aware that the amounts of bankers' balances actually held were far in excess of these needs; to some observers they represented "funds not needed by business" in the countryside, while to others they were funds "taken away from legitimate business."[28] Adopting the latter position, the 1913 *Pujo Report* suggested a remedy:

> The most effective way of keeping these funds at home, where they could perform their legitimate function of supplying the needs of trade and commerce in the section from which they are drawn, would be to limit the proportion of resources that may be loaned by any bank on stock-exchange collateral.[29]

But the Money Trust investigators went on to note that "Banks, like individuals, will use their money where it can be employed to the best advantage within legal limits. No currency system can or ever will be devised that will prevent that result."[30]

The theoretical analysis in the second section of this article provides a way of reconciling these positions. It suggests that the country banks were employing their funds to the best advantage both in the country and in the cities, and that this was consistent with an economically efficient allocation of funds. The latter result would apply only if the country banks could practice price discrimination, though not necessarily perfect price discrimination, within their local markets, but because of restricted entry and the personal character of the bank loan market this condition probably applied in many country banking

28. B. H. Beckhart and James G. Smith, *The New York Money Market, Sources and Movements of Funds* (New York: Columbia University Press, 1932), p. 184.
29. Quoted *ibid.*, p. 164.
30. *Ibid.*

markets during the late nineteenth century. Moreover, the theory is entirely consistent with – indeed, even explains – higher average loan rates in the country than in the cities, which was a problem many contemporaries sought to solve.

Conclusion

In tracing the consequences for late nineteenth-century bank behavior of entry barriers created by Federal banking legislation in the 1860's, this article is an attempt to explain several phenomena which puzzled contemporaries and later scholars. Interregional and city-country interest rate differentials persisted because of variations in the degree of monopoly power possessed by bankers in different areas. When barriers to entry were eroded, competition became more uniform and bank interest rate differentials narrowed, often rather sharply. In addition, the large amounts of net bankers' balances that, at all times in these years, country banks in high-interest areas held on deposit in banks in the cities where interest rates were lower, were shown to be related to variations in banking competition as well as to the transfer mechanism established by the national bank reserve system.

These features of post–Civil War banking development have important implications for larger financial and economic trends. Within a context of restricted bank entry, they promoted the mobilization of bank funds and, if the price discrimination theory of bank behavior correctly describes the situation of the typical country banker, they also encouraged an economically efficient allocation of those funds. The behavior of bankers' balances in particular offers a useful insight into how the problem of capital supply for developing industries and industry-related activities during the postbellum era was solved in part, as well as why in those decades the industry–agriculture balance in the economy underwent rapid change.

VI

Populism

"A reappraisal of the causes of farm protest in the United States, 1870–1900"

by Anne Mayhew

The last third of the nineteenth century has long been seen as a period of agricultural distress and unrest, the "age of agrarian discontent." Farmers argued that they were discriminated against by the monopoly power of railroads, milling companies, commodity buyers, meat packers, and money lenders. They maintained that the monopoly power exercised by these groups depressed farm prices and reduced farm profits. Many farmers attempted to change their economic situation by direct political action through groups like the Grange, the Greenback Party, the Farmers Alliance, and especially the Populist Party.

For decades, historians accepted the complaints of the farmers at face value. Then in 1966, Douglass North provided empirical evidence that rejected the farmers' complaints about prices, freight costs, and interest rates. Others have corroborated and extended these findings, showing that the real income per capita of farmers rose consistently throughout this period. Anne Mayhew's "A Reappraisal of the Causes of Farm Protest in the United States, 1870–1900" examines the agrarian unrest in light of this new evidence. She argues that much of the protest by farmers can be explained as a response to commercialization. They were not objecting to the prices they faced per se, but "to the increasing importance of prices."

This essay differs from many of the others in that it relies on secondary sources (articles, books, etc.) rather than primary sources (records from the nineteenth century).

Mayhew's penetrating interpretation poses many unanswered questions:

- Mayhew defines a commercial system as one that depends on purchased inputs, with a consequent necessity of the sale of outputs. What exactly is "dependence on purchased inputs?" What is a useful benchmark for dependence – 1 percent, 50 percent, 100 percent?

- What percentage of output is sold by a "commercial" farmer? What percentage of output was sold by these farmers? Mayhew does not attempt to measure either of these levels.
- What quantitative measures would help prove or disprove Mayhew's theory?
- Once a farmer owns his land, he no longer needs to pay for this input. Could you assume that this farmer is no longer a part of the commercial system?

Subsequent to Mayhew's essay, researchers have sought to assess more carefully the economic circumstances of the farmers and to tie them even more directly to political protest.

Mayhew argues that "in the absence of the protests we would lack evidence that economic conditions were deteriorating during this period." Does her explanation rule out the crisis-response explanation? Mayhew's argument implicitly states that commercial farmers face greater risk. Subsequent research has sought to appraise this risk quantitatively, tying it to protest. Robert McGuire (1981) finds a strong correlation between protest activity and random variations in price and yields at the state level. Using data from futures markets, Dennis Halcoussis (1993) finds that the median loss of Kansas farmers due to forecasting errors peaked during the Populist period. James Stock (1984) links farmer indebtedness and fear of foreclosure directly to political unrest. In this revised view, farmers protested most loudly when prices moved adversely.

Why did political activism emerge in this period? There were agricultural crises before the late 1800s, after all. Dennis Halcoussis's answer is insightful: "While it would have been futile to organize in an attempt to control the weather, once enough farmers were participating in a more commercialized system, it made sense to band together to increase control over the economic environment."

Additional Reading

Robert Fogel and Jack Rutner, "The Efficiency Effects of Federal Land Policy, 1850–1900," in William Aydelotte, Alan G. Bogue, and Robert W. Fogel, eds., *The Dimensions of Quantitative Research in History*, Princeton, NJ, Princeton University Press, 1972.

Dennis Halcoussis, "Economic Losses Due to Forecasting Error and the U.S. Populist Movement," Department of Economics, California State University, Northridge, 1993.

Robert Higgs, "Railroad Rates and the Populist Uprising," *Agricultural History*, 44 (July 1970), 291–7.

Robert McGuire, "Economic Causes of Late-Nineteenth Century Agrarian Unrest: New Evidence," *Journal of Economic History*, 44 (December 1981), 835–52.

Douglass North, *Growth and Welfare in the American Past*, New York: Prentice-Hall, 1966.

Fred Shannon, *The Farmer's Last Frontier: Agriculture, 1860–1897*, New York: Harper and Row, 1968.

James Stock, "Real Estate Mortgages, Foreclosures, and Midwestern Agrarian Unrest, 1865–1920," *Journal of Economic History*, 44 (March 1984), 89–105.

15

A reappraisal of the causes of farm protest in the United States, 1870–1900

ANNE MAYHEW

Between 1870 and 1900 American farmers organized in the Grange, the Alliances, and the Peoples (Populist) Party and protested against a variety of economic ills. Economic historians have generally explained the farm organizations and the protests in the same way that the farmers themselves explained them – in terms of low agricultural prices and high costs of inputs resulting in part from the monopolistic organization of the suppliers of those inputs.[1] However, there now exists considerable evidence indicating that the economic conditions of the time were not as the farmers depicted them,[2] thus raising two questions: (1) if the farmers' statements about their economic state cannot be accepted as historical fact, then why were the farmers so angry? and (2) why did they choose to protest the issues which they did?

My purpose in this article is to suggest an explanation of this protest which is consistent with what the farmers said they were protesting *and* with the evidence that farm economic conditions were not deteriorating. It is not my purpose to introduce new data, but rather to reinterpret data from the standard secondary sources. Furthermore, I am concerned

Source: Anne Mayhew, "A Reappraisal of the Causes of Farm Protest in the United States, 1870–1900," *Journal of Economic History* (June 1972), 464–475. Reprinted with permission of the author and the Economic History Association.

1. The two most frequently cited and most detailed accounts of the farmers' organization of this period are John D. Hicks, *The Populist Revolt* (Lincoln: University of Nebraska Press, 1961; first published by The University of Minnesota Press, 1931), and Solon Justus Buck, *The Granger Movement* (Cambridge: Harvard University Press, 1913). Both of these works explain the protests in the farmers' terms, although Buck does note in the first paragraph of his book that ". . . it would be untrue to say that the condition of the American farmers was retrograding in the decade following the Civil War" (p. 3). He does not, however, pursue this argument in the rest of the book. Fred A. Shannon, in his authoritative book on agriculture during this period, *The Farmer's Last Frontier: Agriculture, 1860–1897* (New York, Harper and Row, 1968) explains the protests in the farmers' terms, as do most textbooks.
2. Most of this evidence is presented in Allan G. Bogue, *Money at Interest* (New York: Russell & Russell, 1955) *passim*, and Douglass North, *Growth and Welfare in the American Past* (Englewood Cliffs: Prentice-Hall, Inc., 1966), ch. ii.

only with the farm protests of the Midwest – the area for which we have the best studies of farm conditions during this period.[3]

The problem of explaining the farm protests

Midwestern farmers said they were being unfairly treated by railroads, moneylenders, manufacturers and retailers of farm equipment, banks, and other "middlemen" who by virtue of monopolistic position and undue influence on government policy were able to deprive the farmer of what should have been his share of rising American income.[4] Economic historians have generally taken the farmers' complaints, along with the long-run changes in the position of American agriculture, as sufficient explanation of the farm protests. The usual reasoning is that rapid increases in acreage under cultivation, increasing per acre productivity, and low income elasticity of demand for agricultural products meant that many farmers could not operate their farms at a profit and it was the railroads, middlemen, and moneylenders who had the unpleasant task of making this fact clear to the farmers.[5]

But, were farm economic conditions deteriorating? Douglass North rejects the farmers' complaints about prices and freight and interest rates as sufficient explanation of the protest.[6] He does so because: (1) agricultural terms of trade were rising, though erratically, throughout the period; (2) between 1865 and 1900 railroad rates were falling rapidly (though less rapidly in the area west of Chicago than in the eastern part of the country); and (3) the burden of indebtedness and high interest rates has been exaggerated.[7]

It could certainly be argued that the farmers' statements about the conditions they faced cannot be so easily dismissed as they are by North. The data on railroad freight rates used by North are those provided by Shannon, but Shannon argues that the apparent fall in freight rates may be misleading since farmers probably often paid more than the railroad's

3. Although it is frequently emphasized that Southern farmers faced a different set of problems in the post–Civil War period from the set faced by their counterpart in the Middle West, the protests of the two groups are usually explained in the same terms, perhaps because in an effort to forge a broader alliance the leaders of farmgroups emphasized the common plight of all American farmers (and occasionally of workers, too). Ignoring basic differences in problems faced and solutions desired may be good politics, but it is not necessarily good history.

4. Cf. Buck, *The Granger Movement*; Hicks, *The Populist Revolt*; and Norman Pollack, *The Populist Mind* (New York: The Bobbs-Merrill Company, Inc., 1967).

5. This, with variations, is the standard explanation found in textbooks; e.g., Ross M. Robertson, *History of the American Economy* (2nd ed.; New York: Harcourt, Brace World, Inc., 1964), pp. 260–264.

6. North, *Growth and Welfare in the American Past*, pp. 137–148.

7. Ibid., pp. 137–142.

stated annual average rate.[8] He also argues that the data on prices received by farmers may be misleading because farmers often received less than the prices stated as paid.[9]

Finally, it might be objected that North does not show that farm incomes were *not* falling, and so fails to deal with a central point in the argument that farmers were protesting worsening economic conditions. What he does suggest is that even though, with statistics now available, we cannot be sure of what happened to farm income, land values and farm mortgage foreclosure rates do not suggest a "pattern of long-run continuous farm distress."[10] The question of what happened to farm incomes remains unanswered.[11]

Whatever the case, it is puzzling that farmers began to complain about railroad rates, interest rates, and problems of obtaining credit in a period when freight rates and interest rates were falling rapidly and when, according to Bogue, credit was easily available.[12] Why had farmers not protested earlier when transporting goods and borrowing money cost far more, and when it was far more difficult to transport goods any distance or to borrow money at all? It is also puzzling that earlier fluctuations in prices did not provoke farmer protest.

It is frequently argued that the protests of 1870–1900 were simply one manifestation of a general long-term protest by farmers against their peculiarly hard lot.[13] The fact remains, however, that farmers between

8. Shannon, *The Farmer's Last Frontier*, p. 300.
9. *Ibid.*, p. 292.
10. North, *Growth and Welfare in the American Past*, p. 146.
11. Using Frederick Strauss and Louis H. Bean's estimates of gross farm income as given in *Gross Farm Income and Indices of Farm Production and Prices in the United States, 1869–1937* (Washington: G.P.O., 1940), p. 23, and the increase in the number of farms as reported by the Censuses for 1870, 1880, and 1890. *Historical Statistics of the United States*, 1789–1945 (Washington: G.P.O., 1949), Series E 1–5, it is easy to determine that gross per farm income declined during the period. This fact, combined with Theodore W. Schultz's estimates in *Agriculture in an Unstable Economy* (New York: McGraw-Hill Book Company, Inc., 1945), p. 68, of low income elasticity of demand for agricultural products have seemed to be strong evidence that farmers must have suffered declining incomes. However, total output of the major Midwestern crops grew steadily, exports of those crops increased rapidly, and the Midwest provided an increasing share of the total U.S. production of wheat, corn, and meat. Thus, it is not clear that *Midwestern* farm incomes were failing during this period. It remains possible that gross per farm income declined in the U.S. as a whole but did not decline in the Midwest. Of course it is possible that with improving terms of trade for agriculture, real incomes of Midwestern farmers were rising even if their money income was falling.
12. Bogue, *Money at Interest*, pp. 1–6, 262–276.
13. See, for example, Shannon, *The Farmer's Last Frontier*, pp. 3–4: Carl C. Taylor, *The Farmers' Movement, 1620–1920* (New York: American Book Company, 1953), pp. 1–12; and Lance E. Davis, Jonathan R. T. Hughes, and Duncan M. McDougall, *American Economic History: The Development of a National Economy* (3rd ed.; Homewood: Richard D. Irwin, Inc., 1969), pp. 367–368.

1870 and 1900 protested as they had not before. Before the Civil War farm protest was sporadic and most farm organizations are devoted to improving agricultural practices.[14]

Furthermore, when American farmers in other periods protested, it is easier to identify the economic causes than it is for the period of 1870–1900. In the case of the Whiskey Rebellion – which was a protest against economic conditions – there is little doubt about why the farmers were angry. A tax was imposed on their "cash crop" and they protested that tax. Similarly, in recent times, there can be little doubt that the farm bloc programs of the 1920s and 1930s were a direct consequence of deteriorating agricultural conditions and the measures proposed by the farmers were in fact designed to alleviate those conditions. By contrast, in the case of the protests between 1870 and 1900, it is difficult to find a direct connection between the actual conditions on the farms and the farmers' specific complaints.

Actually, in the absence of the protests we would lack evidence that economic conditions were deteriorating during this period. Even without the Whiskey Rebellion we would know that a tax had been levied on whiskey and that whiskey was the major "cash crop" of the then "Western" farmers. In more recent times and without knowing that farmers exerted pressure for agricultural relief, we could determine that farmers had a rough time in the 1920s and 30s. But if farmers had not protested between 1870 and 1900, the story of agriculture during that time would probably be written quite differently. It would probably be noted that a lack of rainfall in the newly settled Plains States, combined with wide fluctuations in prices of agricultural products, caused some hardship, but otherwise the Midwest would probably be described as an area in which farmers were able to enjoy a less rapid fall in prices received than in prices paid, rapidly falling costs of transportation and credit, and new marketing opportunities abroad as well as in this country. But the farmers did not see their situation this way and it remains to explain why they did not and why they had the grievances that they did.

North proposes that the protest can be explained in terms of the opening of fertile lands throughout the world: the development of an international market for agricultural products caused fluctuations in prices which the American farmer could not understand.[15] Agricultural prices did fluctuate during this period, and they did fluctuate in response to changes in the supply from newly opened agricultural lands, but this was not a new phenomenon. Prior to 1870, agricultural prices

14. Taylor, *The Farmers' Movement*, p. 71.

15. North, *Growth and Welfare in the American Past*, p. 142.

fluctuated and new land was brought into cultivation in the United States. Why did not these earlier fluctuations in prices and changes in supply cause protest?

While the farmers may have found the international market and its effects on them difficult to understand, this does not explain why the farmers were so angry with the specific groups with which they were angry. I am not arguing that North is wrong in suggesting that the farmer did not understand the relationship between the prices he received and the weather in Australia, but I am arguing that this lack of understanding does not explain why he took his frustrations out on railroads, bankers, and middlemen.

North also argues (as do many others) that the farmer was responding to his changing place in American society:

> As though these woes [of participation in an international market] were not enough for the nineteenth century farmer, this was the era when he was becoming a minority in America. Throughout all of our earlier history, his had been the dominant voice in politics and in an essentially rural society. Now, he was being dispossessed by the growing industrial might of America and its rapid urbanization. The farmer keenly felt his deteriorating status. His reading matter was full of warnings and complaints against the evils and moral decay of the city and its malign influence over the countryside. His disenchantment was an inevitable component of the vast and complex economic-sociological phenomenon that was taking place.[16]

The problem is to explain how this dispossession was made real to the individual farmer. What was he afraid of? How did he know his status was deteriorating? The problem is also to explain why the farmer led in placing the blame specifically on monopolists. The farmer was not protesting some abstract change in his position – he was specifically angry with railroad companies, banks, mortgage companies, and middlemen who were "exploiting" him. Articles about the evils of cities do not drive people to the picket lines – or to the Grange meeting.[17]

The protest as a reaction to commercialization

My hypothesis is that we can explain much of the protest – we can explain what the farmer was mad about and why he was mad at

16. *Ibid.*, p. 145.

17. We all know that many of the American voters who are excited by the campaign slogan "Law and Order" are not concerned with the preservation of domestic tranquility by protecting or extending formal or substantive due process. A statement that these voters are reacting to "a complex economic-sociological phenomenon" would strike most of us as correct – *but* not a sufficient explanation of how residents of Cicero came to associate "Law and Order" with keeping Cicero white, nor even an explanation of why they are concerned at all. North's comments do not tell us why the farmers were up in arms nor why "Destroy Monopoly Power" was the "Law and Order" cry of the late nineteenth century.

"monopolists," "middlemen," and "moneylenders" – as a response to commercialization. The argument is that the farmers were objecting to the *increasing importance of prices*; that they were protesting a system in which they had to *pay* for transport and money rather than the specific *prices* of transport and money.

So as not to be misunderstood, let me emphasize here that I am not suggesting that American farmers before 1870 were not "economic men" responding to economic stimuli. Certainly the farmers of this early period moved West, cleared land, improved their farms, sought markets, and in a variety of other ways tried to increase their incomes. But response to economic stimuli and efforts to increase incomes are not sufficient to produce a commercial system.[18] By a commercial system I mean one in which there is dependence upon purchased inputs and a consequent necessity for sale of output. My hypothesis – put slightly differently – is that the protest was a reaction to new, technologically superior inputs which replaced traditional inputs and which could be acquired *only* with money, and a reaction to the new need for cash to buy consumer goods which could not be supplied on-the-farm in the Plains area.

In the economic history literature very little is made of the possibility that the farm protests were a response to commercialization.[19] The reason, I suspect, is that commercialized agriculture was and is assumed to have been the standard form of agricultural organization from early in American history. This is assumed because of the rapid transition to production for the market which followed the opening of transportation facilities. As rapidly as canals, rivers, and railroads became available to farmers, agricultural products flowed into the cities and farmers began purchasing manufactured goods from the cities on a large scale.[20]

The rapidity with which American farmers shifted from self-sufficient

18. A willingness to adopt new techniques and a desire for economic improvement are not characteristics found only in commercial systems, as the histories of Africa, Asia, and the American Indians illustrate. The rapid spread of cassava in Africa after its introduction from South America, maize in India, and the horse among the Plains Indians of the U.S. all took place in non-commercial societies.

19. In Samuel P. Hays, *The Response to Industrialization* (Chicago: The University of Chicago Press, 1957), p. 27 and in Taylor, *The Farmers' Movement*, p. 492, commercialization is cited as a cause of the agrarian unrest. Although some economic historians such as Edward C. Kirkland in *A History of American Economic Life* (4th ed.; New York: Appleton-Century-Crofts, 1969), ch. xv, do mention adjustment to commercialized agriculture as a problem for late nineteenth century farmers in the U.S., they do not use this adjustment as a major part of their explanation of the protests.

20. That this was the case is shown in Thomas S. Berry, *Western Prices Before 1861* (Cambridge: Harvard University Press, 1943), and Douglass C. North, *The Economic Growth of the United States, 1790–1860* (Englewood Cliffs: Prentice-Hall, Inc., 1961).

farming to production for the market has been an important theme in the treatment of American economic history, perhaps because it has seemed important to emphasize that the United States did not have the problem of "peasant" farmers who resisted change.[21] But to argue that production for the market increased rapidly as transportation facilities improved *is not the same* as to argue that all, or even most, American farmers before 1860 had been involved in commercialized agriculture.

Large numbers of farmers kept moving westward in advance of well developed means of transporting agricultural products to market. Gates holds that one of the problems of those farmers moving into the Middle West was the lack of markets:

> If the farmer's need for credit was acute, his need for markets was equally serious. Self-sufficiency, if attainable, was not the goal of intelligent farmers, instead they planned to produce something they could trade – better still, something they could sell. Though necessity forced them to produce much that they consumed, even though that required an inefficient expenditure of labor, they continually struggled to wrest from their land a marketable surplus. Commercial farming developed rapidly in the Middle West.[22]

Though commercial farming may have developed rapidly, and though farmers may have been eager for opportunities to produce for the market, Gates is not describing farmers involved in commercial system. Farmers who need markets and struggle to produce a "marketable surplus" are not commercial farmers. Commercial farming may have developed rapidly in the Middle West; according to Gates' description commercial farming was not common when farmers first moved into the area. Again, Bogue's description of "commercial" farming in Illinois and Iowa in the 1850s in fact indicates at most a casual reliance on markets. He says,

> There was a limit beyond which the farmer could not draw grain to market profitably. Some have placed this at forty miles. But we must remember that the farmer decided among alternatives, rather than on the basis solely of labor cost. If the pioneer farmer had nothing more remunerative to do, he might haul grain considerably farther than forty miles, provided, of course, that spring or fall pasturage was available for his workstock along the way. Yet, there was a definite limit to the amount of time that could be spent on long trips to market or shipping point. At least one historian has argued that commercial agriculture could not develop in many districts of Illinois before

21. One of the major themes of Norman Pollack in *The Populist Response to Industrial America* (Cambridge: Harvard University Press, 1962) is that neither Grangerism nor Populism were "Luddite" responses to technology. There can be little doubt that he is correct and that historians have been correct in their insistence that the U.S. did not have a "peasant sector" which was resistent to new technology and new and profitable opportunities for disposal of produce. But absence of a "peasant problem" is not proof of commericalization.
22. Paul W. Gates, *The Farmer's Age: Agriculture, 1815–1860* (New York: Harper & Row, 1968), p. 413.

the railroad age because they lay isolated from shipping points on river or canal. Actually, there was no district of Illinois so isolated in 1850 that farmers there could not market their grain in the form of pigs or cattle. And farmers in new communities with few transportation outlets might find a considerable market for some years in supplying newcomers who proposed to settle there. Pioneer farmers deep in central Iowa discovered buyers long before the railroad came, among the members of the Mormon migration, the gold seekers, and later settlers bound for the plains or the far West.[23]

It seems highly unlikely that commercial farmers would or could depend on those passing through for markets. Nor does the following description, given by Gates, of the farmers who moved into the Middle West indicate that they would have provided much of a market for agricultural products: "Few farmers had anything more to invest in their lands than their labor. Little actual money was brought into new communities by immigrants, who had generally exhausted their resources on moving themselves and their families to the new El Dorado."[24]

These descriptions of farming in the Middle West prior to 1870 are not descriptions of farmers who depended on markets for disposal of their produce; rather, they are descriptions of farmers who were quick to take advantage of opportunities to market goods as they arose, as they did after 1870. Similar descriptions of pre-1870 farming operations can be found in many sources and all indicate a willingness to take advantage of opportunities to sell produce, but they do not provide a picture of farmers who devoted most of their time and land to growing crops which they planned to sell.

If large numbers of American farmers did not produce primarily for the market prior to the Civil War, neither did they pay for most of their inputs. The farmer in this early period, even if he had quite limited amounts of capital, could move on West, obtain land, and improve it with his own and his sons' labor. Gates speaks of the farmer's problems with credit prior to 1860, but as he describes the problem it is not clear that farmers *had* to have credit, or any large amount of capital, to survive, or even to prosper:

Little actual money was brought into the new communities by immigrants. . . . Capital goods, however, were brought: household effects, a plow, an ax, a shovel, a hoe, perhaps a few chickens, a hog, a cow, and horses or oxen. Most farmers were not able at the beginning to pay for their land, much less to stock or equip it, and they made their start either as squatters or by buying land on credit. In the goods economy the pioneer's capital was chiefly his labor. If, however, he could obtain credit for supplies, he could

23. Allan G. Bogue, *From Prairie to Corn Belt, Farming in Illinois and Iowa Prairies in the Nineteenth Century* (Chicago: The University of Chicago Press, 1963), p. 123.

24. Gates, *The Farmer's Age*, p. 403.

utilize his own labor to better advantage, create a productive farm more rapidly, and hasten the process of capital formation.[25]

The farmer *could*, according to Bogue, "if he had nothing more remunerative to do," and "if spring and fall pasturage for his workstock was available along the way," haul his produce to market. He did not *have* to do so and he did not *have* to pay for transport. He *could*, according to Gates, improve his farm more rapidly if he *could* obtain credit, but he did not have to do so. That many did borrow money and that many did take advantage of opportunities to sell goods does not mean that it was necessary to do so in order to be a good farmer and a respected and self-respecting citizen.

From the description of farming operations during this period it seems likely that a very large number of American farmers were in the position of the person who buys an Irish sweepstake ticket. If he wins it will make a big difference in his life, but if he does not win not much is lost. Any payoff to the lottery ticket is a good thing. The farmer who was lucky enough to be able to sell a "marketable surplus" was happy to do so. But, in the absence of major commercial obligations and given the possibility of continuing or even expanding his operations, he did not have to sell much and the prices he received for what he did sell, even if lower than he would have liked, were not important enough to his operations to warrant putting much energy into protest. Given a high degree of self-sufficiency, prices paid and received and cost of transport and credit are not vital.

As people and railroads moved into the Middle West after the Civil War, all of this changed. The irony of a Homestead Act in a country where land suitable and available for homesteading had virtually disappeared has been noted. There is also irony in the fact that the problems about which the farmers in the post–Civil War period were agitated were a result of the solution of the earlier problems of lack of credit and markets. The railroads provided marketing opportunities, and, as Bogue describes it, money for land mortgages poured in from the East.[26]

It is surprising that the farmer borrowed and that he shifted rapidly to production for the market. Had he not done so he would have been ignoring opportunities for which all writers on earlier periods in American history agree that American farmers were eager. But even if he was not eager, he probably had very little choice. As the plains were settled, farmers found it increasingly difficult to be self-sufficient because of the limited range of crops which could be grown, and

25. *Idem.*
26. Bogue, *Money at Interest*, Cf. pp. 262–276.

increasingly difficult to get along without credit because of the need to purchase land to add to that which could be claimed under the Homestead Law.[27]

In addition, the farmer who was not able to participate successfully as a commercial farmer could not claim to be a success when many around him were succeeding as commercial farmers. Even if he were able to eke out the sort of living for himself and his family which had previously been enjoyed by the majority, he could no longer count himself a success. There was a new test by which the farmer had to judge himself – the test of business success. And, as Schumpeter put it, "Business success and business failure are ideally precise. Neither can be talked away."[28]

Whether trapped in or enjoying an opportunity to take advantage of commercial operations, the farmer faced a new situation and new problems. He had to pay for credit, he had to pay for land, and he had to pay for what Bogue calls "his other needs." To do so he had to sell enough at a high enough price. If he could not do so – even though he might be as good a farmer as he had been earlier – he was in trouble. Once the farmer assumed obligations which required him to buy inputs and to sell a major part of his produce he was caught up in a commercial system.

From the farmers' vantage point the crimes of those who were "exploiting" them were not limited simply to charging too much and paying too little. They also forced him to live in a "coldly economic" world. Bogue suggests that a major reason for the dislike of the money-lender was the necessity of providing him with information on the farm to be mortgaged and with records or information on the farm's operation. He says that, "One of the less advertised functions of the mortgage companies was to assist in teaching business methods to reluctant farmers. The efforts to enforce prompt payment and other business procedures appeared to be no more than petty tyranny to many borrowers."[29]

It is not unreasonable to suppose that the farmers also found the railroad agent, the equipment salesman, and the grain elevator operator tyrannical because they did not respond, as the country store owner had earlier, to tales of a bad year, family illness, or other such problems. If the commercial system was a new thing for the farmer, he would be

27. *Ibid.*, pp. 274–275.
28. Joseph A. Schumpeter, *Capitalism, Socialism, and Democracy* (3rd ed.; New York: Harper & Row Publishers, 1950), p. 74.
29. Bogue, *Money at Interest*, p. 275.

likely to perceive the immediate demands of the local agent of the land mortgage company only as evidence of tyranny and evil intent.

Whereas markets and opportunities to borrow money had earlier seemed to the farmer to be solutions to his problems, now these same opportunities brought other problems. The farmer could quite plausibly conclude that "someone" must be exploiting him; that someone must be charging him too much and paying him too little. "Obviously" those who bought his produce, and those whom he had to pay for money, transport, and equipment, must have gained an "unfair" advantage.

Furthermore, in these circumstances, it is not surprising that the farmer attributed the unfairness to the acquisition of "monopoly power." Not only was the farmer frequently in the position of having only one supplier of an input or one buyer of his crops with whom to deal, but, perhaps more importantly, "In the Anglo-American world monopoly has been cursed and associated with functionless exploitation ever since . . . the sixteenth and seventeenth centuries . . . [and] nothing is so retentive as a nation's memory."[30] It is easy enough to see why the farmers were angry with "monopolies," bankers, and middlemen, so long as we do not require that the historical record verify the reasons given by the farmers for their anger.

Conclusion

The hypothesis that the agrarian protest movement in the Middle West from 1870 to 1900 was a reaction to the commercialization of agriculture allows a reconciliation of the protesters' claims about what they were protesting and North's interpretation of the economic conditions which the farmers actually faced. Even though interest rates were falling, they were "too high" for the farmer who expected only benefits from the opportunity to borrow money. Even though the prices he received were falling less rapidly than the prices he paid, the farmer protested about his "deteriorating" economic position because he was locked into a system where his success or failure now depended on prices – a system where, even if he was a "good farmer" in pre-1860 terms, he might fail because he was a "bad businessman" in late nineteenth-century terms.

Viewing the farm protest as a reaction to commercialization of agriculture also allows greater precision in explaining the protest as a "reaction to the changing place of the farmer in American Society." As agriculture was commercialized the farmer was drawn into the rapidly developing commercial-industrial economy and was no longer exempt from the pressures and consequences of changes in that economy.

30. Schumpeter, *Capitalism, Socialism and Democracy*, p. 100.

"The 'Wizard of Oz' as a monetary allegory"

by Hugh Rockoff

You may know and love the children's classic *The Wizard of Oz*, but you've probably never suspected that it contained an account of the political battles over late-nineteenth-century monetary policy. As Hugh Rockoff describes the action, L. Frank Baum's characters are symbols of various political factions and figures, and the story is also an informed comment on the battle over free silver in the 1890s.

With Dorothy representing America, Rockoff tells the tale of William Jennings Bryan (the Cowardly Lion) and the Populist free silver movement of 1896 (the tornado from the Midwest) battling the defenders of the gold standard. The tale touches on the impact of monetary events on the working man (the Tin Woodman) and the farmer (the Scarecrow). Each felt the impact of the deflation of the late nineteenth century, and each felt that Washington (the Emerald City) should alleviate the monetary problems that existed. The leading thinkers of the day portrayed Bryan and the Populists as monetary cranks, but Rockoff argues that the advocates of free silver had a strong argument on both theoretical and empirical grounds.

The free silver movement implicitly accepted the quantity theory of money. This theory is based on the identity

$$\text{Money} \times \text{Velocity} = \text{Price} \times \text{Output}$$

and assumes that the velocity of money is stable. Thus, if they could increase the supply of money (on the left-hand side of the equation), nominal income (on the right-hand side) would also rise. Some economists accept an almost automatic link between changes in the money supply and changes in nominal income. Milton Friedman, the father of monetarism, argues that "inflation is always and everywhere a monetary phenomenon." To many economists, however, these positions are very controversial.

Enjoy your reading and ponder these questions:

- Suppose that an increased money supply did lead to inflation; how would this have solved the farmers' perceived dilemma?
- These days, it is rare to hear someone promote inflation; why did the Populists champion it?

- Rockoff states that in some ways inflation was a substitute for rain. What is the economic sense of this statement?

Additional Reading

Milton Friedman, "The Crime of 1873," *Journal of Political Economy*, 98 (December 1990), 1159–94.

Milton Friedman and Anna Schwartz, *A Monetary History of the United States, 1867–1960*, Princeton, NJ: Princeton University Press, 1963.

Richard Timberlake, "Repeal of Silver Monetization in the Late Nineteenth Century," *Journal of Money, Credit, and Banking*, 10 (February 1978), 27–45.

16

The "Wizard of Oz" as a monetary allegory

HUGH ROCKOFF

The *Wonderful Wizard of Oz*, perhaps America's favorite children's story, is also an informed comment on the battle over free silver in the 1890s. The characters in the story represent real figures such as William Jennings Bryan. This paper interprets the allegory for economists and economic historians, illuminating a number of elements left unexplained by critics concerned with the politics of the allegory. It also reexamines Bryan and the case for free silver. Far from being monetary cranks, the advocates of free silver had a strong argument on both theoretical and empirical grounds.

I. Introduction

The *Wizard of Oz* is perhaps the best-loved American children's story. The movie, starring Judy Garland, Bert Lahr, Ray Bolger, and company, is an annual television ritual. The book on which the movie is based, L. Frank Baum's *The Wonderful Wizard of Oz*, however, is not only a child's tale but also a sophisticated commentary on the political and economic debates of the Populist Era.[1] Previous interpretations have focused on the political and social aspects of the allegory. The most important of these is Littlefield ([1966] 1968), although his interpretation was adumbrated by Nye (1951), Gardner and Nye (1957), Sackett (1960), and Bewley ([1964] 1970). My purpose is to unlock the re-

Source: Hugh Rockoff, "The 'Wizard of Oz' as a Monetary Allegory," *Journal of Political Economy* (August 1990), 739–60.

I must thank Marcia Anszperger, Michael Bordo, Charles Calomiris, Stephen DeCanio, Stanley Engerman, Milton Friedman, Robert Greenfield, Jonathan Hughes, Fred C. Meyer, James Seagraves, Michael Taussig, Richard Timberlake, Geoffrey Wood, and the participants in a seminar at Rutgers for many useful comments. I owe a special debt to Eugene White not only for his comments but also for encouraging me to put part of Rutgers's "oral tradition" on paper.

1. What follows is based on the book. Metro-Goldwyn-Mayer made numerous changes in the text, some of which, such as changing the silver slippers of the book into the famous ruby slippers of the movie, obscure the allegory.

ferences in the *Wizard of Oz* to the monetary debates of the 1890s. When the story is viewed in this light, the real reason the Cowardly Lion fell asleep in the field of poppies, the identity of the Wizard of Oz, the significance of the strange number of hallways and rooms in the Emerald Palace, and the reason the Wicked Witch of the West was so happy to get one of Dorothy's shoes become clear. Thus interpreted, the *Wizard of Oz* becomes a powerful pedagogic device. Few students of money and banking or economic history will forget the battle between the advocates of free silver and the defenders of the gold standard when it is explained through the *Wizard of Oz*.

This paper also serves a more conventional purpose. William Jennings Bryan and his supporters in the free silver movement, who play a central role in the story, have been treated as monetary cranks even by historians who are sympathetic to them on other issues.[2] Here I show that Bryan's monetary thought was surprisingly sophisticated and that on most issues his positions, in the light of modern monetary theory, compare favorably with those of his "sound money" opponents.[3]

L. Frank Baum's early life proved to be ideal preparation for writing a monetary allegory.[4] Born to a wealthy family in Chittenango, New York, in 1856, Baum while still in his early 20s wrote and produced a successful play that made it to Broadway. In 1882 he married Maud Gage, the daughter of one of the leading suffragettes, Matilda Joslyn Gage. Later Baum and his family moved to Aberdeen, South Dakota, where he viewed at close hand the frontier life that gave rise to the populist movement. He was unsuccessful in South Dakota, where among other things he published a small paper, the *Saturday Pioneer*, and several issues of the *Western Investor*. In 1890, the Baums moved to Chicago. While pursuing a number of jobs, he frequented the Chicago Press Club and met some of the city's leading writers. There he undoubtedly heard a great deal about the battle for the free coinage of silver, especially in 1896 when Chicago hosted the Democratic National Convention at which William Jennings Bryan made his famous "Cross of Gold" speech. Baum's first book of children's stories was published in 1897 and, in 1900, *The Wonderful Wizard of Oz* followed. After moving to Hollywood,

2. For the purposes of this paper, it is sufficient to lump the Populists, free silver Democrats, and other supporters of free silver together. But it should be noted that while the Populist party nominated Bryan, many hard-line Populists advocated more radical measures such as greenbacks or a commodity-backed currency and supported free silver only as the best that could be gotten in the current political climate. See Goodwyn (1976) and the appendix by Yohe (1976) for a detailed discussion of populist monetary ideas and their relationship to free silver.

3. There are many biographies of Bryan. Two of the best, on the issues covered here, are Coletta (1964–1969) and Koenig (1971).

4. This paragraph is based on Baum and MacFall (1961), the major biography of L. Frank Baum.

Baum devoted himself to writing children's stories, the most successful being sequels to his masterpiece.

Table 1 contains data basic to an understanding of the world that produced the *Wizard of Oz*. The key fact was deflation. The gross national product deflator, shown in column 1, fell steadily from the end of the 1860s until the United States returned to the gold standard in 1879. After a brief upsurge the deflator resumed its fall, reaching its nadir in 1896. Farm prices, shown in column 2, fell even more rapidly, also reaching a post–Civil War low in 1896. Thus part of the farm problem was the decline in the relative price of farm products. It is a fair criticism of the Populists, to which Bryan is not immune, that they did not adequately distinguish between general price trends that resulted from relatively slow growth in the stock of money compared with real output and relative price trends that would be impervious to monetary remedies.[5]

Between 1869 and 1879 the stock of money grew at about 2.6 percent per year and real output at about 5.0 percent per year, so the deflationary pressure from the lack of monetary growth is easy to understand. In the same period, high-powered money – gold and silver moneys, other Treasury obligations that could serve as bank reserves, and national bank notes[6] – increased at a rate of only 0.5 percent per year, so the deflation can be traced ultimately to the slow growth in high-powered money. In the following decade, however, the story is somewhat different. High-powered money actually grew at 5.2 percent per year and the total money stock at 7.7 percent, while the rate of growth of real income slowed to 2.7 percent. Since the United States was linked after 1879 to other gold standard countries by fixed exchange rates, one might expect, on the basis of the actual money and real income figures and the velocity trend in the previous decade, a high U.S. inflation rate paralleled by inflation in other gold standard countries. Otherwise rapid U.S. monetary growth would have been cut short by an outflow of gold. But instead all that happened during the 1880s

5. Harvey ([1894] 1963, pp. 198–214), e.g., illustrates the deflation with series on wheat, cotton, and silver. Then in answering the criticism that prices other than wheat had fallen by an equal percentage, he points first to debts but then (p. 214) to a variety of prices – streetcar fares, a hotel room, and so on – that were not fixed in nominal terms.

6. The inclusion of national bank notes in high-powered money is debatable since they were a liability of commerical banks analogous to deposits. But Milton Friedman and Anna Schwartz (who developed the basic series) included the notes in high-powered money, basing their decision on several considerations. The most important was simply that national bank notes were indirectly obligations of the federal government since they had to be backed by federal government bonds.

Table 1. *Prices and related data, 1869–1906*

Year	Implicit Price Deflator (1)	Wholesale Farm Prices (2)	Ratio of Price of Gold to Price of Silver (3)	Percentage Civilian Labor Force Unemployed (4)	Money Stock ($ Billions) (5)	High-powered Money ($ Billions) (6)	Real Income ($ Billions 1869) (7)
1869	100	100	20.7		1.28	.760	7.242
1870	94	88	17.9		1.35	.766	7.369
1871	96	80	17.4		1.50	.778	7.240
1872	91	84	17.6		1.61	.782	8.909
1873	90	80	18.1		1.62	.789	8.958
1874	89	80	18.0		1.65	.795	8.726
1875	87	77	19.2		1.72	.773	8.802
1876	83	70	19.9		1.68	.754	9.411
1877	80	70	18.1		1.65	.758	10.078
1878	74	56	18.1		1.58	.763	10.791
1879	72	56	18.5		1.66	.801	11.902
1880	79	63	18.0		2.03	.949	13.646
1881	77	70	18.3		2.44	1.077	13.911
1882	80	77	18.1		2.63	1.140	14.500
1883	79	68	18.6		2.80	1.186	14.237
1884	75	64	18.6		2.80	1.204	14.555
1885	70	56	19.4		2.87	1.233	14.510
1886	69	53	20.8		3.10	1.213	15.282
1887	70	55	21.1		3.31	1.271	15.656
1888	71	59	22.0		3.40	1.318	15.126
1889	71	52	22.1		3.60	1.342	15.578
1890	70	55	19.8	4.0	3.92	1.390	16.820
1891	69	60	20.9	5.4	4.08	1.461	17.506
1892	66	54	23.6	3.0	4.43	1.533	19.117
1893	68	56	26.4	11.7	4.26	1.561	18.373
1894	64	49	32.8	18.4	4.28	1.582	17.259
1895	63	48	31.7	13.7	4.43	1.499	19.248
1896	61	44	30.8	14.4	4.35	1.451	18.758
1897	61	47	34.6	14.5	4.64	1.554	20.563
1898	63	49	35.5	12.4	5.26	1.682	20.924
1899	65	50	34.7	6.5	6.09	1.812	23.353
1900	68	56	33.7	5.0	6.60	1.954	24.121
1901	68	58	35.1	4.0	7.48	2.096	26.928
1902	70	64	39.6	3.7	8.17	2.168	26.883
1903	71	61	38.6	3.9	8.68	2.278	28.090
1904	72	64	36.1	5.4	9.24	2.423	27.487
1905	73	62	34.2	4.3	10.24	2.489	29.676
1906	75	63	30.9	1.7	11.08	2.646	33.624

SOURCE.—Col. 1: Friedman and Schwartz (1982), pp. 122–23, table 4.8, col. 4 (set equal to 100 in 1869). Col. 2: U.S. Bureau of the Census (1975), pt. 1, ser. E42, p. 200 (linked to ser. E53, p. 201, in 1890). Col. 3: For gold: Jastram (1977), p. 143, table 6; for silver: U.S. Bureau of the Census (1975), pt. 1, ser. M270, p. 606. Col. 4: U.S. Bureau of the Census (1975), pt. 1, ser. D86, p. 135. Cols. 5–7: Friedman and Schwartz (1982), pp. 122–23, table 4.8, cols. 1, 10, and 3, respectively (converted to 1869 dollars).

was a leveling off of prices: the rate of deflation declined from −3.3 percent per year in the 1870s to a modest −0.1 percent per year in the 1880s. In other words, after falling at the relatively low rate of 0.9 percent per year in the 1870s, velocity fell a surprising 5.2 percent per year in the 1880s.

The 1880s were a period perhaps something like the 1980s, in which the economy exhibited a surprisingly strong demand for additional money balances. It would take us too far afield to attempt an explanation of this phenomenon. Suffice it to say that in the 1880s as in the 1980s, there are a number of candidate explanations: interest rates were falling, partially reflecting the fall in prices, but perhaps for other reasons as well; and institutional developments such as the rapid development of the state banking systems may have played a role.

The Panic of 1893 and the subsequent depression were superimposed on these long-term price trends. The depression shows up dramatically in the unemployment data in column 4. Although there is a wide margin of error, it appears that unemployment exploded from 3 percent in 1892 to 11.7 percent in 1893, peaking at 18.4 percent in 1894. The exact cause of the panic is in doubt. One factor was concern over maintenance of the gold standard. In 1890, Congress had passed the Sherman Silver Purchase Act, which provided for the regular purchasing and coining of silver in limited quantities. Silver had been purchased under earlier legislation, but Sherman's act increased the amount. Along with other proposed legislation, it stimulated fears that the United States might leave the gold standard, and this led to a depletion of Treasury gold stocks. In addition, there was a stock market crash prompted by several business failures and a growing tide of bank failures, particularly in the West. Together these developments produced a banking panic, the suspension of gold payments, and a severe depression of an order not seen since the 1830s and not to be seen again until the 1930s.

The response of President Grover Cleveland was to seek (successfully) the repeal of the Sherman Silver Purchase Act. But a brief cyclical expansion that began in June 1894 petered out, the peak coming in December 1895. According to Friedman and Schwartz (1963, p. 111), it was one of the weakest expansions in the cyclical history of the United States. When the Democrats met at Chicago in the summer of 1896 to nominate a candidate for president, the economy, to put it mildly, was in terrible shape and apparently was getting worse. The closest parallel, perhaps, is with 1932. Unemployment was 14.4 percent. This was one of the most famous conventions in American history. The Democrats were locked in a battle between those favoring the gold standard and those favoring a bimetallic standard. After numerous votes, they finally nominated William Jennings Bryan. He and his supporters called for the free and unlimited coinage of silver at mint prices that made the value of 16 ounces of silver equivalent to 1 ounce of gold.

As can be seen in column 3 of Table 1, this ratio was far below the ratio then prevailing in the market, about 31 to 1. Had the United States returned to a bimetallic standard at 16 to 1, there probably would have been some outflows of gold and inflows of silver, although the exact amount is hard to quantify. Critics denounced the plan as wildly inflationary. This criticism was weak on two counts. First, it is unclear that resumption at 16 to 1 would have left the United States with an inflated and purely silver stock of high-powered money. The remonetization of silver by the United States would have substantially increased the world demand for silver and brought the bimetallic ratio down toward the ratio set by the U.S. mint, especially if other countries followed the United States back to the bimetallic standard. Note that as late as 1890 the ratio had been at 20 to 1; the extreme departure of the bimetallic ratio from 16 to 1 was a product of recent events.

Second, some increase in the monetary base was justified. As noted, unemployment stood at 14.4 percent; the business failure rate was 133 per thousand (U.S. Bureau of the Census, 1975, p. 912), one of the highest in the postbellum era. The same could be said for the number of bank suspensions, which stood at 155, down from the record-breaking 496 in 1893 but up from 89 in 1894 and 124 in 1895. Failure rates of the larger, more prestigious national banks paralleled those of the state and private banks (p. 1038). The implicit price deflator was down 10.9 percent and farm prices were down 24.1 percent from 1893 after 3 years of steady deflation. To reject monetary expansion in such an environment because it might be inflationary seems excessive, reminding us of the concerns over inflation voiced by the Federal Reserve in the 1930s. However, despite the appeal of free silver, Bryan lost a bitterly contested election to Republican William McKinley.

Meanwhile, the economy began to improve rapidly. Four years later, when Bryan and McKinley had their second contest, prices were up – farm prices more than the deflator – and unemployment was down to 5 percent. In part, the rapid recovery was caused by the failure of European harvests, which created a strong market for American crops. The U.S. balance of trade turned from a deficit to a surplus, and gold flowed in. The expansion was fueled by a 41.7 percent increase in the stock of money and by a 29.8 percent increase in high-powered money. Increased supplies of gold from South Africa and other areas were now generating a steady rise in the world's stock of monetary gold.

II. From Kansas to Fairy Land

The *Wizard of Oz*, conceived over several years, was written mostly in 1899. It is a cautionary tale, recounting "the first battle" of 1896 (the title of Bryan's [1896] immensely popular account of that election) and warning of the dangers that lay ahead. The story is rich in references to the current scene, but it is not a mathematical puzzle. Baum's main purpose was to tell a good story, and his need for symmetry, interesting characters, and so on took precedence over historical accuracy. Nevertheless, the references to the current scene are sufficiently numerous to make looking for them rewarding and informative. The heroine is Dorothy, a little girl who lives with her Aunt Em on an impoverished farm in Kansas. Dorothy represents America – honest, kindhearted, and plucky.[7] Her best friend is her dog, Toto.[8] The populist movement began in the West, so it is natural that the story begins there. But there may also be a reference here to Kansas City, Missouri, where the Democratic convention of 1900 would be held. In 1900, going "from Kansas to Fairyland" (an early title) meant following the campaign trail from Kansas City to Washington, D.C.

Dorothy is in her home when it is carried by a cyclone (tornado) to the land of Oz. This is Baum's fantasy counterpart to America, a land in which, especially in the East, the gold standard reigns supreme and in which an ounce (Oz) of gold has almost mystical significance. The cyclone is the free silver movement itself. It came roaring out of the West in 1896, shaking the political establishment to its foundations. A cyclone is an apt metaphor. Bryan was first elected to Congress in 1890 and made his first important speech in Congress on the silver question in 1893. Three years later he was the leader of a national movement. Dorothy's house lands on the Wicked Witch of the East. The Witch dries up completely, leaving only her silver shoes. These represent the silver component of a bimetallic standard and are given to Dorothy to wear by the Good Witch of the North, who has been summoned to the scene.[9] The silver shoes have a magical power that the Wicked Witch of

7. Recently, Dorothy has been identified by Leslie Kelsey with the famous populist orator known as the "Kansas Tornado," Mary Elizabeth Lease ("Raise more hell and less corn") (Meyer, 1987, p. 32).

8. Toto represents the Prohibition party, *Toto* being a play on *teetotaler* (Jensen, 1971, p. 283). Prohibitionists' hearts were in the right place on many issues: in addition to opposing alcohol, they supported free coinage of silver in 1896. But they were a minor and eccentric group, always pulling in the wrong direction, and not to be taken all that seriously.

9. Free silver had some support in New England. Bryan's running mate in 1896 was Arthur Sewall, a businessman and banker from Maine. But I have not been able to identify the Good Witch of the North clearly with one particular politician.

the East understood but which the Munchkins (citizens of the East) do not.

On a general level the Wicked Witch of the East represents eastern business and financial interests, but in personal terms a Populist would have had one figure in mind: Grover Cleveland. It was Cleveland who led the repeal of the Sherman Silver Purchase Act, and it was his progold forces that had been defeated at the 1896 convention, making it possible for America to vote for Bryan and free silver. But the American people, like the Munchkins, never understood the power that was theirs once the Wicked Witch was dead. Timberlake (1978) argues that the repeal of the Sherman Silver Purchase Act, rather than the campaign of 1896, was the real end of the possibility of a bimetallic standard. He shows in detail that repeal was a bipartisan movement. He then asks the following question: "Why should anyone then [in 1896] have believed that a Democratic vote would have any greater effect in promoting silver monetization than it had in 1892?" (p. 42). The free silver Democrats had a simple but not naive answer: the Wicked Witch of the East was (politically) dead.

The friendly inhabitants of the land Dorothy enters cannot tell her how to return to Kansas. She is advised to seek the answer in the Emerald City, which can be found at the end of the yellow brick road. The road, of course, is a symbol of the gold standard. Following it will lead to the Emerald City (Washington, D.C.), but the solution to Dorothy's problems will not be found there. Thus the silver shoes and the yellow brick road are Baum's primary symbols of the two metals. But there are many others.

The first person whom Dorothy meets along the way is the Scarecrow. As Littlefield (1968, p. 376) notes, the Scarecrow is the western farmer. He thinks that he has no brains because his head is stuffed with straw. But we soon learn that he is shrewd and capable. He brings to life a major theme of the free silver movement: that the people, the farmer in particular, were capable of understanding the complex theories that underlay the choice of a standard. They did not have to accept a monometallic gold standard simply because the experts said that it was necessary. This attitude is best illustrated in the leading tract of the free silver movement, W. Harvey's *Coin's Financial School* ([1894] 1963). The imaginary Coin is a small boy who conducts a series of lectures in Chicago attended by some of the leading sound money men, including Lyman Gage, a Chicago banker who became secretary of the Treasury, and James Laurence Laughlin, a professor of economics at the University of Chicago. Although first contemptuous of the untutored boy, they gradually find their arguments for a gold standard refuted. Laughlin, for one, was outraged by the use of his name, and a letter by him denying any association with Coin was reprinted in Horace White's answer to Harvey, *Coin's Financial Fool.*

It is one of the ironies of monetary history that William Jennings Bryan gave his 1896 Cross of Gold speech on the South Side of Chicago, only a short distance from the University of Chicago. At the time the university was home to Laughlin, one of free silver's most acerbic critics and a strong opponent of the quantity theory of money, Bryan's basic framework. Later, under Henry Simons, Lloyd Mints, and Milton Friedman, the university's Department of Economics became the intellectual center for the revival of the quantity theory. In *A Monetary History of the United States*, Friedman and Schwartz (1963, p. 134) take a cautious, although ultimately favorable, view of the free silver position when contrasted with maintenance of a monometallic gold standard.[10] They argue that a firm national commitment to either a bimetallic standard or gold would have been preferable to the "uneasy compromise" that existed until Bryan's defeats. But they then consider the effects of an early adoption of a bimetallic standard and argue that, on the whole, the trend of the price level would have been preferable to the trend that actually prevailed. They also suggest, in a cautious way, that the abandonment of a monometallic gold standard might have made sense in the 1890s (p. 115).

Next, Dorothy and the Scarecrow meet the Tin Woodman, Baum's symbol for the workingman. He was once flesh and blood but was cursed by the Wicked Witch of the East. As he worked, his ax would take flight and cut off part of his body. A tinsmith would replace the missing part, and the Tin Woodman could work as well as before. Eventually there was nothing left but tin. This is why the claws of the Cowardly Lion can make no "impression" on him, just as Bryan failed to make an impression on urban industrial workers in the campaign of 1896. But for all his increased power to work, the Tin Woodman was unhappy, for he had lost his heart. As Littlefield (1968, p. 375) points out, this tale is a powerful representation of the populist and socialist idea that industrialization had alienated the workingman, turning an independent artisan into a mere cog in a giant machine. The joints of the Tin Woodman have rusted, and he can no longer work. He has joined the ranks of those unemployed in the depression of the 1890s, a victim of the unwillingness of the eastern goldbugs to countenance an increase in the stock of money through the addition of silver. After his joints are

10. A standard based on government-issued fiat money controlled by a monetary rule was not a politically viable alternative in this period. Interestingly, the position of the radical Populists came closest to this formula, although their rule would have imposed a significant inflation (Yohe, 1976).

oiled, the Tin Woodman wants to join the group to see if the Wizard can give him a heart. He, too, will learn that the answer is not to be found at the end of the yellow brick road.

The last character to join the group is the Cowardly Lion. This character is William Jennings Bryan himself.[11] The sequence is not accidental. Baum is following history in suggesting that the movement was started first by the western farmers, was joined (to a limited extent) by the workingman, and then, once it was well under way, was joined by Bryan. The roaring lion is a good choice for one of the greatest American orators. At the convention of 1896, his stirring speech on the silver plank of the platform, ending with his challenge to the Republicans. "Thou shalt not crucify mankind upon a cross of gold," won him the nomination. In the words of one observer whom Baum may have known, John T. McCutcheon, "When he sat down, the convention went wild. . . . We who watched saw a man march relatively unknown to the platform, and march down again the leader of a national party" (1950, pp. 88–89).

Bryan was a lion, but why a cowardly lion? In the late 1890s; as I noted, the world gold supply began to increase rapidly, reversing the long deflation. As a result, the usefulness of silver as a political issue declined. It was obvious almost immediately after the election of 1896 that Bryan would again be the standard-bearer in 1900. But with the return of prosperity, he continually received advice to soft-pedal silver and concentrate on new issues such as opposition to the trusts and anti-imperialism, which would appeal to the eastern wing of the party, advice that to an extent he heeded. After the successful conclusion of the Spanish-American War, the United States, to retain control of the Philippines, was forced to put down a bloody rebellion. Like many regular Democrats and Republicans, the Populists were opposed to the United States fighting to hold the Philippines. But there were many Populists who were afraid that Bryan would push this issue to the exclusion of silver. They considered this line of action pure cowardice. They wanted the Great Commoner to fight for silver in 1900 as he had in 1896.

The little party heading toward the Emerald City reminds me of "Coxey's army" of unemployed workers that marched on Washington, D.C., in 1894. Jacob Coxey was a greenbacker, and his idea was simple: The federal government should build public works and pay for them by printing money (Hicks, [1931] 1961, p. 322). At the time the idea seemed to be the wildest kind of extremism. But given unemployment

11. The Populists liked to give politicians outlandish nicknames. John W. Daniel, a silver Democrat from Virginia, was known as the "Lame Lion" (Hollingsworth, 1963, p. 54).

of 18.4 percent and the monetary and fiscal options then open to the government, few modern economists would be prepared to dismiss such a proposal out of hand. Indeed, at the height of the Keynesian period, it would have been taken to be the essence of sound macroeconomics. Although the march addressed serious problems, Coxey's army took on an opera bouffe quality. Characters such as "Cyclone" Kirtland, a Pittsburgh astrologer, showed up to take part (Nye, 1951, p. 91). So it is not surprising that Coxey's army should suggest a fairy tale.

Along the way Dorothy and her friends meet a series of challenges that show that each character really has the quality he feels he is missing. The Scarecrow proves intelligent, although he thinks he has no brain; the Tin Woodman proves to be kinder than an ordinary man; and the Cowardly Lion is prepared to fight to the death against the deadly Kalidahs, frightening monsters with the body of a bear and the head of a tiger.[12] The most mysterious challenge is the Deadly Poppy Field. The Cowardly Lion falls asleep in the field and is pulled to safety, but with the greatest difficulty. This is another reference to the dangers of putting anti-imperialism ahead of silver. Poppies are the source of opium, and falling asleep in a field of poppies symbolizes the populist fear that Bryan would fall asleep in the midst of these new issues. Anti-imperialism was predominantly a middle-class and intellectual issue. Bryan's Populist advisers were concerned that if he failed to stress the issues of greatest concern to rank-and-file Populists (particularly silver), he would fail to win the overwhelming support from them that was crucial to his election. It is therefore appropriate that it is the field mice, little folk concerned with everyday issues (such as the price of corn), who pull the Cowardly Lion from the Deadly Poppy Field.

At last the little group arrives at the Emerald City. The Guardian of the Gate assures them that the Wizard can solve their problems. The Wizard has, for example, a pot of courage (a colloquial term for liquor) for the Cowardly Lion. The pot is prevented from overflowing by a plate made of gold, another reference to the gold standard and its effects. But before Dorothy and her friends can enter the city they must don a pair of green-colored glasses. Everyone in the city must wear them and they must be locked on with a gold buckle by order of the Wizard. The conservative financiers who run the Emerald City, in other words, force its citizens to look at the world through money-colored glasses.

Dorothy and her friends are taken to the Emerald Palace, the White House itself, where they must stay the night before they can have their

12. Michael Taussig has suggested to me that the Kalidahs might represent newspaper reporters. Most of the papers were strongly opposed to Bryan and his cause, and they violently denounced the Populists.

audience with the Wizard. Dorothy is led to her room through seven passages and up three flights of stairs. It is not surprising that the layout of the Emerald Palace should reflect the numbers seven and three. The Crime of '73 was a crucial event in populist monetary history. Legislation in that year eliminated the coinage of the silver dollar. At that time the price of silver bullion was well above the traditional mint price, so the decision to eliminate the silver dollar had no immediate impact and aroused little public opposition. But in later years, when the bullion price fell below the mint price, the decision taken in 1873 began to appear as the source of all future difficulties.[13]

The next day Dorothy and her friends are brought to see the Great Oz. First they have to pass through a great hall in which there are "many ladies and gentlemen of the court, all dressed in rich costumes . . . [who] had nothing to do but talk to each other" (Baum, 1973, p. 205), a reference to the bureaucrats to be found in any seat of government, but not amiss in a description of Washington, D.C. One by one, each is taken into a big round room (the oval office?) to meet the Wizard. Each sees a different character: Dorothy sees an enormous head, the Scarecrow sees a lovely lady, the Tin Woodman sees a terrible beast, and the Cowardly Lion sees a ball of fire. Each of them receives the same message: the Wizard will help them, but first they must do something for the Wizard. "In this country," the Wizard explains, "everyone must pay for everything he gets" (p. 208). But who is this Wizard who speaks through various figureheads and adheres to such a purely Republican world view? To a Populist at the turn of the century, there is only one answer: Marcus Alonzo Hanna. A close adviser of McKinley and the chairman of the Republican National Committee, he was, in populist mythology, the brains behind McKinley and his campaigns. It was the money that Hanna raised from giant corporations, according to the Populists, that defeated Bryan. To satisfy the Wizard, the group must travel to the West and destroy his enemy the Wicked Witch of the West. That the Wizard wanted them to leave and go West, there can be no doubt. But that he was really an enemy of the Wicked Witch of the West is another matter. The Wizard does not always tell the truth, a lesson that Dorothy will soon learn.

III. The Wicked Witch of the West

The Wizard's demand is analogous to Hanna's advice to journalists, politicians, and plain citizens to visit McKinley at his home in Ohio. In

13. According to O'Leary (1960), the decision to eliminate the silver dollar was a deliberate attempt to avoid the possibility of a de facto silver standard, based on the understanding that secular forces might undermine the price of silver.

1896, McKinley conducted a "front porch" campaign, extolling the virtues of "sound" money to visiting crowds. If Cleveland was the Wicked Witch of the East, slain in 1896, McKinley in 1896 and 1900 was the very much alive Wicked Witch of the West. Dorothy and her friends must face biblical plagues – wolves, crows, and black bees – thrown at them by the Witch. But they defeat each of them. The Wicked Witch is thus forced to turn to her Golden Cap, another symbol of the gold standard, which gives her the power to call the Winged Monkeys. According to Littlefield (1968, p. 378), the Winged Monkeys represent the Plains Indians, free spirits brought to earth by the relentless western march of the frontier. They, too, cannot avoid the overarching power of the gold standard.

The owner of the Golden Cap is allowed three wishes, but the Wicked Witch of the West has already used two, one to drive the Wizard out of the West and one to enslave the yellow Winkies. Although Hanna was a westerner living in the East, he had not really been driven out. Here Baum has departed, apparently, from a strict allegory.[14] But the enslavement of the yellow Winkies is clear enough. After winning the Philippines, the United States, as I noted above, had to put down a bloody rebellion to maintain control of the islands. The Wicked Witch of the West's enslavement of the yellow Winkies is a not very well disguised reference to McKinley's decision to deny immediate independence to the Philippines. To a modern ear there is a condescending tone to "yellow Winkies," but clearly Baum was sympathetic to the plight of the Philippines (and to the Plains Indians).[15]

The Wicked Witch commands the Winged Monkeys to attack Dorothy and her friends. They drop the Tin Woodman on jagged rocks and pull out the Scarecrow's straw. The Lion is taken to the castle and penned up. Dorothy is taken there as well and made to do household chores. The Witch covets Dorothy's silver shoes, for the Witch knows their power. At last she devises a scheme: she trips Dorothy over an invisible iron bar and snatches one of the silver shoes. The Wicked Witch is greatly pleased with this trick, for she realizes that with the silver shoes divided, Dorothy cannot use them. This refers to McKinley's

14. This is one of the few points at which the allegory does not work straightforwardly. I would be interested in hearing alternative interpretations of this piece of Oz history.

15. Several readers of a previous draft suggested that there might also be a reference here to the plight of Asian immigrants in California. The coincidence of the events in the Philippines with the composition of the *Wizard of Oz* leads me to discount this possibility. But the analogy is broadly consistent with the populist view of the relationship between western financial interests and the immigrants. But although sympathetic, the Populists supported efforts to limit Asian immigration on the grounds that it undermined the wages and working conditions of native Americans; support for unrestricted immigration generally came from the Republican side.

position on silver. McKinley and the Republicans in 1896 did not argue that only gold monometallism would do. Their position was that bimetallism should be reestablished, but only after an international agreement. The Republicans argued that this would raise the world demand for silver sufficiently to prevent the United States from being flooded with silver and protect the dollar from being devalued when bimetallism was reestablished. This position had a number of respectable academic supporters, and McKinley followed through on his promise to support an international conference on bimetallism. But the Populists believed, perhaps correctly, that this was merely so much talk designed to hide the real intention of the Republicans: to maintain a monometallic gold standard. Most of Bryan's Cross of Gold speech and much of his campaign in 1896 were devoted to attacking the Republican position on international bimetallism.

Dorothy is so angry with the Wicked Witch for tripping her that she pours a bucket of water over her. To her surprise, the Witch melts away. For Littlefield (1968, p. 379), to whom the Wicked Witch represents the malign forces of nature in the West, the point is that all it takes is some water to make the dry plains bloom. In the 1890s the "rain line" moved east, causing farmers in Kansas, Nebraska, and the Dakotas who had moved west in the 1880s, on the basis of a few good years, great hardships in addition to those generated by the depression in agricultural prices. Kansas was one of the areas hardest hit. To the western farmer, it appeared that what he needed to get out of debt was some good rain and some good crops.

Inflation was to some extent simply a substitute for rain. But the usefulness of inflation to the farmer depended in large measure on its effects on farm debt. Although the percentage of farmland that was mortgaged was low for the nation as a whole, western farmers, especially in certain areas, were heavily mortgaged. Kansas had one of the heaviest levels of indebtedness, with 60 percent of taxed acres under mortgage (Emerick, 1896, p. 603). But not all the indebted farmers would have benefited from inflation. One of the most telling criticisms of free silver was that the prospect of inflation would lead to the renewal of mortgages at higher interest rates; many farmers would be no better off than before. One important statement of this point was made by Fisher (1896). His paper, one of the most influential in the history of monetary economics, argued that anticipated increases in the rate of inflation would be reflected in higher interest rates, although he acknowledged that as a historical matter debtors did tend to lose during periods of deflation and gain during periods of inflation.

Fisher pointed out that most farm mortgages were relatively short. He gave 4.67 years as the average length so that the typical mortgage had only 2.33 years left. It is obvious that a large proportion of existing mortgages would mature, and have to be renewed, between the time when free silver became a fait accompli and when farmers saw any benefits in the form of higher farm prices. The expected inflation would be incorporated in interest rates, so for many farmers there would be little or no debt relief. Bryan was aware of this argument but had no convincing answer. In his Madison Square Garden speech, he tried to meet this criticism by arguing that the lag between the election and the adoption of free silver could be shortened by calling a special session of Congress (1896, p. 336).[16] But he quickly moved on to other issues.

With the Wicked Witch dead, Dorothy is able to free her friends. Tinsmiths repair the Tin Woodman, and he is given a new ax. The handle is made of gold, and the blade is polished until it "glistens like burnished silver." The new ax is a good symbol of a point often made by the Populists: that they did not want to replace a gold standard with a silver standard; they wanted a genuine bimetallic standard. In *Coin's Financial School*, Harvey likened the gold standard to a one-legged man and the bimetallic standard to a two-legged man. Baum's image is even more vivid. The Tin Woodman is also given a silver oilcan inlaid with gold and precious stones, just the thing to prevent a recurrence of unemployment. Toto and the Cowardly Lion are given gold collars without any silver, and the Scarecrow is given a walking stick with a gold head. Here Baum did not follow through explicitly on the bimetallic theme (although given the purpose of a collar this may not be surprising), and we are not told what the stick itself was made of. Bryan frequently received gifts of this sort to portray the battle of the standards. There was an ink bottle made of gold and silver, a gold pen with a silver holder, gold-headed canes like the one given to the Scarecrow, and so forth (Bryan, 1896, pp. 537, 619–620).

The advocates of a gold standard argued that bimetallism was unworkable because a rise in the bimetallic ratio could produce an outflow of gold and an inflow of silver that left only silver in circulation; a fall in the ratio might leave only gold in circulation. There could be alternating gold and silver standards, but there could not be a true bimetallic standard in the sense of two metals circulating side by side, except in the accidental case in which the mint ratio was equal to relative prices in world markets. Although not always consistent, the Populists at times made correct counterarguments. First, with a nation as large as the

16. The Madison Square Garden speech was Bryan's most complete analysis of the money issue during the campaign. The speech, eagerly anticipated after his stirring Cross of Gold speech in Chicago, was expected to be filled with fire and brimstone. Instead, to allay fears of his radicalism, he wrote a detailed defense of free silver, treating his audience to a lecture on the quantity theory of money, the meaning of the purchasing power of money, and related issues.

United States on the standard, the world ratio might adapt to the U.S. ratio, and gold and silver might circulate simultaneously for a long period of time. Second, the really important things about a standard are the implications for the stock of money and the price level. Under a bimetallic standard, a decline in the production of one monetary metal would not necessarily imply a drastic fall in the supply of money because the other metal was ready to fill the gap.

These arguments were laid out clearly by William Stanley Jevons and other scholars whom Bryan read. The extent of the increase in price stability to be expected is debatable. Fisher ([1922] 1971, pp. 325–326), who accepted the theoretical argument and had his own gift for the telling analogy, likened the benefits from a bimetallic standard to "two tipsy men locking arms. Together they walk somewhat more steadily than apart, although if one happens to be much more sober, his own gait may be made worse by the union." In short, bimetallism offered no more than an "indifferent remedy" to the problem of long-term price instability.[17]

IV. The Discovery of Oz the Terrible

Dorothy and her friends return to the Emerald City confident that the Wizard will grant them their wishes. But they soon unmask the Wizard and learn that he is nothing but a humbug who has been fooling the people. It is clear that the Wizard has been lying, but how much of the story that he now begins to tell is true is open to question. He claims to be from Nebraska, Bryan's state. But this is doubtful. There may be a reference here to Hanna's own transition after the election of 1896. He entered politics behind the scenes and soon became the sinister figure of populist mythology. Shortly after the election, he was appointed to the Senate from Ohio. But to win a full term, he was forced to take to the stump. Here he was a surprising success. His down-to-earth "I'm just a common man" (Baum, 1973, p. 264) style was a hit, effective even with farmers and workers. If I read Baum correctly, he accepts this transformation, up to a point. The Wizard is to be accepted as an ordinary man, but that does not mean that we can believe everything he says. With a little shrewd psychology, the Wizard solves the problems of Dorothy's friends. The Scarecrow is given brains in the form of a mixture of bran and pins and needles (to be sharp-witted), the Tin Woodman is given a heart lined with silk and filled with sawdust, and the Lion is given courage in the form of a green liquid. But Dorothy still cannot get back

17. Fisher, although mildly sympathetic to bimetallism, was strongly opposed to its adoption in 1896 at the ratio of 16 to 1.

to Kansas. The Wizard promises to take her in a hot air balloon. But at the last moment, the line holding the balloon breaks and the Wizard is carried away, leaving Dorothy behind. The promises of the Wizard of Oz (like those of the newly reformed Hanna) are partly hot air.

Dorothy then decides to seek out Glinda, the Good Witch of the South. The South was generally sympathetic to free silver, so it is not surprising that it is ruled by a good witch. All her friends join Dorothy, including the wise Scarecrow, who has been made ruler over the Emerald City. The inhabitants of the city are proud to have the Scarecrow as their leader because it makes them, as far as they know, the only city to be ruled over by a stuffed man. Along the way, Dorothy and her friends encounter the Dainty China Country, a land in which the inhabitants are actually figurines made of bone china. To enter the Dainty China Country, the party must crawl over a high wall that has been likened to the Great Wall of China (Hearn 1973, p. 303). Once inside, Dorothy and her party accidentally damage some of the figures, and after a China Princess explains how delicate the figures are, Dorothy and her friends decide to leave so that they will do no more damage. The attitude of the China Princess has been compared to that of the Dowager Empress of China, Tzu Hsi. Chinese resistance to the West culminated in the Boxer Rebellion in the summer of 1900. But, as Hearn notes (p. 311), all the damage in Baum's story is done by the foreign invaders. This point of view, like Baum's attitude toward the Winkies, is a reflection of his populist anti-imperialism.[18]

After further adventures the party reaches Glinda, the Good Witch of the South, where, incidentally, the favorite color is red, like much of the soil in the American South. Glinda solves all the party's remaining problems. The Scarecrow returns to rule the Emerald City, the Tin Woodman becomes ruler of the Winkies, and the Cowardly Lion becomes ruler of a jungle. The populist dream of achieving political power with the help of the South is realized. Dorothy is told how to return to Kansas. All that is necessary is that she click the heels of her silver shoes together three times. The power to solve her problems (by adding silver to the money stock) was there all the time.

When Dorothy awakes in Kansas, she finds that the silver shoes have disappeared, just as the silver issue was disappearing in the late 1890s.

18. China, as well as several other Asian nations, was on a silver standard during the period 1879–96 when the United States, along with the rest of the gold bloc, was experiencing deflation (Fisher, 1971, pp. 243–245). The silver standard countries experienced, predictably, a mild inflation. Bryan and his allies in the free silver movement, however, do not appear to have made much use of the argument, perhaps because they wanted to avoid being labeled as inflationists or because they did not want to reinforce the argument that it was the "advanced" countries that were moving to the monometallic gold standard.

As Littlefield (1968, p. 380) notes, another lesson here may be that the battle for silver added a measure of excitement to the lives of the westerners, even if in the end the battle could not be won. In any case, Baum's observation that the silver cause would become a distant memory proved to be true. The Gold Standard Act, committing the United States firmly to the gold standard, was passed in 1900.

V. Some thoughts for the skeptics

There is always a danger that a critic may see symbols where the author has merely placed the concrete reference points of his story. Baum left no hard evidence that he intended his story to have an allegorical meaning: no diary entry, no letter, not even an offhand remark to a friend. But this need not be conclusive. He probably considered his references to current events to be a series of sly jokes, like the puns that dot the text, rather than something to be worried about by future generations. The creative process, moreover, is highly complex. An author's experience may be transformed in ways he is only dimly aware of, before it issues forth in a work of art. The critic may be uncovering elements beyond the explicit intentions of the author.[19]

There is, moreover, considerable circumstantial evidence for the populist interpretation. It has been recognized independently by a number of thoughtful readers. It is consistent with what we know of Baum's politics, for although he was not an activist, it is known that he marched in torchlight parades for Bryan and voted Democratic (Baum and MacFall, 1961, p. 85). References to current affairs appear in a number of his later works. The most obvious are a comic opera Baum worked on in 1901, *The Octopus* or *The Title Trust*, and *The Marvelous Land of Oz* (1904), which was a satire of the suffragist movement.

An allegorical interpretation of a story can be viewed as something like a model in economics. The test of an economic model is whether it can be extended in a "natural" way to explain additional phenomena. Here I have tried to extend Littlefield's populist interpretation by using what we know of populist monetary thought to explain additional episodes in Baum's story. That this can be done with a relatively moderate amount of pushing and pulling strengthens the case for the populist interpretation. If this interpretation is right, then Baum's story gives us some real insight into how a detached but informed Populist

19. Just how complex that process can be is illustrated by Lowes's (1927) account of how Samuel Taylor Coleridge's imagination fashioned some of his most memorable poetry from the books he had been reading.

viewed free silver. In any case, economists should not have any difficulty accepting, at least provisionally, an elegant but controversial model.

VI. Williams Jennings Bryan and free silver

Bryan was not a deep or original thinker; he was a politician with a gift for the telling analogy in an age of high oratory. But historians have been too hard on Bryan the monetarist, influenced more perhaps by their antipathy to the religious beliefs that engaged his attention in later years or other aspects of the populist creed than to a real examination of his monetary views. An early statement by Bryan, to the effect that he was for silver because Nebraska was for it and he would look up the arguments later, has been often quoted against him. But he did his homework better than most politicians. He read Jevons, Laughlin, and other scholars well enough to understand the case for a bimetallic standard and for expanding the stock of money in periods of deep depressions. He understood the rudiments of the quantity theory of money, including the relationship between velocity and the rate of price change. He understood the mechanics of a bimetallic standard. He recognized that a bimetallic standard could keep both metals circulating side by side for long periods of time and that the problem of alternating metallic flows was secondary, in any case, to the problem of maintaining price-level stability. If he sometimes claimed too much for monetary expansion, he was at least on as strong a theoretical basis as his critics.[20]

Not all economists who started from the quantity theory agreed that an inflation resulting from the free coinage at 16 to 1 would restore prosperity. Clark (1896a, 1896b) imagined a stagflation: prices would rise, alleviating debt burdens as the advocates of free silver claimed, but the uncertainty would rock credit markets and produce a business "convulsion." The counterclaim that an increase in the stock of money generated by the introduction of large elements of silver into the monetary base would have effects similar to a sudden increase in gold – that prices and real output would both rise – was soundly based on historical experience and an interpretation of the quantity theory of money acceptable to many monetary economists even today.

Changing the monetary constitution to cure the depression opened the door to discretionary policies. There was a danger that milder recessions would be met with changes in the mint prices or other

20. In a series of recent papers, Milton Friedman has reexamined the case for free silver. He agrees that the general case for bimetallism, as opposed to a monometallic gold standard, was strong (1990*a*), and he argues that returning to a bimetallic standard at 16 to 1 would have made sense in 1873 (1990b). But he argues that it would have been a mistake to return at 16 to 1 in 1896 (1989).

devices. Clark (1896a) speculated that the transitional inflation would encourage farmers to go further into debt. The inflation would end and farmers would again be agitating for monetary expansion to alleviate their new debt burdens. The only bailout the second time around would be paper money. Bryan and his allies recognized the danger of a discretionary policy. It was one reason they gave for rejecting the greenback and commodity-backed standards favored by radical Populists. But in the circumstances of 1896, using reentry to the bimetallic standard at a ratio that overvalued silver as a substitute for a central bank operating in its role of lender of last resort made a good deal of sense. It is only because we now know that rising gold supplies would solve the monetary problems of the day, a fact not known at the time, that we can be sure that Bryan's reforms were unnecessary.

Bryan was aware that the expansion of gold supplies had undermined the case for free silver. But as he noted (1900, p. 179), the expansion of gold supplies had dramatically vindicated his basic framework: the quantity theory of money. The stock of money had risen rapidly, and prices, employment, and real output had responded. The case for a bimetallic standard, moreover, remained intact, according to Bryan. For one thing, the monetary stringency that followed the Boer uprising in South Africa showed that the gold standard was vulnerable to threats to the supply of gold (pp. 171–172). More fundamentally, the increased supplies of gold might be exhausted, and prices could again head down.

Others were observing the trend in prices, associating it with rising gold supplies, and concluding that this supported the quantity theory. But if others saw the logic, Bryan still had the gift for expressing his point with a simple metaphor:

> Suppose the citizens of a town were divided, nearly equally, on the question of water supply, one faction contending that the amount should be increased, and suggesting that the increase be piped from Silver Lake, the other faction insisting no more water was needed; suppose that at the election the opponents of an increase won (no matter by what means); and suppose, soon after the election, a spring which may be described as Gold Spring, broke forth in the very center of the city, with a flow of half as much water as the city had before used; and suppose the new supply was turned into the city reservoir to the joy and benefit of all the people of the town. Which faction would, in such a case, have been vindicated?
>
> Just such a result had followed a similar increase in the nation's supply of money to the joy of all – thus proving the contentions of the bimetallists. (Bryan and Bryan, 1925, p. 471)

Is it any wonder that in an age in which politicians would be willing to describe monetary policy in such wondrous terms, Baum would incorporate the monetary controversies of the day in his fairy tale?

References

Baum, Frank Joslyn. and MacFall, Russell P., *To Please a Child: A Biography of L. Frank Baum, Royal Historian of Oz*. Chicago: Reilly & Lee, 1961.

Baum, L. Frank, *The Wonderful Wizard of Oz*. New York: Hill, 1900. Reprinted in *The Annotated Wizard of Oz*, edited by Michael Patrick Hearn. New York: Potter, 1973.

———, *The Marvelous Land of Oz, Being an Account of the Further Adventures of the Scarecrow and the Tin Woodman* . . . Chicago: Reilly & Britton, 1904.

Bewley, Marius, "Oz Country." *New York Rev. Books 3* (December 3, 1964): 18–19. Reprinted as "The Land of Oz: America's Great Good Place." In *Masks and Mirrors: Essays in Criticism*. New York: Atheneum, 1970.

Bryan, William Jennings, *The First Battle: A Story of the Campaign of 1896*. Chicago: Conkey, 1896.

———, *The Second Battle; or, the New Declaration of Independence, 1776–1900*. Chicago: Conkey, 1900.

Bryan, William Jennings and Bryan, Mary Baird, *The Memoirs of William Jennings Bryan*. Chicago: Winston, 1925.

Clark, John B. "The After Effects of Free Coinage of Silver." *Polit. Sci. Q.* 11 (September 1896): 493–501. (*a*)

———, "Free Coinage and Prosperity." *Polit. Sci. Q.* 11 (June 1896): 248–258. (*b*)

Coletta, Paolo E., *William Jennings Bryan*. 3 vols. Lincoln: Univ. Nebraska Press, 1964–1969.

Emerick, C. F., "An Analysis of Agricultural Discontent in the United States. II." *Polit. Sci. Q.* 11 (December 1896): 601–639.

Fisher, Irving, *Appreciation and Interest*. Publications of the American Economic Association, Vol. 11. New York: Macmillan, 1896.

———, *The Purchasing Power of Money*. 2nd ed. New York: Macmillan, 1922. Reprint. New York: Kelley, 1971.

Friedman, Milton, "William Jennings Bryan and the Cyanide Process." Manuscript. Stanford, Calif.: Hoover Inst., 1989.

———, "Bimetallism Revisited." *J. Econ. Perspectives* (1990), in press. (*a*)

———, "The Crime of 1873." *J.P.E.* 98 (December 1990), in press. (*b*)

Friedman, Milton and Schwartz, Anna J., *A Monetary History of the United States, 1867–1960*. Princeton, N. J.: Princeton Univ. Press (for NBER), 1963.

———, *Monetary Trends in the United States and the United Kingdom: Their Relation to Income, Prices, and Interest Rates, 1867–1975*. Chicago: Univ. Chicago Press (for NBER), 1982.

Gardner, Martin and Nye, Russel B., *The Wizard of Oz and Who He Was*. East Lansing: Michigan State Univ. Press, 1957.

Goodwyn, Lawrence, *Democratic Promise: The Populist Moment in America*. New York: Oxford Univ. Press, 1976.

Harvey, William, *Coin's Financial School*. Chicago: Coin, 1894. Reprint. Edited by Richard Hofstadter. Cambridge, Mass.: Harvard Univ. Press, 1963.

Hearn, Michael Patrick, ed., *The Annotated Wizard of Oz*. New York: Potter, 1973.

Hicks, John D., *The Populist Revolt: A History of the Farmer's Alliance and the People's Party*. Minneapolis: Univ. Minnesota Press, 1931; Lincoln: Univ. Nebraska Press, 1959.

Hollingsworth, Joseph Rogers, *The Whirligig of Politics: The Democracy of Cleveland and Bryan*. Chicago: Univ. Chicago Press, 1963.

Jastram, Roy W., *The Golden Constant: The English and American Experience, 1560–1976*. New York: Wiley, 1977.

Jensen, Richard, *The Winning of the Midwest: Social and Political Conflict, 1888–1896*. Chicago: Univ. Chicago Press, 1971.

Koenig, Louis W., *Bryan: A Political Biography of William Jennings Bryan*. New York: Putnam, 1971.

Littlefield, Henry M., "The Wizard of Oz: Parable on Populism." *American Q.* 16 (Spring 1964): 47–58. Reprinted in *The American Culture: Approaches to the Study of the United States*, edited by Hennig Cohen. Boston: Houghton Mifflin, 1968.

Lowes, John Livingston, *The Road to Xanadu: A Study in the Ways of the Imagination*. Boston: Houghton Mifflin, 1927.

McCutcheon, John T., *Drawn from Memory*. Indianapolis: Bobbs-Merrill, 1950.

Meyer, Fred M., "Oz in the News." *Baum Bugle* 31 (Autumn 1987): 32.

Nye, Russel B., *Midwestern Progressive Politics: A Historical Study of Its Origins and Development, 1870–1950*. East Lansing: Michigan State College Press, 1951.

O'Leary, Paul M., "The Scene of the Crime of 1873 Revisited: A Note." *J.P.E.* 68 (August 1960): 388–392.

Sackett, S. J., "The Utopia of Oz." *Georgia Rev.* 14 (Fall 1960): 275–291.

Timberlake, Richard H., Jr., "Repeal of Silver Monetization in the Late Nineteenth Century." *J. Money, Credit and Banking* 10 (February 1978): 27–45.

U.S. Bureau of the Census, *Historical Statistics of the United States, Colonial Times to 1970*. Washington: Government Printing Office, 1975.

Yohe, William P., "An Economic Appraisal of the Sub-Treasury Plan." App. B in *Democratic Promise: The Populist Moment in America*, by Lawrence Goodwyn. New York: Oxford Univ. Press, 1976.

VII

Women in the economy

"The changing economic role of women: A quantitative approach"

by Claudia Goldin

Women have always worked. Despite this continuity, there have been profound changes in the economic roles of American women in the past three centuries. In colonial America, the work performed by women in the home and the field helped ensure the survival of the family. Child rearing, housework, food processing, cloth and apparel manufacture, candlemaking, and a variety of farm chores were the primary responsibility of women. Outside the home, positions as domestics or farm servants were sometimes taken, especially by unmarried women. Market activity also included the sale of handicrafts and household manufacture.

In the antebellum period, factory production emerged and greatly expanded employment opportunities for women in the Northeast. Women played a major role in a number of industries, especially textiles. Opportunities for women continued to increase in the late nineteenth century with the rising demand for clerical workers. However, by 1890, only 19 percent of adult women participated in the labor market. Forty percent of single women took part, but only 4.6 percent of married women did. This is where Claudia Goldin's history picks up.

Goldin examines the movement of women into paid employment between 1890 and 1980 in "The Changing Economic Role of Women: A Quantitative Approach." She focuses on white married women because of "their numerical importance among all women, and because changes in their economic role have had repercussions transcending the economic sphere."

Goldin demonstrates that the economic behavior of married women after World War II was a result, in part, of their earlier work experiences as single women. In addition, she quantifies three broad factors that played an important role in the long-term changes in the economic role of these women: cohort-specific effects, point-in-time effects, and a trend toward higher participation over time that persists even after the other effects are included. This quantitative explanation makes use of the variation in participation rates across age groups and over time.

Consider these questions:

- Historians ceaselessly debate the roles of continuity and change. Was the impact of World War II on female labor force participation one of continuity or change?
- What might explain the positive coefficient on the time trend variable?
- Can changing social attitudes among men and women and changing household production technology be included in Goldin's framework?
- Where are the forces of supply and demand in this model?
- Goldin's methodology allows one to project labor force participation rates into the future. Do the equations predict recent changes?

Goldin has greatly expanded on this work in her book *Understanding the Gender Gap* (1990). She reworks the key tables of this essay to develop a more complex model and tackles a number of other issues, including gender-based discrimination, the political economy of "protective" labor legislation, and changes over time in the male-to-female earnings ratio.

Additional Reading

Nancy Folbre and Barnet Wagman, "Counting Housework: New Estimates of Real Product in United States, 1800–1860," *Journal of Economic History*, 53 (June 1993), 275–88.

Victor Fuchs, *Women's Quest for Economic Equality*. Cambridge, MA: Harvard University Press, 1988.

Claudia Goldin, *Understanding the Gender Gap: An Economic History of American Women*. New York: Oxford University Press, 1990.

Claudia Goldin and Kenneth Sokoloff, "Women, Children, and Industrialization in the Early Republic: Evidence from the Manufacturing Censuses," *Journal of Economic History*, 42 (December 1982), 741–4.

Alice Kessler-Harris, *Out to Work: A History of Wage-Earning Women in the United States*. New York: Oxford University Press, 1982.

Valerie Kincade Oppenheimer, *The Female Labor Force in the United States: Factors Governing Its Growth and Changing Composition*. Berkeley: University of California Press, 1970.

17

The changing economic role of women

A quantitative approach

CLAUDIA GOLDIN

In the early nineteenth century only a small fraction of women in the United States worked in the agricultural, industrial, and service components of the market sector. Within agriculture the wages of females relative to those of men were exceptionally low. But, wherever industry spread, relative wages for females increased, and their employment appeared linked to the diffusion of the factory system. The female labor force that expanded in the nineteenth century was primarily young and unmarried. It was not until the twentieth century that married women entered the market sector in any substantial way, first in the 1920s when young, and later, in the 1940s and 1950s, in their post-child-rearing years. Impressive gains in the participation of married women in the labor force were eventually achieved, with particular age groups affected during particular decades. This article explains the timing and the form of this expansion in the market role of married, white women in the United States.[1]

The focus is on those who are married because of their numerical importance among all women, and because changes in their economic role have had repercussions transcending the economic sphere. Single women are not, however, ignored. The labor force, education, and home experiences of young, single women have profoundly influenced their economic roles when married and have also affected the economic roles of their mothers. My methodology stresses a life-cycle approach to understanding change in the economic role of married women. Change

Research for this article had been supported by N.S.F. Grant #SOC78-15037 and is part of the author's monograph, in progress, *Economic Change and American Women: An Economic History*.

Source: Reprinted from *The Journal of Interdisciplinary History*, XIII (1983), 707–733, with the permission of the editors of *The Journal of Interdisciplinary History* and the MIT Press, Cambridge, Massachusetts.

1. Goldin and Kenneth Sokoloff, "Women, Children, and Industrialization in the Early Republic: Evidence from the Manufacturing Censuses, 1820 to 1850," National Bureau of Economic Research Working Paper, no. 795 (1981), forthcoming in *Journal of Economic History*.

during one part of the life cycle can affect employment in another part. Thus different cohorts at any point in time may respond differently to the same set of factors. The analysis is limited to the economic behavior of white women, because the labor force participation of black women has differed in significant ways from that of white women even in analyses accounting for income, education, and family size. Most studies of this phenomenon have concluded that white and black married women differ substantially in their labor supply functions.[2]

The use of labor force participation rates as an indicator of economic and social change has some limitations. It does not fully capture changes in occupations and in work conditions, nor does it fully reflect the alteration in economic roles as individuals move from the nonpaid to the paid sector. But these changes seem adequately proxied by variations in labor force participation rates. Indeed, Lewis, an eminent student of development, has commented that "the transfer of women's work from the household to commercial employment is one of the most notable features of economic development."[3]

Whereas economists and sociologists have concentrated on the causes of the progressive entry of women into the labor market, the historical literature has focused on the social impact of such change. The most immediate impact has been on the family itself. Thus, notes Degler, "[w]ork for money, as opposed to work for family, generates different attitudes and relationships among family members," and, to Chafe, "the

2. See the discussion in Goldin, "Female Labor Force Participation: The Origin of Black and White Differences, 1870 and 1880," *Journal of Economic History*, XXXVII (1977), 87–108.

3. A more comprehensive measure of market work for married women including boardinghouse keepers, industrial homework, etc., is being constructed as part of Goldin, *Economic Change and American Women*. Labor force participation is used in this article as the primary indicator of the economic role of women in the market economy. Several empirical and theoretical issues arise, however, when using such a statistic. The distinction made here, an extension of that made in our national income accounts, is between work for pay, which is generally part of the market sector, and work at home or within the voluntary sector, which is not. This distinction, although generally useful, is not immune to problems, particularly regarding the type of work that women have generally pursued. How participation in the market economy is measured is another issue. The current definition of the labor force includes those seeking work but not currently employed, together with those at work. Prior to 1940, the definition used was whether or not the individual listed an occupation on the population census questionaire. There has been concern that participation rates for married women have been understated in the past because of the reluctance of women to state an occupation, particularly when the work was performed in the home or done intermittently. These problems, however, have not significantly biased the data. The labor force participation rates of married women from census data in the early period seem consistent with those from, for example, studies of working-class families around 1900. The change in the definition also has not altered the meaning of the data. W. Arthur Lewis, "Economic Development with Unlimited Supplies of Labour," in A. N. Agarwala and S. P. Singh (eds.), *The Economics of Underdevelopment* (London, 1958), 404.

growing employment of married women after 1940 exerted a considerable influence on the distribution of tasks and authority within the family." Beyond the family lies change in social roles and in ideology. Although it is clear that economic change altered family life, the relationship between economic change and social norms has been less obvious. That the feminist movement did not spring from the rapid rise in female labor force participation in the 1950s has appeared paradoxical to some. Nor did the earlier feminist movement of the 1920s result in a radical altering of the market role of women.[4]

Although economic change need not have altered ideology, prevailing social norms may still have been a critical force in defining and containing the economic role of women. To many, the pervasive ideology inhibiting work for married women was the notion that such work was harmful to the family. Others stressed what Martineau noted was a particularly American sentiment, that a "husband's hair stands on end at the idea of [his wife's] working." But if the impediments to economic change for women were primarily ideological, then only a major break with the past, such as that effected by war, could have redefined economic roles. With some exception, there is general agreement with Chafe's view that World War II was that "watershed event." It "radically transformed the economic outlook of women" with an impact greater than even "the implementation of a well-developed ideology." Change, in this context, was catastrophic, not cumulative.[5]

There has been virtual unanimity that little progress in the economic role of married women was achieved prior to World War II, with most adopting Oppenheimer's division of the twentieth century into two distinct periods. The earlier, pre-1940 period witnessed the evolution of work for single women. Beginning with the initial adoption of the factory system early in the nineteenth century, the labor force participation of single women expanded almost steadily until about 1940. This widening of an economic role for single women carried with it important implications for married women. With more daughters in the labor force

4. Carl Degler, *At Odds: Women and the Family in America from the Revolution to the Present* (New York, 1980), 362; William H. Chafe, *The American Women: Her Changing Social, Economic, and Political Roles, 1920–1979* (New York, 1972), 222, 188.

5. E.g., Degler, *At Odds*, 362–394. Alice Kessler-Harris, "Women's Wage Work as Myth and History," *Labor History*, XIX (1978), 287–307, provides an insightful interpretation of the historical commentary about working women in light of such ideological considerations. Harriet Martineau, *Society in America* (New York, 1837), II, 227; Chafe, *American Woman*, 195, 135. One exception to Chafe's view can be found in D'Ann Campbell, "Wives, Workers, and Womanhood: America During World War II," unpub. Ph.D. diss. (Univ. of North Carolina, 1979). Maurine Weiner Greenwald, *Women, War, and Work: The Impact of World War I on Women Workers in the United States* (Westport, Conn., 1980), emphasizes some of the less obvious changes in the female labor force resulting from that war.

there were fewer compelling reasons for their mothers to leave the household. But work for single women not only precluded that for married women, it may also have made future change more difficult. Tentler and others have argued that the manufacturing jobs given to single women were sufficiently arduous, dead-end, and sexually segregated that they reinforced the prevailing notion that the proper and preferred role for married women was in the home. Furthermore. Rotella's study of the emerging clerical sector reminds readers that this impressive transformation of women's jobs from 1870 to 1930 almost universally involved single, and not married women.[6]

Even for those who view World War II as initiating change in the economic role of married women, the continued increase in labor force participation rates has demanded further thought. Most of the explanations for change in the more recent period have come from economists. Historians have been understandably hesitant to analyze these recent, and thus brief, trends. Although economists are not unanimous as to the precise line of causation, most have isolated a similar set of critical variables. But within the small group of noneconomists who have studied this topic, there is less consensus. Oppenheimer, a sociologist, emphasizes the demand side. The increased demand for labor in the post-1940s, combined with a relative short-fall of young, single women, led employers to seek a new pool of labor – older married women. Chafe, however, stresses family decision making, and thus labor supply factors. In his view, the post-war period gave rise to a new standard of living which made two primary earners per family a necessity. This reliance on changing consumption norms does not explain why such change occurred, nor, more important, why older and younger married women increased their roles in the labor force at different times.[7]

The framework employed in this article, in its emphasis on the life cycle of women, is a departure from that in the literature just summarized. Although change in the labor force participation rates of married women did accelerate after World War II, many of the pre-

6. Valerie Kincade Oppenheimer, *The Female Labor Force in the United States: Factors Governing Its Growth and Changing Composition* (Berkeley, 1970). See Winifred D. Wandersee, *Women's Work and Family Values, 1920–1940* (Cambridge, Mass., 1981), on changes from 1920 to 1940. Goldin and Sokoloff, "Women, Children, and Industrialization," and Goldin, "The Work and Wages of Single Women: 1870 to 1920," *Journal of Economic History*, XLI (1981), 81–89, discuss the evolution of work for single women. Leslie Woodcock Tentler, *Wage-Earning Women: Industrial Work and Family Life in The United States, 1900–1930* (New York, 1979); Elyce Rotella, *From Home to Office: U.S. Women at Work, 1870–1930* (Ann Arbor, 1980).

7. Oppenheimer, *Female Labor Force*, 261; Chafe, *American Women*, 174–195. On changing consumption norms see also Wandersee, *Women's Work and Family Values*.

conditions for this expansion had been set decades before. The education, home roles, and occupations of single women, and the fertility behavior of married women, had lasting impacts on their later response to economic factors. The increased role of single women in the labor force prior to 1940, either in the manufacturing or in the clerical sectors, influenced the labor force patterns of these women at other points in their life cycles. New social norms of the 1920s may have influenced the decisions of many young women to delay leaving the labor force until their first pregnancy, rather than with marriage. Although this change may have affected only a small percentage of women, it may have provided that critical break on which future changes were founded. This point echoes and extends one made by Durand who, writing in 1948, was sensitive to the changes made from 1900 to 1945, and noted that "each successive generation of women seems to have retained the greater propensity to be in the labor force which it developed in early adulthood." Thus the historical evolution of market work for married women and the related changes in social roles and norms must be viewed by considering women at every point in time to have had important past histories of their own.[8]

The incomplete nature of the data presently available cautions against forming rigid notions about the determinants of long-term change in the economic role of women. But despite the deficiencies of the data, the empirical results that follow are striking and persuasive. They indicate that long-term changes in the economic role of white married women have been the result of three sets of factors: cohort specific effects, primarily predetermined (education and fertility); point-in-time factors, under the assumption of exogenous wages (full-time earnings and unemployment rate); and a time trend, which probably proxies long-run changes in the structure of the economy, such as the growth of the service sector. Thus this almost century-long experience has had remarkable structural continuity, with political and social factors operating through variables such as education, income, and fertility rather than directly affecting this process.

Dimensions of change: The data

Census marshals were first instructed to collect data on the occupations of women and children in 1860, and even though data on female

8. John D. Durand *The Labor Force in the United States, 1890–1960* (New York, 1948), 124. On the role of past events in determining marriage, fertility, and labor force participation, see Sheila K. Bennett and Glen H. Elder, Jr., "Women's Work in the Family Economy: A Study of Depression Hardship in Women's Lives," *Journal of Family History*, IV (1979), 153–176.

employment were collected for the decades from 1860 to 1880, the printed census returns for these years yield only scant indication of how the national figure varies by age, race, nationality, and marital status. Trends in the labor force participation of women in the market economy can, at present, be calculated only for the period since 1890, although such data stratified by age, race, national origin, and marital status are not even conveniently available in the printed censuses for 1900 to 1930.[9]

I have produced a matrix of cross-section and time-series labor force participation rates by marital status, age, race, and national origin for 1890 to the present which covers cohorts born from 1816–1825 to 1946–1955. Figure 1 is part of this larger matrix and summarizes the expansion of the labor force participation of white married women born from 1866 to 1955. Each set of solid (or dashed) lines represents the participation rate of a particular birth cohort and traces its market role as it matured. Cross-section data can also be read from this figure by connecting the relevant points on the cohort lines; for example, the data for 1970 are given by the dotted lines.[10]

Several aspects of the data in Figure 1 should be recognized. The format used is termed an "experiential" one in that the connected points represent participation rates for members of a birth cohort extending over its married life and reflect the actual experience of a cohort. There are, however, changes in the composition of each cohort as it ages that should be addressed. Individuals born in a particular year enter these data when they marry, and therefore as the cohort ages the size of this group changes. Furthermore, individuals who married late may have had different work histories than those who married early, and individuals who were widowed early and who exit from the data set may also differ. The geographical location of these cohorts also changed through time, as the population in the United States became more urbanized.

9. For data on the 1820 to 1850 period see Goldin and Sokoloff, "Women, Children, and Industrialization," which uses manufacturing census information; Thomas Dublin, *Women at Work: The Transformation of Work and Community in Lowell Massachusetts, 1826–1860* (New York, 1979), which uses firm records and the population census for 1860. There are several studies which have sampled the 1870 and 1880 censuses, among them Goldin, "Female Labor Force Participation"; Tamara K. Hareven and Maris A. Vinovskis, "Patterns of Childbearing in Late Nineteenth-Century America: The Determinants of Marital Fertility in Five Massachusetts Towns in 1880," in Hareven and Vinovskis (eds.), *Family and Population in Nineteenth-Century America* (Princeton, 1978), 85–125.

10. Goldin, *Economic Change and American Women*. Juanita M. Kreps and R. John Leaper, "Home Work, Market Work, and the Allocation of Time," in Kreps (ed.), *Women and the American Economy: A Look to the 1980s* (New York, 1976), construct cohort female labor force participation rates but do not derive them conditional on marital status.

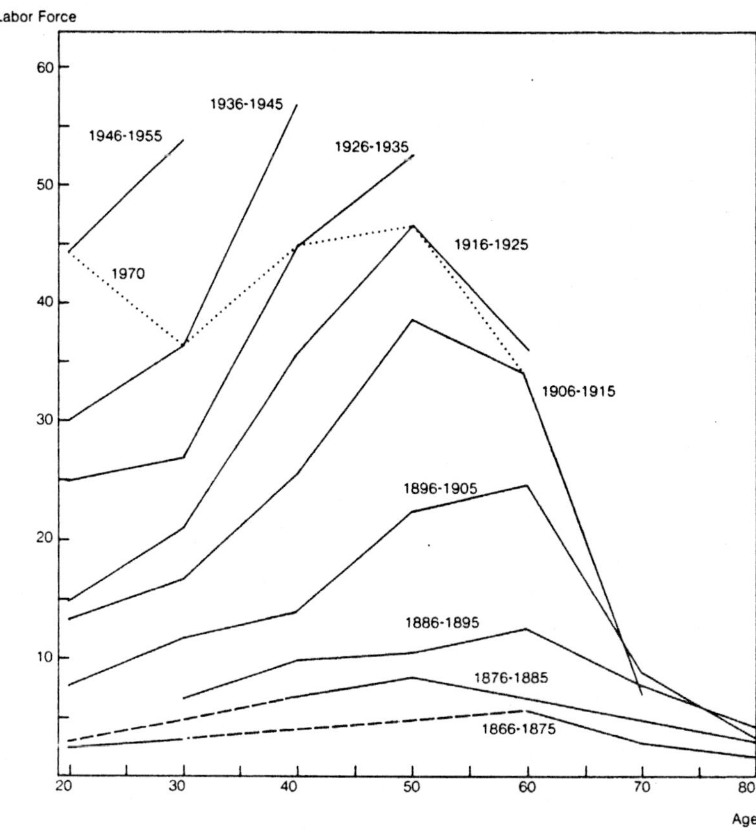

Figure 1. Labor force participation rates of cohorts of white, married women, born 1866 to 1955: Entire U.S.

Dashed lines denote missing data. Data for 1890 to 1920 are for native-born women with native-born parents. Dotted line is 1970 cross section.
Source: Derived from population census data. Data appendix on request from author.

Despite these considerations the data in Figure 1 have a more or less transparent interpretation – for every cohort born since 1855 participation in the labor force has increased within marriage, at least until about age fifty-five. Despite the currently popular notion that married women universally experience interruptions in their work careers, the majority who have entered the labor force after their children began school had not experienced labor force work since they were single, if even at that time. The notion of interrupted work careers has arisen, in part, from the pattern of double-peaked labor force participation characteristic of cross-sectional data for women's work experiences in most contemporary developed nations. This pattern emerged in the United States in 1950 and is illustrated by the dotted line in Figure 1 giving participation rates for the cross section of married women in 1970. At that time the labor force participation rate for married women of fifteen to twenty-four years old was higher than for those twenty-five to thirty-four years old, and this rate rose again with those aged thirty-five to forty-four. Such a bimodal or double-peaked pattern has indicated to some an exiting of women from the labor force with the birth of their children and a later reentrance as their families matured.

But the actual labor force experience of these cohorts of women has universally consisted of increasing labor force participation rates until about age fifty-five. For reasons discussed later, each successive decade brought an expanded participation of married women in the market economy. Thus the cohort participation rates are substantially different from the cross-sectional ones. No generation of young women could have predicted solely from the experiences of their elders what their own work histories would have been. Indeed, in 1930 a cohort of twenty-year-old daughters born in 1910 would have been off by a factor of 3.6 in predicting their own participation rates in twenty-five years, had they simply extrapolated from the experiences of their forty-five-year-old mothers born in 1885. Had they, with more quantitative sophistication, partially utilized the model presented in the next section and recognized education and fertility differences between their and their mothers' cohorts, they would have been off by a factor of 2.1, considerably less. The remainder of the differences between these groups was accounted for by changes over time in the structure of the economy and thus economic opportunities for women and, among other factors, in increases in the earning capabilities of women.[11]

Interruptions in the work careers of women have been central to explanations for differences in the training and occupations of women relative to men. These cohort data do not eliminate entirely the notion of career interruption, but alter its significance and meaning. The large increases over time in labor force participation mean that many women

11. The daughter's labor force participation rate was about 32% when she was 45 years old, whereas the mother's was only about 9%. The daughter, however, had 39% more years of schooling than her mother and, on average, 28% fewer children. Using the coefficients from Table 1 column (2) yields an expected labor force participation rate of 15.3% had the daughter extrapolated only on the basis of these two differences in the experience of her cohort and that of her mother. That is: $d\log FLFP = (0.891)d\log SCH - (0.723)d\log CHILD = (0.891)\log(11.5/8.3) - (0.723)\log(2.3/3.2) = 0.53$. Therefore, these two factors served to increase FLFP by 1.7 times, ($e^{0.53} = 1.7$), or from 9% to 15.3%. (See Table 1 for variable name definitions.)

must have entered the work force when older with very little, if any, work experience after marriage. Because a very high percentage of women worked at some time prior to marriage, many who worked when married were returning to occupations that they had when single. Because the clerical labor force, for example, consisted primarily of single women in the pre-1940 period does not mean that it was an entirely unimportant factor in shaping the labor force experiences of married women later in the century.[12]

In terms of time-series trends, participation rates increased for married white women in all age groups, except the very oldest, in every decade. Increases were slight, however, for most cohorts until the 1920s and then again in the 1940 and 1950 decades. Young, married women experienced somewhat larger increases than did older women during the 1920 to 1930 period. But from 1940 to 1960 participation rates for older women, say over thirty-five years, rose dramatically, and from 1960 to 1980 the rates for younger women, say those under thirty-five years, experienced similar increases.

These time-series trends can be seen more clearly with reference to Figure 2, which shows labor force changes over time for married women both twenty-five to thirty-four years old (younger) and forty-five to fifty-four years old (older). It is more evident from Figure 2 than it was from Figure 1 that the greatest expansion in the labor force participation of older women occurred in the World War II and post-war periods, when that for younger women increased far less. The younger women, however, have had relative expansions in their market work activity both in the earliest periods drawn and in the most recent ones. Such differences in labor market activity by age were explored by Easterlin whose explanation of them stressed a relationship between cycles in the economy and changes in birth rates.[13]

The cohort experiences and time series graphed in Figures 1 and 2 are for the entire United States, and thus, it might be claimed, reflect in large measure the long-run movement of the population out of agricultural and non-farm rural areas. But similarly constructed data for urban areas only (not shown) are virtually identical to the total data for the period after 1950 and differ before 1950 only with respect to the greater increase in the labor force participation of young married women in urban areas from 1920 to 1930. This increase in young married

12. On the implications of career interruptions see Jacob Mincer and Solomon Polachek, "Family Investments in Human Capital: Earnings of Women," *Journal of Political Economy*, LXXXII (1974), S76–S108.

13. Richard Easterlin, *Birth and Fortune: The Impact of Numbers on Personal Welfare* (New York, 1980).

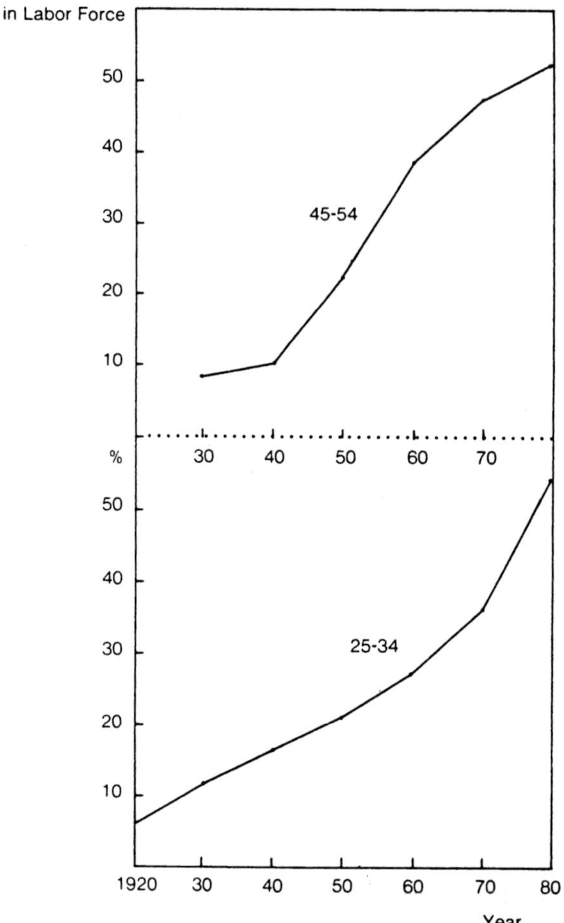

Figure 2. Labor force participation rates for two age groups of white, married women, 1920 to 1980: entire U.S.

Source: Fig. 1. Data appendix on request from author.

women in the labor force of the 1920s suggests that they were either progressively exiting from the labor force after their first pregnancy or delaying their first birth. The urban data also indicate that within cities there were few substantial differences by nativity in average labor force participation rates of married women, a result which would have been difficult to demonstrate in the context of the national figures.

Each cohort has been influenced in its decision to participate in the labor force both by economic and social conditions at a particular date

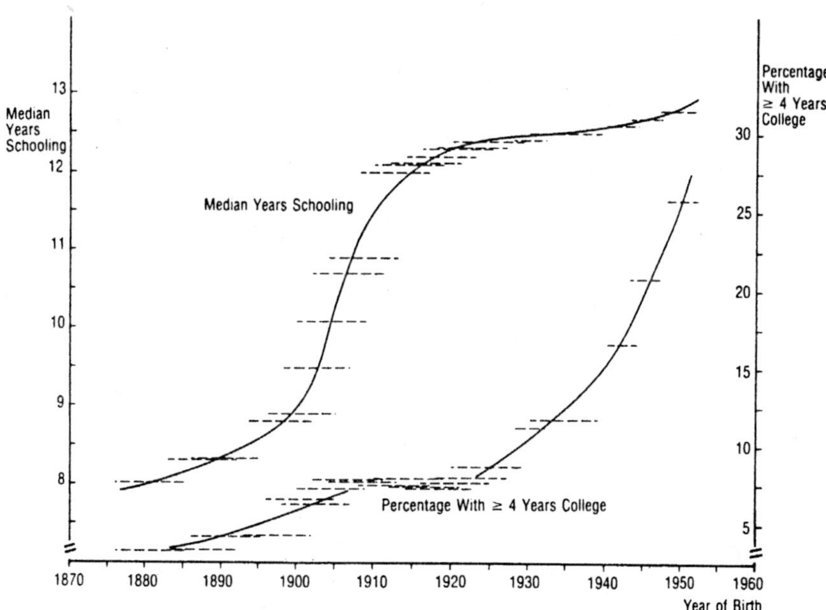

Figure 3. Educational attainment for cohorts of white women born 1876–1952.

Horizontal lines indicate the width of the birth cohorts for which data on educational attainment are given.
Source: U.S. Bureau of the Census, *Current Population Reports*, Series P-20 for years 1940, 1947, 1962, 1966, 1968, 1970, 1972, 1974, 1977. Data appendix on request from author.

and by aspects of early socialization and training carried with it through time. Of the factors which may have differentiated one cohort's work history from another, three relate to their early experiences: schooling, work in the market economy, and work in the home.

The median years of schooling for female cohorts born from 1876 to 1952 and the percentage with four or more years of college are given in the left and right-hand graphs of Figure 3. The data on median years of schooling show a remarkable rise in the educational attainment of young American women beginning approximately with the cohorts born between 1900 and 1910. During a very brief period young women had increased their years of education by about one third, from about nine years to twelve years. This rapid rise in years of schooling was a product of the increase in high school education, with these individuals leaving school from 1915 to 1928. The cohort that achieved this educational transformation was precisely that which experienced substantial increases in its labor force participation both during its early years and even more so at the time, during the 1950s, that it was forty to fifty years old (see Fig. 1).[14]

Not only was the educational attainment of the cohort born from 1900 to 1910 a break with prior experiences, but it also achieved a high rate of labor force participation when single. The labor force participation rate of native-born white, single women of fifteen to twenty-four years old was 30 percent in 1890, 33.5 percent in 1900, 45.1 percent in 1920, and about 40 percent from 1930 to 1960. Thus this cohort carried with it through time a labor market experience and education that differed considerably from those of prior generations of young women. It was also a cohort that was employed to a large degree in the clerical sector when it was single and when that sector employed young single women almost exclusively.[15]

Cohorts of women born around the early twentieth century were able to achieve both an increase in their educational attainment and an increase in their labor market experience when single, by spending considerably less time "at home," ostensibly helping their mothers. In 1880 over 50 percent of all unmarried urban daughters between sixteen and twenty-four years old (white with American-born parents) were full-time workers in their parents' households. By 1900 about 30 percent were, and by 1930 practically no post-adolescent single women were either not in school or not in the labor force. This shift away from home chores by teenaged girls and young women may have been an influential factor both in delaying the entrance of older married women into the labor market and in encouraging labor market work for these younger women when they married.[16]

After the initial schooling increase with the cohorts born from 1900 to 1910, median years of education increased only gradually, with the exception of the most recent cohorts. Changes in the educational attainment of the most recent cohorts can be seen more clearly on the right-hand portion of Figure 3, which graphs the percentage of women

14. The increase in effective years of schooling would be even greater if days attended and expenditures per pupil were incorporated. Years of schooling for males did not rise as dramatically over the same period.

15. On this point see Rotella, *From Home to Office*; Goldin, "The Historical Evolution of Female Earnings Functions and Occupations," National Bureau of Economic Research Working Paper, no. 529 (1980).

16. The 1880 data are for Philadelphia and are from Goldin, "Household and Market Production of Families in a Late Nineteenth-Century City," *Explorations in Economic History*, XIV (1979), 111–131. The 1900 data were computed from labor force and schooling data for Boston, Chicago, New York, Philadelphia, and St. Louis in *Population Census, 1900* (1902), Pt. 2 and the related volume *Women at Work* (1904); those for 1930 were computed from labor force and schooling data on the same cities in *Population Census, 1930* (1933), II, V. Data are in an appendix available upon request from the author.

with four or more years of college. This indicator increased most rapidly with cohorts born after 1940, precisely those with substantially higher labor force participation in the most recent decades.

Yet another factor influencing the future labor force participation of these cohorts is fertility, although it might best be viewed as jointly determined with the work history. The well-known cycles in fertility which have marked the twentieth-century experience began with the trough produced by the cohorts born between 1905 and 1914. The peak of this cycle was achieved by the cohorts born from 1928 to 1932. Although it is still too early to know, another trough may have been produced by the cohorts born between 1948 and 1952. The relationships between education and fertility data are suggestive. Changes in schooling, by affecting early work experience and social norms, may have influenced fertility, although a complete model of fertility change must also incorporate an explanation for the "baby boom" of the post–World War II period.[17]

The data on the schooling, market work, and home work of post-adolescent daughters have suggested that experiences early in the life cycle of women may have greatly affected their market involvement when older. The data on educational attainment indicate that increases in median years of schooling were discontinuous and that certain cohorts experienced rapid increases in years of schooling. These same cohorts also had more years of labor market experience when young, but far less experience in household production than prior cohorts. Their early socialization may have provided a change in focus with that of past generations. The cohorts whose schooling and early labor force experiences rapidly approached contemporary levels were precisely those whose labor market participation rates, both in their early and in their later married years, substantially increased over previous levels. These cohorts also had smaller families than did those who were born before or, for some time, after. Recent changes in the percentage of women completing college may have affected the current labor force and fertility behavior of young married women.

The profiles of labor force participation for cohorts of white married women born from 1866 to 1955 show an unbroken upward trend to about age fifty-five. But there were distinct changes in participation rates during particular decades and for particular cohorts. The increases in labor force participation with age for each cohort appear to reflect two

17. For data sources see notes and sources for Table 1, CHILD variable. Deborah Dawson, Denise Meny, and Jeanne Clare Ridley, "Fertility Control in the United States Before the Contraceptive Revolution," *Family Planning Perspectives*, XII (1980), 76–86, examine the fertility experience of the cohort of females born from 1901 to 1910.

complementary sets of factors: those affecting point-in-time experiences, such as economic upturns or downturns, and those concerning characteristics that each cohort retained with it through its life cycle. The estimation in the next section addresses how much of the increase over time in labor force participation was due to increases in wages, employment opportunities, and changes in societal norms, and how much to changes in cohort specific factors.

Explaining change in the labor force participation of married women

Two distinct but complementary theories of change in the economic role of married women have been offered by economists. One, due to Easterlin, stresses the concept of relative income and the importance of fertility decisions; the other, associated primarily with Mincer, stresses the value of time and the importance of changes in female wages.[18]

As part of a more comprehensive theory of demographic, social, and economic change in the twentieth century. Easterlin has distinguished between changes in the labor force participation rates of younger and older women. The fertility rate is the prime determinant of changes in the economic behavior of both groups, but the mechanism of change is through alterations in the relative income of younger men, presumably the prospective husbands of the younger women. Relative income is a critical concept in this analysis, and Easterlin defined it as income in comparison to what one had anticipated earning, perhaps relative to the incomes of older cohorts. Thus, the children of the baby trough of the 1920s and 1930s married in the relatively prosperous post–World War II era. These young men were from a relatively small cohort and thus commanded relatively high incomes. They married young and had large families. The fertility rate rose, the labor force participation rate of younger women rose only slightly, but that of older women increased greatly. Older women were close substitutes for younger women, whereas older and younger men were presumably poor substitutes for each other. Younger women had small increases in their labor force participation rates for two reasons: they were raising larger families; and their husbands had relatively high incomes, generally a factor deterring female labor market participation.[19]

18. Easterlin, *Birth and Fortune*; Mincer, "Labor Force Participation of Married Women: A Study of Labor Supply," in H. Gregg Lewis (ed.), *Aspects of Labor Economics* (Princeton, 1962), 63–105.

19. See also Easterlin, "What Will 1984 Be Like? Socioeconomic Implications of Recent Twists in Age Structure," *Demography*, XV (1978), 397–432; *idem, Population, Labor Force, and Long Swings in Economic Growth* (New York, 1968). Richard Freeman, "The Effect of Demographic Factors on Age-Earnings Profiles," *Journal of Human Resources*, XIV (1979), 289–318, has

The recent baby slump and large labor force increases by all age groups of married women have been viewed by Easterlin as rooted in the relatively lower incomes of the young cohorts in the 1970s. These lower incomes were produced by two coincident factors: large cohorts born in the post–World War II period have depressed the earnings of young men relative to old men; in addition, the economy was generally depressed in the early and mid-1970s. Young men, faced with relatively lower incomes (again, relative to what they might have expected) married later, and had smaller families. Easterlin's formulation has pointed to critical differences in the determinants of work for younger and older women, as well as the importance of perceived changes in standards of living. But his implicit model is a highly complex one and difficult to test over long periods of time.

Mincer's explanation of secular changes in labor force participation rates of married women is an application of neoclassical labor economics. He had set out to resolve a paradox which Long had noted earlier, that despite increases in real family incomes, which should have reduced market work for women, the labor force participation of married women rose steadily from 1890. Long had used cross-section estimates of economic concepts termed income and substitution coefficients to predict time-series changes in participation rates. But he found that the cross-section income effect was so strong that it offset changes from all other possible variables, particularly the substitution effect.[20]

The solution to Long's paradox was Mincer's recognition that the cross-section income effect might be a gross overstatement of the income effect in a time-series context. The cross-section income estimate was overstated for use in predicting time-series, because it reflected, in large measure, variations in income arising from transitory, not permanent factors. The time-series and cross-section results could, to some degree, be reconciled by correcting the income effect coefficient. The income and substitution coefficients estimated by Mincer from a cross section of cities in 1950 were -0.53 and $+1.52$, respectively (where incomes and wages are in 1949 dollars $\times 10^{-2}$), and the elasticities, measured about

provided independent and substantiating evidence for the theory concerning both changes in relative incomes and the greater substitutability between older and younger women than between older and younger men.

20. Mincer, "Labor Force Participation." Clarence Long, *The Labor Force Under Changing Income and Employment* (Princeton, 1962). The "income effect" refers here to the change (generally a decrease) in labor time with an increase in income. For example, in most cross sections married women with husbands whose earnings are high tend to work fewer hours or days per year during their lifetimes. The "substitution effect" refers to the change in labor time with a change in the wage rate, generally, positive. For example, in cross sections individuals with high actual or anticipated wages work more hours or days per year or more years within their lifetimes.

the mean, were −0.83 and +1.50, respectively. Because variations in incomes across cities presumably arise from permanent and not transitory factors, the estimated income effect would be applicable for predicting the trend in labor force changes over time. But when applied to the wage and earnings data for 1890 and 1980 that underlie the regressions presented in Table 1, the Mincer estimates severely overstate changes in labor force participation from 1930 to 1940 for both younger and older women, and severely understate the increases in the labor force participation of older women from 1940 to 1960. However, over the entire period from 1890 to 1980 Mincer's coefficients do account for 62 percent of the change for women twenty-five to thirty-four years old.

One might track the turning points with better precision by taking into account changes in unemployment and in fertility, particularly as the latter affected younger women. Although Mincer had found these variables to have no statistical significance, Cain's reworking of Mincer's data concluded the reverse. The more extensive cross-section estimates of Bowen and Finegan are consistent with those of Cain, yielding a negative impact for increases in unemployment, and thus account better for the 1930 and 1950 data. These estimates do not, however, account for a greater percentage of the change over the entire period, primarily because the effect of the female wage is smaller in the Bowen and Finegan study than it was in Mincer's. In addition, the impact of changes in the number of children is too small in the Bowen and Finegan study to increase the predictive power of their equation over the entire time period.[21]

In the years since Mincer's influential paper was written, there have been advances both in the estimation of coefficients and in the recognition of the complexity of change in the labor market participation of married women. This body of research has suggested a set of variables to include in a model of long-run economic change, and the discussion above of life-cycle effects has suggested some extensions. But rather than applying cross-section coefficient estimates to time-series data, as Mincer had done, I have used a pooled time-series and cross-section model directly to confront the sources of long-run change.[22]

21. Glen G. Cain, *Married Women in the Labor Force: An Economic Analysis* (Chicago, 1966), 22–24; William Bowen and T. Aldrich Finegan, *The Economics of Labor Force Participation* (Princeton, 1969).

22. An excellent introduction to the literature which extended Mincer's work on labor supply is James J. Heckman, Mark R. Killingsworth, and Thomas MaCurdy, "Empirical Evidence on Static Labour Supply Models: A Survey of Recent Developments," in Zmira Hornstein, Joseph Grice, and Alfred Webb (eds.), *The Economics of the Labour Market* (London, 1981), 73–124. I am aware of only one other time-series analysis of labor force participation rates for women: June A. O'Neill, "A Time-Series Analysis of Women's Labor Force Participation," *American*

The variables of the preceding discussion can be divided into two groups, isolating the impacts of two sets of factors: (1) those influencing change over time for any particular cohort (point-in-time factors) and (2) those differentiating each cohort's experience from any other (cohort specific factors). Such a procedure enables a full analysis of the cohort and cross-sectional data given in Figure 1.

The first set of factors, which accounts for within cohort effects, includes the full-time earning capacity of women (*FEARN*), the income of other family members (*MEARN*) proxied by the actual income of all labor force participants or of males, and the unemployment rate (*UN*). Depending on the degree of precision used in stratifying the labor force data, factors such as the urbanization rate (*URB*) or merely a time trend (*TIME*) are needed to account for long-term structural change in the economy. Relative prices for market goods which had been primarily home produced and for labor-saving capital equipment are also important indicators, but are not readily available for the full period considered. The data in Figure 1 allow for, at most, nine equations of the general form of (1), one for each of the nine cohorts to explain ($LFPR_{i,t}$) the labor force participation rate of cohort i at time t:

$$LFPR_{i,t} = f(FEARN_t, MEARN_t, UN_t, TIME \text{ or } URB_t) \quad (1)$$

where t = year, i = cohort, for all i.

The second set of factors, which accounts for cross cohort effects, includes schooling attainment (*SCH*) and fertility (*CHILD*). Additional aspects of early socialization, work experience, and the time allocation of older children in the household cannot at present be incorporated. As summarized in equation (2) there are eight years of data, one for each of the census years from 1890 to 1980 (with the exception of 1910):[23]

$$LFPR_{i,t} = g(SCH_i, CHILD_i) \quad (2)$$

where i = cohort, for all t.

By pooling the cross-section and time-series data one can estimate a model of the form:

$$LFPR_{i,t} = h(FEARN_t, MEARN_t, UN_t, TIME \text{ or } URB_t; \; SCH_i, CHILD_i) \quad (3)$$

for all i,t.

Economic Review, LXXI (1981), 76–80, which covers the 1948–1978 period and runs separate regressions by age and marital status. Although O'Neill's study does not include the same variables and its coefficients are not expressed as elasticities, the estimates presented below in Tagble 1 appear generally consistent with those of O'Neill.

23. The 1910 data, because they included women in agricultural activities not included in other census years, have been omitted from the entire analysis.

The data underlying Figure 1 contain thirty-six observations on $LFPR_{i,t}$, beginning with fifteen to twenty-four year olds in 1890 from the birth cohort 1866–1875, ending with those twenty-five to thirty-four year olds in 1980 from the birth cohort 1945–1955, and omitting women over sixty-five years old. The data for the SCH_i variable are contained in Figure 3. Procedures for obtaining $FEARN_t$, $MEARN_t$, UN_t, URB_t, and $CHILD_i$ are described in Table 1. All earnings are expressed in constant dollars, female earnings are for full-time employment, and male earnings adjust for unemployment. This asymmetry in measuring female and male earnings is deliberate and reflects the notion that women condition their labor force decisions on actual family income but determine hours or days worked by considering their full-time wage. Unemployment is included as a separate factor, a possibly discouraging element in labor force decisions.

Several variables are added to test hypotheses raised earlier and to account for differences among groups. A dummy variable for the oldest age group, women between fifty-five and sixty-four years, is included (*OLD* Dummy). An interaction between fertility and a dummy variable for women in their childbearing years ($CHILD \cdot YOUNG$) is added to test whether increased fertility lowers a cohort's labor force participation rate only when it is young or whether family size has a more enduring impact. A dummy variable for 1950 (*WAR* Dummy) is included to test whether the increase in participation rates from 1940 to 1950 was due primarily to conventionally measured factors or whether the war had some residual impact.

The functional form used is double log (natural) and is given by:

$$\begin{aligned} \log LFPR_{i,t} = {} & \beta_0 + \beta_1 \log FEARN_t + \beta_2 \log MEARN_t \\ & + \beta_3 \log UN_t + \beta_4[\log URB_t \text{ or } TIME] \\ & + \beta_5 \log SCH_i + \beta_6 \log CHILD_i \\ & + \sum_j \alpha_j D_j + \epsilon_{i,t} \end{aligned} \tag{4}$$

where all variables are defined above, the D_j are various dummies and interaction terms, and $\epsilon_{i,t}$ is the error term, assumed uncorrelated within cohorts and among years.[24] The results are given in Table 1, where the coefficients, with the exceptions of the dummy variables and the time trend, are elasticities, the magnitudes and signs of which are generally

24. A logit form for the equations in columns (2) and (4) of Table 1 yielded virtually the same elasticities, evaluated at the mean of the labor force participation rates.

within the range of estimates from disaggregated studies. Although I discuss below the deficiencies of data and modeling, these estimates can, with caution, be employed to understand some of the sources of long-term change. The relative influences of cohort specific and point-in-time effects can be disentangled, and the role of special influences, such as World War II, can be assessed.

It can be seen in Table 1 that the impact of the female wage is strong, as suggested by cross-sectional studies such as Mincer's, with an elasticity of about 0.7 to 1. The role of a husband's or a family's income is insignificant, but unemployment generally has the predicted and somewhat significant discouraging impact. Because of the collinearity between female and male earnings over time, the equations were also estimated without the latter variable, as in columns (2) and (4). The cohort influences on schooling and fertility are both of the predicted sign, with elasticities around 0.9 for years schooling and −0.7 for average number of children.

The coefficients on the fertility and age interaction (log *CHILD* · *YOUNG*) and on fertility (log *CHILD*) alone indicate that labor force participation for a cohort remains significantly affected by its fertility experience beyond the period of childbearing and child-raising. The cohort does experience a greater impact from changes in fertility when it is young, but the effect is not contained in those years. Indeed, the elasticity with respect to number of children is reduced by only 20 percent for women above thirty-five years old.

Sources of long-term change in female labor force participation, derived from the regressions and the data underlying them, are given in Table 2. Point-in-time effects, which might also be thought of as demand-side factors, principally the rise in the earning ability of women, have exerted a powerful influence on participation rates, accounting for about one third of the total change from 1900 to 1980 or from 1920 to 1980. The impact of changes in education and fertility, termed cohort specific factors, have provided from 28 to 34 percent of the long-term movement. These cohort specific factors might also be thought of as supply-side factors. The time trend, which may be picking up either demand or supply factors, has accounted for about the remaining third.

I have shown elsewhere that, in the early twentieth century, earnings for women over their own life cycles in manufacturing jobs first rose sharply with age and then declined. Furthermore, such a decline persists even after adjusting for various factors, such as days worked per year, work experience, and marital status. But work in the clerical sector, at a somewhat later date, did not exhibit such a pattern. Instead, its age–earnings or experience–earnings profile was flatter and did not peak

Table 1. *Explaining variations in the labor force participation of white married women, 1890 to 1980, for age groups 15–24 to 54–65*

Dependent Variable = Log (Labor Force Participation Rate) for cohort i at time t. 't' statistics are given in parentheses below the coefficients. Independent variables are defined in the text and in the SOURCES. Number of Observations = 36 for all four regressions

	(1)	(2)	(3)	(4)
Constant	−9.112	−9.300	−11.070	−11.496
	(−3.53)	(−3.14)	(−6.52)	(−6.66)
Log FEARN	0.658	0.673	1.008	1.097
	(1.37)	(1.50)	(2.84)	(5.22)
Log MEARN	−0.015		0.040	
	(−0.07)		(0.17)	
Log UN	−0.078	−0.074	−0.003	−0.012
	(−1.32)	(−1.47)	(−0.05)	(−0.33)
Log SCH	0.892	0.891	0.957	0.945
	(3.48)	(3.48)	(3.80)	(3.74)
Log CHILD	−0.718	−0.723	−0.707	−0.711
	(−4.64)	(−4.75)	(−4.50)	(−4.57)
Log CHILD · YOUNG	−0.171	−0.173	−0.183	−0.182
	(−2.89)	(−2.95)	(−3.15)	(−3.18)
OLD Dummy	−0.312	−0.312	−0.305	−0.307
	(−5.46)	(−5.47)	(−5.33)	(−5.37)
TIME	0.014	0.014		
	(1.88)	(1.56)		
Log URB			0.794	0.688
			(1.73)	(1.44)
WAR Dummy		−0.001		−0.024
		(−0.14)		(−0.42)
R^2	0.990	0.990	0.989	0.989

NOTES AND SOURCES:

LFPR = labor force participation rate of white (native-born) married women for cohort i at time t, from Fig. 1.

FEARN = a weighted average of the annual full-time female wage in manufacturing and that in the clerical sector where weights are the share of female employment in each sector. Wages are from Rotella, *From Home to Office*; Paul F. Brissenden, *Earnings of Factory Workers, 1899–1927* (Washington, D.C., 1929); M. Ada Beney, *Wages, Hours, and Employment in the U.S. 1914–1936* (New York, 1936); U.S. Bureau of the Census, *Historical Statistics*, Series D838; U.S. Bureau of the Census, *Current Population Surveys*, Series P-60, 1945–1980. The wages are deflated to 1967 = 100 using the B.L.S. C.P.I., *Historical Statistics*, Series E135. For each year t, wages are an average of (t − 3) to (t − 1).

MEARN = male earnings adjusted for unemployment and are deflated to 1967 = 100. From Stanley Lebergott, *Manpower in Economic Growth: The American Record Since 1800* (New York, 1964), Series A-17, 524, non-farm wages for 1900–1960; Series A-19, non-farm wages for 1890–1900; *Current Population Surveys*, Series P-60, for urban white males, 1960–1980. For each year t, wages are an average of (t − 3) to (t − 1).

UN = national unemployment rate, five year average for (t − 6) to (t − 1), from *Historical Statistics*, Series D 85–86.

SCH = median years schooling for cohort i, from Fig. 3.

within the relevant range. It is possible, therefore, that an extensive participation of married women in the labor force had to await the emergence of such an occupation, the earnings profile of which did not decline at older ages. The time trend variable may be picking up changes in the structure of the economy which increased the demand for occupations in the clerical sector. It may also be picking up changes in social and individual norms and ideals.[25]

The twentieth century has been punctuated by two wars and one protracted economic depression, and change over this time in the economic role of married women has frequently been attributed directly to these events, apart from their indirect impact through such factors as economic variables. But the regressions in Table 1 indicate that change over the twentieth century has had a certain structural stability. The impact of World War II, for example, appears to have worked primarily through conventionally measured variables rather than as a separate factor, as can be seen by the insignificant coefficient on the variable (*WAR* Dummy).[26]

As encouraging and useful as this exercise may be in interpreting the past, it is not without problems regarding both the data and the underlying model. Several omitted variables have already been isolated.

25. Goldin, "Historical Evolution of Female Earnings Functions."

26. However Judith M. Fields, "A Comparison of Intercity Differences in the Labor Force Participation Rates of Married Women in 1970 with 1940, 1950 and 1960," *Journal of Human Resources*, XI (1976), 568–577, demonstrates that cross-sectional data yield vastly different labor–supply relationships over time. Although it is likely that the recent period demands more diligent modeling of factors relating to investment in human capital, differences among these decades may also be a function of greater geographical mobility in the later period.

CHILD = average number of children born to white women in cohort i over its life cycle. Cohorts born 1865 to 1924 from *Historical Statistics* (Washington, D.C., 1976), Series B42–48, 53; cohorts born 1928 to 1952 from U.S. Bureau of the Census, *Current Population Reports*, Series P-20, No. 341, "Fertility of American Women" (1978).

CHILD · YOUNG = Child · dummy variable for women 15 to 34 years old.

OLD = dummy variable for women 55 to 64 years old.

TIME = number of years from 1890

URB = percentage of U.S. population living in urban areas at time t, from *Historical Statistics*, Series A 57–72.

WAR Dummy = dummy variable for 1950.

Table 2. *Explaining long-term change in female labor force participation rates*

TIME INTERVAL	1900–1980	1920–1980	
AGE GROUPS	25–34	25–34	35–44
Point-in-time factors	0.96 (30%)	0.66 (29%)	0.66 (33%)
Cohort specific factors	1.00 (31%)	0.77 (34%)	0.56 (28%)
Time trend	1.23 (39%)	0.81 (36%)	0.81 (40%)

NOTES AND SOURCES:

The numbers in this table give the values of dlog FLFR predicted by the equation in Table 1, column (2). The time intervals and age groups given were dictated by the available data underlying Table 1, e.g. there are no data for 1910. The figures in parentheses give the percentage of the predicted change in dlog FLFP explained by the set of variables in each row. The definitions of each row are:

Point-in-time factors = 0.673 dlog FEARN − 0.074 dlog UN

Cohort specific factors =
0.891 dlog SCH − 0.723 dlog CHILD − 0.173 dlog CHILD · YOUNG

Time trend = 0.014 dTIME

Note that all three sets of factors fully exhaust the relevant variables in the regression in Table 1, column (2).

The income data are not age or race specific over the entire period for males or females, and although the fertility data are for white women, they are not specific to native-born women. The use of a time-trend or urbanization variable disguises the need for better indicators of economic structural change that have affected the demand for female workers. In terms of the model, the framework implies that female earnings are exogenous. Although this might be an acceptable assumption for the earliest periods, it becomes less viable as the percentage of females in the total labor force rises. The complexities raised by Easterlin concerning the endogeneity of fertility and the use of a relative income concept are further issues with which to contend.

Finally, nothing has been said about the constraints facing married women in the labor market. The occupations in which married women have been employed expanded greatly over the period analyzed. Whereas it was commonplace earlier in the century for women to be dismissed from their jobs upon marriage, particularly from teaching and clerical sector positions, this prohibition slowly disappeared. But its relaxation has been linked to certain economic factors, and thus its presence may not have been solely a function of social norms. One study of the local employment practices of a school board has found a marked increase in married women hired during the tight World War I labor market. In addition, unemployment in the 1930s led to a rationing of jobs among women by marital status. But there have been no quantitative studies of the precise impact of such practices, the ways in which they were relaxed, and how changes in the interval between marriage and first pregnancy, for example, affected them.[27]

The concentration in this article on economic role and, more specifically, on labor market participation, should not be interpreted to mean that society has measured the worth or position of individuals only in this manner. Nor do I mean to imply that men and women have had the same treatment or experience in the labor market. The focus on labor market participation stems from the notion that such a convenient measure conveys information. It may in some economies convey information about the harshness of life, but it may in others point to deeper social and economic change. Work for married women in the American past has frequently meant, as it has for men, economic necessity. But it has also implied, with more and more frequency, economic autonomy. The emergence of such independence and control has carried with it further implications, such as the formation of wider and less family-dependent social networks, a greater chance for marital dissolution, and the possibility of less constrained and structured sex roles. Across a wide variety of countries, the emergence of married women in the paid labor force has carried with it similar implications for social and economic change, and thus an explanation for changes in female labor force participation has been a topic of great importance.

In explaining the labor force behavior of married women, economists have stressed contemporaneous variables, primarily income, wage rates, family size, and unemployment. But precedents for economic change within the life cycles of individual cohorts, although harder to isolate, also merit inclusion. I have made a strong case for viewing individuals through time as having important past experiences. A pooled cross-section and time-series model was estimated across the years 1890 to 1980 to explain variations in female labor force participation, including at most five age groups in each year and using both cohort specific and point-in-time independent variables. The primary findings were that there apparently was structural stability in the process of change over the

27. Robert Margo and Rotella, "Sex Differences in the Market for School Personnel: Houston, Texas, 1892–1923," unpub. ms. (1981).

past century. Despite the importance of the female earnings variable and the time trend, the role of education and fertility in accounting for between cohort differences was significant, and these are only two of the variables that might capture aspects of a cohort's past.

VIII

The Great Depression

Monetary forces and the Great Depression: Milton Friedman and Anna Jacobson Schwartz versus Peter Temin

The Great Depression of the 1930s ranks as one of the greatest disasters in American history. The economy shrank for four years, and output languished far below its potential throughout the decade. Consequently, millions were unemployed or depended on public assistance. Investment not only failed to rise, it did not even keep up with depreciation. No area of economic activity was unaffected by the Depression.

The explanation for a disaster of this magnitude will be of profound importance. As Bernanke (1986, 82) puts it, "seismologists learn more from one large earthquake than from a dozen small tremors. On the same principle, the Great Depression of the 1930s would appear to present an important opportunity for the study of the effects of business cycles on the [macroeconomy]." Thus, macroeconomists have searched, and continue to search, for possible causes. One leading explanation (the monetary hypothesis) views an exogenous reduction of the money supply as the primary culprit; another prominent interpretation (the spending hypothesis) blames the collapse of the economy on an exogenous fall in spending on capital goods, consumer goods, and exports. For some economists, the validity of the Keynesian school and the monetarist school rests on which of these explanations of the Great Depression is correct.

The chief standard bearers of the monetary hypothesis are Milton Friedman and Anna Schwartz, authors of *A Monetary History of the United States, 1867–1960* (1963). "Since its publication, Friedman and Schwartz's *Monetary History* has defined much of the research agenda for the study of connections between financial markets and real activity during the Depression" (Calomiris, 1993, 63). The essay "Factors Accounting for Changes in the Stock of Money" is one of the most important parts of their book. It shows that in the years from 1929 to 1933, there was a drastic drop in the money stock. Friedman and Schwartz explore the subcomponents of the money stock, and carefully tie dramatic drops in the deposit–reserve ratio and the deposit–currency ratio to financial events.

At all points they underline the errors of the Federal Reserve. In the next section of *A Monetary History*, Friedman and Schwartz argue that the banking failures were not due to bad loans and a collapsing economy but rather to the "cycle of fear" in the banking system, especially the drop in the value of banks' assets as they were forced to dump these assets on the market to supply additional currency to depositors.

Peter Temin's "The Fall in the Demand for Money," an excerpt from his book *Did Monetary Forces Cause the Great Depression?* (1976), questions the validity of the monetary hypothesis. He argues that Friedman and Schwartz have ignored the falling demand for money. He examines interest rates, the "price" of money, and finds that they fell. Likewise, he fails to find any strong sign of credit rationing that might reverse his interpretation of movements in the interest rate. The explanation for the decline of money balances lies in changes in the demand for money, not changes in the supply, says Temin.

Both of these essays attempt to explain the same phenomenon: the decline in the stock of money. Friedman and Schwartz argue that a fall in the *supply* of money is the key to the Great Depression. Temin rejects this and argues that a decline in the *demand* for money led to a decline in the quantity of money supplied. The two essays presented here represent a small but important part of the larger debate about the causes of the Great Depression. Because of the complexity of the debate and of the economy, each essay encompasses a whole range of economic indicators and issues.

Reading these essays is extremely valuable because they demonstrate the rigorous examination required for each explanation. Each story must not only explain the decline in GNP, it must adequately explain changes in the stock of money, each of its components, the deposit–currency ratio, the deposit–reserve ratio, various interest rates, and much more. Life is messy, but this shouldn't stop you from keeping the central question in mind as you sort through this maze of indicators and issues.

The debate continues. Temin's central criticism of Friedman and Schwartz concerns the movement of interest rates. Thomas Mayer (1978) points out that it is the *real* interest rate, not the *nominal* interest rate, that matters. When deflation occurs, it is possible for nominal and real interest rates to move in opposite directions. In fact, it is *expected* real interest rates that matter rather than *realized* real interest rates. The key question becomes whether (and how much) deflation was anticipated or unanticipated. How are expectations about inflation to be inferred? Several recent articles have attempted to measure these expectations, but they have reached differing conclusions about deflationary expectations during the critical period.

Until recently, this debate has been a classic case of differences of opinion being amplified, while agreements are hushed up. However, Christina Romer (1993, 26) argues that a consensus is at hand that combines the two explanations. "The fact that prices and wages were not perfectly flexible in the 1920s and 1930s means that movements in the aggregate demand had real effects. . . . The evidence suggests that domestic spending shocks related to the stock market crash were crucial in the first year of the Depression, while monetary shocks were important in later years."

Explanations of the causes of the Depression must also explain its length. As surveyed by Charles Calomiris (1993), a new paradigm is emerging that helps explain how monetary shocks and other disturbances during the early phase of the Depression had long-run effects largely because they destroyed much of the institutional structure of the credit market and rearranged the balance sheets of borrowers. The regulatory mistakes of the government, including those of the Reconstruction Finance Corporation, the National Industrial Recovery Act, and the Interstate Commerce Commission, may also explain the duration of the Depression. In addition, a more complete understanding of the causes of the Depression must emphasize the importance of international events, especially the workings of the gold standard in the transmission of the Depression.

Additional Reading

Ben Bernanke, "Employment, Hours, and Earnings in the Depression: An Analysis of Eight Manufacturing Industries," *American Economic Review*, 76 (March 1986), 82–109.

Charles Calomiris, "Financial Factors in the Great Depression," *Journal of Economic Perspectives*, 7 (Spring 1993), 61–85.

Barry Eichengreen, *Golden Fetters: The Gold Standard and the Great Depression, 1919–1939*, New York: Oxford University Press, 1992.

Milton Friedman and Anna Schwartz, *A Monetary History of the United States, 1867–1960*, Princeton, NJ: Princeton University Press, 1963.

Thomas Mayer, "Money and the Great Depression: A Critique of Professor Temin's Thesis," *Explorations in Economic History*, 15 (April 1978), 127–45.

Christina Romer, "The Nation in Depression," *Journal of Economic Perspectives*, 7 (Spring 1993), 19–39.

Peter Temin, *Did Monetary Forces Cause the Great Depression?* New York: Norton, 1976.

Peter Temin, "Transmission of the Great Depression," *Journal of Economic Perspectives*, 7 (Spring 1993), 87–102.

18

Factors accounting for changes in the stock of money

MILTON FRIEDMAN and
ANNA JACOBSON SCHWARTZ

The factors accounting for changes in the stock of money during the four years from 1929 to 1933 are strikingly different from those in the other periods we have examined. Generally, the pattern for high-powered money has impressed itself most strongly on the total stock of money, the behavior of the two deposit ratios serving mainly to alter the tilt of the money stock relative to the tilt of high-powered money. That relation holds in Chart 1 only for the period up to October 1930, the onset of the first banking crisis. Thereafter, the two deposit ratios take command. High-powered money moves in a direction opposite to that of the total stock of money, and not even most of its short-term movements leave an impress on the stock of money.

From August 1929 to March 1933 as a whole, the change in high-powered money alone would have produced a rise of 17½ per cent in the stock of money. The change in the deposit-currency ratio alone would have produced a decline of 37 per cent; the change in the deposit-reserve ratio, a decline of 20 per cent; interaction between the two ratios, a rise of 10 per cent; these three converted the 17½ per cent rise that high-powered money would have produced into a 35 per cent decline in the stock of money.[1] For a more detailed examination of these changes, we

Source: Friedman, Milton, and Schwartz, Anna Jacobson, "Factors Accounting for Changes in the Stock of Money" from *The Great Contraction*, 1929–1933.

1. The trough of the money stock was reached in April 1933. Although the percentage decline from Aug. 1929 to Apr. 1933 is only slightly larger than from Aug. 1929 to Mar. 1933 (35.7 rather than 35.2 per cent), the percentage changes in the money stock each determinant would have produced if it alone had changed over the longer period show larger differences: 13, −35, −19, and 9 per cent, in the order shown in the text. The reason is that the return flow of currency after the banking holiday reduced high-powered money substantially and also raised the deposit-currency ratio from Mar. to Apr. 1933.

   The numerical values of the contributions of the determinants during the contraction, dated as ending in Mar. and in Apr. 1933 are in Table 1.

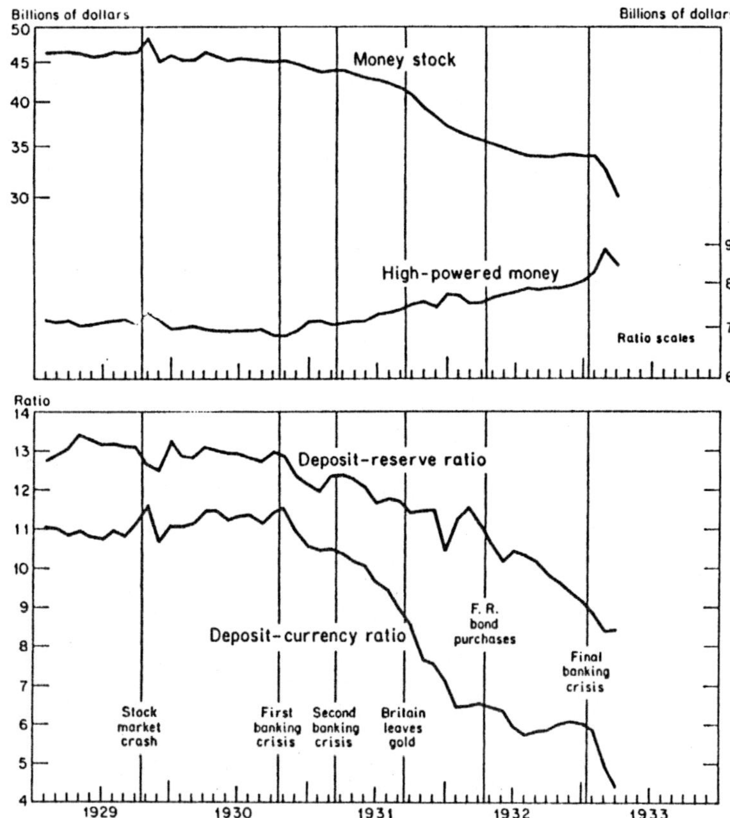

Chart 1. The stock of money and its proximate determinants, monthly, 1929–March 1933.

Source: *A Monetary History of the United States, 1867–1960* (Princeton University Press, 1963), Table A-1, pp. 712–713, col. 8, and Table B-3, pp. 803–804, cols. 1, 2, 3.

consider separately each of the periods distinguished in the preceding section and marked off on our charts.

The stock market crash, October 1929

Before the stock market crash, all three determinants of the money stock, and hence also the money stock itself, had been roughly constant. The constancy in high-powered money reflected a rough constancy in each of the categories into which we have divided the corresponding assets of the monetary authorities: the gold stock, Federal Reserve

Table 1. *Change in money stock that would have been produced by indicated determinant if it alone had changed*

Proximate Determinant	*Rate of Change Per Year (per cent)* Aug. 1929– Mar. 1933	Aug. 1929– Apr. 1933	*Fraction of Total Change* Aug. 1929– Mar. 1933	Aug. 1929– Apr. 1933
High-powered money	4.6	3.2	−0.37	−0.28
Deposit-reserve ratio	−6.2	−5.9	0.52	0.49
Deposit-currency ratio	−13.0	−11.8	1.07	0.98
Interaction	2.6	2.3	−0.22	−0.19
All	−12.1	−12.0	1.00	1.00

Detail may not add to total because of rounding.

private claims, and other physical assets and fiat of the monetary authorities (see Chart 2B). However, the constancy of Federal Reserve private claims conceals a not uninteresting detail, brought out by Chart 3, which shows the components of Federal Reserve credit outstanding. The total was roughly constant because a decline in bills discounted was offset by a rise in bills bought. The reason for the divergent movements was the simultaneous rise in August 1929 of the New York Reserve Bank's discount rate from 5 to 6 per cent and the decline of its buying rate on bills (bankers' acceptances) from 5¼ to 5⅛ per cent. Their effect was to make it profitable for banks to get funds from the Reserve System by creating acceptances and selling them to the Reserve Banks rather than by increasing their own indebtedness.

When the crash came, there were widespread attempts by holders of securities to liquidate them and by banks and other lenders outside New York to reduce their loans. As in all such cases, the position of the collection of participants is different from that of any one participant. Long-term securities cannot, on net, be liquidated in a short interval but only transferred from one holder to another. The widespread attempts to liquidate simply reduced prices to a level at which intended purchases matched intended sales.

Loans on securities, especially call loans, are a somewhat more complex affair. In large measure, what is involved is also a transfer of debts from one lender to another, rather than a change in total. But, in addition, the total can be altered much more rapidly. Aside from default, one way is by a transfer of other assets, as most directly when a borrower transfers money to a creditor and reduces his own money balance, or more indirectly when a borrower acquires cash by selling the security serving as collateral to someone else who draws down a money balance to acquire it. Another way is by what is in effect mutual cancellation of reciprocal debts. The most obvious but clearly insignificant example involves the cancellation by two borrowers of loans they have made to one another. A less obvious but more important example involves a longer chain, say, a corporation lending on call in the stock market and simultaneously borrowing from a bank. If the bank takes over the call loan in discharge of its loan to the corporation, the total of the two kinds of debt outstanding is reduced. The total can also be altered by creation of debts; for example, if a corporation lending on call in the market is willing to accept a note from a bank or – more realistically – a deposit in that bank in return for the corporation's claim. In that case, the total of the two kinds of debt is increased.

The essential point for our purpose is that the demand for liquidation of security loans involves one of three arrangements: (1) finding someone willing to take over the loans which, as for securities, can be done by a change of price, that is, a rise in interest rates; (2) finding someone willing to acquire assets for money to be used by the borrower to repay his loan, which can be done by lowering the price of the assets; or (3) arranging for more or less roundabout mutual cancellation or creation of debts, which involves changes in the relative prices of the various assets. The pressure on interest rates and on security prices can be eased by any measure that enhances the supply of funds in one of these forms to facilitate the liquidation of loans in one of these ways.

The situation was eased greatly at the time of the stock market crash by the willingness of New York banks to take over the loans. In the first week after the crash, those banks increased their loans to brokers and dealers by $1 billion and the rest of their loans by $300 million.[2] In large measure, this involved a creation of debts. The former lenders, the "others" for the accounts of whom the New York banks had been making loans, accepted deposits in New York banks as repaying their loans, and the New York banks in turn took over the claims on the

2. For the data on New York City weekly reporting member bank loans to brokers and dealers in securities, see *Banking and Monetary Statistics*, Board of Governors of the Federal Reserve System, 1943, Table 141, p. 499, and, for quarterly estimates of the total of such loans by all lenders, see *ibid.*, Table 139, p. 494. Although both tables show similar captions for the principal groups of lenders – most of whose funds were placed for them by the New York banks – except for loans by New York City banks for their own accounts, the breakdowns are not comparable. In the weekly series, "out-of-town domestic banks" include member and nonmember banks outside New York City and, to an unknown amount, customers of those banks, whereas in the comprehensive series that category is restricted to member banks outside New York City. Similarly, "others" in the weekly series cover mainly corporations and foreign banking agencies, but in the comprehensive series include also other brokers, individuals, and nonmember banks.

For loans except to brokers and dealers by New York City weekly reporting member banks, which also increased in the week after the crash, see *ibid.*, p. 174.

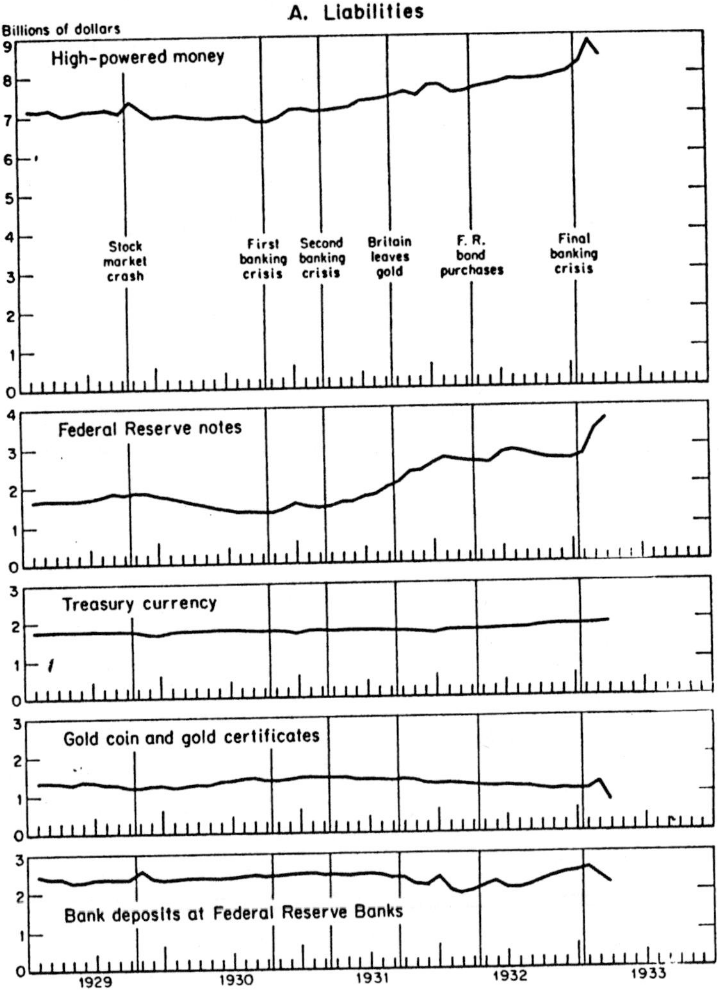

Chart 2. High-powered money, by assets and liabilities of the Treasury and Federal Reserve banks, monthly, 1929–March 1933.

Note: Federal Reserve notes, Treasury currency, and gold coin and certificates are outside the Treasury and Federal Reserve Banks.
Source: A. Liabilities. *A Monetary History*, Table B-3, pp. 803–804, col. 1 (high-powered money); Table A-2, pp. 739–740, col. 2 (bank deposits at Federal Reserve Banks); *Banking and Monetary Statistics*, pp. 411–412 (Federal Reserve notes, Treasury currency, gold coin and gold certificates), plus $287 million deducted by Federal Reserve added back to gold coin, seasonally adjusted by us.

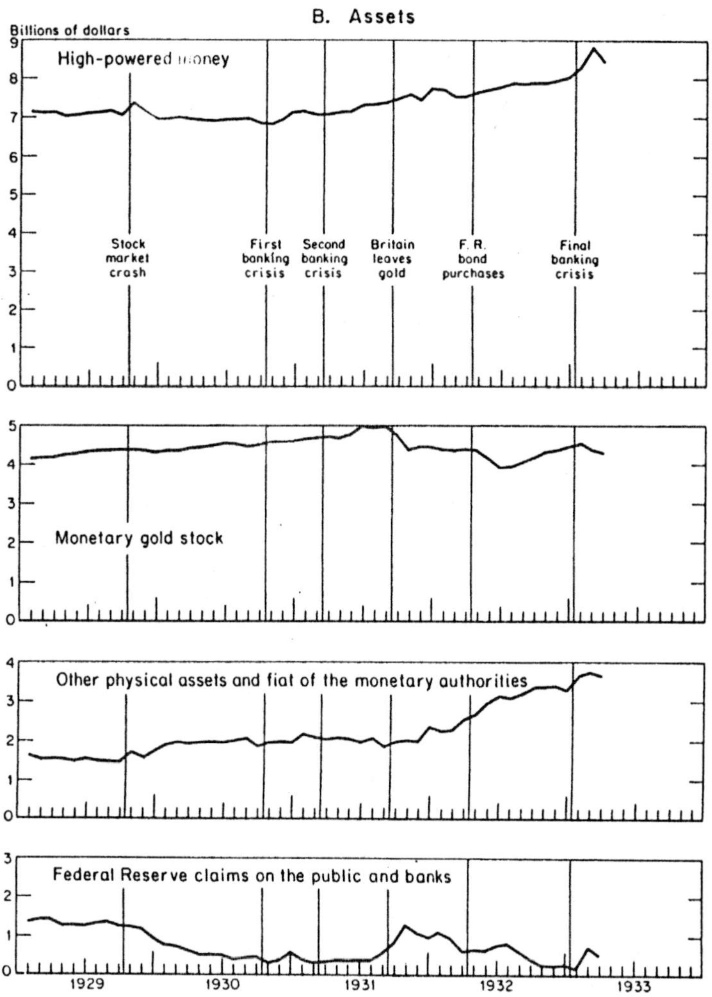

Chart 2. (concluded)

B. Assets. *Ibid.*, p. 537 (monetary gold stock) plus $287 million deducted by Federal Reserve added back, seasonally adjusted by us; pp. 375–376, Federal Reserve credit outstanding and System holdings of U.S. government securities were each corrected for seasonal movements, and the latter subtracted from the former (Federal Reserve claims on the public and banks); high-powered money minus monetary gold stock minus Federal Reserve claims on the public and banks (other physical assets and fiat of the monetary authorities).

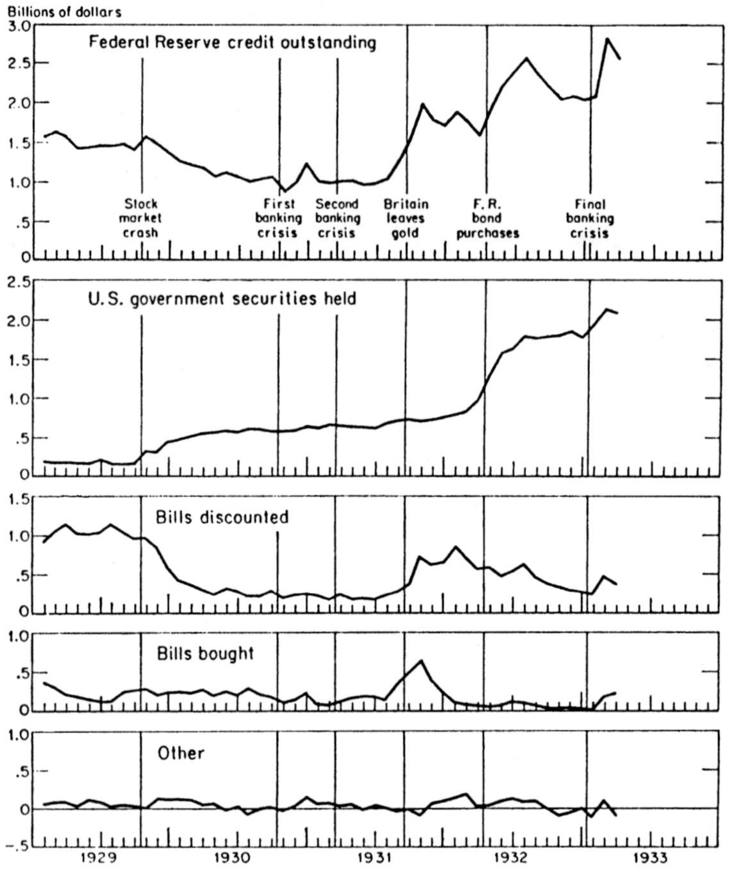

Chart 3. Federal Reserve credit outstanding, by types, monthly, 1929–March 1933.

Source: *Banking and Monetary Statistics*, pp. 375–376 (Federal Reserve credit outstanding; U.S. government securities held; bills discounted; bills bought), seasonally adjusted by us. "Other" obtained as a residual. All seasonal adjustments are by Shiskin-Eisenpress method.

borrowers without pressing for their immediate payment. That is the reason the monetary effect of the crash shows up in our money stock series as a sharp increase in demand deposits and the reason the increase was in New York City. Indeed, the increase in our estimates understates the magnitude of the action of the New York banks. Some of the loans taken over were for the accounts of out-of-town banks and were matched by an increase in interbank deposits of $510 million in New York City weekly reporting member banks. But our money stock estimates exclude interbank deposits.

To be able to expand deposits, the New York banks had to be able either to raise the ratio of deposits to reserves or to acquire additional reserves. The first was impossible because New York banks had no excess reserves. Indeed, the ratio of deposits to high-powered reserves was lower in New York than in the rest of the country because of the higher legal reserve requirements imposed on banks in central reserve cities. Therefore the increase in deposits in New York relative to deposits in the rest of the country in October 1929 produced a decline in the average deposit-reserve ratio for the country as a whole. Accordingly, the New York banks had to and did acquire additional reserves, as the bulge in high-powered money shows. They did so in the week of the crash partly by borrowing from the Federal Reserve Bank of New York, which, in Harrison's words, kept its "discount window wide open and let it be known that member banks might borrow freely to establish the reserves required against the large increase in deposits resulting from the taking over of loans called by others;"[3] and partly by virtue of the purchase by the New York Bank of about $160 million of government securities. That purchase was far in excess of the amount the System's Open Market Investment Committee had been authorized to purchase for System account. It was made by the New York Bank on its own initiative for its own account without consulting either the Open Market Investment Committee or the Board. Though subsequently ratified, it was, the occasion for another battle in the struggle between the Bank and the Board, which had important effects on Federal Reserve policy during the rest of the contraction.

3. *The George Leslie Harrison Papers on the Federal Reserve System.* Harrison was a deputy governor (1920–1928), the governor (1928–1936), and president (1936–1941) of the Federal Reserve Bank of New York. Harrison's personal files, covering the period of his association with the Bank (1920–1940), contain many official memoranda and other documents. Items are identified by the titles of sections of the Papers, as follows: Conversations, 1926–1940 (cited as Harrison, Conversations); Office Memoranda, 1921–1940 (Harrison, Office), both records of conversations, with some duplication; Miscellaneous Letters and Reports, 1920–1940 (Harrison Miscellaneous), copies of correspondence with the Federal Reserve Board and others; Open Market Investment Committee, 1928–1940 (Harrison, Open Market), minutes of regular meetings of the executive committee, memoranda, correspondence, resolutions; Governors Conference, 1921–1940 (Harrison, Governors), detailed agenda for meetings; Discussion Notes, 1930–1940 (Harrison Notes), minutes of meetings of the board of directors of the Federal Reserve Bank of New York and of the executive committee; Special Memoranda, 1933–1940 (Harrison, Special), discussions of policy questions prepared by the Bank's research staff. Harrison, Miscellaneous, Vol. I, Letter, dated Nov. 27, 1929, Harrison to all governors. During the week ending Oct. 30, 1929, discounts increased $200 million at all Reserve Banks, of which $130 million was the increase in New York City weekly reporting member bank borrowings from the New York Reserve Bank.

The actions taken by the New York Reserve Bank were timely and effective. Despite the stock market crash, there were no panic increases in money market rates such as those in past market crises, and no indirect effects on confidence in banks which might have arisen if there had been any sizable defaults on security loans. Harrison himself expressed the view that "it is not at all unlikely that had we not bought governments so freely, thus supplementing the reserves built up by large additional discounts, the stock exchange might have had to yield to the tremendous pressure brought to bear upon it to close on some one of those very bad days the last part of October."[4] Harrison may have overstated the case – he was, after all, writing in defense of the actions the New York Bank had taken – but that is by no means certain.

In the month following the crash, there was a reversal. Deposits declined, as more lasting arrangements for the transfer and reduction of stock market loans replaced the temporary shift of many of those loans to New York banks. The changes in deposits produced a decline in the deposit-currency ratio, following the rise in October, and a decline in the deposit–reserve ratio milder than that in October. High-powered money also declined as a result of a reduction in bills discounted and in the gold stock, generally attributed to the withdrawal by foreigners of funds from the New York money market.[5] The net effect was to leave the stock of money after the crash at a lower level than before. At the end of November 1929, the stock of money was $1.3 billion, or 3 per cent, less than it had been at the end of September. By the end of December, most of the loss had been made up; the stock of money was about $0.5 billion, or 1 per cent, less than in September. These changes were concentrated in demand deposits. From December 1929 to October 1930, the stock of money fluctuated around a roughly constant level, though with a mild downward trend. In October 1930, the stock of money was almost the same as it had been in November 1929 and nearly 2 per cent below its level at the end of December 1929.

For the period from August 1929 to October 1930 as a whole, the money stock declined by 2.6 per cent. High-powered money alone

4. *Ibid.*, letter, dated Nov. 27, 1929, Harrison to all governors.

5. The return flow of foreign funds gave temporary relief to the foreign exchanges, which had been under pressure during the period of speculation. Foreign currencies had depreciated vis-à-vis the dollar, while foreigners were remitting funds to the security markets here. Before the peak in stock prices in 1929, the prices of those currencies had declined to the United States' gold import point. After the crash, the return flow of funds raised their prices to the gold export point. For example, the pound was as low as $4.845857 in Sept. 1929 and in Dec. was as high as $4.882010 (the figures are noon buying rates for cable transfers to New York, from *Commercial and Financial Chronicle*, Sept. 21, 1929, p. 1969; Dec. 27, 1929, p. 4017).

declined by 5 per cent. However, the deposit-currency ratio rose by about 7 per cent, enough to offset a minor decline in the deposit-reserve ratio as well as half the decline in high-powered money. In October 1930, the deposit–currency ratio stood at the highest level reached at any time in the 93 years covered by our data, except only for a fractionally higher peak reached in the month of the stock market crash. As we noted earlier, the public was clearly not greatly concerned at the time about the safety of bank deposits. But the high ratio made the System peculiarly vulnerable to the development of any such concern, as the following years were to demonstrate so tragically.

The decline in high-powered money occurred despite an increase of $210 million in the gold stock and of $470 million in the fiat of the monetary authorities. The latter increase reflected mostly a rise in government securities held by the System, i.e., the substitution of noninterest-bearing for interest-bearing government debt. Those expansionary factors were more than offset by a decline in Federal Reserve private claims of $1,020 million – $100 million in bills bought and $920 million in bills discounted and other claims (see Chart 2B). Ultimately then, it was the failure of the Reserve System to replace the decline in discounts by other credit outstanding that was responsible for the decline in the stock of money.

The decline in discounts took place despite sharp reductions in discount rates – at the New York Bank, from 6 per cent to 2½ per cent in June 1930. [See Chart 4 on p. 601.] The successive declines in discount rates – the first of which came in November 1929, three months after the date set by the National Bureau as the reference cycle peak – though sharp and rapid by earlier standards, took place during a time when there was a sharp decline in the demand for loans and an increase in the demand for assets regarded as safe. Both made for a sharp decline in market interest rates. Though the discount rate fell absolutely, it probably rose relative to the relevant market interest rates, namely, those on short-term securities with essentially zero risk of default. Hence, discounting became less attractive. It is perhaps worth noting that this is not merely a retrospective judgment. The New York Reserve Bank favored more rapid reductions in the rate than those made. Harrison said in May 1931 that "if there had been no Federal Reserve System in October, 1929, money rates would probably have come down more rapidly than they had." In September 1930, Adolph Miller of the Federal Reserve Board said at a meeting with all the governors, "Money is not really cheap nor easy." In mid-1930, Harold L. Reed, in the second of his two excellent books on the Federal Reserve System said: "In the writer's opinion, however, there was much stronger ground for holding that the rate reductions had been too gradual and long delayed" than that they had been too rapid.[6]

As the near-constancy of the deposit–reserve ratio indicates, there was no tendency of banks to accumulate excess reserves. It has been contended with respect to later years (particularly during the period after 1934, when large excess reserves accumulated) that increases in high-powered money, through expansion of Federal Reserve credit or other means, would simply have been added to bank reserves and would not have been used to increase the money stock. In other words, a rise in high-powered money would have been offset by a decline in the deposit–reserve ratio. We shall argue later that the contention is invalid even for the later period. It is clearly not relevant to the period from August 1929 to October 1930. During that period, additional reserves would almost certainly have been put to use promptly. Hence, the decline in the stock of money is not only arithmetically attributable to the decline in Federal Reserve credit outstanding; it is economically a direct result of that decline.

Onset of first banking crisis, October 1930

The onset of the banking crisis is clearly marked in all three proximate determinants but particularly in the deposit ratios (Chart 1). From a peak of 11.5 in October 1930, the ratio of deposits to currency declined sharply – a decline that was to carry the ratio, with only minor interruptions along the way, to a low of 4.4 in March 1933. The deposit–reserve ratio likewise began a decline that was to carry it from a level of 12.9 in October 1930 – the all-time high was 13.4 in April 1929 – to a level of 8.4 in March 1933. These declines brought the deposit–currency ratio back to its level at the turn of the century and the deposit–reserve ratio to its level in 1912. They thus wiped out the whole of the much heralded spread in the use of deposits and "economy" in reserves achieved under the Reserve System.

The decline in the stock of money as a result of the banking crisis – a decline of slightly more than 3 per cent from October 1930 to January 1931, or more than in the preceding fourteen months – was clearly a result of the declines in the two deposit ratios, since high-powered money rose by 5 per cent. As Charts 2B and 3 show, the rise of $340

6. . . . The quotation from Harrison is from Harrison, Notes, Vol. I, May 21, 1931; from Miller, Charles S. Hamlin, Hamlin Papers, Manuscript Division, Library of Congress, Diary, Vol. 18, Sept. 25, 1930, p. 86; from Reed, *Federal Reserve Policy, 1921–1930*, New York, McGraw-Hill, 1930, p. 191. This may not have been Miller's view earlier in the year. In May, Hamlin reported, "Miller said the Federal Reserve Bank of New York was obsessed with the idea that easy money would help the business recession" (Hamlin, Diary, Vol. 17, May 9, 1930, p. 151).

million in high-powered money, seasonally adjusted, was produced partly by an inflow of $84 million of gold[7] – the source that had always been the major reliance in pre–Federal Reserve crises – partly by an increase of $117 million in Federal Reserve credit outstanding. The increase in Federal Reserve credit consisted partly of a rise of $41 million in government securities, the balance of a rise in float. A rise in discounts just about offset a decline in bills bought. There was a brief spurt of roughly $200 million in bills discounted in the two weeks after the failure of the Bank of United States, but it does not show up in the seasonally adjusted end-of-month figures plotted in Chart 3.

The rise in Federal Reserve credit certainly helped to offset some of the immediate effects of the banking crisis. But the movement was minor in magnitude. Many an earlier year-end shows rises of comparable magnitude and, even at its peak in December 1930, seasonally adjusted Federal Reserve credit was only 84 per cent of its level in the summer of 1929 when the System was seeking to curb speculation. The one other measure taken by the System in reaction to the banking crisis was a reduction in late December 1930 in the New York Reserve Bank's discount rate to 2 per cent – to reassure the public.[8]

The rise in Federal Reserve Bank credit was temporary. After December 1930, discounts declined, bills bought were allowed to run off without replacement, while government security holdings increased by only a small fraction of the combined decline in discounts and bills bought. High-powered money rose in January 1931, only because a continued gold inflow offset the decline in Federal Reserve credit. It declined in February despite continued gold inflow, and rose slightly in March along with a minor rise in Federal Reserve credit and the gold stock. The decline in Federal Reserve credit from December 1930 to March 1931 was greater than the gold inflow. In effect, the System was not only sterilizing the gold inflow but exerting a contractionary influence greater than the expansionary influence of the gold inflow.

Despite the reduction in high-powered money in February 1931, the money stock rose a bit because of a rise in both deposit ratios, as the

7. The gold inflows reflected partly the Hawley–Smoot Tariff Act passed in June 1930, which raised the tariff to the highest level up to that time in U.S. history; partly the reduction of U.S. lending abroad, and the continuance at a high level of interest and dividends on investments abroad and of war debt payments; partly the consequence of U.S. deflation on imports and exports.

8. Governor Harrison wrote, "he had been urged from many quarters to make a reassuring statement which might aid in quieting the banking situation. Such a statement was practically impossible because to be strong enough to do any good it would run the risk of being contradicted by any small bank failure which might thereafter occur. The rate reduction, apart from other reasons, served as a method of stating to the public that money was freely available" (Harrison, Open Market, Vol. II, Jan. 21, 1931).

wave of bank failures died down and confidence in banks was somewhat restored. As suggested earlier, if the rises in the deposit ratios had been reinforced by a vigorous expansion in high-powered money, instead of being offset by a reduction, the ground gained might have been consolidated and extended.

Onset of second banking crisis, March 1931

The onset of the second banking crisis is clearly marked in Chart 1 by the renewed decline in the deposit ratios and the beginning of a decline in the money stock at the fastest rate so far in the contraction. In the five months from March to August, to exclude wholly the effects of Britain's departure from gold in September, the stock of money fell by 5¼ per cent, or by almost exactly the same percentage as in all the preceding nineteen months of the contraction. This was at the phenomenal annual rate of 13 per cent, yet the rate was soon to rise still higher.

As after the first banking crisis, the decline in the stock of money was entirely a consequence of the fall in the deposit ratios. High-powered money rose, this time by 4 per cent from March to August, and so offset nearly half the contractionary effect of the declining deposit ratios. There were, however, two differences between the second banking crisis and the first one some six months earlier.

(1) This time, the rise in high-powered money was produced almost entirely by the continued gold inflow, whereas earlier there had been at least a temporary increase in Federal Reserve credit, which helped to absorb some of the initial effects of the crisis. Federal Reserve credit remained almost perfectly stable, rising slightly only in July and August 1931. Despite the unprecedented liquidation of the commercial banking system, the books of the "lender of last resort" show a decline in bills discounted from the end of February to the end of April – a period when the usual seasonal movement is upward – and a rise from April to the end of August that made the whole increase from February to August less than the usual seasonal increase; they show irregular increases and decreases in bills bought, with the total at the end of August $75 million higher than at the end of February, but still below its level at the turn of the year; and they show an increase of $130 million in government securities purchased, the whole of the increase beginning late in June. Of this increase, $50 million was a purely technical move rather than a reaction to domestic financial difficulties: it simply offset other reductions in credit outstanding. The remaining $80 million represented a deliberate, if timid, move to contribute ease.[9]

9. Federal Reserve Board, *Annual Report* for 1931, pp. 7–8. These figures are all as of Wednesdays. Of the $130 million of government securities purchased, $80 million was for System account

(2) The second crisis lasted longer. In late 1930, there were signs of improvement after two or three months. On this occasion, as Chart 1 shows, the deposit–currency ratio – the most sensitive indicator of the public's attitude toward banks – not only continued to fall but fell at an increasing rate. There was no sign that the crisis was drawing to an end when Britain's departure from gold intensified it.

Aside from the modest open market purchases in July and August, the only other domestic action of the System relevant to the money stock was a further reduction in the discount rate of the New York Reserve Bank to 1½ per cent in May – before the sharp June increase in bank failures. As we have seen, the reduction did not stimulate borrowing. On a different front, potentially of great consequence for the domestic money stock, the System participated in loans to foreign banks as part of an international effort to avert financial catastrophe abroad.[10]

Britain's departure from gold, September 1931

In the few months after the departure of Britain from the gold standard, the proximate determinants of the money stock plotted in Chart 1 continued the pattern of the preceding five months, but the pattern was even more emphatic. The stock of money fell still faster: in the five months from August 1931 to January 1932, it fell by 12 per cent – compared with 5 per cent in the preceding five months – or at the

and $50 million for the New York Bank's own account (Harrison, Open Market, Vol. II, minutes of June 22 and Aug. 11, 1931, Open Market Policy Conference meetings; Miscellaneous, Vol. I, letter, dated July 9, 1931, Harrison to Seay; Notes, Vol. I, July 16, 1931, and Vol. II, Aug. 4, 1931). The latter purchase was made to offset the effect of the transfer of foreign-held balances from the acceptance market to Federal Reserve Banks.

10. During the second and third quarters of 1931, the Federal Reserve Bank of New York in association with other Federal Reserve Banks purchased prime commercial bills with guaranteed repayment in gold from the Austrian National Bank, the National Bank of Hungary, the Reichsbank, and the Bank of England. The credit agreements with the Federal Reserve Banks at their separate maximums aggregated about $156 million and were renewed several times. Reserve Bank holdings of bills payable in foreign currencies increased from $1 million at the end of March to $145 million in August (Federal Reserve Board, *Annual Report* for 1931, pp. 12–13).

See also Harrison, Miscellaneous, Vol. I, letter, dated July 9, 1931, Harrison to McDougal; Open Market, Vol. II, minutes of meeting, Aug. 11, 1931; and Notes, Vol. I, June 1, 15, 22; July 13, 16, 1931; Vol. II, July 28, 30; Aug. 4; Sept. 24, 28, 1931, for discussion of the foreign credits. One of the directors of the New York Reserve Bank, Charles E. Mitchell, was quoted as saying, "In all of these cases, he was concerned about the soundness of the operation to be undertaken by the Federal reserve banks which, in their domestic business, take as few chances as possible," and "the thing which bothered him with regard to these foreign credits was the risk involved when, at home, the Federal reserve banks take no risks" (Harrison, Notes, Vol. I, June 22, 1931).

annual rate of 31 per cent – compared with 13 per cent. High-powered money again rose, this time by about 4½ per cent, and again offset only part, and this time a smaller part, of the effect of the declines in the deposit ratios, particularly the deposit-currency ratio. The banks were so hard pressed to meet the demands of their depositors that, try though they did, they were able to do little to lower the ratio of their deposit liabilities to their reserves. That had to wait for a more propitious time, which is why the most rapid decline in the deposit–reserve ratio came later when the decline in the deposit–currency ratio had tapered off, and the slowest decline came earlier when the deposit–currency ratio was declining fastest. As we shall see in later chapters, much of the adjustment on the part of the banks did not come until after the end of the business contraction and the beginning of recovery. The timing relations between changes in the two deposit ratios during the 1931–1932 segment of the contraction repeated the tendencies we have observed in each earlier banking crisis.

The major difference, aside from scale, between the five-month period, August 1931–January 1932, and the preceding five months is the source of the rise in high-powered money, which does not show up in Chart 1 but does in Charts 2B and 3. Up to August 1931, high-powered money had risen chiefly as a result of gold inflows. The period after Britain's departure from gold saw a sharp outflow, particularly in September and October 1931, large enough to offset the gold inflows during the earlier segments of the contraction. High-powered money rose because Federal Reserve credit outstanding rose. Federal Reserve credit rose primarily because of the sharp rise in discounts as banks, having no other recourse open to them, were driven to borrowing from the Reserve System, despite the unprecedentedly sharp rises in discount rates in October 1931. Bills bought increased substantially in September and October, but then were allowed to run off so that, by January 1932, they had fallen below their level at the end of August 1931. All told, from August 1931 to January 1932, the rise of $330 million in high-powered money was accounted for by a rise of $560 million in discounts, $80 million in government securities, $270 million in other assets of the monetary authorities, offset by a decline of $580 million in the gold stock.

During those five months when high-powered money rose by $330 million, currency held by the public increased by $720 million. The extra $390 million had to come from bank reserves. Since banks were unwilling and unable to draw down reserves relative to their deposits,[11] the $390 million, amounting to 12 per cent of their total reserves in

11. At the end of Jan. 1932, their excess reserves totaled $40 million.

August 1931, could be freed for currency use only by a multiple contraction of deposits. The multiple worked out to roughly 14, so deposits fell by $5,727 million or by 15 per cent of their level in August 1931. It was the necessity of reducing deposits by $14 in order to make $1 available for the public to hold as currency that made the loss of confidence in banks so cumulative and so disastrous. Here was the famous multiple expansion process of the banking system in vicious reserse. That phenomenon, too, explains how seemingly minor measures had such major effects. The provision of $400 million of additional high-powered money to meet the currency drain without a decline in bank reserves could have prevented a decline of nearly $6 billion in deposits.

In discussing the 1907 crisis [in an earlier section,] we showed how the rise in deposit ratios had made the banking system more vulnerable to an attempted conversion of deposits to currency. The situation in 1931 was even more extreme. At no time in 1907 did the public hold more than $6 in deposits for every $1 it held in currency; in March 1931, when the second banking crisis began, it held over $10 in deposits for every $1 of currency, an amount it succeeded in reducing to under $7 by January 1932. In 1907, the banks owned less than $9 in deposits for every $1 of high-powered money they held as reserves; in March 1931, they owed more than $12. The more extensive use of deposits – widely regarded during the twenties as a sign of the great progress and refinement of the American financial structure – and the higher ratio of deposits to reserves – widely regarded as a sign of the effectiveness of the new Reserve System in promoting "economy" in the use of reserves – made the monetary system much more vulnerable to a widespread loss of confidence in banks. The defenses deliberately constructed against such an eventuality turned out in practice to be far less effective than those that had grown up in the earlier era.

When bank failures tapered off in February and March 1932, the deposit–currency ratio temporarily stopped falling. However, high-powered money declined by $160 million in those two months, despite a dwindling of gold outflows, mainly as a result of changes in Reserve Bank credit: a decline of $280 million in discounts, and a continued decline of $50 million in bills bought, while government security holdings rose by about $180 million. Discounts declined because banks took advantage of the pause in the demands on them to repay some of their borrowings. They followed that course despite a reduction in the New York Bank's discount rate to 3 per cent in February. The banks took advantage of the pause also to strengthen their reserve position somewhat, so the deposit–reserve ratio fell slightly from January to March 1932. The result was that the stock of money continued to decline, though at a slower pace. In these two months it fell by another 2 per cent, an annual rate of 13 per cent, which can be described as moderate only by comparison with the preceding 31 per cent annual rate of decline.

Beginning of large-scale open market purchases, April 1932

The beginning of the purchase of government securities on a large scale by the Federal Reserve System in April 1932, involving purchase of $350 million during that month (see Chart 3 for seasonally adjusted end-of-the-month figures), had no immediate effect on the behavior of the stock of money. It declined another 4½ per cent for another four months, or at an annual rate of 14 per cent. The decline then slowed up sharply, the money stock falling one-half of 1 per cent in the two months from July to September 1932, or at the annual rate of 3 per cent. From September on, it rose mildly until January 1933, when the money stock was one-half of 1 per cent higher than in September 1932, implying an average rate of growth of about 1¾ per cent per year.

The reason the bond purchases had no greater effect to begin with is that they were offset in part by a renewed outflow of gold and the rest was more than offset by continued declines in the deposit ratios. From April to July 1932, when Reserve System holdings of government securities went up by roughly $1 billion, the gold stock fell by about half that amount, most of the outflow going to France. At the same time, a renewed flurry of bank failures in June produced a further appreciable decline in the deposit–currency ratio, and the continued efforts of the banks to strengthen their position produced a further decline in the deposit-reserve ratio.

The gold drain ceased in mid-June and was replaced by an inflow. Over the rest of the year, the gold stock rose by $600 million, bringing the gold stock in January 1933 above its level a year earlier. Reserve System bond purchases ceased in August 1932. Discounts and bills bought fell from July on, so that total Federal Reserve credit outstanding reached a peak in that month and fell by $500 million from then to January 1933. Nonetheless, high-powered money continued to rise at roughly a constant rate from April 1932 to January 1933 because of the reversal of the gold flow, plus an increase of $140 million in national bank notes. The latter increase was due to an amendment attached to the Home Loan Bank Act of July 1932, which broadened the range of government bonds eligible as security for national bank notes.[12] Once

12. The amendment permitted use for a period of three years of all government bonds bearing interest at 3⅜ per cent or less, including future bond issues during the period. From August

the deposit–currency ratio reached its trough in July 1932, the rise in high-powered money plus the rise in the deposit–currency ratio were enough to offset the continued fall in the deposit–reserve ratio and produce the pattern of change in the money stock already described.

The form taken by the improvement in the banking position, recorded in the deposit–reserve ratio, is worth noting because it presaged a development that was to be important in the next few years. Banks began to accumulate substantial reserves in excess of legal requirements. Since the Reserve System regarded the so-called "excess reserves" as a sign of monetary ease, their accumulation contributed to adoption of the policy of keeping total government securities at the level reached in early August. Excess reserves were interpreted by many as a sign of lack of demand for bank funds, as meaning that monetary authorities could make "credit" available but could not guarantee its use, a position most succinctly conveyed by the saying, "monetary policy is like a string; you can pull on it but you can't push on it." In our view, this interpretation is wrong. The reserves were excess only in a strictly legal sense. The banks had discovered in the course of two traumatic years that neither legal reserves nor the presumed availability of a "lender of last resort" was of much avail in time of trouble, and this lesson was shortly to be driven home yet again. Little wonder that the reserves they found it prudent to hold exceeded substantially the reserves they were legally required to hold.[13] As noted above, their reaction was the same as in earlier crises, only greater in magnitude in response to the greater severity of the crisis.

The banking panic of 1933

The final banking crisis, which terminated in the banking holiday early in March 1933, was in most essential respects a duplicate of the two preceding ones but still more drastic. The money stock fell 12 per cent in the two months from January to March 1933, or at an annual rate of decline of 78 per cent. For reasons we discuss in detail in the next chapter, our estimates overstate the decline in the stock of money, but hardly any reasonable allowance for error could cut the rate of decline to

1929 up to July 1932 there was a slight increase – $60 million – in national bank notes in circulation, as national banks exercised somewhat more fully their right to issue on the security of three government bond issues bearing interest at 2 per cent, which had the circulation privilege.

13. See Chap. 8, sect. 1, for evidence on this view. In Dec. 1932, Governor Meyer said that "if the banks knew that there was going to be a constant amount of excess reserves over a long period, that amount could be relatively small and still be more effective than a much larger but uncertain amount. We have not obtained the full effect of recent large excess reserves because of uncertainty as to our future policy" (Harrison, Notes, Vol. III, Dec. 22, 1932).

less than the 31 per cent rate of decline from August 1931 to January 1932. As in the earlier crises, high-powered money rose, primarily as a result of a rise in discounts and a lesser rise in bills bought. Chart 3 shows an appreciable rise in government securities. This rise is produced by the seasonal adjustment. There is no rise in the original figures. The early months of the years before 1933 were generally characterized by a decline in the Reserve portfolio of government securities in response to the return flow of currency from circulation usual at that season. In 1933, there was, of course, a drain of currency rather than a return flow: government securities were nevertheless reduced in January by $90 million, but then raised in February by $70 million, to a level at which they also stood at the end of March. Seasonal adjustment of the figures converted the decline in January and the modest rise in February to appreciable increases, and raised the original March figure only slightly less.

The banking holiday in March renders all the money figures non-comparable with earlier ones, so we consider the change from January to February alone, as an approximation of the decline up to the bank holiday. In that one month the money stock fell 4½ per cent, or at an annual rate of 56 per cent. Currency held by the public rose by over $600 million, high-powered money by $535 million – almost the same. But even the remaining $65 million which had to be supplied from bank reserves, plus the scramble by banks for reserves, produced a decline in deposits of over $2 billion in that one month, or nearly 7½ per cent of the already shrunken total. This time the multiplier was not 14 but 29.

The major monetary difference between the final banking crisis and the earlier ones was that for the first time the internal drain in part clearly took the form of a drain of gold coin and certificates. As Chart 2A shows, the volume of gold coin and certificates had risen mildly in 1930 but then had been constant or declining until the onset of the final crisis. In January 1933, the amount of gold coin and gold certificates outside the Treasury and Federal Reserve Banks was $420 million less than at its peak in December 1930, $340 million less than at its previous January peak in 1931. The decline was apparently in some measure the result of a deliberate policy on the part of the Federal Reserve System of adding to its gold reserves by paying out Federal Reserve notes instead of gold certificates where feasible, a reversal of the policy adopted during the twenties to keep down the apparent reserve ratio.[14] Though the total of gold coin and gold certificates declined,

14. Gold certificates in circulation declined in all but three months in 1931 and 1932 – when the certificates may have been paid out partly because of a shortage of other forms of currency, as in

the amount of gold coin alone increased by nearly $120 million, from $65 million in April 1931 to $181 million in December 1932. That increase may have reflected a preference for gold coin in the earlier period, though to some extent it must reflect the growth of all forms of currency as opposed to deposits. But if it does reflect a preference for gold, that preference was not sufficiently widespread or dramatic to attract much attention. In February and March 1933, the situation was entirely different, as shown by the sharp spurt in gold coin and certificates in early 1933 in Chart 2A. Fears of devaluation were widespread and the public's preference for gold was unmistakable. On February 23, 1933, Harrison told the directors of the New York Reserve Bank, "there is little that foreigners can do to hurt our gold position, . . . the real danger comes from domestic sources."[15]

Feb. and Mar. 1933 before the bank holiday – for a net change of $460 million. Although there is no acknowledgment in the *Annual Report* for 1931 and 1932 that such a retirement policy was in effect, it is significant that the *Federal Reserve Bulletin* (Nov. 1931, p. 604) contains the following comment:

> In considering the gold position of the country, it should be noted also that there are $1,000,000,000 of gold certificates in circulation, a large part of which can be retired by the Federal reserve banks by substituting an equivalent amount of Federal [reserve] notes. The retirement of gold certificates would increase the gold holdings of the reserve banks, and of this increase 40 per cent would be required as reserves against the additional Federal reserve notes and 60 per cent would be added to the system's excess reserves.

15. He went on to say, "During the last ten days out-payments of gold coin at this bank, and, probably, at all of the Federal reserve banks have been heavier than in any recent similar period. This movement represents something more than the hoarding of currency, which reflects a distrust of banks; it represents in addition a distrust of the currency itself and it is inspired by talk of devaluation of the dollar and inflation of the currency" (Harrison, Notes, Vol. III).

Harrison made efforts to get banks to discourage hoarding. He suggested that they refuse to provide facilities for storage of gold and to grant loans against the collateral of an equivalent amount of gold. With respect to the first, he suggested that banks impose no obstacles to the acquisition of gold but make no offer of safe-keeping facilities; with respect to the second, he advised banks to decline a loan to buy gold on the ground that it was a loan for a capital purpose. He said, "I saw no occasion for a member bank, in these times particularly when so many people who needed credit for business purposes could not obtain the credit, to make loans to their customers for the purpose of buying gold to hoard. It was nothing but a speculative loan gambling on our going off the gold standard" (Conversations, Vol. II, Feb. 9, 1933). Direct pressure had come full circle.

19

The fall in the demand for money

PETER TEMIN

The outstanding volume of the principal short-term credit instruments in the years around 1929 is shown in Table 1. Commercial paper and bankers' acceptances were used to finance domestic activity and international trade. Brokers' loans were used to finance purchases of other financial assets. And loans by commercial banks included both commercial loans – serving the same purposes as commercial paper – and stock exchange loans. Since most of the brokers' loans listed came from banks, there is substantial double counting in that category.

Most short-term credit was extended in these years in the form of bank loans. These loans were issued in a wide variety of localities and in widely varying circumstances. We cannot hope to describe fully the changes in this variety of local markets. Instead, we look at the rates on bank loans for New York City, which can be expected to reflect any monetary stringency that existed. This rate moved closely with the rates in other cities, although it is somewhat lower than rates charged by smaller banks.[1]

In addition to this interest rate, we will examine the rates on the other instruments listed in Table 1. Although the amounts outstanding of these other instruments were smaller than the volume of bank loans, the movements of rates in these markets can be expected to reflect the changes in monetary conditions in the economy. Since we are looking for evidence of stringency, not following a causal pathway from the money supply to the rest of the economy, we do not have to restrict ourselves to the short-term instruments used most widely.

These interest rates are graphed on a monthly basis for the interwar period in Figures 1 and 2. Weekly observations are available for some of the interest rates shown, but the weekly patterns do not show any

1. Board of Governors of the Federal Reserve System, *Banking and Monetary Statistics*, Washington, D.C., Government Printing Office, 1943.

Table 1. *Volume of short-term credit outstanding, 1928–1932 (millions of dollars)*

	1928	1929	June 1930	1931	1932
Commercial Paper	503	274	527	298	103
Bankers' Acceptances	1,026	1,113	1,305	1,368	747
Brokers' Loans	4,900	7,070	3,795	1,600	335
U.S. Bills and Certificates	1,252	1,640	1,420	2,246	3,341
Loans by Commercial Banks	34,035	35,738	34,539	29,166	21,806

SOURCE: *Banking and Monetary Statistics*, pp. 19, 465–66, 494, 511.

movements not present in the monthly data. Three rises can be seen clearly in these rates, in 1920, 1929, and 1931. They are not present in all of the rates, but the movements of the various rates are sufficiently similar to allow us to group these three years together as periods of some monetary stringency. In addition, the magnitudes of the rises in 1920 and 1929 are sufficiently similar that there is no reason apparent in these data to think that either of these periods of stringency was worse than the other.[2]

It is possible, in other words, that the downturn in 1929 was caused in part by monetary stringency. The Federal Reserve was trying to tighten up in order to dampen or break the stock-market boom. Many observers, including Keynes, thought that this action would have consequences for the economy as a whole.[3] But, it must be remembered, this is the answer to the wrong question. While the downturn originating in 1929 is interesting, we are trying to discover why the downturn was so much larger and more sustained in the few years just after 1929 than in the other interwar depressions. The interest-rate rises in Figures 1 and 2 are similar in the periods just preceding the first two downturns. They suggest that the monetary stringency in 1929 was no larger than in 1920. Why should the effects have been so much larger?

This question can be posed rather differently. We have been looking for evidence of monetary restriction. Let us turn for a minute to the actual mechanism by which such a restriction causes changes in the economy. The mechanism has been specified in slightly different ways by different authors, but it always involves changes in interest rates and

2. The monetary restriction in 1929 may have been more severe than the one in 1920 if the demand for money was also falling at that time. As noted above, interest rates show only the net effect of the two movements. But if the demand for money was falling more rapidly in 1929 than in 1920, then this is the phenomenon that needs to be explained.

3. John Maynard Keynes, *Treatise on Money*, 2 vols. New York: Harcourt Brace, 1930.

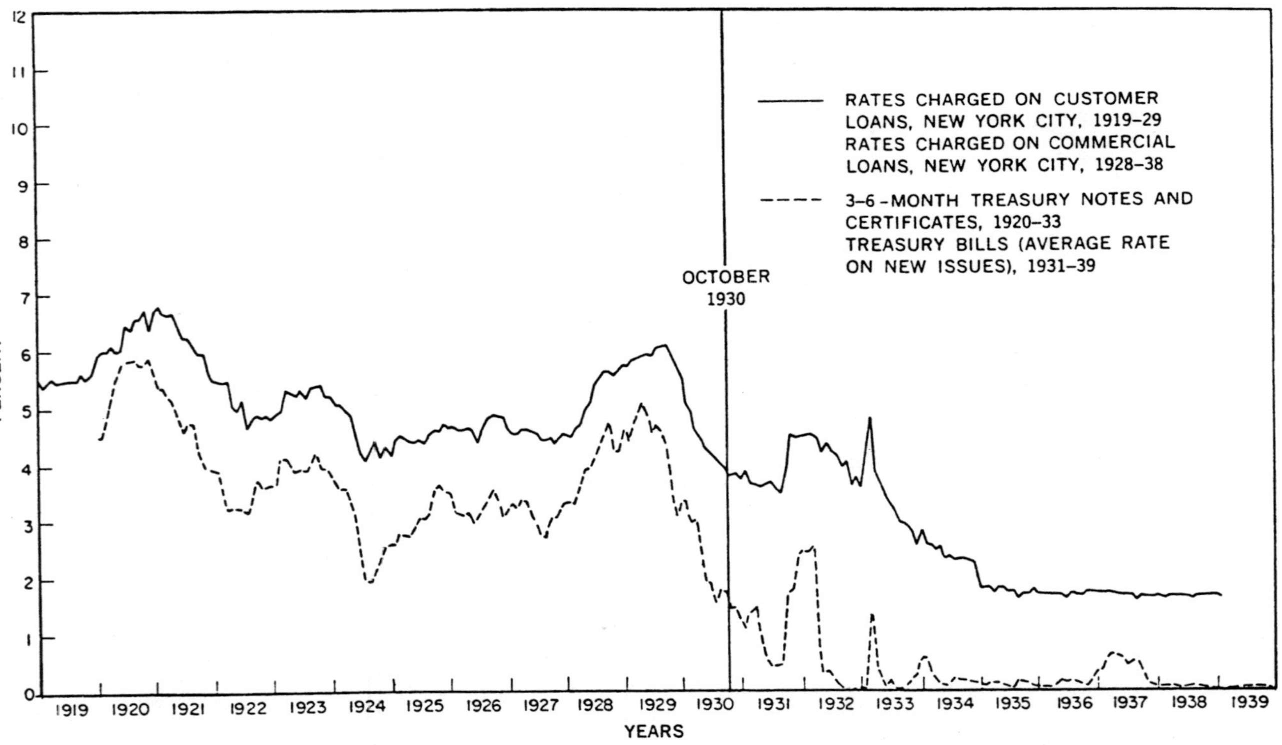

Figure 1. Two short-term interest rates, monthly, 1919–1939.

Source: *Banking and Monetary Statistics*, pp. 450–451.

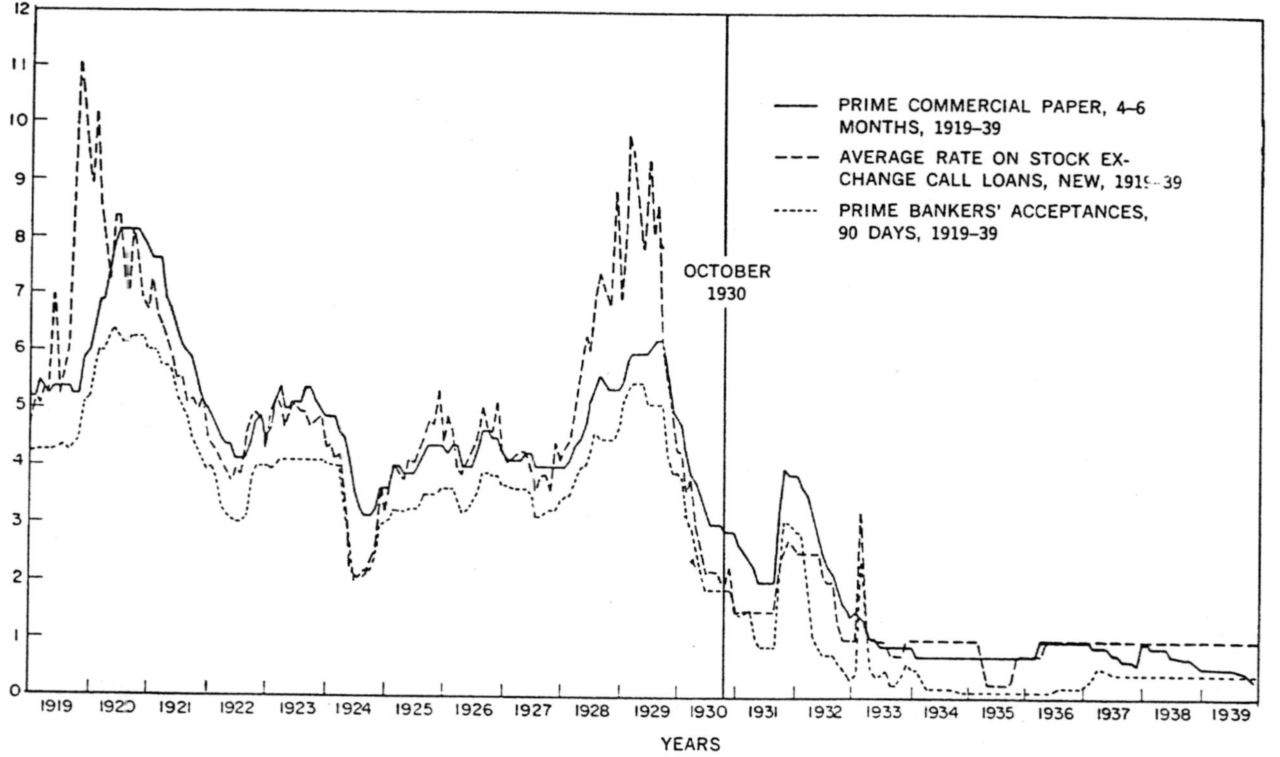

Figure 2. Three short-term interest rates, monthly, 1919–1939.

Source: *Banking and Monetary Statistics*, pp. 460, 463–464.

changes in actions in response to the changes in relative prices that the changes in interest rates represent.[4] It is hard to believe that the cause of the Great Depression was the minor change in relative prices visible in the short-term interest rates in 1929. The only large change in interest rates was in the rate for stock exchange loans which had little effect by itself on the economy as a whole. And if one looks at long-term rates . . . there is no evidence of a rise at all.

Even the money hypothesis does not assert that the monetary stringency in 1929 was severe enough to cause the entire depression. The argument is that an ordinary downturn was turned into a rout by the bank panic late in 1930. The monetary stringency that distinguished the Great Depression from other depressions therefore came at the end of 1930 and the beginning of 1931, according to this story. The rise in interest rates that was generated by this stringency should be apparent in the data. It may not be an actual rise in the interest rates, since the decline in income in 1930, coming in part from the previous monetary stringency in 1929, was acting to lower interest rates. But we should be able to see an interruption in the downward trend of interest rates, an interruption that should be quite marked if the effects of the panic were important for the economy.

This temporary reversal of trend should be apparent even though a decline in the supply of money stemming from a banking panic is not precisely analogous to the open-market sales analyzed in most theoretical discussions. After an open-market sale, there is both a reduced supply of money and an expanded supply of government debt. The price of government securities falls for two reasons. As people try to rebuild their diminished money balances, they sell assets that resemble money, that is, government debt. And as people try to reduce their excessive holdings of government debt, they offer this debt for sale.

When the supply of money falls for other reasons, such as a banking panic, the latter influence on interest rates is absent. Interest rates nevertheless rise as people attempt to regain their lost money balances by selling other assets. While the effect on interest rates of a given reduction in the supply of money may not be as great when this change results from a banking panic as when it results from an open-market sale, the effect should be easily apparent if the reduction had any important macroeconomic impact.

Yet a glance at Figures 1 and 2 is sufficient to show that no such interruption of trend is visible at the end of 1930. There is, in other

4. Compare Milton Friedman and Anna J. Schwartz, "Money and Business Cycles," *Review of Economics and Statistics*, 45 (February 1963), 32–78, and Frank de Leeuw and Edward Gramlich, "The Federal Reserve-M.I.T. Model," *Federal Reserve Bulletin*, 54 (January 1968), 11–40.

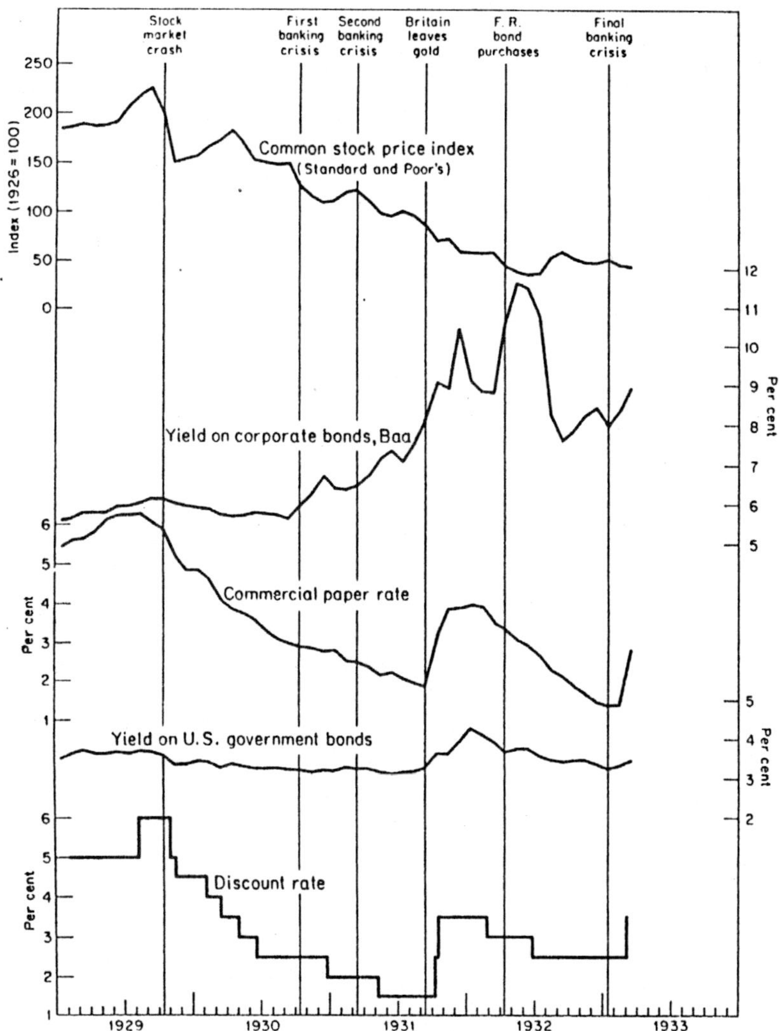

Chart 4. Common stock prices, interest yields, and discount rates of Federal Reserve Bank of New York, monthly, 1929–March 1933.

Source: Common stock price index, Standard and Poor's, as published in *Common Stock Indexes, 1871–1937* (Cowles Commission for Research in Economics, Bloomington, Ind., Principia Press, 1938), p. 67. Discount rates, *Banking and Monetary Statistics*, p. 441. Baa corporate bonds, *Banking and Monetary Statistics*, pp. 448, 464, 468. U.S. Government bonds, *Federal Reserve Bulletin*, Dec. 1938, p. 1045; Feb. 1940, p. 139. Commercial paper, *Historical Statistics*, 1949, p. 346, averaged annually.

words, no evidence in the interest rates of the monetary stringency cited in the money hypothesis as the cause of the Great Depression. We must conclude that the money hypothesis has failed its most important test. There is no reason to think that the monetary stringency in 1929–30 was more severe than in other interwar depressions and no evidence that the bank failures in 1930 created such a stringency. The money hypothesis, therefore, gives no reason why the downturn following 1929 differed from the other interwar downturns.

Friedman and Schwartz appeared to recognize this, in a somewhat indirect way. They commented that "The onset of the first liquidity crisis [in October 1930] left no clear imprint on the broad economic series shown in Chart 29 [that is, personal income, industrial production, and the wholesale price index]."[5] They also said, to be sure, that the effects could be seen in the Baa interest rate, but their argument connecting the crisis and this interest rate has been shown to be invalid. They did not say where else the imprint of this crisis can be found.

There is one way, however, in which a decrease in the supply of money could have affected the economy without leaving traces behind of the sort we have been discussing. We have assumed throughout this discussion that the various markets involved were functioning properly, that is, that a condition of excess demand or supply resulted in a change in the appropriate price. But there are some markets and some times where imbalances between supply and demand are reconciled by means other than price changes. One way of dealing with an excess demand is by rationing, allocating the scarce supplies among users on some basis other than who can and will pay a higher price. It is possible that credit was being rationed in 1931, and we must ask if there is any evidence that it was.

Rationing in the credit market is always hard to detect after the fact. If we find records that a particular firm was refused a loan in early 1931, we may or may not have found evidence of rationing. Not every attempt to get more money succeeds – or should succeed – even in perfect markets. The price at which the firm wished to borrow may not have been high enough to compensate the lender for the risk involved in the loan, and the firm may not have wanted to pay a higher cost. This is how the market clears in a functioning market; demanders who cannot pay the higher price drop out of the market. The question is not whether a particular borrower could borrow at the market price. It is whether the market price could rise.

Two reasons may be given why the interest rate might not have risen

5. Milton Friedman and Anna J. Schwartz, *A Monetary History of the United States 1867–1960*. Princeton: Princeton University Press, 1963, p. 313.

in response to a shortage of credit. There might have been legal or administrative barriers to raising interest rates. Or there might have been legal or administrative barriers to furnishing credit to the people who wanted it.

It is absurd to think that there were legal or administrative reasons why interest rates could not have risen in late 1930 or early 1931. Short-term interest rates had fallen sharply in 1930 and were far below the levels of the 1920s. They could have risen again had conditions warranted. In fact, they did so at the end of 1931 in response to the reactions of the Federal Reserve to the European currency crisis.[6]

It is equally hard to think of reasons why potential borrowers or potential sellers of assets should have been barred from doing so. We can go further than this and say that the potential demanders of money had ample supplies of other financial assets which they could have sold if they had wanted to. In addition, they bought and sold these assets in ways consistent with the existence of a free market in them. This is not to say that they could have raised all the money they wanted by selling these assets. It is probable that if everyone had decided to sell government bonds, for example, the price of government bonds would have fallen, and people would have suffered a capital loss in the course of, or perhaps even instead of, acquiring money. But in that case, their efforts to sell would have been reflected in price movements, and our previous discussion would have found evidence of them. We are looking now for evidence that people were precluded from selling financial assets or acquiring financial liabilities for reasons independent of prices.

Table 2 shows a simplified national balance sheet for 1929. The data are drawn from Goldsmith's massive studies and official banking data.[7] These data are far and away the best compilation of financial data for this period, but they are not without their problems. In order to obtain the coverage and consistency he desired, Goldsmith had to make many assumptions in his treatment of the data that readers of his work find questionable or obscure. This procedure is inevitable in any massive compilation of data, and the resultant data must always be seen as approximations or as point estimates of the true number. We do not know the variance of these estimates, and it may be quite large. We will be on safe ground, therefore, only if we restrict ourselves to questions

6. Interest rates had not fallen much before 1929, but there is no reason to think that they could not have risen farther in that year if the pressure on the financial markets had been greater. The inference that roughly equal rises of short-term interest rates indicate roughly equal amounts of pressure thus is not negated by legal or administrative constraints.

7. See the sources for Table 2.

Table 2. *U.S. national balance sheet, 1929 (billions of dollars)*

	Nonagricultural Individuals		Nonfinancial Corporations		Commercial Banks		Federal Reserve Banks		Federal Government		All Other	
	A	L	A	L	A	L	A	L	A	L	A	L
TANGIBLE ASSETS	157.6		121.3						5.0		138.6	
FINANCIAL INSTRUMENTS												
Cash					16.2		3.1				6.8	22.1
Currency and Demand Deposits	8.6		7.4			20.8		4.3	.2	.4		
Time Deposits	19.2					19.2						
Interbank Deposits						4.7						
Bank Float						4.0						
Other Deposits	11.3		1.4			.3			.1	.2		
Securities												
U.S. Government	5.1		3.2		4.7		.5		.1	17.5	3.9	
State and Local Government	7.6		.6		2.1						6.6	16.9
Corporate and Foreign Bonds	24.1		.5	36.3	5.6						7.9	1.8
Common and Preferred Stock	138.3		42.3		1.2						4.9	
Life Insurance	15.9										1.7	17.6
Other Securities		1.7					.4				9.8	8.5
Loans												
Discounts by Federal Reserve						.6	.6					
Consumer Loans		6.4	4.0		2.0						.9	.5
Commercial Loans				9.4	17.0							7.6
Security Loans		11.6	2.0	.6	8.3						6.0	4.1
Mortgages		18.0		11.2								7.6
Farm	3.6				.9				1.2		3.9	9.6
Residential	8.5				3.1						13.3	
Nonresidential	5.0				2.2						4.7	
Other Loans	1.2	4.1	21.9	16.1	2.5				.2		7.4	13.0
OTHER INTANGIBLES	42.1		23.4	22.8		7.4	.9	.7	1.4		1.3	
NET WORTH		406.2		131.8		8.8		.4		−9.9		120.4
TOTAL	448.1	448.1	228.1	228.1	65.8	65.8	5.5	5.5	8.2	8.2	217.7	217.7[a]

[a] Statistical discrepancy of $12.0 billion in liability total – sum of individual items is $229.7 billion.

Sources: Raymond W. Goldsmith and Robert E. Lipsey, *Studies in the National Balance Sheet of the United States*, 2 vols., Princeton, NJ: Princeton University Press, 1963; Raymond W. Goldsmith, *A Study of Savings in the United States*, 3 vols., Princeton, NJ: Princeton University Press, 1955; United States Bureau of the Census. *Historical Statistics of the United States, Colonial Times to 1957*, Washington, D. C., Government Printing Office, 1960. Data are from Goldsmith and Lipsey, 1963, vol. II, pp. 78–79, with the following exceptions: Commercial bank data from Goldsmith, 1955, vol. I, pp. 383, 385–386, 409; Commercial bank net worth from *Historical Statistics*, p. 632, and Federal Reserve Balance Sheet from *Banking and Monetary Statistics*, Table 86, pp. 331–332.

involving large changes in the variables and gross comparisons between them.

Net worth of individuals was about $400 billion in 1929, of which roughly $150 billion was composed of tangible assets. The remaining $250 billion represents the difference between the financial assets and the financial liabilities of individuals. The money balances held by individuals were less than $10 billion if a narrow definition of money (M_1) is used and less than $30 billion if a broader definition (M_2)

is used.[8] In either case, money balances constituted a small part of individuals' financial portfolios. Individuals who were short of money, therefore, had the option of selling other financial assets to get more money. We do not know that they wanted to do this, and if everyone wanted to do this, each individual would have found his ability to do so limited. Nevertheless, the possibility was there, and if people tried to use it we should observe either changes in the composition of individuals' portfolios or changes in the relative prices of financial assets or both.

Nonfinancial corporations had a net worth of approximately $130 billion in 1929, of which almost all was in the form of tangible assets. They held approximately $100 billion of both financial assets and financial liabilities. Their money holdings were less than $10 billion (whether M_1 or M_2 is meant), representing only a small part of their financial portfolios. If corporations wished to acquire more money, they had the options of selling other financial assets or increasing financial liabilities. If they exercised either of these options, relative prices might change. This could prevent them from altering the composition of their portfolio and could change prices so that they no longer desired to do so. If it did, the evidence should have been visible in the interest rates.

Tables 3 through 5 contain flow-of-funds data for the sectors distinguished in Table 2.[9] These data show the value of changes in the various portfolios, not the change in the value of the portfolios. To cite the most important example, the net additions to individuals' holdings of common stocks in 1930 and 1931 shown in Table 3 do not mean that the value of common stocks held by individuals rose. This value fell sharply in these years as the prices of stocks fell. Despite the fall in price, however, the value of total purchases of common stocks by individuals exceeded the value of total sales by individuals in these years. This difference is shown in the table.

It can be seen from Table 3 that nonagricultural individuals had net financial investments of almost $8 billion in each of the years 1929, 1930, and 1931. (The last of these years was only slightly lower than the others and far above 1927 and 1938.) In other words, the sum of their net purchases of financial assets and net redemptions of financial liabilities was almost $8 billion in each of these years.[10]

8. M_2 was only $20 billion more than M_1 in 1929 (Milton Friedman and Anna J. Schwartz, *A Monetary History of the United States, 1867–1960*. Princeton, NJ: Princeton University Press, 1963, p. 712) so only $20 billion of the $30 billion of "other deposits" could have been in M_2.
9. Unincorporated businesses are taken from the "all other" category in Table 2.
10. As the wealth data used in the estimation of consumption functions show, their net wealth did not increase at the same time because the net purchases were more than offset by declines in the values of assets already in their portfolio, stocks in particular.

Table 3. *Flow-of-funds data for nonagricultural individuals, 1927–1932 (billions of dollars)*

	1927	1928	1929	1930	1931	1932
Net Financial Investment	4.9	1.7	7.9	7.9	7.2	2.5
Change in Assets	9.3	7.1	9.5	5.3	3.3	−.7
Change in Liabilities	4.4	5.4	1.6	−2.7	−3.9	−3.2
Assets						
Currency and Demand Deposits	2.7	−1.9	−.8	−.3	−1.5	−1.3
U.S. Government Securities	−2.4	−1.1	−.4	−.1	.8	.7
State and Local Bonds	.4	.4	.5	.6	1.8	.1
Corporate and Foreign Bonds	2.0	1.6	.7	.7	.6	−.4
Common Stocks	1.0	2.5	4.1	.9	.1	—
Mortgages	1.2	1.6	1.9	.8	−.2	−.2
Life Insurance	1.2	1.2	1.0	.9	.8	.3
Other	3.2	2.8	2.5	1.8	.9	.1
Liabilities						
Mortgages: 1–4 Family	1.6	1.7	1.3	.1	−.5	−1.0
Mortgages: Multifamily	.7	.8	.7	.4	—	−.1
Borrowing on Securities	1.3	1.6	−1.3	−2.1	−2.0	−1.0
Consumer Debt	.2	.8	1.0	−.7	−1.2	−1.3
Other	.6	.5	−.1	−.4	−.2	.2

Sources: All data are from Goldsmith (1955, vol. 1).

Despite the near-constancy of net financial investment, the net purchases of assets by individuals fell sharply in 1930 and 1931. At the same time, individuals stopped acquiring new financial liabilities and began to reduce the financial liabilities they had. They stopped increasing their borrowing against securities in 1929, against commodity purchases in 1930 (consumer debt), and against houses in 1931. They were increasing their financial leverage through 1929; they decreased it in the following years.

Starting in 1928, individuals reduced their money balances in each year shown. This, of course, was a net movement. Individuals were receiving income from many sources, including sales of financial assets. They added this income to the monetary balances they held at the beginning of the year and spent the resulting balances for goods, services, and assets of all sorts. If the money left over at the end of the year was less than the amount at the beginning of the year, the entry in Table 3 is negative. Obviously we cannot say that the decrease shown in Table 3 was used to buy commodities or to buy financial assets. We can say that there does not seem to be any legal or administrative reason – as opposed to reasons derived from prices, incomes, and expectations – why they could not have attempted to increase their money balances by selling

Table 4. *Flow-of-funds data for nonfinancial corporations, 1927–1932 (billions of dollars)*

	1927	1928	1929	1930	1931	1932
Net Financial Investment	−4.2	−3.0	−4.6	−2.8	−2.2	1.5
Change in Assets	.5	2.6	1.1	−1.0	−2.8	−1.1
Change in Liabilities	4.8	5.7	5.7	1.8	−.6	−2.7
Assets						
Cash	—	1.2	—	−.2	−2.1	−.4
U.S. Government Securities	.1	.3	−.1	−.5	−.3	.1
Consumer Loans	—	.5	.6	−.5	−.6	−.9
Other	.4	.6	.6	.2	.2	.1
Liabilities						
Bonds	2.1	.7	.2	1.6	.6	−.3
Common Stock	.8	2.3	3.6	1.1	.3	.1
Mortgages	.8	.8	.9	.5	−.1	−.4
Commercial Loans	−.2	.6	.3	−1.4	−1.9	−1.5
Other	1.3	1.3	.7	—	1.7	−.6

Sources: All data are from Goldsmith (1955, vol. 1).

other financial assets or by refraining from purchasing as many of these assets as they did in 1930 and 1931.

In fact, the changes shown in Table 3 are quite consistent with the hypothesis that individuals were reacting to changes in prices, incomes, and expectations in this period. They reduced their leverage and their rate of acquisition of long-term financial assets in response to the increase in the risk of these assets. They reduced their money balances and their rate of acquisition of other short-term assets in response to the fall in income and the consequent need for working balances. They reduced their money balances, therefore, because their demand for money fell – not because of a restriction of supply. The evidence from quantities is consistent with the evidence from interest rates.

Nonfinancial corporations had very different financial structures than individuals. Their financial flows are shown in Table 4. They had negative net financial investment for every year shown in Table 4 except 1932. They were acquiring more financial liabilities than financial assets in these years, although this phrase must be interpreted to mean that they were reducing their financial liabilities more slowly than they were selling financial assets in 1931.

The difference in financial behavior between the late 1920s and the early 1930s that was shown in Table 3 for individuals is also visible here. Nonfinancial corporations were acquiring financial assets in the years before 1929; they were decreasing their holdings of financial assets after then.[11] Three different financial assets were affected. Consumer loans rose in the twenties and fell in the thirties. This change can be understood as a result of the volume of trade; it tells us nothing about the desire of corporations for financial assets. Corporations bought government securities in the 1920s and sold them in the 1930s. This movement suggests that corporations reduced their desires to hold financial assets in the 1930s, but the movement is too small and indefinite to provide a basis for such a conclusion. And corporations kept stable money balances in the late 1920s, reducing them in the early 1930s. This movement is the one we are interested in.

The question at issue is whether corporations decreased their money balances because their expenditures were falling or whether their expenditures were falling because their money balances were falling. We have found already that the evidence of interest rates is consistent with the first alternative. We are asking here if the movements of quantities suggest that the connections between money balances and expenditures went through channels that did not affect interest rates. In short, is there evidence of credit rationing?

Commercial loans were falling at the same time as money balances. It is possible that they were being rationed. But if they were, it does not follow that this rationing would have prevented corporations from making expenditures. Corporations were issuing both stocks and bonds in 1930 and 1931. They issued more bonds in 1930 than in any other year shown except for 1927. No rationing is possible in the markets for these assets; they are organized along impersonal lines. If corporations had wanted more cash, they could have sold more stocks or bonds.

Nevertheless, it is hard to understand why businessmen preferred to sell low-priced bonds and stocks in 1930 and 1931 rather than to take out bank loans.[12] The paradox can be resolved by assuming the existence of credit rationing. Perhaps corporations did not borrow from banks in 1930 and 1931 because banks would not lend. This presumption, however, has its own difficulties. Most short-term credit was extended through bank loans, as Table 1 shows. If access to these loans was restricted by rationing, corporations would have tried to get the funds they were denied in this market from other sources. They might have sold more stocks and bonds than they would have otherwise. But these

11. This process of simultaneously acquiring financial assets and liabilities was noted with suspicion by George A. Eddy, "Security Issues and Real Investment in 1929," *Review of Economics and Statistics*, 19 (May 1937), 79–91.

12. One possible argument is that corporations thought that short-term interest rates were going to rise. While direct evidence on these expectations is lacking, the evidence on expectations presented above suggests strongly that businessmen were not anticipating the kind of strong upsurge in business that would cause short-term interest rates to rise sharply in 1930 or 1931.

are long-term liabilities for corporations. To replace bank loans, at least some corporations would have wanted to borrow on a short-term basis. Being denied access to banks, they would have tried to sell commercial paper or bankers' acceptances. As Table 1 demonstrates, the market for these assets was very small compared to the volume of bank loans outstanding. Even if only a few corporations switched into these markets in response to credit rationing, the increased supply of commercial paper and bankers' acceptances should have lowered their price and raised their yield dramatically. There is no reason why the interest rates in these markets could not have risen in 1930 and 1931. Their failure to do so – as shown in Figure 1 – implies that credit rationing by banks was not diverting demands for funds into these markets. In fact, the fall in interest rates for commercial paper relative to interest rates on commercial bank loans is precisely contrary to what we would expect if the latter market was rationed while the former one was free. There is no evidence, therefore, of binding credit rationing by banks.

A better way out of this dilemma is to assume that corporations had separate demands for long-term and short-term liabilities. In other words, the demands for different parts of their financial portfolios were determined by different variables.[13] Corporations continued to issue bonds and stocks in 1930 and 1931 to raise long-term funds for investment. They issued fewer bonds and stocks as their capital investment fell, retiring more bonds than they issued in 1932. They decreased their bank loans in 1930 and subsequent years because of the fall in sales and inventories. And they were not subject to rationing by banks that led them to try alternative methods of raising short-term funds.

Data for the net financial flows of unincorporated businesses are shown in Table 5. Credit rationing by banks could not have been very important for unincorporated businesses for the simple reason that changes in their cash holdings and bank debt were small relative to other changes in the financial flows of these firms. As with individuals and corporations, 1929 marked a dividing line for unincorporated businesses. Accounts receivable from customers had been declining slowly before 1929; they began to fall rapidly in 1930 and continued to fall for the next few years. This movement dominates all other financial movements of these firms.

Negative net financial investment therefore does not mean the same thing for unincorporated businesses as it did for nonfinancial corporations. Corporations were borrowing to finance real investment. Unin-

13. Recent work on corporate financial structures bears out the hypothesis. See Barry Bosworth, "Patterns of Corporate External Financing," *Brookings Papers on Economics Activity*, 2 (1971), 253–79.

Table 5. *Flow-of-funds data for unincorporated businesses, 1927–1932 (billions of dollars)*

	1927	1928	1929	1930	1931	1932
Net Financial Investment	−.5	−.7	−.6	−1.9	−2.8	−1.5
Change in Assets	−.3	−.1	−.1	−2.4	−3.6	−2.3
Change in Liabilities	.2	.6	.5	−.5	−.8	−.7
Assets						
Receivables (nonfarm)	−.2	−.2	−.2	−2.0	−2.5	−2.0
Cash	−.2	—	.2	−.3	−.9	−.1
Other	.1	.1	−.1	−.1	−.2	−.2
Liabilities						
Bank Debt	−.2	.1	.1	−.7	−.8	−.6
Other	.4	.5	.4	.2	—	−.1

corporated businesses were decreasing their lending to customers. As the total volume of purchases fell in the early 1930s, the demand for consumer credit fell also, and firms found themselves with smaller sales and smaller accounts receivable. The decrease in their bank debt and cash balances undoubtedly was a response to the decline in their business.

The data on financial flows therefore does not provide evidence of important credit rationing by banks. If individuals had wanted more cash, they could have refrained from buying the financial assets they were buying in the early 1930s. If nonfinancial corporations had wanted more cash and been refused credit by banks, they would have gone into other short-term capital markets, leaving some evidence of this displaced demand behind. The lack of such evidence in markets like the one for commercial paper shows that there was no such displaced demand. And it is highly unlikely that unincorporated businesses were displeased by the decline in bank credit extended to them. It was both small and almost certainly desired by the firms themselves in response to the fall in their sales.

This is not to say that credit rationing was absent in the early 1930s. No evidence has been presented here on the actual extent of credit rationing. But the credit rationing present in 1930 and 1931 – if it existed – did not restrict the overall supplies of money available to firms and individuals by avenues independent of interest rates. Individuals were buying financial assets (other than money) throughout the early 1930s in a manner that is inconsistent with the notion that they were short of cash. Corporations were not seeking alternative sources of short-term credit as they would have done if they had been suffering from rationing by banks. And unincorporated businesses were suffering from a loss of business, not credit.

Having said this, however, it is worth saying also that the evidence on financial flows is consistent with the hypothesis that there was in fact no credit rationing in the early 1930s. Nonagricultural individuals who had been increasing their leverage in the late 1920s, reduced their leverage in the early 1930s as their expectations about the gains to be gotten from purchasing financial assets such as common stocks changed dramatically. Nonfinancial corporations reduced the rate at which they issued their long-term liabilities in response both to the decline in the prices of common stocks and in the perceived opportunities for profitable investment in plant and equipment. Unincorporated businesses found their loans to customers falling with sales. All of these groups reduced their cash balances and bank debt in the early 1930s in response to the fall in income.

We conclude, therefore, that there is no evidence that the banking panic of 1930 had a deflationary effect on the economy. Instead, the data are consistent with the hypothesis that the demand for money was falling more rapidly than the supply during 1930 and the first three-quarters of 1931. They are consistent with the spending hypothesis, not the money hypothesis about the cause of the Depression.[14]

14. It should be remembered that the data suggest that the downturn in 1929 may have been caused in part by a monetary restriction. They do not suggest that the monetary pressure in the early 1930s was more severe than the pressure in other interwar depressions.

Appendix: Basics of regression

Cliometrics is the explicit use of economic theory and measurement in the study of economic history. As the essays in this reader demonstrate, cliometrics has become a dominant method among economic historians. One of the central tools of cliometrics, and of all econometrics, is regression analysis. Multiple regression analysis is a means of fitting economic relationships to data. It lets us quantify economic relationships and test hypotheses about them.

Examine the data plotted in Figure A.1 for the Michigan furniture industry in 1889. Each dot on the scatter plot represents one worker. Clearly, there is a relationship between age and earnings. If we could draw a line through the scatter of points summarizing what is going on, the line would have an upward slope, since earnings generally rise with age. This is exactly what regression analysis does – it selects the line that provides a best fit to the data.

Estimating this line must begin with some economic theory. Most models of the labor market assume that wages are based on the value of the worker's contribution to output. Furthermore, in many jobs, productivity of young adults rises with maturity and experience. The theory, therefore, says that earnings depend on (rise with) age. Earnings are the dependent variable; age is the independent variable. It would be foolish to argue that the causation runs the other way, that age depends on or is caused by level of earnings. We can write this simple model mathematically as

$$\text{Earnings} = b_0 + b_1 \cdot \text{Age} + e$$

or more generally as

$$Y = b_0 + b_1 \cdot X + e$$

In the equation, b_0 and b_1 are the parameters or coefficients to be determined from the data. Here b_0 is the intercept term, and b_1 is the slope term in the equation of the line. The error term, e, represents the collective influences of any omitted variables that may also affect

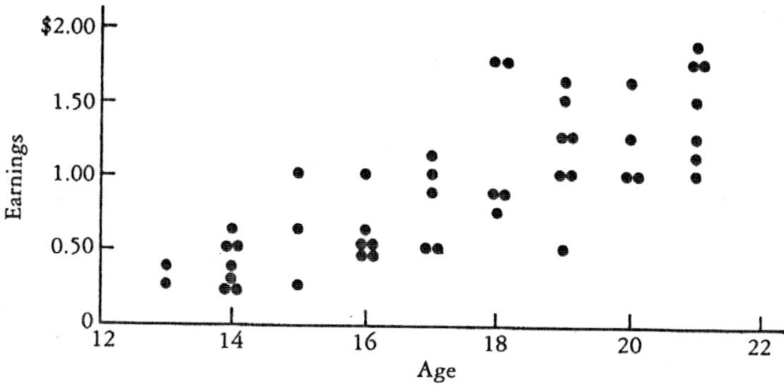

Figure A.1. Age and wage (dollars per day) Michigan furniture workers, 1889.

earnings. It recognizes that not every case will fall on the line.

Some criterion for a best fit is needed to choose values for the regression parameters, b_0 and b_1. The criterion most often used is to minimize the sum of squared differences between the actual values of Y and the fitted values for Y obtained after the equation line has been estimated. This is called the "least-squares criterion." If we denote the estimated parameters for the model by $\hat{b}_0$ and $\hat{b}_1$, then the fitted values for Y are given by

$$\hat{Y} = \hat{b}_0 + \hat{b}_1 \cdot X$$

For each data point, the regression residual is the difference between the actual and fitted values of the dependent variable. The parameter values are chosen so that when all the residuals are squared and then summed, the resulting sum is minimized.

In the data from the scatter plot given previously, the result of fitting this equation using the least-squares criterion is

$$\text{Earnings} = -1.73 + 0.145 \cdot \text{Age}$$

where earnings are the dollars per day of furniture workers in Michigan in 1889 and age is in years. These data are used in Whaples (1992).

The slope parameter, $\hat{b}_1$, is of the most interest. It indicates that among young male workers below age twenty-two, a one-unit (i.e., one-year) increase in the age of the worker generally led to a $0.145 per day increase in earnings. The average daily earnings of this group was $0.89 (in 1889 dollars). Often the intercept is economically meaningless. This intercept literally tells us that a zero-year-old worker is predicted to have negative earnings. However, the intercept is important for fitting the best line through the data.

The beauty of computers is that they can easily think in many dimensions, so a more complicated model of earnings can easily be constructed, one that allows for many independent variables to influence the dependent variable and examines the impact of a change in each of the independent variables while holding the other independent variables constant. For example, the same data yield this regression line:

$$\text{Earnings} = -1.666 + 0.151 \cdot \text{Age} - 0.116 \cdot \text{Immigrant}$$

It indicates that, after controlling for age, immigrant workers earned \$0.116 less per day than nonimmigrant workers. Independent variables like this immigrant variable, which take on only two values (which = 1 if a condition holds and = 0 if it doesn't hold) are known as "dummy variables."

Our estimates of the true (but unknown) underlying parameters depend on the set of observations we use. We generally cannot observe every occurrence (e.g., only some farmers' account books have survived, or the 1910 U.S. census of population is so huge that only a small but representative fraction has been computerized). (The number of observations used in the regression's sample is often noted by the letter N.) If we could collect more and more samples and generate further estimates, the estimates of each parameter would follow a probability distribution. The probability distribution can be summarized by a mean and a measure of dispersion around that mean, a standard deviation referred to as the "standard error of the coefficient."

For any particular sample, least-squares estimates provide the best guess of the true underlying parameter. However, once we have information about the probability distribution for each coefficient, we can make statistical statements about our knowledge of the true parameters. Error terms are often assumed to be normally distributed. The normal distribution has the property that the area within 1.96 standard errors of its mean is equal to 95 percent of the total area. Thus, given our parameter estimate, $\hat{b}$, we can construct an interval around $\hat{b}$ within which there is a 95 percent probability that the actual parameter lies. That confidence interval is given by

$$\hat{b} + 1.96 \cdot (\text{standard error of } \hat{b})$$

Therefore, we should not only look at the point estimates of the coefficients, but also examine their standard errors. If the 95 percent confidence interval contains 0, then we cannot be certain that the true parameter b is different from 0. If we cannot be sure that the parameter is different from zero, then we cannot be sure that a relationship between the dependent and independent variables actually exists.

Regression printouts and tables report either the standard error of $\hat{b}$ or the t-statistic. The t-statistic is defined as

$$t = \frac{\hat{b}}{\text{standard error of } \hat{b}}$$

If the t-statistic is less than 1.96 in magnitude, the 95 percent confidence interval around $\hat{b}$ includes 0, and there is at least a 5 percent chance that b equals 0. We therefore say that our estimate is not statistically significant. On the other hand, if the absolute value of the t-statistic is greater than 1.96, we reject the hypothesis that $b = 0$ and call our estimate statistically significant.

Using the data on Michigan furniture workers again:

$$\begin{array}{rllll} \text{Earnings} = & -1.666 & + \; 0.151 \cdot \text{Age} & - \; 0.116 \cdot \text{Immigrant} \\ & (0.306) & (0.017) & (0.087) \\ t = & -5.44 & 8.77 & -1.33 \end{array}$$

In this case, we are fairly confident (more than 95 percent confident) that earnings do climb with age, but we are not confident that immigrants actually earn any less (or more) than nonimmigrants. It is important to consider the "economic significance" of a coefficient in addition to its statistical significance. Suppose that the immigrant coefficient was statistically significant. Would the coefficient be economically significant as well? Would this 11.6 cent per day difference in earnings be economically important? This question cannot be answered by a computer. This is the historian's job.

The last thing to pay attention to in a regression table is the measure of the goodness of fit. This measures how much of the variation in the dependent variable has been explained by the variation in the independent variable(s). Goodness of fit is usually measured using the r-squared (R^2) or adjusted r-squared. This measure ranges from 0 (when the regression explains none of the variance) to 1 (when it explains all of the variance). A high R^2 by itself does not mean that the variables actually included in the model are the appropriate ones, because R^2 varies with the types of data being studied. Time-series data will often yield much higher R^2 values than cross-sectional data. In addition, if the theory underlying the equation is not valid, the equation could still yield significant coefficients with a high R^2, even though the results are meaningless. The adjusted-R^2 values from the preceding equations are 0.623 and 0.630. Adding the immigrant variable helps explain a small fraction of the variance in wages.

To summarize, these questions must be answered when examining a regression table:

1. What is the underlying theory? What is the dependent variable, and how is it assumed to be related to the independent variables?
2. What are the slope coefficients? How much does the dependent variable rise or fall when the independent variables change by one unit?
3. Are the slope coefficients statistically significant? Can we be sure that the coefficient is different from zero? Is the magnitude of the t-statistic greater than 1.96?
4. What is the R^2? How much of the variation in the dependent variable has been explained?

References

Robert Whaples, "Using Historical State Bureau of Labor Statistics Reports in Teaching," *Historical Methods*, 25 (Summer 1992), 132–6.

Glossary

axiom of indispensability the idea that there would have been little or no economic growth in the nineteenth century without the railroads

backward linkage the positive impact of improvements in one industry on other industries that supply it with inputs

balance of trade the difference between the money value of a country's merchandise exports and the money value of its merchandise imports

bank notes paper currency issued by banks

bimetallism the use of two metals, usually gold and silver, as a legal monetary standard

c.i.f. cost, insurance, and freight

Cobb–Douglas production function an equation that shows physical output as the product of inputs and is usually written algebraically as $Q = AL^aK^b$, where Q is output; L and K are the inputs (in this case, labor and capital, respectively); and A, a, and b are constants. A is called "total factor productivity." This form of the production function suggests that labor and capital can be substituted for one another

cohort a group of people sharing a particular statistical or demographic characteristic, especially a group born at the same time

consumer surplus the area below the demand curve and above the market price, traditionally used to represent the welfare gain or loss associated with a change in market price

cost per ton-mile rate charge in transportation indicating the cost of transporting one ton one mile

cross section an analysis that compares different cases (e.g., groups or individuals) at a given point in time

currency ratio the ratio of specie in the hands of the public to currency

demand a schedule that indicates the quantity of a good that is desired to be purchased at various prices in a given time period

demand deposit funds held at a bank with a withdrawal notice period of less than seven days, especially checking deposits

deposit ratio the ratio of bank reserves to bank demand deposits

diminishing returns successive increases in one input will lead to smaller and smaller increases in output as long as other inputs and technology are held constant

durable goods goods that have a relatively long expected work life (e.g., machines, equipment, appliances)

economic growth increase in the aggregate level of economic activity, usually measured by changes in GNP

economic model a simplified picture of economic reality; an abstract generalization showing the interrelationships between a few economic variables

economies of scale as the size of the production unit increases, greater subdivision and specialization of the production process may be achieved, leading to lower per unit costs

equilibrium a situation in which there is no tendency for change (e.g., a price at which there is no shortage or surplus)

excise tax a tax levied within a country on the production, sale, or consumption of certain goods or services

exploitation utilization of an input without giving a just or equivalent return

financial intermediaries institutions that receive funds from households and firms and make them available for investments

f.o.b. free on board; cost excluding insurance and shipping charges

forward linkages the positive impact of improvements in one industry on other industries that consume its outputs

free banking free entry into the banking business; anyone could set up a bank, as long as the note issue was backed by securities on deposit with the state banking authority

general equilibrium the state of the economy in which all markets (goods, capital, labor, land, financial assets, money, etc.) are in equilibrium. General equilibrium analysis examines how changes in one type of market influence the others

gross national product (GNP) the total value of all goods and services produced for final sale in a given year

high-powered money currency held by the public, plus vault cash of banks, plus deposit liabilities of the Federal Reserve System to banks

labor force participation rate the ratio of the number of people employed or actively seeking work to the total number of people of working age in the population

monetary policy collective power of the Federal Reserve System to influence output and unemployment by controlling credit conditions and the money supply

monopoly a market in which there is only one seller

national income total income paid to the factors of production, including wages, interest, rent, and profit

natural monopoly an industry in which economies of scale are great enough that one firm can produce a product at lower average cost than multiple firms can

nominal used to designate variables that have not been adjusted for inflation

normative economics an economic statement with value judgments incorporated into the analysis, that is, what "ought" to be

open market operations the buying and selling of U.S. government securities by the Federal Reserve

opportunity cost the implicit cost of choosing one alternative rather than another; foregone costs of other choices represent opportunity costs

pareto efficiency an optimum position that exists when it is impossible, through a change in resource allocation, to make any individual better off without making another worse off

partial equilibrium an equilibrium in one particular market or sector of the economy

positive economics an economic statement that can be verified by observations, that is, a statement about what "is"

present value the current value of assets or income that will be accumulated in the future

price discrimination the selling of a product at different prices to different buyers when the price difference is not due to differences in the cost of producing the product for the different buyers

principal–agent refers to a situation whereby the principal (e.g., employer) attempts to design a contract that motivates the agent (e.g., employee) to act in the principal's interests. Problems arise when imperfect information prevents an individual's actions from being observed or inferred, thereby affecting the payoff in a given relationship

production function schedule showing the maximum amount of output that can be produced from any specified set of inputs, given the existing level of technology

rate of return percentage of an investment yielded as profit

real used to designate variables that have been adjusted for inflation

reserve requirement the specified minimum percentage of its deposit liabilities that a bank must keep on deposit with the Federal Reserve Bank or in vault cash

specie tangible form of money, usually gold or silver

supply a schedule of quantities that sellers are willing to sell at various prices in a given time period

tariff government tax on imports of foreign goods

terms of trade ratio of prices received to prices paid

time series analysis that compares cases through time

total factor productivity a weighted index of the ratio of outputs to inputs used to measure differences in productivity

value added the value of output minus intermediate production expenses (materials, etc.); measures the net contribution to output at each stage of production

velocity of money the number of times the supply of money changes hands in a given time period

Name index

Subject index